Ancient Rome

Ancient Rome

Duncan Hill

PaRragon

Bath · New York · Singapore · Hong Kong · Cologne · Delhi · Melbourne

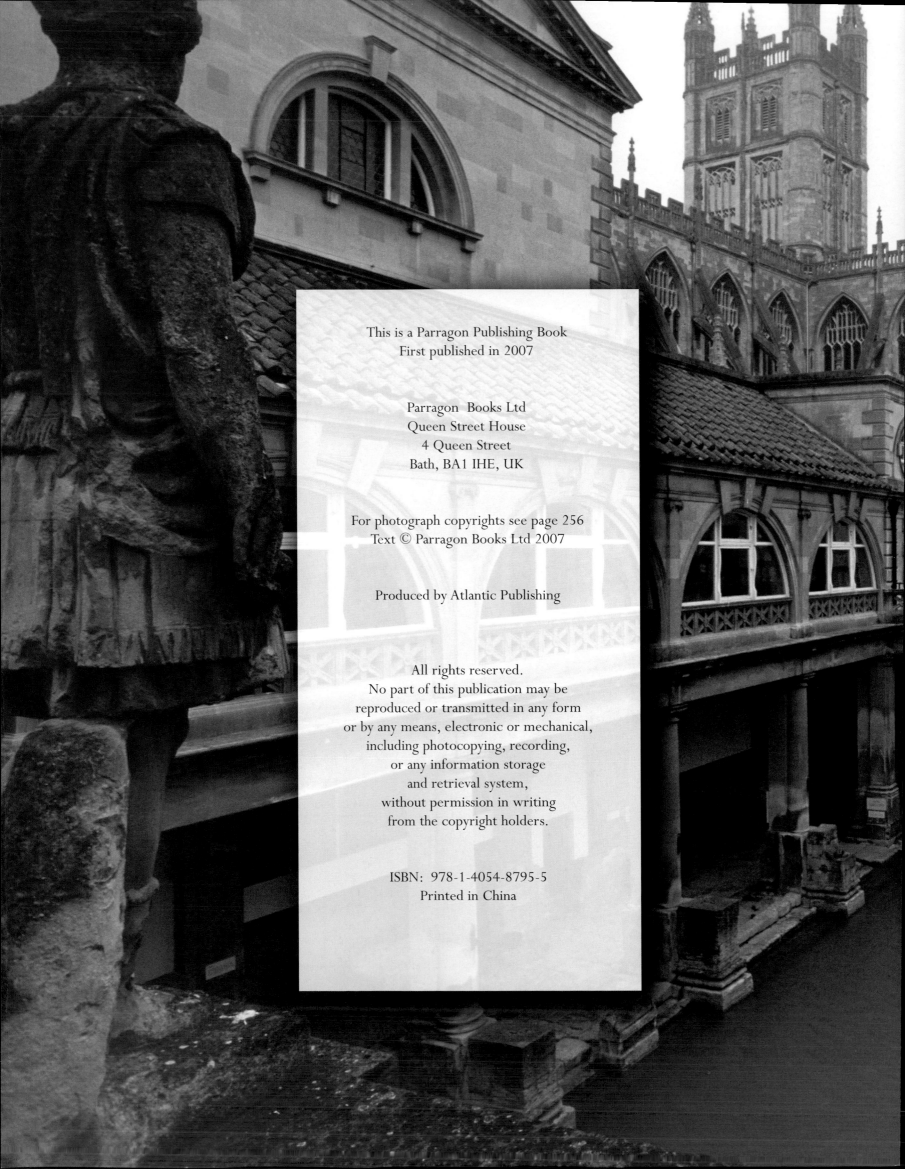

This is a Parragon Publishing Book
First published in 2007

Parragon Books Ltd
Queen Street House
4 Queen Street
Bath, BA1 IHE, UK

For photograph copyrights see page 256
Text © Parragon Books Ltd 2007

Produced by Atlantic Publishing

ISBN: 978-1-4054-8795-5
Printed in China

Contents

Introduction

The rise of Rome from provincial settlement to imperial power is an epic story that reads like fiction rather than fact. Fable does indeed play a part: Romulus is said to have slain his twin brother Remus and founded the future city-state, both infants having survived abandonment on the banks of the Tiber thanks to the nurturing milk of a she-wolf.

When myth is stripped away, what remains is hardly less extraordinary. Despite possessing few strategic advantages, Rome mastered Italy, then looked outward. At its height the Empire encompassed territories from the Rhineland to Egypt, Britain to Armenia. Over two million square miles fell within Rome's orbit.

Conquest on such a scale required a formidable military machine, yet the Empire was not wholly underpinned by compulsion. The Romans were a largely civilizing force, urban and literate, a people who replaced tyrannical monarchy with citizenship, and who were proponents of selfless discipline, loyalty, and order.

Rome is also associated with opulent decadence, particularly after power passed from the republican institutions into the hands of autocratic military commanders. During some reigns the Empire flourished; others were blighted by intrigue and blood-lust. Caligula, who appointed his favorite horse a consul, was just one emperor who fell victim to an assassin's hand.

Ancient Rome traces all facets of one of the world's great civilizations, from the legends surrounding Rome's foundation to the strife that precipitated the Empire's collapse. It describes a remarkable imperial power that left an indelible mark on the lands it occupied. The face of Europe today would be radically different were it not for the rich cultural, technological, linguistic, and administrative legacy bequeathed it by the Romans.

The Roots of Rome

Origins

The vast Roman Empire, which at its peak stretched all the way from Britain in the west to Arabia in the east, had humble origins in the Latin-speaking settlements, collectively called Latium, surrounding the River Tiber.

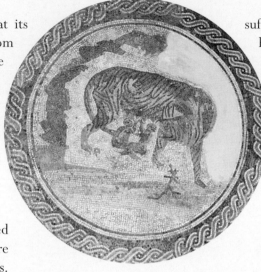

Importance of the Tiber

The banks of the Tiber proved perfect for agricultural use and were well-defended by the nearby hills. The location further benefited from the river itself, which provided ready access to the sea for trade with seafaring merchants, but was sufficiently distant to protect the settlements from seafaring enemies. In their ideal location, the Latin settlements were able to develop during the early centuries of the first millennium BC.

Rome was among the younger of these Latin settlements, its foundation was dated by Roman historians to approximately 750 BC, but without

Floor mosaic depicting the story of Romulus and Remus. The myth of the noble-born twins, saved from being killed at birth and raised by a she-wolf on the Palatine Hill, gave Rome, once one of the lesser Latium settlements, a grandeur to legitimize the city's domination of its neighbors.

sufficient archaeological evidence, this has proved impossible for modern historians to verify. In spite of its relative youth, over the following centuries Rome was able to rise, dominate, and conquer its neighboring Latin settlements, to become the region's supreme ruler.

Romulus and Remus

The uncertainty surrounding the city's origins, combined with the need of Roman writers to provide a less modest account of the origins of their mighty civilization, led to the emergence of the famous legend of Romulus and Remus.

The tale originates at the time when the ruler of Alba Longa, Numitor, had just been overthrown by his younger brother, Amulius. Alba Longa was the main city-state of Latium, and according to Virgil's *Aeneid*, the kings of the city had origins among the ancient Trojan people. Virgil's protagonist, Aeneas, was thought to have fled amidst the legendary Battle of Troy and settled in the region.

The rolling countryside surrounding Rome provided a fertile land for agriculture to support the growing population of the city.

Birth of a legend

Desperate to maintain his grip on power, Amulius sought to eradicate Numitor's descendants before they were even born. He forced his niece, Numitor's daughter, Rhea Silva, into becoming a Vestal Virgin so that she would never have children. However, Amulius' plan failed. The God of War, Mars, raped Rhea Silva and she conceived as a result. Numitor was to have not just one male heir, but two, because Rhea Silva gave birth to twin boys, named Romulus and Remus.

Anxious that Numitor's grandsons might challenge his rule, Amulius ordered that the newborn twins be disposed of. However, the servant tasked with killing the boys could not carry out the assignment and left them afloat on the Tiber, where they were spared by the river god, Tiberinus. Romulus and Remus were subsequently raised by a she-wolf on the Palatine Hill, until a shepherd, Faustulus, found them and adopted them as his own sons.

Both grew up into a life of banditry, but their noble birth meant they were natural leaders and amassed a following among fellow bandits and exiles. This brought them into conflict with authorities of Alba Longa and eventually with Amulius himself. During one of several scuffles with Alba Longa, Remus was captured, which encouraged Romulus to raise an army to free his brother and take the city. Romulus' forces were victorious, and Amulius was executed.

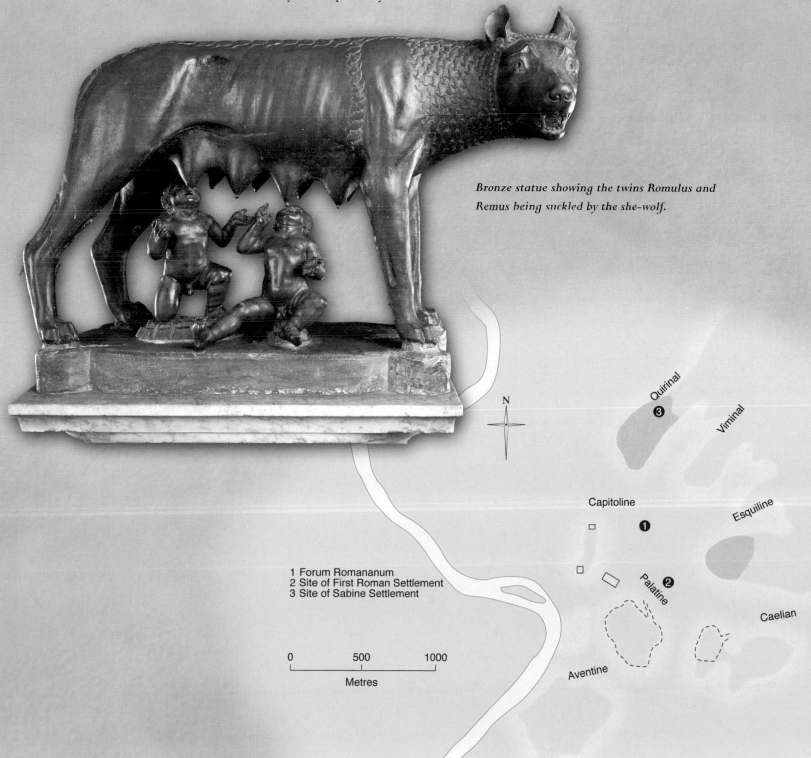

Bronze statue showing the twins Romulus and Remus being suckled by the she-wolf.

1 Forum Romananum
2 Site of First Roman Settlement
3 Site of Sabine Settlement

0   500   1000

Metres

Romulus emerges triumphant

The twins were jointly offered the crown of Alba Longa, but refused, in favor of re-enthroning their grandfather, Numitor. With the threat from Alba Longa removed, the two brothers took their followers and sought to establish their own settlement close to where they had been raised. However, Romulus and Remus disagreed as to where their settlement ought to be situated. Romulus insisted on the Palatine Hill, where the she-wolf had nurtured them, while Remus stood firm for the Aventine Hill because it offered a superior strategic position. The disagreement was deferred to the gods, who found in favor of Romulus.

Work began on the Palatine Hill, but ungracious in his defeat, Remus attempted to obstruct the process and demonstrate that Romulus' location was not as defendable as his own. Angered by his brother, Romulus killed Remus and proclaimed himself king. In 748 BC the new settlement was named "Rome" in his honor, and one of the greatest Empires the world has ever seen was begun.

The Sabine Women

Rome would not have lasted more than a generation, were it not for some underhand tactics by Romulus. Romulus' group of bandits, outcasts, and exiles was, by its very nature, dominated by males, and suffered from a perilous lack of females. To compensate, Romulus invited the Sabine, a small civilization with a settlement on the nearby Quirinal Hill, to join the Romans for a religious festival. Rather than showing hospitality, the Romans stole their womenfolk and returned them to Rome to become wives for Roman citizens. Inevitably, war broke out between the Sabine and the Romans.

Ruins of a palace on the Palatine Hill. The decision to build the settlement of Rome on the Palatine Hill, where the she-wolf had nurtured the infant twins, led to a fierce disagreement between Romulus and Remus. Arbitration by the gods found in Romulus' favor but Remus continued to obstruct the building work. Angered by his brother's recalcitrance, Romulus killed Remus, and proclaimed himself king.

ROOTS OF ROME

- Roman territory, 298 BC
- Samian League, 298 BC
- acquired by Rome to 263 BC
- Roman colonies, 272 BC
- Roman controlled by 270 BC
- Carthaginian possessions, c. 260 BC

Tarpeia's Treachery

The Romans were thought to have been well-defended by an outpost on the Capitoline Hill, but the Sabine were able to capture the hill. According to legend, this was because the daughter of the commander of the outpost, Tarpeia, was given to greed. In exchange for payment, she opened the city gates to the Sabine. Instead of rewarding her, the Sabine army, repulsed by her treachery, brutally murdered her. The steep face of the Capitoline Hill overlooking the Roman Forum, was subsequently named the Tarpeian rock, and became an execution site, to highlight her dishonor.

War with the Sabine

Romulus marched an army to stem the Sabine advance and met his foe in the swampland between the Capitoline and Palatine Hills, the site upon which the Roman Forum would later stand. The Sabine were initially successful, but Romulus regrouped his forces ready for another attack. Just as the two sides were about to go into battle, the captured Sabine women ran onto the battlefield and implored their fathers and husbands to stop fighting. Persuaded and touched by the bravery of the Sabine women, the Roman and Sabine armies not only made peace, but also agreed to unification. The king of the Sabine was to rule alongside Romulus, and Rome underwent its first expansion, stretching from the Palatine Hill to the Quirinal Hill. The Capitoline Hill, lying in the middle of the two settlements, was chosen as the political center of Rome. A few years after unification, the Sabine king, Tatius, was killed and Romulus became the sole king of the expanded settlement.

Ruins of a structure on the Palatine Hill, the first of Rome's "seven hills" to be settled.

The Sabine Women by Jacques-Louis David. The Sabine women who had been captured and taken to Rome, ran onto the battlefield and implored their Sabine fathers and Roman husbands to stop fighting. Convinced and touched by the bravery of the Sabine women, the armies not only made peace, but also agreed to political unification.

Roman Monarchy

King Romulus

It is difficult to verify the elements of truth in the Romulus and Remus story. However, available evidence suggests Romulus was the first king of Rome and this myth probably developed in order to provide a back-story for him, in order to ground the foundations of Rome in the grandiose world of gods and heroes.

King Romulus

Under Romulus' rule, Roman society was delineated into three tribes, Roman, Sabine and Etruscan, a civilization immediately to the north of Rome. Each of the three tribes was politically represented in an assembly, the *comitia curiata*, which was established in order to restrict the king's powers. Legislation that the king wished to pass traditionally had to be ratified by the *comitia*. However, in spite of the restrictions posed by the *comitia*, Romulus was able to circumvent the elected bodies because the king was able to monopolize the ability to interpret the will of the gods. His rule was further backed up by the creation of his own personal bodyguard called the Celeres.

Under Romulus, a forerunner of the Roman Senate was created, as one hundred patricians, or heads of noble families, were established as an advisory council for the king. This was later expanded to two hundred, as an extra one hundred patricians were brought in from the Sabine population.

The Death of Romulus

In 715 BC King Romulus vanished. Senators said they had seen him ascend to heaven, but the most likely explanation is that the Senate had him killed. In keeping with the myth that Romulus had been carried up to heaven, the senators rapidly deified him as the god Quirinus and built a temple in his honor on the hill where the ascension had reportedly taken place. This hill, the one upon which the Sabine settlement had been situated, was named the Quirinal Hill in honor of the new god.

Left: Undated engraved illustration of an ancient coin which depicts the deified Romulus as Quirinus.

Above: Remains of a street and its buildings in the port of Ostia.

Opposite right: Floor mosaic showing the head of the god Oceanus, an important god for a state with a growing dependence on trade around the Mediterranean.

Opposite left: Ruins of Ostia, the first port of Rome, established during the reign of Ancus.

Numa Pompilius

The Roman Monarchy was not hereditary; rather, the best man for the job was selected by the senators. This meant that there was a period in between successive monarchs when Rome would have had no king at all. This period was called an "interregnum." During this time the senators took turns at being an "interrex." The interrex would rule for several days before being replaced by a fellow senator until a suitable candidate could be found.

After the first interregnum, Numa Pompilius was chosen to succeed Romulus. Numa was a wise choice because he was a Sabine, and thus this helped smooth the absorption of the Sabine into Rome. As Numa was such a well-respected king, it was widely believed that he was being advised by the clever water nymph, Egeria. Numa's reign was a long and peaceful one, lasting approximately forty years, until his death of old age in 674 BC.

War and Peace

After Numa, there were five further Roman kings who ruled until 510 BC. The peaceful reign of Numa gave way to the more militaristic tenure of his successor, Tullus Hostilius. His reign was marred by war with a former ally, Alba Longa, as well as with the Etruscans. So ruthless was Tullus Hostilius that he reputedly had the king of Alba Longa torn in two by chariots. This famous punishment was to highlight the perils of indecision; the king of Alba Longa had held back in Rome's war against the Etruscan city-state of Fidenae so that he could enter on the winning side. When Rome won, Tullus was so infuriated that he meted out this harshest of penalties. Fearing that too much warfare had meant that Tullus had ignored and angered the gods, the senators opted for a more serene heir, Ancus Martius. Ancus was the grandson of Numa Pompilius, and is thought to have been a similarly peaceable ruler as his grandfather. Under Ancus' reign, Rome established the first port at Ostia, where the River Tiber met the sea.

Assassinations

Ancus' appointed heir was an emigrant from the Etruscan cities in the north, called Tarquinius Priscus. Ancus' biological sons were never satisfied with his appointment as king and even forty years into his reign, they colluded to have him assassinated. The king was murdered in 579 BC but Ancus' sons were unable to get themselves elected as king. Instead, Tarquinius' wife was able to secure the succession for her son-in-law, a former slave, named Servius Tullius.

Servius Tullius undertook the first Roman census, and is widely accredited with the establishment of the class system of Ancient Rome. He replaced Romulus' *comitia curiata* with a reformed *comitia centuriata* based upon this new census information. The new *comitia* no longer excluded poorer members of Roman society, called plebs. Instead both the patrician and the plebeian classes were represented.

Although the wealthier patrician class was still able to maintain control of Roman government, they were nevertheless angered by the populist reforms of Servius Tullius. Together with his own daughter, a handful of patricians murdered the king. To dispose of the body, his daughter arranged for a chariot to drive it into the ground, and in addition conspired to have her husband, Tarquinius Superbus, named king in her father's stead.

The last Monarch

Tarquinius Superbus was the son of Tarquinius Priscus, but had been overlooked by the Senate in favor of Servius. He set about establishing absolute despotism by ignoring the *comitia* and purging the Senate of all men loyal to his predecessor. He executed Romans and embarked upon wars unimpeded, enraging not just the Senate but the general population as well.

In 509 BC dislike of the king erupted into outright rebellion. Tarquinius' son, Sextus, raped a noblewoman named Lucretia. The Romans drove Tarquinius from the city, only to have him attempt to stage a comeback after appealing for help from the Etruscan city of Clusium. Tarquinius was able to use his Etruscan roots to encourage the king of Clusium's assistance.

Desperate to avoid a resumption of the despotic monarchy, the Romans held off the Etruscan invasion and Tarquinius was doomed to die in exile in Etruria. The overthrow of the king signaled the end of the period of Roman Monarchy and ushered in the era of the Roman Republic.

Crown of golden ivy leaves.

Above: Panel painting of a Roman citizen. Under Servius Tullius, himself a former slave, the poorer classes, the plebs, gained representation. Despite these reforms, the patrician classes, who believed themselves to be descended from the original inhabitants of Rome, were still able to maintain control over the government.

The Etruscan Civilization

Before the rise of Rome, the Etruscan civilization dominated the north and central regions of the Italian peninsula. Relatively little is known about them, but they are believed to have wielded considerable influence over Rome in its formative years.

Where did the Etruscans come from?

It was long thought that the Etruscans were immigrants to Italy. The great historian, Herodotus, claimed that they originated amongst the Lydian people of Asia Minor (modern Turkey). He believed that the Lydian king split the population in two and sent half to build a new life in Italy under the command of his son, Tyrrhenus, after whom the Tyrrhenian Sea was named. The remainder of Lydians were allowed to stay in Asia Minor under the king's control. Herodotus' theory is not universally accepted. Many historians believe that the Etruscans were native to the peninsula and that Etruscan culture simply emerged when the Ancient Greeks and Carthaginians began to influence the pre-existing bronze-age tribes.

City-states

In the eighth century BC, the Etruscans developed a series of city-states in the north west of the peninsula, in what is modern Tuscany. The cities, which included Clusium, Veii and Perusia, were first linked together by a monarch but then later by a league. Each Etruscan city retained a degree of independence, which made it very easy for its enemies to divide and conquer them at a later stage.

The Etruscans were not simply urban dwellers, they were farmers, artists, and merchant seamen as well. It is believed that the Etruscans traveled large distances in the name of trade and established links across the Mediterranean.

Influence on Rome

Rome emerged at a time when the Etruscans dominated the surrounding regions. The extent of Etruscan influence over early Rome is not known because the Roman records for the period were lost when the Gauls sacked the city in 390 BC. The last three Roman kings were Etruscan, so a direct link between Rome and Etruria is almost certain. It is likely that the Romans learned a good deal from the Etruscans, from road building, sewage systems and gladiator fights to metalwork and sculpture.

Rome rapidly eclipsed the Etruscan city-states, which soon fell under Roman domination. Etruscan culture was gradually eroded and lost, but it was not until Sulla became dictator that the civilization was completely wiped out as a consequence of supporting Marius in the civil war.

The ruins of an Etruscan settlement at Cerveteri.

Roman Republic

Governing Rome

The government of the Roman Republic was founded upon the ashes of the Roman Monarchy. To avoid a return to the tyranny of King Tarquinius Superbus, a new form of leadership emerged.

Two-man rule

Rome was no longer to be led by one man, but two. They were called consuls, and by ruling together they were able to ensure that the will of one man was counterbalanced by that of the other. This was achieved through providing both consuls with a right of veto over the decisions of the other. Another way the system was designed to safeguard against despotism was to limit the terms of each consul to just one year, although they could be re-elected. This was changed in the second century BC when consuls were restricted to serving just one term. In the late Republic, however, these restrictions were flouted by powerful, ambitious men, who wanted to serve as leader for longer.

Consuls

The consuls were appointed by the *comitia centuriata*, an assembly that met annually to appoint the magistrates for the following year. It was presided over by the outgoing consuls. Decisions in the assembly were taken by a vote; citizens were organized into blocs, within which they were able to vote as a unit. There was a property qualification to be eligible to vote in this assembly and voting rights were staggered according to wealth; the most affluent citizens were given a disproportionately large influence over the assembly. The property qualification meant that the assembly was dominated by soldiers, who were expected to have a certain level of wealth to become soldiers in the first place. In addition to the consuls the *comitia centuriata* also appointed censors, *praetors,* and *aediles.*

Above: Part of the Forum, at the base of the Palatine Hill that became the center of Roman government. It was a complex of government buildings, temples, and private homes.

Below: Fragment from a sarcophagus which depicts the procession of the consuls of Acilia.

Censors

Censors were in charge of enumerating the population to see who could vote in the *comitia centuriata* elections and what voting rights they would have. In addition, the censor was tasked with maintaining public morality and could also instigate public works; for example, it was the censor, Appius Claudius, who commissioned the construction of a road from Rome to Capua, called the Appian Way, as well as Rome's first aqueduct, the Aqua Appia. *Praetors* were in control of law and justice but they also performed the role of minor generals when Rome was at war. *Aediles* managed the city of Rome; their responsibilities included the running of the markets, the temples, and the public games.

The Senate

The Senate managed to withstand the transition from the Monarchy to the Republic and in fact it became stronger as a result. The Senate continued to be an advisory body, as it had been to the kings, but in reality it had gained considerably more power. It set the agenda of the government and made recommendations to the magistrates who would take the executive decisions. Although the Senate was only dispensing advice, the magistrates almost always adhered to their suggestions (until the last century of the Republic). This effectively meant that the Senate had indirect executive powers. If a magistrate went against the Senate in a manner that was perceived to threaten the Republic, the Senate had the power to overturn his law. Senators were unpaid, but the position was highly prestigious and offered the opportunity for a man to carve out a power-base built upon the patronage of other citizens. This meant that senators became incredibly powerful and wealthy, but it also meant the Senate was often dogged by corruption. Senators were appointed for life, but could potentially be expelled by the censor, who was in charge of maintaining public morality. If a senator was believed to have acted indecently, the censor could remove him from the Senate.

Above: Ruins of the Capitol.
Below: A column base lies in the ruins of the Forum.

Patricians and Plebs

The patricians were the traditional elite of Ancient Rome. They were a group of several leading families who held a monopoly of power during the Roman Monarchy and the early Republican period. The word stems from the Latin for "fathers." They believed that their ancestors were the original inhabitants of Rome and wished to maintain the privileges they had built up over the years.

The remainder of Roman citizens were the plebeians. This term is relatively indiscriminate because plebs ranged from self-sufficient tradesmen to the urban poor who required handouts of free corn just to survive. They were marginalized from power by the patricians who frowned upon any kind of relationship between patricians and plebeians; intermarriage was strictly forbidden.

Over time the plebs sought to erode the political privileges given to the patricians and gain some of it for themselves. In the mid-Republican era, they had achieved this and the patrician class lost much of its power, although it managed to maintain its prestige.

For a time the patricians and the plebeians were both happy with the status quo, but in the second century BC, the rich began to get richer while the poor were getting poorer. This once again polarized the two groups and set Rome on a path of violence and anarchy that would eventually spell the end of the Republic.

Above: Fresco portrait of Terentius Neo and his wife found in a house in Pompeii. It is believed that the house belonged to the magistrate Terentius Neo and his brother Terentius Proculus, a baker. By the time of the first century AD, the class stystem of plebs and patricians had broken down.

Left: Pair of gold lionhead earrings.

Power to the plebs

The fact that these political institutions clearly favored the patricians did not go unnoticed amongst the plebs. Frustrated by their relative disenfranchisement, the plebs sought to gain political equality and used their superior numbers to that end. Knowing that Rome could not function without them, they literally abandoned the city on several occasions to force the patricians into conceding to their interests. This action was known as secession and it was used as a political weapon for the first time in 494 BC. On that occasion, the patricians were forced to allow the establishment of a plebeian council to encourage the plebs to return to Rome. The plebeian council was able to manage the affairs of the plebs through so-called plebiscites, but it had no jurisdiction over the lives of the patricians. The plebs also gained political representation at this time with the creation of the post of plebeian tribune. Initially the role had little power besides bringing the interest of the plebs to the government. However, over time, the role amassed more power, and eventually the plebeian tribune was granted the power of veto over anything suggested by the Senate that was considered counter to the interests of the plebs.

In 449 BC, the plebs again withdrew from the city in protest at the arbitrary legal system. The law had favored the patricians and the majority of the plebs were ignorant as to their rights, which had allowed patricians to gain the upper hand in trials. The patricians were left with little option but to appease the plebs; to entice them to return to Rome, the "Twelve Tables," a codified list of laws, was displayed in the Forum for all to see. This served to make Rome a more just society than it had been, although the judicial system was still far from fair.

Above: Carved gemstone ring with Roman portrait.

Below: Panel inscribed with the names of members of the Roman Senate.

The plebs continued to knock down the barriers that prohibited them from political power. In 367 BC, the Licinio-Sextian Law allowed plebs to be appointed as consuls, the first one being elected in 366.

Plebeian consul

The law stipulated that one of the two consuls should always be of plebeian origin. In 366 BC, a popular assembly, the *comitia tributa*, was formed. It was designed to appoint the ten plebeian tribunes as well as plebeian *aediles* and *quaestors*, who were officials in charge of financial affairs. Unlike with the *comitia centuriata*, there were no financial requisites upon the electorate and all Roman citizens were each allowed an indirect vote within a unit called a tribe. There were thirty-five tribes in total and each tribe had one vote within the committee. Although this was more democratic than the *comitia centuriata*, it still had its own disadvantages; the city of Rome had only four out of the thirty-five voting tribes, which did not reflect the population distribution. This meant that the individual vote of a resident of the city was not as significant in the popular assembly as the individual vote of a rural Roman. In 339, the popular assembly was given the power to circumvent the *comitia centuriata* and pass some of its own laws, provided they were agreeable to the Senate.

Balance of power

The plebs finally achieved something near political equality in 287 BC, after a long and hard-fought campaign. In this year, the plebs once again seceded from the city of Rome and forced the patricians to give them even more powers. The resulting Hortensia Law made plebiscites legally binding on all Roman citizens, not just the plebs; furthermore it gave the plebeian council the power to make laws without the Senate's agreement.

These changes might seem revolutionary, but the reality was somewhat more conservative because the patricians continued to be deeply involved. Laws were usually drafted by patricians and the Senate's approval was almost always solicited before the plebeian council pushed ahead.

Rome had somehow struck a balance between the plebs and the patricians for the first time, leading to a golden age for the Republic's political institutions. Such equilibrium lasted for over a century, but was eventually destroyed by a social crisis, which once again encouraged the plebs to push for even more power.

Above: Statues from the House of the Vestal Virgins in the Forum.

Below: View of the ruins of the Forum.

A Roman Villa

In the second century BC the wealthy urban elite of Rome seized upon the opportunity provided by a rural depression to push the traditional Roman smallholders off the land, and carve up large swathes of countryside for themselves. These new urban landowners began building second homes on their large country estates as retreats from their hectic lifestyles in the city.

Away from the bustle

Over time Rome became even busier as ever more smallholders were alienated from their land and pushed into the city to find work. Faced with Rome's growing population and the increasingly bustling atmosphere, many more affluent Romans sought sanctuary in a second home in the countryside. A villa culture quickly emerged; soon it became fashionable for all wealthy Romans to own one, or more, such properties.

Villas were usually set in many acres of land which the villa owner would put to agricultural use to make money. Although the farms were usually located very close to the villa, they were not always considered to be a part of the tranquil, rural idyll, and the villa was usually kept separate.

The farm would supply the villa with its food, wine, and olive oil, but otherwise most landlords were quite content to keep themselves and their villa apart. Agricultural labor was left to slaves and an administrator was usually appointed to manage the farm in the owner's absence.

Above: Detail from a fresco showing a garden scene with birds. The plastered walls in the villa's interior were painted, sometimes just with color washes, sometimes with decorative designs of pillars and geometric figures, but by the first century AD the fashion was for realistic frescoes.

Left: Mosaics on the interior walls of a villa at Pompeii.

Hypocausts

Many Roman villas had their own heating system called a *hypocaust*. The word *hypocaust* means "heat from below." Underfloor heating would have been especially welcome in the provincial villas in the northern provinces that were inhabited during the colder, winter months.

The way in which the *hypocaust* system worked was quite simple. The floor of the building was raised above ground level on a series of short pillars, leaving a void beneath the floor. At one end of the villa a fire in a small chamber just below floor level was maintained by a household slave. The hot air from the fire would be drawn through the void below the floors. In many *hypocaust* systems, hot air was channeled from the underground chamber into ducts between the walls of the villa, heating the walls as well.

Ingeniously, and efficiently, the same fire which heated the air for the *hypocaust* also heated water for the villa's baths and other hot water requirements.

Millefiori glass bowl from Alexandria. This may have been used as tableware or for purely decorative purposes in the villa.
Below: Diagram of a Hypocaust for heating a bath at a villa.

Below: A hypocaust at the Chedworth Roman Villa in the Cotswolds once trapped heat under the floor for use in a room or baths.

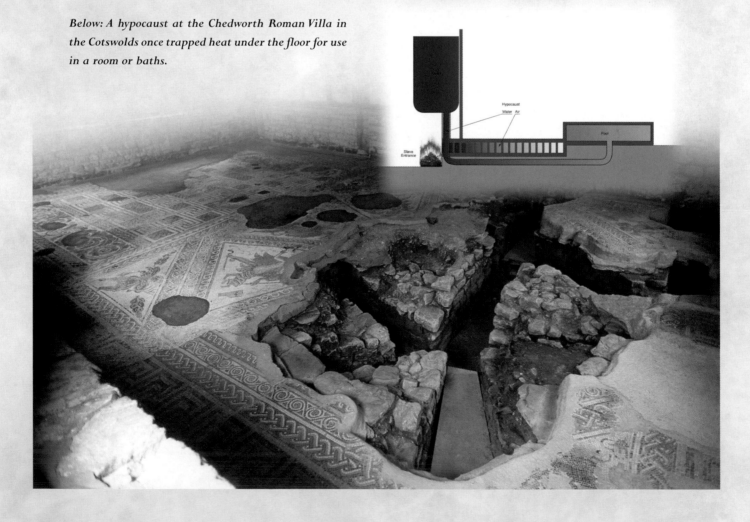

Lavish and extensive

Initially, Roman villas tended to be relatively conservative in size and decoration, but they soon became lavish and extensive as the Roman rich vied to outdo one another. Once the elite were made even richer by the plunder brought back from Rome's foreign conquests, they could afford to build larger and more extravagant villas.

Traditional Roman villas were largely similar in design to the houses that wealthy Roman families owned in the city, although they usually had much more space. Most villas were entered through an impressive tree-lined and colonnaded forecourt, which removed the need for the large atrium that townhouses would have had. The atrium was the customary place in which the family would meet guests and clients. Since most of these meetings would take place in the city home, there was less necessity for such a space in the country home and many villas would have had no atrium at all.

Al fresco dining

The villa would have all the facilities of the townhouse, including a lavish internal garden, bedrooms, kitchens and an outdoor dining room, which would be used more than the one in the city because Romans tended to visit the villa when the weather was better suited to *al fresco* dining.

Like Roman townhouses, Roman villas were sparsely furnished. The main item of furniture was a long couch, which was used for both dining and sleeping. Villas usually had very few tables on display because most were portable so that they could be moved between rooms to wherever they were needed, and stored out of sight when they were not. Roman villas were rarely cluttered; most possessions were hidden away in large wooden chests.

The property's isolated setting required it to have many additional amenities that were not common in town-houses; these included private baths, temples, and bakeries. Most villas would also have a water supply and drainage system to meet the needs of the household, the baths and the farms.

Ruins of a section of Hadrian's Villa, a lavish country residence to the north-east of Rome, near Tivoli.

Seafront villas

As demand for villas grew, many were built without farmland attached or with just a sufficient amount of land to meet the needs of the villa. It became common for villas to be built along the seafront, where the cool sea breezes would contrast favorably with the stuffy heat of the Roman summer.

The Bay of Naples, to the south of Rome, became a particularly popular location for coastal villas, and a great number were discovered in the ruins of Pompeii and Herculaneum. Of all the towns in the Bay of Naples, the resort of Baiae was the one that became most linked with villa culture and the hedonism that became associated with the Roman upper classes.

Julius Caesar built a villa in the town, which encouraged many of Rome's elite to buy summer homes there. Baiae remained popular over the years for its medicinal sulfur springs, cool climate, and rich vegetation.

Fresco showing a seaside villa.

Villas across the Empire

Over time, villas were built across the entire Empire, as native elites and Roman administrators sought to emulate the lives of their counterparts in Rome. Provincial villas were often fashioned in the style of Roman architecture and were designed with all the amenities enjoyed by their Roman counterparts, including central heating systems, Roman artwork, bathhouses, bakeries, and temples.

Outside of Italy, villa culture often had a distinctively different character, especially in the less urbanized provinces of Gaul and Britannia. In such places, villas were used less as a rural getaway and more often as a permanent residence. This meant that the villas were not usually kept separate from the surrounding farmland and were often integrated with the local economy.

Gold oil Lamp
from Pompeii.

Mosaics

Floor mosaics have been discovered in the ruins of villas across the Roman Empire. Many have remained in excellent condition and usually prove to be among the most interesting finds at an excavated villa. Mosaics comprise many small fragments of stone or glass, called *tesserae*, arranged in intricate patterns on a bed of wet plaster.

Mosaics depended upon the personal taste of the owner of the villa, as well as the fashions of the day. A guilloche pattern of interwoven rope was especially popular, but a variety of shapes and patterns can be found. Numerous pictorial mosaics have also been discovered; most consist of a single image, often of animals or gods, but some comprise elaborate scenes, such as men hunting, gladiators dueling, or an illustration of a famous myth or legend.

Frescoes

Some Romans chose to have mosaics on their walls as well, but frescoes were more common. A fresco is a type of mural; the term is derived from the term "fresh" because the artist would apply the paint directly on to wet plaster. This technique allowed the paint to permanently bond with the wall and has meant that several examples have lasted until this day, although many have faded over the centuries.

Unfortunately, the walls of most villas have either been demolished or collapsed over time, but volcanic ash prevented this from happening to the villas surrounding Pompeii and Herculaneum. As a result, some of the best examples of villa frescoes are to be found at these sites.

Inside a house in the ruins of Ostia. Richly decorated floor mosaics were an obvious sign of the villa owner's wealth.

War of Expansion

From the its modest origins on the Palatine Hill to its position at the heart of
Italy Rome underwent several centuries of aggressive expansion, so that by 270 BC the Romans
held full control of the Italian peninsula south of the River Arno.

Dominating Latium

Initially Rome had to gain domination of Latium. In 493
BC, the city joined the Latin League, a union of Latin-
speaking settlements, for the purposes of common trade
and protection.

Alba Longa was the chief city of the Latin League and
Rome had to stand in its shadow. It was not until the
reign of Tullus Hostilius, when he reputedly ordered that
the Alban king be torn in two, that Rome was able to
dominate the League for the first time.

The Latin War

After this time, states of the Latin League were only able
to challenge Roman dominance once. In 340, they tried
to exploit Roman weakness to stage the "Latin War." This
lasted for two years until Rome was eventually
successful; the Latin League was dissolved and its
members were subsumed into the Roman state as
municipia, with full citizenship rights.

Triumph over the Etruscans

In addition to dominating its neighboring Latins, Rome
faced challenges from the various small tribes which
littered central Italy. During both the Monarchy and the
early Republic, successful wars continued intermittently
with the Etruscans and the Sabine as well as the
neighboring Aequi and Volsci. Rome's crowning
achievement in these infant years of the Republic was
perhaps its defeat of the nearby Etruscan city of Veii in
396 after a decade-long siege.

The city of Veii was razed to the ground, and its
population killed or sold into slavery. The victory
presented Rome with both short- and long-term
economic gains. In the short term, there was plunder
sent back to Rome, but in the longer term, Rome had
removed a key trading rival from central Italy and
heralded the decline of the neighboring Etruscans.

*Detail from the Palestrina Mosaic showing
the Nile river delta during the flooding
season. Palestrina was a town in what
is now the Lazio region which
fought in the "Latin Wars"
against Rome.*

Humiliation by the Gauls

Roman glory was short-lived, as they suffered a humiliating defeat at the hands of the Gauls, just a few years later in 390 BC. The Gauls, a group of tribes which inhabited the region of Western Europe in the area centralized on modern-day France, had been pushing into Etruria in the preceding decades and in 391 threatened the Etruscan city of Clusium. The city appealed to Rome for assistance, an indication of Rome's new, powerful regional status.

The Romans sent a delegation to negotiate with the northern invaders, but this came to nothing when a member of the Roman delegation killed one of his counterparts from Gaul. This resulted in the ire of the Gauls who, under the leadership of Brennus, marched on Rome, defeating the Roman Army in the Battle of Allia and capturing the city.

Bas-relief from a metope (a section of a frieze) depicting a combat scene.

Reconstruction

Rome was exceptionally fortunate. Although much was destroyed and looted, the city was not totally razed to the ground and a war indemnity was paid to encourage the Gauls to withdraw from the city without murdering or enslaving the population.

The following years were spent rebuilding the city structures and defences, as well as Rome's regional prestige. Efforts also had to go into satisfying the increasing demand for land and food as Rome's population grew, an imperative which would take them into further conflict.

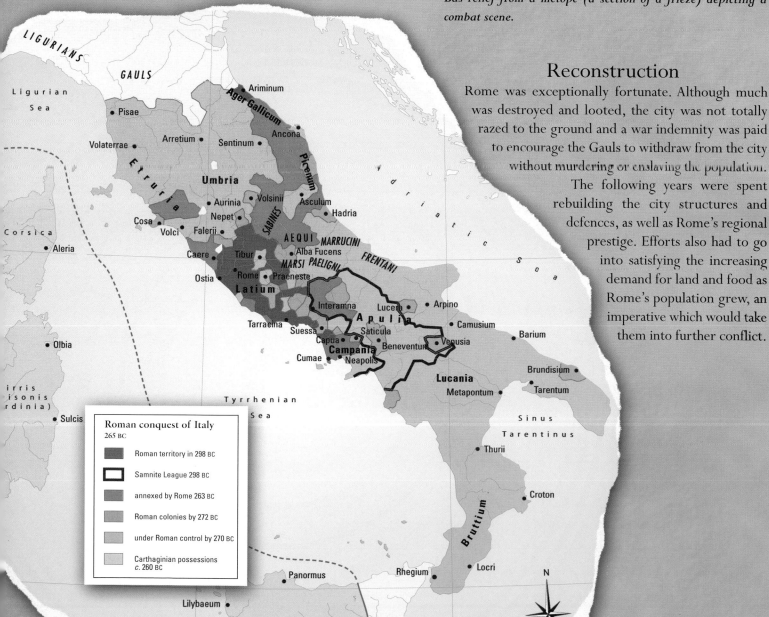

Roman conquest of Italy
265 BC

- Roman territory in 298 BC
- Samnite League 298 BC
- annexed by Rome 263 BC
- Roman colonies by 272 BC
- under Roman control by 270 BC
- Carthaginian possessions *c.* 260 BC

War with the Samnites

Roman expansion in the fourth century BC brought them into conflict with the Samnite tribes of the Apennine Mountains. The Samnites were a strong military nation and engaged the Romans in three prolonged wars, the first beginning in 344 BC, and the last not ending until 290.

During the Second Samnite War, in 321, the Romans suffered a humiliating defeat in the Battle of the Caudine Forks, which gave the Samnites the upper hand for several years.

The third and final war began in 298 when the Samnites enlisted help from a number of Rome's other enemies, including the Celts and several Etruscan cities.

In 295, the Battle of Sentium became the defining moment in that war. Vast numbers of men perished on both sides, but the Romans came out of the battle in the best shape, which allowed them to crush the Samnites once and for all. Victory against the Samnites handed Rome the control of central Italy.

Maintaining new territories

Rome had learned the lesson from the "Latin War" that it was important to avoid uprisings in conquered territories when the city was distracted and appeared weak, in this case from its ongoing wars of expansion. Thus it was crucial that the Romans consolidated the land they had already conquered.

This gave rise to prudent occupation policies. Troublesome areas were totally and brutally suppressed, while less unruly occupied peoples were met with a benevolent response and were allowed to continue much as before, with the understanding that they were now subject to Roman authority.

In addition, colonization tactics were employed to dilute the native populations of a territory with Roman citizens, so as to obstruct any united uprising against Roman rule in the future.

These shrewd occupation tactics, employed during the early days of Rome, continue to be reflected in the policies of nations across the globe in our modern world.

Detail from a sarcophagus relief which shows horse chariots in use.

Expanding southward

During the third century BC, Rome began an expansion into southern Italy. This demarcates an important shift in the nation's history. Rome was no longer facing wars against the smaller tribes of central Italy, instead it moved into competition with some of the greatest powers in the ancient world, Carthage and Greece.

Among Rome's first forays into the region was a response to the request for assistance from the city of Thurii against the Greek Lucanians. Rome sent a fleet to investigate, which was promptly sunk by Tarentum, the leading Greek city-state on the Italian peninsula.

Pyrrhic victories and defeats

In 280 BC, fearing that the rise of Rome would eat away at Greek dominance in southern Italy, Tarentum paid for Pyrrhus, king of Epirus, to come to their rescue. Pyrrhus brought with him an army of 25,000 men, as well as a number of elephants, a war weapon the Romans did not have, and which proved decisive in scaring the Roman Army from the field in the initial battles.

Pyrrhus won one of the first great battles at Asculum in 279. However, Pyrrhus' victory was at a huge cost to his own army, which resulted in the phrase "pyrrhic victory," for a victory that comes at such a high price.

In addition to fighting the Roman advance, Pyrrhus attempted to assist Greek cities in Sicily against the Carthaginians menacing from the west of the island. Dividing his troops allowed Rome time to rejuvenate its forces and march further south, eventually besieging Tarentum in 275 BC. Despite successes in Sicily, heavy losses in the south of Italy encouraged Pyrrhus to withdraw his forces back to Greece, leaving Tarentum to fall to the Romans.

Above: Coin depicting warrior with shield and hatchet.

Right: Wall fresco depicting a bust of the mythical warrior figure, Hercules. The cult of Hercules was adopted from the Greek, Heracles, early in Rome's history, perhaps as early as the sixth century BC. Hercules embodies all the masculine virtues.

The Mercenary War

The financial indemnity imposed by the Romans, combined with the economic pinch from years of warfare, ensured that Carthage retreated from the international scene to deal with more pressing domestic concerns. A "Mercenary War" broke out between 240 and 238 BC. It was started by mercenaries, employed by the Carthaginians during the First Punic War, who had not been paid as a result of Carthage's dire financial situation. Although the war was primarily confined to North Africa, mercenaries also became troublesome on the island of Sardinia, which was still nominally under Carthaginian control. Unable to police Sardinia as well as North Africa, Carthage could do little but watch the Romans step in and annex the island.

The Saguntum Crisis

In the 230s, with the Mercenary War won, Carthage returned to the international scene, desperate to regain its former glory and fulfil its imperial ambitions. Rather than challenging Rome for its former possessions in Sicily and Sardinia, Carthage looked elsewhere, to the Iberian Peninsula, in what is modern-day Spain. The Carthaginians had already settled the coastal regions in the south of the peninsula before the war, but between 237 and 219, they moved deeper into the interior, consolidating control over the region at the expense of the local Celtic tribes.

Carthage's resurgent expansionism was not unremarked in Rome. But the Romans were busy conquering the Gallic tribes to the north of the River Arno and expanding toward the Alps, capturing Mediolanum,

modern-day Milan, in 222 BC. Therefore, the Romans resolved to make an agreement with the Carthaginians. Carthage would not expand north of the River Ebro, and Rome would not expand south of it. Ostensibly, this handed control of the Iberian Peninsula to Carthage.

However, the agreement was worth very little. Carthage's invasion of Spain had helped her recover financially and politically from the first Punic War, and Roman-Carthaginian rivalry over the Mediterranean once again began to flare up.

The flashpoint was to be the city of Saguntum, located south of the Ebro, in Carthage's sphere of influence. Rome provocatively established a protectorate over the city, and Carthage responded by laying siege to it in 219. When the city finally capitulated to the Carthaginians, Rome once again declared war.

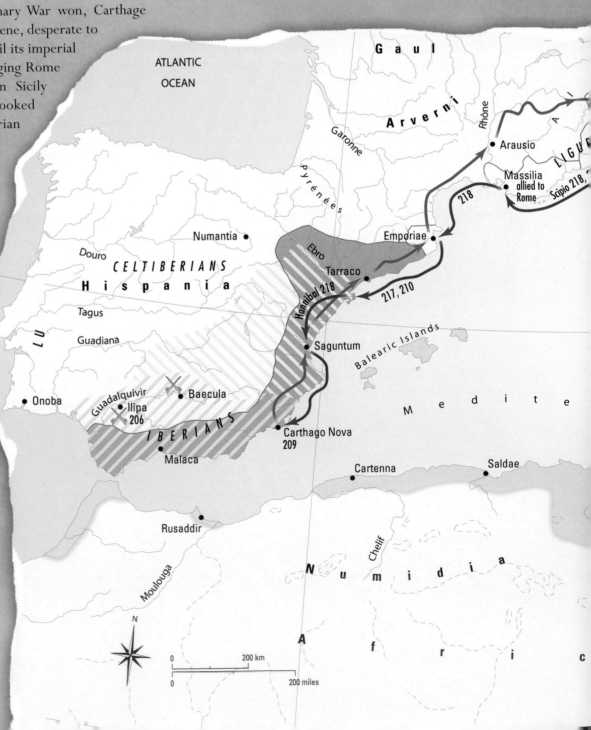

The Second Punic War

The second Roman-Carthaginian conflict was certain to be different to the first because of Carthage's new European base in Spain and also because of its new general, Hannibal Barca, who had been appointed in 221 BC. Hannibal was vehemently anti-Roman and it was said that he had sworn an oath never to make peace with Rome.

Hannibal's advance

Hannibal resolved to take the fight to the Roman heartland in the Italian peninsula. From his position in Spain, he determined to execute an overland invasion, which required his forces to traverse both the Alps and the Pyrenees, a spectacular feat that was to become legendary. In 218 Hannibal crossed the River Ebro with in excess of 100,000 men and a number of elephants. After crossing the Pyrenees, Hannibal had to fend off the local tribes that were hampering his progress, before crossing the Alps into Italy. Only three quarters of the men who had started the journey with Hannibal made it to Italy. Many had died along the treacherous route, but many had been strategically left behind by Hannibal who was unsure of the loyalty of some of his forces.

The Romans did not hinder Hannibal's advance from Spain to Italy. The Roman Army could have routed him in the Rhone valley but was distracted by rebellions in Cremona and Placentia. Desperate to halt Hannibal's remarkable progress, a Roman Army, commanded by consul Publius Cornelius Scipio, tried to defeat Hannibal's force before it had a chance to recuperate from its arduous journey across the Alps. In October 218, the Romans engaged Hannibal in the Battle of Ticinus, which resulted in a Carthaginian victory, in spite of the troops' fatigue.

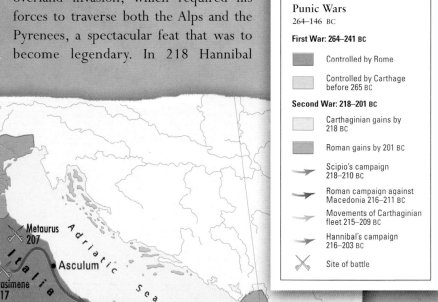

Punic Wars
264–146 BC

First War: 264–241 BC

- Controlled by Rome
- Controlled by Carthage before 265 BC

Second War: 218–201 BC

- Carthaginian gains by 218 BC
- Roman gains by 201 BC
- Scipio's campaign 218–210 BC
- Roman campaign against Macedonia 216–211 BC
- Movements of Carthaginian fleet 215–209 BC
- Hannibal's campaign 216–203 BC
- Site of battle

Two elephants walk below a ruined arch during a British Alpine Expedition to reconstruct Hannibal's journey across the Alps.

Hannibal

Hannibal Barca, son of the Carthaginian general Hamilcar Barca, is often cited as one of the greatest military commanders in history, most notably for his inspirational strategies and tactics. The name Barca is actually an epithet meaning "lightning," although his descendants continued to use it as a surname.

Legend tells that at the age of nine, Hannibal asked his father if he could join a mission to create a military base in Hispania. His father agreed but only after Hannibal had sworn that he would make the Roman Republic his lifelong enemy.

Like father, like son

Hamilcar, like his son, was a great and well-respected general who had several military successes before he was finally killed in combat. After Hamilcar's death in 229 BC, his son-in-law Hasdrubal the Fair took command but was murdered in 221. Hannibal then became commander of the Carthaginian Army. He had no doubt inherited many of his father's characteristics, immediately embarking on a

First-century BC sculpture of the head and shoulders of the Carthaginian general, Hannibal, who attacked Rome in 218 BC.

series of aggressive attacks that culminated in his famous journey across the mountains to fight the Romans on their home ground.

End to his career

Hannibal's military career finally ended at the Battle of Zama on October 19, 202. He then successfully transferred his skills to the position of "suffet" or chief magistrate. To this position he brought authority and power, pushing through several important and popular reforms. In 195, after the Romans demanded his resignation from the by now client state of Carthage, he went into exile and continued to work with various military campaigns before poisoning himself in 183 in order to avoid certain capture by the Romans; he was sixty-four.

For many years after his death the name Hannibal Barca was synonymous with fear and terror throughout the Roman Empire. The expression "Hannibal *ad portas*" (Hannibal is at the Gates) was coined by Romans and used in times of anxiety or disaster.

Painting from the Renaissance period depicting Hannibal fighting a Roman legion near the Alps.

A resounding blow to Rome

Although the victory at Ticinus was only a token one, and the Roman Army was able to regroup to fight another day, it was also an important one because many north Italian tribes opted to switch sides and join Hannibal, and in doing so, replenished the ranks of his depleted army. The Roman commander Scipio's army retreated to the River Trebia where he was joined by the army of his co-consul, Sempronius, from Sicily. Sempronius insisted upon a direct attack on Hannibal, a plan which Hannibal discovered and pre-empted with his own invasion of the Roman camp early in the morning in December 218 BC. He was able to catch the Romans unprepared for the campaign, both cold and hungry, and dealt a resounding defeat; Scipio and Sempronius lost an estimated 30,000 men.

A war of attrition: "Fabian Tactics"

In the wake of the humiliating defeat, the Senate recalled the consuls and replaced them with two new ones, Gaius Flaminius and Gnaeus Servilius Geminus, who fared little better against Hannibal. Desperate to score a victory, Flaminius allowed his legions to be lured into an ambush in the Battle of Lake Trasimene. Hannibal's Army used the lake to enclose the Romans by denying them an escape route. Once penned in, Hannibal's forces proceeded to butcher their enemy in what was another decisive Carthaginian victory. Flaminius was killed in action and the fearful Senate elected a dictator, Fabius

Maximus. His response was to avoid pitched battles with Hannibal and instead try to wear down his army through a prolonged war of attrition. This strategy continues to be known as "Fabian tactics" in his honor, or rather his dishonor because Maximus' fellow Romans often expressed contempt for such a seemingly un-heroic strategy, especially because Hannibal was able to push further south as a result.

Funerary stele showing a warrior on horseback.

The dictatorship was ended, and Maximus was replaced with consuls Lucius Aemilius Paullus and Gaius Terentius Varro, who opted for a more active approach to Hannibal as a contrast to Maximus' unpopular policies. Their humiliation in the Battle of Cannae in 216, where Rome suffered its worst defeat of the war, seemed to vindicate Maximus' strategy. Rome had amassed a superior-sized army and the consuls thought they could defeat Hannibal.

Ruins in the port of Ostia. Although now inland, this would have been an important port in the strategy against the Carthaginians.

Rome loses allegiance

In the face of the consuls' strategy, Hannibal used military genius to defeat the larger Roman Army. He lured them in to his own lines and then outflanked his enemy using a crescent formation. The Romans were encircled by the Carthaginians, who once again completely destroyed their enemy. The Battle of Cannae could have proved a decisive turning point in the war, because a number of southern Italian tribes detached from their allegiance to Rome and expressed loyalty to Carthage instead. This led Hannibal to resolve to press further south to consolidate control there, rather than march on Rome.

Scipio drives the Carthaginians from Spain

Although the Romans had stumbled from one humiliation to another during the first years of the war, there was an ongoing success story in Spain. In 218 BC, an army under Gnaeus Scipio, brother of the general at Trebia, crossed into Spain with the aim of denying Hannibal his Spanish base for future resource and finance replenishment. Battles continued in Spain until 211 when Scipio was defeated and killed. In 209 he was replaced by his brother's son, named, like his father, Publius Cornelius Scipio. Over the following three years Scipio managed to drive the Carthaginians out of Spain and returned to Italy in 205. The loss of Spain was a blow to Hannibal. He no longer had a semi-independent base and had to pay greater heed to the interests of Carthage itself. Carthage's paramount concern was defence of its heartlands and this was exploited by Scipio who resolved to send an army to conquer the capital city itself. In 204, he reached North Africa and this meant that Hannibal was recalled from Italy. He had to abandon his gains in the south and his years of campaigning became redundant as he returned to Carthage the following year, 203 BC.

Carthage sues for peace

The endgame of the second Punic War was the Battle of Zama in 202. After so many defeats in Italy, the Romans overcame the Carthaginians in this North African campaign, and Carthage sued for peace. The treaty imposed by Rome was an even greater punishment than in the first war. Carthage was forced to pay 10,000 talents and its naval capacity was restricted to just ten ships for the sole purpose of combating piracy. In addition, the treaty stipulated that should Carthage ever wish to raise an army, it would need to gain permission from Rome first. Essentially, Carthage's power had been well and truly eclipsed by Rome, but it would be another fifty years before the death blow was dealt.

Left: The remains of a Roman road crossing the Sierra de Gredos, mountains in central Spain. During the war with Carthage, Spain was an important battleground and when Scipio drove the Carthaginians out of Spain in 205 BC it was the beginning of the end for Hannibal's campaigning.

The Third Punic War

In the aftermath of the second war, Hannibal reinvented himself as a statesman, to the alarm of Rome, who demanded that he be handed over to them. Rather than giving himself up or precipitating a war, Hannibal went into exile, crossing the various kingdoms of the Middle East for over a decade until the Romans ordered the king of Bithynia to give him up. He obliged, but Hannibal committed suicide in 183 BC to deny the Romans the pleasure of humiliating him before killing him.

"Carthage must be destroyed"

Carthage itself outlived Hannibal by almost forty years. The Romans never got over their fear and mistrust of Carthage, despite its weakened status. Cato captured the popular sentiment by ending every speech to the Senate with the words "Carthage must be destroyed." In spite of this ingrained hostility, the die was cast by neighboring Numidia rather than Rome itself. Numidia shrewdly antagonized the Carthaginians by attacking their cities, knowing that Carthage could not do anything about it because they first had to get permission from Rome. Numidia had helped Rome in the Battle of Zama and so Rome always favored the Numidians in such disputes. In 150, Carthage finally rose to the bait and resolved to disregard Rome's restrictions and repel the Numidians. This placed them in violation of the treaty and Rome demanded an impossible price for peace; all Carthaginians would have to abandon Carthage and move into the African interior. Unable to comply with this unreasonable request, the Carthaginians had no option but to resort to yet another war with Rome.

Rome gains a foothold in Africa

The Third Punic War lasted from 149 to 146 and was essentially a battle for Carthage itself. In 146 when Rome was eventually successful it literally wiped Carthage of the face of the map. The city was completely razed to the ground and the whole area was sown with salt so that nothing else would ever grow and the city could never re-emerge. Most of the population was killed and the remainder sold into slavery. Rome occupied Carthage's former territories and gained itself a foothold on the African continent. However, Carthage did not entirely disappear because a new Roman settlement was eventually built upon the site and Tunis, the capital of Tunisia, stands nearby the ruins of Carthage to this day.

The Romans were so thorough in expunging the Carthaginians from history that relatively little is known about them, in spite of their crucial importance in the western Mediterranean before the rise of Rome. Much of our knowledge comes from Rome itself and therefore much is assumed to be biased and unreliable.

Above: Wall fresco of a gladiator with a lion.

Left: Detail of a gladiator and a leopard from a mosaic of battling gladiators.

Wild cats, such as lions and leopards, are recurring images in Ancient Rome. They are part of the exotic appeal of Africa and their strength and aggression being controlled by Romans is a powerful metaphor.

Granary of the Empire

Northern Africa was a vital source of grain, which earned it the title "the granary of Rome," but in reality, it exported grain right across the Empire. The grain supply was extremely important to Rome because the masses were appeased with free handouts, which thousands relied on for survival. When Vespasian overthrew Vitellius in 69 AD, he first took Alexandria in Egypt to gain command of the grain supply, prudently aware that a grip on this commodity was vital to controlling Rome.

Africa's resources

Not only were Rome's northern African territories important as a source of grain, they also provided a number of other valuable resources. Africa replaced Spain as Rome's chief source of oil, used for a wide variety of purposes in everyday Roman life. Hunting was a popular activity and northern Africa was a major source of various animals for the games in Rome and other parts of the Empire. A trade in ivory from elephant tusks also emerged in the region. North Africa also developed considerable importance in the fishing industry; not only in fishing itself, but in the salting of fish, as well as making *garum*, a popular fish sauce.

Egypt and Cyrenaica retain independence from Rome

The Hellenic rulers of Egypt's Ptolemaic dynasty maintained their independence much longer than most of their Greek neighbors. Egypt played an important role in the last civil war of the Roman Republic, when Mark Antony entrenched himself there with the Egyptian queen, Cleopatra. In 30 BC, Octavian defeated Mark Antony, forcing the suicide of both Antony and Cleopatra. Octavian murdered her son and turned Egypt into a province under the direct control of the Emperor.

Neighboring Cyrenaica, was originally under the control of the Egyptian king, but it was turned into a separate province at the end of the first century BC for the king's son, Ptolemy Apion to rule. Ptolemy Apion bequeathed the province to Rome upon his death in 96 BC.

Although Cyrenaica and Egypt were relatively peaceful under Roman occupation, antagonisms between the Greek, Jewish, and Christian population simmered beneath the surface. Fighting between Greeks and Jews forced the Romans to annex Cyrenaica outright in 74 BC and a Jewish Rebellion in 116 AD, caused great loss of life, not least during the brutal counterinsurgency launched by Trajan, and continued by Hadrian.

The Severan Forum of Leptis Magna, Libya. Leptis Magna was the birthplace of Emperor Severus who made his African hometown a flourishing metropolis. It was one of the three cities, with Sabratha and Oea, which came to make up Tripoli, Libya.

African Cities

Leptis Magna: birthplace of Severus

The Emperor Septimius Severus made his African hometown, Leptis Magna, a flourishing metropolis, rivaling the Empire's many great cities. He built a new forum with a splendid colonnaded street leading up to an improved harbor.

The city's fertile hinterland had allowed Leptis Magna to thrive even before Severus became Emperor at the end of the second century AD. The city had undergone significant development during the Augustan age and Hadrian had built a vast bathing complex over fifty years before Severus became Emperor.

Carthage rises from the ruins

When the Romans defeated the Carthaginians after the Third Punic War, their city was razed to the ground and it was alleged that salt was sown into the earth so that nothing else could grow on the spot. Utica replaced Carthage as the main city in the region and became the capital city of Roman Africa. However, the ruined vicinity of Carthage proved too good a source of grain for the Romans to pass over and a new colony was founded on the site on the orders of Augustus.

Timgad and Antinopolis

The most notable cities founded by the Romans in North Africa were Timgad in Numidia and Antinopolis in Egypt. Trajan had built Timgad in 100 AD as a military colony to settle his veterans. The city was situated in a strategically beneficial area to deter an insurrection by the native Berber population. The city is remembered for its exceptionally square shape and gridiron street plan, which testifies to its functional, military origin.

Antinopolis was founded by Hadrian on the site where his lover, Antinous, drowned in the Nile. The city was developed in the Hellenic style Hadrian so adored, and functioned largely as a shrine to his lost lover. Antinous was deified and a temple was built in the city in his honor.

Mosaic which shows a reclining nude holding a basket from the entrance to the women's baths in the Musée de Timgad in Algeria.

Mummified crocodile from Ancient Rome— a testament to the influence of Egypt on the Romans.

Conquest of Greece

While Rome contended with its Carthaginian rival in the western Mediterranean, politics in the East became increasingly tumultuous. After the death of Alexander the Great in 323 BC, his vast Macedonian Empire fell into decline, resulting in the emergence of a number of smaller, rivalrous Greek states.

The first Macedonian War

Rome had already expressed a limited interest in the eastern sphere during the interlude between the first and second Punic Wars when it conquered Illyria, which lay on the opposite coast of the Adriatic to Italy. Roman expansion into the region alarmed the Macedonian king, Philip V, who entered into an alliance with the Carthaginians against Rome during the Second Punic War in 215 BC. The alliance meant that Rome and Macedon were now at war, but with Hannibal running amok across the Italian Peninsula, Rome responded by allying with Macedon's rival, the Aetolian League. This was a shrewd move because it kept the Macedonians in check without Rome having to deflect troops from the defence of Rome. In 206, however, the weary Aetolians agreed to a peace and the first Macedonian War ended, with very little Roman involvement in the process.

A second war with Macedonia

Macedon was not spared direct Roman involvement in the Second Macedonian War, which lasted from 200 to 196 BC. With the war in the West won, Rome would have probably begun looking to expand into the prosperous East at some point, and a call for assistance from smaller Greek states provided a pretext. Philip V had attempted to reassert Macedonian control over the eastern Mediterranean in order to regain something of the former glory Macedon enjoyed during the days of

Alexander the Great. Fearful of such Macedonian expansionism, two smaller Greek states, Rhodes and Pergamum, appealed to Rome for help, and the war began. There was one decisive battle in the conflict, in 197 at Cynoscephalae. The Romans won, and imposed a heavy indemnity, which was to mark the eclipse of the once great Macedonian Empire for ever.

With Macedon pacified, Rome withdrew its troops out of respect for its Greek allies, but this did not mean that Rome had no political interests in the region, as the king of the Seleucid Greeks, Antiochus III, discovered to his misfortune. With the decline of Macedon as a regional hegemonist, Antiochus decided to expand into the region. This brought him into conflict with Rome who returned to the region and expelled the Seleucids in the Battle of Thermopylae in 191. The Romans may not have maintained an army in Greece, but Rome was there to stay.

In 333 BC Alexander of Macedonia (Alexander the Great) won a great victory against the Persian king, Darius III at Issus, a site close to present-day Iskenderum in Turkey. Alexander was revered in Rome as a great military strategist. At the Battle of Issus Alexander's men were outnumbered by three to one. The defeat was the first for Darius, pictured here in his Battle chariot, and marked the beginning of the end of Persian power in the region. This mosaic was found in the House of the Faun in Pompeii.

Macedonia challenges again

After Philip V of Macedon died in 179 BC, his son, Perseus, became king. Perseus, like his father, had delusions of Macedonian grandeur and attempted once again to reassert Macedonian control over Greece. He went on a charm offensive with neighboring Greek states, but this aroused the suspicion of Pergamum, which again called upon Rome. In 171 BC, the Romans declared war for the third time, fearing that Macedon might be able to resume its position and wrestle political domination of Greece from Rome. The decisive battle was in 168 at Pydna. In the aftermath of another Roman victory, Rome ensured that Macedon would not be able to challenge it again by dividing the territory into four and enslaving thousands, including the Macedonian elites.

Rome crushes Macedonia and its allies

Two decades later, while Rome was distracted, an imposter pretending to be the son of King Perseus, claimed the Macedonian throne. Rome invaded and saw off the challenger by 148, but its patience with Macedon had evaporated and it was incorporated as a province of Rome. With a permanent Roman settlement to the north, other Greek states were alarmed and the Achaean League in the south declared war. This act achieved nothing; it gave Rome cause to expand its control even further to the south in crushing the League.

By 146 Greece was essentially overrun by Rome. The Romans ensured the compliance of the remaining Greek states by making an example of the wealthy city of Corinth in that year. Corinth was a member of the Achaean League and in retribution for declaring war the Romans burned the city to the ground, killed all the men and sold all the women into slavery. Brutal as it was, it was an effective symbol that ensured obedience from Greece for many years.

Above: A large marble head sits near the Baths of Hadrian in Aphrodisias, an ancient Greco-Roman city in the Anatolian uplands of Turkey.

Right: Marble relief sculpture with scenes from Cumae. In the eighth century BC, the Greeks had established the colony of Cumae, in the area around the Bay of Naples.

Hellenization of Rome

Greek culture, education, and values began to have a direct impact upon Rome. The invasion of the Greek city states of southern Italy had begun this process of Hellenization, but it was not until the invasion of Greece that the impact became profound. Greek culture was more extravagant than the Romans were used to; Romans had traditionally emphasized qualities such as duty and frugality. For example, one of the early Republic's great figures was a Roman named Cincinnatus who responded to the call of duty, stopped farming during a time of crisis and became dictator for a few weeks. When the crisis was resolved he returned to his farm to live a simple life. In contrast to Cincinnatus' example, the invasion of Greece ushered in an era of ostentatious living that was to define Rome during the Empire.

New fashions and foods

Greek life infused into Roman life in many different ways. Romans sought out Greek art and treasures for their homes and Greek architectural styles became increasingly popular, especially Greco-pillars. Greek foods and fashion began replacing Roman foods and fashions and it was around this time that Roman men, in line with their Greek counterparts, preferred not to sport beards.

Greek intellectuals find a home in Rome

Rome was also a magnet for Greek intellectuals who were in demand as tutors for young Romans, or welcomed into Roman academic and political circles. In addition, Greek doctors found ready employment; for example, the Greek physician, Galen, moved to Rome during the late Republic and his ideas on medicine became sacrosanct for hundreds of years.

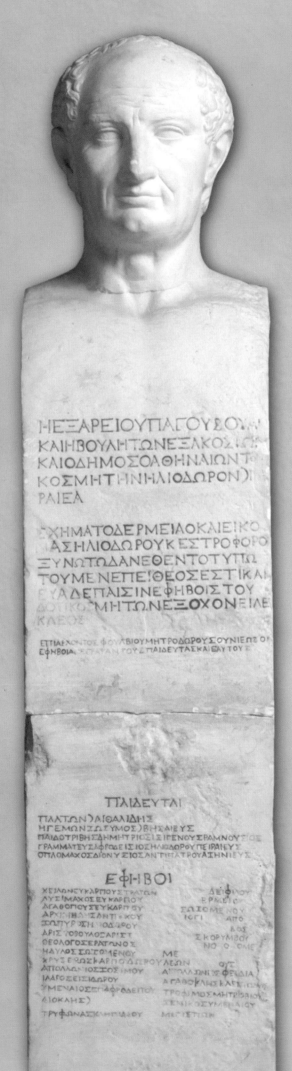

Left: Directional pillar with the bust of the Greek writer Heliodorus.

Below: Roman fresco painting depicting the Greek story of the sacrifice of Iphigenia. Roman life became increasingly influenced by Greek culture and lifestyle.

Alexander of Macedonia

Alexander III of Macedon, who lived between 356 and 323 BC, is remembered as one of the most successful generals of all time. He conquered a vast Empire, spanning from Greece all the way to the Himalayas in northern India.

Formidable enemy

The Persian Empire, which had hitherto been the leading power in the Middle East, was Alexander's most formidable enemy. After crossing into Asia Minor, his army won a score of battles and sieges, which brought Judea, Egypt and the area of modern Turkey quickly under Macedonian control.

In 331 Alexander and his men pushed eastward, soon overrunning Mesopotamia and Babylon before capturing the Persian capital, Persepolis in 330. He maintained his eastward momentum into the Hindu Kush until the Himalayas prevented him from marching further east. Thus, he turned into India, maintaining that southward advance until 325 when he started tracking back to the west.

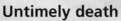

Untimely death

Alexander died unexpectedly in 323 AD at just thirty-two years old. With his passing, his vast Empire was fragmented among his various generals and friends; the all too brief glory days of Macedon were over.

Revered by Rome

Alexander the Great was a contemporary of the early days of Rome. While he was invading much of the known world, Rome was engaged in a war with the Samnites for dominance of the southern Italian peninsula.

Throughout the Ancient Roman civilization, Alexander became a revered icon, especially for the Emperors, who sought to emulate both his success and the magnitude of his legacy.

The historian Suetonius records that Julius Caesar was jealous of Alexander's accomplishments and that the Emperor Caligula took to wearing Alexander's breastplate, which he had taken from the dead king's tomb at Alexandria. In the second century AD, the Emperor Trajan was encouraged by Alexander's triumphs to push into the East, until old age forced him to halt his ambitions at the Persian Gulf.

Medicine

Roman Medicine was greatly influenced by the Ancient Greeks. Based upon a mixture of limited scientific knowledge and religious convictions, many of their ideas seem ridiculous today. Nevertheless, Roman medicine continued to dominate its field for more than a century after the collapse of the Empire.

Faith Healing

Religion played an important role in Roman medicine. Many Romans believed that illnesses were an indication of the disapproval of the gods and therefore many treatments involved a patient attempting to regain favor with the gods through worship and piety.

It was also believed that ill-health was caused by evil spirits and thus sufferers would resort to alms and spells to drive them out. Many illnesses would eventually subside and it would appear that the spiritual treatment had worked.

The god Asclepius was particularly revered by the sick. He was originally the Greek god of healing, but his cult was adopted by the Romans. People would make a pilgrimage to one of his temples, called *Asclepions*. At these sanctuaries it was believed that Asclepius would visit and cure the patient in a dream.

Evidence suggests that the *Asclepions* had many successful cases—of course unsuccessful patients would have been less readily recorded, but the strength and endurance of the cult is testament to the widespread belief that this method of healing worked. Initially, Romans would visit the more established Asclepions in Greece, but later a temple was built on the island in the River Tiber, in Rome.

Brass balance scales found at the ruins of Aphrodisias, an ancient Greco-Roman city in the Anatolian uplands of Turkey. These could have been used by a doctor to weigh out "medicines" for a patient.

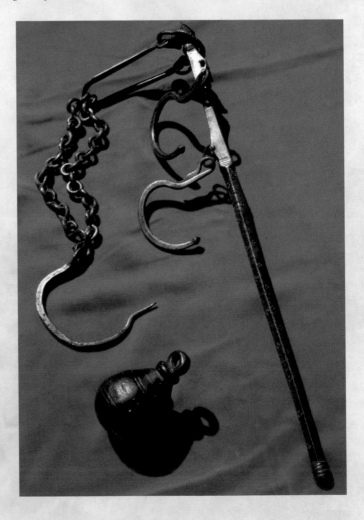

Statue of the god, Asclepius who was revered by the sick. He was originally the Greek god of healing, but his cult was adopted by the Romans.

Visiting the doctor

Asclepius was not the only Greek import; most doctors working in Ancient Rome were of Greek origin. During the Republic, medicine was not a highly regarded profession because most doctors were slaves or freedmen. The onset of the Empire elevated their position because doctors gained the support of Augustus. He kept a personal physician and professionalized their role in the military.

Wealthy Romans could afford to call a doctor to their house, but the poor—if they could afford treatment—would have to visit the doctor. Without free healthcare, a number of "quacks" established practices in Rome to provide a cheap service, to poor Romans, that was of little or no help whatsoever. This unfortunate state of affairs was redressed in 100 AD, when the government assisted the poor in paying for healthcare.

A scientific approach

Doctors emphasized a variety of preventative measures to maintain public health. They recommended balanced diets, exercise and clean living, much the same as a doctor would today. However, when it came to treatments, the doctors were not so well informed; they subscribed to the Greek notion of four humors. The idea, begun by Empedocles and applied to medicine by Hippocrates, argued that the body comprised four fluids, (blood, black bile, yellow bile, and phlegm), that were in harmony with the four elements of nature, (air, earth, fire and water). Those who favored a scientific approach to medicine believed that all disease was caused by an imbalance in one of the four fluids in the body. The symptoms the patient exhibited would explain which fluid was in excess—for example, flu was the result of too much phlegm. Doctors would prescribe treatments designed to restore balance, such as blood-letting, which aimed to reduce the amount of blood in the body.

Galen

Many Greek ideas were translated into Latin by the famous doctor, Galen. He mixed Hellenic medicine with the concept of a single Creator, which later made his theories palatable to the Christian and Islamic faiths. Supported by these two powerful religions, Galen's work meant that Greco-Roman medicine was able to dominate its field for more than one thousand years.

Surgery

While Roman medicine was relatively primitive, Roman surgery was exceptionally advanced. Galen pioneered the field and encouraged students to take whatever opportunity they could to see the inside of the human body. Although dissection was discouraged, the Romans were able to gain a working knowledge of anatomy by studying human skeletons without dissecting the body first. However, because Romans were very strict about burying their dead, only the unburied corpses of executed prisoners were readily available, which made the study of anatomy particularly gruesome. Galen also advocated other, less sinister methods, such as dissecting the body of an ape, rather than a human, and looking at the inside of the body through the wounds of gladiators and soldiers.

Roman surgeons met with a reasonably good success rate. They could perform basic operations such as amputations, but were also adept at more skilled procedures, such as trephination and cataract surgery. In a trephination operation, a hole was bored into the skull using a small drill to relieve pressure on the brain; records would suggest that this painful-sounding operation met with relative success.

Many Greek ideas were translated into Latin by the famous doctor, Galen. Galen mixed Hellenic medicine with the concept of a single Creator, which made his theories palatable to the Christian and Islamic faiths. Supported by these two powerful religions, Galen's work meant that Greco-Roman medicine was able to dominate its field for more than one thousand years.

The Late Republic

Social Crisis

Impressive victories, expanded territories and accumulated wealth had transformed Rome by the time of the late Republic. The city itself had become a busy metropolis with the largest population in the world, but such rapid change was threatening the very existence of Roman society.

Although victory in the Second Punic War set Rome on a path to longer-term greatness, in the short term, it created problems for the state. The army used in the war came from the *adsidui* class. This was a Roman citizen classified as a landowner because they owned in excess of a given amount of land. In the fighting against Carthage, Rome sustained heavy casualties, which decimated the numbers of the *adsidui*. Not only did this class have to face the loss of a substantial number of men, but the war itself ravished much of the land in Italy, exacerbating the problem confronting rural Romans.

Rome's rich treasury

While the Roman countryside was entering crisis, the city itself was entering something of a golden age. Plunder, trading monopolies and hefty war indemnities had glutted Rome's treasury. The prosperity of Rome acted as a magnet to people wishing to escape the rural depression and the city was flooded with people, and the population boomed. However, Rome offered little salvation to these newcomers because its affluence was narrowly distributed.

Opposite above: Gold fibula, or pin, from Pompeii. This type of decorative brooch would have been worn by the wealthy. While it has a functional purpose, to secure clothing, the richness of the material and the design would have been a statement of status.

Opposite below: Via Appia, the Appian Way, was seen as a symbol of the Republic. The road began in the Forum and ran all the way to Brindisi on the south-east coast of Italy. Begun at the end of the fourth century BC, it was an important factor in establishing and maintaining Roman order and control.

Growing gulf between rich and poor

The gulf between rich and poor citizens was growing, and the situation was only getting worse. Rome's new super-rich were able to buy up vast swathes of the countryside, amassing large estates. In doing so, they alienated many of the remaining *adsidui* from the land, and brought in slaves to work on these farms, with the result that the landless Romans had to migrate to the city to find work. But the city was not always a saving grace for these Romans because Rome's conquest had resulted in the acquisition of huge numbers of slaves. The slaves did all the menial jobs leaving the poor Romans plunging even further into destitution.

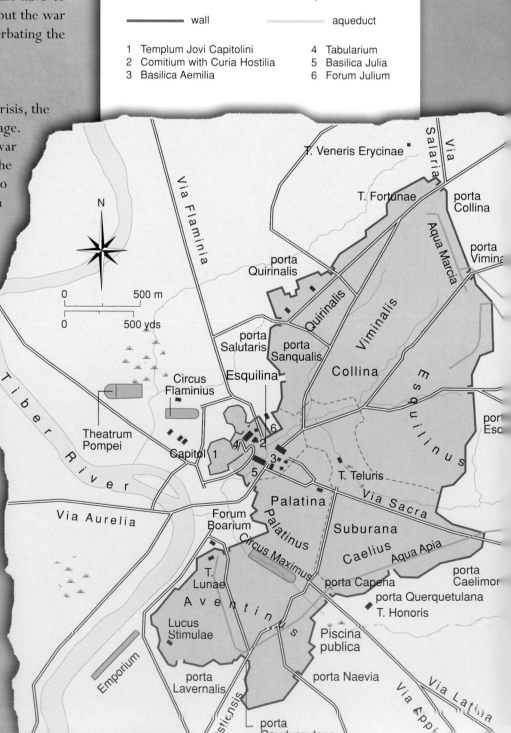

Rome in the Late Republic

———— wall   ———— aqueduct

1 Templum Jovi Capitolini
2 Comitium with Curia Hostilia
3 Basilica Aemilia
4 Tabularium
5 Basilica Julia
6 Forum Julium

Social reform

As Rome's society became increasingly polarized, so too did Rome's political scene. The *Populares*, or popular faction, advocated policies to help Rome's new poor residents. The members of this faction were still aristocratic but they took a populist stance, either because they were genuinely interested in social reform or because they were trying to secure a popular support base outside the Senate. Their political opponents were known as *Optimates*, meaning the "Big Men," who were more reactionary in outlook and did not wish to see the progressive policies of the *Populares* implemented. These men were often senators who wished to extend the power of the Senate to control of the popular assemblies.

Tiberius Gracchus' plans

The immigration and poverty problems facing Rome did not go unnoticed by these factions. In 133 BC, an ambitious plebeian tribune, Tiberius Gracchus, proposed agrarian reforms to put the former *adsidui* back on the land by redistributing the large estates. Many of the senators were owners of these properties and responded to Tiberius' agenda with outright hostility. Tiberius marched ahead with his plans, using the power of the plebs to circumvent the Senate and land reform got underway.

The senators got their revenge through a smear campaign against Tiberius; they convinced the people that he held the ulterior motive of becoming king and was simply using land reform as a means to that end. Fear of monarchy had been ingrained in the Roman psyche since the days of Tarquinius Superbus and huge numbers of people turned against Tiberius. The Senate was able to mobilize the people to its advantage on this occasion and Tiberius was killed, but he had already opened "Pandora's Box," unleashing social discontent and upsetting the delicate equilibrium that had existed between the people and the Senate; this was the beginning of the end of the Republic.

The herald of turbulent times

Reform did not cease with the death of Tiberius; in 126 BC, his brother Gaius assumed the role of tribune and pursued a similar agenda. Gaius Gracchus attempted to

introduce a grain subsidy so that poorer Romans could afford food, but this, together with his other populist policies, incurred the anger of the senators and reactionary Roman aristocrats. However, they could do little about his threat because Gaius had a strong popular base; he was even re-elected as tribune in 122.

His downfall came when he alienated that base by proposing to extend Roman citizenship to other Latins. The senators were able to find common cause with the plebs, as neither wished to see Roman citizenship expanded. Gaius' attempts to win another election were thwarted and the Senate, alleging that Gaius would mount an imminent coup, established a state of emergency. The Senate encouraged its followers to give Gaius the same treatment as had been extended to his brother, and he and thousands of followers were duly murdered. Such political violence heralded the dawn of one of the most turbulent periods in Rome's history.

Rural Life

Initially, most Romans lived in rural areas as smallholder farmers, but over time, they were pushed off the land and into the city as wealthy landowners amassed vast estates. While this meant that most Romans were urban residents, across the Empire, the vast majority of people continued to live in rural settings.

Mosaic showing workers using horses and cattle to thresh wheat.

Early Republic smallholders

In the early days of the Roman Republic most landowners were smallholders who grew just enough food for the needs of their family. Any additional produce could be exchanged or bartered with neighboring farmers. There was no necessity to provide Rome with vast quantities of grain because the city's population was relatively small, and most people had access to their own farms close to the city.

Whenever Rome went to war, the Army was made up exclusively from the ranks of these landowning Romans; army recruitment was not open to the landless, urban class that emerged over time. As soon as a campaign or war was completed, a landowner was demobilized and could return to his duties at the farm.

The loss of a generation of farmers

At first, Rome won many of its wars and the system seemed to work well, but when Rome lost, the pitfalls inherent in its recruitment system quickly emerged.

When Hannibal invaded Rome through the Alps in 218 BC, his army wrought such havoc over Italy and killed so many Roman soldiers, that an entire generation of landowners was lost over the course of the war. This resulted in a sea change in the countryside; bereaved families found life extremely difficult without the help of their husbands or fathers and were often forced to sell their farms to ensure survival. They found willing buyers as a new class of super-rich emerged in Rome, made wealthy by the plunder from defeated cities in Carthage and Greece.

Large estates

Over time, more land was concentrated in fewer hands as most of the remaining smallholders were forced to sell to the large landowners. The old smallholdings gradually disappeared as the countryside was divided up into large estates called *latifundia*.

The new landowners were absentee owners, who spent most of their time living and working in Rome. As the land was simply a means of income the owner would appoint a manager to run the farm in his place. When the landowner did visit, it was usually to spend time in his villa, away from the city, and not to do any faming.

With the establishment of these large estates, agriculture underwent a degree of marketization. Agricultural produce was no longer grown simply for personal use, instead it was destined for the marketplaces of Rome, where the population had swelled as the dispossessed smallholders had converged on the city.

Mosaic from a Roman villa in Piazza Armerina, Sicily, depicting a man restraining an ostrich.

Emerging capitalist economy

With the new landowners desiring to see a profit from their estates, a capitalist economy emerged in the countryside. To keep the cost of production low, slaves were brought in for farm work. The abundance of slaves meant very little investment was made in labor-saving devices.

The exceptions to the rule were the use of oxen-driven reapers to mow the harvest and a mechanical wine press. However, both of these processes still required considerable input from the slaves. Rural slaves were less well treated than their urban counterparts because household slaves could build up a close relationship with the family they served. In the countryside, by contrast, the slave was under the control of the farm manager, usually a freedman or a highly-regarded slave, whose concern was to impress the landowner with his management skills. This meant the manager usually prioritized production levels over the wellbeing of his expendable workforce.

Ram's head wine press in the Villa of the Mysteries at Pompeii.

Slave labor

This use of slave labor on absentee landlord farms effectively spelled the demise of the traditional Roman farmer, who could not compete with the cheaper slaves for jobs on the estates. The handful of remaining smallholders who had held out against the onset of the *latifundia* were eventually forced to sell out because they could not contend with the new, capitalist environment of the countryside.

Smallholder farming was not entirely lost to Ancient Rome because army veterans were granted small plots of land upon their retirement as a bonus for good and loyal service. During the Republic many of these soldiers were given land in Italy, but over time, as space became limited, most were settled in the provinces instead. Cities such as Timgad in Numidia and Italica in Hispania were set up for the purpose of accommodating veterans, where they could act as a supplementary army in case of any provincial unrest.

The main crops grown on the latifundia were fruit, vegetables, and cereals, most of which went directly to the markets in Rome. However, olives and grapes were first turned into wine and olive oil.

Winemaking became a particularly lucrative industry, with many large estates desperate to own and grow their own vines. Wine was consumed on a great scale in Rome, where it was the staple drink. It was drunk throughout the day because most Romans preferred it to the water (although they usually diluted their wine with water anyway).

Most wine was grown from wild grapes, which grew naturally across the Mediterranean at the time. The grapes were collected and then sent to be pressed; most farms used a mechanized press, called a torculum, but some opted to use the more traditional method of trampling the grapes with bare feet.

The grapes were stored and fermented in ceramic containers called amphorae. To give the wines individual tastes, a variety of flavors would be sought by adding herbs, spices, honey, or even salt.

Winemaking became such a popular enterprise that the Emperor Domitian was forced to legislate against it, to encourage the estates to invest in other produce.

Army recruitment reformed

The reform offered by the brothers of the Gracchi family had not lifted Rome from its crisis, and after the death of Gaius Gracchus the reactionary *Optimates* dominated the Roman political scene for over a decade. During this time, Rome was busy in wars against Numidia in Africa and Germanic tribes, the Teutones and the Cimbri, to the north. Soldiers for the Army still came from the *adsidui* classes, but their declining numbers meant that the Army was denied many new recruits and the wars in Africa and Germany were dragging on.

It fell to Gaius Marius, an aristocrat affiliated with the *Populares*, to raise Rome out of its quagmire, both at home and abroad. He did this by creating a standing army and opening recruitment to all Romans. In the short term this helped the Romans to defeat their enemies in Numidia by 105 BC and in Germany by 101 by replenishing the Army with better-skilled, new recruits. In the longer term a career in the armed services offered a way out of destitution for the poor Roman citizens.

Gaius Marius' foreign victories helped him to amass a popular following leading him to an unprecedented sixth consulship in 100. Although ostensibly allied to the *Populares*, it is clear that Marius' foremost concern was his own power. When popular reforms, such as further reducing the price of grain, were called for by the plebeian tribune, the Senate refused and violence between the factions broke out. In spite of his allegiance, Marius favored the Senate in this instance. By opposing the plebeian tribune, Marius alienated his support base and prudently chose to retire from political life in 100.

The Social War

Marius was not gone for long; nine years after he disappeared from the political scene, he re-emerged to fight in the Social War. The conflict was effectively a civil war because it was fought between Rome and its allies on the Italian Peninsula.

In addition to the strife associated with the proletarianization of the rural Romans, there was growing discontent amongst Rome's Italian allies because they had to pay all the taxes, while Roman citizens were exempt. This anger was compounded by the fact that while Roman citizens had a say in how that revenue was spent, as non-Romans, the allies had no say whatsoever.

In line with the interests of Rome's allies, and picking up where Gaius Gracchus had left off, the tribune in 91 BC, Marcus Livius Drusus, had suggested that citizenship rights be extended to these long-time allies. But just as had happened to Gracchus, few Romans, rich or poor wished to extend citizenship rights and the proposal was rejected.

The majority of the allies broke with Rome and formed their own independent confederacy with its seat of government in the town of Corfinium. A war was inevitable. Rome budged on the citizenship issue, prudently offering it to any ally that did not take up arms against it. This helped to isolate and weaken its enemy and handed Rome victory by 88 BC.

Lucius Cornelius Sulla

The war heralded the emergence of Lucius Cornelius Sulla. Sulla had so distinguished himself in the war that he earned the grass crown, one of Rome highest military honors. An additional reward was his election as consul in 88 BC. This appointment enraged Marius who believed he should have been given the consulship instead. Sulla had served under Marius but the pair had fallen out during the campaign against the Numidians in Africa. Marius evoked his old alliance with the *Populares*, getting the plebeian assembly to name him consul in Sulla's place. This political uncertainty sparked a wave of violence in the city and Sulla, with fewer loyalists on hand, was forced to flee the city.

Opposite: Ruins of the Forum where the tribunes and senators met.

Left: Directional pillar with the bust of the Greek Sosistratus.

Below: Amphitheater at Leptis Magna. In about 23 BC the Punic city became part of the Roman province in North Africa. It is the site of some of the most lavish and best-preserved remains from the Roman period.

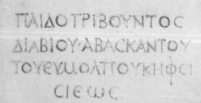

Sulla marches on Rome

Sulla's forces were not in the city because they had just finished campaigning in the Social War. However, this meant that they were easy to group and Sulla was quickly ready to march on the city. Marius fled to Africa leaving the city open for Sulla to reclaim the consulship, where he exacted a brutal retribution on Marius' followers and thousands of people were killed.

With his reign of terror complete, Sulla left the city to embark on a campaign against Mithridates in the East. Mithridates was the king of Pontus, who had made successful gains in Roman Asia and had been treated as a liberator by the local tribes. While Sulla's back was turned Marius returned with the help of Lucius Cornelius Cinna, and began a reign of terror of his own against Sulla's followers. Marius regained the consulship in 86 BC but died soon after. However, Marius' friend, Cinna, became consul and ensured that Sulla's supporters were kept out.

Pompey "the Great"

After exacting heavy-handed retribution in the East, Sulla made a quick peace with Mithridates so that he could return to Rome and regain his power. His return was not easily achieved as Marius' supporters had ruthlessly purged Sulla's support in the city, but was aided by the help of two young generals, Marcus Licinius Crassus and Gnaeus Pompeius Magnus (Pompey). Pompey gained his title "the Great," during Sulla's second march on Rome, in honor of his pacification of Marius' supporters in Sicily and North Africa.

The death of Sulla

In a bid to end the violence and chaos Sulla was appointed dictator. From this position he exacted one of the most brutal purges Rome had seen to date. Many thousands were killed and their assets went to the state, making Sulla even wealthier. As an affiliate of the *Optimates*, he extended the ranks of the Senate at the expense of the popular assembly and doubled the number of senators. In 81 BC, with his enemies disposed of, Sulla announced an end to the dictatorship and arranged for his appointment as consul in 80. At the end of his one-year term he went into retirement and died in 78 BC. However, the political violence did not end once Sulla and Marius were off the scene. On the contrary, it had only just begun.

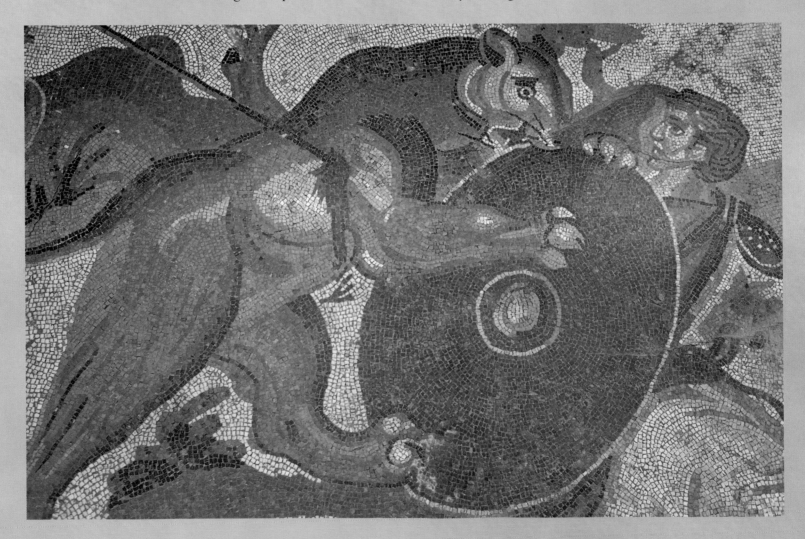

The First Triumvirate

When Sulla retired from the dictatorship it seemed that the *Optimates* had won the war. Sulla's reforms had severely undermined the plebeian tribune, a key support base for his rivals, the *Populares*. In contrast, the Senate now stood as the most powerful governing body in Rome.

Resistance against the *Optimates*

The *Populares* were much weakened during Sulla's reign of terror, but Marius' supporters still existed. Quintus Sertorius, a Marian by virtue of his animosity toward Sulla, refused to acknowledge the Senate's authority and joined with the native Lusitanian tribe in the west of the Iberian Peninsula against Rome. He ruled much of the peninsula during the 70s and, together with exiles and natives, he held off the Roman counterinsurgency. Pompey was sent to crush his rebellion in 76 BC, but did not succeed until 72 when Sertorius was assassinated. In spite of his lucky break, Pompey was lauded as a hero in Rome.

Challenge to the Senate

The supremacy of the Senate was challenged more directly in Rome itself, when Marcus Aemilius Lepidus, the consul in 78 BC, tried to undermine the political arrangement and reinstate the tribunate's powers using his army. This attempt was also thwarted by Pompey, and Lepidus was forced to flee to Sardinia. With Marius' supporters unable to restore the powers of the tribunate, it fell to three powerful individuals, Marcus Licinius Crassus, Gnaeus Pompeius Magnus (Pompey) and Gaius Julius Caesar to balance the power of the Senate.

Left: Marble statue from the ruins of the port of Ostia.

Far Left: Roman bridge at Alcantara in the province of Caceres in Spain. It was from Spain that the Marian resistance to the power of the Senate came. Pompey failed to put down an uprising by Quintus Sertorius who refused to acknowledge the authority of Rome.

Opposite: Mosaic, depicting a hunter fighting a lion, from the Piazza Amerina in Sicily. The island of Sicily and northern Africa, like Spain, were regions where it was difficult for the authority of the Senate to hold sway.

Crassus and Pompey

The oldest of the three men was Crassus. Born in 115 BC, he had become incredibly wealthy as an ally of Sulla's and a participant in the confiscations of land and riches that accompanied the reign of terror. He was not as well known for his military skill as Pompey but he had successfully put down a slave rebellion in 71.

Spartacus

The rebellion began in 73, when gladiators broke out of a school in Capua. They were led by Spartacus, a slave from Thrace, and in their quest for liberty camped out on Mount Vesuvius before destroying two Roman legions. Success brought ever more slaves to their side but they were held in the toe of Italy by Crassus' forces. Although the slaves were able to break out of the siege, they were routed by Pompey's legion which had just returned from Spain. It was Crassus who dealt the final blow and Spartacus was probably killed in battle. Thousands of slaves were captured and Crassus made a brutal example of them, having each one of them crucified along the Appian Way, the Roman road from Rome to Capua.

Both Crassus and Pompey were credited with their victories on behalf of Rome and jointly offered the consulship in 70. The two men openly disliked one another, but they were the richest and most powerful men in Rome and had to work together if they wanted to succeed. To challenge one another would have been extremely costly.

Caesar emerges

For much of the 60s Pompey was away campaigning in the East, engaged in the third war against Mithridates of Pontus. During this time Julius Caesar emerged on the political scene. Caesar had a privileged early life, but as a child his family had lost its wealth and as a result Caesar developed frugal habits, which later helped ingratiate him with the poor.

His background meant that he did not have sufficient funds for a dazzling political career but he tied himself to the wealthy Crassus, who valued Caesar as an orator. Crassus was linked with the *Optimates* but Caesar was clearly allied to the *Populares*; Marius was his uncle by marriage and his wife was the daughter of Cinna, Marius' closest ally. In addition to Crassus' backing, Caesar was able to establish an independent political and economic base of his own when he was elected *pontifex maximus*, chief priest, in 63, and to a governorship in Spain in 62.

Pompey returns

In 62 BC, Pompey returned from the East. He had successfully defeated Mithridates and his popularity became unassailable. Crassus and Caesar were anxious as to how his return would affect their positions in Roman politics and society. Fortunately for them, the Senate was also concerned for Pompey's return; they feared that he might re-establish a dictatorship like Sulla. As a result, the Senate tried to weaken Pompey by failing to grant land for his veterans.

A frustrated Pompey decided that the only way of circumventing the Senate was to ally with the two other most powerful individuals in Rome, Crassus and Caesar. Together they were able to challenge the authority of the Senate by using Caesar's popularity to gain a support base amongst the plebs.

The Triumvirate gains power

Although their authority was never official, this Triumvirate, or rule of three, was able to undermine the Roman government, weaken the Senate and pave the way for the age of the Emperors. The Triumvirate was always an icy arrangement because of Pompey and Crassus' dislike of one another, but this was to some extent smoothed over by Pompey's marriage to Caesar's daughter.

The Triumvirate's power was increased with Caesar's appointment as consul in 59, but with Caesar away conquering Gaul in the early 50s, the Triumvirate began to break down as the antagonism between Crassus and Pompey began to re-emerge. Caesar called the men together at Luca and agreed that they should both stand for the position of consul once again in 55. The meeting thinly patched over their differences until 54 when Caesar's daughter, who was also Pompey's wife, died in childbirth and the familial bond between the two men was broken.

Death of Crassus

In 53 BC the final blow was served to the Triumvirate when Crassus was captured in battle against the Parthians in the East. Legend has it that he was executed by having molten gold poured into his mouth, an end perhaps befitting a life of incredible wealth.

The united power of these three titans helped to erode the power of the Senate and remove it from the perch upon which Sulla had left it. With the Senate weakened and Crassus dead, the future of Rome was to be decided by Caesar and Pompey.

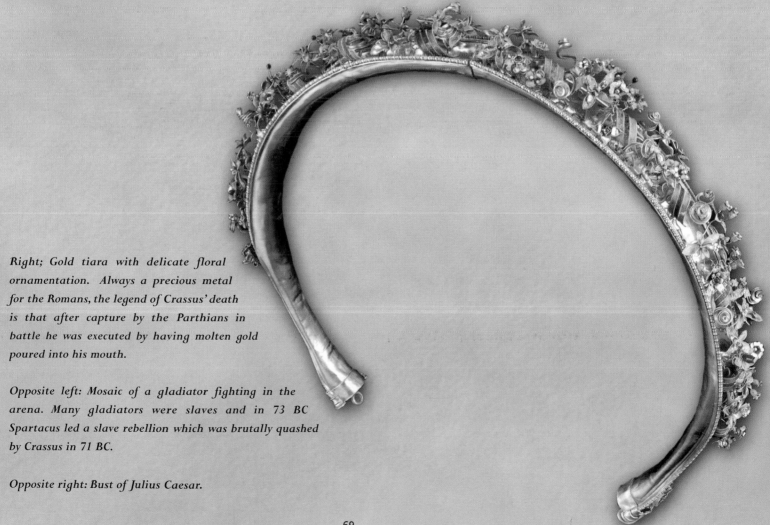

Right; Gold tiara with delicate floral ornamentation. Always a precious metal for the Romans, the legend of Crassus' death is that after capture by the Parthians in battle he was executed by having molten gold poured into his mouth.

Opposite left: Mosaic of a gladiator fighting in the arena. Many gladiators were slaves and in 73 BC Spartacus led a slave rebellion which was brutally quashed by Crassus in 71 BC.

Opposite right: Bust of Julius Caesar.

Germany under the Romans

The Romans did not have any substantial contact with the Germanic tribes of north eastern Europe until the end of the second century BC, when the Cimbri and the Teutons migrated south-westward towards Gaul. The German migration caught the attention of Rome because it caused displacement among the settled Celtic tribes of the region. Rome finally decided to deal with the threat when the Germans invaded the lands of the Taurisci, a Roman ally.

Battles with the Germanic tribes

The Germanic invaders won the first two encounters, crushing the Roman Army at the Battle of Noreia in 112 BC and completely annihilating them at Arausio in 105. Arausio provided Rome's greatest military defeat since the Battle of Cannae against Hannibal, more than a century beforehand.

The tables were turned when Gaius Marius was put in charge of the campaign. Fresh from defeating Jugurtha, the king of Numidia, and with an army which he had professionalized, his fighting force swiftly defeated the Teutons in 102 and then the Cimbri in 101. The two tribes were almost wiped out; the men were slain in battle and the women and children committed mass suicide to avoid being sold into slavery.

The Roman advance

After the defeat of the Cimbri and the Teutons other Germanic tribes made incursions into Gaul. During Caesar's Gallic campaign, he was forced to deal with these menaces and undertook punitive expeditions against the Usipi, Tencteri, and the Suebi.

It is thought that Caesar had hoped to establish a more permanent Roman presence in Germania, but he believed the task difficult because the Germans were warlike and could not be civilized—unlike the Gauls, who he thought were warlike, but could be civilized. The civil war with Pompey and his subsequent assassination scotched any plans to invade Germania, and the Roman border remained at the Rhine.

Roman coin depicting a female head with a crown of oak leaves.

The remains of a fourth century Roman city gate, the Porta Nigra, stand near the center of Trier in modern Germany. Trier, known as Augusta Treverorum, the capital of Roman Belgica, became an important town after Diocletian's division of the Empire.

Augustus takes control

When Augustus came to power, he rearranged the Roman provinces, creating Germania Inferior and Germania Superior on the west bank of the Rhine. Germania Inferior was the territory at the mouth of the Rhine, in the location of the modern Netherlands. Germania Superior was upstream in what is today western Germany and eastern France. The capital of Germania Superior was based at Moguntiacum (Mainz).

Augustus was not content to maintain the status quo and dispatched his stepsons, first Drusus and then Tiberius to push further into Germany. Drusus arrived in 12 BC and succeeded in advancing across the Rhine to the River Elbe by 9 BC. Tiberius then consolidated the new Roman position.

Massacre forces a retreat

However, the local tribes resented the Roman occupation and conspired to repel the invaders. A romanized German, Arminius, of the Cheruscan tribe befriended the governor, Quinctilius Varus and convinced him of a rebellion in a remote part of the province. Varus set off with three legions to defeat the insurgency, but in reality, it was a trap. The Romans were led into an area of hills and marshes in the Teutoburg Forest, where an alliance of German tribes completely wiped them out. The destruction of three legions shocked and wounded Roman pride and forced Rome to abandon the Elbe frontier for safety behind the Rhine.

Rhine border

By 16 AD, the Romans had recovered their lost territory and re-established the border at the Elbe under the command of Tiberius' highly popular adopted son, Germanicus, under whom they took back much of the territory they had lost earlier.

These victories reinvigorated Roman morale, but Tiberius considered operations in Germany too costly. He withdrew Roman forces to the Rhine, which was established, for the most part, as the permanent border for the remainder of the Empire. The Romans did continue to occupy some territory on the eastern bank of the River Rhine; without the natural defence of the river, they fortified their positions with an extensive series of man-made defences called *limes*.

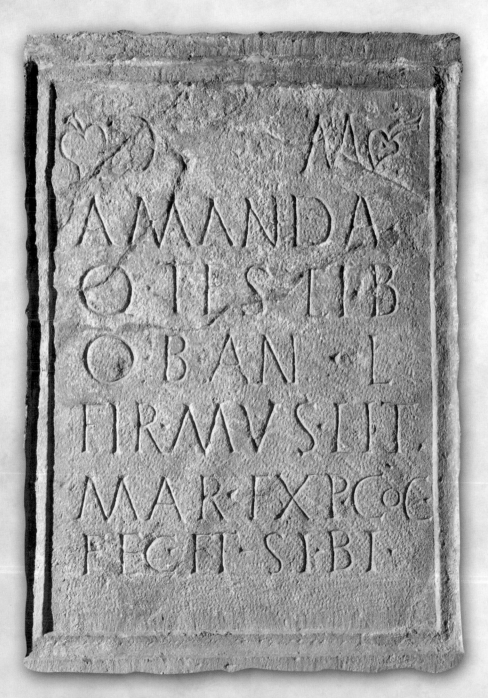

Carved Roman tombstone from Chiemgau in Germany.

The Invasion of Gaul

Caesar sought military glory in order to improve his own standing within the Triumvirate and within Roman politics as a whole; pacifying the supposedly hardy Gallic and Germanic warriors to the north provided the perfect opportunity for him to achieve this.

Caesar makes his name

After his stint as consul in 59 BC, Caesar became the governor of three of Rome's northerly provinces, Cisalpine Gaul, Illyricum, and Transalpine Gaul. The influence of the Triumvirate over Roman politics was so great that it was able to secure Caesar an exceptionally long period as governor. Throughout the 50s, Caesar was handed control of the border provinces between the Roman Empire and Gaul; a perfect springboard for a campaign to make his name.

Caesar's pretext to intervene in Gallic affairs was delivered to him when the Helvetii planned a massive migration into Gaul. The Helvetii were a Gallic tribe, who lived in the south of Germania, where they were terrorized by the local Germanic tribes. Hemmed in by the Romans to the south and the Germans to the north, the Helvetii resolved to migrate to Gaul. Caesar refused to permit this migration because he feared it would destabilize Gaul and remove a very important buffer between the Roman Empire and the Gallic Tribes.

In spite of Caesar's orders, the Helvetii began their migration through Geneva, in Transalpine Gaul. This was routed by Caesar's forces and the Helvetii were forced to find a route that did not pass through Roman territory. The Helvetii passed through the land owned by the Aedui, who appealed to Caesar for help. Caesar obliged and decisively defeated the tribe in the Battle of Bibracte, where he slaughtered the majority of the tribe; those who survived were forced to return to their homeland.

Rome's increasing influence in Gaul

Caesar's defeat of the Helvetii pleased several of the Gallic tribes, who requested his help against another menace: the Germanic Suebi tribe. The tribe had been intervening in Gallic politics by shoring up the Averni tribe against the Aedui. Caesar obliged this request and marched on the Suebi, encountering them in the Battle of the Vosges in 58 BC. The result was another Roman victory and the Suebi were forced back across the Rhine into Germania.

Ruins of a necropolis in Alyscamps, just outside the ancient city walls of the French town of Arles. Roman cities usually forbade burials within the city.

The Dying Gaul. This is a Roman copy of a lost Greek statue but serves the purpose of making the enemy seem both noble and brave, thus emphasizing the might of the Romans' victory. The figure shows the Gaul naked, apart from his neck torc, with his weapons beside him. Julius Caesar, governor of Gaul for several years, records that the Gauls went into battle in just such a manner.

Caesar invades Britain

Caesar's increasing influence over Gaul caused concern in a number of tribes in the far north. Communally known as the Belgae, from the region of modern-day Belgium, they intended, in early 57 BC, to mount a surprise attack on the Romans, but Caesar pre-empted them and destroyed the tribes one by one before they could join forces against him. In 56, Caesar moved in to attack the Veneti of modern-day Brittany, before crossing the *Mare Britannicum* (English Channel) in 55, and again in 54, to upset supply routes to northern Gaul and dislodge the Belgae tribes who had settled there.

Insurrection in Gaul

Caesar's foray into Britannia was halted as insurrection once again reared in Gaul. A Belgae tribe, named the Eburones, under the leadership of Ambiorix, had risen up against the local Roman garrison. The Eubrones exacted a humiliating defeat over the Romans and, buoyed by their success, many other natives joined the rebellion against Rome. Caesar was furious; he brought in new legions and brutally suppressed the uprising, such that the Eburones were completely destroyed. Although peace had been forcibly returned to Gaul, it was short-lived as a new insurrection was brewing.

In early 52, taking advantage of the distraction caused to the Roman Army by revolt in the north, tribes in the south-central regions of Gaul rose up against Roman dominance. The insurrection was led by a chieftain of the Averni named Vercingetorix. The rebellion enjoyed several successes owing to the insurgents' use of guerilla tactics, scorched-earth policies, and superior knowledge of the local terrain.

Each victory encouraged more tribes to join the uprising. Caesar grouped his forces in the north and marched on the rebels, taking the town of Avaricum, which had not been razed by the rebels; once inside, the Romans slaughtered the entire population. The Romans scored ever more victories in minor engagements that took place across the region and Vercingetorix lost a number of his key men and the rebels were forced to regroup at Alesia.

Built in the late first century BC by the Roman general Agrippa, this temple sits in the town of Nîmes in France. Its rededication as a Christian church in the fourth century AD probably helped in its preservation.

Battle of Alesia

Alesia was a stronghold for the Gallic insurgents because it was a hilltop fort surrounded by rivers, making it easily defensible. When Caesar arrived in pursuit, he discounted a direct attack because the fort was so well defended; instead he opted to besiege the fort and starve the Gallic rebels out. Vercingetorix's men held on for a time but were forced to try and break the siege to escape the fort. This was a failure, as the superior Roman Army and cavalry were able to rout the breakout and slaughter thousands of the rebels, forcing the remainder to retreat to the fort. Vercingetorix was left with little option but to capitulate to the Romans. Most of the rebels were sold into slavery, and Vercingetorix was kept in prison for five years so that he could be paraded in Rome upon Caesar's victory against Pompey. After this five-year wait, he was executed.

Gallic rebellion ended

Although the rebellion continued, Vercingetorix had proved to be a unifying figure and without him, the insurgents were divided. This made them perilously weak and allowed the Romans to isolate individual tribes and destroy them. Although Caesar was exceptionally ruthless, he did use a mixture of benevolent policies to co-opt the strategically important tribes. By 51 BC, the Gallic rebellion was over because the natives were exhausted; towns and villages were destroyed and it is estimated that at least one third of the population of Gaul was killed in the fighting. Back in Rome, Caesar was not seen as a butcher; his popularity was rising meteorically, to the concern of his old ally, Pompey.

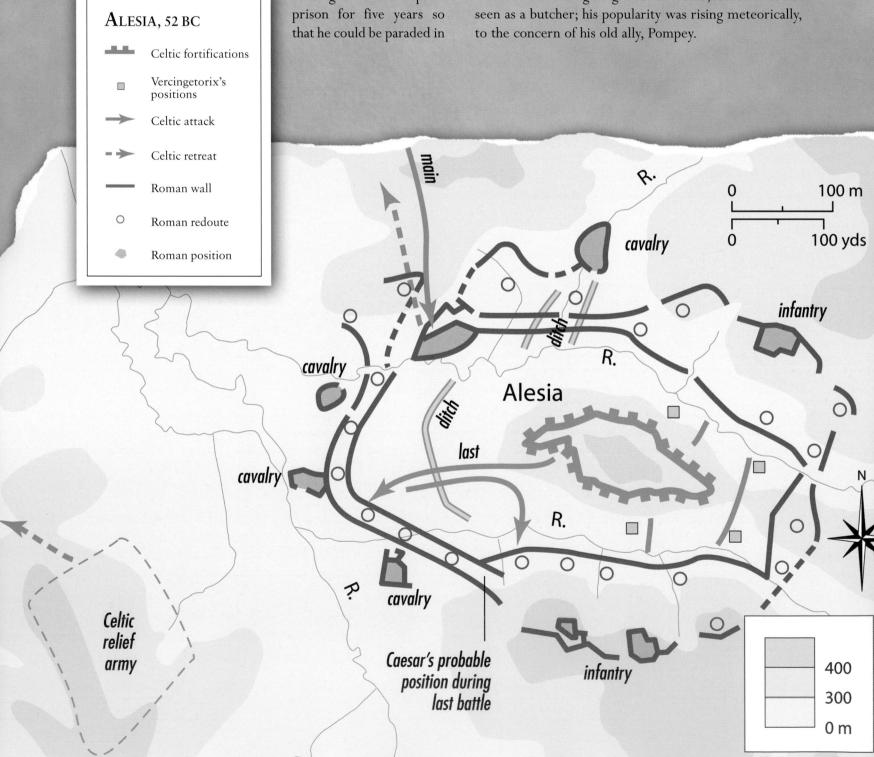

ALESIA, 52 BC

- Celtic fortifications
- Vercingetorix's positions
- Celtic attack
- Celtic retreat
- Roman wall
- Roman redoute
- Roman position

Apollo

It was from the Greeks that the Romans adopted the god Apollo. The cult of his worship appears in Rome as early as the fifth century BC, and during the Punic Wars the Apollonian Games was instituted.

Augustus develops the cult

Under the reign of Augustus, the importance of Apollo as a Roman god developed. Following the Battle of Actium, at which Augustus defeated Mark Antony, he built and dedicated a new temple to Apollo. The temple, on the Palatine Hill, was dedicated in 28 AD, although the exact site is uncertain because there are no extant remains.

Head from a statue of the god Apollo found at Pompeii.

The myth of Apollo

In mythology, Apollo was the son of Jupiter and Leto, and Diana's twin brother. He was god of the sun, archery, music, and poetry, and is often depicted playing a lyre. As father of Asclepius, he was also seen as the god of healing who taught medicine to mankind.

It was believed that one of his most important roles was to harness four horses to his chariots, with which he would then drive the sun across the sky each day. Mythological symbols for Apollo include the laurel tree, the crow, and the dolphin.

Athleticism

Images of Apollo show him to be a beautiful, eternally youthful man, athletic in build and action. The Greeks held the Pythian Games every four years at Delphi, in honor of his slaying of Python. While these games stemmed from Greek mythology and culture, the Romans also held games in Apollo's honor.

Although its precise site is unknown, Augustus built a temple in honor of Apollo on the Palatine Hill. There are no remains of the temple, which was dedicated in 28 BC. The area has been developed over the years, including the Farnese Gardens (pictured here), designed in the Renaissance by Vignola for Cardinal Alessandro Farnese.

Slaves

Slavery was commonplace in Ancient Rome. As the Republic won ever more wars, increasing numbers of slaves from all over the Roman world filled the city of Rome and the surrounding countryside. Rome's greatness was founded on the back of many of these faceless individuals who struggled to build glorious public works, toiled in the farms or performed household functions for Roman citizens.

A wide range of duties

Slaves performed a wide range of duties; they were not simply laborers and cleaners, but were also tutors, nurses, cooks, and gladiators. The worst job a slave could have was to be sent to work in the mines, where the work was grueling and life expectancy was short. The best job for a slave was to work in a family home, but this of course depended upon the nature of the family; some owners were exceptionally harsh, including Cato the Elder, who publicly advocated showing little compassion to slaves, but many were reasonably compassionate and a slave would be able to establish a friendly relationship with a family over the years. In fact, household slaves were treated as the masters for the duration of the Roman festival of Saturnalia. The extent of the role reversal varied, some masters simply waived punishments, while others got fully involved and waited on their slaves.

The Servile Wars: slave rebellions

For the most part, slaves acquiesced to their lot; however, there were three unrelated uprisings by slaves in the later Republic, called the Servile Wars. The third Servile War is the most famous of the three. It was led by Spartacus, a slave-gladiator, originally from Thrace.

The rebellion began in 73 BC, when Spartacus and fellow gladiators decided to fight for their own freedom and overran the gladiator school in Capua where they were held. After killing the guards, they broke out and ran amok in the south of Italy. The rebellion quickly spread as the story of the self-emancipation of the gladiators inspired other slaves to abandon their owners and join the uprising. With a growing force, the rebels occupied Mount Vesuvius and managed to destroy two Roman legions sent to subdue them. These successes encouraged yet more slaves to join their cause.

Above: A gladiator fights a leopard. Most gladiators were slaves. Spartacus was a slave who in 73 BC led a rebellion by slave-gladiators which lasted for two years, before being brutally crushed by Crassus.

Below: Panel painting depicting dancers. Slaves also took on roles as entertainers.

Spartacus' revolt is crushed

Spartacus' initial plans had been to escape across the Alps outside Roman territory, but as his army scored ever more victories against the Romans, he was encouraged to stay in Italy and fight.

The Senate sent Crassus to deal with Spartacus once and for all, but his forces did not perform well against the rebels. Crassus, desperate for victory and glory, employed one of the most brutal disciplinary methods to get his army into gear: decimation. Decimation was when every tenth soldier was killed as an example to the rest of the troops.

With a newly disciplined fighting force, Crassus was able to hem the rebels in to the toe of Italy. The slaves managed to break out of the siege, but they were marching headlong into Pompey's forces, who had come all the way from Spain. Trapped between Pompey and Crassus, the slaves had little choice but to fight. It was Crassus' army that dealt the final blow and Spartacus was probably killed in the battle.

Thousands of slaves were captured and Crassus made a brutal example of them, having each one of them crucified along the Appian Way, the Roman road from Rome to Capua.

Better treatment

In general, slaves were treated better during the Empire than during the Republic. Claudius introduced new laws to prevent inhumane treatment of slaves and later in the Empire slaves were even allowed to take their masters to court.

Slaves were not necessarily condemned to lifelong service; they could be emancipated. Manumission could occur in several ways: they could buy their freedom from their owner; the owner could release a slave from service upon the master's death; or the owner could choose to willingly free the slave while he was still alive, perhaps as a reward for good service.

An emancipated slave was called a "freedman." There were relatively few restrictions on freedmen; they could own land and their children were granted Roman citizenship. In fact, freedmen became an important part of Roman society. During Claudius' reign, freedmen held the most senior posts in his civil service.

Below: Captured Dacian workers as depicted on Trajan's column. Most slaves came from Roman-occupied lands throughout the Empire.

Death of the Republic

Twilight of the Republic

The Triumvirate had undermined the control of the Senate and the death of
Crassus had left just two rival contenders to fill the vacuum. The ensuing battle between
Caesar and Pompey was to be the endgame of the Roman Republic.

An alliance of convenience

Caesar and Pompey's alliance had largely been
one of convenience. Caesar had been a
traditional ally of the *Populares*, while
Pompey was affiliated with the
Optimates. Nevertheless, both men
had found common ground in
opposing the intransigence of a
bloated Senate, and Pompey
joined Caesar in drawing support
from the general population of
Rome. However, at the end of the
50s, Caesar's successes in Gaul were
beginning to eclipse Pompey's support
amongst the masses, forcing him to
fawn on the Senate in order to shore up
his own position against Caesar's rocketing
popularity.

The Senate did not trust
Pompey, but in 52 BC he was
appointed the sole consul so
that he could deal

*Sculpture head of Pompey the Great
whose head was offered to Julius Caesar
on a plate by Ptolemy of Egypt.*

with civil unrest and factional fighting that had been
getting worse since the time that Marius and Sulla
had begun undermining Roman government.
By successfully restoring order, Pompey
was able to get back into the Senate's
good graces and undermine Caesar
from within the system.

"The die is cast"

The opportunity to do just that came
in 50, when Caesar's tenure as
proconsul expired. Caesar wished to
continue his popular and successful war
in Gaul and therefore he needed to be
granted another consulship. This placed
him at the mercy of Roman politics, and
therefore provided the Senate and Pompey
with a chance to undermine their mutual
rival. They insisted that Caesar
could not apply for the
consulship in absentia and must
return to Rome. This meant
abandoning his army, which
would have placed him in a
perilously weak position. Caesar decided upon a
compromise, but illegal, solution; he would return
to Rome, but bring his army with him. In
January 49 Caesar ordered his troops to cross
the Rubicon, a river demarcating the border
between Gaul and Italy, and war between
Pompey and Caesar was begun.

*This well-preserved Roman building on
the Nile-island temple complex at Philae
in Egypt was left unfinished.*

Civil War

As Caesar marched on Rome, Pompey decided his best option was to abandon the city so he could group his forces and present a more formidable challenge. He went first to Brundisium and then fled across the Adriatic to Dyrrhachium. After capturing Rome, instead of going straight for Pompey, Caesar went to Spain to defeat Pompey's army stationed there. This was a shrewd move because Pompey's Spanish army might have advanced on Italy while Caesar was dealing with Pompey in the East.

After overcoming Pompey's army in Spain, Caesar traveled to Dyrrhachium to face his rival directly. The first battle against Pompey did not go well for Caesar; Pompey had amassed as many as 45,000 men and was able to fend off Caesar's attack in January 48 BC. Pompey, however, failed to consolidate his gains and Caesar's army was able to escape to fight another day.

During 48, Pompey had naval superiority in the Adriatic, meaning that Caesar's supply lines were stretched to near breaking point and his troops went hungry and thirsty. Pompey was happy to let Caesar's armies run themselves down, but his senatorial colleagues were spoiling for a fight and encouraged him to attack Caesar prematurely. The result was the Battle of Pharsalus in August 48 where Caesar correctly anticipated Pompey's tactics and won. Caesar believed that Pompey would try to flank to the right of Caesar's forces with his cavalry, so Caesar simply took a gamble by shoring up the defences on his right wing, but leaving the rest of his line gravely weak. The gamble paid off; Pompey attacked to Caesar's right, handing Caesar victory in the most important battle of the conflict.

Pompey flees to Egypt

In defeat, Pompey fled Greece for Egypt with Caesar in pursuit. As soon as he arrived, the Egyptian Pharaoh, Ptolemy, had him murdered to curry favor with Caesar. He hoped that Caesar might help him solve a dynastic conflict between him and his co-ruler, Cleopatra, who was both the Pharaoh's sister and wife. Ptolemy believed Cleopatra was overshadowing him and wished to dispose of her.

THE ROMAN EMPIRE, 55 BC

the first Triumvirate

- Caesar
- Pompey
- Crassus
- other Roman possessions
- allied to Rome

Pompey's head on a plate

When Caesar arrived in Alexandria in pursuit of his enemy, Ptolemy had Pompey's head presented to him as a gift. This gesture not only shocked Caesar, but deeply upset him as well; after all, despite their recent differences, Pompey was his one time colleague and father-in-law. As a result of Ptolemy's barbarity, Caesar sided with Cleopatra in the dispute between the warring Egyptian siblings and Ptolemy was ousted.

Soon after, with Cleopatra as sole ruler of Egypt, she and Caesar began an affair. Cleopatra claimed to have to have borne a son by Caesar, whom she named Caesarion. He later became co-ruler of Egypt with his mother, and it was Cleopatra's intention that he would succeed his father as ruler of Rome. However, when Octavian, Caesar's adopted son, defeated Cleopatra, he ordered Caesarion's execution because he viewed him as a potential rival.

Pompey's Pillar in Alexandria stands surrounded by Egyptian statues of female sphinxes. The pillar was erected in 300 AD in honor of the Roman Emperor Diocletian, who saved Alexandria from famine. The pillar's name was given by medieval travelers under the misapprehension that Pompey's head was buried beneath it.

Caesar triumphant

In 47 BC, after leaving Egypt, Caesar went to the Middle East to challenge Pharnaces, the son of Mithridates, in the battle of Zela. Pharnaces had exploited Rome's distraction with the civil war to seize more territory in the East. Caesar's victory over Pharnaces was so swift that he boastfully coined the phrase "*veni, vidi, vici*" (I came, I saw, I conquered). Caesar scored another success at Thapsus the following year. He faced the remainder of Pompey's allies who had fled to North Africa after the battle of Pharsalus and the death of their leader. Caesar won at Thapsus and forced the opposing general, Cato the Younger, to commit suicide. Thapsus had almost wiped out the opposition to Caesar, but Pompey's sons had been able to escape to Spain for one last stand. The battle, which took place at Munda in 45, was yet another success for Caesar. It was to be the last military challenge posed to his rule; Caesar had won the war.

Board Games

Ivory dice excavated from Pompeii.

Romans played a variety of board and dice games including *Latrunculi*, a tactical chess-like game played out on a board grid and using sixteen pieces. The aim was to capture the opponent's pieces, the game concluding when all the pieces had been taken. Excavated *Latrunculi* pieces have been made from stone and colored glass. The boards themselves were mostly made from wood, and occasionally stone or marble.

Dice, or *Tesserae*, played by adult Romans, proved to be a favorite form of gambling. Despite the fact that games of chance were forbidden by Roman law, except at Saturnalia, they appear to have been widespread, with gambling houses, brothels, and taverns playing host to these activities. Most dice were made from bone or ivory, or more commonly wood.

The Lines of the Twelve Philosophers

Duodecim Scriptorum (also known as *XII Scripta*) was a board game thought to be a predecessor of modern backgammon. The board was marked out with three rows of twelve spaces and the aim was to move all one's pieces to the final square on the opposite side of the board. As three dice were used, the game was considered to be gambling by the Roman authorities and therefore illegal. In an effort to disguise the true game, it is thought that some boards were made with letters replacing the squares on the board. This game was then known as "The Lines of the Twelve Philosophers," although it was almost identical to *Duodecim Scriptorum*. Tabula is thought to have

evolved from this game as it uses the same number of pieces and three dice.

Bones and stones

Calculi, or *Ludus Calculorum*, was a simple game, similar to the game "five in a row." Played by two people on a board of any size, the winner was the first person to make five stones in a row, horizontally, vertically, or diagonally.

Tali is the Latin name for knucklebones, and is so called because the pieces would originally have been made from the knucklebones of sheep and goats. The game originated in Ancient Egypt and was played in Greece as *Astragali*. Romans played with pieces made from a variety of materials, including gold, silver, marble, ivory, and wood. Four pieces would be thrown in the air and fall onto one of four sides, each of which would have a value. *Tali* was a form of gambling; it was superseded by dice as the preferred game in later Imperial Rome.

A third century AD Roman mosaic from El Djem, Tunisia, shows three men seated at a table, playing dice.

Julius Caesar: Dictator for Life

Like Sulla, Caesar ostensibly adhered to the pre-existing governing structures of Rome. But in reality, the Republic was in tatters. Caesar was appointed dictator for life and took to wearing purple robes, a tradition previously upheld only by the old Roman kings.

Roman crown with ivy and berries. Although Julius Caesar refused the title of "King," in the senate he sat on a throne wearing a laurel crown.

Below: An inscribed tablet lies in the ruins of the Forum.

Refuses title of "King"

He may have refused the actual title of king, which would have been an obvious deathblow to the Republic, but he did sit on a throne wearing a laurel crown while in the Senate. During 45–44, Caesar's cult of personality blossomed; coins were marked with his face and the month of July was named in his honor. Caesar's power began to know no bounds when he began appointing people to government positions rather than have them elected.

Caesar controls the Senate

Given his affiliations with the *Populares* and his military campaign against senatorial forces, it might have been expected that a victorious Caesar would have castrated the Senate as Sulla had neutered the Tribunate. But Caesar did not have to resort to the political machinations of his

predecessors because he had dealt the decisive blow to his rivals on the battlefield. This meant that Caesar believed he could maintain the Senate as a governing institution but replace reactionary senators who had once sat in it.

Although he appointed some of his own men to these positions, he also allowed many of the pre-existing senators to keep their jobs; this was adroit because it meant the Senate did not need to be rebuilt from scratch. With the Senate seemingly compliant, Caesar even resolved to increase its membership from six hundred to nine hundred because he argued that an Empire the size of Rome's required a larger assembly.

Populist reforms

The quest for personal power was not Caesar's only goal; after capturing Rome in 49 BC, he embarked on a series of social reforms in line with his populist views. For example, the wealthy were to be held more accountable for crimes against the plebs and a quarter of debts for all Romans were to be canceled because interest rates had spiraled out of control during the civil war.

In addition, Caesar instigated a number of public building works, which provided employment for a number of poor Romans. However, Caesar did not get carried away with social reforms, and many of his policies were distinctly moderate in character; he stopped short of canceling all debts and slashed in half the number of the population receiving corn benefits. Such policies were not necessarily designed to be popular, but rather to be of wider benefit to the health of the Roman economy.

Benefits to the legions

Caesar also ensured his legions were well cared for. At the time of his victory, he gave each soldier a massive cash bonus and ensured that land was found for his retiring veterans, by establishing new colonies across the Roman world. Among the most famous of these were the rebuilt cities of Corinth and Carthage, the two cities most harshly treated by the Roman Republic. In addition to Caesar's veterans, poorer Romans and emancipated slaves or "freedmen," came to settle in these new frontiers.

Alarm at Caesar's autocratic rule

In hindsight, Caesar's biggest mistake was to assume that the Senate, purged of the elements that outwardly opposed him, could be made compliant. But this was not the case; members of the aristocratic Senate became increasingly alarmed by Caesar's autocratic rule with its monarchical trimmings.

A group known as the "Liberatores" plotted to murder Caesar, and on the Ides of March, (the fifteenth day), they succeeded. The senators lured Caesar into the trap on the pretext that they wished him to read through a petition they had written and the dictator was stabbed to death. Chief among the conspirators were Marcus Junius Brutus and Gaius Cassius Longinus, both conservatives who had originally been affiliated with Pompey but had been magnanimously, if foolishly, pardoned by Caesar.

Upon Caesar's death Brutus proclaimed the regained freedom of Rome, but this was highly premature; the struggle had not been won and in many ways it was only just beginning.

Bust of Julius Caesar. After winning the civil war, Caesar returned to Rome and began to amass substantial personal powers. Alarmed senators plotted and carried out his assassination on the Ides of March 44.

Antony and Octavian

Mark Antony, who had stuck by Caesar throughout the campaign against Pompey, maneuvered to take charge immediately after the assassination of his colleague. However, Caesar's will revealed that he had had another heir in mind: his nephew and adopted son, Octavian.

Octavian challenges Mark Antony

After the assassination of his uncle/father, Octavian returned from his studies in Illyria to Rome. Upon his return he discovered an ambitious Mark Antony planning to shore up his position by occupying Cisalpine Gaul and ingratiating himself with Cleopatra in Egypt.

The Senate feared that Antony was attempting to make himself dictator and encouraged the eighteen-year-old to challenge Antony so they could play the two leadership contenders off against one another. Their first encounter came just a year after Caesar's assassination, when Octavian joined the Senate's forces and the two consuls in the Battle of Mutina against Antony. The senatorial forces were victorious, but the two consuls were killed in the fighting and Octavian all of a sudden found himself at the head of an army.

The death of both consuls meant that the consulship had come up for grabs and Octavian demanded his own appointment. His demand was refused by the Senate which was not willing to see him become a dictator. With his new army, Octavian simply marched on Rome and took the consulate by force.

New alliances

Like Pompey, two decades earlier, Octavian's initial support for the Senate was destroyed because the Senate was unwilling to see him become too powerful. His solution to the intransigent Senate was the same as Pompey's; to build an independent power base outside the Senate by throwing in his lot with his powerful rivals. In Pompey's case this had been Julius Caesar; in Octavian's it was his former enemy, Mark Antony, and also Aemilius Lepidus, a close associate of Caesar, with a large army.

Right: Cleopatra had relationships with both Julius Caesar and Mark Antony. With Caesar she had a son, Caesarion, whom she intended would succeed his father. Her relationship with Mark Antony was a personal affront to Octavian whose sister, Octavia, was married to Antony.

Antony and Lepidus had already joined forces and added to Octavian's strength, as well as his status as Caesar's adopted son; the three could dominate Roman politics and marginalize the Senate. The result was that a Second Triumvirate was formed at a meeting in Bononia (Bologna) in 43 BC.

The Second Triumvirate

Unlike the first Triumvirate, the second gained official status because the Senate, too weak from years of fighting and purges, was unable to challenge the combined will of the three men. The second Triumvirate was restricted to a five-year tenure, although there seemed little anyone but the triumvirs could do to police such terms. Although consuls continued to be appointed, their role was marginalized by the triumvirs and at various times one of the triumvirs doubled up in the position of consul.

Avenging Caesar

The three men had their close personal links to Caesar in common and therefore the first task of this three-man dictatorship was to hunt down Caesar's assassins and avenge his death.

An angry mob had forced the chief culprits, Brutus and Cassius, to flee Rome because they did not share the opinion that Caesar's death had liberated the population. The assassins settled in the East where they were hunted down by Antony and Octavian, while Lepidus had remained in Rome in a dual role of triumvir and consul.

Revenge was served in the Battle of Philippi, in Macedonia, in 42 BC. In the first encounter, Antony's forces defeated Cassius', but Brutus was able to overcome Octavian. However, disaster struck for the assassins when incorrect intelligence led Cassius to

believe that Brutus had also been defeated. Cassius duly took his own life, leaving Brutus to face Antony and Octavian on his own. In the second encounter Brutus was defeated and forced to commit suicide before being captured.

Death of Cicero

The conquest of Brutus and Cassius was not the end of the retributions; back in Rome, the triumvirs were content to use their hunt for co-conspirators as a pretext for purging their political enemies. Obvious foes such as the famous philosopher and political theorist, Cicero, who had openly and very publicly opposed Caesar and Antony, were hunted down and killed.

However, the triumvirs were not particularly discriminate in the purge; even Antony's uncle, Lucius Julius Caesar, an ally of Julius Caesar, was killed. In total, well over one thousand enemies of the triumvirs were proscribed; the majority faced death and only the lucky few managed to survive. Not only did the purge shore up the Triumvirate in itself, but the confiscated wealth of the proscribed men lined the triumvirs' pockets giving them an even stronger base against the remnants of Roman government.

The second Triumvirate, like the first, was largely a marriage of convenience. The three men were not the best of friends, and the dislike between Antony and Octavian was particularly palpable.

Above: The famous philosopher and political theorist, Cicero, who had openly and very publicly opposed Caesar and Antony, was hunted down and killed as part of the second Triumvirate's plan to avenge Caesar's assassination.
Left: Bust of Mark Antony.

Division of the Empire

The triumvirs did try to patch over their differences. For example, in 40 BC, when Octavian arranged the marriage of his sister, Octavia, to Mark Antony, but mutual antagonism meant that conflict was always around the corner. To keep each other at arm's length, the triumvirs divided the Empire into three spheres of influence. Octavian took the West and Antony the East, while Lepidus acquired North Africa. Infighting was largely averted and the Triumvirate was given a second five-year term in 38.

Octavian and Lepidus clash

During the second term the second Triumvirate quickly came undone. Octavian's and Lepidus' relationship was immediately severed when Octavian believed that Lepidus was conspiring to take control of Sicily. Lepidus had brought his legions from Africa to assist Octavian in dislodging Pompey's son, Sextus, who had based his armies there. Octavian feared that Lepidus' assistance was a ruse to bring his own legions to Sicily and keep them there. To pre-empt this eventuality, Octavian encouraged Lepidus' legions to switch loyalties to him.

This was not an easy task but Octavian was able to win the legions over because he was the son of Caesar, and moreover, because Caesar was in the process of deification, Octavian was even able to claim that he was the son of a god. Octavian cast Lepidus, now bereft of his armies, out of the Triumvirate, but was merciful with his colleague; Lepidus was allowed simply to quietly retire and even keep his post as *pontifex maximus*.

Preparation for war

The relationship of the remaining two dictators also soured, although it had never been very good in the first place. Antony's ambition once again flared when he married and had children with Cleopatra of Egypt. This move was a political threat to Octavian because Antony had become the king of Egypt, and had additionally gained important influence over Greece, owing to the Hellenistic origins of Cleopatra's dynasty.

Concurrently, Antony tried to weaken Octavian by asserting that Caesar and Cleopatra's son, Caesarion, should become ruler in Octavian's stead. Besides the political threat, Octavian also had a personal gripe with Antony; his marriage to Cleopatra was humiliating to his Roman wife and children, who were also Octavian's sister and nieces. The personal and the political combined to make Octavian prepare for war. To convince the Senate to support him, he illegally read Antony's will, which indicated that he would divide the East up among Cleopatra's children and wished to be buried in Alexandria instead of Rome. An outraged Senate gave Octavian the necessary backing for a war.

Left: The temple site on the island of Philae in the middle of the River Nile was associated with the Egyptian goddess Isis, who was associated with the Greek goddess Aphrodite, whom the Romans worshiped as Venus.

The last civil war of the Republic

In 32 BC, Octavian declared war on Cleopatra and, by extension, on Antony. Although he had the backing of the Senate, not all senators were on Octavian's side and a number went to join Antony in Egypt. Both sides amassed vast armies of men but the decisive encounter was to happen at sea in the Battle of Actium in 31.

Octavian's forces had naval superiority and won the day, in part due to Octavian's competent general and lifelong friend, Marcus Vipsanius Agrippa. Antony's ship managed to escape back to Egypt but his legions in Greece were left behind. They had little choice but to defect, but the mastery shown by Agrippa at Actium was encouragement for many generals to do so willingly. Octavian found himself in charge of the vast majority of the Roman Army and began his march on Alexandria overland.

Octavian allied with his cousin, Lucius Pinarius, who was governor of Cyrenaica, the Roman province immediately to the west of Egypt. Together, the two armies pinned Antony's forces in Egypt and eventually trapped Antony in Alexandria.

Antony and Cleopatra commit suicide

In 30 BC, Antony committed suicide by falling on his sword and soon after Cleopatra followed suit, allegedly allowing an asp to bite her, but it has not been ruled out that Octavian actually murdered her. What is known is that she outlived Antony by a few days, during which time she tried to negotiate with Octavian to spare the life of her son by Caesar, Caesarion. However, the negotiations failed because Octavian feared "too many Caesars" and had Caesarion, a potential political rival, pre-emptively murdered.

With the death of Caesarion, who had reigned jointly with his mother, the Egyptian throne was presented to Octavian who became not just the ruler of Egypt, but the master of the entire Empire.

Above: Roman coin, depicting a crocodile, marking the defeat of Cleopatra.

Right: Bronze head of Augustus at about the age of 30. The sculpture was found in Meroe in the Sudan. Augustus, meaning "majestic," was the name given to Octavian by the Senate in 27 BC.

Dealing with excess

As there was so much food served at the banquet, it was usual for much of it to be uneaten. It was commonplace for guests to take food home with them at the end of the evening for the second breakfast the following day.

However, not all Romans stopped eating when they were full; although it was not a common practice, some purged their stomachs during the meal, by inducing vomiting, and then carried on eating.

Whether they took home the leftovers, or carried on eating, it was polite for a guest, upon finishing the meal, to show appreciation of the food by belching.

Slaves' jobs

Slaves were worked hard during a banquet, not only would they prepare the meal, but they would also attend to the diners' needs during the meal. When the guests first arrived, in preparation for eating, their hands would be washed by slaves. As Romans usually ate with their fingers, this hand-washing process was repeated between each course.

Slaves were also responsible for bringing dishes to and from the table as well as pouring the wine. In some houses, slaves were expected to fan the guests throughout the meal, which would have been a long and tedious job.

Amphorae storage jars from Ostia. Romans stored many foodstuffs in amphorae—large, conical vessels—which were often buried in the ground to help preserve the goods.

Seafood was usually eaten by wealthier Romans, but a sauce called liquamen made from fermented fish was popular with all classes.

Food for the poor

The majority of Romans were not wealthy enough to afford the lavish banquets and extensive cuisine enjoyed by the rich. Breakfast and lunch usually consisted of bread made from the free grain handed out to all citizens by the government.

As with their wealthier counterparts, poorer people would take their main meal of the day in the evening, although it consisted only of bread and vegetables. Ordinary Romans seldom ate meat or fish because it was very expensive. The poorest only usually ate meat when an animal was sacrificed to the gods; as only the internal organs were required for the religious ceremony, the meat from the animal was distributed among the needy.

Hunting was a favorite occupation among the rich and in many cases would provide food for the table. Here a hunter with a dog kills a boar.

Street vendors

Most Romans lived in crowded, multi-story tenement buildings which, to reduce the risk of fire, were not equipped with stoves. Instead of cooking at home, Roman women had to go out and buy the evening meal from vendors on the street. Any leftovers from dinner were eaten for breakfast or lunch the next day.

There were exceptions to these norms; some people chose to buy lunch or an afternoon snack from a food vendor, especially the ones surrounding the entrances to the public baths. Some families even opted to cook in their own apartment, disregarding the risks and often sparking dangerous fires.

Public fountains

Ordinary Romans mostly drank water from public fountains throughout the city. These fountains were connected to an aqueduct, which brought fresh water through a system of underground pipes.

In addition to drinking water, most Roman men also drank wine throughout the day. Roman women were forbidden from drinking wine but, for wealthier women this rule became slightly relaxed over time. The wine consumed by the rich and the poor differed sharply in quality, but all classes shared the opinion that it was uncouth not to dilute their wine with water.

Julio-Claudian Emperors

Augustus

Octavian emerged as the great winner after more than a century of turmoil. Following his defeat of Antony and Cleopatra in 30 BC, he ruled for a long period over a relatively serene Empire and laid the foundations for a new golden age.

Octavian becomes Augustus

To all intents and purposes Octavian was the first of the Roman Emperors. In 27 BC he ostensibly restored the Roman Republic but this was more of a token gesture because he continued to amass more power for himself. In the same year the Senate honored Octavian by renaming him "Augustus," meaning "majestic" and gave him the status of *princeps* or "first citizen." This gave him a specific position in Roman government, whilst superficially adhering to the overarching Roman Republic. In fact, the Emperors were to continue to pay lip-service to the Republic and disguise their despotic rule until Diocletian came to power in 284 AD.

Augustus was very quickly made a dictator and a consul for life and accumulated even more functions when he was granted the powers of a tribune, allowing him to set the agenda of the Senate and wield an absolute veto against all laws. He was handed control over all proconsuls, which gave him the right to manage the affairs of the entire Empire and he was also given exclusive *imperium*, or authority, over the city of Rome. After the death of his former colleague in the Triumvirate, Lepidus, in 12 BC, Augustus also acquired the role of *pontifex maximus*.

Gold coin with portrait of Augustus.

Creation of the Praetorian Guard

Although Augustus created a ruthless personal bodyguard, the Praetorian Guard, to ensure his own safety and authority, his success in gaining absolute power was largely a result of his relative moderation. After generations of civil wars and anarchy, Romans were happy to accept Augustus' rule in exchange for stability and the rule of law that he offered. The streets of Rome were cleared of the gangs that had menaced them for so long, and Rome regained its peace and prosperity.

Statue of Augustus as pontifex maximus, *the head of the state religion.*

A return to "family values"

Augustus' emphasis on frugality and a return to family values also chimed well with ordinary Romans, who had detested the ostentatious lifestyles that the city's rich had enjoyed during the late Republic. Such was his stress on modesty that he even had his own daughter exiled from Rome as punishment for her hedonistic lifestyle.

The Senate, which had traditionally been reluctant to accept any curbs on its own power, also provided very little resistance to Augustus because purges and warfare had transformed it into a relatively benign institution. Octavian further benefited from the support of the Army, whose continued loyalty was assured by generous offers of land to veterans. Moreover, the size of the Army was greatly reduced and the legions dispersed across the Empire so that it would not have been easy to mount an effective challenge to Augustus' rule, even if the Army had wished to do so.

Marble pillars lie within a ruined room in the Forum. Augustus famously boasted that he found a city of brick and left it a city of marble.

Rome regenerated

With increased stability and security in Rome, a regeneration of the city got underway. Augustus famously boasted that he found a city of brick and left it a city of marble. This might have been an exaggeration but he did make a number of upgrades to the city.

One of his first works, the Forum Augustus, was begun in 42 BC after the Battle of Philippi but not completed until 2 BC. The Forum was complete with a temple to Mars, the god of war, an offering to thank him for victory against Caesar's assassins.

During Augustus' reign, the Campus Martius underwent particular development; Augustus had the Senate build the peace altar to commemorate the return of peace in Rome and additionally he convinced his general, Agrippa, to build the Pantheon on the site. The original building was destroyed in a fire, but its replacement, built during the reign of Hadrian, still stands to this day.

Another prominent addition to the city was the temple of Julius Caesar, built by Augustus to honor his deified adoptive father. Not only did Augustus oversee the construction of a number of buildings, he also set a fashion for later Emperors, who took to building grandiose public works, especially forums, which were usually named after the Emperor who had commanded their construction.

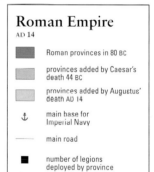

Roman Empire
AD 14

- Roman provinces in 80 BC
- provinces added by Caesar's death 44 BC
- provinces added by Augustus' death AD 14
- ⚓ main base for Imperial Navy
- main road
- ■ number of legions deployed by province

Ostia: the port of Rome

It is believed that Ostia was founded in the seventh century BC by the fourth King of Rome, Ancus Martius, although so far remains have only been excavated dating back to the fourth century BC.

Series of walls from Ostia showing different styles of brickwork.

The town was located at the mouth of the River Tiber, 18 miles west of Rome, and almost certainly developed to defend the capital from anyone entering via this waterway.

A naval base

In the third century BC it was mainly used as a naval base where the *quaestor classici* (officer taking care of the fleet) operated during the Punic Wars against Carthage. It was from Ostia that Scipio sailed in 211 BC when he set off to defeat the Carthaginians in the Second Punic War. Inhabitants of the town were not involved in the fighting, as they were needed to keep the harbor running.

The second century BC saw it emerge primarily as an important commercial harbor with many goods from the colonies passing through the port on their way to Rome. The *quaestor* was now responsible for the import of grain.

Independence and renovation

The town was attacked by Marius in 87 BC and again by pirates in 67 BC so was rebuilt by the statesman Marcus Tullius Cicero, with additional protective walls. Also around this time Ostia ceased to be governed by Rome but was able to have its own government.

Under Augustus and his son Tiberius much of the renovation of the town began. During the reign of Claudius (41–54 AD) a new port was built at Portus. It was constructed about one mile north of Ostia and therefore created a new, separate settlement. Trajan later enlarged Portus with the construction of a hexagonal basin designed to withstand erosion from the waves. After the harbor was completed there was a great building boom in the city, with much of this work supervised by Hadrian and Antoninus.

Ruined entrance to a house, domus, *in Ostia.*

Rise and decline

Local government in Ostia consisted of two magistrates called *duoviri* who were in power for a year and presided over the city council. Two quaestores aerarii handled the city's finances, the *curator operum publicorum et aquarum* looked after the public buildings and water supply, and the *quaestor alimentorum* helped poor children. These served a population in the first century AD which had risen to fifty thousand, a figure that included seventeen thousand slaves, who came mainly from Egypt and the Middle East.

However, in the second half of the third century, along with the rest of the Western Roman Empire, Ostia began a slow decline. Buildings that collapsed were not rebuilt, and Portus was beginning to gain in importance. The town was now mainly a residential area with some expensive habitations built between the third and fifth centuries, probably for merchants working in Portus.

Interior of a bakery at Ostia, showing the bread ovens.

In the eleventh century, marble and other materials taken from Ostia were used for magnificent new buildings, including the Leaning Tower of Pisa, which gives a clear indication of how neglected the city had become. In 1461 Pope Pius II visited the city and commented on the vast areas of ruins; it was in this condition the city remained until the end of the nineteenth century.

Uncovering Ostia

Occasional and spasmodic excavations of the city began in the 1700s with the Roman archaeologist Rodolfo Lanciani starting his work in the 1800s.

Dante Vaglieri began to systematically excavate the city in 1907, although he died six years later. Guido Calza took over, but unfortunately, during the age of fascism, the buildings were uncovered too quickly, without a systematic study of the layers that would have provided a greater understanding of the history of the town. During this time some of the ruins were rebuilt or renovated, so it is the case that some buildings, such as the Theater, are largely 1930s reconstructions.

Excavations have, however, shown an urban structure typical of Roman town planning, with the Forum at the center, crossed by the Cardo and Decumanus. Close by is the Temple, built under Tiberius and dedicated to Rome and Augustus. The Basilica, used for the administration of justice, and the Curia, normally used for council meetings (although Ostia's was probably used as a temple) were constructed at the beginning of the second century when Hadrian was responsible for building the Capitolium. This was the largest temple in the city, with impressive Corinthian columns, dedicated to Jupiter, Juno and Minerva. There were also many cult buildings, dedicated to the different divinities located around the town.

Nowadays Ostia is actually five miles from the shoreline as major silting of the Tiber estuary took place between the Middle Ages and the nineteenth century.

Carved stone sarcophagus from Ostia.

Tiberius

The ultimate death blow to the Republic was Augustus' longevity. He ruled Rome for more than forty years, during which time his autocracy was accepted as the norm and the days of Republican control gradually slipped from the living memory of most Romans.

Augustus' succession

Despite, or perhaps because of, his long reign, Augustus had gone as far as appointing a successor in his stepson Tiberius. Tiberius had not been the first choice of heir; Augustus had earlier chosen to adopt his grandsons. However, his longevity meant that he outlived several of these potential heirs, and it was Tiberius who ended up in pole position at the end of Augustus' reign.

Accusations have been made with regard to Augustus' wife, Livia Drusilla. It has been suggested that she had a number of rival heirs disposed of so that her son, Tiberius, would inherit. Tiberius had shored up his position by marrying Augustus' widowed daughter, Julia, after the death of her first husband, Agrippa.

The reclusive Emperor

Tiberius had large shoes to fill, and although he did a competent job, he is seen as a rather lackluster emperor. He did not like public life and had a history of reclusive behavior; before he became heir apparent he had secluded himself on the island of Rhodes and even as Emperor, after 26 AD, he retreated from Rome to live the rest of his days on the island of Capri.

With the Emperor out of the city, the ambitious head of the Praetorian Guard, Lucius Aelius Sejanus, tried to gain power for himself. Early in Tiberius' reign, Sejanus had convinced him to build a large camp to concentrate all the Praetorian Guard in one location, which was, in part, a ruse to allow Sejanus to secure his own power base. He spent the 20s purging Rome of his personal opponents, and is even the chief suspect in the murder of Tiberius' son, Drusus in 23.

Bust of Tiberius, a largely unpopular Emperor who spent much of his reign away from Rome, secluded on the island of Capri.

Tiberius acts to secure his position

Sejanus was becoming so powerful that he began to worry the Emperor, who became convinced of a conspiracy against him. Tiberius secretly replaced Sejanus as head of the Praetorian Guard with Naevius Sutorius Macro, who assisted the Emperor in organizing the execution of Sejanus in 31 AD. What followed was a plethora of treason trials, which amounted to more than just a purge of Sejanus' allies.

After the relative calm of Augustus' rule, Tiberius was beginning to return to the terrifying political tactics of the late Republic, hinting at the brutal despotism that would plague Rome in the not too distant future.

Family intrigue

Another intrigue that plagued Tiberius' reign was that of the family of his adopted son, Nero Claudius Germanicus. Germanicus was the son of Tiberius' older brother who had died relatively young. When Augustus had adopted Tiberius, he instructed that Tiberius in turn must adopt Germanicus.

Germanicus was quite different in character to Tiberius; he was exceptionally popular, brave, and handsome. He was a successful general, and in 16, restored the Roman frontier in Germany at the River Elbe, earning him the name Germanicus. The border had been catastrophically lost in the Battle of Teutoburg Forest in 9 AD, where almost three legions were completely wiped out. Germanicus' success in 16 was seen as glorious retribution for Rome's humiliating defeat, making him ever more popular with ordinary Romans, such that calls for him to replace Tiberius as Emperor began to emerge.

Right: Arch of Germanicus. This triumphal arch in the French town of Saintes was built at the entrance to a bridge where the main Roman road crossed the Charente. The arch was moved and rebuilt on its present site in the nineteenth century when the old Roman bridge was demolished.

Mysterious death of Germanicus

In 18 he was transferred to Asia, where he died under mysterious circumstances that led many Romans to believe in a conspiracy theory that Tiberius had murdered his adopted son.

Germanicus' widow, Agrippina the Elder, allowed this conspiracy theory to blossom across Rome, seriously damaging Tiberius' reputation. When she returned from Asia to Rome, she proved more of a nuisance to the Emperor by joining a group of senators opposed to both Sejanus and Tiberius.

Tiberius as tyrant

The Emperor eventually had Agrippina exiled from Rome, together with her two eldest sons. The three of them died in exile, probably through suicide, but many Romans chose to believe Tiberius had murdered them.

The fate of the popular Germanicus and his family, combined with treason trials and his lengthy absence from Rome, did little to endear ordinary Romans to their Emperor with the result that Tiberius is remembered as a tyrant.

Caligula

Agrippina's youngest son and three daughters were deemed less of
a threat to Tiberius and they escaped death by being sent to live with their grandmothers.
After 31 AD, the only surviving boy, Gaius Germanicus (Caligula), was then taken to
live with his adoptive grandfather, the Emperor, on Capri.

"Little Boot"

Caligula got his nickname, meaning "little boot" from his
father's soldiers during the German campaign of 16 A D.
He was so called because his mother used to dress the
boy in a little soldier's outfit, complete with little boots.

On Capri, the boy was reared as an heir, but faced
competition from Tiberius' biological grandson, Tiberius
Gemellus. Gemellus was the son of Drusus, who had
been murdered by Sejanus. Gemellus' mother was also
dead, having been implicated in the plot to kill his father
and executed. Like his orphaned cousin, the parentless
Gemellus was also raised on Capri as a potential heir.

Caligula becomes Emperor

When Tiberius died in 37 AD, he did not choose between
them and appointed both as his heirs. However, any
uncertainty was swiftly overcome by Naevius Sutorius
Macro who had become powerful since helping Tiberius
defeat Sejanus. He found in favor of Caligula, whom he
believed would better suit his own career plan. Caligula
duly became Emperor in 37, but Macro had made a
mistake; a paranoid Caligula later had both him and
Gemellus murdered.

Initially, for the Romans, who had tired of
Tiberius' absentee rule and treason trials, Caligula had
shown promise. His popularity was assured as a member
of the admired and much-pitied Germanicus family and
he was able to bask in the reflected glory of his father's
military success. He was welcomed to Rome by citizens
yearning for change and initially he did not disappoint; he
reduced taxes, he offered amnesty for political prisoners,
and put on grandiose public events.

*Right: Mosaic depicting death
as a skeleton with scythe, from
the floor of a Pompeian villa.
The motto reads "know
thyself."*

*Opposite below: Sculpture bust
of Caligula. After contracting
a mental illness, Caligula
became a cruel and capricious
Emperor, prone to humiliating
his Senators, and proclaiming
himself a living god.*

Reign of Terror

However, that was all set to change by the end of the first year of his reign when Caligula contracted a mental illness. After this time, Caligula became a depraved and capricious Emperor who exacted a heinous reign of terror against his people. He famously remarked, "Let them hate me, so long as they fear me," and he kept to his word.

He shunned Augustan frugality in favor of lavish spending, which meant he was always short on money. To compensate he insisted that all wealthy Romans had to appoint him as their heir and then ordered them killed to get his hands on their fortune faster. When this did not cover his expenditure, he placed the burden on ordinary Romans by raising taxes on absolutely everything.

Caligula was a megalomaniac; he believed that he was a living god and had a total disregard for the rule of law. He intimidated and humiliated people for his own amusement. His senators suffered his whims the most, for they were arbitrarily ordered to commit suicide or

The Arch dedicated to the Emperor Caligula in Pompeii.

run alongside his chariot and their wives were even forced into prostitution.

However, the plebs did not escape; it was rumored that whenever there were insufficient prisoners to fight lions in an arena, he would arbitrarily throw spectators in to make up the numbers, and was not averse to beating ordinary Romans who had mildly irritated him.

Of all his crazed acts, the one most remembered is that he made his horse a senator, and even tried to get the Senate to grant it a consulship.

Assassination of Caligula

Caligula's outrageous behavior left severe discontent brewing beneath the surface. A conspiracy to murder the Emperor was swiftly underway and found a willing and able executioner in Cassius Chaerea, the commander of the Praetorian Guard. Cassius had been a colleague of Caligula's father Germanicus, but Caligula saw this as no reason to show respect. Instead, Caligula always mocked and degraded Cassius by insinuating that he was a eunuch. As head of the Praetorian Guard Cassius was an ideal candidate because he could get up close to Caligula. In 41 AD, at his wits' end, Cassius, in league with the conspirators, assassinated Caligula and his entire family.

Divorce

In the early days of the Republic a husband could divorce his wife without providing just cause. In the mid-Republic, husbands were expected to give greater justification, but it was still relatively easy for them. If a husband decided to divorce his wife, he would have to return her and her dowry to her former *paterfamilias*.

During the reign of Augustus, the husband no longer had to issue grounds for a divorce, but by this time, the wife could also break with her husband. These changes came about because it was expedient for the Emperor to introduce them; he wished to marry Livia Drusilla, who was married and pregnant by another man. In spite of Augustus' increased toleration, women were made to feel greater consequences of a divorce; they could not expect the return of a complete dowry and unfaithful wives were forbidden to remarry.

Children need to be accepted

Soon after the birth of a child, the *paterfamilias* had to officially welcome the baby into the family by taking it into his arms. If he refused then the child had to be disposed of; a slave would leave the baby on the roadside, where it would die of exposure. It is unknown how prevalent such infanticide was, but it was commonly practiced with disabled children.

Given the high infant mortality rate, it is unlikely that many healthy children would have been killed, but if a poor Roman household had too many mouths to feed, they may have been faced with little option but to reject the baby.

If the baby was accepted, the birth was celebrated for eight days with feasts, prayers, and visits to the temple. Over the course of the celebrations, the baby would be given a name and presented with a lucky charm to ward off evil spirits during its childhood. The Ancient Romans suffered from an incredibly high infant mortality rate, which meant that couples had as many children as possible to increase the likelihood of one or more surviving.

At the age of seven most children were sent for some form of elementary schooling, but before that much time would be spent in the home. During these formative years, Roman children would enjoy a variety of

Above: Detail of a fresco painting from the Oplonti Villa, depicting a birdbath and foliage.

pastimes, such as leapfrog, hopscotch, seesaw, and hide and seek, which are still give pleasure to children today. The toys of Roman children also resemble modern toys: miniature carts, hoops, board games, balls, and rag dolls made from papyrus; all seem to have been popular.

Coming of age

A Roman boy came of age at fourteen and was recognized as a citizen in his own right. The boy would have had considerable practice at adulthood before the age of fourteen, because fathers were expected to take their young sons under their wing and show them how to behave and how to operate in the family business.

To mark his passing in to adulthood, the boy would sacrifice his childhood lucky charm and don the toga of an adult male. He would then march toward the forum to add his name to the list of citizens and visit the temple. On the march, he would be accompanied by all the available adult males his family knew, to give the impression that the boy was strong and supported. The celebrations would continue into the evening, when a large banquet would be held to mark the occasion.

The client system

A wealthy Roman male usually had a wide network of clients, for whom he also had acted as their patron. This was an additional family of sorts, based on loyalty rather than blood and was a fundamental social relationship, especially during the Republic. It was a mutually beneficial arrangement; a patron could command loyalty, while a client would be rewarded with food and money for his support.

Each morning, before starting the workday, a client would put on his finest clothes and go to his patron's home to salute him in the atrium of the house. In exchange for his troubles, the client would be given food and money for the day.

There were also longer-term benefits to be had by a client; patrons would ensure that he and his family received a proper burial, legal aid, and financial help. This, in part, made the client system a social welfare network, whereby a wealthy private citizen would provide the services that most governments would provide today.

Mutually beneficial

However, the motivations were not necessarily altruistic; for his part, a patron received a good deal of support in exchange for his patronage. Clients provided a ready and loyal support base in case a patron decided to run for

office or was undertaking a military campaign. The patron could mobilize his clients to go onto the streets and support him for whatever purpose he required.

Often patrons would be the clients of an even wealthier man themselves, which meant that in the event of civil war, Rome could be quite quickly polarized along the lines of the client system; the would-be ruler could count on the support of not just of his client, but of his client's clients as well.

The bond between a client and patron was not broken upon the death of either man because his heir was expected to continue the link. This meant that the client system endured for centuries and a wealthy family could retain their status in society for many generations.

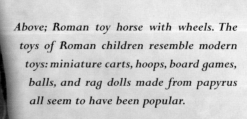

Above; Roman toy horse with wheels. The toys of Roman children resemble modern toys: miniature carts, hoops, board games, balls, and rag dolls made from papyrus all seem to have been popular.

Left: Imperial cameo of Livia, wife of Augustus and her son, Tiberius.

Death Rites

The ruins of a Roman necropolis at Carmona, Spain.

Preparing the body

Professional undertakers would prepare the funeral, which began with the dead body being washed and covered in oil. In some cases embalming was also part of the preparation. The deceased was then dressed in what had been, in life, their finest clothes, and a coin was placed under the tongue as a payment for Charon, the ferryman, who took souls across the River Styx into the underworld.

After the body had been prepared it was put on display for people to come and pay their last respects; if the person was particularly popular or high-ranking, the body could lie on display for a number of days.

Once everyone had paid their respects, a funeral procession made its way to the burial site, with family, friends, clients, and even hired mourners in tow.

Roman law forbade the burial of bodies or cremated remains anywhere within the city limits. Thus the procession has to make its way beyond the city walls. As the funeral party could not wander too far through the countryside, most people were buried alongside the major roads out of the city.

Death was a commonplace occurrence in Ancient Rome: infant mortality was high; contracting illnesses and diseases that are considered easily treatable today could result in death; and for women, death in childbirth was not unusual. Thus, the fear being unmourned was probably greater than the fear of death itself.

Family duties

It was considered imperative to give the dead a proper send-off. Families had a duty to organize at the very least decent funeral for the deceased. Trades and craftsmen, as well as soldiers, could pay into a group fund which would provide for a fitting funeral when they died.

A collection of Roman tomb artifacts. Roman bodies would be buried or entombed with artifacts for use in the next life.

Cremation and inhumation

Roman funeral practices changed throughout the long span of Ancient Rome. During the Republic, most bodies were buried. At the burial site the body would be inhumed, sometimes simply wrapped in a shroud, but wealthier people could afford a coffin made from wood, lead, or stone. The deceased would be buried with objects for the afterlife; these could be marks of offices held during life, or personal items such as mirrors, jewelry or jars of food, drink, or perfumes.

During the Empire period, for reasons of health and space, cremation became the norm. The objects for the deceased present at an inhumation were also part of the cremation ceremony and would be burned with the body. The ashes were placed in a container fashioned from a range of materials, some of which were made specifically for this function, but some of which seem to have been made for other purposes. The vessel containing the ashes was then buried.

Grave markers

Many graves were marked by some sort of tombstone. A few, made from stone have survived. There are some that are inscribed with names of the dead, others with bas-reliefs which may indicate aspects of the person's life.

Fayyum mummy portraits

A collection of interesting grave goods is the mummy portraits from Fayyum. These are a large number of paintings on wooden panels, each of which depicts the face of the deceased on whose mummy it is laid.

Produced in Egypt between the first and the third centuries AD, when Egypt was a Roman province, the naturalistic paintings show, in vivid detail, the fashions and styles of the time.

Christian burial

Burial once again became popular in the late Empire with the advent of Christianity and the belief that the body had to be preserved for the afterlife.

A Roman mummy portrait from the Fayyum, Egypt, shows a woman with dark wavy hair wearing gold earrings and necklace set with gems and a gold fillet.

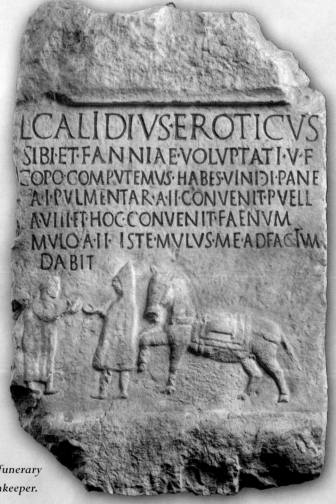

Found near Isernia, this funerary stele is a memorial to an innkeeper.

Claudius

Caligula's rule highlighted the inherent pitfalls of imperial rule;
namely that too much depended upon the character of the Emperor himself.
The system may have seemed to work under Augustus, but his successes resulted from his moderate
nature and the system offered no safeguards against tyrannical rulers like Caligula.

Praetorian Guard maintain control

Such drawbacks were not overlooked by the Senate, who hoped that Caligula's assassination might result in the restoration of the Republic. However, this proved to be wishful thinking; the Praetorian Guard was unwilling to let this happen because its own power was tied to continuation of imperial control.

The Guard opted to replace Caligula with another Emperor, but one who they thought could be molded as they saw fit. This next Emperor, Tiberius Claudius Drusus, was found quivering behind a curtain in the royal household when the Guard went about their purge of the royal family following Caligula's murder.

Related to Augustus

Claudius was well connected to the Emperors; he was Augustus' step-grandson, Caligula's uncle and the brother of Germanicus. The circumstances of his accession to the throne meant that he was never adopted into the Julian family and remained a member of the closely related Claudian family. During his reign, Claudius did try to shore up his links with the Julian family by pushing the idea that his father was the biological son, and not simply the stepson, of Augustus. He furthered this link during his reign by taking up Julius Caesar's unfinished business and successfully invading Britain.

Claudius the historian

Claudius was always considered to be a peripheral member of the imperial family, who was not expected to amount to very much. Although he was clever and became a budding historian, the imperial family kept him out of public office and prohibited him from fulfilling his potential. Caligula had brought him to the fore by giving him a consulship in 37 AD, but this was simply because he was the brother of Germanicus and was no indication that Claudius had finally gained respect. On the contrary, Caligula loved to torment his uncle and make public jokes at his expense.

The imperial family's marginalization of Claudius was a key to his survival because he had managed to slip

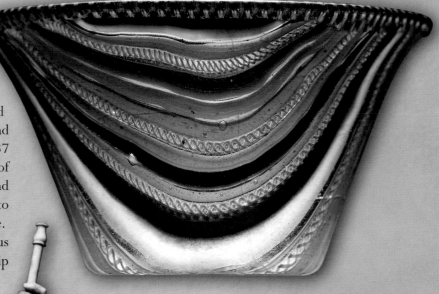

under the radar and escape not only Caligula's paranoia but the subsequent purge against the imperial family.

Return of the rule of law

It thus came as a surprise to many Romans that Claudius became an efficient emperor. He oversaw a return of the rule of law and peace to Rome after Caligula's excesses and Tiberius' treason trials.

Two famines struck Rome during Claudius' rule, which encouraged him to construct a new harbor at Portus, near Ostia and to embark upon agrarian reform.

Domestically, Claudius is best known for his bureaucratic reforms; he reduced the burden of responsibility on the principate by establishing an imperial civil service. This was placed in the hands of Claudius' freedmen (emancipated slaves), especially Polybius, Narcissus, Calistus, and Pallas, who each amassed a great deal of power and wealth for themselves. Claudius had been careful not to antagonize the Senate but they were shocked and appalled by the power wielded by these freed slaves. This led to several attempts on Claudius' life, none of which was successful.

Above: First-century ribbon glass bowl.

Left: Sculpture of Claudius and Eagle.

Opposite: As a result of two famines during his reign, Claudius organized the construction of a new harbor at Portus, close to Ostia. The port of Ostia is well-preserved and the ruins are open to visitors.

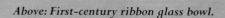

Nero

Claudius had intended that he be succeeded by his own son,
Britannicus, but events conspired against him and Nero took the imperial crown.

Unlucky in marriage

Claudius married four times, but only two of his marriages coincided with his time as Emperor. His third wife, Messalina, was his first empress. She was a notorious woman—known to be unfaithful to Claudius on frequent occasions. In 48, a coup attempt, which she had orchestrated, was foiled by Claudius' freedmen and she was duly executed. However, Messalina had done Claudius one service; she had given him a direct male heir, Britannicus, who was born in 41 AD.

Agrippina the Younger

After Messalina's death, Claudius married his niece, Caligula's sister, Agrippina the Younger, who campaigned to have her own son, Lucius Domitius Ahenobarbus, named Emperor instead of Britannicus. Her machinations succeeded and Lucius was adopted by Claudius as his main heir and renamed Nero Claudius Caesar Drusus. Claudius thought this a prudent move in case he should die suddenly when Britannicus was too young to take power.

In 54, Britannicus neared the age of adulthood and Claudius was planning to replace Nero with Britannicus as heir, but he died before he could change his will. As a result, Nero became Emperor. It was widely speculated that Agrippina had arranged Claudius' murder in order to deny him the chance to change his will. This theory is not unreasonable; she certainly had the motive and the drive. With Nero as Emperor, she persistently meddled in imperial affairs and effectively made herself co-ruler with her son—her face even appeared alongside Nero's on coins at the time.

Right: Portrait bust of Nero.

Opposite above: Fresco showing a sleeping lunatic.

Opposite below: Cameo showing Claudius and his wife Agrippina, his brother Germanicus and his wife Agrippina the Elder.

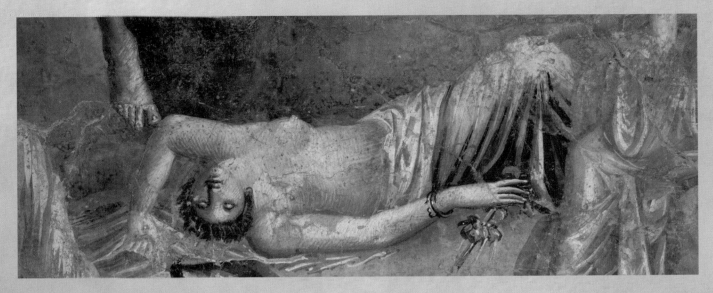

Nero and his overbearing mother

For the first five years Nero's reign was greatly influenced by others; besides his mother, his tutor, Seneca, and the head of the Praetorian Guard, Burrus, had a good deal of influence. It is thought that it was these two men who encouraged Nero to dispose of his overbearing mother.

Initially Nero attempted to marginalize Agrippina, but this did not work and he realized he would have to kill her instead. He first determined a discreet method—he set her aboard a boat he knew not to be seaworthy in the hope she would drown. However, Agrippina did not prove to be such an easy target and she managed to swim to safety after the boat sank, leaving Nero with little choice but to deal with his mother directly.

Nero gains control

In 59 AD he ordered her murder and she was duly beaten to death. Seneca and Burrus thought they stood to gain from the removal of the domineering Agrippina, but the real winner was Nero, who no longer wished to share his power.

His opportunity for exclusive control came in 62, when Burrus died. As Praetorian Prefect, he posed the greatest threat to Nero's position and with him out of the picture, Nero moved against Seneca and reigned supreme from 62. Although Burrus' death might have been a stroke of luck for Nero, it was thought at the time that he might have poisoned the Praetorian Prefect.

Seneca was allowed to return to his writings but an increasingly paranoid Nero believed that Seneca was plotting to kill him. Without giving him a trial, Nero ordered Seneca to commit suicide in 65.

Nero the performer

It was Nero's love for entertainment that really defined his rule; he liked to stage great public events and even shocked Roman opinion by performing in many of them himself. He was an avid sportsman and participated in chariot races at a time when charioteers were slaves. He even entered numerous competitions and always won, but his victory was largely due to bribes and intimidation of the other competitors rather than his own sporting prowess.

His love of sports encouraged him to stage his own version of the Olympics, called the Neronia Games and to construct an artificial, salt-water lake in order to re-enact famous naval battles.

Nero also loved to act and often took to the stage for lengthy periods of time, forbidding any member of his audience to leave the room. The Roman historian Suetonius wrote that people used to pretend they were dead so they could be carried out before he had finished.

Violence and intimidation

Nero's childlike love for entertainment did not preclude him from acts of sheer cruelty. As his reign progressed he became increasingly poorer and resorted to violence and intimidation to replenish his treasury. He brought back the treason trials of Tiberius and, like Caligula, he found ways to get his hands on the inheritances of the rich.

He became deeply unpopular, not only because of his despicable treatment of his mother, but also his disregard for his wife, Octavia. Nero wished to marry another woman, named Poppaea, so connived to divorce his wife and banished her from Rome.

Octavia was the daughter of Claudius and was popular with the people of Rome, who were outraged at her exile. So great were the protests that Nero, at Poppaea's request, agreed to have his wife murdered.

One of the greatest criticisms of Nero was the Golden House he ordered be built; not only did it seem frivolous and greedy, but its construction was seen to profit from the land cleared by the Great Fire of Rome.

Revolts outside Rome

As people turned against Nero within Rome, the final blow was dealt from without. The Roman governor of Gaul, Gaius Julius Vindix, rose up in revolt against Nero's rule.

Nero was relatively unperturbed by the challenge, which he thought would be easy to overcome. However, he was not so confident when Servius Sulpicius Galba, his governor of Spain also rose up, allying himself with Vindix against Nero. Galba's insurrection encouraged more defection; two high-profile legates in control of the armies in North Africa and Lusitania joined him.

Nero loses support

As the list of his enemies grew, ever more of his allies in Rome began deserting Nero. The Senate even allied itself with Galba's forces and declared Nero an enemy of the people. Ordinary Romans began declaring support for the rebellion against him, largely because the grain supply to the city had began to dry up.

Forces loyal to Nero did manage to crush Vindix's rebellion in Gaul, but the death blow had already been dealt. Even the Praetorian Guard abandoned Nero, who could no longer hold on to power, even through the use of force.

With no allies left, Nero fled from the palace and had little option but to commit suicide. With his death, the great Julio-Claudian dynasty came to an end.

Above: Decorative fresco depicting an acrobatic entertainer.

Great Fire of Rome

In 64 AD a fire broke out near the Circus Maximus in Rome. It spread quickly because most Romans lived in tightly packed, flammable tenement buildings called *insulae*.

The fire raged for nine days and destroyed a large portion of the city. Although the exact proportion is unknown—estimates range from one tenth to as much as two thirds of the city—a large part of Rome was devastated by the fire. These figures do not indicate how many people lost their homes or livelihoods because the tenements were so densely populated.

The fire sparked rioting in the city from angry residents, many of whom blamed Nero for having ordered the fire for his own amusement. Others believed that if he had not started it, then he certainly relished it; "Nero fiddled as Rome burned" became a popular saying. However, Nero was not in the city at the time so he could not have started the fire himself and he did not seem to delight in the fire and resolved, rather, to help the victims. Nero took it upon himself to rebuild Rome and ensure that the new buildings adhered to fire-safety regulations.

Nevertheless, the charges against Nero were not entirely untrue, because he was known to have seen a silver lining in all the destruction; the fire had cleared a space in central Rome for him to build a vast, ostentatious palace — the "Golden House." Regardless of the accuracy of the charges, the fact that Romans were so quick to blame Nero gives a good indication of how the public felt about their Emperor.

Nero was not sheltered from these criticisms and quickly found someone else to blame for the fire: the Christians. The Christians were a young sect that had originated in Judea during the reign of the Emperor Tiberius. They were peripheral in Rome at the time, but they were widely disliked by Romans and thus proved a useful scapegoat for the Emperor. Nero's punishment was state-sponsored persecution of all Christians, who were killed in an assortment of barbaric ways. However, he may have shifted the blame for the fire, but he still failed to endear himself with the Roman population.

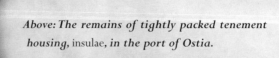

Above: The remains of tightly packed tenement housing, insulae, *in the port of Ostia.*

Left: Tripod for burning coal. While wealthy homeowners would have underfloor heating through a hypocaust, poorer Romans used open braziers which were a frequent source of house fires.

The Baths

As very few Roman houses had facilities for bathing, most cities, towns, settlements and even forts were equipped with a communal bathhouse. They served a dual purpose; the baths, or *thermae*, were not only a place to get clean but also a place to talk business or politics, to gossip and socialize, and also to relax.

Time to visit

For much of the Republic period, there was an entrance charge for attending the baths—later it became free. However, even when charged for it was relatively cheap.

Children were admitted free and although women had to pay more than men, it was still within the reach of most citizens. Paying everybody's entry to the baths for a day was a way in which wealthy politicians would try to persuade people to vote for them.

Men and women did not bathe together, but visited at separate times, although some places had separate facilities. Women visited the baths in the morning and often took their children with them. Most Roman men only worked until the early afternoon. After work they would visit the baths, sometimes staying there until the close at sunset.

Section of the one of the bath complexes at Hadrian's Villa.

Working up a sweat

Although some people would go straight to the bathing pools, it was usual to take part in some form of exercise before bathing. There were spaces set aside for this—*palaestrae*. Men would wrestle, lift weights, engage in fencing and ballgames. Women would exercise with light weights and balls, or might play a game called *trochus* which used a hooked stick to roll along a metal hoop.

Bathing procedure

When ready for the baths the bather would go first into the *tepidarium*. This, as the name suggests, was a lukewarm room designed for relaxation. The bather would then progress to the *caldarium*, a hotter room, where oils were applied to the body. The oils were used as a cleansing agent—the Romans did not have soap. A metal tool called a strigil was then used to scrape off the oil and dirt; this was not an easy process and slaves were often employed to perform this procedure.

After the oil treatment, the bather would then dip in a hot pool in the *caldarium*, before proceeding to the cooler *frigidarium* for a plunge into a very cold pool.

Bas-relief of a gorgon's head.

Mosaic depicting a woman exercising with a ball. Women were able to attend the baths. They would usually visit at separate times from the men, although some complexes had separate areas for men and women. Both sexes would engage in some form of exercise before bathing.

After completing the bathing process the bather could finish off with a massage or, in some of the more luxurious bathhouses, a beauty treatment.

A growing pastime

During the Republic, bathhouses were relatively small, but during the Empire, a number of vast complexes were built at the expense of the Emperor or a wealthy citizen. General Marcus Vipsanius Agrippa, a friend and ally of the Emperor Augustus, built the first of these large public baths in 25 BC.

Baths of Caracalla

Other emperors followed suit, most notably Caracalla, whose baths, built between 212 and 219 AD could hold 1,600 people at a time. The Baths of Diocletian were even larger. Opened in 306, these baths are thought to have accommodated up to 3,000 bathers. Large parts of both these emperors' baths are either well-preserved or have been subsumed into later structures.

Throughout the Empire, huge bathing complexes were built across the Roman world. In the early second century Emperor Hadrian built an extravagant complex in the North African city of Leptis Magna which became, like many of these developments, the social hub of the city.

Above: Vestibule of the public baths at Herculaneum.

Extensive facilities

The large bathing complexes that developed during the Empire period, were about more than just bathing, they provided a host of leisure facilities. They had gymnasiums where a visitor could take exercise, libraries for reading and writing, and food stalls to sit around and eat.

There were usually extensive and lavish gardens to walk around, and sometimes a theater; the baths of Caracalla were so extensive that they even had a stadium.

As women could attend the baths for only a few hours each morning, it tended to be the men who enjoyed the luxuries of these complexes. After bathing, men often stayed into the evening. Here they would spend the time using the wide range of facilities on offer—maybe listening to a concert, playing board games with friends, reading or eating and drinking, perhaps discussing business.

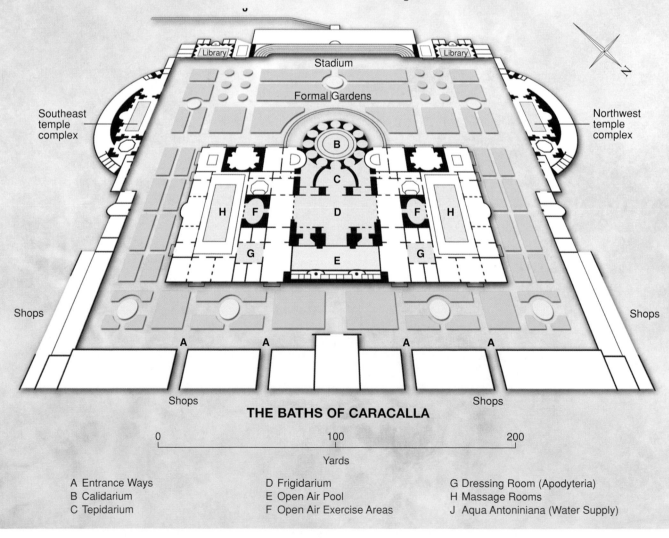

THE BATHS OF CARACALLA

0   100   200

Yards

A Entrance Ways
B Calidarium
C Tepidarium

D Frigidarium
E Open Air Pool
F Open Air Exercise Areas

G Dressing Room (Apodyteria)
H Massage Rooms
J Aqua Antoniniana (Water Supply)

Ceiling fresco in the caldarium of the Oplonti Villa depicting a nude woman riding a scorpion-tailed bull.

Free baths

Before Agrippa built his baths, the citizens of Rome were served by a number of smaller bathhouses, which charged a small entrance fee. This meant that the rich could go every day, but the poorer Romans could visit less frequently.

Agrippa was the first to stop charging customers an entrance fee to visit his baths and all the large bathing complexes built subsequently followed his example and waived the admission fee.

However, the smaller bathhouses continued to charge entrance fees and were still patronized by the rich.

Heating the baths

The grandiose public baths needed a vast amount of water to function. Specially diverted or extended aqueducts were usually needed for the purpose.

Once the water had reached the baths, it was necessary to get each room to the right temperature. Using the unique Roman heating system of the *hypocaust*, it was possible to heat these vast areas, with their numerous different chambers.

Beneath the building an underground furnace called a *praefurnium* was kept alight by slaves, who worked under unbearably hot conditions. The floor of baths was raised on pillars, allowing the hot air created by the furnace to circulate underneath and heat the floor. Sometimes the floor got so hot that bathers were provided with wooden-soled shoes.

The *praefurnium* would also be used to heat the water for the bath in the *caldarium*. A similar system was used to heat Roman villas, albeit with a much smaller fire.

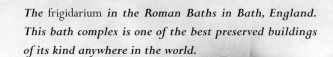

The frigidarium *in the Roman Baths in Bath, England. This bath complex is one of the best preserved buildings of its kind anywhere in the world.*

69AD:
The Year
of Four
Emperors

Galba hacked to death

Otho was the legate of Lusitania and had accompanied Galba on his march into Rome. He had hoped to be rewarded by being adopted as Galba's son and heir, but the elderly Galba instead adopted Lucius Calpurnius Piso, a young man of no particular note. Otho conspired with the Praetorian Guard to overthrow Galba and succeeded. On January 15, 69 AD, Servius Sulpicius Galba was hacked to death in the Forum by a group of soldiers. Piso was killed shortly afterward, and Galba's head was put on a stick and paraded about for others to mock.

Detail from the frescoes at the Oplonti Villa which shows a bird eating figs.

Otho and Vitellius battle for the title

Otho set about trying to rule Rome, but by early spring of 69, it was clear even to Otho that Rome had two Emperors, one proclaimed in Rome and one proclaimed in Germany. Otho tried to negotiate with Vitellius, offering the hand of his daughter, to little avail; Vitellius had already begun his march on Rome.

Otho had fewer men at his disposal but had little option than to meet the challenge. He marched his troops north, where they encountered Vitellius' men on April 14 in the Battle of Bedriacum. Vitellius, trailing the legions from Germay, had military superiority and won the day, leaving Otho with little option but to commit suicide.

With Otho defeated, and Vitellius marching on Rome, the Senate was presented with no choice but to accept the appointment of Vitellius as the third Emperor in just over three months.

Below: This nineteenth century drawing depicts the assassination of the Emperor Vitellius by army officers loyal to Vespasian. Vitellius was the last of the short-lived successors to the Emperor Nero, who ruled for just eight months.

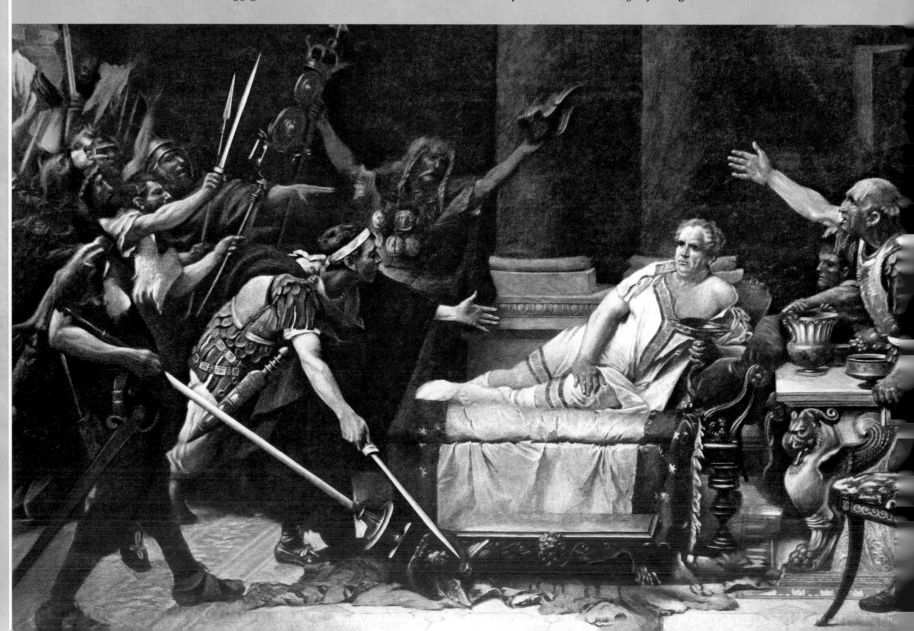

Vitellius as Emperor

Vitellius entered Rome and began the, by then, ritual purges to shore up his authority. The violence of the purges was reflected in the everyday brutality and licentiousness of the legions he had brought with him. He also replaced the existing Praetorian Guard with his own men.

As Emperor, he seemed to have met his own desires before he sought out the problems facing Rome. He is reputed to have been exceptionally gluttonous and was said to invite himself to several expensive banquets a day at different houses. And indeed, surviving images of him show him to be someone who ate to excess.

While the German legions at Vitellius' command had been sufficient in overcoming Otho, they were not adequate to control the entire Empire. Legions in the East had a distinct distaste for Vitellius and began declaring their support for a highly popular general, Titus Flavius Vespasianus (Vespasian).

A new challenger for the title

Vespasian had initially made his name as a general in Britain, where he had successfully invaded the south-west of the island. Toward the end of Nero's rule, he had become extremely popular with the military, and the Roman public, for successfully putting down a rebellion in Judea.

The war against the Jews had distracted Vespasian's army from the tumultuous politics of Rome, but at the beginning of July, his forces declared him Emperor. He was assisted by the governors of Syria and Egypt, as well as Roman legions in the provinces along the River Danube.

Vitellius' enemies presented an attack on two fronts: the Danubian legions attacked from the north, and those from the Middle East attacked from the south. The decisive blow was dealt against Vitellius in a second Battle of Bedriacum in September 69. Vespasian's forces were free to march on Rome, where they killed Vitellius in the Forum and then dumped his body in the Tiber.

Portrait bust of Vespasian, who became the fourth Emperor during the turbulent year, 69 AD.

Flavian Emperors

Vespasian

After the personal excesses of the Julio-Claudian Emperors and the civil wars of 69 AD, Vespasian and the Emperors that succeeded him were a breath of fresh air. Peace became a key feature for over a century, as three stable imperial dynasties ruled over a secure and relatively calm Empire.

Vespasian's early career

Vespasian was born in 9 AD, at the end of the Augustan period. He distinguished himself in military service in Britain, leading the conquest of the south-east of the island as well as the Isle of Vectis, present-day Isle of Wight, just off the south coast of Britain.

Despite his lauded background, when Nero ascended the throne, he fell out of favor with the imperial family, because Nero's mother and de facto co-ruler, Agrippina, had a distinct dislike for him. In order to survive he went into retirement.

Insulting Nero

This was a prudent move because Agrippina was soon disposed of and Vespasian was able to re-emerge on the political scene and was granted a governorship in North Africa in 63.

However, his rehabilitation was short-lived because he fell asleep during one of Nero's music recitals, which deeply insulted the Emperor and Vespasian once again found himself discharged. Given Nero's excesses, this was a relatively lenient punishment.

Proclaimed Emperor

Vespasian was not in the political wilderness for too long, because he was considered the perfect candidate to deal with the revolt against Roman rule in Judea. It was while fighting in the counterinsurgency against the Jews that Vespasian was pronounced Emperor by his men, and he returned to defeat Vitellius and take Rome.

Vespasian was more similar to Augustus than any of the Julio-Claudian Emperors had been: he was parsimonious; he commanded respect rather than fear; and he also sought to stabilize the Empire after years of conflict. In terms of dealing with old conflicts and wounds, he took a just approach. He sorted through backdated legal claims, paid and rewarded the soldiers and most importantly, he refused to reintroduce purges to settle scores against his old political enemies.

Right: Coin from the reign of Vespasian, showing his portrait.

Opposite above: Detail from a fresco in the Oplonti Villa, depicting an insect hovering over some berries.

The Emperor and the mule driver

It seems that Vespasian's only negative quality was a tendency toward miserliness. One famous account of this was when Vespasian's mule driver slowed down his carriage and the Emperor quickly realized this was part of an elaborate fraud. He knew that the mule driver would have been paid to slow down so that a citizen would have time to approach the Emperor for a favor. In spite of his wealth and position, Vespasian only agreed to the plan if the mule driver gave him a fifty percent cut of his fee.

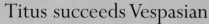

His meanness prevented a return to the excesses of Caligula and Nero, but it did not preclude him from spending vast sums of money on construction. He continued the work of Nero in reconstructing Rome after the Great Fire, and personally inaugurated the rebuilding of the Capitol.

He also extended the *pomerium*, the sacred boundary of the city of Rome. This enlarged the city in order to reduce the problem of overcrowding. One of his grandest and most enduring constructions was the great Flavian Amphitheater, or Coliseum, which still stands to this day.

Titus succeeds Vespasian

Upon Vespasian's death of a fever in 79 AD, he was succeeded by his biological son, Titus Flavius Vespasianus. His accession to the throne met with almost universal objection because Titus had a reputation for cruelty, greed, immorality, and excessive behavior.

When his father had returned to Rome from Judea in 69, Titus had carried on the counterinsurgency against the Jewish Revolt. Although he was thanked for his pacification of Jerusalem and Masada, he gained a reputation for ruthlessness. There was concern that Titus might undo his father's good work and plunge the Empire back into insecurity and chaos.

After his death, Vespasian was deified. In the right of the picture are the ruins of a temple dedicated to him in the Forum. The structure on the left is the remains of the Temple of Saturn.

Titus

With a reputation for cruelty and immorality,
it came as a surprise to many Romans to discover that they had misjudged Titus.
He was affable, generous and wholesome; he threw spectacular games for the citizens of Rome;
always heard every petition presented to him, and emphasized public morality and respect.
Titus' reign was quickly marred by natural disaster.

The eruption of Vesuvius

In the first year of his reign, Mount Vesuvius erupted, completely destroying the towns of Pompeii and Herculaneum. Titus acted quickly to help the victims; he established a committee of former consuls to arrange the relief effort.

While Titus was away visiting the region and assessing the devastation caused, a fire broke out in Rome, destroying several important buildings, most notably the original Pantheon, which had been built by Augustus' general, Agrippa. The newly rebuilt Capitol was also burned down, as well as a number of houses.

Titus' generosity

Titus excelled in bringing relief to the city in a way that Nero had never done when rebuilding after the Great Fire of Rome. Generously, he stripped his private holdings to refurnish public buildings in Rome, put a great deal of his own money into the relief effort, and re-housed the homeless in properties owned by families who had perished in the Vesuvian eruption. When a further disaster struck in the shape of an outbreak of plague, he dealt with that in a similar manner: using all means at his disposal to cure people and prevent its spread to others.

An early death

In 81 AD, just over two years into his reign, Titus fell ill and, at the premature age of forty-one, he died. Although he died from fever, Titus' appointed heir, his brother Domitian, was blamed for having murdered the Emperor.

This idea of a conspiracy against Titus was not entirely far-fetched; Domitian had very publicly plotted against his brother while he was alive: for example, by inciting the Army to revolt. Although he was aware of his brother's scheming, Titus forgave him and continued to treat him with dignity and respect.

With such a short reign, Titus' time as Emperor was very much defined by the three catastrophes that struck. However, they failed to overshadow his rule because he proved so adept at coping with them, such that he is remembered as one of Rome's greatest Emperors; the same cannot be said for his brother Domitian.

Above: Mount Vesuvius overshadows the ruins of Pompeii.

Left: Under the shadow of Vesuvius, a concrete cast at Pompeii captures the moment of death of a Pompeian caught in the mountain's violent pyroclastic flow in 79 AD. The bodies of those who died in the hot flow of ash and mud left hollows, and poignant casts like these were made as the positions of the bodies were discovered by archaeologists.

Pompeii and Herculaneum

On August 24, 79 AD, Mount Vesuvius erupted catastrophically, burying the towns of Pompeii and Herculaneum under piles of ash. Both towns were preserved under layers of ash, mud and rock for years, before they were both rediscovered in the eighteenth century.

Pompeii's early years

The settlement at Pompeii was founded just to the south of Mount Vesuvius by the Oscan civilization in the eighth century BC. The Greeks occupied the settlement during the sixth century, before it was taken over by the Samnites in the fifth. It is even thought that the Etruscan peoples might have controlled the town at one stage.

In 290 BC, after Rome's victory in the Samnite Wars, the town became an ally of Rome, but rose up in protest against Roman rule during the Social War of 91 BC. The war was short-lived; Lucius Cornelius Sulla's forces quickly conquered much of the Campania region and Pompeii had little choice but to capitulate. The town was turned into a Roman colony and renamed Cornelius Veneria Pompeianorum in honor of Sulla and Venus, the goddess he admired.

Villas of the powerful

The supporters of Sulla, the *Optimates*, were deeply involved in the politics of the town during the later Republic, and at this time many large villas were built by them in and around Pompeii. A number of army veterans were also awarded land close to the town. Amenities associated with Roman town life, such as bathhouses, and amphitheater, temples, and an odeon were built at this time.

As part of romanizing Pompeii, the state religion was established in the town. The principal Samnite shrine was turned into a temple to the deities of the Capitoline Triad, Jupiter, Juno, and Minerva.

Right: Portrait of Aulus Gabinius from Herculaneum.

Changes in the Empire period

The onset of the Empire subjected the town to several changes as the ruling elites, who had been linked to Sulla, were replaced with allies of the imperial family. The imperial cult was added to list of Roman deities worshiped in the town and a temple to the Emperor Vespasian was built in the forum shortly before the town's destruction. A number of other honors were paid to the Emperors, including a statue of Augustus in the forum and an arch to commemorate Nero's reign.

Domitian

Titus Flavius Domitianus' reign got off to a reasonable start; he inaugurated public works, gave generously to the citizens of Rome, and presided over social and legal reforms.

Establishing popularity

Like Nero, Domitian loved public games and in 86 AD established his own version of the Olympics, the Capitoline Games, a no-expense-spared event, which made good use of the new Coliseum, built on the orders of his father, Vespasian.

Unlike his father and brother, he did not ascend to the imperial title with an already distinguished career, so he sought to compensate with a successful campaign in Germany. He was so pleased with his triumph in the north that he gave himself the name "Germanicus," but his glory was short-lived.

Agricola removed from Britain

Another general, Agricola, began to steal the limelight. Agricola, the governor of Britain, was becoming popular as a result of his victories against the exotic Caledonians in the north of Britain, so Domitian jealously recalled him from service. Upon Agricola's return to Rome, the Scottish Highlands were abandoned and he was forced into anonymity, while Domitian continued to try to make a name for himself as a general.

He campaigned against the Dacians, a Danubian tribe, from what today is Romania, and against a Germanic tribe called the Chatti, with some degree of success, but these were never the victories that he proclaimed to great fanfares in Rome.

The Coliseum where Domitian held his lavish version of the Olympic Games, the Capitoline Games.

Greed and cruelty come to the fore

As Domitian's reign progressed he became increasingly cruel and avaricious. His own domestic entertainments and his foreign enterprises had taken their toll on his personal treasury, so Domitian resolved to recoup his monetary losses through confiscations. Thus he revived the reign of terror of his predecessors and proscribed senators and wealthy Romans so that he could get his hands on their fortunes. He also took more money from the Jews by tightening Vespasian's tax against Jews to include anyone even vaguely connected with the Jewish race.

His cruelty was not simply driven by the need for money, he seems to have had a sadistic side to his character; on more than one occasion, he condemned a man to death, then insisted on spending a pleasant day with him, before having the execution carried out in the evening.

His jealousy also seems to have been a factor in his cruelty; in addition to his petulant response to Agricola's victories, he also had the governor of Britannia, Sallustius Lucullus executed for naming a new type of lance after himself. Domitian's oppressive ways inevitably gained him powerful enemies among the senators and the wealthy of Rome. This led to several conspiracies but it was his own household staff who eventually killed him in 96 AD. With Domitian's death, the Flavian dynasty came to an end.

Above: The ruins of the excavated Roman Vindolanda Fort on the route of Hadrian's Wall in the rolling hills of Northumberland, England. A reconstruction of a stone wall with a turret and a timber milecastle have been added to the original found ruins.

Decorative stone cornice from the Forum in Rome.

One hundred days of celebration

To celebrate the opening of the Coliseum in 80 AD, Titus lavished on the citizens of Rome one hundred days of grand events; besides the normal gladiator shows he flooded the amphitheater and staged a mock sea battle, then drained it again in order to stage an extensive hunt for wild animals.

Roman historian Dio Cassius, writing in the following century, claimed that in the course of Titus' celebrations over 11,000 animals were killed. Once the inaugural festivities were concluded, the Coliseum mostly hosted gladiatorial contests and hunts.

A decorative capital displayed in the interior of the Coliseum.

Gladiators need to please the crowd

Gladiators were expected to exert themselves in the arena. If they failed to put on a good enough show, they faced execution. When a gladiator had been defeated, he was allowed to request mercy from the Emperor, or whoever was presiding over the games—their decision was often based upon what would be the most popular with the crowd.

Victorious gladiators were rewarded with fame and money. An additional reward was emancipation, especially enticing given that most gladiators were slaves or prisoners.

Hypogeum

The underground chambers or *hypogeum* were completed by Vespasian's younger son, the Emperor Domitian. Wild animals, weapons, slaves, prisoners, scenery, and other props were kept under the ground. When needed, the props and the animals were heaved to the surface by a system of weights and pullies.

The present-day façade of the Coliseum is not what the Roman citizens who flocked to Emperor Titus' hundred days of celebrations for the inauguration of the Flavian Amphitheater would have seen. This is the inner wall, less decorative than the outer wall which has largely disappeared and is extant in only a few places around the 600-yard perimeter.

Detail of a mosaic depicting a gladiator fight.

Animal hunts

The arena of the Coliseum was used for a number of displays and shows. Gladiatorial battles were popular, as were animal hunts, or *venatio*. A huge variety of wild beasts was used, mainly imported from Africa and stored in the *hypogeum*. Elephants, big cats, giraffes, crocodiles, and hippopotamus are among some of the animals hunted in the arena.

Elaborate sets were constructed with moveable trees and buildings into which the animals would be introduced and the hunters would stalk their prey. For the urban-dwelling Romans this would all add to the exotic experience of the *venatio*.

Over five hundred years of use

The Coliseum remained in use for its original purpose for over five hundred years. Gladiatorial contests seem to have died out during the fifth century AD but wild animal hunts continued into the sixth century. Throughout that period it saw a number of repairs and restorations as the building suffered damage through fire, earthquake, or deterioration over time.

Interior view of the walls of the Coliseum.

Hunting baths at Leptis Magna take their name from the frescoes that adorn their walls. It has been suggested that the frescoes indicate that the baths were owned by a guild of local hunters who supplied wild beasts to the Coliseum and other amphitheaters of the Roman Empire.

Five Good Emperors

Nerva

The three emperors of the Nervo-Trajanic Dynasty, together with the first two Antonine Emperors are called the "Five Good Emperors." In an era, already defined by relative peace and stability, these Emperors stand out as the best Rome ever had. One reason for this was because each heir was adopted, allowing the best man for the job to be chosen.

A hasty appointment

Domitian was murdered without an heir so Marcus Cocceius Nerva was hastily appointed to the imperial throne to avoid a political vacuum, which could have meant recourse to unrest and violence.

Despite the haste of his appointment, Nerva was deemed the most suitable candidate because he was a popular member of the Senate, but he was also a respected member of the Flavian courts. Domitian had marginalized Nerva in the last years of his campaign, but Flavian supporters were satisfied that his appointment would guarantee the safety of their person and their interests.

There is no doubt that Nerva was a "stop-gap" Emperor; he was in his sixties, was known to be in ill-health and most importantly he had no male heir. He was simply a temporary arrangement to hold the Empire together while a suitable candidate could be found.

Nerva provides domestic stability

Nerva styled his rule on that of Augustus'—he quickly set to work expunging the legacy of Domitian; the Jewish tax was relaxed, political prisoners were freed and Domitian's laws were revoked. After Domitian had extorted money by every underhand means possible, Nerva reintroduced fiscal health through more legitimate channels; he tightened the public purse and sharply reduced the amount of public games and building works.

Nerva's reign provided domestic stability, which made him popular in Rome, but not necessarily with the troops. To appease the Army, Nerva appointed a successor with a military pedigree; however, it came as a surprise to many Romans that his chosen heir was not, strictly speaking, an Italian.

Main: Theater at Merida in Spain. The town was originally named Emerita Augusta. Spain was the birthplace of Trajan, the first non-Italian emperor.

Above left: Amber ring, showing the head of a woman, produced during Trajan's reign.

Trajan

Marcus Ulpius Trajanus was born in Italica (Seville) in the Roman province of Hispania. Although his family were originally from Italy, they had settled in the Iberian Peninsula long before, making Trajan the first Emperor from outside of Italy. His family had an impressive military reputation, which endeared Trajan to both the Praetorian Guard and the Army.

Trajan's father had been governor of Syria and he himself had come to the fore by helping Domitian in his Dacian Wars. In 91 AD, Trajan was granted his first consulship and managed to avoid the reign of terror that Domitian unleashed back in Rome.

Co-ruler with Nerva

Nerva ensured a smooth transition of power by allowing Trajan to rule alongside him whilst he was still alive. However, when Nerva died in early 98 Trajan was preparing for another war against the Dacians. He did not return to Rome immediately, but continued his preparations for more than a year. When he did return, he made a great show by entering the city on foot, a very humble gesture, which gained him the support of ordinary Romans.

Trajan's military success

Trajan was a highly successful Emperor; he sought to expand the Empire and succeeded. Between 101 and 106 he picked up where Domitian had left off and mounted a campaign against the Dacians. Domitian had never achieved a decisive outcome, but Trajan certainly did—the Dacians were beaten and Dacia was turned into a province of the Empire.

The following year, the Empire underwent further expansion when the king of Rome's client state, Nabatea, died. Trajan opted to annex the region, creating a new Arabian province within the Empire.

In 107, with Dacia and Nabatea under his belt, Trajan returned to Rome to begin a seven-year stint as a "civilian Emperor." He set to work on a number of construction projects, especially a widespread road- and bridge-building program.

Ruins in the Forum. Trajan established a large, new forum in Rome, the Trajan Forum, complete with a new shopping center and a monument to celebrate his victories in Dacia—"Trajan's Column."

Roman Spain

The direct Roman presence in Hispania (the Iberian Peninsula) began in 218 BC during the Punic Wars, when troops moved in to dislodge the Carthaginians established there. By 206, the Romans had made important gains, moving into the peninsula as the Carthaginians moved out. The Roman conquest took almost two centuries, until Augustus decided to occupy the peninsula once and for all.

Crushing opposition

In 29 BC, after defeating Antony and Cleopatra, Augustus sent his prized general, Marcus Vipsanius Agrippa to Spain to crush all tribes opposed to Roman rule. Chief among the dissident tribes were the Cantabri of northern Spain.

The Cantabri were skilled fighters and the Romans campaigned for ten years, bringing in a number of legions, as well as the Army. The campaign lasted so long that Augustus himself intervened on occasion to try to bring a swift victory, but to little effect. In 19, the Cantabri finally fell to the Romans and with them, the entire peninsula came under Roman control. Resistance did continue for a time, but it was limited because all the Cantabri males were wiped out; they were either killed by the Romans, or they killed themselves.

Bronze coin showing the gate to Augustus Emerita, the city of Merida in modern Spain.

Occupation strategies

Even before the entire peninsula had been pacified, Hispania was divided into two provinces of the Empire, Hispania Ulterior in the south and west, and Hispania Citerior in the north and east.

Augustus made some modifications by dividing Hispania Ulterior in two; the province of Baectia was established in the south and Lusitania was created on the Atlantic Coast, in a position corresponding with modern day Portugal. Augustus kept Hispania Citerior intact, but renamed it Tarraconensis.

Economic contributions

Hispania's economy was predominantly based on agriculture and mining. Initially, Rome relied on Hispania as a ready source of oil for cooking, cleaning, and lighting. However, North Africa began to replace the Spanish provinces as a source of oil during the Empire.

Farmers on the peninsula continued to produce fish sauce and wine, although Italy was still a major source of these two sought-after commodities, and it was rather Hispania's metal wealth that kept the Romans interested. Tin, silver, iron, lead, copper, and even gold were mined on the peninsula.

Magnificent Roman aqueduct near Nerja, Andalusia, Spain.

Political contributions

In addition to its metals, Hispania proved to be a rich source of good Emperors—two of Rome's most famous, Trajan and Hadrian, were born on the peninsula. In addition Galba, Emperor for a brief time in 69 AD, began his rebellion against Nero from his post in Hispania.

Galba's revolt was not a new departure for the province. The peninsula had already developed a reputation for insurrection in 83 BC, when Quintus Sertorius broke with Rome and ruled Hispania for over a decade. Sertorius, a supporter of Marius and the *Populares*, stood opposed to the government of Sulla and his *Optimates* in Rome. He allied with the local tribes, especially the Lusitanians, and took control of Hispania Ulterior and much of Hispania Citerior.

Battleground for Pompey and Caesar

The *Optimates* sent Pompey to deal with the rebellion, but he was unable to bring Hispania back under the control of Rome. In 72 BC, the uprising collapsed because Sertorius' forces had been worn down by years of war, and his native allies had proved unreliable.

The peninsula was brought back under the control of Rome, but Pompey had many forces deployed there, with the consequence that Hispania was later to become a battleground between the forces of Julius Caesar and Pompey. Caesar's last war against Pompey loyalists took place in Hispania, at Munda in 45 BC.

Developing Spanish cities

Most of the cities in Hispania pre-dated the Romans, Gades (Cadiz), for example, had been Hannibal's operational base before the Romans had invaded and the name of Carthago Nova (Cartagena) reveals its Punic origins.

Rome developed its own cities on the peninsula, most notably Tarraco, the provincial capital of Tarraconensis, which sat at the mouth of the River Ebro.

Silhouette of the colonnades of the Roman theater in Merida, Spain.

Although the settlement certainly pre-dated the Romans, it was not significantly developed until their arrival. The Romans gave the city an amphitheater, and aqueduct an even a large circus for chariot racing.

Establishing new settlements

While Tarraco was simply developed by the Romans, Italica, near Hispalis (Seville), was actually founded by them. The town was established by Scipio Africanus in 206 BC to settle soldiers who had fought for him on the peninsula during the Punic Wars.

For much of its history, the town was largely eclipsed by Hispalis until its two most famous sons, the Emperors Trajan and Hadrian, invested considerably in its regeneration. Of the two, Hadrian took the greatest interest, which meant that much of it was built in his favored Hellenic style. One of his greatest gifts to the town was an amphitheater capable of seating 25,000 people—just half the capacity of the Coliseum; an incredible gift for a city with a population a fraction of the size of Rome's.

Arches of the aqueduct that runs through the city of Caceres in Spain.

Trajan's Forum

Trajan established a large, new forum in Rome, the Trajan Forum, complete with a new shopping center and the famous "Trajan's Column"—a one-hundred-feet-high pillar designed to commemorate his victories in Dacia.

    He also inaugurated the construction of a new aqueduct and a new public baths in Rome, as well as a new harbor at Ostia to increase the grain supply to Rome. His administration was particularly successful because he was courteous towards the Senate, employed first-rate administrators and allowed women an important role in public life.

A return to army life

After seven years of civilian life, Trajan was itching to return to the army. His opportunity came in 113 AD, when a dynastic dispute in Armenia provided him with the pretext to invade Parthia, Rome's long-time rival in the East. Trajan was highly successful; his troops easily overran the Parthians, quickly occupied their capital, Ctesiphon, and declared Mesopotamia as a Roman province.

    The addition of Mesopotamia saw the Empire reach its greatest-ever extent, stretching all the way from the Atlantic Ocean to the Persian Gulf.

Detail from the carvings on Trajan's Column.

Ruined building in the preserved remains of the port of Ostia. Trajan instigated the building of a new harbor at the Roman port to increase the grain supply to Rome.

Trajan relished his time with the army, and it was said that, had he not been so old, he would have pressed on through Persia, in the footsteps of Alexander the Great.

Popular with the people

Trajan was one of Rome's greatest Emperors and was exceptionally popular in his own time because he had managed to strike a perfect balance of providing glorious victories without impinging upon the lives of ordinary Romans.

Hadrian

In 117 AD, Trajan died, and Publius Aelius Hadrianus (Hadrian) was declared Emperor in his place. Officially, it was stated that Trajan had adopted Hadrian on his deathbed, but a number of people cried foul play.

Arguments in the Senate

It was believed that Trajan's wife, Plotina, had tampered with the adoption after Trajan's death so that Hadrian, her favored candidate, could take power. There were heated arguments in the Senate, but Hadrian's supporters won out; Hadrian became Emperor and several of the dissenters, namely four ex-consuls, were executed.

In spite of the questionable circumstances of the adoption, Trajan had certainly groomed Hadrian as a potential successor by advancing his political career and establishing a close relationship with him.

Reducing the frontiers

Hadrian's imperial policy was dramatically different to his predecessor's; Trajan emphasized expansionism, while Hadrian focused upon defence and consolidation. Hadrian believed the Empire to be overstretched so some of Trajan's territorial gains were quickly reversed under Hadrian. Troops were recalled

Coin depicting the head of Emperor Hadrian.

from the East, Mesopotamia was put in the hands of client kings and expansion was halted in Britain, Germany and North Africa. The aim was to reduce the Empire to a more manageable size, and to revert to naturally defendable frontiers.

Hadrian seeks support

These seemingly inglorious policies did little to endear Hadrian to the Army. He was already suffering a lack of popularity in the Senate, where it was believed that the execution of four popular ex-consuls was too high a price to pay for Hadrian's succession.

Hadrian was forced to seek support among ordinary Romans; he canceled all debts, which was an extremely popular gesture and certainly helped to win him the hearts and minds of his subjects. He further pleased the public by placing a strong emphasis on culture and entertainment as well as initiating a large number of civic building projects right across the Empire.

A section of the ruins of Hadrian's Villa, a country retreat built by the Emperor at a site near Tivoli, a day's march from Rome.

Hadrian's travels

During his reign, Hadrian traveled to almost every corner of his Empire, where he micromanaged the affairs of each province, and sometimes even each fort.

His first trip, which began in 121 AD and lasted four years, encompassed visits to Britannia, Hispania, and Mauretania in the West, as well as Galatia, Asia, and Syria in the East. While he was in Britannia in 122, the Emperor commissioned the construction of the famous 75-mile-long defensive wall which bears his name.

Hadrian's second trip took him to North Africa in 128, and the third and final trip from 128 to 132 took him exclusively to the East of the Empire, where much of his time was spent in Greece. Hadrian was an admirer of Hellenic culture; he took to following Greek fashions and spent a considerable amount of money on improvements and gifts for Athens.

Lover drowned

Hadrian's lover, Antinous, usually escorted the Emperor on his travels, but in 130, disaster struck when they were in Egypt. Antinous drowned whilst swimming in the Nile. Hadrian was devastated; Antinous was deified and statues of him were built across the Empire, and even a city, Antinopolis, was founded in his honor.

Below: Archway entrance into the complex of Hadrian's Villa, just outside Tivoli, 18 miles north-east of Rome.

Right: Head of Antinous, the lover of Emperor Hadrian, who drowned while swimming in the Nile. After his death, Antinous was deified and statues of him erected throughout the Empire.

The Second Jewish Revolt

In 130, before reaching Egypt, Hadrian's travels took him to the province of Judea where his decisions and actions were to have long-reaching effects.

Initially, Hadrian had been relatively tolerant of the Jews, and boasted of plans to rebuild Jerusalem after it had been largely destroyed by the Roman Army in 70 BC, after an uprising against Roman rule. However, outrage spread among the Jewish population when it emerged that the city would be renamed Aelia Capitolina and a temple dedicated to Jupiter would be constructed on the site of the main Jewish temple.

The population rallied under the leadership of Simon Bar Kokhba and a revolt broke out in 132. The rebels were highly successful at first, but eventually capitulated to the Roman counterinsurgency, and by 135 the revolt had collapsed. The rebellion led Hadrian to believe that Judaism was inherently troublesome, so he sought to stamp it out; those lucky enough not to have been killed were forced out of the region as slaves or exiles. Judea was romanized, leaving the Jews without a homeland for more than eighteen hundred years.

Hadrian's Villa

In 118 AD, work was begun on a villa for Hadrian's personal use. He disliked the imperial palace on the Palatine Hill and wished to build a retreat outside the city. His villa, *Villa Adriana* in Italian, was located just outside Tibur (Tivoli), a town 18 miles from Rome.

As his reign progressed, more and more time was spent there, until eventually he governed the Empire from the Villa. As a result there was a large court in permanent residence, with a postal service directly linked to Rome.

The villa was so extensive that it would have appeared more like a small town, complete with theaters, libraries, bathhouses, swimming pools, and an infirmary.

A carefully chosen site

The site was carefully chosen; it was on a hillside surrounded by two tributaries of the Aniene that flowed into the Tiber, providing an easy means of transport between the Villa and Rome. There was also a plentiful supply of water from the aqueducts serving Rome—essential to fill the number of baths in the Villa. Quarries were also available nearby for the building materials required, including travertine, lime, pozzolana, and tufa.

Construction took place between 118 and 138 AD, probably in two distinct and separate phases, with the buildings laid out to follow five alignments. Unusually the planners did not use the usual rigid Roman town planning patterns but instead mapped the structures along the natural terrain.

Caryatids line one of the sides of the water of the Canopus, an artificial pool, named after the canal at Alexandria.

Looking toward the Euripus, the semicircle of arches with statues at one end of the Canopus.

Inspired by Hadrian's travels

Covering an area of at approximately 50 acres, and containing over thirty separate buildings, there is evidence of many different types of architecture, all inspired by Hadrian's travels. He was widely acknowledged to be a gifted architect in his own right and was no doubt responsible for many of the stunning ideas, and often emulated a particular place or building he had seen with a building or garden design.

Although inspired by various types of architecture, the methods used were very much Roman, with buildings constructed in *opus mixtum*, a technique invented by Roman builders that combined cement, tufa blocks, and bricks. The bricks were often stamped with the names of the Roman consuls in the year of production, giving archaeologists a perfect dating tool for each individual wall and structure.

The imperial palace was built on top of an older villa dating back to the first century BC. This was the nucleus of the residence, and the *cryptoporticus* can still be seen with its intricate mosaic decorations.

Mosaic from Hadrian's Villa depicting a theater mask.

Significant features

Close by is the Maritime Theater, named after the patterns used, based on marine themes. There is a circular island in the center with a small Roman house, complete with baths and an atrium. It is surrounded by a lake and was probably used as a retreat for the Emperor—dating shows that it was one of the first structures to be built.

The *Pecile* is a huge courtyard surrounded by four porticoes, measuring approximately 750 by 325 feet with a 325 by 80 feet pool inside. The north side would have acted as a *porticus miliaria*, planned to a specific length that measured the distance advised by doctors for a healthy walk (*ambulatio*) at the time.

One of the best-preserved features is the *Canopus*, a long pool surrounded by a colonnade, based on the canal stretching from Alexandria to *Canopus*.

There were three sets of baths in the residence with the Small Baths being one of the most luxurious spaces inside the villa. These were beautifully decorated in marble, with intricate architecture, and no doubt used by the Emperor.

The Maritime Theater was actually a small villa surrounded by a moat. During Hadrian's day the moat was crossable only by a portable wooden bridge, giving the appearance of an unapproachable island home and offering a peaceful retreat.

Other occupants

The villa is served by a warren of underground tunnels, used to transport servants and goods around, while the higher-ranking residents used the roads above.

After Hadrian died in 138, Antoninus, his adopted successor, continued to use the residence, as did Marcus Aurelius. Wall paintings found from the third century also show that it was occupied under the Severans.

However, Constantine I did not use it and had many valuable objects removed to Constantinople. It fell into ruins and was then an easy source of marble and other building materials needed for new constructions.

Reconstruction of Doric colums in a corridor area.

Discovery and decimation

Pietro Ligorio and other humanists began to excavate the villa in the sixteenth century, a time when it was officially identified as Hadrian's residence. An eminent architect, he discovered the fountains and *nymphaeums* with all the statues and decorative work.

Ironically his discovery led directly to the decimation of the villa. In the seventeenth and eighteenth centuries the land was divided, with the owners removing any remaining valuable objects, such as statues or mosaics, which were dispersed through Europe; many ended up in papal collections that can now be viewed in museums.

Excavation finally began in the late nineteenth century after Italy was unified. The site became protected and Pietro Rosa began a systematic and scientific exploration. This work was then continued by Lanciani, Aurigemma and Vighi, along with many foreign academies centered in Rome.

Hadrian's Villa is now a UNESCO World Heritage Site and widely regarded as one of the most stunning Roman excavations, giving a privileged insight into the interests and lifestyle of the Emperor.

View down the Canopus *to the* Serapeum, *a hemispherical dome, the interior of which was decorated with paste glass mosaics.*

The Arts

Much of early Roman art was influenced by the Etruscans and then the Greeks. When Syracuse in Sicily fell to the Romans in 210 BC, many Greek works of art, particularly sculptures, were plundered and brought back to Rome. Collecting Greek sculptures became a major occupation, and later, as Greek artists moved nearer to the center of the Republic, works were commissioned in the Greek style.

Roman realism

The style of Greek classicism gradually gave way to Roman realism and many of the sculptures which survive today are un-idealized portraits of real Roman people. Busts or portrait sculptures were often made to display in the home. Larger pieces, made to signify importance or power—often of gods and goddesses, emperors, or heroic soldiers—were erected in prominent places around Rome, and other towns and cities throughout the Republic, and later the Empire.

This bust of Emperor Caracalla shows the realism which was a feature of Roman sculpture.

Bas-relief sculptures—shallow carvings—were used to decorate arches, columns, and temples; a magnificent example of this is Trajan's Column which stands in Trajan's Forum in Rome.

Most Roman sculpture was made in marble or bronze, although there is some evidence that more common and less expensive materials, such as terracotta, were used and painted over.

Fresco painting

Very few paintings from Roman times have survived to date. Most of the images rendered in two dimensions during the period were wall frescoes, where paint is applied to the walls of houses and other buildings. As most of these structures have been destroyed or buried, so the paintings have perished.

Much of our knowledge comes from the well-preserved houses of Pompeii and Herculaneum, buried under feet of ash after the eruption of Vesuvius in 79 AD. One of the most stunning examples of mural work can be seen in the Villa of the Mysteries just outside Pompeii. Here, the fresco runs for fifty-five feet around the four walls of a room, depicting life-sized figures in a Dionysian initiation rite.

The Romans' interest in nature and daily life is evident in the paintings of landscapes and in portraiture. The artists of the time had mastered the technique of perspective, and by painting onto the walls were able to create the illusion of windows looking out onto gardens. Paint was applied to wet plaster and it is thought that this has helped preserve the colors and detail of many of the murals that have been uncovered.

Sculpture of a reclining figure from the port of Ostia.

Mosaics endure

Unlike painting, mosaics were more easily preserved and numerous examples of this art form can be found throughout the countries of the old Empire, although the quality of preservation varies.

An invention of the Greeks, mosaics were first worked in black and white, with color making an appearance in the Western Empire and Africa at a later date. Traditionally, mosaics were laid on the floor, using tesserae, small tiles of colored stone and glass, laid on mortar. The excavations of Pompeii and Herculaneum have revealed that wall mosaics were also popular.

Melodies without harmonies

Very little is known about the music of Ancient Rome, although it was probably influenced by the Greeks and likely to have been played as simple melodies with no harmonies. Music was played on many occasions: at private and public functions, funerals, religious ceremonies, and at gladiatorial games.

The Romans possessed stringed instruments such as the lyre, lute and kithara; wind instruments were also played, using a reed. A double-reed instrument, known as an *aulos*, sounded rather like a clarinet, and a form of bagpipe, called an *ascaules*, was played. There were also drums, cymbals, and castanets.

Roman writers

Throughout the Roman Republic and Empire periods, writers produced numerous works of literature in the form of poems, plays, history and comedies. Many have survived today and the Latin language itself continued for many centuries as the written medium around much of Western Europe.

Wall fresco which depicts a horned theater mask.

Early Latin literature, up until the first century BC, can be exemplified by the comedies of Plautus and Terence. From about 100 BC to the beginning of the first century AD, The Golden Age produced poets such as Virgil and Ovid, the prose of Julius Caesar and historical works by Livy. This was succeeded by The Silver Age, when Pliny the Elder and the Younger were writing, along with Petronius and Juvenal.

Theater at Ostia. Most plays were staged in a semi-circular theater, rather than the circular or oval amphitheaters which were used for gladiatorial contests, animal hunts, and other grand public displays.

Antoninus

The first Antonine Emperors upheld the good governance of the Nervo-Trajanic rulers and perfected it. Although the dynasty was sullied by Commodus, who reverted to the capricious megalomaniacal ways of the Julio-Claudians and set the Empire on a path to its eventual downfall, the first of the Antonines, Antoninus the Pius was a "good Emperor."

Death of Hadrian

Hadrian had firsthand experience of the problems that arose when an Emperor did not appoint a clear successor. He wished to avoid making the same mistake as Trajan and in 137 AD, he adopted Titus Aurelius Fulvus Boionius Antoninus, a man just ten years his junior.

Antoninus was a prudent choice because he came from a family of consuls and was sure to be an acceptable candidate to all parties, which meant he could maintain peace and stability in the Empire. In 138, Hadrian died at his Villa in Tivoli, and Antoninus became Emperor in his stead.

The Senate was not disposed to deify Hadrian, but Antoninus insisted on this and presided over the funeral of his adopted father. Respectfully honoring Hadrian in this way earned Antoninus the name "Pius." a name he lived up to as Emperor. Hadrian was entombed in a grand mausoleum that still stands today, called the Castel Sant'Angelo.

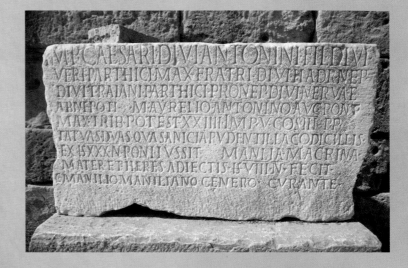

Stability a priority

Antoninus was in advanced years when he became Emperor and although he was not expected to live long, he ruled Rome for twenty-three years.

Unlike his predecessors, he did not impose his personality on the Empire, but ruled modestly and frugally. This made him a rather uncontroversial character who made few enemies during his reign.

His chief policy was to maintain stability, which was achieved by keeping Rome's finances in check. Antoninus opted for austere economic measures and cut back luxury public spending, reducing the amount of civic construction.

In his foreign policy, Antoninus was less conservative. He is most famous for extending north of Hadrian's Wall in Britannia. He added an extra one hundred miles to the Empire when he ordered the construction of a second defensive wall, the "Antonine Wall," which stretched from the Firth of Forth to the Firth of Clyde.

Above: Inscribed stone tablet probably from the reign of Antoninus. Found in the ruins of Sabrath, one of the three cities which made up ancient Tripoli (Three Cities). The text makes reference to Nerva, Trajan and Hadrian, Antoninus' three predecessors.

Bust of Antoninus Pius, the first of the Antonine Emperors and one of the "five good Emperors."

Marcus Aurelius

Hadrian had first noticed the promise in a young Marcus Aurelius and had encouraged
Antoninus to adopt him. Antoninus, already having a familial link to Aurelius as
his uncle by marriage, happily complied.

Dual rulers

Following Aurelius' adoption, he effectively ruled
alongside the ageing Antoninus and was ready to assume
control upon the Emperor's death in 161 AD. However,
he was not to rule alone. Hadrian had convinced
Antoninus to adopt a second heir, Lucius Ceionius
Commodus Verus (Lucius Verus).

Worried that Verus was similar in character to the
errant Julio-Claudian Emperors, the Senate tried to
overrule his appointment after Antoninus' death.
However, Aurelius held firm to Antoninus' and Hadrian's
wishes and convinced the Senate that Verus should
rule alongside him. To strengthen the relationship
between the two Emperors, Aurelius married his
daughter to Verus, a gesture which confirmed Aurelius as
the senior partner.

War with Parthia

The first concern facing the co-rulers was a new war
with Parthia in the East. Since Hadrian had pulled out of
the region following Trajan's successes, the Parthians had
once again begun meddling in the affairs of Armenia.
Neither Emperor had military experience, but Lucius
Verus was sent to lead the campaign.

Although Verus frittered away much of his time
behind the frontline, the Romans defeated the Parthians
and the Emperors were able to take credit for their first
military victory.

Celebrations were short-lived because plague
spread across the Empire and killed scores of people.
One of its victims was Verus himself, who died in 169 at
just thirty-nine years old. Aurelius became the sole
Emperor and moved to pacify the Germanic tribes for
much of the following decade. In 177, he decided to
revert to diarchic rule and appointed his son, Lucius
Aelius Aurelius Commodus as a co-ruler.

Meditations

Marcus Aurelius is best remembered for his book,
Meditations. The work offers an important contribution to
Stoic philosophy, which had a profound impact over
Aurelius' life. It also acts as an insightful autobiographical
account of his life. Aurelius had a favorable reputation at
the time, which has largely endured, but is somewhat
tarnished by his occasional persecution of Christians.

*The column of Marcus Aurelius. Modeled on Trajan's Column
Marcus Aurelius' celebrates his triumph over the Germanic tribes.*

Commodus

When Marcus Aurelius died in Vindobona (Vienna) in 180 AD, his biological son and successor, Commodus, had already had three years experience of ruling alongside his father as co-Emperor.

Unfitted to the role

However, such experience seems to have counted for very little and Commodus proved himself to be a poor emperor. With his accession to the imperial role, the line of "Good Emperors" came to an end.

Aurelius is often blamed for reverting to a dynastic succession, rather than appointing the best person for the job. It is worth noting that each of the five "Good Emperors" was adopted, not the biological son of the previous Emperor.

Pleasure of the imperial position

Although his father, Marcus Aurelius, had invested the last years of his life in pacifying the Rhine and the Danube borders Commodus had little interest in these wars. He quickly concluded a treaty with his father's enemies so that he could return to Rome and enjoy the pleasures that the imperial position opened to him.

It is reputed that he was debauched, avaricious, and cruel. He was so convinced of his physical prowess that he believed that he was a reincarnation of Hercules—a number of statues show him masquerading as Hercules in a lion skin and carrying a club.

He further outraged Roman opinion by participating in gladiator fights—a sport usually undertaken by slaves. He has often been likened to Caligula because he and Aurelius were another example of a popular father and megalomaniacal son pairing.

Commodus' wayward behavior eventually resulted in his murder in 192. His rule had signaled the end of the Pax Romana, a two-hundred-year period of relative peace and prosperity, and pushed Rome headlong into a period of crisis.

Portrait bust of Commodus.

Above: A tumbled Corinthian capital lies in the ruins of the Therma in the Antonine Baths in Carthage.

Education and Thought

During the early Republic most children were educated at home by their parents. Mothers would teach their children until the age of seven, at which time a son's development would be transferred to his father's charge, while the mother would continue to teach her daughter.

Fathers taught their sons all they would need to know for everyday life in Roman society; a son would even receive clients with his father as practice for when he himself would become a patron. While boys learned a whole range of disciplines, girls were usually only instructed in the domestic tasks expected of them once they were married.

Greek schools

After the conquest of Greece, many Roman children received a Hellenized education, which meant sending children out to school for their academic development. Between the ages of seven and twelve, Roman children went to elementary school, called a *ludus*, where a Greek teacher, who was often a slave, taught them.

Ancient Rome had a relatively high literacy rate, which indicates that a significant proportion of the population would have received elementary schooling, despite having to pay fees.

Roman mosaic depicting the academy of Plato. Greek thinkers like Plato had a huge influence on Roman thought.

Class sizes would have been very large to keep the costs sufficiently low for ordinary Romans to have been able to afford them.

Rich and poor

The poorest Roman children would not have been able to go to school because families could not afford either the cost of sending them in the first place or the cost of the child not working.

Richer families often preferred not to send their children to school, but rather to bring a tutor, called a *paedagogus*, into their home. Like an elementary school teacher, tutors were usually Greek slaves. However, they would be exclusively attached to one family and would become a member of the household staff like the other slaves.

Further education

At the age of twelve, ordinary Roman children, lucky enough to have gone to school, would go out into the workplace. For the boys of richer families there would be an opportunity to go on to further education at a *grammaticus*. At these secondary schools, lessons were given in both Latin and Greek; pupils were expected to study and recite various works of classical literature, ranging from Homer to Virgil. After completing secondary school, a handful of the wealthiest boys were sent for further education where they were taught rhetoric, in practice for a career in politics or law.

Girls from richer families were not allowed to receive a secondary education but were instead expected to get married.

Literature

As with education, Roman literature drew greatly on the influences of the Ancient Greeks. At the end of the third century BC, Plautus began adapting Greek comedies into Latin, and Ennius, who is widely regarded as the father of Latin poetry, began styling his own works on those of the Ancient Greeks.

The end of the Republic and the beginning of the Empire is considered to be the Golden Age, when Latin literature came into its own, (albeit still intensely influenced by Homer). The seminal work of this time was Virgil's nationalist epic, *the Aeneid*, which developed the legend that the Romans were the descendants of the people of Troy.

Virgil and Horace

The poem took Virgil ten years to write and had only just been completed at the time of his death in 19 BC, which meant he had no time to revise the piece. *The Aeneid* was popular with Augustus because it chimed well with the traditional values he was trying to reintroduce. Augustus wanted more of the same and encouraged Virgil's patron, Gaius Cilnius Maecenas, to find more of these aspiring Latin poets. Virgil introduced him to Horace, who was to become another celebrated "Augustan Poet" and coined the famous nationalist phrase *"Dulce et decorum est pro patria mori"*—"It is sweet and proper to die for one's country."

Fresco painting from Pompeii of a young woman holding a stylus. It is suggested that the picture portrays Sappho, the famous Greek poet who was born on the island of Lesbos in the late seventh century BC.

Ovid banished

The support of Maecenas and Augustus certainly helped make the Golden Age, but not all of the great poets of the era met with the Emperor's approval; Ovid was banished by Augustus to a life of exile on the Black Sea. The reasons for this are not clear, but it is believed that the liberal nature of some of Ovid's love poems did not sit easily alongside the Emperor's drive for family values.

Livy's History

The Romans were accomplished historians, a trait which has allowed modern readers unprecedented insights into the civilization. The most famous was Titus Livius (Livy), an Augustan historian who wrote a grand historical survey of Rome from its foundations to the rule of Augustus.

Livy's history was written over one hundred and forty-two books, but unfortunately only thirty-five survive. Tacitus and Suetonius picked up where Livy left off and wrote about the lives of the early Emperors in their books *Annals* and *The Twelve Caesars*, respectively.

Emperor's accounts

Dio Cassius' *Roman History* spanned an even longer period; he began his study at the time of Aeneas and ended it in 229 AD during the reign of Alexander Severus. Although it covers a significant time period, the earlier sections in *Roman History* are less detailed than Livy's work and the book is most useful for its accounts of the later Emperors.

Many Romans enjoyed writing histories; Caesar's *Gallic Wars* and *Civil War* provide his perspective on the histories of the war in Gaul and the war against Pompey. Even the Emperor Claudius took to writing history in his youth, but his works have, unfortunately, been lost.

The Neumagen School Relief. This bas-relief, depicting students and their teacher is housed in the Roman Archaeological Museum (Landesmuseum) in Trier, Germany.

Fresco depicting a meditating Philistine.

Economy

Roman trade and industry was largely an internal affair; little was needed from outside and most trade and industry occurred within the Empire. Rome owed this self-sufficiency to an abundance of natural resources, a complex network of roads across the Empire and above all, the exploitative use of slave labor.

Moving materials round the Empire

The roads allowed cargo to be transported from one part of the Empire to the other; they connected merchants in Britannia with those in Egypt, although much of the trade was destined exclusively for Rome. Transporting goods across land was slow but steady because horses, camels, donkeys, or people were required to haul the cargo over the long distances. Towns along the trade routes felt the economic benefit of these traders and couriers passing through, and grew in importance as a result.

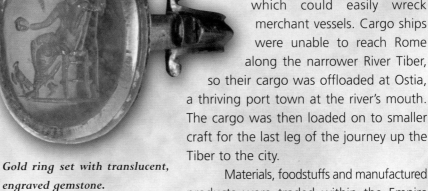

Gold ring set with translucent, engraved gemstone.

When there was a need to transport heavier cargo, there was little option but to do so by sea. This was hazardous. Even if the Roman Navy could guarantee safety from pirates, it could not safeguard against bad weather, which could easily wreck merchant vessels. Cargo ships were unable to reach Rome along the narrower River Tiber, so their cargo was offloaded at Ostia, a thriving port town at the river's mouth. The cargo was then loaded on to smaller craft for the last leg of the journey up the Tiber to the city.

Materials, foodstuffs and manufactured products were traded within the Empire and the Romans rarely resorted to importing from without. One of Rome's few notable exceptions was silk from China. Romans did not have the resources to manufacture silk, which made it an exotic and luxurious commodity, enjoyed only by the richest citizens. Silk initially reached Rome through the Parthian Empire, but after Trajan extended Roman territory to the Persian Gulf, the Romans were able to develop direct links with China.

Street in the remains of Ostia, Rome's port. Cargo ships were unable to reach Rome along the narrow River Tiber, so the cargo was offloaded at Ostia. It was then transferred onto smaller craft for the last leg of the journey up the Tiber to the city.

An economy built on slave labor

Slavery was vital to the Roman economy; by using people as mere commodities, the Romans were able to drastically reduce the cost of production of all they grew, made, mined, and transported. Although slaves provided free labor in theory, many owners chose to provide some form of payment to give slaves an incentive to work hard. Even limited funds would have been sufficient incentive because when slaves earned enough money they were able to buy their freedom.

During the late Republic and early Empire, the Roman economy thrived because fresh sources of slaves were made available by successful Roman conquests. Rome had a particularly bountiful supply in 146 BC, when the cities of Carthage and Corinth were both destroyed and all the surviving inhabitants were sold into slavery. The crucial role played by slaves was revealed when the Roman economy went into decline in the third century AD, once Rome had stopped expanding and the supply of slaves had dried up.

Keeping the country fed

Agriculture was the mainstay of the Roman economy. Grapes and olives were staple crops, but grain was by far the most important. Around the Empire, most grain was grown and used at a subsistence, or local level, but Rome's demand outstripped the supply capabilities of its hinterlands and it was forced to import grain on a large scale from North Africa, which earned the name "the Granary of the Empire."

This grain supply to Rome was of vital importance because a considerable proportion of the city relied on a free corn-dole to survive. Even after Caesar and Augustus reduced the number of people receiving free grain, it remained important to keep supply ahead of demand, to keep the prices low for ordinary Romans.

Mining conditions

Mining was an important industry, as a number of different metals were required to make a whole range of everyday items including coins, weapons, jewelry, piping, ornaments, and paint. Mining was among the worst jobs available in Ancient Rome, so slaves were used for the task. With such an abundant supply, merchants did not need to worry about the terrible working conditions.

Slaves were forced to endure long hours of backbreaking work in cold, cramped, dark underground mines, which were prone to flooding and collapse. During the later Empire, when slaves became less plentiful, better working conditions were introduced to help extend life expectancy so that fewer slaves could work more years to compensate for the shortfall.

The Romans mined a variety of metals right across the Empire, especially in Hispania, where lead, iron, tin, silver, copper, and gold could be found. Rome's manufacturing industry was relatively low-key. Basic goods such as glass, pottery, weapons, jewelry, and textiles were manufactured on a small scale, although a large glassworks has been discovered at Colonia Agrippina (Cologne) in Germany.

Ruins of Las Medulas mine in Spain. It was the most important gold mine in the Roman Empire. Mining techniques, requiring vast amounts of water to eat away the hillside, led to the construction of a 60-mile-long system of channels to import water to the area, which is now a World Heritage site.

Taxing the population

In the early days of the Republic, Roman citizens were very lightly taxed on their land and possessions, even during times of war. Following a number of successful conquests, Roman citizens were no longer taxed at all; instead the occupied peoples of the Empire were forced to shoulder the tax burden.

During the period that Roman citizens had paid tax, they were counted by a census; however, the Romans were unable to conduct accurate censuses of their provinces. Instead they had to rely on a system of tax farming, which essentially privatized the collection of taxes—allowing tax farmers called *publicani* to impose additional fees on top of the taxes so they could take their cut.

At the start of the first century BC, Rome's Italian allies became so angered by having to pay tax, while the neighboring Romans did not, that they declared a breakaway Republic. A short war followed during which Rome annexed large parts of the peninsula and agreed that most Italians could stop paying tax.

The rest of the Empire was not afforded the same luxury, although Emperor Augustus did scrap the abusive system of tax-farming. By compiling better census data, Augustus introduced direct taxation; on the one hand this meant that individuals could no longer be exploited by the *publicani*, but on the other, it allowed him to introduce a regressive head tax where everybody paid the same amount, irrespective of their personal wealth or income.

Roman money from the reign of Nero.

Chamber in the remains of the Forum in Rome. Most towns had at least one forum which was a political and economic meeting place for the citizens.

Early currency

In the early days of the Roman Republic, the Roman economy relied upon a direct exchange of goods or services, with one of the key units of payment being livestock. As Rome expanded, this system proved less practical and a new one, based upon payments in lieu, was developed.

The early Romans would exchange lumps of bronze, called *Aes rude*, for the goods and services they needed. Although this system was more efficient than the previous one, it still had its own impracticalities; the worth of the lump was in its weight, which required a weigh-in each time anyone carried out a transaction. Moreover, the system was open to easy forgery.

Coinage systems

At the start of the third century BC, war brought Rome into contact with the Greeks in the south of Italy and their system of using coins as currency. Rome began to adopt these Greek practices and established mints in its own territory.

Although bronze initially continued to underlie Roman currency, it was quickly replaced by silver coins, called *denarii*. The *denarii* was the foundation of the Roman economy for centuries, although it was significantly devalued over time.

Gold coins (*aureii*) were less readily available, especially during the Republic. The Emperors later took to minting gold coins to pay for costly foreign wars, but Augustus stipulated that they could only be made in Rome.

Economic inflation

The *denarii* became progressively weaker over time and although in 215 AD, Caracalla tried to reform the silver coinage by creating a new unit, the *antoninianii*, Rome slid into decades of political and economic chaos.

During the crisis of the third century, a rapid succession of ambitious army generals tried to appoint themselves Emperor using troops to back them up. To buy the loyalty of troops, the would-be Emperors took to minting their own coins, which led to inflation and a decline in central control of the money supply.

Diocletian brought about political stability at the end of the third century and with it, he returned Rome to economic health. He increased the value of Roman coinage by insisting on a greater rate of metal purity in the coins and then imposed strict limits to stop the value of the currency from fluctuating in the future.

Cornices with inscriptions lie in the Severan Basilica of Leptis Magna. The birthplace of Severus, Leptis Magna in North Africa had a number of lavish building works constructed in it during his reign.

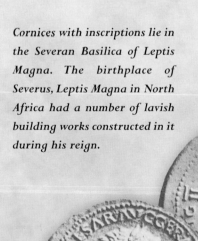

Severus and his legacy

Severus

Commodus' reign upset the momentum of the Empire; within months of his death,
Rome had once again reverted to civil war. Respite was briefly offered by the stable, if ruthless,
reign of Septimius Severus. But after his death, Rome slid into five decades of disorder.

Publius Helvius Pertinax was appointed Emperor upon the death of Commodus. Like Nerva, he was in advanced years, making him very much a "stop-gap" arrangement. Pertinax tried to restore the Empire to economic health and saw the need to reduce the bonuses and rewards paid to the Army. This was an unwise move; the Army believed the cuts were politically motivated and the Emperor was murdered just a few months into his reign.

Buying control

Without an obvious heir to Pertinax, the Praetorian Guard saw the perfect opportunity to sell the principate to the highest bidder. Didius Julianus' offer of 25,000 *sestertii* won the auction and the Senate was forced to recognize his authority.

However, this appointment was not widely accepted and three other men were emerging as contenders for the throne: Pescennius Niger, governor of Syria; Clodius Albinus, governor of Britannia; and Septimius Severus, who had command of the troops in Pannonia.

Pannonia was the closest of the three provinces to Rome, so it was Severus who posed the most immediate threat to Julianus. After marching on Rome, Severus gained the crucial support of the Praetorian Guard and the Senate. He brought Julianus' two-month reign to a conclusion by ordering his execution, and then set himself against his rival contenders, Niger and Albinus.

Civil war ensues

Severus first concluded an expedient peace with Albinus to secure the West while he went to war with Niger in the East. By giving Albinus the conciliatory title "Caesar," Severus hinted that he would appoint Albinus as his heir. This placated Albinus who agreed not to declare his own imperial ambitions, giving Severus a free hand to deal with Niger in the East.

Niger was quickly defeated and killed at the Battle of Issus in 194 AD—on the same field where Alexander the Great had scored an historic victory against the Persians in 333 BC.

Many of Niger's forces fled into neighboring Parthia to escape Severan punishment. However, Parthia was too weak to act as a safe haven and in 195, Severus chased Niger's troops into the region and mercilessly hunted them down.

With the last vestiges of Niger's support removed, his province, Syria, was broken up, and the East was pacified.

Detail from a glass cameo amphora depicting cupids.

Bust of Emperor Septimius Severus.

In 196 AD, confident of his power in the East, Severus then turned his attentions to the West, when he reneged on his unwritten understanding with Albinus by appointing his own son as his heir. This was a veiled challenge, which Albinus took up. He declared himself Emperor while in Britannia and crossed with his troops into Gaul to begin the march on Rome.

Albinus advanced only as far as Lugdunum (Lyon), where Severus had come out to meet him. The resulting battle was closely fought, but Albinus was murdered, leaving Severus as the unchallenged ruler of the Roman world.

A popular but ruthless leader

Severus accrued a reputation for ruthlessness during the civil war, which he continued to live up to. Soon after Albinus was defeated, Severus invaded Parthia and captured the capital, Ctesiphon. Here, the male population was butchered, the women and children were sold into slavery and Upper Mesopotamia was reincorporated into the Empire.

Despite such ruthlessness, Severus became popular in Rome because he reintroduced stability. He shored up his authority by disbanding the Praetorian Guard and replacing them with a personal bodyguard comprising his loyal army officers.

Lavish construction work

Severus was the first Roman Emperor from Africa. He had been born to a romanized family in Leptis Magna, a city that had come to prominence under the Carthaginians. He lavished a great deal of attention on the city and helped regenerate it to become a leading metropolis in the Empire.

Nor did he overlook his adopted home of Rome. Severus is remembered for contributing a number of new buildings, most notably the Arch of Septimius Severus, built at the entrance to the Forum to commemorate his victories over the Parthians.

Frigidarium of the Hadrianic Baths in Leptis Magna, Libya. Leptis Magna was the birthplace of Septimius Severus, who lavished a huge construction program on the city during his reign.

Caracalla

Before being succeeded by his sons, Caracalla and Geta, Severus spent the last years of his reign campaigning against the "barbarian" tribes in the north of Britain, where he died in 211 AD.

The Antonine Wall had been abandoned but the Romans had not retreated to the safety of Hadrian's Wall. Although Severus scored several victories, he realized that advances offered little solution to the Caledonian menace. He resolved to revert to Hadrian's line of defence, and had the wall repaired and brought back into action. Severus never returned to Rome; he died in Eburacum (York).

Warring heirs

Severus' rule provided temporary stability for the Empire, but the appointment of both his sons, Septimus Bassianus Caracalla and Lucius Septimus Geta as his heirs, seems to have lacked forethought.

Severus knew that his sons did not get on and must have expected some sort of trouble in the future. The initial plan was to divide the Empire between them, but Caracalla prevented this by murdering his brother and reigning supreme.

Caracalla did not stop at fratricide; during his reign, thousands were killed during his terror campaign. He spent much of his time away from Rome, fighting wars, and much of the legislation he passed was designed to benefit the military.

Of his more populist acts, Caracalla granted Roman citizenship to all freeborn men of the Empire. He also commissioned the construction of an extensive bathing complex in Rome, which housed 1,600 bathers at a time. Extensive remains of the complex are still visible today.

Bust of the Emperor Caracalla. After his father Severus' death, he succeeded to the imperial position with his brother Geta, becoming supreme ruler when he murdered Geta.

Ruins of the Severan Basilica in Leptis Magna, Libya.

Caracalla's death

Caracalla was murdered in 217. For all his shortcomings, he had provided a relative degree of stability for the Empire.

His Praetorian Prefect, Marcus Opellius Macrinus, was widely believed responsible, but he proclaimed himself Emperor and managed to find a scapegoat for Caracalla's murder. Macrinus was not well liked. He did not ever visit Rome and his military campaigns were rather lackluster.

The Severan women

The females of the marginalized Severan family used Macrinus' unpopularity to their advantage—they plotted a coup to return a Severan to the throne. In 218 AD they claimed that Caracalla's cousin, Elagabalus, was in fact his illegitimate son and proclaimed him Emperor.

The unpopular Macrinus was executed by his troops and the seventeen-year-old Elagabalus became Emperor. Much of his power was vested in his mother, Julia Soaemias, and his grandmother, Julia Maesa; Elagabalus is remembered for little other than his decadence and his promiscuity.

Julia Maesa in control

It became clear that power really lay with Julia Maesa. In 222, when the family was divided by a dispute, Julia Maesa had Elagabalus, her grandson, and Julia Soaemias, her daughter, killed and promoted another grandson, Alexander Severus, to the position of Emperor.

When he assumed the imperial title, Alexander was even younger than his cousin, Elagabalus, had been. This allowed the overbearing Julia Maesa to continue ruling the Empire. Her authority was shared with her other daughter, Alexander's mother, Julia Mamaea.

End of the Severan dynasty

Unlike her unfortunate sister, Julia Mamaea outlived her mother, who died in 226, and continued to dominate imperial politics until the end of Alexander's reign.

Alexander never proved much of a tactician and his troops murdered him in Germany in 235, after several mediocre campaigns. His mother, who usually accompanied him to the front, suffered the same fate.

With Alexander's death, the Severan dynasty was brought to an inglorious and bloody conclusion.

Women's Lives

The rights of Roman women seem very limited when they are judged by modern standards, but Roman women did enjoy greater freedoms than their counterparts in contemporary civilizations. By any standards, Rome was a highly patriarchal society where a woman's chief function was to have children and maintain the home. Men were supported by the law in this regard—if a woman could not, or would not, have children, her husband was free to divorce her.

Nevertheless, women in Ancient Rome were not simply considered instruments of reproduction, they played important roles in raising children and supporting their husband. Over time, some of the patriarchal barriers that Roman society threw in their way were overcome, and a handful of women even enjoyed especially prominent positions in society.

Wife and mother

Roman women spent their lives under the complete control of their fathers until they were married, when authority was transferred directly to their husbands. Women were married between the ages of twelve and fifteen to men who were usually several years older; after the wedding, they were expected to reproduce. As infant mortality was high and many children died before reaching adulthood, a woman would spend a large portion of her life having as many children as possible. The frequency and number of pregnancies and births endured by Roman women meant that it was relatively common for women to die in the process.

Household roles

In the Roman family, it was the woman who was responsible for the formative years of the children; she would usually give them a basic education before they went to elementary school at the age of seven. This differed from Ancient Greece, where the men were in charge of education.

Most women did not work and were charged with keeping the house instead; in richer households this meant managing the slaves; in poorer ones, it meant doing the work themselves. Some poorer women had little choice but to seek paid work as midwives, hairdressers, or dressmakers. It is likely that many women would have also assisted their husbands in a family shop or workshop. Although wealthier women did not work, the wives of politicians did assist their husbands through providing support and sometimes offering opinions.

Fresco showing a woman pouring perfume into a vial.

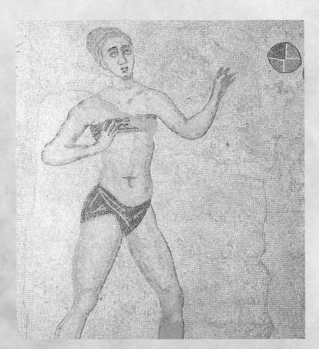

Detail from a mosaic in the Villa Romana del Casale in the Piazza Armerina, Sicily, Italy, depicting a young woman exercising.

Limited lives

Women's lives were confined by a variety of restrictions. They were also not allowed to vote, run for political office, or own property. They were often not free to make purchases without the agreement of their husband or father, and drinking wine was punishable by death. Perhaps most restrictive of all was that women were inferior before the law, especially during the early Republic.

There were some exceptions, notably the Vestal Virgins, who were fortunate enough to be outside these restrictions because they were free of the control of their paterfamilias (father of the family). Some women were also able to channel their political ambitions through their husbands or sons.

Personal freedoms

Although they were stifled publicly, Roman women enjoyed a relatively high degree of personal freedom. They were allowed to leave the house without their husbands, and could visit the baths—albeit for a limited time in the morning—as well as the theater and even the games.

During the late Republic, these freedoms became more commonplace, as Rome underwent a social transformation and the stuffier constraints of the early Republic were lifted. Women enjoyed greater independence and better treatment before the law. Moreover, with the death of almost a generation of landowning Romans in the Second Punic War, many Roman women found themselves taking over the roles traditionally played by their husbands.

Constraints re-imposed

These newfound freedoms for women led to a sharp decline in the birth rate. This led the Emperor Augustus to curb many of the freedoms women had enjoyed. They were expected to stay at home more, so constraints were imposed on their attendance at the games and the theater, and tougher laws were re-imposed on adultery. These were expedient measures to restore the birthrate, because as soon as a woman had more than three surviving children, she was allowed to resume her relatively independent lifestyle.

An intricately adorned gold necklace.

Powerful women

Although men dominate the history of Rome, a few women were able to make a name for themselves, especially during the Empire, when the mothers, wives and even grandmothers of Emperors involved themselves in affairs of state.

Perhaps the most prominent woman in Ancient Rome was Livia Drusilla, the wife of Augustus. It is believed that she had considerable influence over her husband's decisions and enjoyed a good deal of independence from him—she even had clients of her own. Livia publicly supported her husband's attempts to re-impose family values and portrayed herself as an image of frugality and traditional womanhood. However, she is also remembered for being privately ambitious; she is thought to have tampered with Augustus' succession and removed all competition to her son, Tiberius. Livia became the first woman to join the Imperial Cult when Claudius deified her in 42 AD.

Agrippina and Poppaea

Nero's mother, Agrippina the Younger, had less discreet ambitions—it is thought that she murdered her husband Claudius, so that her son, Nero would inherit the throne. Agrippina then proceeded to rule alongside her son—going so far as to have coins minted with her head on. She became such a nuisance to Nero that in the end he resolved to kill his own mother to get her out of the way.

Nero continued to be influenced by women, when his second wife, Poppaea, stepped up to fill Agrippina's shoes. She is thought to have had a good deal of power—even encouraging Nero to murder his popular ex-wife. However, Poppaea faced the same fate as his mother; she died when an angry Nero kicked her in the stomach while she was pregnant.

Women of the Severan Family

In the third century, the women of the Severan Dynasty managed to maintain a lengthy grip on power. Julia Donna, the wife of Septimius Severus exerted considerable influence over her husband, which was then transferred on to her son, Caracalla, after Severus' death. She accompanied both Emperors on campaigns which took her from Britain in the West to Parthia in the East.

When Caracalla was overthrown, Julia Donna killed herself, but her sister Julia Maesa kept the ambition of the Severan women alight. She overthrew the incumbent ruler, Macrinus, and together with her equally determined daughter, Julia Soaemias, placed her grandson, Elagabalus on the throne. After Elagabalus proved to be a weak ruler and a liability, Julia Maesa conspired with her other daughter Julia Mamaea to kill Elagabalus and Julia Soaemias, and place another grandson on the throne.

Fresco painting of a female saint with a mirror.

Virtuous women

Although most famous women of Ancient Rome are remembered for their political roles, a small number are remembered for either their virtue or their vice. Cornelia Scipionus Africana, the mother of the Gracchi brothers, was considered so honorable that a statue was erected in her memory in Rome in the first century BC.

At a time when social norms were breaking down and many women were seeking greater freedom, Cornelia lived the life of a traditional Roman woman; she was pious and frugal as well as being a devoted wife and mother—she even bore her husband twelve children, although only three survived to adulthood.

During the Roman Monarchy, the son of King Tarquinius Superbus raped a Roman noblewoman called Lucretia. She reported the crime to her family, having them swear to punish the prince; she then committed suicide out of respect for her own virtue and her husband's honor.

Both Lucretia and Cornelia became role models for Roman women, but there were also women who became infamous and served as a lesson for how women should not behave.

Treachery and inconstancy

Tarpeia was the original wayward woman; right at the dawn of Rome, it is believed that she opened the gates of a well-defended Roman fortress for the Sabine enemy to enter, provided they gave her their jewelry in exchange. Her behavior was considered so treacherous that even the Sabine soldiers, who stood to gain from her treason, were repulsed; each took a turn at striking her with a shield until she was killed.

The only child of Augustus, Julia the Elder, is also remembered for her vice; at a time when Augustus was emphasizing family values, she was scandalizing public opinion with stories of drinking alcohol and extramarital affairs (she was married to the future Emperor Tiberius at the time). Julia was fortunate not to have been executed by Augustus, her paterfamilias; instead, she was exiled to an inhospitable island. Her story reveals something of the double standards men held toward women, because Augustus was notorious for scandalous behavior himself.

Above: Faustina the Younger, wife of Marcus Aurelius often featured on coins symbolizing various virtues. Here she is depicted holding a globe and cornucopia, symbolizing constancy.

Right: Roman funerary inscription for a female medic, Asyllia Polla.

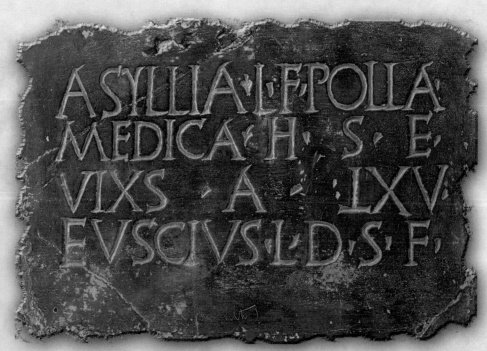

"Soldier Emperors"

After the death of the last Severan Emperor in 235 AD, the Empire was plunged into five decades of chaos as a number of ambitious men vied for the top job.

Anarchy

Signs of an impending crisis had been evident for some time: the previous five Emperors had been assassinated; plague was devastating population numbers; and the Roman economy was pounded as trade began to break down across the Empire.

With the legions, the Senate and the Praetorian Guard providing opposing support bases for a range of contenders, the result was a rapid series of imperial successions. During this period, a number of so-called "Soldier Emperors" struggled for power, but none proved able to lift Rome out of its malaise.

Maximinus Thrax

The first of the soldier Emperors was Maximinus Thrax. He was elevated to the imperial position by the Praetorian Guard. However, he was despised by the Senate; not only was he from a low socio-economic background, but he had never set foot in Rome. During his reign, a revolt in the province of Africa resulted in the ageing governor, Gordian, being proclaimed Emperor by the troops there.

Gordian, father and son

Gordian was of advanced age, so his son, Gordian II, was pronounced co-Emperor. The Senate leapt at the opportunity to support a challenge to Maximinus Thrax and backed the Army's insurrection. However, political support from the Senate did little to safeguard against the governor of the neighboring province of Numidia, who was allied to Maximinus Thrax. He invaded Africa, defeated the Gordians' troops, killed Gordian II, and forced the elder Gordian to commit suicide.

Two new Emperors

Senators realized that their defiance of Maximinus would not go unpunished and swiftly appointed two new Emperors, Pupienus and Balbinus, to replace the Gordians. The co-Emperors abided by the interests of the Senate and defeated Maximinus Thrax, who was killed by his own men.

In spite of their victory, Pupienus' and Balbinus' positions were not safe; the plebs disliked the appointment of two patrician Emperors and called for their overthrow. The Praetorian Guard, who also disliked the men, obliged the people; Pupienus and Balbinus were murdered and were replaced with Gordian III.

Bas-relief cut into a rockface showing Shapur I receiving submissions from the defeated Emperors Philip and Valerian. This is a symbolic representation as Philip was one of the seven Emperors who reigned in the nine years following Gordian III's death. Valerian is the standing figure whose uplifted arms are being grasped by the victorious Shapur.

Valerian

Less than four years had elapsed between the murder of Alexander Severus in 235 AD and the accession of Gordian III, but in that time, Rome had six different Emperors.

This was a trend that was set to continue. In the decade following the death of Gordian III in 244, Rome had seven different Emperors. Such rapid turnover was only halted in 253, when Valerian acceded the throne as co-Emperor with his son, Gallienus.

A decaying Empire

Two decades of decay within the Empire had encouraged challenges from without. When Valerian came to power, a new Persian Empire, called the Sassanids, were pushing in from the East, while the Alamanni and the Franks, two Germanic tribes, were threatening in the West. To counter these menaces, Valerian took to the East, while Gallienus managed the West.

In 256, the Sassanids took the city of Antioch from Rome and also overran Armenia, a Roman client state. After Valerian dispatched himself to the region, the Romans scored a number of successes, including the recapture of Antioch.

Valerian humiliated

When Goths invaded Asia Minor in 258, Valerian became distracted and diverted his forces from the Persian front. The Sassanids, under the leadership of Shapur I, defeated a weakened Roman Army at the Battle of Edessa in 259 AD, and managed to capture Valerian in the fighting.

Rather than killing the prisoner straight away, the Persians humiliated the Emperor, who was forced to kneel as a footstool for the Persian king. Eventually, Valerian was murdered, but his body was skinned and stuffed, so that even in death he could be kept as a trophy to the might of the Sassanids.

After Valerian's death, Gallienus continued to rule Rome for a further eight years. Such durability was rare in the third century, but Gallienus faced his share of usurpers. Zenobia, the client Queen of Palmyra, formed her own breakaway "Palmyrene Empire" in the east, while Postumus, one of Gallienus generals in Germania, proclaimed himself ruler of a breakaway "Gallic Empire" in the west.

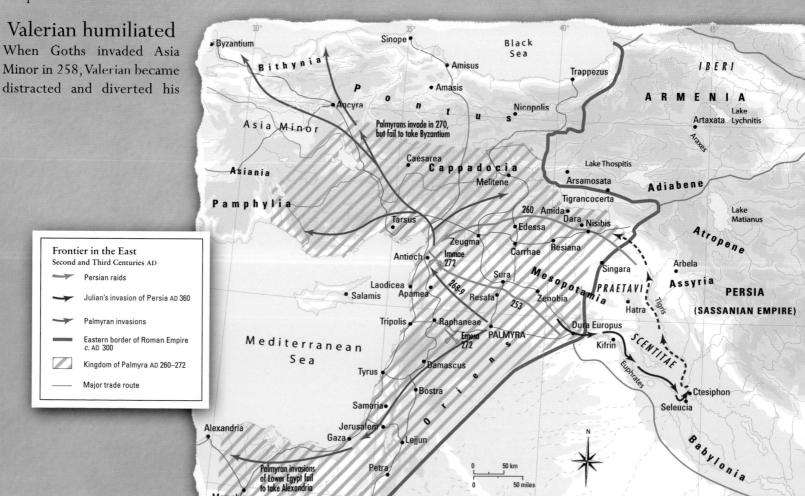

Frontier in the East
Second and Third Centuries AD

→ Persian raids

→ Julian's invasion of Persia AD 360

→ Palmyran invasions

— Eastern border of Roman Empire *c.* AD 300

▨ Kingdom of Palmyra AD 260–272

— Major trade route

Aurelian

In 270 AD, Lucius Domitius Aurelianus
(Aurelian) came to power. He ruled for a
relatively long period of five years, during
which time he restored the Empire
by defeating, and re-incorporating,
the Gallic and Palmyrene Empires back
into the Roman Empire.

"Restorer of the world"

As well as his successes in re-establishing the Empire,
he successfully dealt with the Alamanni. This Germanic
tribe had been such a great threat to Rome that Aurelian
had ordered the construction of new defensive walls
around the city.

Having re-established some degree of security and
stability to the Empire, the Senate proclaimed him
"Restituor Orbis"—"restorer of the world."

Conspiracy against Aurelian

In 275, Aurelian prepared to move
against the powerful Sassanid Empire,
but fell prey to a conspiracy en-route.
His secretary plotted against him and
managed to convince the Praetorian
Guard that Aurelian was going to
order their executions. This
encouraged the Guard to move
pre-emptively against the Emperor
and in Caenophrurium, Thrace,
they murdered him.

The death of Aurelian was
yet another disaster for the
Empire; the crisis deepened as a
further six Emperors followed
over the next decade.

*The Arch of Titus, constructed at the
eastern end of the Forum in Rome.*

Feats of Engineering

Driven by military need and imperial expansion, the Romans became skilled constructors, building many structures which are visible today, and engineering solutions to many of the problems they faced in their building programs or everyday life.

Early roads

The Romans may not have been the first civilization to develop roads, but they were certainly unparalleled in terms of the extent of their network and the sophistication of their building techniques. Roman roads were not surpassed until the invention of Macadam in the nineteenth century, and many of the routes developed still form the basis for roads in use today.

It was from the Etruscans and the Greeks that the Romans learned the art of road building. In the early days, most of the roads they developed were on a small scale and in urban centers.

It was not until 312 BC that the first major Roman road was constructed between Rome and the city of Capua in the south. The road was named the *Via Appia* (the Appian Way), after the censor, Appius Claudius, who ordered its construction. In the short term, the road was designed to strengthen Rome's link with Capua, its ally in the second war against the Samnite tribe. In the longer term, the road paved the way for Roman hegemony, and expansion in Campania.

The Romans mastered the techniques for the construction of arches and domes. This dome is from the nymphaeum *at Hadrian's Villa.*

The Appian Way

After defeating the Samnites, the Romans began to dominate the region by establishing colonies and forging alliances with the independent Campanian city-states. Once the Romans had penetrated further southward, the Appian Way was extended beyond Capua to nearby Beneventum, where a Roman colony was founded on the site of an ancient settlement.

At the start of the third century BC, the Romans pushed further south, threatening the Greek city-states along the coast. In this, the Appian Way proved to be a vital supply route for the Roman Army in the resulting "Pyrrhic Wars" against the Greeks. After the Greeks were defeated in 275 BC, a further extension of the Appian Way to Brundisium, on the south-east coast, took place. From here sea crossings could be made to Greece.

Decorative cornice from Ostia.

Military origins

After the construction of the Appian Way, the Romans continued to build roads across their growing Empire. They were primarily constructed for military purposes, namely transporting men and supplies quickly to the frontlines, or to troublespots within Rome's occupied territories. As the roads were developed with marching soldiers in mind, they were built very wide, direct and straight.

Over time this developed into a major road network crisscrossing the Empire and linking cities as far and wide as Lugdunum (Lyon) in Gaul with Carthage in North Africa. Even Britannia, separated from the rest of the Empire by sea, was carved up by a system of Roman roads. Rome sat at the hub of this vast network, giving rise to the saying that "all roads lead to Rome."

Civilian use

Although the military were given primary use of the roads, a good deal of civilian traffic developed as well. Traders and travelers from across the Empire used the roads to get from one place to another. Most people preferred to travel by these overland routes than by sea, where passengers faced the very real threat of drowning in a storm.

With so many people using Roman roads in need of refreshments and places to stay, many towns and villages grew up along the roadside to catch passing trade.

To allow people to navigate the roads, milestones or *milliaria* were put up every one thousand paces to let people know how far, and in which direction, the nearest town or city was. Most of these milestones also made reference to the distance to or from Rome.

Road construction

The Roman government paid for the construction of roads, which were built by the legionaries, often assisted by slaves. Although Rome tried to standardize road building across the Empire, the roads usually depended upon the available time, material and space. Road construction at the frontiers was more improvised than for those closer to Rome.

To build a new road, surveyors would first plot the best possible course for the road, and plan its route in detail. Once this was calculated, the legionaries would dig down to the bedrock to establish a firm base for the road; they would be guided by rods planted along the route where the road was to be built. If it was available, a layer of sand was placed on top of the bedrock and then covered with a layer of stone

A street in Pompeii.

and gravel mixed in cement. The surface of the road, comprising large stone slabs would sit in the cement mix. The road was built on a very slight gradient so that any rainwater would run off into drainage ditches at the side.

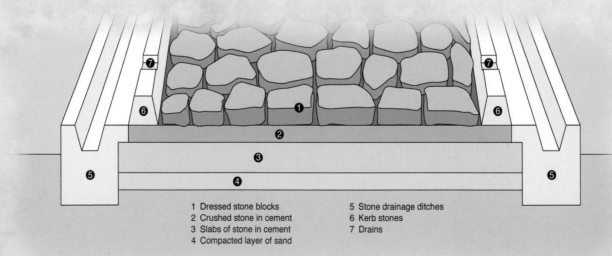

1 Dressed stone blocks
2 Crushed stone in cement
3 Slabs of stone in cement
4 Compacted layer of sand
5 Stone drainage ditches
6 Kerb stones
7 Drains

Postal Service

The road network was also used by couriers, established under Augustus, who acted as an early form of postal service. These couriers were allotted for official business only and were used to transport messages from Rome to the generals, governors, and forts across the Empire. A network of relay stations was established so that as soon as one rider began to tire, another could take over. This meant that official correspondence was able to cover a vast distance in a short space of time.

The postal service made communications much quicker across the Empire, which allowed the Emperors' wishes to travel with greater ease and meant they did not necessarily have to rule from Rome. During Hadrian's rule, when he retired to his villa at Tibur outside Rome, the postal service provided him with a quick and easy connection to the city.

Sanitation

Although the Romans' understanding of medicine was relatively primitive and many basic diseases were not properly treated, their understanding of hygiene was exceptionally advanced. Through relatively sophisticated sanitation systems, they were able to prevent many diseases, and maintain high levels of public health.

Wall from a building in Ostia.

One of Rome's most exceptional engineering feats was the development of the aqueduct. The innovation of a system to bring fresh water to a city was first made in the East, but the Romans refined and developed the idea.

Bringing water

The first Roman aqueduct was built at the command of the censor, Appius Claudius, in 312 BC. Before that time, the population of the city had used water from the Tiber and nearby springs, but the river had become polluted and the springs did not meet the needs of the increasing numbers. Over the centuries, eleven aqueducts were built to serve the city of Rome alone, and others appeared across the Empire.

Aqueducts were principally a system of underground pipes, which brought water from its source in the mountains down to a city. The system simply relied on gravity taking its course and the pipes were set at a slight gradient to assist the flow. A benefit of the use of underground conduits was that it prevented the water from becoming contaminated by animals or dust, and also protected from heating by the sun.

Spectacular structures

The spectacular, arched structures that are most readily associated with Roman aqueducts were only built when the aqueduct encountered a river valley or a low plain. Such features disrupted the gradual downward flow of the water and so the over ground section of the aqueduct was built to compensate.

Cisterns and pipes

Once the water reached the city, it was stored in a cistern called a *castella*, where it was distributed to the city through a network of pipes. The cisterns were usually located on the highest ground outside the city to allow the pipes to run water down into the city by gravity.

Pipes directly supplied the imperial residence, and some public amenities, and richer Romans paid for the pleasure of having pipes bring water directly to their homes. Private Roman baths also paid for their own water pipes from the cisterns, but the larger public baths were usually served by their own aqueduct. These aqueducts did not usually come all the way from the source, but were spurred off a main aqueduct specifically for use at the baths. The poor did not enjoy such a luxury; they had to get their water from one of the public fountains that could be found all over Roman cities.

Removing waste

Long before the first aqueduct was built, the Romans had developed a sewage system to take excess water, together with human waste, away from the city. Rome's first sewage system, the *Cloaca Maxima*, (Greatest Sewer) was built during the sixth century BC, at the time of the Roman Monarchy. The ruling monarchs at the time were Etruscan and it is believed that the *Cloaca Maxima* was influenced by Etruscan designs.

The sewers probably originated as a system which comprised an open channel of waste and water that flowed into the River Tiber. An open sewage system was not only highly unpleasant, but it also took up a lot of space; the solution was to cover up the sewers and build over them.

Left: The latrines of the Hadrianic Baths in Leptis Magna, Libya.

Below: The Pont du Gard—an aqueduct spanning the River Gardon in France.

A boost to public health

The underground sewage system provided an excellent boost to public health, but large openings were still necessary to allow surface water to run off into them. The stench near to these openings became unbearable when the sewage did not flow quickly enough into the river. This problem was overcome once the aqueducts were built and excess water stored in the cisterns could be used to flush out the sewers and move the waste away from the city quickly.

The considerable public health benefits offered by the sewer system in Rome was undermined by a shortage of drains. Bathhouses, public toilets, and the houses of the rich were usually equipped with drains that took waste directly to the sewers. However, the majority of the population did not have immediate access to drains to the sewers. Their waste was left to run down the streets and into the openings in the sewage system designed for run-off water.

Although most Romans frequently used public toilets, it was not always practical and many people opted to use chamber pots, which they emptied onto the streets. These public latrines are a part of the Hadrianic bathing complex in Leptis Magna, North Africa.

Public toilets

Although there were public latrines, it was impractical for Romans to make several trips there each day, especially as, in the early period, there was an entrance fee. Thus, urine was often among the surface run-off. When a chamber pot was filled, it would be emptied in the street; often its contents were simply ejected through the window of one of the Roman tenements, onto the street below.

In spite of the popular use of chamber pots, Romans did make regular use of the public latrines. The toilets were communal, so customers would sit and catch up with friends, almost as if they were at the baths.

Urine was regularly used to stiffen clothes in the process of cleaning them, which meant that some people were actually employed to collect urine from the streets and from the public toilets. Although it was widely agreed that this was among the nastiest of jobs, the thrifty Emperor Vespasian saw it as an opportunity for extra revenue and introduced a tax on urine. In honor of his tax, French public urinals became known as *vespasiennes* in the twentieth century.

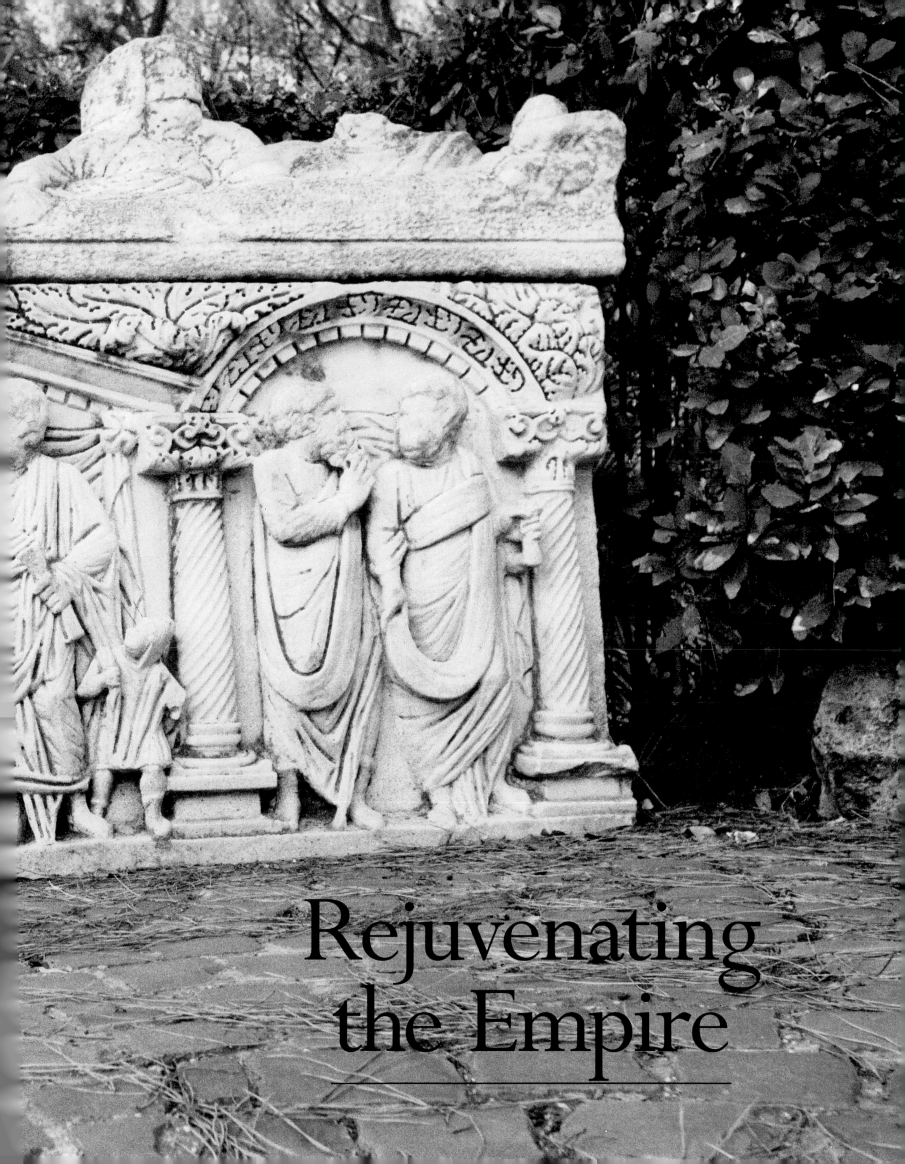

Rejuvenating the Empire

Diocletian

The long period of anarchy following the death of Aurelian finally came to a conclusion
with the accession of Diocletian. He brought about much-needed reforms,
which gave the Empire a new lease of life.

Humble origins

In 284 AD, Diocletian, an Illyrian of humble origins, was pronounced Emperor by his troops in Nicomedia. In early 285, he defeated the incumbent ruler, Carinus, and moved to unify the Empire.

Diocletian encouraged a more obvious form of despotism; he was to be known as "*dominus*"—meaning lord, instead of "*princeps*" meaning first-citizen. Augustus and his successors had been careful to maintain the pretence that Republican institutions were not contravened by their rule; Diocletian and his successors no longer adhered to such fiction.

The Tetrarchy

Diocletian's most famous political reform was his institutionalization of the system of co-Emperors. One Emperor was charged with the West, while the other controlled the East and each Emperor appointed a junior Emperor to assist him—the result was a rule of four men called a "Tetrarchy."

Not only did the Tetrarchy ensure easier and better management of the Empire, it also provided a clear system of succession because the junior Emperor could take over on the death of the senior one, removing any uncertainty over succession, and putting an end to the instability of the preceding decades.

Diocletian appointed Marcus Aurelius Valerius Maximianus, a fellow Illyrian, as his co-Augustus in 287 and gave him control of the western half of the Empire, while Diocletian looked after the affairs of the East. In 293, Galerius and Constantius were appointed as Caesars to Diocletian and Maximianus respectively.

The Tetrarchy allowed the rulers to deal with several problematic fronts simultaneously, helping to end the incursions by the Alamanni and the Sassanids, thwart revolts in Britannia, Mauretania, and Egypt, and restore order within the Empire.

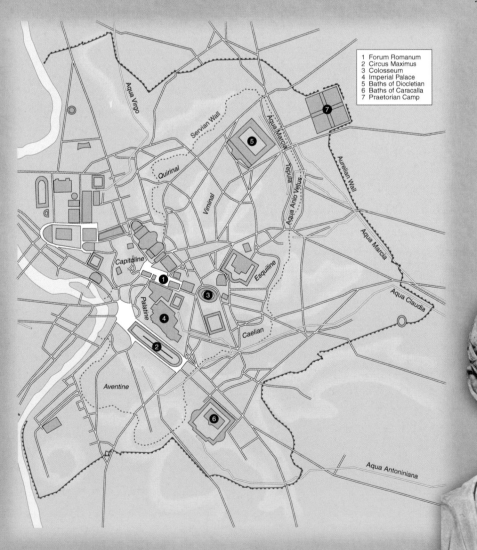

1 Forum Romanum
2 Circus Maximus
3 Colosseum
4 Imperial Palace
5 Baths of Diocletian
6 Baths of Caracalla
7 Praetorian Camp

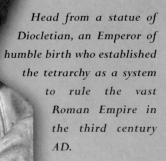

Head from a statue of Diocletian, an Emperor of humble birth who established the tetrarchy as a system to rule the vast Roman Empire in the third century AD.

Restoring order

Diocletian introduced bureaucratic reforms to bring the Army under control and decrease the number of challengers for the imperial title. He doubled the amount of provinces in order to reduce the number of men under the command of one general, although to maintain efficiency the smaller provinces were grouped into dioceses—a new administrative unit that was later adopted by the Christian Church. In addition to the Army, a civilian militia was established to increase defence in border regions.

One of the underlying problems of the decades of anarchy had been a growing economic crisis. Diocletian attempted to bring hyperinflation under control, firstly by strengthening

Stone sculpture from the third century AD *depicting two of the four Tetrarchs at the west entrance to the Basilica San Marco in Venice, Italy.*

the price of gold, and when that failed by introducing price-fixing using the Edict on Maximum Prices of 301. This edict insulated the poor from the harshness of the devastated economy in the short term. However, this strategy offered no long-term solution and encouraged the emergence of a vast and expensive black market.

Persecution of the Christians

Diocletian was a strong believer in traditional, pagan Roman religion. He identified with Jupiter, while Maximianus found affinity with Hercules, and he expected to be treated somewhat like a god. Christian monotheism could not be reconciled with Diocletian's religious views and he resorted to persecuting the sect as a result. Christians were banned from the Army, terrorized, and often forced to worship Roman gods.

In 305, Diocletian abdicated in favor of his junior Emperor, and encouraged his co-Emperor to follow suit. He retired to the Illyrian town of Spalato (Split), and lived just long enough to see his political system unravel.

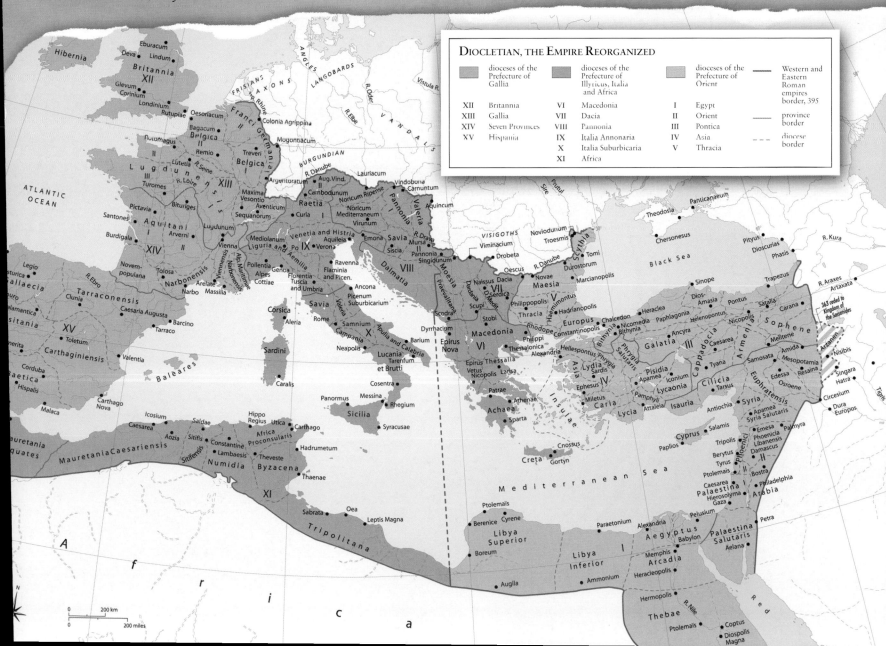

DIOCLETIAN, THE EMPIRE REORGANIZED

▢ dioceses of the Prefecture of Gallia	▢ dioceses of the Prefecture of Illyricus, Italia and Africa	▢ dioceses of the Prefecture of Orient

— Western and Eastern Roman empires border, 395

— province border

--- diocese border

XII	Britannia	VI	Macedonia	I	Egypt
XIII	Gallia	VII	Dacia	II	Orient
XIV	Seven Provinces	VIII	Pannonia	III	Pontica
XV	Hispania	IX	Italia Annonaria	IV	Asia
		X	Italia Suburbicaria	V	Thracia
		XI	Africa		

Urban Life

Across the Roman world, it is estimated that as many as one in every ten people lived in urban areas. In a culture which emphasized social interaction and activities, urban living provided a perfect platform for Roman values. Additionally, the city offered a more reliable and plentiful supply of jobs than in rural areas. This acted as a magnet, pulling people in to the cities.

Insulae—a space-saving solution

Most people in Rome lived in tenement buildings called *insulae*. At times in Rome's history, more than one million people needed housing near the city center because they had no means of transport to live further out. This made land expensive and forced the Romans to build upward, in order to provide affordable housing for ordinary people.

This problem of space was not exclusive to Rome and *insulae* were built in towns across the Empire, albeit to a lesser extent. Some of the best ruins of the tenements are to be found at Ostia, the bustling harbor that linked Rome with the sea.

Overcrowding

These tenements were exceptionally overcrowded; often an entire family would be forced to live in just one room. They were also densely packed together and some were as high as seven stories, which placed them in serious danger of collapse.

Fire was an additional hazard because the upper floors were made of wood, and there was a serious risk of it catching alight when people were cooking. This was probably the cause of the Great Fire of Rome in 64 AD, which burned for nine days through these tightly packed, wooden tenements.

To try to prevent such calamities, the Emperor Augustus introduced legal restrictions on the height of *insulae*; they could be no higher than 65 feet. He also introduced a night watch to keep a look out for fire. Both Nero and Trajan imposed even stricter height limitations.

A plaque on a wall in a Pompeii street depicts two porters bearing an amphora hung from a pole indicating that the use of porters is obligatory.

Remains of tenements, or insulae, in Ostia, the port of ancient Rome.

Living above the shop

The ground floors of *insulae* were usually used as shops and the living quarters were located on the upper floors. With the threat of fire and collapse, as well as a precarious staircase, the higher, wooden floors were the least desirable place to live in the building.

Most apartments had small, open windows, but some of these openings looked onto an internal courtyard, which would not have allowed in much light. It is even thought that some homes might have had no access to natural light at all.

Middle-class Romans also lived in *insulae*, but unlike the poorer citizens, they would have been able to afford better apartment blocks in which they would have occupied more than one room.

A model of how Roman insulae *might have looked. Many would have been several stories higher than this. Additional floors were constructed with wood, which was a perennial fire hazard.*

Domus

Wealthy Romans could afford to live away from the crowded tenements in their own single-story houses, called a *domus*. Many of these were located on the Palatine Hill, away from the plebs and close to where the Emperor's palace stood.

The front door of these houses opened onto an atrium, where guests were received, and a shrine to the household and ancestral gods was located. The ceiling in the atrium was open to the elements to allow sunlight, and more importantly rainwater, to enter the house. Rainwater was also collected from the roofs of these houses which were slanted to channel water through the opening in the atrium ceiling. The water would be caught in a small basin on the floor below, and put to good use around the house.

The remains of Trajan's Market, a large shopping complex commissioned by Emperor Trajan, alongside the construction of his Forum.

Layout of a *domus*

All the main rooms in the *domus* were located off the central atrium, including the study or office at the back where the head of the family would conduct business. The atrium was flanked by the family's bedrooms, which were usually small and functioned only as a sleeping chamber.

This type of Roman home tended to be sparsely furnished, giving the illusion that the house was larger than it actually was. However, it would be elaborately decorated to convey an impression of grandeur.

Entertaining al fresco

To the rear of the house was a small walled garden, where much of the entertaining was done and many meals were enjoyed al fresco. Originally, the garden would have been relatively understated, but during the late Republic, many families preferred to model their gardens on the

Decorative oil lamp from Pompeii.

Hellenic style, complete with columns, expensive frescoes, and exotic fauna. If it was too cold, or even too hot, to eat outside, then a *domus* had a separate dining room.

The house also had a simple kitchen with a stove, where the slaves would work. Some houses also rented out their frontages as shops.

Employment in the city

Much of the backbreaking and menial work in Rome was done by slaves, which meant that ordinary Roman citizens had to seek employment elsewhere. Most men worked as traders, such as bakers, fishmongers, and wine vendors. Others worked as craftsmen or carpenters, making clothes, trinkets, furniture, or utensils.

Shops and workshops would usually be based on the ground floor of the *insulae* and the family and employees would normally live in the same building, often in cramped conditions behind the shop. These workers were often members of guilds, which served as social clubs, as well as looking after the communal interests of the industry.

Street and temple ruins in Ostia.

Working practices

Roman women, however poor, were not usually expected to work, but it is likely that many would have assisted their husbands. Sons would usually follow their fathers into the family business, although after the Army was opened up to ordinary Romans, many would follow a military career instead.

Ordinary Romans worked a strict six-hour day, which began at dawn and left the afternoon free for leisurely pursuits, especially a trip to the baths, the games, or the races. Some traders opened their shops again in the early evening to catch a last bit of trade before Rome settled down for the evening.

High status jobs

Employment as a trader or craftsmen was considered beneath patrician Romans, whose job options were almost exclusively limited to the interconnected fields of politics, law, and the Army. Their jobs were not strictly regimented, but like plebeian males, the afternoon was usually spent at the baths, where they would continue to talk politics.

With the rich limiting their employment options and the poor unsuitably skilled, slaves had to undertake highly skilled professions, such as teachers, doctors, surgeons, and architects. Technically, any money the slaves made went directly to their masters, but they were mostly allowed to keep a percentage as an incentive to work hard. When they had earned enough money they could buy their freedom. Many continued to work in the same profession after their emancipation, meaning that highly skilled jobs became the preserve of these freedmen and their progeny.

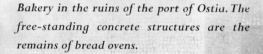

Bakery in the ruins of the port of Ostia. The free-standing concrete structures are the remains of bread ovens.

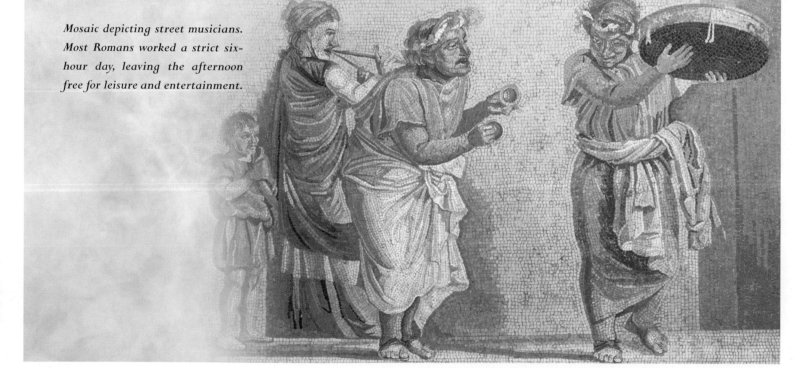

Mosaic depicting street musicians. Most Romans worked a strict six-hour day, leaving the afternoon free for leisure and entertainment.

Clothing and fashion

Roman clothing was relatively plain and straightforward, so most Romans tried to follow the latest fashion for haircuts, jewelry, and cosmetics. Such accessories reflected a person's social status; rich Romans would bejewel themselves and adopt elaborate hairstyles, while poorer Romans tried to follow whatever trends they could afford.

The Toga

The toga was the standard Roman dress worn by all male citizens from the earliest days of the Republic. It consisted of a long woolen sash, which was wrapped carefully around the body. These garments were usually hot and uncomfortable, making them particularly impractical for soldiers or workers. As a result, the toga was usually saved for special occasions, and a less cumbersome cloak was worn. However, wealthy Romans would usually wear a toga in public to show that they did not have to work.

Different togas were worn at different stages in life; boys would wear a *toga praetexta*, with a purple hem, and would only be able to wear an adult's plain, white *toga*

virilis at fourteen, when they had come of age. When men were in mourning, they were expected to wear a dark gray *toga pulla*. For a time, a general celebrating a great military victory was allowed to wear a purple toga, until that privilege was reserved only for the Emperor. Thus, however unwieldy they might have been, togas were considered a mark of honor for many Romans, because non-citizens were forbidden from wearing them.

Female *stola*

Women quickly developed their own shapely, and less heavy, version of the toga called the *stola*, which did not need to be wrapped around the body. The *stola* was a rectangular-shaped, long-sleeved dress, which covered both shoulders and ran down to the ground. Women often wrapped a shawl called a *palla* over the top of the *stola* to complete their outfit. If a woman was from a particularly wealthy family her *palla* might have been made of silk, an exceptionally rare commodity, imported all the way from China.

Gold cameo ring with profile portrait of a man wearing a diadem.

Tunics

In the early Republic, togas were usually worn directly over undergarments, but this was incredibly uncomfortable, especially because togas were made from wool, which often irritated the skin. Roman men and women began to wear a tunic under their togas or *stolas*.

Ordinary Roman men, who only wore a toga occasionally, wore a tunic most of the time. During the summer when it was hot, just one tunic would suffice, but several tunics were layered on to keep warm in winter.

Men's tunics comprised two rectangles of wool sewn together; they were usually short-sleeved and tied with a belt so as to make the garment stop at the knees. Women's tunics were longer in both the sleeve and the length. The tunics worn by slaves had stripes running down the sides to indicate their social status.

To clean the woolen material used in their clothing, the Romans would visit a fuller. First the clothes were stiffened using urine and then rubbed with special clay called "fuller's earth" to remove any impurities before being washed in water. It was also the fuller's job to prepare the cloth used to make clothes, by stretching and dyeing it. A Roman woman would then use the cloth to make clothes for her family.

Footwear

Roman footwear was relatively uniform for men and women. In their own home or at the houses of friends or family, Romans wore informal, open-toe sandals. Soldiers wore a form of booted sandal called *caligae*. Outside of the home, Romans wore *calcei*, leather shoes, which covered the feet entirely; it was rare for Romans to leave the house with their sandals on and only *calcei* would ever be worn with a toga.

Although Romans did not wear socks with their shoes, many took to using some kind of material to prevent rubbing because fashion demanded that shoes be worn tightly.

The Emperor Gaius Julius Caesar Germanicus became known as Caligula, meaning "little boot," because his mother used to dress him up in a miniature soldier's outfit, including a small pair of these boots.

A female figure from the frescoes in the Villa of the Mysteries in Pompeii shows typical Roman dress of the first century AD.

Statue of Helena which shows the drapes of the stola and the palla.

Hairstyles

During the Republic, Roman haircuts were relatively unremarkable because most men wore short hair while most women simply tied their hair into a bun. During the Empire, women's tastes became more ostentatious and dyes, products, and wigs became popular.

Although the majority of Roman women had dark hair, many sought to be blonde or red-headed, either by using dyes or by cutting the hair from north European slaves to turn into wigs or extensions.

During the Flavian Dynasty, it became popular for women to have an elaborate hairstyle, involving several layers of mounted ringlets at the front of the head. Such a fashion could only be followed by the wealthy because it required women to visit a hairdresser, or to own a slave who could perform the extensive and time-consuming curling and pinning involved.

Men's haircuts remained largely unchanged until the second century AD, when Hadrian popularized a trend for curled hair when he had his own hair carefully styled into ringlets using heated tongs.

Beards

Few Roman men shaved during the early Republic because it was not fashionable, and the Romans did not have the necessary equipment. That changed in the third century BC, when Romans came under the influence of the Greeks in the south of the Italian peninsula, where shaving was more commonplace. Roman men would not shave themselves because shaving equipment was still relatively primitive; instead they would visit a barber, particularly one with a reputation for smoothness.

The shaved-look remained popular for several centuries, although men often decided to sport a short, tidy beard. When Emperor Hadrian came to the throne, he reintroduced the beard, allegedly because he wanted to hide a slight disfigurement to his face. The beard remained popular until the time of Constantine the Great, when shaving became fashionable again.

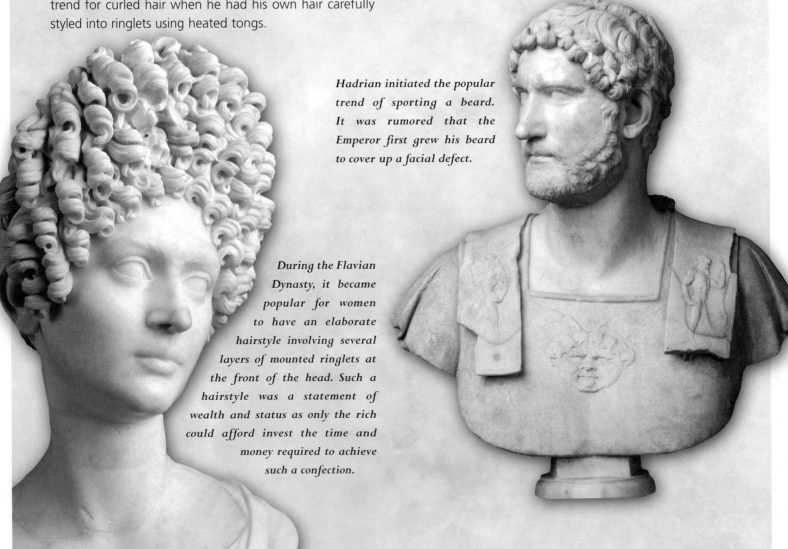

Hadrian initiated the popular trend of sporting a beard. It was rumored that the Emperor first grew his beard to cover up a facial defect.

During the Flavian Dynasty, it became popular for women to have an elaborate hairstyle involving several layers of mounted ringlets at the front of the head. Such a hairstyle was a statement of wealth and status as only the rich could afford invest the time and money required to achieve such a confection.

Jewelry and Make-up

Signet rings

Roman men usually limited themselves to one piece of jewelry, a signet ring with a personalized engraving, which allowed the owner to make a seal by dipping the ring in melted wax. Signet rings were initially made of iron, but later gold rings became standard. Over time, richer Roman men took to wearing more than just one ring, probably because the fact that the majority of Roman men wore one ring meant that wearing more would be an outward sign of the owner's wealth.

Unlike their menfolk, Roman women wore a good deal of jewelry—especially rings, necklaces, earrings, bracelets, brooches, and hairpins. Most wedding rings were made from iron, which was the main metal used in jewelry in the early Republic. As Rome expanded and gained access to more materials, gold and silver jewelry became extremely popular, and remained so for the duration of the Empire. However, this did not preclude some women from seeking other types of jewelry, fashioned from materials such as mother-of-pearl or bone.

As with the men, Rome's wealthiest women liked to show off their riches; in order to stand out in a society in which most woman owned at least some jewelry, the wealthiest women liked to have their jewelry encrusted with rare gems such as sapphires, rubies, and emeralds.

Crushed snails and ants

Roman women desired to appear paler than they actually were. Many achieved this look simply by staying out of the sun, but make-up was always on hand to help them look even paler. Powdered chalk, or even poisonous white lead, was applied to give the necessary light complexion to the face and arms, and crushed snails were applied as a face cream. The fair-skinned appearance could be accentuated by darkening the eyebrows with crushed ants or ash. Reddish clay or dye was applied as a blusher and a lipstick, in order to complete the desired facial appearance.

Gold necklace with gemstones found at Pompeii.

Complex and intricate gold earring with five pendants.

Constantine and the Christian State

Constantine

Diocletian's tetrarchical rule quickly broke down and Constantine emerged as the sole ruler of the Roman world. He attributed his victories over his rivals to the divine intervention of the Christian God. Christianity was favored over Roman paganism and eventually became the state religion.

Breakdown of the Tetrarchy

Diocletian's abdication in favor of his second-in-command, Galerius, was the beginning of the end for the Tetrarchy. In the West, Maximianus had also stepped down to allow Constantius to become Augustus in his stead. It was supposed to be a managed transfer of power.

In 305 AD the two junior Emperors, Constantius and Galerius were proclaimed Augusti in place of Diocletian and Maximianus. However, the following year, Constantius died at Eburacum (York) in Britannia and the Tetrarchy faced a serious crisis.

Diocletian had, in part, established the Tetrarchy to ease the succession process, with the junior Emperors taking power upon the death of the senior. But things did not go according to Diocletian's plan when the troops declared Constantius' son, Flavius Valerius Constantinus (Constantine) as Augustus, despite the fact that he had not been named as the vice-Emperor.

The serving vice-Emperor, Flavius Valerius Severus, declared power for himself in Rome, but he was defeated by another would-be ruler, Maxentius, the son of Maximianus. The East faced a similar breakdown when Galerius died in 311 and the territory was carved up between two prominent individuals, Licinius and Daia.

Battle for the Western Empire

In October 312, the battle between Constantine and Maxentius for the western portion of the Empire took place at the Milvian Bridge on the River Tiber.

En route to the battlefield, Constantine believed he had a divine vision that encouraged him to go into battle under the banner of Christianity. He obliged the vision and entered the battle under the sign of the Christian cross.

Although considerably outnumbered, Constantine managed to defeat Maxentius, who drowned when the bridge across the river collapsed while he was still on it.

Constantine's surprise victory, and the circumstances of Maxentius' death, convinced some people of a divine intervention by the Christian God.

The Gate of Diocletian on the temple island of Philae in the River Nile.

The Edict of Milan

Following his victory, Constantine marched on Rome, where the people and the Senate readily accepted him as Emperor. Although he was not yet a Christian, he legislated to protect them from persecution.

In 313 AD he passed the "Edict of Milan," which stipulated that the Roman government would tolerate all religions. The agreement was co-signed by Licinius, who had allied with Constantine against Daia, his rival in the East. Licinius was firm in his pagan beliefs, but signed the edict to gain Constantine's support for his war against Daia, who had been persecuting the Christians. With Constantine's backing, Licinius was soon victorious over Daia and Christians were freed from tyranny across the entire Empire.

Constantine favors Christianity

The alliance between Licinius and Constantine gradually broke down as Constantine turned ever more to Christianity. At the dedication of the Arch of Constantine —a memorial to his triumph against Maxentius—he refused to make the traditional sacrifice to the pagan gods. In addition, state funds were channeled into the Christian Church at the expense of pagan temples.

Constantine's preference for Christianity over the traditional Roman gods frustrated the Senate, which looked to Licinius to help rid them of the heretical Constantine.

A Holy War

In 316, war broke out. Although it was essentially a power struggle between the two men, Constantine and Licinius, it was also a holy war between Christianity and Roman paganism. Neither man was able to score a decisive victory, so they reverted to an uneasy peace for seven years.

When Licinius began persecuting Christians another war became inevitable. This war ended in Constantine's favor after the Battle of Chrysopolis in 324, leaving him as the sole ruler of the Roman world.

Constantine's Arch, erected next to the Coliseum in Rome, stands as a memorial to his triumph over Maxentius, a victory which paved the way for him to assume sole command of the Roman Empire.

Constantinople: A New Capital

For much of Roman history, Rome was the most important city in the world.
During the late Republic and early Empire period, the city had been made rich by the plunder
from wars and occupied lands. Incredibly, the population had exceeded one million people and
the city had become a hub for trade and transport across the Empire.

Rome declines

During the political crisis of the third century, the city had slipped into decline, as its economy stagnated because new sources of revenue became scarce. Trade through the city also began to dry up, as Rome was fast eclipsed by the East, where the economy flourished.

Rome's saving grace was the fact that it remained the political center of the Empire, but even this was eroded when Diocletian introduced his reforms; the Western Ruler governed from Mediolanum (Milan), which was closer to the troublesome borders in the north,

Gold solidus depicting Emperor Constantine.

and the Eastern Ruler held his court at Nicomedia, in what is now the north-east region of Turkey.

A decisive break with Rome

Constantine made the decisive break with Rome when he moved the capital of the Empire to Byzantium, modern-day Istanbul, which he renamed Nova Roma (New Rome).

Rome was considered too far from the new economic and cultural center in the east of the Empire. Although Byzantium was favored because Constantine had studied there, it was certainly a better location for the capital.

It brought the government closer to the geographical center of the Empire, within easier reach of the trouble spots in both the East and the West. Furthermore, the city was situated in a perfect position to control much of the overland trade that passed between the East and West.

Lavish imperial capital

Cities across the Empire were forced to hand over treasures to make Nova Roma a lavish imperial capital. Although Rome maintained some prestige, there is little doubt that it became eclipsed as aristocrats, entertainers and merchants moved to the new capital.

After Constantine's death, Nova Roma was renamed "Constantinople" in his honor.

CONSTANTINOPLE

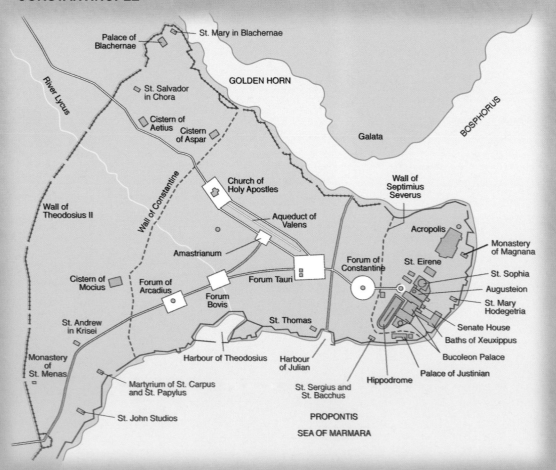

Venus

The daughter of Dione and Jupiter, Venus was one of the most important Roman goddesses, mainly associated with love and beauty, and seen as the mother of all Roman people.

Unfaithful lover

Married to Vulcan, the god of fire and blacksmiths, she was sometimes unfaithful; lovers included Adonis and Mars.

Venus' particular cult began in 293 BC when the oldest-known temple dedicated to her was built and inaugurated on August 18—the festival of *Vinalia Rustica* was then observed on this anniversary each year.

Temple of Venus and Rome

Venus is so closely identified with Rome that the largest temple in Ancient Rome was the "Temple of Venus and Rome." This structure, located at the eastern edge of the Forum, close to the Coliseum, was commissioned by Emperor Hadrian. Work began on construction in 121 AD and it was dedicated in 135, with the work being completed in the reign of Antoninus Pius.

Venus was very closely linked to the Greek goddess Aphrodite, taking over many of her myths.

Torso and head from a statue of Venus.

Statue of Mars from the Canopus at Hadrian's Villa. Mars was one of Venus' lovers.

Julian

Establishing Christianity

In 325 AD, Constantine convened the council of Nicaea to discuss matters of doctrine and practice in the Christian Church. It had far-reaching effects and the agreed statement of belief still underlies Christianity today. Constantine took to building churches, most significantly, the Church of the Nativity in Bethlehem and the Church of the Holy Sepulcher in Jerusalem, on the spots where Jesus is believed to have been born and to have died. Constantine went even further in the application of Christianity, crucifixion was abolished as a means of punishment and markets and offices were closed on a Sunday, the Christian holy day.

In spite of the changes he brought to Roman society, there is considerable debate as to whether Constantine was a true Christian, or whether the religion proved politically expedient. Although he continued to exhibit some impious behavior, notably having Licinius, his wife and one of his sons disposed of rather than forgiven, he was sufficiently convinced by the religion to have himself baptised shortly before his death in 337.

The forces of paganism

While Constantine had made Christianity widely acceptable, it was not yet secure in its position as the orthodox religion of Ancient Rome; just over twenty years after Constantine's death, the forces of paganism were once again on the march.

Constantine had left the Empire to his three sons, who divided it up amongst them. However, infighting between the three rulers, as well as challenges from other family members and usurpers plunged the Empire back into division and chaos. The power struggle was eventually won by Constantine's nephew, Flavius Claudius Julianus (Julian), who became the sole ruler of Rome in 361.

He is known as Julian the Apostate because he brought back the traditional pagan gods of Rome and began to move against the Christians. A fully-fledged restoration was halted in 363, when Julian was killed in battle against the Persians. He was to be the last pagan Emperor of Ancient Rome—in 380, the devoutly Christian Emperor, Theodosius, acceded to the throne and made Christianity the official state religion.

The Missorium of Theodosius is a votive platter that was made to commemorate the tenth anniversary of his reign. These platters were made on significant occasions and given away as gifts. Since the platter was found in Spain and it has been suggested that the soldiers may be German, the cosmopolitan nature of the Empire is indicated.

Detail from the base on which the Egyptian obelisk is mounted shows Emperor Theodosius at the races.

Theodosius

Unlike Julian, the next Emperor, Flavius Jovianus (Jovian), was a Christian.
The war against the Persians that had cost Julian his life was quickly ended when
Jovian agreed to withdraw from several provinces in the East.

On his return to Constantinople, Jovian died in his sleep after less than eight months as Emperor. Officially he is thought to have suffocated on the fumes from a charcoal brazier nearby, but many people suspected foul play.

A return to diarchic rule

Flavius Valentinianus (Valentinian I) succeeded him and quickly resorted to a diarchic system of rule because he believed that the Empire was to be too large to govern alone. He appointed his brother, Valens, to rule the East while he took charge of the West. Valentinian proved a capable ruler and strengthened Rome's frontiers along the Danube and the Rhine, as well as in North Africa.

However, Valens proved to be less capable than his brother in the West. He ineffectively managed the challenges posed by the Persians and the Visigoths against him, and at one stage he even contemplated handing over control to a usurper, named Precopius, rather than stand and fight him.

Years of instability

In 375 AD, Valentinian died and his young sons, Gratian and Valentinian II took his place as rulers in the West. Three years later, Valens was killed in battle against the Visigoths at Adrianople. Gratian appointed Theodosius, the son of one of his father's greatest generals, as Emperor in the East.

Eight years after his appointment of Theodosius, Gratian was murdered at the hands of Magnus Maximus, a usurper who had been proclaimed Emperor by the troops serving under him in Britannia. Maximus had crossed into Gaul where he trapped and killed Gratian at Lugdunum (Lyon).

Theodosius refused to recognize Maximus' claim and continued to acknowledge Valentinian II as the rightful Western Emperor. Angered by this affront, Maximus invaded Italy to unseat Valentinian. Theodosius came to his rescue and swiftly defeated and killed Maximus.

Theodosius emerges as sole Emperor

To safeguard against future threats, Theodosius placed Valentinian under the protection of a Frankish soldier named Arbogast. When Valentinian was found hanged in 392, Arbogast claimed that the Emperor had committed suicide. However, Theodosius believed that Arbogast had murdered him; a suspicion that appeared to be confirmed when Arbogast appointed one of his allies, Eugenius, as Emperor in the West.

Theodosius promptly invaded from the East and defeated Arbogast at the Battle of the Frigidus River. He took up control of the West and became the sole ruler of the Roman world for three years until his death in 395.

Theodosius was a Christian and had curtailed the practice of traditional Roman religion during his tenure as Emperor in the East. In 391 AD, he took a further step by confirming Christianity as the official state religion across the Empire. His death marked the permanent division of the Empire, when his sons Arcadius and Honorius took control of the East and West respectively.

This Egyptian obelisk from Karnak was raised, on the instructions of Theodosius, in the Hippodrome (or racetrack) in Constantinople.

Religion

Genius and *juno*

The earliest form of Roman religion was animistic in character. Romans strove to please spirits they believed inhabited everything around them. Every place and object had its own spirit or *numen*, as did every person. People believed they were watched over by the spirits of their ancestors, called *genius* and *juno* for men and women, respectively.

Three prominent gods

Early in Rome's history three gods, Mars, Quirinus, and Jupiter, came to prominence. It is thought that their importance was a result of the Sabine influence over Rome during the earliest years of the city.

Mars, the god of war, played a vital role in the story of the origins of Rome—he was thought to have been the father of Romulus and Remus. Quirinus, who watched over the people and government of Rome was the deified Romulus, and Jupiter was the leader of all the gods.

All three gods were worshiped at a temple on the Capitoline Hill, and were known as the Capitoline Triad. These new gods did not replace the traditional spirits, but both sets were worshiped alongside one another.

Etruscan influence

During the Roman Monarchy period, Rome came under the influence of the Etruscan civilization and the Capitoline Triad underwent a transformation. Jupiter remained at the pinnacle of Roman religion, but Mars and Quirinus were replaced with Juno and Minerva. Juno was the wife of Jupiter, and Minerva, their daughter, was the goddess of wisdom.

The religious ideas of the Greeks, who had settled in the south of the Italian peninsula, also infiltrated Roman beliefs. Roman gods traditionally had very limited or abstract characteristics, and it was under the influence of the Greeks that the Romans created a mythology surrounding their gods.

The characters of many Roman gods were borrowed from Greek gods, thus Jupiter began to share characteristics with the Greek god Zeus, Mars with Ares, and Minerva with Athena. This process, called syncretism, was applied to most Roman gods. However, reflecting Roman values, their gods displayed a distinctly frugal nature, not shared by their Greek counterparts.

Ara dei Gemelli *from Ostia. This altar is dedicated to Silvanus, the ancient Italian god of nature and forests.*

Pontifex Maximus

The worship of these gods was part of an organized state religion. The faith was guided by a college of pontiffs, an assembly of the highest-ranking priests in Ancient Rome, who were charged with the control of all of the gods combined. It was the college's duty to ensure that each god was happy.

The college was presided over by the chief priest or *pontifex maximus*; originally this position was open exclusively to patricians, but after the third century BC a plebeian Roman could also hold the office.

Although the chief priest initially had a wholly spiritual function, during the late Republic, the position was increasingly politicized—for example, Julius Caesar was the *pontifex maximus* during the first Triumvirate. During the Empire, the role of chief priest was taken over by the Emperors.

Representing the gods

Each god had its own temple and each temple had its own priests, or *flamines*, who were exclusively dedicated to one god. While the college was tasked with managing

Fresco painting from Pompeii showing the Punishment of Eros. The gods of Ancient Greece and their associated myths were important in the development of Roman religious beliefs, and while Roman gods might share some characteristics with their Greek counterparts, their mythological lifestyle were considerably more frugal.

the affairs of all the gods, the *flamines* would be present to represent their particular deity. The most important priests represented one of the three gods of the Capitoline Triad. With the exception of the priestesses to Vesta, the goddess of the hearth, all priests were men.

Vestal Virgins

The priestesses to Vesta were called the Vestal Virgins because they were ordered to remain celibate for the entire thirty years they were in service. The virgins were tasked with keeping the sacred fire of Vesta burning in the temple.

The vestals were extremely privileged because they were no longer under the control of their fathers, which meant they could vote and own property. Vestals were highly regarded in Roman society, so many patrician families wished to see their daughter become one of six vestals. Vestal Virgins were appointed by the *pontifex maximus*, who chose them by drawing lots.

Although Vestal Virgins had considerable advantages in society, there were also downsides—if a Vestal Virgin failed to remain celibate, the punishment was to be buried alive.

Detail of the altar to Matronae Aufaniae from the monument of Vettius Severus.

The Imperial Cult

Several Emperors were deified after their death. The trend began with Julius Caesar and was continued by his successor Augustus.

Initially, the government was quite discerning about which Emperor could become a god. Claudius, Vespasian, and Titus were believed to have earned their divinity, while the less deserving, Caligula and Nero, were overlooked. After the accession of Nerva to the throne, deification became commonplace, unless the Emperor had been particularly unpopular or brief.

Worship of the Imperial Cult became commonplace during the Empire and a number of Emperors even believed themselves to be living gods. This was evident in Commodus, who thought he was the embodiment of Hercules, and the Emperor Diocletian found affinity with Jupiter. However, no Emperor promoted the idea of imperial divinity more than Caligula—he even ordered that his statue be placed in the temples of the monotheistic Jewish worshipers.

The pyramid of Caius Cestius is a funerary monument which contains a burial chamber.

Christianity comes to Rome

Christianity started out as a marginal, often persecuted, sect but ended up as the official state religion.

As Christians grew in number, they became more prominent in society and managed to gain influence over the Emperor Constantine. Vaguely convinced by its teachings, Constantine decided to march into a battle under the banner of Christ. The odds were heavily stacked against Constantine, but he won a surprise victory and assumed it to be the result of divine intervention.

Constantine immediately released the Edict of Milan, which professed tolerance toward Christianity, and during his reign he increasingly favored the religion. At the end of his life, Constantine was baptized and most of his successors were Christians.

One exception was the Emperor Julian, who tried to reinstate the traditional Roman gods, to little avail. In 380 AD, Christianity was made the state religion and the Imperial Cult and the traditional, polytheistic Roman religion came to an end.

Pantheon

The Pantheon

The Pantheon is undoubtedly the best-preserved Roman building in the world today, largely because it was saved from ruin by the Christian Church. The Pantheon was commissioned soon after the defeat of Antony and Cleopatra in 28 BC, by Marcus Vipsanius Agrippa, the famous general, and friend of the Emperor Augustus. The name Pantheon means "temple to all Gods," which explains the function of the structure.

Agrippa's Pantheon is not the one that still stands. It was destroyed in a fire in 80AD during the reign of Titus. However, Hadrian began the rebuilding process after he came to the throne in 118 and the building that can be seen today dates from 126AD. Hadrian had a habit of not putting his name to his buildings, so the inscription on the portico still dedicates the building to Agrippa. It translates as, "Marcus Agrippa, son of Lucius, built this during his third consulship."

Right: Interior of the Pantheon.

Below: Aerial view of the Pantheon in Rome.

The Pantheon is a marvellous feat of ancient engineering. It is a huge domed structure, approximately 150 feet at both the maximum height and diameter. It was the largest domed building for over a millennium. Thick walls and innovative concrete has allowed the building to remain standing. In the center of the dome, there is a large eye, or *oculus*, designed to let light from the sun enter the building.

Most impressively, the Pantheon is still functioning in a somewhat similar capacity to that originally intended for it; it continues to be used as a place of worship by the Christian Church.

Collapse of Empire

Barbarian attack

After the death of Theodosius in 395 AD, the division of the Roman Empire became permanent. While the East flourished, the West fell into decline. Sensing weakness, various "Barbarian" tribes picked away at the decaying West, and carved up the spoils between them.

The Visigoths

The endgame of the Roman Empire had begun with the migration of the Germanic Visigoths into Roman territory in 376. They were refugees who had fled attacks from the Huns, tough warriors from Central Asia.

Distracted by a war against the Sassanid (or Persian) Empire, the Roman Emperor, Valens, predecessor of Theodosius, had allowed the Visigoths to settle in Roman territory. It was hoped these peoples could replenish the Army legions and act as a bulwark against further invasions by the Huns.

Exploiting the refugees

The men tasked with the resettlement exploited the refugees, by taking whatever possessions they had and leaving them worse-off than before they had entered Roman territory. Outraged, the Visigoths took up arms against the Romans, running amok over the Balkans. Valens had to take troops from the Eastern theater to pacify the refugee army, but they defeated the his men at the Battle of Adrianople; Valens was killed the process.

The war had gone so badly for the Romans, that the new Emperor, Theodosius, had to agree to let the Visigoths settle in Thrace, as an ally of Rome. Allowing the Visigoths to establish an autonomous state within the Empire offered a clear display of quite how weak Roman power had become. This lesson was not wasted on the Visigoths, who pushed for more.

Visigoths lay siege to Rome

In the early fourth century, under the leadership of Alaric, the Visigoths menaced Greece and Illyricum, and also carried out raids into Italy. He tried to march on Constantinople, but the attack was averted when the Eastern Emperor offered him control of Illyricum instead. In 408, Alaric pushed into Italy once again and laid siege to Rome.

Again, the Visigoths were offered compensation, and the city managed to pay him off, but he returned the following year, and again in 410. On this last occasion the Visigoths actually entered the city—the first foreign army to do so in eight hundred years. The Visigoth Army plundered the city for three days, but owing to their Christian beliefs, they practiced relative restraint.

Above: Although the Visigoths have a reputation as a "barbarian" race, they were a Christian and civilized people. These gold crowns are an example of their metalworking skills.

Right: Alaric's entrance into Rome. The Visigoths became the first foreign army to capture Rome in eight hundred years when they plundered the city in 410 under the leadership of Alaric.

Peace treaty

Alaric moved his troops out of Rome into the south of Italy, where he prepared an invasion of North Africa. He died before the invasion could be carried out and his successor, Athaulf, moved the Army into the south of Gaul, where he hoped to settle.

However, the Visigoths had taken the Emperor Theodosius II's sister, Galla Placidia, hostage and were pursued by the Roman Army. Athaulf and his Visigoths were pushed into Spain. They later traded the return of Galla Placidia in exchange for peace. The treaty allowed the Visigoths to settle in northern Spain and southern Gaul.

Breaching the Rhine

While Rome had to deal with the Visigoths in the Balkan region, the Huns continued to menace the Germanic tribes of northern and eastern Europe. This forced many of these tribes to push westward. In the winter of 407 AD, these Germanic tribes—the Vandals, the Suebi and the Alans—made use of the cold weather to cross the frozen River Rhine into Roman territory.

The "barbarians" crossed near Moguntiacum (Mainz), where the Roman defences were weaker. They pushed into Gaul and crossed into the Pyrenees.

Weighed down by the difficulties posed by the Visigoths in Italy, attacks against Roman authority in Britannia and a parlously weakened Western Empire, there was little the Romans could do to stop the Huns' advance.

Control of North Africa

Moving south, the "barbarian" tribes gained access to the Mediterranean. Here they resorted to piracy to fund their migrations. In 429, under the leadership of Gaiseric, the Vandals crossed the Mediterranean into Africa, the home of Rome's grain supply. Within just ten years, the Vandals had captured Carthage and the whole of North Africa had been conquered. Emperor Valentian III was forced to concede that the land was no longer subject to Roman rule.

Ruins from the port of Ostia which by the fifth century AD had declined in importance, although it was here that the Vandals landed in 455 AD to begin their march on Rome.

Control of the "granary of the Empire"

Although the Vandals' control of North Africa threatened the grain supply which was vital for the Eastern Empire, there was little to be done to confront the challenge this posed. Constantinople was distracted by the invasion of the Huns.

In the early fifth century, the Huns had settled near to Roman territory on the east side of the River Danube. The Eastern Roman Emperors were happy to pay them tribute to keep them at bay.

Attila the Hun

However, in 434 AD, a ruthless new leader named Attila emerged. He demanded double the amount of money from the Romans, but was refused by the Emperor, Theodosius II, in Constantinople. The Huns crossed the Danube and exacted a brutal reign of terror in the Balkans, razing several Roman cities and butchering the populations.

By 443, the Huns had marched on Constantinople itself. They were unable to take the city, because it was too well defended by its great walls, but they had a sufficient psychological effect on Theodosius II to force him to negotiate terms. In the end, the Eastern Empire agreed to triple the tribute paid to the Huns and secede territory in the Balkans.

High price of deterrence

The Eastern Empire paid a high price to deter the Huns, but the poorer relation in the West did not have the same luxury and paid an even higher price. After agreeing terms with the Eastern Empire, the Huns set their sights on the Western Empire. Attila's army, together with an assortment of barbarian allies, crossed the Rhine in 451 and laid waste to several Gallic cities.

The Hun advance was only halted when it encountered the Roman Army at the Battle of Chalons. This battle is generally perceived as a Roman victory, albeit a pyrrhic one; thousands were killed on both sides. It was to be the last battle the Western Roman Empire would win.

When the Huns retreated across the Rhine, the Romans were too weak to go in pursuit. Consequently, the Huns undertook further attacks in Italy, and planned another march on Constantinople, but Attila died in 453 before he could carry it out.

The end of the Western Empire

After Attila's death, the threat from the Huns dissipated, but Italy was by no means safe, because the Vandals picked up where the Huns had left off. In 455, still under the leadership of Gaiseric, the Vandals landed at Ostia and marched into Rome. The city was completely sacked, leaving the Western Roman Empire in tatters.

In 476, Italy fell under the control of a barbarian named Odoacer, as the Visigoths moved in to occupy the peninsula, and the Empire in the West had reached a conclusion.

Farmers harvest their crop near the ruined city walls of Constantinople (Istanbul, Turkey) constructed by Emperor Theodosius II. During the fifth century the wall was constructed to keep out the raiding army of Attila the Hun. Theodosius also employed mercenary Viking warriors to help defend the city. In 447 most of the wall was destroyed by an earthquake. Wall construction began immediately to repair the damage before raiders could attack the city. The task of maintaining the wall was continued by successive Emperors.

GERMANIC KINGDOMS,
c. 500

movements of peoples

→ Huns

→ Slavs

→ Germanics

→ Celtics

COLLAPSE OF EMPIRE

N

Arctic Circle

Norwegian
Sea

Faeroe Islands

FINNO-UGRIANS

C E L T

North
Sea

JUTES

SCANDINAVIANS

Baltic
Sea

ANGLO-SAXONS

ANGLES
SAXONS

FRISIANS

SLAVS

FRANKS

BURGUNDIANS

KINGDOM OF THE
THURINGIANS

VANDALS

FRANKISH KINGDOM

ALEMANNI

Lutetia

ATLANTIC
OCEAN

Namnetes

KINGDOM OF
BURGUNDY

KINGDOM OF
THE OSTROGOTHS

SUEVES

HUNS

VISIGOTHS

Pavia

Arelate

Ravenna

Spalatum

EAST
ROMAN EMPIRE

Marcianopolis

Naissus

BASQUES

Massilia

Adriatic Sea

Adrianople

KINGDOM
OF THE
SUEVES

Rome

Constantinople

Toletum

KINGDOM OF THE VISIGOTHS

Corsica

Salonica

Aegean
Sea

Lisbon

Valentia

Balearic Is.

Sardinia

Smyrna

Hispalis

Carthago
Nova

KINGDOM
OF THE VANDALS

Panormus

Sicily

Athens

M e d i t e r

Hippo Regius

Carthage

r a n e a n

Crete

VANDALS

S e a

B E R B E R S

Black Sea

Byzantium

Eastern Roman Empire

After the collapse of the Western Roman Empire, the Eastern Roman Empire continued to function.
The Emperor, government, and people still considered themselves part of the Roman Empire,
but in reality the East had evolved into something new: the Byzantine Empire.
The classical world had ended and the Middle Ages were beginning.

Gold cup from sixth century Byzantium.

Dawning of the Byzantine Empire

The "Byzantine Empire" is a construction of historians. In reality the Empire was the Eastern Roman Empire. However, any claim to being "Roman" had been weakened by the loss of the city of Rome, and the later replacement of Latin with Greek as the principal language. Over time, historians adopted the term 'Byzantine Empire' as a label for the East, coining the term from the name of its capital city, Byzantium, known also as Constantinople.

The precise date at which the Byzantine Empire began is debatable. The earliest proposed date is the division of the Empire by Diocletian at the end of the third century, but at this time the East was still integrated politically with Rome and court was held at Nicomedia, not Byzantium.

Another proposed start-date is in 330 AD, during the reign of Constantine, when Nova Roma (New Rome) was established on the site of Byzantium and was lavished with all the attentions of the Emperor. However, the most widely accepted date is 476 AD when the "barbarian" king, Odoacer, took control of Rome and Italy, effectively severing the link between East and West.

A "barbarian" Emperor

Odoacer had continued the pretence of being the Roman Emperor by resuming the Senate and holding public games, but there was little chance of a rapprochement between East and West because Odoacer was not a Roman citizen. Although Zeno, the Emperor in the East, initially acknowledged him, the relationship was not strong.

Unwilling to engage in open warfare to reclaim the West from the pretender to the imperial role, Zeno instead encouraged Theodoric, the king of the Ostrogoths, to go to war against Odoacer in exchange for control over the Italian peninsula.

Theodoric defeated and killed Odoacer, and ruled Italy in his place; Rome had simply replaced one "barbarian" with another, more amenable, one. In theory, Theodoric was under the influence of the Emperors in the East, but in reality, by paying lip-service to Constantinople, he maintained a strong degree of independence.

Mosaic from San Vitale Cathedral in Ravenna, Italy, depicting the Byzantine Emperor Justinian.

Justinian

Despite the uneasy relationship with Byzantium, Theodoric ruled over a relatively peaceful and stable Italy, but order began to break down when he died in 526 AD.

Justinian moves to take control

The new Byzantine Emperor, Justinian, decided to take advantage of the unrest in the West, to make one last bid to control the former Western Empire.

His first move was to dispatch a small force to retake North Africa in 533, where the Vandal king had been persecuting Christians who held different doctrinal beliefs to those held by the Vandals. The mission was led by Belisarius, a general who had made his name suppressing an extremely violent riot in Constantinople which erupted as a result of a chariot race.

North Africa regained

Belisarius and his men faced only limited resistance in North Africa because the Vandal forces were preoccupied in Sardinia. What troops the Vandals had to hand were sent from Carthage to engage the Byzantine Army ten miles south of the city itself. The battle is referred to as "The Battle of *Ad Decimum*," meaning "the battle at the ten-mile post."

Although the Vandals, lead by King Gelimer, were in a strong position, the result was an easy victory for the Byzantines. Belisarius and his men were able to re-occupy Carthage, defeat the remainder of the Vandal forces in the Battle of Tricamerum, and take back the province of North Africa in the process.

Minarets in present-day Istanbul, formerly known as Byzantium or Constantinople. By the end of the fifteenth century, the city had fallen to the Islamic Ottoman Empire, after more than one thousand turbulent years, during which it had been subject to attack, siege, and decline.

Rome recaptured

Justinian then ordered Belisarius to push on into Sicily and Italy to take advantage of Theodoric's death to annex the peninsula. Belisarius marched through southern Italy and, by the end of 536, even captured Rome. The Byzantine troops had faced little resistance because the ruling Ostrogoths were distracted by the Franks, whom Justinian had encouraged to invade from the north.

In January 537, after paying a large indemnity to the Franks, the Ostrogoths were free to march south to try to reclaim Rome. They laid siege to the city for more than a year, but failed to break the will of Belisarius' smaller force. The siege was only broken when Constantinople sent more men to relieve Belisarius' beleaguered troops in early 538. The tables were quickly turned and the Byzantine force laid siege to the Ostrogoth capital at Ravenna in 540.

By 554, Justinian's army, supported by thousands of mercenaries, had succeeded in redeeming a sizeable amount of territory in the West; as well as Italy, Sicily, and North Africa, the Byzantines occupied Sardinia, Corsica, and southern Spain.

Despite the immense gains, it quickly became apparent that Constantinople could not hope to hold on to the West for long because its army had become dangerously overstretched, and opposition was galvanizing.

Over the following two centuries the Empire was attacked by a host of enemies, including Magyars, Slavs, Bulgars, Persians, Avars, Lombards, Goths, and Arabs, forcing it into retreat.

Legacy

In the centuries following Justinian's death in 565 AD, the Byzantine Empire ebbed and flowed, intermittently gaining control of territory in Italy. For the most part, the Empire was restricted to the Balkans and modern Turkey. Rome became something of a backwater, as its population plummeted to just tens of thousands, a far cry from the height of the Empire when more than a million people crammed into the city.

Charlemagne: Holy Roman Emperor

Justinian's war against the Ostrogoths had ravaged the Italian peninsula. After the Byzantines and the Ostrogoths were pushed out, the Lombards, a Germanic people from northern Europe, moved in. The Lombards did very little to regenerate Italy, and were eventually ousted by the Franks, another Germanic tribe, at the end of the eight-century. The Frankish king, Charlemagne, was rewarded with the title "Emperor of the Romans" by the Pope, and became the first of the Holy Roman Emperors.

After Charlemagne's death, his territories were split in half, with the Franks continuing to control the area of Roman Gaul, and the Holy Roman Empire being carved out of northern Italy and Germany.

A Holy Roman Empire

The creation of a Holy Roman Empire was partly an attempt to rekindle the Western Roman Empire. The Emperors were appointed by the Pope, and ruled over vast swathes of central Europe for almost a millennium, until Napoleon reorganized the region in 1806. However, the Holy Roman Empire was really quite different to the Roman Empire; it was a confederation of small states and principalities, and it was centered on Germany, neither of which had been true of Ancient Rome.

The Byzantine Empire continued the Roman Empire in the East for many centuries. Over time it grew gradually weaker as new, powerful tribes moved into the region under the banner of Islam. At times only Constantinople's near-impenetrable walls kept the city safe. The city was sacked in 1204 during the fourth crusade, which set in motion a steady decline as the population plummeted. Two and a half centuries later, in 1453, Constantinople finally fell to the Ottomans and the Byzantine Empire passed into history.

Ruins of a great hall at Emperor Hadrian's Villa, just outside Tivoli, Italy, one of the many wonderfully preserved structures which give us an insight into the way in which the peoples of the Ancient Roman civilization lived.

Ruins of a carved column sitting on the Palatine Hill, where Rome's first settlement was established.

Italy divided

In the West, Italy remained divided for centuries, ownership of the land being carved up between foreign invaders, wealthy families, and the Catholic Church. After a series of wars and a conscious nationalist effort, Italy was reunified during the nineteenth century.

Much of the reunification task was completed by 1861, but Rome still remained elusive because it was under papal control, backed by French support. Paris finally removed its backing in 1870 and Italian troops took the city.

Italy was unified as a nation; Rome was established as the capital, and once again placed at the heart of a short-lived Empire, ruling over parts of Africa, the Balkans, and Greece.

Relics of Rome

The array of fascinating Roman relics that litter Europe, North Africa and the Middle East strike awe into the millions that visit them each year. But the Romans have bequeathed so much more to us than just ruined buildings; we continue to be influenced by Roman politics, law, time, literature, town planning, sanitation and road building. Even Roman education and medicine, which are now largely discredited, were upheld until very recently.

The political systems of the Roman Republic have influenced the American and French systems among many others, and the word "Caesar" was still evident in the German "Kaiser" and Russia "Tsar" until these positions were abolished during the First World War.

The Romans were also largely responsible for the removal of the Jews from Judea, an act that was to have fateful consequences in the twentieth century, and which still impacts international relations to this day.

Legacy of language

One of Rome's greatest legacies is its language; Latin forms the root of a number of European languages, including Italian, French, Portuguese, Spanish, and Romanian. Even the Germanic English language, that has replaced Latin as the *lingua franca* of our time, owes much of its vocabulary to Latin words.

Rome's other greatest legacy is religion; since Jesus' disciple, Saint Peter, was crucified in the city, Rome became an important religious center of the Christian Church. The Bishop of Rome, later called the Pope, could claim to be the successor of Saint Peter, which meant that through the centuries he retained an important role, despite the relegation of Rome to the sidelines.

Over time, theological and political differences led to a split between the Christian Churches of the East and West and the Pope became the highest authority of the western, Catholic Church. Today the Catholic Church has the most followers of all the world's religions; one in every six people in the world is thought to be Catholic. At the heart of such a massive religion, the city of Rome has been able to retain its position at the center of the world, long after the Roman Empire disappeared.

Rome remains an important international city, where the ruins of Ancient Roman lie alongside modern building.

Ancient Rome Timeline

ROMAN MONARCHY 753–509 BC

753 BC Traditional Date for the foundation of Rome.

According to Roman mythology founded by Romulus and Remus. In a dispute over who should rule, Romulus killed Remus, gave the city his own name and went on to reign for the next 38 years.

715 Numa Pompilius elected as king.

From the Sabine tribe, he created the Roman Senate.

673 Reign of Tullus Hostilius.

During his reign, the Curia Hostilia (the Senate House) was built.

642 Reign of Ancus Marcius.

617 Reign of Lucius Tarquinius Priscus.

Also known as Tarquin the Elder, he was responsible for the building of the Circus Maximus and the construction of the city's first sewer system.

578 Reign of Servius Tullius.

534 Reign of Lucius Tarquinius Superbus.

The last Roman king whose reign was characterized by bloodshed and violence.

509 Violation of Lucretia, by king's son, Sextus Tarquinius.

Uprising by Lucius Junius Brutus against Tarquin dynasty and their expulsion.

ROMAN REPUBLIC 509–27 BC

509 BC Establishment of the Roman Republic.

War with the Etruscans begins and lasts 13 years.

495 Temple of Mercury built.

494 1st Tribune of the Plebs (the People) established.

449 The Twelve Tables codified – the ancient laws comprising the foundation of Roman law.

They were said to have been written on 12 ivory tablets and placed in the Forum for all Romans to read.

445 Marriage permitted between patricians and plebeians.

433 Temple of Apollo built.

396 Roman soldiers are paid for the first time.

390 Roman Army defeated at the Battle of Allia. Sacking of Rome by Gauls.

388 Temple of Mars built.

387 The city walls built.

344-41 First Samnite War.

Between the Republic and the tribes of Samnium. The three Samnite Wars, extending over 50 years, involved almost all of the Italian states and concluded with the domination of the Samnites by Rome.

329 Circus Maximus completed in Rome.

326-04 Second Samnite War.

With victory, Rome increased its colonisation and control of most of central and southern Italy.

312 Building of the Appian Way.

The Via Appia was the most important of all Roman roads, running from the Forum Romanum out of the city walls, south and east to Brindisi (Brundisium). Construction of first aqueduct, Aqua Appia.

298-90 Third Samnite War.

After Rome's great victory at Sentinum in 295 BC it emerged as the dominant force throughout the Italian peninsula, except for the extreme south and the Po Valley.

280-75 The Pyrrhic War.

The Empire fought the Greek ruler, Pyrrhus of Epirus. With the surrender of Tarentum to the Romans at the end of the war, Pyrrhus returned to Epirus and Rome won control over the whole of Italy.

C270 Minting of the first Roman coinage.

First gladiatorial games in Rome.

264-41 First Punic War against Carthage (now Tunisia).

Rome emerged victorious in the battle for supremacy in the western Mediterranean Sea and won Sicily.

218-02 Second Punic War (the "War against Hannibal").

216 Hannibal invades Italy and inflicts defeat on the Romans at Cannae.

215-05 First Macedonian War.

212 New denarius coin introduced.

206 Carthaginians defeated in Spain.

Spain becomes two Roman provinces.

204 Scipio invades Africa.

202 Scipio defeats Hannibal at Zama.

204-169 Career of Plautus, a comedic playwright, attaining huge popularity in the Republic.

200-196 Second Macedonian War.

The Roman victory meant Macedonian control of Greece was ended.

121 Gaius Gracchus murdered after proposing to extend Roman citizenship.

112-01 War against Germanic tribes – the Cimbri and the Teutons.

111-05 War against Jugurtha, King of Numidia.

107-86 Gaius Marcus elected consul seven times.

91-98 Social War between the Republic and its Italian allies over citizenship reforms.

The end of the war saw citizenship extended in some form to much of Italy.

88-85 First Mithridatic War.

171-67 Third Macedonian War.

The Kingdom of Macedon was destroyed at the Battle of Pydna in 168 BC.

149-46 Third Punic War against Carthage.

Resulted in complete destruction of Carthage, the Carthaginian population being sold into slavery and the annexing by Rome of the province of Africa.

149-48 Fourth Macedonian War.

Macedon was defeated and became a Roman province.

133 Murder of the tribune Tiberius Gracchus after proposing land reform.

126 Gaius Gracchus (Tiberius' brother) becomes tribune.

88-86 Civil War between Sulla and Marius.

83-72 Sertorius' rebellion in Spain.

82 Sulla appointed dictator of Rome, with total control of the city and Empire of Rome.

He instituted a reign of terror, proscribing his political opponents and ordering the execution of 1500 nobles.

79 Sulla resigns dictatorship.

73-71 Slave rebellion led by Spartacus, brutally put down by Crassus.

63 Consulship of Cicero.

Catiline conspiracy – an attempt by Lucius Sergius Catiline to overthrow the Republic and the power of the Senate. Julius Caesar appointed chief priest/pontifex maximus.

60 First triumvirate of Pompey, Julius Caesar and Crassus.

58-50 Caesar fights Gallic wars and conquers Gaul.

55-54 Caesar's first expeditions to Britain.

53 Crassus defeated and killed in a campaign against the Parthian empire.

Triumvirate collapses.

49 Caesar crosses the Rubicon in a deliberate act of war against Pompey and the Republicans.

49-45 Civil war.

48 Pompey killed in Egypt.

46 Reform of the Roman calendar.

45 Caesar defeats the Republicans and declared dictator of the Roman Republic for life.

44 Caesar assassinated on the Ides of March (15th).

44-42 Third Roman civil war between the assassins of Caesar (Cassius and Brutus) and Caesar's heirs – Octavian and Mark Antony.

43 Second triumvirate between Octavian, Mark Antony and Lepidus.

42 Caesar's death avenged at the Battle of Philippi by the defeat of Cassius and Brutus.

Murder of Cicero.

41 Triumvirs divide up Empire – Octavian in West, Antony in East, Lepidus in North Africa.

Mark Antony joins Cleopatra in Egypt.

32 End of peaceful relations between Octavian and Mark Antony.

Octavian declares war on Cleopatra.

31 Octavian defeats Antony and Cleopatra at the Battle of Actium.

30 Mark Antony commits suicide.

Cleopatra commits suicide.

27 The end of the Roman Republic.

THE ROMAN EMPIRE
27 BC–476 AD

27 BC Octavian becomes sole ruler of Rome and named Princeps or "First Citizen" Augustus.

Agrippa's Pantheon built.

25 Baths of Agrippa built.

19 Virgil's Aeneid completed.

Livy's history of Rome Ab Urbe Condita written. Death of Virgil.

16-6 AD Campaigns against the Germanic tribes and conquest of the Danube provinces.

2 Forum of Augustus completed.

Ovid's Metamorphoses published.

2 AD Augustus adopts Tiberius.

Tiberius was the son of Augustus' wife (Livia Drusilla) from her first marriage. When Augustus' adoptive heirs Gaius Caesar and Lucius Caesar died, Tiberius was recalled to Rome and became Augustus' heir apparent.

6 Judea becomes a Roman province.

8 Exile of Ovid.

9 Battle of Teutoburg.

Three Roman legions lost. The outcome of the battle defined the Rhine as the boundary of the Roman Empire.

14 Death of Augustus.

Tiberius becomes Emperor.

17 Death of Livy.

Death of Ovid.

19 Death of Germanicus.

Tiberius had been compelled by Augustus to name Germanicus as his heir.

23 Tiberius' natural son, Drusus, dies.

26 Tiberius governs Rome by proxy from self-imposed exile in Capri.

Pontius Pilate appointed prefect in Judea.

31 Death of Sejanus.

A confidant of Tiberius, Sejanus' influence increased further on his betrothal to the Emperor's niece, Livilla. He plotted to seize power but was discovered, arrested and condemned to death.

37 Death of Tiberius.

Caligula becomes Emperor.

41 Assassination of Caligula by Praetorian Guard.

Claudius becomes Emperor.

43 Conquest of Britain.

54 Nero becomes Emperor.

60-61 Boudica's uprising.

Queen of the Iceni tribe in Norfolk, she led a revolt against the Roman forces. Boudica was ultimately defeated at the Battle of Watling Street, but not before she had destroyed the cities of Camulodunum (Colchester), Londinium (London) and Verulamium (St. Albans), killing tens of thousands in the process.

64 Fire in Rome.

Large proportion of the city was destroyed. In the aftermath, Nero found a scapegoat in the form of the small Christian sect in the city. On his orders, Christians were thrown to the lions and many others were crucified.

65 Suicides of Seneca and Lucan.

A statesman who influenced the early years of Nero's rule, Seneca was accused of being involved in a plot to kill the emperor. Nero ordered him to commit suicide, and it is reported that he died a slow and painful death. The poet Lucan was also implicated in the conspiracy and committed suicide at the age of 25.

66-73 First Jewish-Roman War.

Also known as the Great Revolt. Sparked by persecution of their race, it ended in defeat for the Jews: Jerusalem was looted and destroyed and Jews were killed on a massive scale or enslaved.

68 Nero commits suicide.

End of the Julio-Claudian dynasty. Succeeded by Galba.

68-69 Civil war and the Year of the Four Emperors.

Galba succeeded by Otho, Vitellius and finally Vespasian. Vespasian becomes the first ruler of the Flavian Dynasty.

79 Titus becomes Emperor.

Pompeii and Herculaneum destroyed by the eruption of Vesuvius. Death of Pliny the Elder at nearby Stabiae.

80 The Coliseum in Rome completed.

Capable of holding more than 50,000 spectators it was used for gladiatorial contests. Fire engulfs Rome, destroying Agrippa's Pantheon.

81 Domitian becomes emperor.

96 Domitian killed. End of Flavian Dynasty.

Nerva becomes Emperor – first of the "Five Good Emperors," known for their moderate rule.

97-109 Letters of Pliny the Younger published.

These included an account of the eruption of Vesuvius and the death of his uncle Pliny the Elder. The nine published books gave an insight into everyday life in first-century Rome.

98 Trajan succeeds Nerva as Emperor.

Born in Spain, Trajan was the first non-Italian to become Emperor. During his reign the Empire grew to its maximum boundary.

101-102 First Dacian War.

105-106 Second Dacian War.

Dacia was conquered and annexed as a province of Rome.

112 Trajan's forum and column completed and dedicated.

Death of Pliny the Younger.

113-16 Trajan's war against the Parthian Empire.

Parthian capital Ctesiphon captured. Mesopotamia becomes Roman province. Empire reaches Persian Gulf.

117 Hadrian becomes Emperor.

118-134 Hadrian's Villa built at Tibur.

c119 Biographies of Suetonius on The Twelve Caesars published.

Under Hadrian, Suetonius became his secretary, but was dismissed in 122.

122 Building of Hadrian's Wall begun in Britain.

On a visit to Britain in 122, Hadrian decided the wall was needed to protect the province from possible invasion from the tribes in Caledonia (now Scotland).

132-35 Second Jewish Revolt

The building of a pagan temple in Jerusalem sparked the second Jewish-Roman War. The revolt was eventually crushed after three years, and it is thought that hundreds of thousands of Jews were slaughtered. Hadrian took draconian measures to outlaw Judaism – prohibiting Jews from entering the holy city, romanizing Judaea and renaming the region Syria Palaestria.

138 Antoninus Pius becomes Emperor.

142 Construction of the Antonine Wall begins.

Made from turf and stone and stretching 37 miles, it was built to replace Hadrian's Wall to the south. Despite the 19 forts built along its course, it came under many attacks, and was abandoned soon after Antoninus' death.

161 Marcus Aurelius becomes Emperor.

162-66 Campaigns against the Parthian Empire (now Iran).

168-80 Campaigns against Germanic tribes on the Republic's border with the Danube.

180 Commodus becomes Emperor.

192 Commodus murdered.

Pertinax briefly Emperor. Replaced with Didius Julianus.

193 Septimius Severus becomes Emperor.

His reign begins with immediate opposition: Pescennius Niger was proclaimed Emperor by the Syrian legions, and Clodius Albinus was hailed as Emperor by his own troops.

194 Niger defeated by Severus at the Battle of Issus.

197 Clodius Albinus defeated and killed at the Battle of Lugdunum.

211 Caracalla and Geta proclaimed joint emperors after the death of their father, Septimius Severus.

Within months of accession, Caracalla had Geta assassinated.

212 Roman citizenship granted to freemen throughout the Empire.

217 Caracalla murdered by Praetorian Guard on the order of Macrinus.

Macrinus declared Emperor.

218 Macrinus defeated and killed outside Antioch.

Elagabalus becomes Emperor.

222 Elagabalus murdered.

Alexander Severus becomes Emperor.

235 Maximinus Thrax becomes the first of the "Soldier Emperors."

238 Gordian I and II proclaimed joint Emperors but reigned for less than 40 days.

Succeeded by Pupienus and Balbinus as joint emperors but were themselves killed by the Praetorian Guard. Maximinus assassinated by the Praetorian Guard. Gordian III declared Emperor.

244 Marcus Iulius Philippus becomes Emperor.

249 Philippus killed in battle with Decius.

Decius becomes Emperor.

250 Persecution of Christians.

251 Decius killed in battle with the Goths.

Gallus becomes Emperor with his son Volusianus.

252 Romans defeated at Barbalissos by Shapur I of Persia.

253 Gallus and Volusianus killed.

Aemilianus becomes Emperor for 3 months. Valerian and Gallienus become joint emperors.

257 Valerian captured by Shapur I of Persia.

Gallienus continues to rule.

258 Goths invade Asia Minor.

260 Postumus declares break away "Gallic Empire" in the West.

267 Zenobia forms break away "Palmyrene Empire" in East.

268 Gallienus murdered.

Claudius II becomes Emperor.

269 Postumus killed.

Victorinus proclaimed Emperor in Gaul and Britain.

270 Claudius dies of plague.

Aurelian becomes Emperor. His reign was known for reunification of the Empire. Victorinus murdered. Tetricus I proclaimed Gallic Emperor.

271 Campaigns against Vandals, Juthung and Sarmatians.

272 Palmyra retaken.

Dacia abandoned.

273 Gallic Empire reincorporated by Aurelian.

274 Tetricus defeated by Aurelian.

275 Aurelian murdered by Praetorian Guard.

Tacitus becomes Emperor.

276 Tacitus dies.

Probus becomes Emperor and re-establishes security of the Empire's frontiers.

282 Probus killed by own troops when they changed sides in support of Carus.

Carus becomes Emperor.

283 Carus dies whilst invading Persia.

Numerian, his son, becomes Emperor.

284 Diocletian becomes Emperor, bringing the period of anarchy for the previous 50 years to an end.

287 Diocletian appoints Maximian as Emperor in the Western Regions.

Diocletian takes Western Regions. Carausius revolts and declares himself Emperor in Britain and Northern Gaul.

293 Establishment of Tetrarchy: Two Caesars appointed to each Augustus: Galerius to Diocletian, Constantius Chlorus to Maximian.

Carausius murdered by Allectus. Allectus declares himself Emperor in Britannia.

296 Constantius Chlorus defeats Allectus and returns Britannia to the Empire.

301 The Edict on Maximum Prices issued.

303 Diocletian's Edict Against the Christians.

Persecution of Christians increases.

305 Diocletian and Maximian abdicate.

Constantius and Galerius become Augusti (Emperors) of West and East respectively. Severus and Maximinus appointed Caesars.

306 Constantius dies.

Constantine, Severus and Maxentius all declared Emperor of West.

307 Severus defeated and killed by Maxentius.

Maximian comes out of retirement to rule with Maxentius.

308 Diocletian persuades Maximian to step down.

Licinius appointed Emperor in the East.

310 Maximian captured by Constantine and commits suicide.

311 Galerius dies.

Licinius and Maximinus Daia rule in the Eastern Region.

312 Battle of Milvian Bridge – Constantine defeats Maxentius and becomes sole Emperor in West.

313 Edict of Milan – legalized Christianity in the Empire.

Maximinus Daia dies.

314 Licinus defeated at Cibalae by Constantine.

316 Diocletian dies.

324 Licinius defeated by Constantine for third time and abdicates.

326 Crispus executed on the order of his father, Constantine.

330 Constantinople becomes capital of the Roman Empire.

337 Constantine I dies.

His sons succeed him: Constantine II and Constans (West) and Constantius (East).

340 Constantine II killed by his brother at Aquileia.

350 Magnentius proclaims himself Emperor in the West.

Constans is captured and killed.

353 Magnentius defeated by Constantius II and commits suicide.

Constantius II now sole Emperor with Julian and Gallus appointed as Caesars in West and East respectively.

361 Constantius dies.

Julian named as his successor. Attempts to reintroduce pagan religion.

363 Julian invades Persia and is killed in battle.

Jovian declared Emperor.

364 The Empire again divided into East and West.

Valens Emperor in the East. Valentinian Emperor in the West.

380 Theodosius I becomes Emperor.

He reunited the two parts of the Empire, but after his death they split again, this time permanently. Makes Christianity official state religion.

410 Sacking of Rome by Alaric.

455 Sacking of Rome by Vandals.

475 Romulus Augustulus becomes Emperor of Western Empire.

476 Romulus Augustulus abdicates.

Traditional date for the fall of the Western Roman Empire.

The Roman

Emperors

276-82	Probus
282-83	Carus
283-84	Carinus
283-84	Numerianus
284-86	Diocletian

West		East	
286-305	Maximian	286-305	Diocletian
305-06	Constantius Chlorus	305-11	Galerius
306-07	Severus		
306-12	Maxentius	309-13	Maximinus
307-24	Constantine		
324-37	Constantine I		

West		East	
337-40	Constantine II	337-53	Constantius II
337-50	Constans		
350-353	Magnentius (usurper)		
353-61	Constantius II		
361-63	Julian		
363-64	Jovian		

West		East	
364-75	Valentinian I	364-78	Valens
375-83	Gratian	379-92	Theodosius I
375-92	Valentinian II		
383-88	Magnus Maximus (usurper)		
392-94	Eugenius (usurper)		
392-95	Theodosius		

West		East	
395-423	Honorius	395-408	Arcadius
423-25	Iohannes (usurper)	408-50	Theodosius II
425-55	Valentinian III	450-57	Marcian
455	Petronius Maximus		
455-56	Avitus		
457-61	Majorian	457-74	Leo
461-65	Librius Severus		
467-72	Anthemius		
472	Olybrius		
473	Glycerius		
473-75	Nepos	474-91	Zeno
475-76	Romulus Augustulus	475-76	Basiliscus

Places to Visit

Roman ruins are spread throughout Europe, the Middle East, and North Africa.
Here is just a limited selection of the most impressive Roman sites to visit.

Algeria
Djémila ● Timgad

Britain
Bath ● Hadrian's Wall ● London
St. Albans ● York

Croatia
Split

France
Nîmes ● Arles ● Orange

Germany
Saalburg ● Trier

Israel
Caesarea ● Masada

Italy
Herculaneum ● Ostia ● Pompeii ● Ravenna
Rome ● Tivoli

Jordan
Jerash

Lebanon
Baalbeck

Libya
Leptis Magna ● Sabratha

Spain
Italica ● Merida ● Segovia ● Tarragona

Syria
Bosra ● Palmyra

Tunisia
Carthage ● Dougga ● El Djem

Turkey
Aphrodisias ● Ephesus ● Istanbul

Opposite above: The best-preserved Roman Baths can be found at Bath, England, a day trip from London.

Opposite center: The ruins of Ostia, the ancient city-port of Rome, are among the finest and most extensive in the world. Despite suffering a natural decline, the ruins are almost as impressive as the better known Pompeii and Herculaneum, which were frozen in time by the eruption of Vesuvius in 79 AD.

Opposite below: This remarkable amphitheater, the largest in Africa, can be found at El Djem, Tunisia.

Above: This spectacular temple, the Maison Carrée, in Nîmes, France, explains why the city is sometimes called the "Rome of France." However, Arles, with its magnificent amphitheater, is also a strong contender for this title.

Center: The view from within the Coliseum in Rome is equally as breathtaking as the view from without.

Below: The Canopus is among the many spectacular sights at Hadrian's Villa at Tivoli near Rome.

Index

Acknowledgments

All photographs copyright Corbis© except the following:

G.N.Photography:

1, 3, 9, 14, 15t, 16t, 17l, 19b, 22t, 23b, 26t, 26b, 29b, 31t, 31b, 37b, 41b, 45b, 64, 67r, 75b, 96b, 97b, 101t, 102t, 102b, 103t, 103b, 114, 116l, 116r, 117t, 118, 119, 125t, 126, 134l, 134r, 135t, 135b, 142, 149t, 151, 154, 155b, 156t, 156b, 157b, 158t, 158b, 159tr, 160, 162r, 163, 165t, 165b 166t, 167b, 168l, 169t, 169b, 170b, 171t, 171b, 172b, 173b, 180b, 182b, 190r, 196, 197t, 197b, 199, 202, 206b, 208b, 209t, 214, 217, 219l, 222, 226, 229, 236l, 236r, 238b, 240l, 240c, 241t, 242b, 243b, 244b, 245t, 245b, 246c, 246t, 247b, 249t, 249b, 250c, 251c, 251b.

Cartographica:

14, 33, 42, 60, 74, 83, 86b, 101, 121, 189, 195, 205, 231

Thanks also to John Dunne and Mark Brown for the design;
Simon Taylor and Gordon Mills for the diagrams;
Sarah Rickayzen and Alison Gauntlett for their supplements;
Sunny Dhillon, Ryan Near, Guy Nettleton, Jo Newson, Cliff Salter,
Richard Betts and Jill Dorman.

MAKING SCHOOLS SAFER AND VIOLENCE FREE

Critical Issues, Solutions, and Recommended Practices

Edited by Hill M. Walker and Michael H. Epstein

8700 Shoal Creek Boulevard
Austin, Texas 78757-6897

This text has been adapted from material that previously appeared in the *Journal of Emotional and Behavioral Disorders*.

pro·ed

© 2001 by PRO-ED, Inc.
8700 Shoal Creek Boulevard
Austin, Texas 78757-6897

Library of Congress Cataloging-in-Publication Data

Making schools safer and violence free : critical issues, solutions, and recommended practices / edited by Hill M. Walker, Michael H. Epstein.
      p.   cm.
    Includes bibliographical references.
    ISBN 0-89079-856-7
    1. School violence—United States—Prevention.   2. Schools—United States—Safety measures.   3. Schools—United States—Security measures.   4. School discipline—United States.   I. Walker, Hill M.   II. Epstein, Michael H.

LB3013.3.M27   2001
371.7'82'0973—dc21
                                          00-059247
                                              CIP

Printed in the United States of America

1 2 3 4 5 6 7 8 9 10   04 03 02 01 00

Contents

Preface

THE UNITED STATES CURRENTLY FAR outranks all other developed countries in its rate of interpersonal violence, which is defined as murder, aggravated assault, rape, and robbery (Grossman, 1995). The U.S. per capita homicide rate for men of ages 15 to 24 far surpasses that of any other developed nation (Osofsky, 1997). According to the U.S. Centers for Disease Control, gunshot wounds are now one of the leading causes of paralysis among today's young people. In addition, 4,000 to 5,000 children and youth die each year in tragedies involving firearms. The optimistic reports in the media about recent declines in youth violence and crime notwithstanding, the toxic impact of the violent images and risk factors and outcomes that fuel youth violence and pervade our daily lives continue unabated.

The limits of believability surrounding the forms and levels of youth violence are constantly challenged. Now the landscape of youth violence includes a Michigan first grader who brought a pistol to school in February 2000 and murdered a classmate. The number of school shootings involving multiple murders and injuries, which culminated in 15 dead and 23 wounded in the April 1999 Columbine, Colorado, tragedy, escalated dramatically in the last half of the 1990s. Very recently, three young girls in Indiana were discovered to be plotting the drowning death of a classmate. These developments make us wonder about the conditions out of which this epidemic of violence in our society arises and how and when it will abate. Firm answers to these questions remain elusive; however, the demand for solid information on the prevention of youth violence is currently one of our highest national priorities.

The root causes of youth violence are very likely embedded in our culture and society. They will be extremely difficult to change, both in the short- and long-term. As a society, we need to reduce the risk factors that negatively influence vulnerable children and youth in the direction of violent and destructive behavior (Walker & Walker, 2000). Among others, these include *(a) easy access to weapons, especially handguns*; *(b) early involvement with drugs and alcohol*; *(c) association and affiliation with antisocial groups*; and *(d) pervasive exposure to violence in the media* (American Psychological Association, 1993; see Kashani et al. in this volume for a detailed discussion of youth violence risk factors).

The impact of these risk factors is increasingly reflected in the violent and destructive behavior of many at-risk students in today's school settings. The anger, social fragmentation, and acceptance of violent forms of behavior that are rampant in our society are spilling over into the schooling process in most unfortunate ways. Many schools are now finding it necessary to teach violence-prevention skills as part of the daily school curricula. Many schools in chaotic urban neighborhoods have turned themselves into fortresses in order to secure the premises. School systems are investing in security technology at an unprecedented rate (National Institute of Justice, 1999). Our schools are no longer the safe havens they once were in which students were free to develop socially and academically without having to be concerned about their personal safety. Now, many students are psychologically victimized by their fears on the way to and from school and even during school hours. Parents increasingly express grave concerns about the ability of schools to protect their children from the possibility of violence and other forms of destructive behavior.

There are four major sources of vulnerability to a school's safety and security:

1. the design, use, and supervision of school space;
2. the administrative operation of the school;
3. the neighborhoods and community served by the school; and
4. the attitudes, beliefs, and behavioral characteristics of the students enrolled in the school. (See Sprague & Walker, 2000, for a detailed discussion of risk factors in each of these areas.)

The content of this book focuses on the knowledge base relating to the fourth area—school safety—and the behavioral inclinations and potentials of students who bring a diverse array of risk factor influences with them to the schooling process. We currently know a tremendous amount about how to make schools safer, less violent, and more effective. The chapters herein and the authors who have contributed them represent the state of the art in our thinking and knowledge about how to achieve this most important societal goal.

In the opening chapter, Kimberly Hoagwood of the National Institute of Mental Health provides an important analysis of the research base on youth violence and directions for future research on this topic. Michael Furlong and Gale Morrison review the knowledge base on violence in schools and clarify definitions, concepts, and studies of the school setting that advance our understanding of school violence and its associated risk factors. Frank Gresham, Kathleen Lane, and Katina Lambros describe the unique educational and service challenges of children and youth who demonstrate conduct problems and attention-deficit disorders. Alan McEvoy and Robert Welker provide a critical review of the interconnections among antisocial behavior patterns, academic failure, and school climate. Javad Kashani and colleagues cogently frame the risk factors associated with youth violence and offer several broad-based solutions. Mitchell Yell and Michael Rozalski offer a review and analysis of the legal issues involved in the prevention of school violence. The remaining nine chapters focus on tools and strategies for intervening effectively at the individual student, small-group, and school-wide levels in the prevention of school violence and in the creation of safe, effective schools with positive climates. We think the material herein will be of significant value to educators and related service professionals who must daily face the daunting challenge of educating and protecting students in the context of schooling.

H.M.W.
M.H.E.

References

American Psychological Association. (1993). *Violence and youth: Psychology's response. Volume I: Summary report of the American Psychological Association Commission on Violence and Youth.* Washington, DC: Author.

Grossman, D. (1995). *On killing.* Boston: Little, Brown.

National Institute of Justice. (1999). The appropriate and effective use of security technologies in U.S. schools: A guide for schools and law enforcement agencies. Washington, DC.

Osofsky, J. D. (Ed.). (1997). *Children in a violent society.* New York: Guilford Press.

Sprague, J., & Walker, H. M. (2000). Early identification and intervention for youth with antisocial and violent behavior. *Exceptional Children, 66,* 367–380.

Walker, H. M., & Walker J. E. (2000, March). Key questions about school safety: Critical issues and recommended solutions. *National Association of Secondary School Principals Bulletin,* 46–55.

Research on Youth Violence:

Progress by Replacement, Not Addition

KIMBERLY HOAGWOOD

*A riot is at bottom the language
of the unheard.*
—Martin Luther King

*The merest glance at history would tell
us that our certitudes are temporary.*
—Doris Lessing

HEADLINES AND ACCOMPANYING media voycurism have reduced the problem of youth violence to its simplest common denominator. Single-factor explanations abound, usually accompanied with single-digit finger-pointing. Blame is laid at the feet of the gun seller, the drug dealer, the parole officer, the absent parent. To paraphrase H. L. Mencken, for every problem there is a solution, which is neat, plausible, and wrong.

If a society is to seriously address problems of youth violence, it must seek to understand its causes and intervene without delay. If it prefers to promote violence, it can engage pollsters, pundits, and media experts to decry it while simultaneously advertising it. Eliminating youth violence will require stepping outside the narrowing and popularized frameworks that provide unidimensional and generally individualized explanations and, instead, thinking deeply about the transactional meaning of youth violence in a violent society.

Research investment on youth violence by the National Institutes of Health (NIH) has supported studies on correlates, consequences, prevention, and treatment of antisocial behavior. The social and behavioral sciences have tackled the problem of youth violence with a vengeance, and this work has yielded a vast amount of descriptive information about the manifestations of antisocial behavior, its prevalence and incidence, and the pattern of risk factors that place some children on trajectories that end in the adult criminal system. There is now ample consensus among social scientists that certain risks (such as academic failure, early psychiatric problems, and language delays) are highly correlated with poor outcomes. Many social scientists believe that the characteristics of children, families, and neighborhoods associated with later antisocial behavior syndromes can be specified and that the more persistent and difficult-to-treat behavior patterns

are often established early. A resounding call for preventive efforts has hailed from many quarters.

Not surprisingly, when preventive actions are called for, schools become a focal point. A free, appropriate public education is guaranteed for all children. Children spend almost as much time in school as they do watching television. Moreover, when children have mental health needs, it is the schools that provide services, not the mental health system (Burns et al., 1995). Schools are the hub of many communities, particularly in rural areas, so it is understandable that if preventive efforts targeted towards early intervention are to succeed, schools must be involved.

At the same time, the host of social ills besieging children in this country, from homelessness to domestic violence to HIV to child neglect and abuse, place unprecedented pressures on schools to, in essence, become surrogate guardians for many children. Balancing the needs of these children against the mandate to educate and now to meet academic standards set by state agencies is a formidable task, and schools are finding their curricula bulging with special units on what are sometimes seen as nonacademic and irrelevant frills—social skills training, anger management, conflict resolution, and safe sex, to name a few.

In a recent review of the distribution of research grant emphases in the area of violence, several NIH institutes classified their studies into one of three categories: (a) preintervention studies, which included risk or protective studies, population-based epidemiological studies, or basic prevention development; (b) efficacy studies, which included laboratory trials of the impact of specific preventive or treatment interventions targeted at disruptive behavior disorders, including conduct disorder; and (c) effectiveness research, which included studies of the effectiveness, dissemination, or transportability of interventions into community (nonacademic) settings. Approximately three quarters of the grants fell into the category of preintervention studies. The remainder were thinly spread between studies of the efficacy of specific interventions and (even more thinly) studies of their effectiveness in diverse communities.

The articles in this special double issue are addressing the very important questions that characterize the latter two categories of study: the impact, efficacy, and effectiveness of violence prevention programs delivered in the schools and the organizational factors, including climate, culture, and context, that enable programs to have tenure beyond the life of the research teams who study them.

In fact, the articles here reverse the trend that has constituted what Felton Earls recently called "the implicit logic of violence prevention" (NIH, 1999). While in the past, theories and interventions were formulated on the assumption that individual behavior or attitudes needed to be the first target, followed by an outward expansion towards communities, Earls suggested that it is not only possible but necessary to reverse the logic. The strongest factors influencing behavior are extra-individual, not intra-psychic. Advances in research methods designed to assess the impact of social settings and social networks have made

such techniques available for studies of community-level interventions. In fact, had these techniques and methods been available three decades ago when community activism was at its height, one wonders whether more progress might have been made in building an evidence base for community interventions to stem violence. Several of the articles in this double issue specifically address issues of community milieu, school climate, social interactional variables, and other "extra-individual" influences that affect the implementation and impact of evidence-based intervention programs.

A second corrective balance provided by this issue is the explicit contribution to the evidence base through inclusion of rigorously examined school service programs. The preventive and intervention programs demonstrate, through carefully crafted designs, clear reductions in youth violence and associated antisocial behaviors. This is noteworthy because the fugitive literature (i.e., not peer reviewed) is filled with anecdotal reports of poorly designed evaluations where outcomes are often positive but their meaning is unascertainable. Even worse, the majority of school programs currently in use across the country that are aimed at reducing violence in youth are completely untested, so outcomes of these programs are not even known.

This is an important corrective because the promotion of untested practices can be worse than harmless; it can be dangerous. Del Elliot (NIH, 1999) pointed out that 95% of programs being used to reduce violence in communities have no scientific evidence for their effectiveness. The dangers of implementing popular but undocumented services has been recently demonstrated. An important article by Dishion, McCord, and Poulin (1999) reported that peer group interventions (including counseling sessions and summer camps run and supervised by adults) significantly increased among high-risk adolescents such problem behavior as substance abuse, delinquency, and violence. They referred to this as "deviancy training" to denote the positive reinforcement that occurs in teen groups via laughter, social attention,

and interest in deviant behavior, which promotes further socially maladaptive behaviors. They also pointed out the need for specificity in targeting interventions to treatment needs: Youth who are depressed and have no comorbid disruptive behavior disorders have been effectively treated in groups using cognitive behavioral interventions (Clarke et al., 1995). Given Dishion et al.'s findings, however, it would be unwise to aggregate youth with disruptive behavior problems in such group treatments.

These so-called negative findings are important not only in pointing practitioners away from bad practices, but also by advancing the science base in very fundamental ways. As Stephen Jay Gould pointed out, the idea of unilinear progress in science is false: "Science advances primarily by replacement, not by addition" (1981, p. 321). If science were linear, then negative findings or disproofs would hamper progress. But, in fact, this is not the case, as the example of deviancy training illustrates.

This issue contributes to the knowledge base on school services by focusing attention on programs with demonstrable impact and on the social context in which the programs are embedded. But as Burns pointed out (1999), although the evidence base is being strengthened, attention must be paid simultaneously to achieving consensus about the criteria to apply to the evidence base, to determine what constitutes evidence and what constitutes clinically significant outcomes. Such criteria are needed for determining when effective programs are ready to be taken to scale and on how grand a scale.

Establishing such criteria will require, among other aims, attention to the degree to which the body of knowledge addresses fundamental questions about causality. Although many theories in the social and behavioral sciences have been propounded over the past two decades to explain the origins of violence, theoretical progress on the causal bases of antisocial behavior has not occurred. Theories ranging from "risky shift" to "cognitive slippage" have come and gone. None have held sway or had staying power. Richters (1993; Richters &

Cicchetti, 1997), whose penetrating work has pioneered new ways of thinking about these problems, pointed out that despite the multiplicative proliferation of theoretical models and descriptive information, progress has not occurred in understanding how the descriptive information about violence should be interpreted: Why do antisocial pathways develop for some children but not for others with the same risk profiles? Why does antisocial behavior remit or change direction in some? Why is such behavior difficult to treat once it has been established? One reason for the lack of progress may be that the methodological traditions, which consistently employ strategies for studying individual differences, presume causal homogeneity. That is, the study designs are crafted to test single multivariate theories, participants are recruited and classified into samples based on phenotypic similarities, and the same variables are assessed on all participants. Estimations of risk are formed on the basis of covariations across participants, and statistical covariation procedures are used to control for the possible influence of nuisance variables. Yet I have never met anyone who believes that violent, delinquent, or otherwise "antisocial" behaviors in children are causally homogeneous. Consequently, there is a mismatch between the methodological traditions widely followed in the social and behavioral sciences, which presume homogeneity, and the expectation that antisocial behavior problems are causally heterogeneous and that, in fact, multiple subtypes and trajectories exist.

AREAS FOR FURTHER REFLECTION

For further progress to be made in understanding, preventing, and treating youth violence, the typical response tends to be "more research is needed." No doubt. Yet, in an age when parenting is less available, when marriage has almost become a thing of the past, and when children are being turned into commodity machines, it may make sense to reflect, as Plotz (1999) pointed out, that America is obsessed with youth because corporations are obsessed with youth: early intervention means netting an eager consumer audience for life. If this is true, then youth violence will be gone only when it is no longer marketable to sell murder, rape, homicide, assault, or violent acts.

Nevertheless, there are many areas in which basic questions about youth violence cannot yet be answered. In addition to the absence of strong, testable, causal theories that take into account the subtypes of antisocial behavior, there are other areas that should be the target of further study.

1. *Mechanisms.* Early onset is an important predictor, yet late onset accounts for the largest percentage of violent behavior. The focus of most research to date has been on markers, not on underlying mechanisms or processes by which aggressive behavior develops. Similarly, no attention has yet been paid to the termination of delinquency, to why some youth divest themselves of delinquent acts and stop their involvement in violence.

2. *Involvement in Gangs.* This is a major risk factor, but almost no researchers have investigated either the mechanisms of transmission of risk whereby some children get involved and others resist, or the efficacy of existing programs for preventing involvement in gangs.

3. *Positive Parenting Strategies.* The risks associated with harsh parenting practices have been amply demonstrated to be predictive of later delinquency, but less attention has been paid to developing specific interventions that promote positive parenting practices in very young children. Such studies are needed.

4. *Environmental Factors.* Programs exist in neighborhoods, communities, and a variety of "host" environments. Little is now known about the ways in which different neighborhood environments moderate, accelerate, or exacerbate the effects of violence. Studies of the ways in which differences in resources affect a neighborhood's ability to mobilize efforts to respond to or reduce violence are especially needed. In addition, socialization processes extend beyond person-to-person exchanges. What aspects of environments socialize aggression? These are questions worthy of investigation.

5. *Organizational Capacity.* As effective interventions are becoming available, the next generation of studies will need to focus on the types of organizational capacities (e.g., strength of leadership, workplace flexibility, employee autonomy) that are necessary to support the implementation of these programs. Issues such as financial capacity, investment of stakeholders, organizational structure, and motivational sustainability are components of capacity that warrant attention.

6. *Fidelity.* Even effective treatments or services cannot be sustained if fidelity to the programs' principles and practices is not upheld. Studies are needed on how to sustain fidelity to treatment models, how to strengthen the quality of the program as delivered, how to maintain integrity as the intervention is implemented in local sites, how to judge when a modification will affect a program, and how much change is legitimate before it interferes with the integrity of the program.

7. *Dissemination and Sustainability.* The transportability of effective services into different schools or community settings is not automatic. An important new area of research involves attention to characteristics of communities, neighborhoods, organizations, schools, clinics, and other settings that will facilitate the long-term sustainability of effective services. Questions such as how much technical assistance to provide and for how long, how and when to certify trainers, and how or why policymakers do or do not adopt effective programs are components of this area of research. Important to this area of research are cost–benefit studies that employ full benefit analyses of programs. Insofar as studies of the effectiveness of services explicitly address issues of transportability, progress in understanding the disseminability of programs will be made.

CONCLUDING REMARKS

The idea of the public sphere, propounded by Habermas (1989), called for a ration-

3

alization of power through democratically driven and mutually constructed discourse. When such a public sphere is created, one can arrive at a "rationally-motivated but not a peremptory consensus" (p. 142). Public concern about the problems of youth violence offer an unprecedented opportunity to galvanize groups of citizens who otherwise might not speak to one another—educators, scientists, policymakers, neighborhood and business leaders, church officials, family advocates—and to mobilize the efforts of all of these groups to reconstruct their communities. The public sphere can be a powerful force for change.

About the Author

KIMBERLY HOAGWOOD, PhD, is associate director of child and adolescent mental health research with the Office of the Director at the National Institute of Mental Health. She is chair of the Child and Adolescent Mental Disorders Research Consortium, a group of interdisciplinary scientists whose mission is to establish research priorities across a range of scientific program areas related to child and adolescent mental health. Dr. Hoagwood is also chief of two research programs:

Child Mental Health Services and Combined Treatment/Service Effectiveness. Among her many publications are articles examining clinical and service effectiveness in children's services, trends in psychotropic medication practices, treatment services for ADHD, and genetic epistemology in the work of Gabriel García Márquez. Address: Kimberly Hoagwood, National Institute of Mental Health, 6001 Executive Blvd., Bethesda, MD 20892.

Author's Note

The opinions and assertions contained in this paper are the private views of the author and are not to be construed as official or as reflecting the views of the Department of Health and Human Services of the National Institute of Mental Health.

References

Burns, B. J. (1999). A call for a mental health services research agenda for youth with serious emotional disturbance. *Mental Health Services Research, 1,* 5–20.

Burns, B. J., Costello, E. J., Angold, A., Tweed, D., Stangl, D., Farmer, E. M. Z., & Erkanli, A. (1995). Children's mental health service use across service sectors. *Health Affairs, 14,* 147–159.

Clarke, G. N., Hawkins, W., Murphy, M., Sheeber, L. B., Lewinsohn, P. M., & Seeley, J. R. (1995). Targeted prevention of unipolar depressive disorder in an at-risk sample of high school adolescents: A randomized trial of a group cognitive intervention. *Journal of the American Academy of Child and Adolescent Psychiatry, 34,* 312–321.

Dishion, T. J., McCord, J., & Poulin, F. (1999). When interventions harm: Peer groups and problem behavior. *American Psychologist, 54,* 755–764.

Gould, S. J. (1981). *The mismeasure of man.* New York: Norton.

Habermas, J. (1989). The public sphere. In S. E. Bonner & D. M. Kellner (Eds.). *Critical theory and society: A reader* (pp. 136–142). New York: Routledge.

National Institutes of Health (NIH). (1999, October 28–29). *Expert Panel on Youth Violence Intervention Research.*

Plotz, D. (1999, September 20). *Slate Magazine.*

Richters, J. E. (1997). The Hubble hypothesis and the developmentalist's dilemma. *Development and Psychopathology, 9,* 193–230.

Richters, J. E., & Cicchetti, D. (1993). Mark Twain meets DSM-III-R: Conduct disorder, development, and the concept of harmful dysfunction. *Development and Psychopathology, 5,* 5–29.

The *School* in School Violence:

Definitions and Facts

MICHAEL FURLONG AND GALE MORRISON

VIOLENCE IS TAKING AN INCREAS-
ing toll on American society generally and on children and adolescents specifically, who are the victims
of more crimes than any other age group
in the United States (Kaufman et al.,
1998; Rennison, 1999). When violence
occurs in the community, and especially
on a school campus, whether by the
hands of another student or by an out-
sider, actions must be taken to ensure the
safety of all students and the staff who
serve them. It is important to promote the
rights, welfare, education, and health of
children and youth by supporting National Education Goal 7 (National Educational Goals Panel, 2000): "Every
school in the United States will be free
of drugs, violence, and unauthorized
presence of firearms and alcohol and will
offer a disciplined environment conducive to learning." As the next millennium
begins, the importance of National Education Goal 7 becomes increasingly apparent.

As researchers, educators, and politicians continue efforts to reduce violence,
it has generally gone unnoticed that the
use and meaning of the term *school violence* have evolved over the past 10 years.
School violence is now conceptualized
as a multifaceted construct that involves
both criminal acts and aggression in

The purpose of this article is to clarify the historical and definitional roots of school violence. Knowledge about this issue has matured to the point where there is a need to refine the definition of school
violence, thereby positioning educators to take the next step in providing effective, broad-based solutions to this problem. The first section provides an overview of the definitional and boundary issues of
the term "school violence" as used in research and applied prevention programs. The second section presents an overview of what is known about the occurrence of violent and related high-risk behaviors on
school campuses. Information about the prevalence of school violence is reviewed to inform and guide
violence prevention programs, emphasizing the need to implement programs that are well linked to
known correlates of school violence. We believe that in addition to identifying the characteristics of both
perpetrators and victims of violence at school, researchers need to examine the contexts in which violence occurs.

schools, which inhibit development and
learning, as well as harm the school's climate. School climate is important, as the
role of schools as a culture and as an organization has not always received attention because of different disciplinary
approaches to studying the problem. Researchers have brought divergent orientations to their work, and these interests
have not always been well coordinated
with the primary educational mission of
schools. An understanding of the multidisciplinary basis of school violence research is necessary in order to critically
evaluate the potential use of programs
that purport to reduce "school" violence.

It was not until 1992 that the label
"school violence" itself was used widely
as a term to describe violent and aggres-

sive acts on school campuses. Citations
in the University of California computer
database of news reports in 5 major national newspapers show that prior to
1992 only 179 citations were listed under
the keyword term "school violence."
Since 1992, there have been 601 school
violence articles in the same newspapers.
Similarly, prior to 1992 only 38 news articles with the words "school violence"
in their title were printed; this compares
to 118 between 1992 and October1998.

Since the 1970s, researchers from various disciplines have also addressed what
is now called school violence but from
different professional perspectives and
from different points of interest. As shown
in Figure 1, citations in the *PsychINFO*
computer database with title or keyword

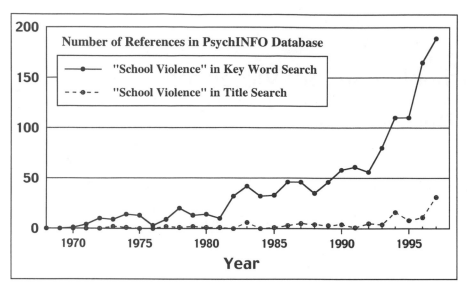

FIGURE 1. Number of citations appearing in *PsychINFO* with the keyword "school violence" and/or including the term "school violence" in the title, 1981 to 1998.

references to school violence were infrequent in the 1960s, grew slowly through the 1980s, and have increased exponentially during the 1990s. Although the *PsychINFO* database does not capture all manuscripts addressing school violence, it does reflect the heightened professional interest in this topic, particularly during the past 10 years.

HISTORY OF THE SCHOOL VIOLENCE CONCEPT

Early interest in school violence focused on youth who committed violence. Violence that occurred on school campuses was primarily a law enforcement issue, and researchers became interested in understanding factors that contributed to the development of antisocial behavior in children (Gottfredson & Gottfredson, 1985; Patterson, DeBaryshe, & Ramsey, 1989). Research also emerged among public health researchers and advocates interested in reducing injury to youth, particularly as it concerned the increase of violence-related injuries and homicides among adolescents during the late 1980s and early 1990s (California Department of Education, 1989; Callahan, Rivara, & Farrow, 1993; Hausman, Spi-

vak, & Prothrow-Stith, 1995; Kann, et al., 1995; Kellerman, Rivara, Rushforth, Banton et al., 1993; Rivara, 1995; Sosin, Koepsell, Rivara, & Mercy, 1995; Spivak, Hausman, & Prothrow-Stith, 1989). The youth/school violence connection was made because schools were the most convenient places to access large numbers of youth for epidemiological surveys of exposure to, involvement in, and perpetration of violence (Dryfoos, 1993).

Professionals developed an increased concern about violence involving youth (not just violence occurring at school) due to an interest in extreme forms of juvenile crime and legitimate concern about substantial increases in youth homicide during the 1980s. Physicians were seeing thousands of youth coming into emergency wards with gunshot wounds, and naturally there was concern about this trend (Prothrow-Stith, 1987), which produced early studies of school weapon possession that were carried out by physicians and others interested in public health injury-prevention models and published in medical, health-focused journals (Kellerman et al., 1993; Kingery, Mirzaee, Pruitt, Hurley, & Heuberger, 1991). In this research tradition, psychologists and psychiatrists inter-

ested in the development and treatment of aggressive, antisocial behavior began to focus on increases of violence involving youth (Cornell & Loper, 1998; Eron, Gentry, & Schlegel, 1994; Slaby & Guerra, 1988; Walker, Stieber, & O'Neill, 1990).

Researchers from health and psychology perspectives who were interested in preventing and reducing youth violence saw schools as logical settings in which to implement programs for reducing violence. In fact, this association was initially formed through the dissemination of an inaccurate interpretation of early youth violence survey results. The early Youth Risk Behavior Surveillance Survey (YRBS; Kann et al., 1995) inquired about adolescents' possession of weapons during the past 30 days. This initial YRBS survey was administered in schools to students, but it did not ask about youths' weapon possession *at* schools. The results were widely reported and showed that more than 20% of high school students reported carrying weapons in the past month. This was a true statement, but it came to be interpreted as meaning that the students were carrying these weapons at school; this was an inaccurate inference. Nonetheless, this "finding" was reported to Congress as fact. At this same time, with the advent of the school crime supplement to the National Crime Victimization Survey (NCVS) in 1989, the link between youth violence/crime and school violence was firmly established.

Initially, educators were not directly included in these inquiries and the discussions and debates they spawned. This is not to say that educational researchers were not cognizant of or were not responding to this topic. Educational administrators expressed their responsibility and concern about school violence over the years but often thought of it in terms of "disciplinary" policies and actions (Baer, 1998), bullying or mobbing behavior (Batsche & Knoff, 1994; Garity, Jens, Porter, Sager, & Short-Camilli, 1997; Limber & Nation, 1998), truancy problems (Johns & Keenan, 1997), crisis response (Poland, 1997), or within the special education context (e.g., students having emotional or behavior disorders; Colvin, Kameenui, & Sugai, 1993; Kerr & Nelson, in press; Morrison, Furlong, & Smith, 1994; Rutherford & Nelson, 1995). Other educators (California Department of Education, 1989; Morrison, Furlong, & Morrison, 1994) focused on school violence by reframing the problem in terms that made sense to educators: avoidance of harm, increased school safety, and viewing violence as a risk factor that negatively affected the learning process (Furlong & Morrison, 1994; Miller, Brehm, & Whitehouse, 1998; Morrison, Furlong, & Morrison, 1994). Some investigators began to view exposure to violence as a development risk factor (Morrison, Furlong, & Morrison, 1994; Resnick et al., 1997; Walker et al., 1990).

Educators' initial lukewarm interest in school violence must be considered within the larger context of a multidisciplinary interest in school violence, the public interest in school violence, and the tendency to sensationalize the issue. From educators' perspectives, increases in youth violence were not always obvious on their school campuses. For example, even recently a national principal's survey found that 90% of all schools had no known felony crimes during the previous year (United States Office of Education, 1998). As another example, in California during the late 1980s, schools were required to report each incident of "school crime" to the State Department of Education. Although it was claimed that the intent of this initiative, promoted by the State Attorney General's Office, was to help schools reduce crime, it was widely interpreted by the press and the community as a potential indictment of schools. Educators, in their opinion, were being asked to be law enforcement agents, and it was unknown how these "crime" data would be used. When the news media used the first statewide school crime report to characterize some schools as high-crime settings, the process broke down and was discontinued. It took 5 years to reestablish this process, now under the framework of the annual California Safe School Assessment (California Department of Education, 1989).

CURRENT USE OF THE TERM "SCHOOL VIOLENCE"

Given these various perspectives of school violence and public policy foci, schools have not been at the forefront of raising public concern about violence and safety issues in schools. Despite the comparatively recent broad use of the term and its lack of clear definition, it is unlikely that "school violence" will be abandoned in favor of another term. Nonetheless, this historical context is important to keep in mind. It is from this perspective that school violence can be understood as a catchall term that has little precision from an empirical–scientific point of view. It is a term that has come to reflect broad community concern about youth violence and how that violence affects the schooling process. School violence has some utility as a policy term because it reflects societal values that schools should be a special place of refuge and nurturance for youth. Acts of violence that threaten the security of schools attack a core value of our social system. Thus, the task of researchers, as we see it, is to study (a) the many complex precursors of violent–aggressive behavior occurring at school, (b) how to prevent it, and (c) how to reduce its impact when it does occur.

Although school violence is a multidimensional construct, there currently exists no definitive statement about its specific dimensions. It has been argued that school violence is composed of the perpetration of violence, violence victimization, antisocial behavior, criminal behavior, fear/worry beliefs, and discipline/school climate, among other aspects. Further complicating the understanding of this term is the political rhetoric that schools are essentially dangerous places and that schools are failing to properly educate today's youth. The lack of clarity in regard to the parameters of school violence has implications for the scientific study of school violence. When researchers say that they are conducting a study of school violence, what do they actually mean? In practice it may mean, for example, that they examine developmental correlates of delinquent behavior

(Resnick et al., 1997), crime on school campuses (Chandler, Chapman, Rand, & Taylor, 1998), victimization experiences (Furlong, Chung, Bates, & Morrison, 1995; Gottfredson & Gottfredson, 1985), school disciplinary practices (Baer, 1998), weapon possession at school (Kingery, Pruitt, & Heuberger, 1996), use of controlled substances at school (Furlong et al., 1997), the influence of delinquent gangs on school (Conly, 1993), conflict resolution approaches (Dusenbury, Falco, Lake, Brannigan, & Bosworth, 1997), or zero tolerance (Morrison & D'Incau, 1997; Skiba & Peterson, 1999), among others. It is this lack of clarity or agreement on definition that fuels the need for further explication of the school violence concept.

SCHOOL VIOLENCE

Given the various definitional and boundary issues of the term, it is necessary to explore specifically what the difference is between "school violence" and "violence in the schools." Getting educators to own their part in preventing school violence may depend on our ability to define and describe the part that "schools" as an organizational and institutional entity play in violence occurring on school campuses.

First, it is important to distinguish between "school" as a physical location for violence that has roots in the community and "school" as a system that causes or exacerbates problems the individuals within it experience. The former happens when students or intruders bring onto school campuses violence stemming from situations outside of the school experience. For example, such a situation occurred in Los Angeles County when a 20-year-old ex-boyfriend of a 16-year-old female student came onto a campus on an early October 1997 morning and used a gun to kill his girlfriend, who just days before had finally been able to move out of an abusive living arrangement with him. In contrast, in response to rejection by a female classmate, two Arkansas boys methodically fired upon their classmates on the school playground. This latter situation arose at least in part from relationships that were developed and broken within the school context, social contexts that educators have the potential to recognize and influence.

In some ways, society has expected a protective bubble to exist between the problems of our communities and the spillover into the school setting. Schools have remained relatively safe environments for teachers and students (Furlong & Morrison, 1994; Garbarino, 1992); however, in some areas, the community norms and behaviors regarding violence have thoroughly invaded the school (Devine, 1995). This is particularly true in urban environments where there is a commitment to subculture norms and values that endorse the use of violence in solving conflicts (Devine, 1995; Wolfgang & Ferracuti, 1967). Hellan and Beaton (1986) note that the influence of the community is greater for crime in high schools, probably due to the intruder problem. Middle school crimes are more influenced by the school environment, especially the ratio of students to teachers. Thus, even in recognizing that schools cannot completely block out the negative community influences in which they are located, the school as an organization can mount, through effective practices, a certain wall of protection.

Owning *School* Violence

As noted previously in this article, educators have been slow to investigate their specific and particular realms of influence on the school violence issue (Haynes, 1996). Although the professions of public health and juvenile justice have been very visible in documenting violent incidents in schools (e.g., Kingery, Coggeshall, & Alford, 1998), educators and public school officials have adopted an understandably defensive stance, relying on the quick fix of physical protection (metal detectors), but try to maintain a focus on their mission of education (Stephens, 1998). The reluctance of educators to enter the conversation has several understandable roots. First, the term *violence* evokes images of crimes and

justice-involved punishments; thus, violent incidents at school can be easily passed on to the juvenile justice system. Educators may rightfully feel that their attention is best kept focused within the educational realm, where the issues of educating today's youth are challenge enough. However, as Braaten (1997) cautioned, "Despite the currently popular rhetoric about 'getting tough' with troubling students and bringing the role of schools 'back to basics,' schools are part of an increasingly complex and diverse society, and must respond to the varied needs students inevitably bring with them" (p. 48).

The ambivalence about owning issues of school violence is seen in role boundary lines drawn by some school personnel. Devine (1995) described schools in which the culture of violence has invaded the school's classrooms and halls and where the teachers' response to behavioral issues has become "hands-off." That is, teachers have defined their role as belonging strictly within the learning/classroom realm. Behavior and social interaction problems are relegated to the security staff, few of whom are prepared to handle these problems within a developmental framework. Similarly, Astor, Pitner, and Duncan (1996) discussed the undefined spaces in school grounds, such as hallways and other unsupervised locations, that are more prone to occurrences of violent behavior because no professional educator (teacher, administrator, support personnel) claims responsibility for that locale as part of his or her assigned duties. Trump (1997) addressed the problem of keeping security issues and security personnel in an unprofessional status, noting that efforts end up being fragmented and ineffective. He argues that school security needs to become part of the central mission of the school, where professional standards and evaluation criteria can be applied to assessing the effectiveness of security professionals. Vestermark (1998) described the inherent tension between police-based and school-based security professionals. Although the former tend to highlight the law enforcement aspects of their role, the latter are more likely to

emphasize their role in the educational process (i.e., supporting the mission of the schools through their facilitation of school proceedings and positive relationships with students).

Thus, the tension about who owns the problem of school violence increasingly plays out in the professional behaviors and role definitions held by educators and "outside" protection personnel. If one embraces a *school violence* rather than a *violence that happens in schools* definition, attention may be refocused on the role that school as a physical, educational, and social environment plays in violence among its participants. Owning school violence as an educational problem also allows the problem of violence to become a topic worthy of classroom and school attention. Epp and Watkinson (1997) eloquently reinforced this focus in suggesting the following:

> School violence is an important component of the daily lives of children in schools. . . . It affects where they walk, how they dress, where they go and who their friends are. As long as teachers treat violence at arms' length, as something that is someone else's problem, they will continue to neglect the opportunity to intervene in a crucial aspect of the children's lives. By ignoring school violence, the name-calling, the shoving, the fighting, the harassment, they are condoning it. Children see teachers walking by, pretending not to notice, and they learn that the way we treat others, the way we interact on the street or in the playground, is nobody's business but our own. Teachers must talk about violence, they must recognize it, examine it, dissect it, and let children see and understand its secrets and its sources. Without this examination it remains an ugly secret that society cannot understand or control. (p. 193)

By adopting educational ownership of school violence, it becomes legitimate to consider the issue within the everyday management of schooling tasks. Threat of physical harm can be interpreted additionally as threat of developmental harm; that is, the threat and reality of physical harm has consequences that suppress the maximal educational growth and development of students. Such a threat lands the issue squarely on the educator's plate of concern. Once this concern has been identified as relevant to the educational mission of the school, then the challenge is in how to weave this concern into the fabric of educational practice. This challenge must be better understood within the context of the impetus for school change.

Defining School and Its Relationship to *School* Violence

The central vision for school change in the 1970s and 1980s was schooling effectiveness, leading to the "school reform," "school change," and "school restructuring" efforts of the late 1980s and 1990s. The schooling effectiveness literature described the school as an organization that impacts student outcomes; that is, effective schools have (a) clearly defined goals in relation to the school mission and philosophy, (b) close monitoring and feedback in regard to progress toward these goals, (c) high expectations for student achievement and clear boundaries for acceptable behavior, (d) high morale among staff and students, and (e) successful and meaningful involvement of parents and the community (Braaten, 1997; Good & Weinstein, 1986; Rutter, Maughan, & Mortimore, 1979). These parameters provide a useful framework for examining school factors as they relate to violence.

It has been assumed and promoted that effective schools are also schools that are safe and are less vulnerable to violence (Morrison, Furlong, & Morrison, 1994). It has been asserted, for example, that students who engage in their schoolwork, are bonded to school, and have multiple opportunities to participate and succeed in academic tasks are less likely to commit acts of violence toward each other, toward school staff, or upon the school itself (vandalism). It also has been noted that schools having low levels of violence tend to have a firm, consistent principalship style, tend to be smaller in size, and have lower levels of crowding (American Psychological Association, 1993; Goldstein & Conoley, 1997; Zwier & Vaughan, 1984).

However, research that specifically ties school factors to levels of violence is sparse and relies on cursory associations without specifically proving the causal relationships. In order to tighten this association, it may be necessary to go to the next level of specification and delineate the specific situations and circumstances that might lead a student to engage in a violent act. For example, a student may react in a violent or aggressive manner in response to bullying, social rejection, public humiliation, perceived lack of fairness in disciplinary actions, and stress. These situations are all tied to contexts, actions, and policies that schools as organizations can effect.

Epp and Watkinson (1997) provided an interesting framework that connects the concepts of "school" and "violence" and facilitates understanding the impact of specific schooling contexts on students from culturally different populations; they refer to it as "systemic violence." Systemic violence has been defined as any institutional practice or procedure that adversely impacts on individuals or groups by burdening them psychologically, mentally, culturally, spiritually, economically, or physically. Applied to education, it means practices and procedures that prevent students from learning, thus "harming them" (p. 1). Examples of systemic violence include but are not limited to exclusionary practices, overly competitive learning environments, toleration of abuse, school disciplinary policies rooted in exclusion and punishment, discriminatory guidance policies, and the like.

This concept of school violence, which is contextually embedded, is a rare focus among the majority of school violence solutions that have focused on the characteristics and developmental patterns of individuals who perpetrate school violence. We have done little to define the contexts in school settings that trigger violence. For violence that occurs in the schools, these contexts are clearly identifiable, yet they have not received much attention. This decontextualized approach to understanding school violence is curious, as violence is usually an interpersonal event arising and resulting from interactions between individuals.

Because of the heterogeneous blending of interests about school violence, it is time for researchers to be more precise about the use of this term or recognize that its primary function should be to motivate researchers to communicate across parallel research traditions and to keep the issues of youth delinquency and antisocial behavior at the forefront of public policy debate. Researchers from outside the education field need to recognize that the interests and needs of schools and educators must be addressed specifically in this process. Schools may have been reluctant passengers on the school violence bus because initial school violence studies were often not empirically based, did not communicate findings to the education community (studies were published in medical and other journals that educators would not consume), did not include educators in the evaluation of school violence reports (Elliott & Tolan, 1999), and sometimes described schools as having such gross problems that there was an "epidemic" of school violence. These dire descriptions were inconsistent with the educator's day-to-day experiences at school, and these statements were interpreted as attacks on the school system itself (Dear et al., 1995). There is no longer any need to engage in alarmist discussion about the school violence problem. What is needed is a thoughtful approach to synthesizing the multidisciplinary knowledge bases that have been created over the past two decades and that promote the agenda of preventing youth crime, delinquency, and violent behavior while at the same time supporting educators' efforts to create a positive learning environment for all students through specific consideration of relevant school contexts.

FACTORS ASSOCIATED WITH VIOLENCE AND RELATED HIGH-RISK BEHAVIORS

The report *Indicators of School Crime and Safety* (Kaufman et al., 1998) provided a snapshot of violence and crime on American school campuses. This was the first of what became an annual school safety and crime scorecard and reported the prevalence of the following types of indicators: (a) nonfatal student victimization (student reports), (b) violence and crime at schools (public school principal reports), (c) violent deaths at school, (d) nonfatal teacher victimization at school (teacher reports), and (e) school environment conditions. Of particular note is the fact that this report systematically emphasized the incidence of these acts both at school and in other locations (while pointing out that even the term "at school" is not uniformly defined in research). Perspective is provided to show that terrible things do happen at schools, but it is emphasized that these events occur more often in other settings. In fact, schools are the safest public setting for children and adolescents (Hyman & Perone, 1998). Enough information is now known about violent and related high-risk behaviors on school campuses that meaningful patterns can be described. The purpose of this section is to provide an overview of the individual factors known to be associated with school violence. It is our assertion that knowledge of these factors is needed to understand the origins of school violence and construct meaningful responses to it.

How Is School Violence Measured?

Recently, researchers have begun to critically examine the procedures used to assess violent incidents on school campuses and how reliability and validity checks of student's self-reports affect school violence incidence rates (Cornell & Loper, 1998; Rosenblatt & Furlong, 1997). When these checks are made, it has been found that the incidence of school violence is significantly higher among those students whose responses fail reliability checks. Cornell and Loper, for example, found that the incidence of fighting at school was 19.2% among students passing reliability checks but significantly higher, at 58.6%, among students failing reliability checks. Ro-

senblatt and Furlong similarly found that self-reported school violence victimization was nearly 100% higher among students whose responses failed prespecified reliability checks than among those students whose responses passed the same reliability checks. Given that almost all basic information about the prevalence of school violence has been gleaned from studies that do not report using any response reliability or validity checks, it is likely that known rates of various types of school violence are overestimates of their true rates.

Most of the databases that provide information about the incidence of school violence have come from public health and criminology disciplines that use an epidemiological model, not the psychometric model that is more familiar to psychologists and educators. Thus, much of what is known and inferred from school violence incidence databases is based on responses to single items with untested properties. The matter of evaluating methodological issues in school violence research is a topic that merits more attention than can be given here, but as a brief example, consider the YRBS item, "In the past 30 days how many times have you brought a weapon to school (gun, knife, or club)?" From a measurement perspective, there is much ambiguity in this question. Do youths responding to this item share a common understanding of what the term "weapon" means? If a student brought a knife to school but did not intend to use it to hurt someone, how would he or she answer this question? Is the intent of the item to place the quality of "weapon" in the object itself or in the behavioral intentionality of the student? Furthermore, combining multiple weapons into one item is not good psychometric practice. And, how is the "past 30 days" time period evaluated compared to the "past 6 months," or "past year" time frames, which have been used in other studies? These measurement issues have not been examined empirically.

It is also important to make the distinction between items that measure violent aggression and those that represent violence victimization. For example, one

item from the NCVS (Chandler et al., 1998) asked respondents if they had damaged anyone's school property; this unambiguously measures violence from a perpetrator's perspective. In contrast, one item from the YRBS asks if the student had "been in a physical fight." This item could reflect predatory aggression or victimization. The context in which a fight occurs is important to know. A fight having its origins in a boyfriend/girlfriend dispute has different implications for schools than fights erupting from racial or ethnic conflict. These contextual variations, unfortunately, are rarely included in school violence prevalence studies. Although research is needed to thoroughly understand the patterns of aggressive behavior and violence victimization, some strong relationships with school violence are known. We now turn our attention to these findings.

Violent and Aggressive Behavior at School

1. *Males are Most Involved in School Violence.* Males are much more likely than females to be physically aggressive at school and to be the victim of attacks. In a national study of deaths that occurred on school campuses from 1993 to 1995, 9 out of 10 of the deaths involved a male as both perpetrator and victim. National studies such as the *National Educational Longitudinal Study,* YRBS, and NCVS, as well as local surveys (e.g., Cornell & Loper, 1998; Furlong, Morrison, Bates, & Chung, 1998; Kingery, Biafora, & Zimmerman, 1996), have all found that males are more involved than females as both perpetrators and victims of school violence, a pattern that is also found in community settings (Rennison, 1999). A side note is that school safety surveys tend to focus on assaultive behavior or high-risk behaviors that could result in physical injury. It is important to recognize that these surveys measure important school violence variables, but they do not measure all types of harmful behavior that occur to students on school property. For example, females do not engage in dangerous physical behaviors as often as males, but they may act in socially aggressive ways more often than males (Crick, 1996). Physical and verbal sexual harassment is another class of behaviors that happen more frequently to females than males (Furlong et al., 1998; Stein, 1998).

2. *Violence Varies by Student Age.* Patterns of school violence and high-risk behaviors are known to vary by the age of the students (Chandler et al., 1998; Furlong et al., 1997). Research examining bullying behavior shows that this form of violence is most frequent among upper-elementary-age students (Batsche & Knoff, 1994). Research with secondary school students has found that some forms of aggressive behavior are higher among junior high school students (e.g., fighting) and that others peak during the high school years (e.g., weapon possession, drug use at school).

3. *Student Experiences Vary by Their Racial/Ethnic Identification.* Most research to date has *not* found extremely large differences in student experiences across racial/ethnic groups. Nationally, one pattern that has been replicated, however, is that African American students report slightly higher rates and Hispanic students slightly lower rates of violence victimization (Chandler et al., 1998). A survey of more than 7,000 California pupils also found this pattern (Furlong et al., 1998). Because some forms of school violence can involve ethnic conflict, it may be helpful to examine student violence experiences by attending to their ethnic and cultural heritage (Kingery, Biafora, et al., 1996).

4. *Student Experiences Differ Slightly by Location of the School.* The school crime supplement of the 1995 NCVS (Kaufman et al., 1998) found essentially no difference in overall victimization prevalence (violent and property combined) in schools located in central city (14.7%), suburban (14.6%), and non-metropolitan (14.3%) locales, despite the finding that crime victimization is typically found to be higher in urban than suburban and rural locales (Rennison, 1999). Although the rates of school violence may not differ strongly by location, differences may occur in specific loca-

tions. In addition, central city areas have larger student populations, so in a given time period, these students may be exposed to a greater number of violent incidents on their school campuses.

5. *Individual Student Attitudes are Associated with School Patterns.* Although perhaps not too surprising, the attitudes held by individual students are associated with their involvement as perpetrators of violence or as its victims. Cornell and Loper (1998) found a significant association between engaging in physical fights and weapon carrying at school and beliefs favoring physical aggression and deriving personal satisfaction from hitting. In another study, Bates, Chung, and Chase (1997) found that students who hold distrusting attitudes and are disconnected from their teachers are more likely to be victims of school violence. Further documenting the importance of examining the characteristics of students involved in school violence, Furlong et al. (1997) found that students reporting frequent substance use at school were more likely to commit aggressive acts *and* to be a victim of others' aggression. This pattern is also strongly supported by results of the annual survey conducted by the Parents' Resource Institute for Drug Education (PRIDE, 1999).

Deaths on School Campuses

Surprising as it may seem, until the release of the 1998 federal school crime and safety index (Kaufman et al., 1998), there was no national reporting mechanism for the shootings, homicides, or suicides that occurred on school campuses. Gathering information from newspaper reports is the way in which deaths on school campuses have been monitored. This effort is carried out by the National School Safety Center, and a comprehensive report for the years 1994 to 1996 was reported in the *Journal of the American Medical Association* (Kachur, 1996). In these 2 years, there were 105 deaths on school campuses nationwide—these included 85 homicides and 20 suicides. Most of these deaths involved the use of firearms. Despite the

justified national attention given to the shootings that occurred during the 1997–1998 school year at several rural schools across America, that year was not the most deadly school year in recent years, a distinction that belongs to 1992 (Kaufman et al., 1998).

Weapon Possession

Other researchers have asked students to report how often they carry various weapons on school campuses, and a few have directly asked about gun possession. Some investigators have also asked students if they have actually witnessed a student with a gun on campus, reasoning that students would be more likely to report that they saw a gun at school than they would be to admit that they personally brought a gun to school. Resnick et al. (1997), in the National Longitudinal Study of Adolescent Health (NLSAH), reported that 12.4% of adolescents report carrying a weapon anywhere in the past 30 days. This compares with 18.4% for the comparable YRBS weapon-carrying item (carrying weapons anywhere, not just on school property; Kann et al., 1998).

Other investigators have focused specifically on gun possession by students at school. Cornell and Loper (1998) found that 8.2% of students in their urban sample said they had carried a gun during the preceding month: 4.0% at school *and* outside school; 3.2% outside of school only; and 1.6% at school only. Other studies using past-30-day time periods have reported school weapon possession rates of between 7% and 15% (Cornell & Loper, 1998; Johnston, O'Malley, & Bachman, 1996; Kaufman et al., 1998). Student reports of school gun possession vary by the community being surveyed and the manner in which the question is asked. Direct comparison between communities is not advised because of the use of dissimilar methodologies, sampling procedures, and response expectation contexts. However, collectively these findings suggest that guns are brought to school by a relatively small group of students who are also likely to carry guns and other weapons in community settings.

The following factors are associated with gun and other weapon possession at school (see Furlong, Flam, and Smith [1996] for a review of gun possession on school campuses).

1. *Self-Reported Gun Possession Rates are Higher in Anonymous Self-Report Surveys.* Paper-and-pencil self-report surveys have produced the highest rates of school gun possession. Data from the *Monitoring the Future* study (MTF; Johnston et al., 1996) showed that between 1994 and 1996 about 3% of twelfth-grade students reported bringing a gun to school at least once during the 4 weeks prior to responding to the survey. See Kingery et al. (1998) and Furlong et al. (1996) for summaries of research about gun possession at school.

2. *Schools are a Barrier to Weapon and Gun Possession.* Educators and parents are legitimately concerned about students bringing guns to school, but it is also important to recognize that every major study about youth weapon possession has found that youth carry weapons more frequently outside of school than at school. The YRBS (Kann et al., 1995, 1996, 1998), for example, has asked about weapon possession on and off school campus on three occasions. For both males and females, weapon possession at school is 3 to 4 times less frequent than outside of school.

3. *Males are Predominantly Involved in Gun Possession.* In the NCVS, data were collected through personal, face-to-face interviews with students ages 12 to 19. In this formal interview context, only 0.1% of all 23,933 students admitted to carrying a gun at school for protection in the preceding 6 months. All of the students who admitted school gun possession were male, and a large majority of them were in the eighth, ninth, or tenth grade. *None* of the 11,602 females interviewed admitted to school gun possession. The NCVS results are likely to underestimate actual gun possession or availability on America's school campuses. Other regional samples using anonymous self-report methods all replicate the strong finding that males are the predominant possessors of weapons at school. However, in regional samples,

some females report bringing weapons to school (Kingery, Pruitt, et al., 1996).

4. *Self-Reported Gang Affiliation is Associated with Gun Possession.* There is some evidence that youths who self-designate themselves as gang members are more likely than non–gang members to bring guns to school. For example, 18.6% of gang members claimed to have brought a gun to school compared to 4.9% of non–gang members (Cornell & Loper, 1998). The NCVS, in 1995, found that students who reported being aware of gangs on their school campuses were significantly more likely to also report being aware of and/or actually seeing guns and other weapons at their school (Kaufman et al., 1998).

5. *Youth Who Own Guns are Disproportionately Involved in Aggressive Behavior at School.* Youth who report owning a gun, as a group, are disproportionately involved in juvenile crimes and in assaultive, aggressive behaviors at school (Callahan et al., 1993). Weapon possession/ownership by any adolescent is a matter of concern, particularly when the youth exhibits other distress signals such as those discussed, for example, in the U.S. Office of Education's *Early Warning/Timely Response* document (Dwyer, Osher, & Warger, 1998). Other researchers have shown that exposure to guns in the home is a high risk factor for being in a physical fight (Kingery, Pruitt, et al., 1996) and for homicide (Kellerman et al., 1993).

6. *Students Who Admit to Frequent Alcohol or Drug Use at School Have Higher Gun Possession Rates.* In a study involving more than 4,000 secondary students in one California county, students who reported using alcohol or other substances at school 7 or more times during the previous year accounted for about 50% of all students who acknowledged frequent school weapon possession (Furlong et al., 1997).

7. *Students Bring Weapons, Including Guns, to School for Protection and Other Reasons.* There is not a lot known about why students specifically bring guns to schools. One regional survey in rural Texas asked students who reported bringing a gun to school during the past

12 months about the reasons why they felt compelled to do this. About half of these gun-carrying students said that it made them feel safer. But, another response should make educators take pause and consider the importance of conflict resolution prevention programs and anger management programs. More than half of these students (55%) reported that they brought the gun to school because they were angry with someone and "I was thinking about shooting him/her" (Kingery, Pruitt, et al., 1996). These findings seem to dispel any notion that the prototypic gun-toting student is acting primarily in a defensive–fearful manner. It is more likely the case, given available data, that these youths are acting in a defensive–aggressive manner. Even more alarming is that only 3% of these gun-carrying students believed that an apology was an effective way to avoid fighting, which compares to 60% for non–gun toting students (Kingery, Pruitt, et al., 1996). This pattern points toward a particularly volatile mix: (a) the combination of concerns about being attacked, (b) the use of weapons as a protective device, (c) angry potentiation to use the gun, and (d) disbelief that apologizing or other nonaggression conflict avoidance strategies are effective.

Gun ownership is known to be much higher among youth who have a history of delinquency, gang membership, and other disorders of conduct (Callahan et al., 1993). Whenever school personnel are concerned about extremely aggressive behavior in a youth, it is advisable to gather additional information about any past involvement in gangs, history of violent offenses, history of selling drugs, and ownership of or easy access to firearms (Furlong et al., 1997). Youth with this kind of delinquency profile are more likely than nondelinquent youth to use guns for self-protection and to bring a gun to school.

8. *Youth Involved with Violence at School May Have Multiple Risk Factors.* Although requiring additional investigation, current research can be interpreted to show that youth who bring guns to school campuses are a high-risk group who usually present with multiple, sig-

nificant risk factors in their lives. Any youth who is caught with a gun at school should be carefully interviewed to ascertain the range of stresses affecting his or her life and how these stresses impact performance in school and the community. Kingery, Pruitt, et al. (1996), in their survey of Texas students, reported that those students who brought a gun to school were much more likely to experience high-risk behaviors, including walking alone through unsafe neighborhoods, using cocaine, getting into fights in the community, and being forced to have sex. These students reported that they often found themselves in settings and situations in which crime and violence were more likely to occur. Being in these settings more frequently than other students, they also were in physical fights more often, perceived more danger in their environments, which in fact may be true, and therefore were more likely to use guns as a means to enhance their sense of self-protection.

Concerns for Safety at School

One marker for the impact of violence on a school campus is to ask students about their level of worry or concern about their personal safety and if they engage in behaviors to limit their exposure to these perceived dangers. Across three national YRBS surveys (Kann et al., 1995, 1996, 1998), about 4% to 5% of secondary school students report that they stayed home at least 1 day in the past month because of safety concerns at school or on the way to or from school. In 1989 and 1995 the NCVS asked students (ages 12 to 19) if they feared being "attacked or harmed" at school. Over this time period (the previous 6 months), more students (6% vs. 9%) expressed feeling this fear (Kaufman et al., 1998). In three other national surveys, students were asked if someone using a weapon at school in the past 12 months had threatened them: MTF (Johnston et al., 1996), the YRBS (Kann et al., 1995, 1996, 1998), and the NCVS (Kaufman et al., 1998). The rates vary widely across these three studies, from a low of 1.3% (NCVS) to a high of 15.2% (MTF). The

reasons for such wide discrepancies are unknown.

The Context of School Violence

Most school violence research to date has focused on univariate relationships that characterize both perpetrators and victims. Researchers are beginning to extend knowledge about the factors associated with school violence that take into account its multidimensional influences, such as developmental patterns, community influences, and behavioral contexts. For example, Lockwood (1997) provides an in-depth evaluation of the social contexts in which youth say violent acts occur ("an act carried out with the intention, or perceived intention, of physically injuring another person" (p. 3). The most frequent violent events involved being "pushed, grabbed, shoved" (55%) and/or "kicked or bit or hit with fist" (67%). Twenty-one percent reported that they had been "beaten up" and 17% had been "slapped." A total of 10% and 8% of these youth reported that they were "threatened with a gun" or "threatened with a knife," respectively. An astonishing 89% of these incidents involved someone they knew personally, but 58% of these were considered to be acquaintances, not friends. In about one half of these incidents, an adult became aware of the event and provided support. In 3 out of 5 events, the youth had a third party present (usually friends and relatives), and the third party often became involved in the event to support the youth. These were time-limited events and were often terminated within 15 minutes.

These events were precipitated by many factors, and there was no one predominant "opening move." Unprovoked touching (13%), interfering with something owned or being used (13%), a request to do something (10%), backbiting (9%), and verbal teasing/rough play getting out of hand (9%) were the primary precipitants in about one half of these events. Of the events that occurred at school, the most predominant physical contexts were the classroom (39%), the hall or stairs (21%), the school bus (11%),

physical education setting (11%), and the cafeteria (6%).

Of particular relevance to violence prevention programs is the finding that in 84% of the events, the youth provided a rationale for their actions that justified their use of violence. These justifications included "retaliation for harmful behavior" (28.8%), the other youth's behavior was offensive (17.7%), "self-defense to stop victimization" (13.6%), and to "help a friend" (12.6%). Unjustified explanations offered included being blinded by anger into action (6.6%) and being "pushed" into violence by another youth (5.6%). In only 1 of these incidents did the youth acknowledge antisocial behavior intentionally: (i.e., wanted money). Lockwood (1997) concluded that most of the violent incidents described by these youth involved situations in which they perceived themselves or others to be victimized and that their actions were justified as retaliation. Not only did they not believe that their actions were inappropriate, but also their value systems required them to retaliate. One can imagine the limited impact that a violence prevention or conflict management program would have on similar youth when these programs emphasize peaceful negotiation while the youth's values promote justified retaliation. This study provides a strong rationale for implementing programs that attend to the social and broader ecological contexts in which violence occurs. Lockwood stresses the need to construct prevention programs that more realistically match the way in which violent acts occur in the lives of youth. Using such a conceptualization, possible intervention points for educators may include the following: (a) Adults are present in about 50% of the aggressive events reported by youth, so adults need to create strategies to respond with an instructional purpose to these incidents; (b) most of these events occurred at school or home, so opportunities for contextualized learning are significant, and adults need to attend to those events, seeing them as an opportunity to teach negotiation skills; and (c) many conflicts begin with mild, but offensive, touching, so programs ought to include components that role-play ways to respond to this touching in a manner that does not escalate into physical fights.

SUMMARY

There are identifiable patterns of an individual's involvement in incidents of school violence. The patterns and trends described should be useful in helping school personnel to be particularly vigilant in their observations and to provide "preventive" support of certain individuals, groups, and situations. Enough is now known about the correlates of violent and aggressive behavior on school campuses to implement meaningful intervention programs. Efforts such as the Blueprint Program created by the University of Colorado Center for the Study of Prevention and Violence (Elliott, 1998) provided detailed descriptions of prevention and intervention programs that have been implemented in schools and have demonstrated effectiveness. These programs can be best implemented when each school considers the identifiable patterns and correlates of school violence. For example, it is quite clear that males are predominantly involved as both perpetrators and victims of violence, which strongly suggests that school-based programs should openly acknowledge the need to specifically examine the behavior of males. Also, school administrators can use current research findings to be specifically vigilant about potential hot spots in their schools that would be the targets of efficient prevention programs. Nonetheless, we caution that there are multiple pathways toward school violence, and these complex relationships have not been fully explored. Educators need to be mindful that their intervention efforts should target not only those youth whose life experiences closely match the correlates of school violence, but also take into consideration the contexts that contribute to or hinder aggressive behavior. This is demonstrated by the findings of a recent National Longitudinal Adolescent Health Survey report (Resnick et al., 1997), in which youth who were connected and bonded to meaningful adults in their lives, at home, and at school, were less likely to commit crimes, use substances, and engage in high-risk behaviors.

Finally, in addition to continuing the collection of detailed and targeted data on this issue, a parallel effort is needed to further define the nature of school violence in order to further understand the specific role that schools as an institution play in the deterrence or exacerbation of student problems that lead to violence. It is through this further explication that the most effective and relevant programs can be guided and implemented.

About the Authors

MICHAEL FURLONG, PhD, is a professor in the APA-approved Counseling/Clinical/School Psychology program at the University of California, Santa Barbara. His research interests include school violence prevention, assessment and treatment of anger, and cross-agency service delivery for youth with emotional and behavioral disorders. **GALE MORRISON**, PhD, is a professor in the APA-approved Counseling/Clinical/School Psychology program at the University of California, Santa Barbara. Her research interests include risk, resilience, and social/emotional adjustment of students at risk for learning and behavior problems, as well as school discipline practices that affect these students. Address: Michael Furlong, UCSB, Education, Santa Barbara, CA 93106. e-mail: mfurlong@ education.ucsb.edu or gale@education.ucsb.edu

References

American Psychological Association. (1993). *Youth & violence: Psychology's response, Volume I: Summary Report of the American Psychological Association Commission on Violence and Youth.* Washington, DC: Author.

Astor, R. A., Pitner, R. O., & Duncan, B. E. (1996). Ecological approaches to mental health consultation with teachers on issues related to youth and school violence. *Journal of Negro Education, 65*(3), 336–355.

Baer, G. G. (1998). School discipline in the United States: Prevention, correction, and long-term social development. *School Psychology Review, 31*(4), 309–318.

Bates, M. P., Chung, A., & Chase. M. (1997). Where has the trust gone? The protective role of interpersonal trust and connections with adults in the school. *The California School Psychologist, 2,* 39–52.

Batsche, G. M., & Knoff, H. M. (1994). Bullies and their victims: Understanding a pervasive problem in the schools. *School Psychology Review, 23*(2), 165–174.

Bender, W. N., & McLaughlin, P. J. (1997). Weapons in schools: Strategies for teachers confronting violence and hostage situations. *Intervention in School and Clinic, 32,* 211–216.

Braaten, S. (1997). Creating safe schools: A principal's perspective. In A. P. Goldstein & J. C. Conoley (Eds.), *School violence intervention: A practical handbook* (pp. 46–57). New York: Guilford.

California Department of Education. (1989). *Safe schools: A planning guide for action.* Sacramento, CA: Author. (Revised in 1995)

Callahan, C. M., Rivara, F. P., & Farrow, J. A. (1993). Youth in detention and handguns. *Journal of Adolescent Health, 14*(5), 350–355.

Chandler, K. A., Chapman, C. D., Rand, M. R., & Taylor, B. M. (1998). *Students' reports of school crime: 1989 and 1995* (NCES 98-241/NCJ-169607). Washington, DC: U.S. Departments of Education and Justice.

Colvin, G., Kameenui, E. J., & Sugai, G. (1993). School-wide and classroom management: Reconceptualizing the integration and management of students with behavior problems in general education. *Education and Treatment of Children, 16,* 361–381.

Cornell, D. G., & Loper, A. B. (1998). Assessment of violence and other high-risk behaviors with a school survey. *School Psychology Review, 27*(2), 317–330.

Crick, N. R. (1996). The role of overt aggression, relational aggression, and prosocial behavior in the prediction of children's future social adjustment. *Child Development, 67,* 2317–2327.

Dear, J., et al. (1995). *Creating caring relationships to foster academic excellence: Recommendations for reducing violence in California Schools, Final Report.* Sacramento, CA: Advisory Panel on School Violence, Commission on Teacher Credentialing.

Devine, J. (1995). Can metal detectors replace the panopticon? *Cultural Anthropology, 10*(2), 171–195.

Dryfoos, J. (1993). Schools as places for health, mental health, and social services. In R. Takanishi (Ed.), *Risk and opportunity* (pp. 82–109). New York: Teachers College Press.

Dusenbury, L., Falco, M., Lake, A., Brannigan, R., & Bosworth, K. (1997). Nine critical elements of promising violence prevention programs. *Journal of School Health, 67*(10), 409–414.

Elliott, D. S. (1998). *Blueprints for violence prevention.* Boulder: Institute of Behavioral Science, Regents of the University of Colorado.

Elliott, D. S., & Tolan, P. H. (1999). Youth violence prevention, intervention, and social policy: An overview. In D. J. Flannery & C. R. Huff (Eds.), *Youth violence: Prevention, intervention, and social policy* (pp. 3–46). Washington, DC: American Psychiatric Press.

Epp, J. R., & Watkinson, A. M. (Eds.). (1997). *Systemic violence in education: Promise broken.* Albany, NY: State University of New York Press.

Eron, L. D., Gentry, J. H., & Schlegel, P. (Eds.). (1994). *Reason to hope: A psychosocial perspective on violence & youth.* Washington, DC: American Psychological Association.

Frammolino, R. (1998). Failing grade for safe schools plan. *Los Angeles Times,* September 6.

Furlong, M. J., Casas, J. M., Corral, C., Chung, A., & Bates, M. (1997). Drugs and school violence. *Education and Treatment of Children, 20*(3), 263–280.

Furlong, M. J., Chung, A., Bates, M., & Morrison, R. (1995). Who are the victims of school violence? *Education and Treatment of Children, 18*(3), 282–298.

Furlong, M. J., Flam, C. S., & Smith, A. (1996). Firearm possession in schools: Disarming the myths. *The California School Psychologist, 1,* 5–14.

Furlong, M. J., & Morrison, G. M. (Eds.). (1994). *School violence miniseries: School Psychology Review* [special issue]. Washington, DC: National Association of School Psychologists.

Furlong, M. J., Morrison, R., Bates, M., & Chung, A. (1998). School violence victimization among secondary students in California: Grade, gender, and racial-ethnic group incidence patterns. *The California School Psychologist, 3,* 71–87.

Garbarino, J. (1992). *Children in danger: Coping with the consequences of community violence.* San Francisco: Jossey-Bass.

Garity, C., Jens, K., Porter, W., Sager, N., & Short-Camilli, C. (1997). "Bully proofing your school:" Creating a positive climate.

Intervention in School and Clinic, 32(4), 235–243.

Goldstein, A. P., & Conoley, J. C. (1997). Student aggression: Current status. In A. P. Goldstein & J. C. Conoley (Eds.), *School violence intervention: A practical handbook* (pp. 3–45). New York: Guilford.

Good, T. L., & Weinstein, R. S. (1986). Schools make a difference: Evidence, criticisms, and new directions. *American Psychologist, 41,* 1090–1097.

Gottfredson, G. D., & Gottfredson, D. C. (1985). *Victimization in schools.* New York: Plenum.

Hausman, A. J., Spivak, H., & Prothrow-Stith D. (1995). Evaluation of a community-based youth violence prevention project. *Journal of Adolescent Health, 17*(6), 353–359.

Haynes, N. M. (1996). Creating safe and caring school communities: Comer school development program schools. *Journal of Negro Education, 65*(3), 308–321.

Hellan, D. A., & Beaton, S. (1986). The pattern of violence in urban public schools: The influence of school and community. *Journal of Research in Crime and Delinquency, 23*(2), 102–127.

Hyman, I. A., & Perone, D. C. (1998). The other side of school violence: Educator policies and practices that may contribute to student misbehavior. *Journal of School Psychology, 36*(1), 7–27.

Johns, B. H., & Keenan, J. P. (1997). *Techniques for managing a safe school.* Denver, CO: Love.

Johnston, L. D., O'Malley, P. M., & Bachman, J. G. (1996). *National survey results on drug use from Monitoring the Future Study, 1975-1995: Volume I Secondary school students* (NIH Publication No. 96–4139). Washington, DC: U.S. Government Printing Office.

Kachur, S. P. (1996). Data on school-associated violent deaths in the United States. *Journal of the American Medical Association, 275*(22), 1729–1733.

Kann, L., Kinchen, S. A., Williams, B. I., Ross, J. G., Lowry, R., Hill, C. V., Grunbaun, J. A., Blumson, P. S., Collins, J. L., & Kolbe, L. J. (1998). Youth risk behavior surveillance—United States, 1997. *Journal of School Health, 68,* 355–369.

Kann, L., Warren, C. W., Harris, W. A., Collins, J. L., Douglas, K. A., Collins, M. E., Williams, B. I., Ross, J. G., & Kolbe, L. J. (1995). Youth Risk Behavior Surveillance—1993. *Journal of School Health, 65,* 163–171.

Kann, L., Warren, C. W., Harris, W. A., Collins, J. L., Douglas, K. A., Williams, B. I., Ross, J. G., & Kolbe, L. J. (1996). Youth risk behavior surveillance—United States, 1995. *Journal of School Health, 66,* 365–377.

Kaufman, P., Chen, X., Choy, S. P., Chapman, C. D., Rand, M. R., & Ringel, C. (1998). *Indicators of school crime and safety, 1998* (NCES 98-251/NCJ–172215). Washington, DC: U.S. Departments of Education and Justice.

Kellerman, A. L., Rivara, F. P., Rushforth, N. B., Banton, J. G., Reay, D. T., Francisco, J. T., Locci, A. B., Prodzinski, J., Hackman, B. B., & Somes, G. (1993). Gun ownership as a risk factor for homicide in the home. *New England Journal of Medicine, 329*(15), 1084–1091.

Kerr, M. M., & Nelson, C. M. (in press). *Strategies for managing problem behaviors in the classroom* (2nd ed.). Columbus, OH: Merrill.

Kingery, P. M., Biafora, F. A., & Zimmerman, R. S. (1996). Risk factors for violent behaviors among ethnically diverse urban adolescents. *School Psychology International, 17,* 171–188.

Kingery, P. M., Coggeshall, M. B., & Alford, A. A. (1998). Violence at school: Recent evidence from four national surveys. *Psychology in the Schools, 7*(2), 137–157.

Kingery, P. M., Mirzaee, E., Pruitt, B. E., Hurley, R. S., & Heuberger, G. (1991). Rural communities near large metropolitan areas: Safe havens from adolescent violence and drug use? *Health Values, 15*(4), 199–208.

Kingery, P. M., Pruitt, B. E., & Heuberger, G. (1996). A profile of rural Texas adolescents who carry handguns to school. *Journal of School Health, 66*(1), 210–214.

Limber, S. P., & Nation, M. (1998). *Bullying among school children.* Washington, DC: Office of Juvenile Justice and Delinquency Prevention.

Lockwood, D. (1997). *Violence among middle school and high school students: An analysis and implications for prevention.* Washington, DC: U.S. Department of Justice, Office of Justice Programs, National Institute of Justice.

Miller, G. E., Brehm, K., & Whitehouse, S. (1998). Reconceptualizing school-based prevention for antisocial behavior within a resiliency framework. *School Psychology Review, 27*(3), 364–379.

Morrison, G., Furlong, M. J., & Smith, G. (1994). Factors associated with the experience of school violence among general education, leadership class, opportunity class, and special day class pupils. *Education and Treatment of Children, 17,* 356–369.

Morrison, G. M., & D'Incau, B. (1997). The web of zero-tolerance: Characteristics of students who are recommended for expulsion from school. *Education and Treatment of Children, 20*(3), 316–335.

Morrison, G. M., Furlong, M. J., & Morrison, R. L. (1994). From school violence to school safety: Reframing the issue for school psychologists. *School Psychology Review, 23,* 236–256.

National Educational Goals Panel. (2000). Goal 7: Safe, disciplined, and alcohol- and drug-free schools. Washington, DC: Author.

Parents' Resource Institute for Drug Education (PRIDE). (1999). *PRIDE survey.* http://www.prideusa.org/press97/ns97t03. htm

Patterson, G. R., DeBaryshe, B. D., & Ramsey, E. (1989). A developmental perspective on antisocial behavior. *American Psychologist, 44,* 329–335.

Poland, S. (1997). School crisis teams. In A. P. Goldstein & J. C. Conoley (Eds.), *School violence intervention: A practical handbook.* New York: Guilford.

Prothrow-Stith, D. B. (1987). *Violence prevention curriculum for adolescents.* Newton, MA: Education Development Center.

Rennison, C. M. (1999). *Criminal victimization 1998: Changes 1997-98 with trends 1993-98* (NCJ 176353). Washington, DC: U.S. Department of Justice, Office of Justice Programs, Bureau of Crime Statistics.

Resnick, M. D., Bearman, P. S., Blum, R. W., Bauman, K. E., Harris, K. M., Jones, J., Tabor, J., Beuhring, T., Sieving, R. E., Shew, M., Ireland, M., Bearinger, L. H., & Udry, J. R. (1997). Protecting adolescents from harm: Findings from the National Longitudinal Study on Adolescent Health. *Journal of the American Medical Association, 278,* 823–832.

Rivara, F. P. (1995). Crime, violence and injuries in children and adolescents: Common risk factors? *Criminal Behavior & Mental Health, 5*(4), 367–385.

Rosenblatt, J. A., & Furlong, M. J. (1997). Assessing the reliability and validity of student self-reports of campus violence. *Journal of Youth and Adolescence, 26*(2), 187–202.

Rutherford, R. B., & Nelson, C. M. (1995). Management of aggressive and violent behavior in the schools. *Focus on Exceptional Children, 27*(6), 1–15.

Rutter, M., Maughan, N., & Mortimore, P. (1979). *Fifteen thousand hours: Secondary schools and their effects on children.* Cambridge, MA: Harvard University Press.

Skiba, R., & Peterson, R. (1999). The dark side of zero tolerance: Can punishment lead to safe schools? *Phi Delta Kappan,* (January), 372–381.

Slaby, R. G., & Guerra, N. G. (1988). Cognitive mediators of aggression in adolescent offenders: I. Assessment. *Developmental Psychology, 24,* 580–588.

Sosin, D. M., Koepsell, T. D., Rivara, F. P., & Mercy, J. A. (1995). Fighting as a marker for multiple problem behaviors in adolescents. *Journal of Adolescent Health, 16*(3), 209–215.

Spivak, H., Hausman, A. J., & Prothrow-Stith, D. (1989). Practitioners' forum: Public health and the primary prevention of adolescent violence—The Violence Prevention Project. *Violence & Victim, 4,* 203–212.

Stephens, R. (1998). *NSSC Web Site.* National School Safety Center. www.nssc1.org

Trump, K. S. (1997). Security policy, personnel, and operations. In A. P. Goldstein & J. C. Conoley (Eds.), *School violence intervention: A practical handbook* (pp. 46–57). New York: Guilford.

United States Office of Education. (1998). *Violence and discipline in U.S. public schools: 1996-97.* Washington, DC: Author.

Vestermark, S. D. (1998). Critical decisions, critical elements in an effective school security program. In A. M. Hoffman (Ed.), *Schools, violence, and society* (pp. 101–121). Westport, CT: Praeger.

Walker, H. M., Stieber, S., & O'Neill, R. E. (1990). Middle school behavioral profiles of antisocial and at-risk control boys: Descriptive and predictive outcomes. *Exceptionality, 12*(4), 43–51.

Wolfgang, M. E., & Ferracuti, F. (1967). *The subculture of violence.* London, GB: Tavistock.

Zwier, G., & Vaughan, G. M. (1984). Three ideological orientations in school vandalism research. *Review of Educational Research, 54*(2), 263–292.

Comorbidity of Conduct Problems and ADHD:

Identification of "Fledgling Psychopaths"

FRANK M. GRESHAM, KATHLEEN L. LANE, AND KATINA M. LAMBROS

Recently, researchers have focused on a group of children and youth who are at high risk for developing a lifelong pernicious pattern of antisocial and delinquent behavior. These children exhibit a behavior pattern characterized by hyperactivity–impulsivity–inattention coupled with conduct problems such as fighting, stealing, truancy, noncompliance, and arguing. These students have been referred to as "fledgling psychopaths" and appear to be highly resistant to interventions. In this article we review the literature on this group of students in terms of epidemiology and prognosis. Procedures for early identification of these students will be described and discussed. Key themes surrounding this early identification process are its proactive nature and resistance to intervention as bases for decision making concerning these students.

VIOLENCE IN AMERICAN SCHOOLS is of great concern to parents, teachers, community members, and law enforcement personnel. Increasingly, many of today's youth are coming to school from backgrounds in which antisocial behavior is normative rather than atypical. These students are highly agitated and invested in antisocial attitudes and beliefs that legitimize violent solutions to interpersonal problems with both peers and adults (Coie, 1985; Walker & Gresham, 1997). These students often perceive the behavior and intentions of others as hostile and specifically threatening against them (Dodge, 1986). This perceptual bias distorts their ability to accurately decode and interpret social behavior of others, and, as a result, these youth frequently decide to react aggressively to situations they view as challenging or threatening (Walker & Gresham, 1997). This *reactive aggression* combined with the easy availability of weapons, drugs, and alcohol yields a volatile mixture that puts our society and schools at risk for serious forms of violence.

Antisocial behavior can be defined as recurrent violations of socially prescribed patterns of behavior and can be characterized by hostility to others, aggressive behavior, defiance of authority, and violations of social norms and mores (Simcha-Fagan, Langner, Gersten, & Eisenberg, 1975). Adolescents with antisocial behavior and aggressive behavior patterns constitute between one third and one half of referrals to mental health clinics, making it the most frequently cited reason for mental health services (Achenbach, 1985; Rogers, Johansen, Chang, & Salekin, 1997). Prevalence rates of antisocial behavior in the general population range between 2% and 6%, which represents between 1.3 and 3.8 million students (Kazdin, 1993; Walker, Colvin, & Ramsey, 1995). Some 55% of all crimes are committed by juvenile delinquents (Foley, Carlton, & Howell, 1996), and in 1993, the Federal Bureau of Investigation (FBI) statistics reported that juvenile arrests made up 15% of all violent crimes (Federal Bureau of Investigation, 1993). Moreover, 87% of incarcerated juvenile offenders between ages 11 and 17 years meet diagnostic criteria for conduct disorder (Eppright, Kashani, Robinson, & Reid, 1993).

Disconcertingly, there are literally thousands of students in the public schools who fit the above profile of an at-risk antisocial youth poorly socialized to the demands of schooling. Many of these students will have contacts with law enforcement early in their lives, some will become habitual delinquents, others will join gangs, and still others will use extreme violence as an instrumental means to attain social goals (Walker et al., 1995). Unfortunately, schools are unprepared and ill equipped to cope effectively with this segment of the school population. Students having the most severe forms of antisocial behavior may hold schools hostage and pose serious and sometimes lethal dangers to staff and peers.

Recently, researchers have focused on a group of children and youth who are at high risk for developing a lifelong pernicious pattern of antisocial and delinquent behavior. These children exhibit a behavior pattern marked by hyperactivity–impulsivity–inattention (HIA) coupled with conduct problems characterized by fighting, stealing, truancy, noncompliance, and arguing. Using terminology from the *Diagnostic and Statistical Manual–IV* (*DSM-IV;* American Psychiatric Association, 1994), these children would be classified as being comorbid for attention-deficit/hyperactivity disorder (ADHD) and conduct disorder (CD). These students have been referred to as "fledgling psychopaths" (Lynam, 1996, 1997) and appear to be highly resistant to interventions.

THE FLEDGLING PSYCHOPATH

The two most common types of behavior problems that bring children to the attention of mental health professionals are excessive violations of social norms, usually involving aggressive and antisocial conduct, and HIA (Hinshaw, 1987). Although these two classes of behavior receive different classifications in *DSM-IV* (i.e., CD and ADHD, respectively), there has been debate over the years as to whether these two domains represent separate entities (Barkley, 1982; Loney & Milich, 1982). Hinshaw's (1987) comprehensive review of ADHD and CD showed that children classified as hyperactive and aggressive overlap considerably. That is, 30%–90% of children in one group could also be classified in the other group using either cutoff scores or cluster analytic methods.

Lynam (1996) identified a subtype of conduct problems, which he referred to as "fledgling psychopaths," based on the dual presence of HIA and conduct problems (CP) or an antisocial behavior pattern. Psychopathy, first described by Cleckley (1976), represents a behavior pattern marked by risk-taking, sensation seeking, and involvement in a variety of criminal activities. Socially, the psycho-pathic individual may be described as egocentric, manipulative, grandiose, and forceful (Lynam, 1996). Psychopaths exhibit shallow emotions, lack empathy, and show little remorse for wrongdoing. In his work with adult offenders, Hare (1981) described psychopaths as among the most violent and persistent of offenders in that they commit more thefts, robberies, and assaults, and escape more often than non-psychopathic offenders (Hare, 1981; Hare & Jutai, 1983; Hare, McPherson, & Forth, 1988).

Children demonstrating the combination of HIA + CP are likely to possess the worst features of both domains because they tend to be more physically aggressive, persist longer in antisocial behavior, display more severe achievement deficits, and have higher levels of peer rejection than children with attention problems or conduct problems alone (Farington, Loeber, & Van Kammer, 1990; Gresham, Macmillan, Bocian, Ward, & Forness, 1998; Hinshaw, 1987; Hinshaw, Lahey, & Hart, 1993). Identification of this comorbid group of children has substantial implications for assessment and intervention in schools.

Prediction of Chronic Offenders

A major goal in working with children and youth who display characteristics of antisocial behavior and concomitant attention–impulsivity problems is accurate early identification of this evolving behavior pattern. Tomorrow's antisocial adults can be found among today's antisocial children, given that conduct problems in childhood are a major risk factor for disorders in adulthood involving aggressive antisocial behavior (Lynam, 1996). In an important longitudinal study, Huesmann, Eron, Lefkowitz, and Walder (1984) followed a group of children who were rated as aggressive by peers in late childhood over a period of 22 years. Their findings showed that aggressive children became aggressive adults, with aggressive men committing more serious criminal offenses and engaging in more spousal abuse, whereas aggressive women were more likely to use severe punishment strategies in disciplining their children.

In a classic longitudinal study, Robins (1966) showed the stability of antisocial behavior among 524 boys in two groups—clinic-referred and control—over a 30-year period. Her findings showed that antisocial boys were arrested and incarcerated more often as adults, had more marital difficulties, were poorer, used excessive amounts of alcohol, and had poorer Armed Services records. These antisocial boys were also more likely to receive a diagnosis in adulthood equivalent to an antisocial personality disorder.

Robins' (1978) longitudinal work strongly suggests two dominant principles concerning the relation between early antisocial behavior and later chronic antisocial behavior: (a) Infrequently, if at all, does antisocial behavior initially occur in adulthood, and (b) less than 50% of children with severe antisocial behavior become antisocial adults, suggesting a limited ability to predict a chronic adult antisocial behavior pattern (Lynam, 1996). In fact, a study by White, Moffitt, Earls, Robins, and Silva (1990) demonstrated that of 209 preschool antisocial children, 85% *did not* develop severe antisocial behavior at age 11.

Part of the difficulty in predicting antisocial behavior in adulthood is due to the relatively *high base rates* of behaviors considered to be characteristic of CD or oppositional defiant disorder. Werry and Quay (1971) used teacher ratings to study a nonreferred group of 1,700 kindergarten through second-grade children and, among boys, found high base rates of: restlessness (50%), attention seeking (37%), disruptiveness (46%), boisterousness (34%), fighting (31%), disobedience (26%), and hyperactivity (30%). In fact, Lynam (1996) suggested that among adolescents,

> . . . delinquency is almost normative; among adolescents (ages 13-18) more than 50% admit to theft, 35% admit to assault, 45% admit to property destruction, and 60% admit to engaging in more than one type of antisocial behavior, such as aggressiveness, drug abuse, arson, and vandalism. (p. 211)

In short, it is extremely difficult to predict an antisocial behavior pattern based on behaviors that have high base rates. This is especially true in longitudinal research in which low base rate behaviors at one developmental level (e.g., early childhood) evolve into high base rate behaviors at a later developmental level (e.g., adolescence).

Review of the Literature

The relationship between conduct problems and HIA problems is complex, and debate has arisen regarding several issues. One key issue addresses whether CP or HIA are truly separate entities that occur together, or do both disorders share similar and overlapping correlates that cannot be separated? Authorities have questioned whether HIA is a "true" diagnostic disorder that remains clearly distinct from other well-established diagnoses such as CP (Szatmari, Boyle, & Offord, 1989).

Hinshaw (1987) provided support for the separation of aggressive, hyperactive, and aggressive–hyperactive subgroups of children; however, he concluded that full syndromal independence has not been substantiated. Additionally, Farrington, Loeber, and Van Kammer (1990) reported that the overlap between CP and HIA may be exaggerated because HIA and CP scales derived from factor analyses often contain overlapping items. Trites and LaPrade (1983) illustrated this overlap in a study involving 9,000 Ottawa children. Six of the 17 items loading on the HIA factor were also among the 14 items loading on the highest CP factor. Of particular significance was that the items with the highest loading did not overlap with one another. Restlessness, fidgeting, inattention, and disturbing other children loaded on the HIA factor. In contrast, stealing, lying, destructiveness, and defiance loaded on the CP factor.

Despite the current debate regarding the independence of these two domains, ample research has indicated a high co-occurrence of CP and HIA (Frick, 1998; Hinshaw, 1987; Lynam, 1996, 1997; Szatmari et al., 1989). According to Frick, ADHD is by far the most common comorbid diagnosis in children with conduct disorders. Rates of HIA in clinically referred children with CP range from 65% (Trites & LaPrade, 1983) to 90% (Abikoff & Klein, 1992). Thus, the majority of children having CP show symptoms of HIA. This relationship is not symmetrical in that there are more children with HIA who do not have conduct problems than there are children with CP who do not have HIA (Frick, 1998; Hinshaw, 1987).

Studies of HIA children have shown that a significant number of children develop conduct problems by adolescence and that children with HIA and CP have more intense antisocial disorders in later life (Biederman, Munir, & Knee, 1987). An examination of hyperactive boys with conduct problems by Satterfield and Schell (1997) revealed that these children are at marked risk for both juvenile and adult criminality in comparison to normal controls. Adult offending was associated with conduct problems in childhood and serious antisocial behavior patterns in adolescence. Children with HIA who did not evidence CP were not at increased risk for later criminality.

Szatmari et al. (1989) indicated that the comorbidity of HIA + CP reflects a true "hybrid" disorder rather than one diagnosis over the other. This is consistent with Lynam's (1996) review in which he contends that children with symptoms of CP and HIA constitute a unique subgroup of fledgling psychopaths, who possess a "virulent strain" of CP. These children seem to be at greater risk for psychopathology and chronic offending.

In order to examine this fledgling psychopath group, it is ideal to have four groups to use in contrast: children with CP only, children with HIA only, children with HIA + CP, and children with neither HIA nor CP (Farrington et al., 1990). A study by Kuhne, Schacher, and Tannock (1997) contrasted 33 ADHD, 46 ADHD + Oppositional Defiant Disorder (ODD), and 12 ADHD + CP children on measures of ADHD aggression, anxiety, parental psychopathology, and social–emotional functioning. Results indicated that the presence of comorbid oppositional or conduct problems in children with attention problems altered the correlates of ADHD across several domains. The ADHD + CP group evidenced higher levels of aggression, higher anxiety, increased maternal psychopathology, and decreased self-esteem. Likewise, Carlson, Tamm, and Gaub (1997) revealed that children with ADHD + ODD received the poorest teacher ratings for problem behaviors on the Teacher Report Form (Achenbach, 1991a). The children in the ODD-only group were rated as learning more, working harder, and being less inattentive than children in the ADHD-only group.

Summary

Researchers have shown that the prognosis for children becomes markedly worse when comorbidity of HIA + CP is present. Comorbid diagnoses are increasing in prevalence and significantly hinder the development and functioning of many children (Loney, 1987; McConaughy & Skiba, 1993). Clearly, additional research is necessary to understand the processes involved in comorbidity. The presence of attention problems in children leads to more severe and maladaptive behavior problems. Earlier onset of problem behaviors, as well as more severe and aggressive behavior, characterize children with both disorders (Walker, Lahey, Hynd, & Frame, 1987). Children with HIA + CP are at heightened risk for the development of future psychopathology, as well as a host of additional adult adjustment problems including substance abuse, unemployment, divorce, accidents, and dependence on welfare (Walker et al., 1987). Moreover, children with HIA + CP evidence a variety of delinquent acts in adolescence, more severe aggression in adolescence, and more violent offending in adulthood than those who are not comorbid for these diagnoses (Loeber, Brinthaupt, & Green, 1990; Lynam, 1996, 1997). What is particularly disturbing about this group is the *impulsive response style* coupled with the tendency to engage in severe aggression and violent offending. Due to the immediate and often dangerous behavior associated with such problem behavior patterns, efforts to correctly identify and subsequently intervene on these behavior patterns are paramount.

DEVELOPMENTAL PATHWAYS TO CONDUCT PROBLEMS

Researchers have described several behavioral sequences that characterize the development of conduct problems in children and adolescents. Specifically, three developmental pathways have been described in the literature: (a) the childhood-onset pathway, (b) the adolescent-onset pathway, and (c) the delayed-onset pathway.

Childhood-Onset Pathway

In the childhood-onset pathway, antisocial behavior begins in early childhood and progresses in frequency, severity, and intensity over the course of a child's development. Children having the childhood-onset pathway initially exhibit behavior problems such as noncompliance, anger, and temper tantrums. Biederman and Cole (1992) suggested that irritability, aggression, and discipline problems can be observed as early as 2 to3 years of age, and these behaviors are associated with conduct problems in later childhood. These behaviors magnify in frequency, duration, and intensity into middle childhood (7 to 10 years of age) and often include lying, physical confrontations with peers, and swearing. By ages 11 through 13 years, a child is engaging in severe antisocial behavior including cruelty to others, truancy, and breaking the law (Frick, 1998). This progression from less to more severe behavior problems is supported in numerous longitudinal studies (Farrington et al., 1990; Hinshaw, Lahey, & Hart, 1993; Loeber, 1982; Moffitt, 1990).

Adolescent-Onset Pathway

In the adolescent-onset pathway, a large number of children exhibit severe patterns of antisocial behavior without a history of prior behavior problems. These children's conduct problems are referred to as "adolescent-limited" (Moffitt, 1993). Such children begin to experience high levels of aggressive and antisocial behavior from ages 12 through 18 years

and show high rates of arrests and convictions that are comparable to those of youth on the childhood-onset trajectory (Frick, 1998). Youth in the adolescent-onset pathway tend to display less aggression, less violence, and less impulsivity than their childhood-onset counterparts. Moreover, these adolescents typically come from less dysfunctional families, have higher levels of social skills, and display fewer cognitive impairments than children with childhood-onset conduct problems. Of particular importance is the differential prognosis for these two groups of youth. The adolescent-onset group is more likely to decrease their high levels of antisocial behavior, whereas the childhood-onset group is likely to continue antisocial and aggressive behavior into adulthood (Frick, 1998; Walker et al., 1995).

Delayed-Onset Pathway

The delayed-onset pathway is particularly valuable in describing the development of conduct problems in girls. Although the childhood-onset and adolescent-onset pathways of conduct problems in boys are well supported in the literature, the distinctiveness of these developmental pathways are less clear in girls (Frick, 1998). Girls often do not display severe conduct problems in early childhood and are more likely to exhibit conduct problems of a less severe nature (e.g., curfew violations, substance abuse) in adolescence (Hinshaw et al., 1993). They do not, however, resemble the adolescent-onset group in any additional characteristics. Instead, this delayed-onset group of girls has more similarities to the childhood-onset group of boys in that they come from dysfunctional families, have higher rates of cognitive dysfunction, and have negative adult outcomes (Robins, 1986; Zoccilillo, 1993). What is interesting about this group of girls is that they do not develop severe antisocial behavior until adolescence, but they come from similar backgrounds (e.g., dysfunctional families, high levels of stress, parental psychopathology) as childhood-onset boys with conduct problems. This delayed-onset group of girls

has not been well researched and warrants further attention.

CAUSAL PATHWAYS TO FLEDGLING PSYCHOPATHY

In light of the above developmental pathways to CP, what causal models explain the development of a comorbid group of children with HIA + CP? Lynam (1996) identified three models that might explain the development of these children: risk-factor model, stepping-stone model, and subtype model.

Risk-Factor Model

The risk-factor model asserts HIA leads to consequences and problems for children that escalate into an antisocial behavior pattern. Patterson (1982), for instance, suggested that coercive child-rearing techniques put children at risk for future antisocial behavior. In Patterson's Microsocial Coercive Family Process model, antisocial behavior progresses from trivial to severe behaviors over time. Typically, this process begins with an unskilled parent trying to care for an infant with a difficult temperament. This sets up a tense and often frustrating series of interactions between the parent and the child (i.e., a coercive cycle). This coercive cycle is repeated literally thousands of times and evolves into a pattern of noncompliance to parental requests and commands, which subsequently develops into an oppositional defiant behavior pattern. Eventually, this oppositional defiant behavior pattern results in more severe antisocial and aggressive behaviors that are characteristic of conduct problems.

Hinshaw (1992) argued that school entry for these children brings academic failure and frustration with academic tasks that results in increases in aggressive behavior. As a result of this increased aggression, peers often reject these children, which often leads to isolation and peer conflicts (Milich & Landau, 1989; Parker & Asher, 1987). Lynam (1996) stated that HIA is but one risk factor among others (e.g., poor or inconsistent parenting, poor school achievement, and peer rejection) and that the child with HIA + CP is no different from other children with conduct problems without HIA.

Stepping-Stone Model

In this model, early onset of HIA leads to Oppositional Defiant Disorder (ODD), which escalates into CD. Moffitt (1993), like Patterson (1982), suggested that a difficult temperament at birth evokes a chain of aversive and problematic parent–child interactions which disrupts the child's socialization. According to the stepping-stone model, early identification and intervention with HIA will prevent ODD and subsequent development of CD (Lynam, 1996). Early interventions that would most likely be effective in interrupting this escalating chain is early prescription of stimulant medication and behavioral parent training (Barkley, 1990).

Subtype Model

Although there is empirical support for both the risk-factor and stepping-stone causal models, these models do not explain why children with HIA only show more deficits in sustained attention than the HIA + CP and CP-only groups. According to Lynam (1996),

> In fact, findings such as these have lead Schachar and Logan (1990a) to raise the possibility that the "mixed clinical presentation of {HIA-CP may be something other than hyperactivity which develops into conduct disorder" (p. 509). Contrary to predictions drawn from the risk-factor and stepping-stone models, children with HIA only appear to possess deficits not seen in those with HIA-CP. (p. 223)

The subtype model suggests that HIA + CP children constitute a unique subgroup that Lynam (1996) calls fledgling psychopaths. According to Lynam, this group of children have a deficit in the ability to inhibit goal-directed behavior in the face of challenging environmental contingencies. That is, fledgling psychopaths are less likely to incorporate new information while engaging in goal-directed behavior. For example, these children would have difficulty in social interactions that change from initially being confrontational to neutral or positive. This difficulty may be due to not attending to social cues in a social interaction and continuing down the confrontations path when social cues suggest the interaction is becoming more positive. Additionally, this group of children is low in "constraint," which may explain their impulsivity and sensation-seeking tendencies.

Lynam (1996) speculated that fledgling psychopaths start out with low levels of constraint, which creates problems in incorporating feedback from the environment. As children, these individuals will exhibit signs of HIA which will develop into ODD behaviors (e.g., non-compliance, arguing, resentfulness) because the child's parents often frustrate or interfere with the child's goal-directed behavior. Upon school entry, the child will have difficulty in remaining seated, being quiet, listening to the teacher, and transitioning among classroom activities. Interpersonally, the child will begin to show signs of CP (e.g., bullying, fighting, stealing) because peers will often interfere with the attainment of the child's interpersonal goals.

In summary, the subtype model of the fledgling psychopath suggests that neither the risk-factor nor stepping-stone model adequately explains the development of this subgroup. It should be noted that currently, the subtype model is speculative and much more research on identification and intervention is needed (Lynam, 1996, 1997). What appears to be needed at this time is a measurement and assessment technology that would reliably and accurately differentiate the HIA + CP group from HIA and CP groups. Lynam (1996) hypothesized that it may be that the HIA + CP group would show more signs of *impulsivity,* whereas the HIA-only group would show more *inattention.* In the remainder of this article, we will present a proposed measurement technology that can contribute toward the accurate and reliable identification of the fledgling psychopath.

PROCEDURES FOR EARLY IDENTIFICATION OF THE FLEDGLING PSYCHOPATH

Given the poor prognosis for remediation and the host of long-term negative consequences facing children who exhibit an antisocial behavior pattern coupled with characteristics of HIA, early identification of these children is crucial. Fortunately, several procedures are available to provide for such early identification of these at-risk children. Walker et al. (1995) suggested 4 criteria for selecting and/or developing screening procedures. One, screening should be *proactive* rather than reactive in order to identify students who are at risk but have not yet developed antisocial behavior patterns. Two, student behaviors should be evaluated using the principle of *multi-operationalism*; that is, students should be assessed using multiple sources (teachers, parents, peers) in multiple settings (classroom, playground, home) using multiple methods (behavior ratings, peer sociometrics, self-reports, records). Three, screening procedures should begin as *early* as possible in the student's educational career, preferably upon school entry, when students are less resistant to intervention. Four, although teacher nominations and rankings are appropriate tools in the initial stage of the screening process, these measures should be supplemented with more *specific and accurate measures* of behavior in later stages of the identification process (e.g., direct observations, school record reviews, ratings by others). A fifth criterion we would add is to establish a link between assessment information and intervention procedures. It is critical that screening procedures provide specific information concerning acquisition and performance deficits in academic and social behavioral domains so that empirically-based interventions can be designed and implemented with appropriate intensity and integrity.

Although by no means an exhaustive list, the following is a description of some procedures and tools that can be used to identify and subsequently intervene with children who are at risk for becoming fledgling psychopaths. The procedures and tools reviewed include many of the required components (e.g., multi-source, multi-setting, multi-method) discussed above. This identification process is perhaps best conceptualized as a multiple gating process similar to the *Systematic Screening for Behavior Disorders* (SSBD; Walker & Severson, 1992). The SSBD uses progressively more labor intensive and expensive assessment procedures as students pass through each gate of the assessment process. Our conceptual model for the early identification of children at risk for fledgling psychopathy is presented in Figure 1.

Stage I: Teacher Nominations

Consistent with the methods used in the SSBD (Walker & Severson, 1992), children at risk for becoming fledgling psychopaths initially could be identified by teacher nominations based on a clear, operational definition of that construct. For example, teachers could be asked to identify 10 students whose behavior patterns most closely match the behavioral profile of the fledgling psychopath. This list of 10 students would then be rank ordered from 1 (*most like*) to 10 (*least like*) the behavior pattern and teachers would select students with Ranks 1–3 as passing the first gate.

The following definition can be used to identify this group of students:

> This behavior pattern refers to aggressive, coercive, impulsive behaviors that are exhibited by students toward the social environment. Students with this behavior pattern show signs of hyperactivity, impulsivity, inattention, noncompliance, and aggressive behavior frequently accompanied by a lack of guilt, remorse, or empathy toward others.

Examples of this behavior pattern include verbal aggression, physical aggression, swearing, defiance toward authority figures, hyperactive behavior, impulsive behavior, inattention, stealing, lack of guilt over misbehavior, absence of empathy toward others, and violation of school rules.

Stage I: Teacher Nominations

- Teachers identify 10 students who most closely match the behavioral profile

  The top one to three students pass through the first gate.

⬇⬇⬇

Stage II: Multi-Informant Ratings

- Teacher Ratings: Teacher Rating Form (TRF), Critical Events Index (CEI)

- Parent Ratings: Child Behavior Checklist (CBCL)

  Students exceeding normative criteria on two subscales from teacher and parent ratings pass through the second gate.

⬇⬇⬇

Stage III: Intensive Assessment

- Direct Observations: Classroom – Academic Engaged Time (AET) & Total Disruptive Behavior (TDB); Playground – Total Negative (TN) and Alone (A)

- Sociometric Assessment: Rejected Sociometric Status

- Functional Assessment Interviews

  Students exceeding specified cut-off scores for AET, TDB, TN, A, and SP pass through the third gate.

⬇⬇⬇

Stage IV: Resistance to Intervention

- Primary Interventions

- Secondary Interventions

- Tertiary Interventions

FIGURE 1. Early identification of children at-risk for fledgling psychopathy.

Stage II: Multi-Informant Ratings

The next step in identifying students who are at risk for fledgling psychopathy is to collect ratings from multiple informants (teachers and parents). We advocate using extant behavior rating scales having excellent psychometric features and substantial empirical support for this purpose. For instance, selected subscales from the Teacher Rating Form (TRF; Achenbach, 1991a) and Child Behavior Checklist (CBCL; Achenbach, 1991b) could be used for this purpose. On the TRF, students can be selected if they receive T scores of 65 or greater on two of the following three subscales: Delinquent Behavior, Aggressive Behavior, and Attention Problems. On the CBCL, students can be selected if they receive T scores of 65 or greater on two of the following three subscales: Delinquent Behavior, Aggressive Behavior, and Attention Problems. Thus, for a student to pass this gate, he or she would have to obtain scores of 65 or higher on at least two TRF and two CBCL subscales. These criteria should identify students scoring at or above the 93rd percentile on these subscales. Lambros (1999) successfully used this method to differentiate fledgling psychopaths from conduct problem-only and ADHD-only groups in a longitudinal follow-back investigation of children in mid-elementary, late elementary, and junior high school.

In addition to the TRF and CBCL, we suggest that teachers complete the Critical Events Index (CEI; Walker & Severson, 1992), a 33-item checklist measuring low frequency, high intensity behaviors. Recent studies have shown the CEI to be highly accurate in identifying students at risk for emotional and behavioral disorders (Gresham, Lane, MacMillan, & Bocian, 1999; Gresham, MacMillan, & Bocian, 1996).

The CEI is nationally standardized and provides cutoff scores for both Externalizers and Internalizers. We recommend that students receiving a CEI score of 5 or more of the following 11 behaviors checked as present pass on to the third gate of this identification process: steals, sets fires, has tantrums, physically assaults an adult, demonstrates physically aggressive behavior with other students or adults, damages others' property, attempts to seriously injure others, ignores teacher warnings and reprimands, uses obscene language, makes lewd or obscene gestures, and exhibits cruelty to animals.

Stage III: Intensive Assessment

The next step in this multiple gating procedure for identifying students at risk for fledgling psychopathy is to move to more extensive and expensive assessment procedures. These multimethod procedures include (a) direct observations, (b) sociometric assessment, and (c) functional assessment interviews. Each of these methods is briefly described below.

Direct Observations. Direct observations of student behavior should take place in both classroom and playground settings. For classroom observations, we recommend the observation of two categories of behavior: (a) academic engaged time (AET) and (b) total disruptive behavior (TDB). The observations should be sampled across different instructional activities and time of the day to ensure a representative sampling of behavior. AET is based on the definition given by Walker and Severson (1992) and may be defined as attending to the material and task, making appropriate motor responses (e.g., writing), and asking for assistance appropriately. AET is a duration recording method that is measured by starting a stopwatch whenever a student is academically engaged and stopping it when the student is not academically engaged. AET is converted to a percentage by dividing the elapsed AET time by the total time observed and multiplying by 100. Walker and Severson recommend that observers select a seatwork period in which at least 15 to 20 minutes of class time have been allocated for independent work on an assigned academic task to collect AET data.

TDB is a class of behavior that disturbs or disrupts the classroom ecology and interferes with instruction. Examples include being out of seat without permission; touching or grabbing others' property; noncompliance with teacher instructions; hitting, biting, choking, or slapping others; any audible noises other than vocalizations; and/or screaming, yelling, cursing, or criticizing others. TDB is measured by duration recording exactly as described for AET. TDB should be measured during a different 15- to 20-minute observation session than the AET recording.

Students at risk for fledgling psychopathy tend to be less academically engaged and engage in higher rates of disruptive behavior. If a student's AET is 50% or less and TDB is 10% or more, the student should be considered at risk for antisocial behavior (Walker et al., 1995; Walker & Severson, 1992).

Playground observations include two categories of behavior: (a) total negative social interaction (TN) and (b) alone. *TN* is defined as behaviors that disturb or disrupt ongoing play activities and involve physical or verbal aggression. Examples include hitting, biting, choking, screaming, cursing, and threatening. *Alone* is defined as behaviors in which the target student is *not* within 10 feet of another student, is *not* socially engaged, and is *not* participating in any activity with other students. TN and Alone are recorded as duration measures exactly like AET and TDB described earlier and should be collected in a 15- to 20-minute observation session.

Antisocial students spend more time alone and are more negative in their social interactions than are nonantisocial students. Based on playground recording, if a target student spends between 12% and 15% of the time in solitary activity (Alone) and engages in negative social behavior (TN) 10% or more of the time, he or she should be considered to be at risk for antisocial behavior (Walker et al., 1995).

Sociometric Assessment. Although a number of sociometric assessment procedures exist, we recommend the peer nomination procedures described by Coie, Dodge, and Coppotelli (1982). In this method, students in the classroom are asked to select from a roster the

3 peers they like most and 3 peers they like least. The number of nominations are summed to yield Liked Most (LM) and Liked Least (LL) scores. Thus, the LM scores represent the total number of nominations a student receives for "Liked Most" and LL scores represent the total number of nominations a student receives for "Liked Least." LM and LL scores are then used to calculate Social Preference (SP) scores and Social Impact (SI) scores. SP is calculated by subtracting the LL score from the LM score ($SP = LL - LM$) and Social Impact is calculated by adding the LM and LL scores ($SI = LM + LL$).

All of the above scores are standardized *within* classrooms (i.e., they are converted to z scores [$M = 0$, $SD = 1$]). These standard scores are then used to classify each student as being *rejected* or *not rejected*. Rejected is calculated by the following: an SP score of less than -1.00, an LL score of greater than 0, and an LM score of less than 0. Being rejected by peers in elementary grades consistently has been shown to be predictive of future antisocial behavior patterns (Asher & Coie, 1990; Coie et al., 1982; Walker et al., 1995). Students obtaining a rejected peer status in addition to the above direct observational criteria are considered to pass this gate.

Functional Assessment Interviews. The functional assessment interview (FAI) has three primary goals: (a) to identify and define specific types of antisocial behaviors, (b) to identify appropriate behaviors that might successfully compete with inappropriate antisocial behaviors, and (c) to obtain preliminary information regarding a possible functional analysis of behavior and formulation of behavioral hypotheses concerning behavioral function. FAIs with teachers, parents, peers, and target students represent important sources of information that can assist in a functional analysis of behavior. We strongly recommend the functional assessment interview protocol described by O'Neill and colleagues (1997) as a model for conducting FAIs with teachers and parents and the student-assisted functional as-

sessment interview described by Kern and colleagues (Kern & Dunlap, in press; Kern, Dunlap, Clarke, & Childs, 1994).

Stage IV: Resistance to Intervention

The concluding phase of this multiple gating model involves conceptualizing students as being at risk for fledgling psychopathy based on the notion of resistance to intervention. Resistance to intervention may be defined as the lack of change in target behaviors as a function of intervention (Gresham, 1991, 1998). Given that the goal of all interventions is to produce a discrepancy between baseline and postintervention levels of performance, the failure to produce such a discrepancy can be used as one basis for making either an eligibility determination or for increased allocation of resources for a particular student. That is, if maladaptive behaviors continue to be exhibited at unacceptable levels subsequent to interventions implemented with integrity, then the student may need the same treatment implemented more frequently and intensely with higher integrity, a more intensive and stronger treatment, and/or a more restrictive placement.

Resistance to intervention has received a great deal of attention over the past 10 years in both the experimental analysis of behavior and applied behavior analysis literatures (see Mace, 1994; Nevin, 1988). Nevin uses the term *behavioral momentum* to explain a behavior's resistance to change. In an analogy to physics, the baseline rate of behavior can be considered analogous to initial velocity and an intervention procedure to external force. Mass, in a behavioral sense, represents the strength of a behavior. Behavioral strength is directly related to the resistance of that behavior to change as a function of intervention. Behaviors with high strength (mass) tend to resist changes in momentum (inertia). As in physics, to change the momentum of high strength behaviors, there must be proportional increase in strength of an intervention (force).

Clearly, the literature on antisocial behavior suggests that these students' be-

havior patterns are well established (high momentum), and they exhibit low frequencies of appropriate behaviors. Moreover, these students' behaviors tend to resist most interventions, particularly those interventions that are not based on empirically established best practices or not implemented with high integrity (Lipsey & Wilson, 1998; Walker et al., 1995). Best practices suggest that multiple interventions of varying force may be required to change multiple behaviors that have variations in behavioral momentum.

A useful model to follow based on the resistance to intervention concept is predicated on the notions of primary, secondary, and tertiary prevention. *Primary prevention* strategies attempt to prevent the occurrence of disorder by removing some risk factor associated with the disorder. Primary prevention approaches are based on the delivery of *universal* interventions in which all students in a classroom or school receive the intervention program. Examples of universal interventions might be a social skills curriculum, schoolwide discipline plans, and drug education classes. *Secondary prevention* strategies are based on the early identification of a problem such as detection of students at risk for fledgling psychopathy such that interventions can be implemented before the problem becomes well established. Secondary prevention strategies are based on the delivery of *selected* interventions in which at-risk children receive interventions such as social skills training, academic remediation or tutoring, or behavioral interventions for inappropriate behaviors. *Tertiary prevention* strategies attempt to limit the pejorative effects of a problem by focusing on rehabilitation efforts. Tertiary prevention efforts are based on the implementation of *indicated* interventions such as parent training, highly individualized behavioral interventions, and teaching of coping and survival skills. Excellent treatments of the topic of levels of prevention can be found in more detailed authoritative sources (Lipsey & Wilson, 1998; Walker et al., 1995; Wasserman & Miller, 1998).

CONCLUSION

In this article we reviewed research showing that students who are at risk for fledgling psychopathy exhibit more severe and maladaptive behavior problems than students having either CD or ADHD in isolation. Fledgling psychopaths exhibit more frequent, severe, and temporally stable behavior patterns marked by an impulsive response style that makes their antisocial behavior at any given point in time unpredictable. The prognosis for students who are comorbid for CD and ADHD is poor, and there is evidence that these students are more resistant to interventions, particularly as they get older (Hinshaw, 1987; Kazdin, 1987; Lynam, 1996, 1997). Students showing the fledgling psychopath behavior pattern are at risk for developing future psychopathology in adolescence and into adulthood as well as additional problems, such as substance abuse, unemployment, divorce, accidents, and welfare dependence (Loeber et al., 1990; Lynam, 1996).

Early identification and intervention with students at risk for fledgling psychopathy is imperative. This early identification process may provide the best means of preventing escalation of this behavior pattern into more severe and resistant forms. As children move into adolescence, this behavior pattern will become more and more resistant to intervention strategies. With younger children, there are numerous opportunities to intervene in multiple settings with multiple change agents such as home (parents and siblings), school (teachers and peers), and individually. In reviewing the treatment outcome literature on antisocial behavior in children, Kazdin (1987) maintained that unless we intervene prior to 8 years of age, we no longer are in the prevention business but rather in the management business. That is, antisocial behavior after age 8 should be considered analogous to a chronic illness (e.g., diabetes) that can be managed with appropriate supports, but not cured.

We described a multiple gating screening process that can be useful in identifying students at risk for fledgling psychopathy. This process uses well-established and empirically validated assessment instruments such as the SSBD (Walker & Severson, 1992), the TRF (Achenbach, 1991a), the CBCL (Achenbach, 1991b), and peer nomination sociometrics (Coie, et al., 1982). It should be noted, however, that the combination of procedures described has not been specifically validated for the identification of fledgling psychopaths and requires future validation work.

In any screening process, the issues of false positive, false negative, and base rates must be considered. A false positive is the inaccurate identification of students as at risk for a problem when they are not. A false negative is the inaccurate identification of students not being at risk for a problem when, in fact, they are. Base rates refer to the prevalence of a problem in a population. In the initial stages of screening (e.g., teacher nominations in the current article), relatively high false positive rates can be tolerated. As students pass through each of the subsequent gates, the false positive rate should decrease because more stringent criteria are required for identification. However, one must be careful because as the false positive rate decreases, the false negative rate can increase. For example, if the base rate for a particular problem is 50%, one can correctly identify those individuals having the problem by simply flipping a coin (i.e., by chance alone). Because the base rate of fledgling psychopathy is low, the identification process will be less accurate.

Besides much needed empirical work in the identification process for fledging psychopaths, there are several practical and ethical questions that should be addressed. First, at what age should we screen children for fledging psychopathy? Should it be in preschool, school entry, or middle childhood? Walker, Severson, and Feil (1994) developed a screening procedure known as the *Early Screening Project* (ESP) that accurately identifies children as externalizers and internalizers as early as 3 years of age. Second, there are some ethical issues involved in the early identification of this group of students. For example, effective intervention programs may be denied for children identified as false negatives, and these same programs may be unnecessarily provided to children who are false positives. The solution to this dilemma would be to increase the accuracy of the identification process. Another ethical issue relates to the possible stigmatizing effects of secondary and tertiary prevention programs. Since primary prevention programs are universal (i.e., all students receive them), the issue of possible stigmatization is moot (LeBlanc, 1998). To date, we have no empirical data to guide us in decision making.

In summary, more empirical work needs to be conducted and replicated before we will have a well validated screening tool for identifying fledgling psychopaths. However, making use of extant assessment instrumentation with excellent psychometric properties represents the first step in this process. We have described these procedures and recommended their use based on what is currently known about the fledgling psychopath.

About the Authors

FRANK M. GRESHAM, PhD, is a professor and director of the School Psychology Program at the University of California–Riverside. His areas of interest include severe emotional and behavioral disorders of children and youth, social skills assessment and training, and behavioral consultation. **KATHLEEN L. LANE,** PhD, is an assistant professor in the Department of Special Education at the University of Arizona. Her interests include severe emotional and behavioral disorders of children and youth, teacher training in special education, and statistical analysis and methodology. **KATINA M. LAMBROS,** PhD, is a postdoctoral research fellow at the University of New Mexico. Her research interests include the comorbidity of emotional and behavioral disorders in children and youth, and behavioral interventions with students having emotional and behavioral difficulties. Address: Frank M. Gresham, School of Education, University of California–Riverside, Riverside, CA 92521.

References

Abikoff, H., & Klein, R. (1992). Attention-deficit hyperactivity and conduct disorder: Comorbidity and implications for treatment. *Journal of Consulting and Clincial Psychology, 60,* 881–892.

Achenbach, T. (1985). *Assessment and taxonomy of child and adolescent psychopathology.* Beverly Hills, CA: Sage.

Achenbach, T. (1991a). *Manual for the Teacher Report Form and 1991 Profile.* Burlington: University of Vermont Department of Psychiatry.

Achenbach, T. (1991b). *Manual for the Child Behavior Checklist and 1991 Profile.* Burlington: University of Vermont Department of Psychiatry.

American Psychiatric Association. (1994). *Diagnostic and statistical manual of mental disorders* (4th ed.). Washington, DC: Author.

Asher, S., & Coie, J. (Eds.) (1990). *Peer rejection in childhood.* New York: Cambridge University Press.

Barkley, R. (1982). Guidelines for defining hyperactivity. In B. B. Lahey & A. E. Kazdin (Eds.), *Advances in clinical child psychology* (pp. 137–175). New York: Plenum.

Barkley, R. (1990). *Attention deficit hyperactivity disorder: A handbook for diagnosis and treatment.* New York: Guilford Press.

Biederman, J., & Cole, M. (1992). A developmental and clinical model for the prevention of conduct disorder: The FAST tract program. *Development and Psychopathology, 4,* 509–527.

Biederman, J., Munir, K., & Knee, D. (1987). Conduct and oppositional disorder in clinically referred children with attention deficit disorder: A controlled family study. *Journal of the American Academy of Child and Adolescent Psychiatry, 26,* 724–727.

Carlson, C., Tamm, L., & Gaub, M. (1997). Gender differences in children with ADHD, ODD, and co-occurring ADHD/ODD identified in a school population. *Journal of the American Academy of Child and Adolescent Psychiatry, 36,* 1706–1714.

Cleckley, H. (1976). *The mask of sanity.* St. Louis, MO: Mosby.

Coie, J. (1985). Fitting social skills intervention to the target group. In B. Schneider, K. Rubin, & J. Ledingham (Eds.), *Peer relationships and social skills in childhood: Issues in assessment and training* (pp. 141–150). New York: Springer-Verlag.

Coie, J., Dodge, K., & Coppotelli, H. (1982). Dimensions and types of social status: A cross-age perspective. *Developmental Psychology, 18,* 557–570.

Dodge, K. (1986). A social information process model of social competence in children. In M. Perlmutter (Ed.), *Minneapolis*

symposia on child psychology (Vol. 18, pp. 77–125). Hillsdale, NJ: Erlbaum.

Eppright, T., Kashani, J., Robinson, B., & Reid, J. (1993). Comorbidity of conduct disorder and personality disorders in an incarcerated juvenile population. *American Journal of Psychiatry, 150,* 1233–1236.

Farrington, D., Loeber, R., & Van Kammer, W. (1990). Long-term criminal outcomes of hyperactivity-impulsivity-inattention deficit and conduct problems in childhood. In L. N. Robins & M. Rutter (Eds.), *Straight and devious pathways from childhood to adulthood* (pp. 62–81). Cambridge, UK: Cambridge University Press.

Federal Bureau of Investigation. (1993). *Age-specific arrest rates and race-specific arrest rates for selected offenses: 1965–1992.* Washington, DC: U.S. Government Printing Office.

Foley, H., Carlton, C., & Howell, R. (1996). The relationship of attention deficit hyperactivity disorder and conduct disorder to juvenile delinquency: Legal implications. *Bulletin of the American Academy of Psychiatry and Law, 24,* 333–345.

Frick, P. (1998). *Conduct disorders and severe antisocial behavior.* New York: Plenum Press.

Gresham, F. M. (1991). Conceptualizing behavior disorders in terms of resistance to intervention. *School Psychology Review, 20,* 348–360.

Gresham, F. M. (1998). Noncategorical approaches to K–12 emotional and behavioral difficulties. In D. Reschly, D. Tilly, & J. Grimes (Eds.), *Functional and noncategorical identification and intervention in special education.* Des Moines: Iowa Department of Education.

Gresham, F. M., Lane, K. L., MacMillan, D. L., & Bocian, K. M. (1999). Social and academic profiles of externalizing and internalizing groups: Risk factors for emotional and behavioral disorders. *Behavioral Disorders, 24,* 231–245.

Gresham, F. M., MacMillan, D. L., & Bocian, K. M. (1996). "Behavioral earthquakes": Low frequency, salient behavioral events that differentiate students at-risk for behavioral disorders. *Behavioral Disorders, 21,* 277–292.

Gresham, F. M., MacMillan, D. L., Bocian, K. M., Ward, S. L., & Forness, S. R. (1998). Comorbidity of hyperactivity-impulsivity-inattention and conduct problems: Risk factors in social, affective, and academic domains. *Journal of Abnormal Child Psychology, 26,* 393–406.

Hare, R. (1981). Psychopathy and violence. In J. R. Hayes, T. K. Roberts, & K. S. Solway (Eds.), *Violence and the violent individual* (pp. 53–74). Jamaica, NY: Spectrum.

Hare, R., & Jutai, J. (1983). Psychopathy and cerebral asymmetry in semantic processing. *Personality and Individual Differences, 9,* 329–337.

Hare, R., McPherson, L., & Forth, A. (1988). Male psychopaths and their criminal careers. *Journal of Consulting and Clinical Psychology, 56,* 741–747.

Hinshaw, S. (1987). On the distinction between attention deficit/hyperactivity and conduct problems/aggression in child psychopathology. *Psychological Bulletin, 101,* 443–463.

Hinshaw, S. (1992). Externalizing behavior problems and academic underachievement in childhood and adolescence: Causal relationships and underlying mechanisms. *Psychological Bulletin, 111,* 127–155.

Hinshaw, S., Lahey, B., & Hart, E. (1993). Issues of taxonomy and comorbidity in the development of conduct disorder. *Development and Psychopathology, 5,* 31–49.

Huesmann, L., Eron, L., Lefkowitz, M., & Walder, L. (1984). Stability of aggression over time and generations. *Developmental Psychology, 20,* 1120–1134.

Kazdin, A. (1987). Treatment of antisocial behavior in children: Current status and future directions. *Psychological Bulletin, 102,* 187–203.

Kazdin, A. (1993). Treatment of conduct disorder: Progress and directions in psychotherapy research. *Development and Psychopathology, 5,* 277–310.

Kern, L., & Dunlap, G. (in press). Assessment-based interventions for children with emotional and behavioral disorders. In A. C. Repp & R. H. Horner (Eds.), *Functional analysis of problem behavior: From effective assessment to effective support.* Pacific Grove, CA: Brooks/Cole.

Kern, L., Dunlap, G., Clarke, S., & Childs, K. (1994). Student-assisted functional assessment interview. *Diagnostique, 19,* 29–39.

Kuhne, M., Schacher, R., & Tannock, R. (1997). Impact of comorbid oppositional or conduct problems on attention-deficit hyperactivity disorder. *Journal of the American Academy of Child and Adolescent Psychiatry, 36,* 1715–1725.

Lambros, K. M. (1999). *Examination of conduct problems and hyperactivity-impulsivity-inattention problems as correlates of fledgling psychopathy: A longitudinal perspective of children at-risk.*

Unpublished doctoral dissertation, University of California, Riverside.

LeBlanc, M. (1998). Screening of serious and violent juvenile offenders: Identification, classification, and prediction. In R. Loeber & D. Farrington (Eds.), *Serious and violent juvenile offenders: Risk factors and successful interventions* (pp. 167–193). Thousand Oaks, CA: Sage.

Lipsey, M., & Wilson, D. (1998). Effective intervention for serious juvenile offenders: A synthesis of research. In R. Loeber & D. Farrington (Eds.), *Serious and violent juvenile offenders: Risk factors and successful interventions* (pp. 313–345). Thousand Oaks, CA: Sage.

Loeber, R. (1982). The stability of antisocial behavior and delinquent child behavior: A review. *Child Development, 53,* 1431–1436.

Loeber, R., Brinthaupt, V., & Green, S. (1990). Attention deficits, impulsivity, and hyperactivity with or without conduct problems: Relationships to delinquency and unique contextual factors. In R. J. McMahon & R. D. Peters (Eds.), *Behavior disorders of adolescence: Research, intervention, and policy in clinical and school settings* (pp. 39–61). New York: Plenum Press.

Loney, J. (1987). Hyperactivity and aggression in the diagnosis of attention deficit disorder. In B.B. Lahey & A.E. Kazdin (Eds.), *Advances in clinical child psychology* (Vol. 10, pp. 99–135). New York: Plenum Press.

Loney, J., & Milich, R. (1982). Hyperactivity, inattention, and aggression in clinical practice. In M. Wolraich & D. Routh (Eds.), *Advances in developmental and behavioral pediatrics* (Vol. 3, pp. 113–147). Greenwich, CT: JAI Press.

Lynam, D. (1996). Early identification of chronic offenders: Who is the fledgling psychopath? *Psychological Bulletin, 120,* 209–234.

Lynam, D. (1997). Pursuing the psychopath: Capturing the fledgling psychopath in a nomological net. *Journal of Abnormal Psychology, 106,* 425–438.

Mace, F. C. (1994). The significance and future of functional analysis methodologies. *Journal of Applied Behavior Analysis, 27,* 385–392.

McConaughy, S., & Skiba, R. (1993). Comorbidity of externalizing and internalizing problems. *School Psychology Review, 22,* 421–436.

Milich, R., & Landau, S. (1989). The role of social status variables in differentiating subgroups of hyperactive children. In L. M. Bloomingdale & J. M. Swanson (Eds.), *Attention deficit disorder* (Vol. 4, pp. 1–16). Oxford, UK: Pergamon Press.

Moffitt, T. (1990). Juvenile delinquency and attention deficit disorder: Boys' developmental trajectories from age 3 to age 15. *Child Development, 61,* 893–910.

Moffitt, T. (1993). Adolescence-limited and life-course persistent antisocial behavior: A developmental taxonomy. *Psychological Review, 100,* 674–701.

Nevin, J. (1988). Behavioral momentum and the partial reinforcement effect. *Psychological Bulletin, 103,* 44–56.

O'Neill, R., Horner, R., Albin, R., Sprague, J., Storey, K., & Newton, J. (1997). *Functional assessment of problem behavior: A practical assessment guide* (2nd ed.). Pacific Grove, CA: Brooks/Cole.

Parker, J., & Asher, S. (1987). Peer relations and later personal adjustment: Are low-accepted children at risk? *Psychological Bulletin, 102,* 357–389.

Patterson, G. R. (1982). *Coercive family processes.* Eugene, OR: Castilia.

Robins, L. (1966). *Deviant children grown up.* Baltimore: Williams & Wilkins.

Robins, L. (1978). Sturdy childhood predictors of adult antisocial behavior: Replications from longitudinal studies. *Psychological Medicine, 8,* 611–622.

Robins, L. (1986). Changes in conduct disorder over time. In D. C. Farren & J. D. McKinney (Eds.), *Risk in intellectual and psychosocial development* (pp. 227–259). New York: Academic Press.

Rogers, R., Johansen, J., Chang, J., & Salekin, R. (1997). Predictors of adolescent psychopathy: Oppositional and conduct-disordered symptoms. *Journal of the American Academy of Psychiatry and Law, 25,* 261–271.

Satterfield, J., & Schell, A. (1997). A prospective study of hyperactive boys with conduct problems and normal boys: Adolescent and adult criminality. *Journal of the American Academy of Child and Adolescent Psychiatry, 36,* 1726–1735.

Simcha-Fagan, O., Langner, T., Gersten, J., & Eisenberg, J. (1975). *Violent and antisocial behavior: A longitudinal study of urban youth.* (OC-CB-480) Unpublished report of the Office of Child Development.

Szatmari, P., Boyle, M., & Offord, D. (1989). ADHD and conduct disorder: Degree of diagnostic overlap and differences among correlates. *Journal of the American Academy of Child and Adolescent Psychiatry, 28,* 865–872.

Trites, R., & Laprade, K. (1983). Evidence for an independent syndrome of hyperactivity. *Journal of Child Psychology and Psychiatry, 24,* 573–586.

Walker, H., & Severson, H. (1992). *Systematic screening for behavior disorders.* Longmont, CO: Sopris West.

Walker, H. M., Colvin, G., & Ramsey, E. (1995). *Antisocial behavior in school: Strategies and best practices.* Pacific Grove, CA: Brooks/Cole.

Walker, H. M., & Gresham, F. M. (1997). Making schools safer and violence free. *Intervention in School and Clinic, 32,* 199–204.

Walker, H. M., Severson, H., & Feil, E. (1994). *Early screening project.* Longmont, CO: Sopris West.

Walker, J., Lahey, B., Hynd, G., & Frame, C. (1987). Comparison of specific patterns of antisocial behavior in children with conduct disorder with or without coexisting hyperactivity. *Journal of Consulting and Clinical Psychology, 55,* 910–913.

Wasserman, G., & Miller, L. (1998). The prevention of serious and violent juvenile offending. In R. Loeber & D. Farrington (Eds.), *Serious and violent juvenile offenders: Risk factors and successful interventions* (pp. 197–247). Thousand Oaks, CA: Sage.

Werry, J., & Quay, H. (1971). The prevalence of behavior symptoms in younger elementary school children. *American Journal of Orthopsychiatry, 41,* 136–143.

White, J., Moffitt, T., Earls, F., Robins, L., & Silva, P. (1990). How early can we tell? Predictors of childhood conduct disorder and adolescent delinquency. *Criminology, 28,* 507–533.

Zoccolillo, M. (1993). Gender and the development of conduct disorder. *Development and Psychopathology, 5,* 65–78.

Antisocial Behavior, Academic Failure, and School Climate:

A Critical Review

ALAN McEVOY AND ROBERT WELKER

EDUCATORS AND RESEARCHERS SEEK-ing to understand the relationship between antisocial behavior and academic failure face a steep challenge. A bewildering array of research on the origins, prevalence, and consequences of antisocial behavior among school-age youth has emerged in recent years (El-liot, Hamburg, & Williams, 1998; Loe-ber & Farrington, 1998; Tonry & Moore, 1998). Concomitantly, argument over ef-fective school and community interven-tions to reduce antisocial conduct among young people is confusing and often con-tradictory. Few studies provide a clear theoretical and empirical basis to guide programs intended to enhance both the academic and the prosocial behavior of students identified as at risk. Because the corpus of literature is immense, no com-prehensive summary of all the relevant findings is manageable. Even a cursory review of the literature, however, points to the need for considering four interre-lated sets of concerns: (a) the relation-ship between academic failure and anti-social behavior, (b) the development of antisocial behavior in children, (c) the climate within which both academic fail-

Researchers have demonstrated a strong correlation between antisocial behavior and academic failure among students. Yet current educational programs designed to modify one or both of these patterns of conduct tend to be limited in at least two fundamental ways. First, they tend to treat conditions associ-ated with academic achievement as separate from those associated with violent or other antisocial be-havior. Second, they often focus narrowly on modifying selected cognitions or personality characteristics of the individual (e.g., changing attitudes and beliefs). Yet both antisocial behavior and academic failure are context specific; each occurs within a climate in which conditions can be identified that reasonably pre-dict problematic behavior and can be modified to reduce such behavior. The success of prevention and intervention programs, therefore, hinges on their ability to identify and modify climates in which aca-demic failure and antisocial behavior emerge. In this article we examine the role of school climate in guid-ing programs designed to reduce academic failure and antisocial behavior among students defined as "at risk." Suggestions are offered for improving such educational programs in a manner consistent with re-search on school climate and effective schools.

ure and antisocial behavior emerge, and (d) the relationship between school cli-mate and school-based violence preven-tion and intervention programming. In this article we examine these concerns and offer suggestions for future inquiry and practice.

ACADEMIC FAILURE AND ANTISOCIAL BEHAVIOR

Academic performance consistently is identified as being inversely related to

antisocial behavior among young people. Poor academic performance co-occurs with or is a predictor of antisocial con-duct (Hawkins, Farrington, & Catalano, 1998; Herrenkohl et al., 1998; Huizinga & Jakob-Chien, 1998; Lipsey & Derzon, 1998; Maguin & Loeber, 1996). In their meta-analysis of studies on the relation-ship between academic performance and delinquency, Maguin and Loeber offered the following findings:

1. Poor academic performance is re-lated to the onset, frequency, persis-

tence, and seriousness of delinquent offending in both boys and girls. Higher academic performance, conversely, is associated with refraining or desisting from offending. Moreover, poor academic performance predicts delinquency independent of socioeconomic status.

2. Cognitive deficits and attention problems are common correlates of both academic performance and delinquency.

3. Interventions that improve academic performance co-occur with a reduction in the prevalence of delinquency.

Maguin and Loeber (1996) tempered these generalizations in two ways. First, the strength of the relationship between academic performance and delinquency, particularly with respect to age and gender, is not clearly established. Second, methodological and conceptual difficulties hinder attempts to ascertain which interventions are effective in enhancing academic performance and reducing delinquency.

Our review of the research supports these concerns and reveals additional conceptual and practical problems. The tendency to treat academic failure as a unitary phenomenon fails to capture the complexity of learning situations. For example, a student's academic performance can vary considerably between content areas (e.g., language arts, science, mathematics, social studies, art) and over time. Poor performance in one content area does not necessarily generalize to other areas. Moreover, many students who experience academic difficulties do not engage in antisocial behavior, and many academically successful students are persistently deviant in their conduct. Seldom do researchers explain those factors that mediate the relationship between academic failure and antisocial conduct for different populations of students at different points in their development. Furthermore, though academic failure may correlate with antisocial conduct in general, it does not predict specific forms of antisocial behavior.

Other variables, particularly family and peer dynamics, intervene to shape the direction and severity of troublesome conduct.

Research supports the general conclusion that the greater the academic quality of the school, the lower the level of school crime and violence (Verdugo & Schneider, 1999). Although interventions that improve academic performance can have collateral effects on reducing antisocial conduct, this finding requires further consideration. Our view is that some academic interventions seem more likely than others to produce desirable social skills. For example, there is little empirical justification to assert that improving an antisocial student's mathematical skills will necessarily direct that student toward prosocial behavior. On the other hand, an emphasis on improving a student's communication skills through reading, writing, speaking, listening, and artistic expression can build that student's repertoire of prosocial skills essential for cooperation. Enhancing communication skills can also provide a student with an "emotional vocabulary" that allows him or her to better identify and talk about troublesome feeling states that might otherwise find expression in antisocial behaviors. Use of writing as a learning tool throughout the curriculum is particularly helpful in this regard. Moreover, *any* academic intervention with antisocial students is likely to have prosocial effects if it functions to establish appropriate bonds between students and their mentors.

Existing research also lacks clarity in how antisocial behavior is conceptualized and measured. There is an absence of agreed-upon valid and reliable instruments for measuring the cluster of violence-related attitudes and behaviors, particularly as these clusters vary by age and by cultural group. Other than offering incomplete "lists" of undesirable behaviors, many studies do not provide clear operational definitions of what is meant by "antisocial" and what is meant by "violent." Not all antisocial conduct is violent. Defying adult authority, running away, being unruly, stealing, or lying may be antisocial but not necessarily vi-

olent. Because violence is multifarious in nature, all expressions of violence cannot be treated as equal. For example, a distinction exists between *initiating* a violent act and *responding* violently when provoked. We should also differentiate among ongoing verbal torment of a victim by a bully, sexual harassment, and physical attacks between two rival gangs. To date, few studies make conceptual distinctions between the various ways in which young people express themselves through violence. One unfortunate consequence of such conceptual ambiguity is a tendency to treat negative *attitudes and values* as indistinguishable from undesirable *conduct*.

An additional conceptual difficulty centers on attributions of causality because risk factors and problem behaviors may be measured at the same time (Kingery, Coggeshall, & Alford, 1999). The research generally suggests that an individual's antisocial conduct is at least partially an outcome of poor academic performance, and often it is. It is equally likely that for many students, poor academic performance is an outcome of their disruptive behavior. To the extent that students begin schooling with aversive behaviors acquired at home, such social skill deficits will affect their ability to attend to and to fulfill academic expectations. Equally important is the social contagion effect of one student's aversive behaviors on the academic performance of others. Because the classroom is a public arena, the time taken to correct one student's behavior negatively influences the allocated instructional time of the teacher and the academic engagement of other students, who are distracted by the interruption. Research consistently supports a direct relationship between student time on task and student academic achievement (Brookover, Erickson, & McEvoy, 1997). Time on task, or academic engagement, is relevant to the academic performance of individual students and to students as a group.

We believe not only that academic failure and antisocial behavior exist in a reciprocal relationship, but also that this reciprocal relationship is context specific. Conditions in the home and conditions in the school can help to predict this relationship. *Antisocial behavior and academic failure reinforce one another within the context of ineffective school practices and ineffective parenting strategies.* Ineffective schooling, for example, can be both a cause and an effect of violent or other antisocial conduct. A pattern of academic failure provides few opportunities for the student to receive positive reinforcement. From the failing student's perspective, school then takes on aversive properties that increase the likelihood of escape, rebellion, uncooperativeness, and other negative behaviors. This cycle often results in school failure, dropping out, and involvement in delinquent groups.

Conversely, ineffective school responses to antisocial conduct have negative implications and influence the academic performance of students in general. One ironic example is assigning a student to "time-out" for a particular misbehavior or for truancy, thus relieving him or her from having to perform an undesirable task (e.g., attend school). Another example is the use of tests as a behavior management tool intended to bring into line poorly motivated, unresponsive, or unruly students. As antisocial behavior increases, school officials may administer even more aversive consequences, thereby increasing the student's antipathy toward requirements of the student role. Students perceived to be at risk of antisocial conduct, particularly boys and impoverished minority students, "are more likely to be punished, excluded, and controlled than to have their problems addressed in a therapeutic manner" (Walker et al., 1996, p. 197).

Two parallel lines of analysis offer promise for developing more effective school-based prevention and intervention programs. The research that advances a developmental perspective on delinquency and the research on effective schools that examines school climate are most relevant. Each line of inquiry emphasizes the climate in which problem behaviors emerge, and each directs interventions toward altering the environments in which children function.

A DEVELOPMENTAL PERSPECTIVE ON ANTISOCIAL BEHAVIOR

Research on correlates of delinquency, including family etiologies and developmental pathways, profiles the origins, direction, and consequences of antisocial behavior in children and adolescents (Catalano & Hawkins, 1996; Hawkins et al., 1998; Kelley, Loeber, Keenan, & DeLamatre, 1997; Loeber, 1996; Loeber, Keenan, & Zhang, 1997; Loeber & Stouthamer-Loeber, 1998; Moffitt, 1993; Patterson, Reid, & Dishion, 1992; Patterson & Yoerger, 1997; Walker, Colvin, & Ramsey, 1995). Researchers note that the development of antisocial behavior in children begins with minor transgressions and gradually advances toward more significant expressions of deviance as they enter adolescence. Early onset combined with progressive deterioration toward more varied and extreme antisocial behaviors characterizes the most seriously delinquent youth.

Research supports a bifurcated categorization of delinquent youth based upon the onset and maintenance of antisocial behavior. Moffitt (1993) identified two distinct groups of antisocial youth: "life-course-persistent offenders" and "adolescent-limited offenders." Similarly, the research of Loeber and his associates (1997) described "experimenters" and "persisters." The adolescent-limited offenders lack a childhood history of antisocial behavior. For them, the onset of antisocial behavior usually does not begin until age 12 or 13, varies according to the situation, and generally ceases by age 18 or 19. In essence, this group experiments with antisocial behavior under certain circumstances—most often in the presence of peers where there is no adult surveillance—but usually abandons this conduct in favor of more rewarding prosocial lifestyles. In contrast, life-course-persistent offenders begin their problematic behavior early. They then move toward varied and ever more serious manifestations of antisocial behavior and express such behavior in multiple settings. Offense seriousness escalates and often persists into adult

criminality. In the absence of effective interventions and rewarding prosocial opportunities, this group of young people poses the most serious threat to schools and to communities.

Conditions in the home help to predict early-onset and chronic antisocial behavior. Patterson and colleagues (Forgatch & Patterson, 1998; Patterson et al. 1992; Patterson & Yoerger, 1997) offered an interactional perspective that sees early-onset and chronic antisocial behavior in children as an outcome of coercive and inappropriate parental family management practices. The following parental behaviors are identified as critical determinants of antisocial behavior in children: (a) frequent use of harsh and coercive discipline (e.g., hitting); (b) being inconsistent in setting rules; (c) infrequent or poor monitoring of children; (d) limited family problem-solving skills, particularly in solving confrontations; (e) low levels of expressed affection and lack of parental involvement with children (lack of bonding); and (f) few positive reinforcements for appropriate behaviors. Personal problems such as substance abuse, depression, and marital strife also interfere with effective parenting.

Ineffective childrearing practices and child antisocial behavior are reciprocally related. Parents use reinforcing contingencies in the natural setting of the home that unintentionally shape the aversive behaviors they would like to end in their offspring (Patterson, 1997). Not only do parents of antisocial children fail to reinforce prosocial behaviors such as nonviolent, cooperative play with siblings, but these children are "literally trained to be aggressive during episodes of conflict with family members" (Forgatch & Patterson, 1998, p. 86). From early on, the child learns that coercive behaviors (e.g., temper tantrums, whining, threats) have functional value "in the sense that they are the only effective means of terminating conflict. Later, the child learns that antisocial acts such as stealing and lying are also functional" (Patterson & Yoerger, 1997, p. 122). In essence,

Over many thousands of trials during family interaction, the problem child learns via negative reinforcement to shut off irritable, aversive intrusions from parents and siblings with his or her own aversive counterattacks. With parents, these attack–counterattack sequences typically occur during discipline encounters and undermine the parents' abilities to socialize and supervise the child properly. (Stoolmiller, Duncan, & Patterson, 1995, p. 237)

Resolving conflict with family members may, therefore, parallel a process of escape conditioning (Patterson & Yoerger, 1997); the child learns to use coercive behaviors in order to escape from an aversive stimulus and then generalizes these learned behaviors to new settings and new relationships, such as those in school. The child's aversive behavior leads to rejection by teachers and prosocial peers. For early-onset antisocial children, this "deviancy training" begins at home in the preschool years and then later is reinforced and sustained in interactions with deviant peer groups and teachers. This developmental continuity places early-onset antisocial children at acute risk for substance abuse, school failure, delinquency, family violence, unemployment, adult criminal conduct, mental health problems, and a range of other nefarious behaviors throughout their life cycles.

The general conclusion that we draw from this research follows. Parents with few appropriate skills for raising and socializing their offspring tend to produce children who are socially unskilled and often hostile in their interactions with others. Because they are socially unskilled and aversive, these children in turn experience social rejection and failure (Patterson, 1997). They are rejected by adults, and they are rejected by their more socially skilled peers. Such rejection further drives these children toward aversive behaviors that are detrimental to academic achievement. Rejection and failure undermine their "social bond" to the school and their commitment to academic success (Catalano & Hawkins, 1996). Many are then drawn to comparably situated peers who also experience rejection and failure and who, in turn, reinforce one another's negative behaviors.

In the absence of effective interventions, the banding together of academically failing and socially rejected peers amplifies deviant behavior and serves as the basis for the emergence of deviant clique structures and deviant subcultures. These deviant subcultures both model and reinforce new and prior antisocial behavior in multiple settings; they set normative standards for those who join; and, finally, they help organize and direct deviant acts. Figure 1 reflects our interpretation of the interactions and reciprocal relationships present in this developmental sequence.

Although inept childrearing practices may set in motion a cascade of unfortunate outcomes, it is dangerous to conclude that poorly skilled parents are abusive or do not care for the well-being of their children. Often these parents believe that coercive practices are necessary to protect their children. Frequently, they model the parenting styles of their own caregivers. Garbarino (1995) described the difficulties of raising children who reside in high-risk, "socially toxic" neighborhoods characterized by high levels of poverty and crime. In order to protect them from drugs, shootings, and gangs and other predators, fearful parents may resort to highly restrictive and punitive measures with their young children (e.g., no outdoor play; threats;

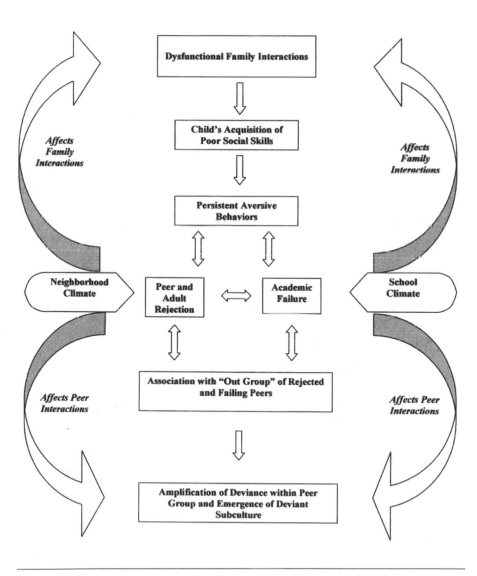

FIGURE 1. Early-onset antisocial behavior developmental pathway.

harsh physical punishments). Such parental behaviors, we believe, often are augmented with messages that condition children to be tough, aggressive, defiant, and distrustful of others. A socially toxic environment, thus, poses a developmental risk to children on two fronts: direct threats to their safety and the absence of normal and predictable opportunities for rewarding prosocial interactions. The resulting undesirable consequence is that attitudes and behaviors learned in order to survive in this socially toxic environment are maladaptive in other settings, such as school.

Despite the significance of current research, important concerns need to be addressed. For example, researchers have focused primarily on the antisocial behavior of boys; they have not offered an empirical basis to determine whether antisocial developmental processes and applied intervention strategies are comparable for girls. Moreover, not all children are affected in the same way by similar social and environmental conditions. The emerging resilient child research indicates that many children who come from disadvantaged homes and neighborhoods still manage to do well academically and socially. We also need to learn more about how patterns of child development vary according to the intensity and type of violence in the families and neighborhoods of children. For example, how does the physical or sexual victimization of children, whether by family members, adults outside the home, or peers, confound our understanding of antisocial development? Do physical, sexual, or psychological forms of child abuse have different developmental consequences for boys than for girls? The influence of media violence on the development and expression of antisocial behavior in various populations is another area of concern. Much more research needs to be done on how structural variables, including poverty and class-based social disadvantages, institutionalized patterns of racial discrimination, and community and neighborhood conditions, interact with family and peer group dynamics to influence child development. We need to know more about

how interventions at the individual and group levels can mediate the negative effects of these structural variables. We also need to know more about how schools affect parenting practices and how parents affect school practices relevant to the prevention and control of antisocial behavior among youth. Longitudinal studies will be required to properly investigate many of these issues.

Despite these concerns, clear advantages emerge when educators and researchers examine antisocial behavior from a developmental perspective. Research can guide the screening and early detection of troublesome behaviors that may progress to more serious transgressions. It can also help to identify coercive climates that produce behavioral transgressions in children. Early detection is critical to devising timely interventions with children and their parents. Another advantage of this research is that it suggests the need for different interventions at different points in the child's antisocial development. An effective intervention that targets a particular behavior at one point in time may not be effective at another. A developmental approach also suggests the need to address both academic skill deficits and social skill deficits as interrelated elements of an overall intervention strategy with antisocial youth. Interventions are unlikely to succeed if they consider the cluster of risk factors as discrete, particularly if they treat the conditions associated with academic success as separate from those associated with antisocial behavior in populations exhibiting both patterns. Many interventions, unfortunately, focus on one or the other rather than both as reciprocally related dimensions that need to be addressed concurrently.

Perhaps the most important implication of a developmental approach is the need to shift away from an overemphasis on the characteristics of individuals, to a greater emphasis on the characteristics of the environments that shape individuals. Both antisocial behavior and academic failure are context specific; each occurs within a climate in which identifiable conditions can help to predict problematic behavior and can be changed to

reduce such behavior. This means that if we wish to change the child, we must alter the interactional dynamic between the child and the environment and not merely change selected cognitions or characteristics of the child (e.g., his or her attitudes and beliefs). Programs that attempt to modify a child's attitudes, for example, will do little to alter the family, school, or peer group dynamics that encourage his or her antisocial behavior and academic failure.

Those calling for school reform often are disappointed with the results of reform initiatives because programs do not affect the environments in which students learn and behave. There is a need to address contextual and developmental concerns that focus on how situations can change individual tendencies and behavior patterns over time. Simply stated, we must change environments rather than focusing only on the "treatment" of individuals. The success of prevention and intervention programs, therefore, will hinge on our ability to recognize and change climates in which academic failure and antisocial behavior emerge and are reinforced (e.g., home, school, community).

EFFECTIVE AND INEFFECTIVE SCHOOL CLIMATES

Both the level of learning and the level of antisocial behavior vary from school to school. Each is related to the climate of a school, which helps to shape the interactions between and among students, teachers, administrators, parents, and the community. School climate consists of the attitudes, beliefs, values, and norms that underlie the instructional practices, the level of academic achievement, and the operation of a school (Brookover et al., 1997). School climate research offers a response to research findings that delineate a direct relationship between socioeconomic status and academic success.

For example, the early research of Jencks and associates (1972) suggested that the academic achievement of children is a function of family background.

Jencks argued that schools do not make a difference in overcoming the deficits that poor children bring to the classroom. Taken as a generalized finding, this research reinforced the stereotype that schools can do little to "change" a child who comes from a "bad" home. One policy implication of this early research is that investing in compensatory and other educational programs for economically disadvantaged children does little to alter their life chances.

School climate research challenges this view by providing examples of high-achieving schools located in the most racially segregated and economically depressed urban areas, where nearly every child masters grade-level objectives. Such schools cannot be accounted for by those who argue that schools do not make a difference. Effective schools share common characteristics, including student perceptions of high expectations for achievement, effective administrative leadership, a shared mission among teachers and staff, a commitment to appropriate assessments, students' sense of efficacy with respect to learning, and student perceptions of a safe environment in which to learn. A widely shared belief—a normative expectation—is that all students will master grade-level objectives regardless of their background. Effective schools exert positive influences on student behavior despite conditions in the home, social status, gender, race, or ethnicity.

Brookover and colleagues (1997) argued that teacher expectations for student performance and teacher judgments of student capabilities influence student achievement levels through their effects on student perceptions. In particular, student self-conceptions of academic ability (i.e., student beliefs about what they are able to achieve) and student sense of academic futility (i.e., student beliefs about whether the school "system" is stacked against them regardless of their abilities or efforts) together affect their decisions regarding academic behaviors (e.g., whether to do assignments). Both are influenced by (and help to influence) teacher expectations and judgments. For example, in research on a sample of Mich-

igan schools that controlled for the effects of race and socioeconomic status, school climate factors, especially students' sense of futility, accounted for 63% of the variation in mean school achievement between low- and high-achieving schools (Brookover & Erickson, 1975).

School practices, such as ability grouping or tracking, dramatically affect student conceptions of ability and sense of futility. For socially marginal and academically failing students, placing them into low-achieving "ability groups" or tracks with low expectations for academic success is especially detrimental to their subsequent school performance and to their nonacademic behavior (Oakes, 1985, 1990). Arguably, both tracking and special "pull out" programs for only those students presumed to be "gifted and talented" have inimical consequences for the overall achievement expectations of a school, for the allocation of resources in a school, and for the distribution of self-conceptions of ability among students. In their review, Brookover and associates offered the following conclusion:

> We know that ability grouping has at least three profoundly negative consequences: it creates conditions for academic and social failure rather than mastery; it heightens tensions between groups, usually along racial and social class lines; and it undermines good citizenship by fostering feelings of injustice and resentment among those denied equal educational opportunity. (Brookover et al., 1997, p. 281)

Tracking is so controversial that many school systems claim to have established policies against it. Nevertheless, a de facto tracking system persists in a number of schools that ostensibly have ended the practice (Oakes, 1994). Tracking systems can persist because of logistical issues surrounding scheduling and the offering of advanced courses to selected students. For example, if an urban school is able to offer only one instrumental music class and one advanced math class for its eighth-grade students, this may mean that students who qualify are automatically placed in the same history, sci-

ence, English, and social studies classes. This virtually locks many of the more advanced students together for special considerations throughout the day.

Although school climate research emphasizes the need to set high performance expectations for teachers and students, caution is in order. Calls for educational accountability over the past two decades have resulted in a move toward enhanced graduation requirements and mandated proficiency tests. Yet higher student performance depends on an interrelated set of requirements that go beyond simply raising the demand level as reflected in high-stakes proficiency tests and more stringent graduation requirements. Equating a climate of expectations for academic achievement to scores on standardized tests can reinforce perceived differences between students who are "ready" for educational work and those who come from family backgrounds that presumably are less supportive of academic achievement. Urban teachers in particular, whose professional success tends to be measured by the percentages of their students who pass standardized tests, can become demoralized and adopt a besieged attitude toward students, parents, and their profession. This accentuates survivalist tendencies, including the tendency to concentrate efforts only on those students and parents who are perceived to "care" about schools and who help to support the teacher's tenuous feelings of efficacy and confidence. In a political world where proficiency tests alone are used as a blanket measure of school success, it becomes possible for those outside of the school system to selectively apply test results to bring sanctions against teachers and schools that are floundering.

Properly understood, school climate research supports the conclusion that affirming interpersonal relationships and opportunities for all to achieve mastery can increase achievement levels and reduce antisocial behaviors. For example, Glasser (1998) documented the transformation of an inner-city, low-achieving school beset with antisocial behavior among its students. The transformation toward academic achievement and prosocial behavior was possible because of a systematic change in the way students and teachers related to one another—a change that began by emphasizing the elimination of coercive practices intended to "motivate" students. An obvious lesson from this study is that changing the climate of expectations, particularly as reflected in standardized test performance, will not be sufficient to change the school climate and achieve desired results. *A change in the demand level must be accompanied by a change in student opportunities for success, along with changes in the relational system in which expectations for behaviors are communicated and reinforced.*

Thus, school climate research is important because it offers clear requirements for building such relationships and opportunities within schools. The first requirement is a safe environment where students and teachers can focus on academic and social skills development. The second is a sequenced curriculum that is understood and supported by faculty and students alike and that demands a high level of mastery from all students. Students do not receive credit for work that fails to demonstrate competence or to meet appropriate standards of performance. Third is a commitment to ongoing assessments that reflect the goals and mission of the school. Such assessments serve the diagnostic function of identifying endemic weaknesses that need to be corrected and building upon skills for learning. The fourth requirement is the elimination of school practices (e.g., ability grouping) that are predicated on the assumption that many students cannot and will not achieve. A final requirement is the affirmation and celebration of achievement for the purpose of enhancing commitment to academic progress for all and to the prosocial mission of the school. An effective school is imbued with an esprit de corps in which every member feels that he or she is a valued participant in working toward meaningful goals.

In summary, school climate research affords several advantages for those investigating the relationship between antisocial behavior and academic failure. It provides a contextual basis for understanding student performance and reveals basic replicable characteristics. Quite simply, the school climate literature emphasizes the capacities of students to succeed, and it avoids the tendency to demonize at-risk students in ways that diminish their chances for success. School climate research provides a basis for assessing which prevention and intervention programs are likely to be effective in addressing the reciprocal relationship that we know exists between academic failure and antisocial behavior.

SCHOOL CLIMATE AND PROGRAM EFFECTIVENESS

We have argued that effective school learning climates have direct, positive effects on the academic achievement and the prosocial behaviors of students. Yet schools, particularly urban schools, are fragile cultures continually beset by disturbances that negatively affect the character of internal social relationships. In turn, these social relationships profoundly influence the manner in which programs that are intended to improve academic achievement or to reduce antisocial conduct are implemented. The relative effectiveness of interventions in a school is circumscribed by the character of relationships among and between those implicated in program implementation. Fidelity of implementation and treatment integrity emerge as key issues in this regard.

Some aspects of school culture seem particularly inimical to fostering relationships essential for effective programming. For example, a widespread sense of futility among students and staff poses a serious impediment. Low rates of daily attendance for students, high rates of teacher and staff absenteeism combined with low levels of commitment, and high rates of teacher and student mobility suggest feelings of alienation. This pattern is common among poorly performing schools beset with low levels of student achievement and high levels of disruptive behavior. Even well-designed interventions may fail if there is poor commitment and a lack of continuity due to absenteeism and mobility.

Another challenge is the limited time and resources directed toward staff development generally and toward program implementation in particular. This includes a failure to provide more than minimal mentoring of new teachers, a tendency to place inexperienced teachers in the most challenging classrooms, and the frequent use of untrained substitutes. It also includes assigning teachers "add on" responsibilities for programs without giving them proper training or reducing their other responsibilities. Because time is a scarce resource, potentially successful practices will receive little support if teachers consider them to be too labor intensive. Often, intervention efforts fail because they are imposed from the top down as an additional responsibility. Those within the school who are expected to implement these programs may not have been given a voice in their design; they have little "buy in" or vested interest in the effort and thus do little to ensure its success. Even when programs are successfully implemented, their effectiveness diminishes over time without ongoing staff development for new teachers and administrators each school year.

Resources and training for school-based counseling and support services now constitute essential elements in most proposed interventions for those defined as at risk. Large caseloads and time constraints on support staff, however, can hamper potentially successful programs. The limitations of school counseling and support services are especially apparent when demands are placed on school officials to "treat" large numbers of students with a history of antisocial conduct (Walker et al., 1995). Unfortunately, the training of school personnel to educate and to cope effectively with these students is often inadequate (Sprague, Sugai, & Walker, 1998). Such training of teachers and others who work with challenging students and their parents may be little more than "baptism by fire" or "sink or swim." Even when special interventions with trained staff are available to students, they tend to be ineffective because they are limited in scope and not sustained over time. As aptly stated by Walker, Stieber, and Bullis,

> Our belief is that most social skills interventions are offered for far too short a time and in an inconsistent instructional manner in order to shape positive behavior. To be truly effective, social skills interventions should be planned and offered in a similar fashion as any other academic course of study and should be considered in terms of years rather than weeks, as is now the norm. (1997, p. 304)

Special support services available to students who have been bullied, sexually harassed or assaulted, beaten, abused, or harmed in other ways are also limited. Few teachers have training in victim assistance issues, yet a student's victimization experiences can have severe consequences on his or her academic performance and on the tendency to behave inappropriately. Seldom is the school able to do more than provide short-term help to such victims other than referral to private practitioners, who may charge a fee for service, or referral to human service agencies with overwhelming caseloads. For many victims of violence, such limited assistance will do little to modify their elevated risk for academic failure or antisocial conduct.

How school officials assess claims of violence in school and how they decide upon appropriate sanctions involving those alleged to be perpetrators of violence further complicates the effectiveness of programs intended to reduce violence. School officials respond to incidents of violence in vastly different ways. There are few clear guidelines on "standards of evidence" and "due process" when an allegation is made, and there may be conflicts over sanctions being either too severe or too lenient. Just as schools are subject to litigation for failure to provide a safe environment, so too do they risk litigation for their responses to those alleged to have violated conduct codes. If school policies are exacerbated by fear, then responses to antisocial conduct can become rigid and excessive.

Schools characterized by low achievement and high levels of antisocial behavior often rely upon suspension and expulsion as preferred means of social control. Although in certain instances the suspension or expulsion of a student is appropriate (e.g., felonies involving assaults on students or teachers), little empirical evidence exists to support the effective use of these measures with most disruptive students. In interactions between adults and students, suspension and expulsion usually exacerbate the difficulties of establishing the bonds necessary to manage behavior and to enhance commitment to academic achievement. Similar to coercive childrearing in the home, coercive school practices can unintentionally reinforce students' antisocial or other dysfunctional escape responses from aversive situations. Walker et al. (1996) argued in favor of providing a continuum of alternative placements for students who exhibit serious problem behaviors. Sustained follow-up of these students, we believe, is also essential once they are returned to their classroom or school of origin. The point is clear: If we wish to modify patterns of antisocial behavior and academic achievement, we must find ways to keep students in school.

We believe that many school-based prevention and intervention programs for students defined as at risk emerge in the absence of a coherent framework that would provide a supportive context for their effective application. In absence of such a clear rationale, program elements may be included in a seemingly random and inconsistent manner. Even a cursory review of the research on school-based violence prevention and intervention programs reveals concerns in this regard. For example, often a lack of coordination is noted between primary, secondary, and tertiary prevention efforts because no comprehensive strategic plan for implementing them exists at either the building or the district level (Walker et al., 1996). The need to screen students in order to appropriately place them into such programs also is evident. Moreover, too often schools take a simplistic approach to interventions, even when the problems they intend to ameliorate are

diverse, severe, and entrenched. This reflects a proclivity among program developers to view student antisocial behaviors as monolithic (as being alike), although clearly they are not.

One such example is the widespread use of "conflict resolution" programs intended to reduce violent encounters between students. Although such programs may be beneficial in helping students to resolve minor conflicts, there is no empirical basis to conclude that they will do much to alter more serious and pervasive problems (e.g., gang violence and patterns of bullying). Conflict resolution programs generally emphasize and teach individual social skills for negotiating disagreements between two parties who presumably are equal in power. Neither gang violence nor bullying fit this model; both involve complex group dynamics, intentions to do harm, and the targeting of victims who do not have the power to resist or negotiate. Claims that a school is addressing a gang problem or a bullying problem via a conflict resolution program are misleading and possibly dangerous. Clearly there is a need to differentiate between types of violence and the levels of risk that are the focus of interventions, as well as address the interface between the two.

Many violence prevention programs are offered for too short of a duration, do not target specific risk factors, and are not coordinated with broader community efforts (Zins, Travis, Brown, & Knighton, 1994). Failure to target specific problem behaviors in specific contexts expends energy and resources in well-intended but diffuse efforts that yield few measurable gains. Comparatively few programs are properly evaluated, particularly with respect to long-term effects. Often, intervention programs claim success if they measure short-term changes in students' cognitions about violence, even though temporary changes in knowledge or attitudes do not necessarily translate into enduring changes in behavior. Moreover, evaluative data often reflect only teacher and staff *opinions* about student behavioral changes, rather than being derived from direct measurement of target behaviors.

Programs that have the greatest likelihood of success are able to evaluate progress on attaining the school's academic and social goals. Ongoing assessment allows for adjustments in programs as aspects of the school's climate change. This requires the school to have in place a system for monitoring students' academic and social behaviors relative to key program goals and a trained staff able to interpret and apply the evaluative data. Unfortunately, in schools already made vulnerable by economic and other conditions beyond their direct control, program assessments and calls for accountability are seen as one more threat to their survival. Too often, evaluative data are so poorly presented to teachers and other staff that the findings are ignored.

Simply stated, formative evaluations may not be perceived as useful by those nonresearchers who are in a position to implement program changes. Moreover, program assessments may overlook what the school is doing well and instead focus on deficits and limitations. This, too, makes it difficult for school staff to accept and act upon research that implies criticism of their efforts. An additional complication is that schools often operate several programs simultaneously. Rarely does the evaluative research differentiate between program effects when multiple programs operate at the same time. As such, arguments over which programs are effective in reducing violence and in promoting academic achievement are confusing. Yet promising practices do exist. A review of research on school-based prevention and intervention programs reveals a core of principles to guide these school practices.

PRINCIPLES OF PROMISING SCHOOL PRACTICES

Although a comprehensive review of all the promising school-based prevention and intervention practices is beyond the scope of this analysis, a brief summary of some of the most central issues is in order. Based on our review of the research, we recommend the following promising practices:

1. *At the district, building, and classroom levels, educators should review practices that are not working to address antisocial behavior and academic problems and eliminate or modify these practices.* We offer two illustrations of questionable practices that are common. First, in violence-prone schools, enhanced physical security of buildings and increased surveillance of students (e.g., cameras, metal detectors, police patrols, random searches) and punishment-oriented responses to rule infractions (e.g., suspensions and expulsions) do little to create a climate of academic success or teach students prosocial skills. Temporary gains in security may, in the long run, be offset by a confrontational siege mentality among students and a reluctance to seek the help of school personnel in order to solve problems. A second example of questionable school programing reflects a misunderstanding of the importance of student "self-esteem." Because many have linked poor student self-conceptions or low self-esteem to both antisocial behavior and academic failure, school programs often reflect a simplistic approach to enhancing students' perceptions of themselves. Simply making a student feel better about himself or herself does not necessarily change undesirable conduct. Concerning academic achievement, Brookover et al. (1997) argued that a specific *type* of self-conception (i.e., a student's self-conceptions of academic ability) must be linked to legitimate mastery of academic skills and content areas. It is inappropriate to communicate that a student's performance is acceptable when he or she lacks the functional competencies required in society, even though such communications may make the student "feel good." There is a clear need to focus our efforts on enhancing student self-control and academic self-efficacy rather than on enhancing diffuse feelings of self-esteem.

2. *Schools should establish appropriate assessment practices for all students directed toward the early identification of problem behaviors and academic skill needs.* Early identification of students defined as at risk is essential to design-ing effective interventions. For those identified with an elevated profile of antisocial or other severe behavioral problems, more comprehensive "functional analysis" has proven to be one of the most rigorous and effective approaches to developing appropriate interventions (Neef & Iwata, 1994; Sprague et al., 1998). In addition, screening for academic skill deficits should rely upon multifactor assessments that allow for the timely modification of instructional approaches. Too often, screening is limited to standardized proficiency tests that are not administered until well into the academic year, thus hindering the development of timely academic remediation. This results in proficiency tests becoming more of a school sanctioning device than a tool for improving instructional practices or determining curricular options.

3. *Develop a schoolwide approach to modifying the learning climate in accord with research on effective schools.* In large measure, this means systematically modifying two interrelated dimensions: changing the way people relate to one another in the school system and changing the nature of the tasks that people are expected to perform in school. A few positive examples include (a) increasing the amount of instructional time (this often requires a change in scheduling practices); (b) substantial use of cooperative learning exercises; (c) use of active learning assignments that encourage students to employ skills to solve authentic "real world" problems; (d) use of service learning to teach both academic and social skills; (e) using "mastery learning" (i.e., small-step, sequential learning with repeated formative evaluations and feedback to students) as an instructional approach; and (f) providing opportunities for teachers to interact and share effective instructional ideas across grade levels and between buildings.

4. *Emphasize staff development as one of the top school priorities, and align staff development to building goals and programs.* Ongoing staff development is essential if programs to reduce antisocial behavior and improve academic success are to be effective. Ultimately, it is the staff that determines how well programs are implemented and whether they are sustained over time. Staff development also should be the vehicle through which each building establishes an accepted system of teacher and school accountability. This implies developing performance standards that are embraced throughout the school, with a means of preparing all staff to meet those standards. This may, for example, involve preparing teachers to collect data from their own classes and assess it in light of agreed upon school performance indicators.

5. *Increase the amount of adult–child contact time.* Research on antisocial children reveals two related problems: lack of bonding with caring adults and lack of adult monitoring and supervising of children. Both problems imply too little time spent between adults and children when they are meaningfully engaged with one another. Opportunities to establish positive, mentoring relationships with children can mitigate the negative consequences of inappropriate family and peer influences. Smaller classes, particularly in the early school years, tend to foster more intimate social bonds and increase the effective monitoring of both academic performance and the acquisition of prosocial skills. Where a reduction in class size may not be possible, extensive after school and summer school programs, particularly those that connect students with community organizations (e.g., Boys and Girls Clubs, Big Brother and Big Sister programs, churches, athletics and hobby groups) can be cost effective. Such programs increase opportunities for children to unite with adults in constructive activities, and they can have the collateral effect of moving children toward academic and social goals in ways that differ from formal instruction.

CONCLUSION

We have argued that patterns of interaction in families, neighborhood characteristics, and school climate are important predictors of both social behaviors and academic behaviors among young people. Because of their mission to educate all children, schools are places in which to concentrate efforts that build the values and skills necessary for young people to be assimilated into society. We believe that the success of these efforts is contingent on our ability to foster positive, supportive, and affective bonds with children. This relational system that circumscribes the lives of children also influences the effectiveness of interventions directed toward those who are most vulnerable.

With an emphasis on the importance of human relationships in mind, we end on a philosophical note. We live in complex times where the stressors on children, and on the adults who care for them, seem to be more complicated with each generation. Educators, in particular, understand the generational quality of their work. Each group of students, with all of their challenges, will be followed by the next group, and the next—perhaps with even greater challenges facing them. Each generation will demand a consistent effort to build relationships and to capture the energy and commitment for success in school and beyond. In such complex times, hope must be a part of the relationships we establish with children. Hope depends on shared purpose, on the belief that the future will be better, and on the belief that our past has had meaning.

About the Authors

ALAN McEVOY, PhD, is a professor of sociology at Wittenberg University and an authority on problems of violence in schools, the home, and community settings. His expertise is reflected in the books and articles he has published on effective schools, youth suicide, rape, child abuse, youth gangs, and strategies for reducing antisocial behavior in schools. He is cofounder of the Safe Schools Coalition and has chaired nearly 20 national conferences on school violence issues. **ROBERT WELKER,** PhD, is a professor of education at Wittenberg University and director of the Wittenberg Center for Professional Development. He is involved in collaborative school reform efforts and has published on topics of teacher professionalism, moral education, and social problems that affect schools, including youth violence. His book, *The Teacher as Expert: A Socio-*

logical and Historical Critique, won the Critics Choice Award in 1993 as one of the top books in the field. Address: Alan McEvoy, Dept. of Sociology, Wittenberg University, Ward St. at N. Wittenberg, Springfield, OH 45501; e-mail: amcevoy@wittenberg.edu

References

Brookover, W., & Erickson, E. L. (1975). *Sociology of education.* Homewood, IL: Dorsey Press.

Brookover, W. B., Erickson, F. J., & McEvoy, A. W. (with Beamer, L., Efthim, H., Hathaway, D., Lezotte, L., Miller, S., Passalacqua, J., & Tornatzky, L.). (1997). *Creating effective schools: An in-service program for enhancing school learning climate and achievement.* Holmes Beach, FL: Learning Publications.

Catalano, R. F., & Hawkins, J. D. (1996). The social development model: A theory of antisocial behavior. In J. D. Hawkins (Ed.), *Delinquency and crime: Current theories* (pp. 149–197). New York: Cambridge University Press.

Elliott, D. S., Hamburg, B. A., & Williams, K. R. (Eds.). (1998). *Violence in American schools: A new perspective.* Cambridge, UK: Cambridge University Press.

Forgatch, M. S., & Patterson, G. R. (1998). Behavioral family therapy. In F. M. Dattilio (Ed.), *Case studies in couple and family therapy: Systematic and cognitive perspectives* (pp. 85–107). New York: Guilford Press.

Garbarino, J. (1995). *Raising children in a socially toxic environment.* San Francisco: Jossey-Bass.

Glasser, W. (1998). *Choice theory: A new psychology of personal freedom.* New York: HarperCollins.

Hawkins, J. D., Farrington, D. P., & Catalano, R. F. (1998). Reducing violence through the schools. In D. S. Eliot, B. A. Hamburg, & K. R. Williams (Eds.), *Violence in American schools: A new perspective* (pp. 188–216). Cambridge, UK: Cambridge University Press.

Hawkins, J. D., Herrenkohl, T., Farrington, D. P., Brewer, D., Catalano, R. F., & Harachi, T. W. (1998). A review of predictors of youth violence. In R. Loeber & D. P. Farrington (Eds.), *Serious & violent juvenile offenders: Risk factors and successful interventions* (pp. 106–146). Thousand Oaks, CA: Sage.

Herrenkohl, T., Maguin, E., Hill, K., Hawkins, J., Abbott, R., & Catalano, R. (1998). *Childhood and adolescent predic-*

tors of youth violence. Seattle: University of Washington, Seattle Social Development Project.

Huizinga, D., & Jakob-Chien, C. (1998). The contemporaneous co-occurrence of serious and violent juvenile offenders and other problem behaviors. In R. Loeber & D. Farrington (Eds.), *Serious & violent juvenile offenders: Risk factors and successful interventions* (pp. 47–67). Thousand Oaks, CA: Sage.

Jencks, C., Smith, M., Acland, H., Bane, M., Cohen, D., Gintis, H., Heyns, B., & Michelson, S. (1972). *Inequality: A reassessment of the effect of family and schooling in America.* New York: Basic Books.

Kelley, B. T., Loeber, R., Keenan, K., & DeLamatre, M. (1997). *Developmental pathways in boys' disruptive and delinquent behavior.* Office of Juvenile Justice and Delinquency Prevention Bulletin, Washington, DC, NCJ 165692.

Kingery, P., Coggeshall, M., & Alford, A. (1999). Weapon carrying by youth: Risk factors and prevention. *Education and Urban Society, 31*(3), 309–333.

Lipsey, M. W., & Derzon, J. (1998). Predictors of violent or serious delinquency in adolescence and early adulthood: A synthesis of longitudinal research. In R. Loeber & D. P. Farrington (Eds.), *Serious and violent juvenile offenders: Risk factors and successful interventions* (pp. 86–105). Thousand Oaks, CA: Sage.

Loeber, R. (1996). Developmental continuity, change, and pathways in male juvenile problem behaviors and delinquency. In J. D. Hawkins (Ed.), *Delinquency and crime: Current theories* (pp. 1–27). Cambridge, UK: Cambridge University Press.

Loeber, R., & Farrington, D. P. (Eds.). (1998). *Serious & violent juvenile offenders: Risk factors and successful interventions.* Thousand Oaks, CA: Sage.

Loeber, R., Keenan, K., & Zhang, Q. (1997). Boys' experimentation and persistence in developmental pathways toward serious delinquency. *Journal of Child and Family Studies, 6,* 321–357.

Loeber, R., & Stouthamer-Loeber, M. (1998). Juvenile aggression at home and at school. In D. S. Elliott, B. A. Hamburg, & K. R. Williams (Eds.), *Violence in American schools: A new perspective* (pp. 94–126). Cambridge, UK: Cambridge University Press.

Maguin, E., & Loeber, R. (1996). Academic performance and delinquency. In M. Tonry (Ed.), *Crime and justice: A review of research* (Vol. 20, pp. 145–264). Chicago: University of Chicago Press.

Moffitt, T. E. (1993). Adolescence-limited and life-course-persistent antisocial behavior: A developmental taxonomy. *Psychological Review, 100,* 674–701.

Neef, N. A., & Iwata, B. A. (1994). Current research on functional analysis methodologies: An introduction. *Journal of Applied Behavioral Analysis, 27,* 211–214.

Oakes, J. (1985). *Keeping track: How schools structure inequality.* New Haven, CT: Yale University Press.

Oakes, J. (1990). *Multiplying inequalities: The effects of race, social class, and tracking on opportunities to learn mathematics and science.* Santa Monica, CA: Rand.

Oakes, J. (1994). More than misapplied technology: A normative and political response to Hallinan on tracking. *Sociology of Education, 67*(2), 84–89.

Patterson, G. R. (1997). Performance models for parenting: A social interactional perspective. In J. E. Grusec & L. Kuczynski (Eds.), *Parenting and children's internalization of values: A handbook of contemporary theory* (pp. 193–226). New York: Wiley.

Patterson, G. R., Reid, J. B., & Dishion, T. J. (1992). *Antisocial boys: A social interactional approach* (Vol. 4). Eugene, OR: Castalia.

Patterson, G. R., & Yoerger, K. (1997). A developmental model for late-onset delinquency. In D. W. Osgood (Ed.), *Nebraska symposium on motivation: Vol. 44. Motivation and delinquency* (pp. 119–177). Lincoln: University of Nebraska Press.

Sprague, J., Sugai G., & Walker, H. (1998). Antisocial behavior in schools. In S. Watson & F. Gresham (Eds.), *Handbook of child behavior therapy* (pp. 451–474). New York: Plenum.

Stoolmiller, M., Duncan, T. E., & Patterson, G. R. (1995). Predictors of change in antisocial behavior during elementary school for boys. In R. H. Hoyle (Ed.), *Structural equation modeling: Concepts, issues, and applications* (pp. 236–253). Thousand Oaks, CA: Sage.

Tonry, M., & Moore, M. H. (Eds.). (1998). *Youth violence.* Chicago: The University of Chicago Press.

Verdugo, R., & Schneider, J. (1999). Quality schools, safe schools: A theoretical and empirical discussion. *Education and Urban Society, 31*(3), 286–308.

Walker, H. M., Colvin, G., & Ramsey, E. (1995). *Antisocial behavior in schools: Strategies and best practices.* Pacific Grove, CA: Brooks/Cole.

Walker, H. M., Horner, R. H., Sugai, G., Bullis, M., Sprague, J. R., Bricker, D., & Kaufman, M. J. (1996). Integrated approaches to preventing antisocial behavior patterns among school-age children and youth. *Journal of Emotional and Behavioral Disorders, 4*(4), 194–209.

Walker, H. M., Stieber, S., & Bullis, M. (1997). Longitudinal correlates of arrest status among at-risk males. *Journal of Child and Family Studies, 6*(3), 289–309.

Zins, J. A., Travis, L., Brown, M., & Knighton, A. (1994). Schools and prevention of interpersonal violence: Mobilizing and coordinating community resources. *Special Services in the Schools, 8*(2), 1–19.

Youth Violence:

Psychosocial Risk Factors, Treatment, Prevention, and Recommendations

JAVAD H. KASHANI, MICHAEL R. JONES,
KURT M. BUMBY, AND LISA A. THOMAS

This article provides mental health professionals with a contemporary review of the youth violence literature by discussing relevant psychosocial risk factors, treatment approaches, prevention programs, and recommendations. PsycINFO, Medline, and manual searches of the literature were conducted to locate the most relevant articles. Preference was given to studies that used rigorous scientific methodology (e.g., adequate sample size, random assignment, control groups) to investigate the topic. It was concluded that violent behavior in youth is linked with multiple psychosocial factors. The most effective treatment and prevention programs appear to be those that simultaneously address the multiple factors related to youth violence. Finally, the authors make recommendations for mental health professionals, law enforcement and juvenile justice personnel, parents, and others who come in contact with violent youth.

VIOLENCE IS PERHAPS ONE OF THE most serious social problems among youths in the United States today. This endemic problem is highlighted by comparisons of juvenile crime in the United States and in Canada. Whereas the arrest rate for property offenses committed by youth in both countries is similar, the arrest rate for violent offenses committed by youth in the United States is twice that of the arrest rate in Canada (Sickmund, Snyder, & Poe-Yamagata, 1997). Federally compiled statistics over the past 10 years have indicated that arrests for juvenile-perpetrated *Violent Crime Index* offenses (i.e., murder and nonnegligent manslaughter, forcible rape, robbery, aggravated assault) rose 183% from 1988 to 1994. During 1995 and 1996, arrests for juvenile violent crime decreased from the previous year (8% and 12%, respectively; Federal Bureau of Investigation, 1989 through 1997). This decrease in the arrest rate is attributed to decreased arrests of younger juveniles and of African American males for gun-related crimes (Office of Juvenile Justice and Delinquency Prevention, 1997). Despite these recent decreases, however,

the arrest rate for juveniles still remains disproportionately high when compared with other age groups (Federal Bureau of Investigation, 1997). These figures reflect only the number of juvenile *arrests* for violent offenses and not the much higher actual rate of violent crime (Dunford & Elliot, 1984). In addition, the very high rate of youth violence during the last decade will likely continue to be high throughout the next few decades for several reasons. First, the number of youth in the population is expected to increase by more than 20% (Reno, 1995). Second, many children and adolescents who commit violent crimes today will continue their criminal behaviors until they reach 40 or 50 years of age, thus increasing the overall rate of violence in

the United States (Farrington et al., 1993). Third, the pendulum is currently swinging away from rehabilitation and toward incarceration of violent youth (Melton, Petrila, Poythress, & Slobogin, 1997). This swing may increase the number of untreated violent youth and adult offenders in the population.

Sadly, with the pervasiveness of violent crime in U.S. society today, many individuals fear walking in their own neighborhoods or leaving their homes unlocked. The quotation, "Nine-tenths of mankind are more afraid of violence than of anything else" (Walter Bagehot, 1880, as cited in Murphy, 1981) may be truer today than when it was stated more than 100 years ago. In addition, beyond these fears and beyond the physical and emotional pain suffered by victims of violent crime are the staggering financial costs to society. It has been estimated that in excess of $60 billion is spent annually on victims' medical treatment and lost productivity, as well as on direct costs to the criminal justice system (Roth & Moore, 1995). The anticipated increase in violent crime committed by youth during the next decade will also be accompanied by an increase in the annual costs resulting from that violence. Thus, considering the extent of the emotional, social, and financial strains caused by youth committing violent crimes today—and the anticipated increase in the very near future—it is imperative that legislators, juvenile justice personnel, and mental health professionals act swiftly to interrupt this dangerous trend by implementing the policies and programs shown to be effective in treating and preventing youth violence. In order for these policies and programs to be effective, they must target the multitude of psychosocial risk factors linked to violent behavior in youth. Clearly, a decrease in the overall violent crime rate is a desirable social goal. Therefore, violent youth, who commit a large portion of the violent acts in the United States, need to be the target population for successful treatment and prevention programs.

When youth violence is brought to the attention of juvenile justice personnel, psychologists and other mental health professionals often become involved. In fact, the juvenile court is the legal system division that most frequently requests the expert opinions of mental health professionals (Melton et al., 1997). These professionals, whether serving as administrators, consultants, or therapists, are therefore in a position to provide effective prevention and treatment programs for violent youth.

The purpose of this article is to review contemporary research on the psychosocial risk factors, successful treatment approaches, and prevention strategies pertaining to youth violence. We used the PsycINFO and Medline databases and manual searches of the literature to locate the most relevant articles. Empirical studies were included in the review

only if they used more rigorous scientific methodology (e.g., random assignment, demographically matched control groups, sufficient sample size) and were conducted on samples of seriously aggressive or violent youth. Theoretical articles were included to provide a context in which the empirical findings can be interpreted or to fill in gaps in the empirical literature. Moreover, recommendations for professionals and nonprofessionals who come in contact with violent youth—and recommendations for future research—were provided. Studies exclusively investigating the psychosocial risk factors and treatment of sexually aggressive youth were excluded. (For a review of this latter topic, refer to Barbaree, Marshall, & Hudson, 1993, or Ryan & Lane, 1997.) Moreover, although biological factors are important to the understanding of youth violence, they are only briefly mentioned in this article. The reader is referred to Scarpa and Raine (1997) for a review of the biological literature.

DEFINITIONS

For this review, the term *youth* will refer to children ages 8 to 17 years. The term *violent* is often used to describe the more serious *aggressive* behaviors that result in the adjudication of the perpetrator in a legal setting (Borduin & Schaeffer, 1998). The U.S. Department of Justice, in the *Violent Crime Index*, categorizes four specific types of violent crime: (a) murder and nonnegligent manslaughter, (b) forcible rape, (c) robbery, and (d) aggravated assault (i.e., unlawful attack for the purpose of inflicting severe bodily injury; Bureau of Justice Statistics, 1996). Because the terms aggressive and violent are often used interchangeably in the literature, this review included recent studies that examined the psychosocial risk factors, treatment, and prevention pertaining to violent and aggressive youth. In addition, the term *risk factors* is often used to collectively describe the characteristics or events that increase the chances for the onset of a problem (e.g., violent behavior). Essentially, risk factors make an individual

more vulnerable to experiencing a problem (Kazdin, 1996). Researchers have also attempted to understand youth violence by identifying *protective factors*, which are characteristics or events that decrease the chances for the onset of a problem (Kazdin, 1996). However, because much more attention has been devoted to the identification of psychosocial risk factors related to youth violence, this review will focus on psychosocial risk factors.

PSYCHOSOCIAL RISK FACTORS

The psychosocial risk factors contributing to violence or aggression in youth have been researched from a variety of theoretical perspectives, including biological, ethological, anthropological, and sociological frameworks. Unfortunately, singular theoretical approaches have largely been insufficient in reliably explaining or predicting such a complex phenomenon as youth violence. The recognition of this complexity has led investigators to explore youth violence within a multidimensional psychosocial framework that includes individual, family, peer, school, and community/cultural variables (Borduin & Schaeffer, 1998; Henggeler, 1989; Kazdin, 1996; Loeber & Farrington, 1998; Ollendick, 1996; Stoff, Breiling, & Maser, 1997). The identification of psychosocial risk factors within this multidimensional framework has served as the basis for interventions and prevention strategies in the mental health field. Finally, it must be acknowledged that the psychosocial factors placing youth at risk for committing violence have been identified from correlational studies; no empirical examinations have led to conclusive identification of specific variables that *cause* youth violence.

Individual Variables

A number of individual or personal characteristics have been associated with violent behavior in youth. For example, a difficult temperament during infancy has been associated with subsequent aggressive behavior during childhood and adolescence. Also, the initiation of delinquent and violent behavior early in a child's life puts him or her at high risk for violent behavior in adolescence and beyond (Howell, 1995). Many developmentalists have suggested that difficult temperament is a product of the interaction between the child's biological predisposition and the parents' behavior toward the child (e.g., Lyons-Ruth, 1996). Indeed, investigators have identified a variety of physiological correlates, such as low resting heart rates (Raine & Jones, 1987), low serotonin activity in the central nervous system (Kruesi et al., 1990), low cortisol (Lahey, McBurnett, Loeber, & Hart, 1995), and high testosterone (Olweus, Mattsson, Schalling, & Low, 1988), in aggressive children and adolescents. Other biological factors, such as perinatal difficulties, minor physical abnormalities, and brain damage, have also been implicated (Howell, 1995).

Cognitive deficits have also been found among youth who exhibit violent behavior. Specifically, violent youth possess lower levels of moral reasoning (Arbuthnot, Gordon, & Jurkovic, 1987), abstract reasoning (Scguin, Pihl, Harden, Tremblay, & Boulerice, 1995), and problem solving (Seguin et al., 1995) than do nonviolent youth. In addition, researchers have consistently identified low verbal IQ scores among aggressive youth (Farrington, 1991). Furthermore, these youth more frequently maintain hostile attributional biases than do their nonaggressive peers. Such biases involve inappropriately interpreting the behaviors of others as hostile in the absence of true hostile intent (Crick & Dodge, 1994). Although we were unable to locate a study describing the diagnostic characteristics of violent youth, our clinical experience has indicated that the young people who appear in juvenile justice and psychiatric settings for violent behavior usually meet the diagnostic criteria of the *Diagnostic and Statistical Manual of Mental Disorders* (4th ed.; American Psychiatric Association, 1994) for Conduct Disorder, Parent–Child Relational Problem, Attention-Deficit/Hyperactivity Disorder (ADHD), or a depressive disorder.

Finally, although they are not psychosocial variables per se, the demographic characteristics of gender and race may serve as risk factors for violence. In 1995, boys under 18 years of age were arrested five times more frequently for violent crimes than were girls in the same age group (Federal Bureau of Investigation, 1996). This gender difference in violent crime has reflected differing socialization practices as well as biological differences (e.g., hormonal, strength, size) between boys and girls (Pepler & Slaby, 1994). A dramatic increase in the rate of violence committed by female juveniles has recently occurred; in fact, this rate of violent offenses has risen to twice that of male juveniles over the past decade (Federal Bureau of Investigation, 1998). This recent increase in violent crimes by girls may be partially attributed to changing societal norms and socialization practices (Eron, 1992).

Race has also been identified as a potential risk factor for youth violence. Of all youth arrested for violent offenses, about one half are African American and about one half are Caucasian; in contrast, of all youth arrested for nonviolent offenses (e.g., theft, arson, vandalism), only one fourth are African American (Federal Bureau of Investigation, 1998; Snyder & Sickmund, 1995). Nonetheless, it is important to keep two important considerations in mind: First, it is unclear whether a disproportionately high number of African American youth are arrested for violent crimes or whether a disproportionately high number of Caucasian youth are arrested for nonviolent crimes. Second, these figures reflect only arrest rates and not incidents of actual crime. It is possible that the high number of African American youth arrested for violent crimes reflects unintentional bias in the arresting practices within the criminal or juvenile justice systems.

Family Variables

A variety of familial factors have been associated with violent behavior among youth. Specifically, a family history of criminal behavior and substance abuse, family management problems, family conflict, and parental attitudes favorable toward crime and substance abuse have been linked with youth violence (Howell, 1995). Further, parents of violent youth have supported aggressive behaviors by failing to reinforce prosocial behaviors (Patterson, 1982) and by modeling aggressive behaviors toward others (Widom, 1989). Moreover, overly harsh parental discipline (Farrington, 1991) and insufficient monitoring (Loeber & Stouthamer-Loeber, 1986) are associated with aggression in youth. Families of aggressive youth also show low warmth (Borduin & Henggeler, 1987), low cohesion (Gorman-Smith, Tolan, Zelli, & Huesmann, 1996), and high levels of marital conflict (Jouriles, Bourg, & Farris, 1991).

Parent–child interactional patterns are also problematic in families of violent or aggressive youth. For example, Patterson (1982) documented that families of aggressive youth often demonstrate a coercive process of interaction that ultimately leads to the development and intensification of aggressive behavior in children. When parents attempt to discipline or confront problematic behaviors, the child or adolescent behaves in an increasingly defiant or aggressive manner. The parents consequently retreat from their efforts to correct the misbehavior; by doing so, they negatively reinforce the child's escalating behavior. Likewise, when the child exhibits severe misbehavior, the parents may respond with overly harsh or abusive discipline that temporarily serves to halt this behavior. The illusory appearance of a cessation serves to reinforce the parents' overpunitiveness. In sum, these familial interaction patterns are bidirectional; the child and the parents ultimately reinforce each other's aversive and maladaptive patterns of responding (Patterson, 1982).

Particularly significant among the psychosocial risk factors at the family level is that of intrafamilial violence (Kashani & Allan, 1998). Specifically, adolescents who were maltreated as children commit more violence than do adolescents who were not maltreated as children. Moreover, those adolescents growing up in homes with multiple forms of violence (e.g., spousal abuse and child abuse) report committing higher rates of violent offenses themselves than do adolescents from homes with less violence (Thornberry, 1994).

School Variables

Several factors related to the school environment have been linked with aggression in youth, including strict and inflexible classroom rules, teacher hostility (Pratt, 1973), and lack of classroom management (Frude & Gault, 1984). In addition, youth in overcrowded schools are more aggressive toward peers than are adolescents attending uncrowded schools (Stephenson & Smith, 1989). Within the classroom, aggressive children have been observed to be more disruptive and off-task than nonaggressive peers (Dodge, Coie, & Brakke, 1982). Furthermore, low academic achievement, academic failure, lack of commitment to school, and school drop-out have been associated with delinquent and aggressive behavior (Hinshaw, 1992).

Peer Variables

Children and adolescents with poor peer relations exhibit verbally and physically aggressive behaviors that ultimately result in their rejection by prosocial peers (Dodge, 1983). Subsequently, these youth tend to associate with other rejected peers, further contributing to the commission of additional aggressive—or other deviant—behavior (Parker & Asher, 1987). Not surprisingly, affiliation with deviant peers has been found to be strongly correlated with antisocial behavior in youth (Borduin & Schaeffer, 1998). Aggressive adolescents become less violent when placed in groups with nonaggressive peers, and they revert to aggressive conduct when placed in groups with other aggressive peers (Feldman, Caplinger, & Wodarski, 1983). Aggressive and other delinquent youth may associate with antisocial peers as a way of meeting needs unfulfilled by their families of origin or by prosocial peer groups. For instance, juvenile gang members have reported that they derive a sense of belonging, purpose, and control over their environment, and that they welcome the structure and discipline that accompany gang membership (Walker, Schmidt, & Lunghofer, 1997).

Community and Cultural Variables

Several community-related variables have been linked with youth violence, such as the availability of firearms (Sloan et al., 1988), drugs (Burkstein, 1994), and alcohol (Moss & Kirisci, 1995). Researchers have found that the number of youth carrying guns or other weapons has increased dramatically over the past 15 years. Whether carrying weapons is perceived as a source of power or protection, or as a means to commit crimes, youth who carry guns or other weapons commit more violent acts (both with and without the use of firearms) than those who carry no weapons (Durant, Getts, Cadenhead, & Woods, 1995). In addition, delinquent youth who use street drugs such as cocaine commit more violent offenses than delinquent peers who do not use such drugs (Kingery, McCoy-Simandle, & Clayton, 1997). Higher rates of aggression have also been found among adolescents who began using alcohol at an early age (Moss & Kirisci, 1995); for those adolescents already prone to aggression, intoxication has been found to have a facilitating effect on their violent acts (White, 1997).

A consistent finding in the literature is that repeated exposure of youth to violence in the media leads to aggressive behavior and attitudes among them (e.g., Donnerstein, Slaby, & Eron, 1994). Decades ago, Albert Bandura demonstrated how social learning plays a role in the transmission of violent behavior when children view a violent model (Bandura, Ross, & Ross, 1961). Repeated exposure to violence through media reporting, such as that which occurred with recent shootings in several U.S. schools, also may serve to perpetuate violent behavior in youth.

Also at the community/cultural level, it has been reported that neighborhoods characterized by poverty, disorganization, much transition, and a low sense of community experience a high rate of youth violence (Hawkins, 1995). Not surprisingly, exposure to violence in the community (e.g., witnessing shootings or experiencing beatings or threats of violence) positively correlates with the frequency of violent adolescent behavior (Farrell & Bruce, 1997).

Summary

Thus, many variables at the individual, family, school, peer, and community/cultural levels are associated with youth violence. Indeed, there is no single formula or combination of psychosocial risk factors that is reliably associated with each violent youth. Therefore, mental health professionals who treat violent youth or advise juvenile justice personnel about the nature of youth violence must consider the multitude of influences at work.

TREATMENT

A wide variety of treatment approaches within cognitive–behavioral skills training, parent training, or family therapy frameworks have been implemented by mental health professionals in an attempt to address one or more of the many psychosocial risk factors associated with youth violence. *Cognitive–behavioral skills interventions* with seriously aggressive or violent youth—such as social skills and problem-solving training, cognitive restructuring techniques, role plays, therapist modeling, and behavioral assignments—can reduce delinquent or aggressive behaviors at home or in school. These approaches attempt to reduce violent behavior by directly addressing psychosocial risk factors within individual youth (e.g., ineffective problem solving, deficits in moral development). Unfortunately, little-to-no significant impact on long-term recidivism (i.e., recurrence of violent offenses) has been demonstrated with these interventions (Borduin, Heiblum, Jones, & Grabe, in press; Kazdin, 1996). *Parent training models*, whereby parents are taught methods for effective communication, conflict resolution, family problem solving, contracting, positive reinforcement, mild punishment, and modeling, are effective in reducing child noncompliance and aggressive behavior among preschool- and school-age children. These models attempt to reduce aggressive behavior by addressing the psychosocial risk factors that occur at the family level (e.g., poor parental monitoring and discipline practices, coercive family interactions). However, only minimal improvements in family functioning occur in families of violent youth, and again, no significant reduction in recidivism rates at follow-up has thus far been demonstrated (Barkley, 1997; Kazdin, 1996).

Functional family therapy (FFT) is a *family treatment approach* that incorporates interventions from systemic forms of therapy (e.g., replacing maladaptive ways of meeting family members' needs for intimacy and support with more adaptive methods), cognitive therapy (e.g., changing faulty attributions and unfair expectations in family members), and behavioral therapy (e.g., having parents monitor and reinforce positive child behaviors). FFT has been used with mildly aggressive youth (Alexander & Parsons, 1982) to reduce aggressive behavior by addressing risk factors at the familial level (e.g., coercive interactions) and at the individual youth level (e.g., hostile attributions). Because FFT addresses more than one type of risk factor, it would be expected to be more effective than either parent training or cognitive–behavioral therapy alone, and this appears to be the case. A few outcome studies have shown that FFT leads to improved family functioning, significant reductions in status offenses up to 2 years posttreatment for delinquent adolescents, and some reduction in rates of aggressive behavior (e.g., fighting; Alexander, Holtzworth-Munroe, & Jameson, 1994). However, no well-controlled outcome studies to date have shown that FFT significantly reduces serious antisocial behavior (e.g., robbery, assault) in youth (Borduin et al., in press).

Overall, the aforementioned approaches have been most effective with younger, nonviolent, or mildly aggressive youth (Henggeler, 1989; Kazdin, 1996). Unfortunately, they have been largely ineffective in reducing or preventing further violence with more serious or chronically violent offenders. As a result, many professionals and nonprofessionals are skeptical that the juvenile justice system and the mental health profession can rehabilitate violent youth (Melton et al., 1997). It has been argued that the approaches previously reviewed have not been successful for two main reasons: First, they have included interventions that focus on only one or two psychosocial risk factors associated with youth violence (e.g., individual cognitions, family relations) and have failed to simultaneously address the many other factors (i.e., peer, school, neighborhood) that contribute to youth violence (Mulvey, Arthur, & Reppucci, 1993). Second, these interventions are not ecologically valid in that they mostly occur in only one location, such as a mental health clinic or juvenile incarceration facility, and fail to affect the other influences on violent behavior (i.e., juvenile's home life, school, or neighborhood; Henggeler, 1989; Zigler, Taussig, & Black, 1992). Fortunately, there have been some notable advances and refinements in the treatment of violent juvenile offenders that compensate for these shortcomings, the most promising of which has been *multisystemic therapy* (MST; Henggeler & Borduin, 1990; Henggeler, Schoenwald, Borduin, Rowland, & Cunningham, 1998). Because MST is the only treatment approach to date that has successfully reduced rates of violent behavior in youth, it is described in detail here.

MST was developed in response to the lack of empirically validated, cost-effective treatment for violent youth behavior. It is a departure from the more traditional approaches such as residential and inpatient treatment, detention and incarceration, and outpatient or clinic-based services typically provided for violent youth (Henggeler, 1997). Occurring in the juvenile's home, school, and neighborhood, MST interventions

are flexibly tailored to the individualized developmental and psychosocial needs of each youth and his or her family. MST comprehensively uses intervention strategies to address the multitude of factors associated with violent youth, targeting the family system (e.g., improving family emotional bonding and parental discipline strategies), the school (e.g., increasing parent–teacher communication and child academic performance), peers (e.g., promoting involvement in extracurricular activities, structured sports, or volunteer organizations), and community agencies (e.g., eliciting help from social service agencies; Henggeler & Borduin, 1990; Henggeler et al., 1998). By making alterations in natural settings, this approach seeks to modify the real-world functioning of violent youth (Henggeler, 1997). Because treatment occurs in the community, MST is significantly more cost-effective than incarceration or inpatient treatment (Henggeler, Melton, & Smith, 1992). Though intensive, the course of MST is relatively brief; in fact, treatment usually involves 20 to 30 sessions and averages of 4 to 6 months (Henggeler & Borduin, 1990; Henggeler et al., 1998).

Success for those involved in MST is operationalized in terms of lower recidivism rates, improved family and peer relations, decreased behavioral problems at home and school, and lower rates of out-of-home placements (Henggeler, 1997). Evidence for the efficacy of MST has been consistently documented through numerous rigorously controlled outcome studies that have measured both instrumental (i.e., self-report questionnaires, observed family interactions) and ultimate (i.e., recidivism) outcomes with several samples of violent youth. Compared with youth involved in more traditional services, youth who participated in MST had significantly fewer arrests, reported fewer criminal offenses, and spent less time in detention at 1-, 2-, and 4-year follow-ups (Borduin et al., 1995; Henggeler et al., 1992; Henggeler, Melton, Smith, Schoenwald, & Hanley, 1993). This success has been attributed to the fact that the interventions that address multiple factors at multiple levels of functioning are individualized, flexible, and occur in the natural environment (Borduin & Schaeffer, 1998).

PREVENTION

The key to effective prevention lies in reducing psychosocial risk factors in the individual, peer, family, school, and community realms (Howell, 1995). To do this, there must exist organized, abundant, and sustained public and private investment of financial and human resources in families, communities, and the systems that support and protect them (Bownes & Ingersoll, 1997). Prevention efforts may be primary, secondary, or tertiary (Kazdin, 1996). Primary prevention and secondary prevention involve helping youth and their families before violent behavior develops or at the first occurrence of violence or aggression, respectively. Tertiary prevention (e.g., MST) involves treatment of youth and their families after violence has become a recurring problem for the particular person.

In a review of promising secondary prevention programs for antisocial or conduct-disordered youth, Kazdin (1996) concluded that a few family-based, school-based, and community-based programs have been somewhat effective in decreasing the number of psychosocial risk factors associated with antisocial behavior and in increasing the overall well-being and adjustment of children and adolescents at risk. He also noted that the evaluations of many of these prevention programs had not included a measure of the impact on recidivism rates. In our literature search, we found only two prevention programs for at-risk violent youth that evaluated or reported the actual effect of the programs on recidivism: the Positive Adolescent Choices Training (PACT) program by Hammond (1991) and the First Step to Success program by Walker et al. (1998).

PACT demonstrated efficacy in the reduction of violent offending among at-risk African American youth by using a 20-session, cognitive–behavioral group training format to teach anger manage-ment, social skills, and conflict resolution techniques. The effectiveness of PACT may be attributed to its direct intervention with psychosocial risk factors within the individual youth and in their relations to peers (e.g., social skills, social problem solving). A 3-year follow-up of middle school students who participated in the PACT program revealed that program participants were arrested for fewer violent offenses than were students in a control group (Hammond & Yung, 1993).

The First Step to Success program targets kindergartners who already show some aggressive or defiant behavior. This program lasts 2 to 3 months and involves specific interventions at school and at home, with close cooperation among the program consultant, the youths, parents, and teachers. Interventions are designed to target a variety of psychosocial risk factors associated with youth violence (e.g., ineffective parental discipline, poor peer relations, deficient academic progress). First Step to Success has been successful in reducing aggressive behavior in kindergartners, and this reduction has persisted into the second grade (Walker et al., 1998). Overall, these two programs appear to be effective in preventing youth violence because they alter several psychosocial risk factors before violent behavior becomes a pattern.

The Office of Juvenile Justice and Delinquency Prevention (OJJDP) has delineated a comprehensive approach to violent crime prevention and intervention among youth in a community. The OJJDP guidelines recommend that prevention efforts (a) address identified psychosocial risk factors, (b) target populations exposed to multiple psychosocial risk factors and communicate effectively with these populations, (c) address psychosocial risk factors early in a child's development, (d) confront the multiple psychosocial risk factors in multiple levels, (e) develop a continuum of prevention services across developmental stages, and (f) involve a team of well-trained and unified service providers (Howell, 1995).

The OJJDP guidelines allow for the analysis of psychosocial risk factors at the individual, family, school, peer, and community levels. Through community planning, the guidelines assist community leaders in reducing psychosocial risk factors for at-risk youth in the community. Other significant aspects outlined in the OJJDP prevention strategy include the assessment of community readiness for such programming, implementation and evaluation of a risk reduction strategy formulated for the specific community, development of a continuum of care, and a strong emphasis on outcome evaluation (Howell, 1995).

To assist communities in carrying out these prevention strategies, the OJJDP has awarded hundreds of Community Prevention Grants throughout the country. This funding has helped support numerous programs that address various risk factors associated with youth violence. These programs include conflict-resolution skills training for youth and their families; parent training; interventions aimed at reducing child abuse and neglect; school-based programs targeting truancy, academic failure, violence, and substance abuse; vocational training programs dealing with job readiness and skill development; neighborhood rehabilitation projects; and gang and gun prevention and intervention strategies (Bownes & Ingersoll, 1997). As previously indicated, however, investigators have only recently begun to evaluate the efficacy of such prevention programs in reducing the actual number of violent offenses committed by participating youth. Given the pervasiveness and staggering costs of youth violence, it is imperative that grants be used to fund only those programs for which long-term effectiveness has been empirically evaluated.

RECOMMENDATIONS

In addition to primary or secondary prevention programs implemented by mental health professionals, U.S. society as a whole must make efforts toward reducing the amount of violent offending. Indeed, the reduction of youth violence is the responsibility of everyone in the community. Several strategies must be taken by policy makers, community leaders, law enforcement personnel, mental health professionals, parents, and other adults to help youth develop a sense of personal accountability for their actions. The guiding force for such strategies should be research that investigates factors that place youth at risk for committing violent acts. The following recommendations are based on this research.

Reduce Media Violence

Movies, the news, prime time television, and even popular cartoons are frequently filled with violent content and thus increase exposure of youth to violence. These programs often show characters, whether real or fictitious, being positively reinforced for aggressive or violent behavior. Also, programs that attempt to highlight the negative consequences of violent behavior may inadvertently sensationalize such violence through repeated publicity and give attention to the offender and to the details of the crime. Although the public needs to be informed of current events, graphic details of violent crimes should not be given repeated, dramatic publicity. Indeed, evidence of the impact and problematic nature of excessive media attention has been documented, whereby adolescents have reported committing homicides to impress peers or to be on television (Kashani, Darby, Allan, Hartke, & Reid, 1997). It is therefore the responsibility of the media and advertisers to limit the amount of violent material to which youth can be exposed and the responsibility of people in the community to ensure that media follow through on this commitment. Initial attempts to inform consumers of the violent and graphic nature of television programming and music have occurred in the form of television rating systems and labels on recorded music. Moreover, parents can limit their children's exposure to media violence by monitoring what their children watch and by providing alternative,

nonviolent activities (e.g., board games, sports, arts and crafts, dancing, reading).

Limit Youth Access to Firearms, Drugs, and Alcohol

Reducing the access of youth to firearms, drugs, and alcohol may have an effect on the reduction of violent crime. This can be accomplished at national and local levels. On a national level, lawmakers must regularly review the effect of laws on the availability of firearms and drugs to youth and modify the laws, if necessary. On a community level, local law enforcement officials, legislators, and parents must unite to make decisions that will limit such access. Community adults not only would be responsible for imposing harsh consequences on those persons (e.g., drug dealers) and local businesses (e.g., liquor stores that sell alcohol to minors) that do not comply, they would also be responsible for educating children and adolescents about the myriad of negative consequences associated with these dangers. Moreover, community leaders need to positively reinforce businesses and young people who comply with the laws.

Involve the Schools

Principals, teachers, and school counselors can help to prevent youth violence by integrating programs similar to First Step to Success and PACT into their curriculum. Although such programs require some funding, the expense is much less costly than the violent acts committed later in adolescence or adulthood. Moreover, school systems need to implement some form of intervention other than suspensions or expulsions for those youth who behave aggressively on school grounds. Prohibiting a violent child from attending school will prevent further violent acts by that youth at the school, but it probably will have little-to-no effect on the rate of violent offending in the community. Indeed, suspension and expulsion probably change only the location of the violent offense. In addition, lack of school attendance and its

consequences (i.e., unstructured time, academic backsliding, decreased opportunities for learning) serve as risk factors for more violence.

When a child or adolescent behaves or threatens to behave violently, it would be helpful for a teacher, counselor, or coach to work with that youth's parent(s) or caretaker and involve the family in interventions that work to reduce violent offending (e.g., MST or First Step to Success interventions). In addition, teachers are invaluable to mental health professionals in identifying those children who show aggressive behavior or other risk factors for aggression. Identification and treatment of aggressive children in their early school years may serve to prevent future violent offending by these youths.

Promote Healthy Family Functioning

Federal, state, and local dollars should fund programs that directly involve the families of youth who are at risk for violent offending. Consistent with the treatment approaches of FFT and MST, parents should be educated and encouraged to do the following:

1. Promote a positive affective climate in the home by modeling values such as respect, trust, and cooperation;
2. Set reasonable and firm limits on their children's behavior;
3. Appropriately reward and punish their children's behavior based on each child's developmental level;
4. Model prosocial behaviors by participating in recreational, athletic, or religious groups, and avoid antisocial activities such as gang involvement and the abuse of alcohol and drugs;
5. Model respectful attitudes toward teachers, police officers, and other authority figures;
6. Successfully negotiate potentially stressful family situations, such as

those that occur in adoptive, foster, and stepfamilies; and

7. Elicit social support from extended family and friends and use this support as a buffer against stress.

Perhaps having new parents attend parenting classes would help parents to actualize these conditions in their families.

Mental health professionals in the community also need to be more proactive in identifying and intervening with parents who are experiencing marital discord in order to decrease the emotional strain placed on youth. Marital interventions may help to keep many families intact and would have the added benefit of increasing the financial resources for the children involved. Moreover, in families in which the parents were never married or have already been divorced, fathers must be encouraged and expected to provide emotional and instrumental support for their children. Many fathers and mothers may need extensive mental health services (e.g., substance abuse treatment, parent training, stress management, problem solving and communication skills training, psychotherapy) in order to help them become effective parents.

Ensure Community Persistence

Many families of delinquent and violent youth contain other family members who also have a long history of involvement with the juvenile and adult legal systems. The youth and adults of these families have learned how to either avoid or "play along" with rehabilitation attempts by local schools, family service agencies, and juvenile courts. What is needed, therefore, is persistence by the school or court personnel in eliciting cooperation from these individuals. These personnel must not limit their services only to families that demonstrate a willingness to cooperate. Even extremely uncooperative families must not be abandoned unless every creative attempt to help them has failed. It has been our experience that this latter group comprises only a very small proportion of the families in need of services.

A Caution

In this section, we offer a number of recommendations to prevent the further spread of youth violence. Of course, any new legislation or agency policy must seek a balance between an individual's personal freedom and the protection of other members of society. Therefore, actions such as reducing violence in the media, labeling youth or their families as "violent" or "at risk for violence" for purposes of treatment or prevention, and limiting access to firearms, drugs, or alcohol will all have potentially constricting effects on the constitutional or civil liberties of youth, their families, or other members of society. Therefore, all societal members must make informed decisions about any laws or policies that, by their nature, call into question the rights of the individual.

Directions for Future Research

Although all of the research reviewed for this article was conducted on aggressive or violent youth, the vast majority of studies involved young people who displayed some variation of just one form of violence (i.e., aggravated assault). There is scant literature investigating the psychosocial risk factors, prevention strategies, and treatment approaches with youth who have committed other violent acts (i.e., murder, rape, and robbery). Future studies need to focus on this latter population to determine if approaches such as MST are effective in treating adolescents who display this more serious violent behavior, or if prevention strategies such as First Step to Success prevent these types of violent behaviors in adolescence and adulthood.

Researchers should also focus their attention on identifying types of psychopathology other than violent behavior. For example, it would be helpful to mental health professionals to know how to identify which violent youth have diagnosable disorders, such as ADHD or a depressive disorder, so that empirically supported interventions can be incorporated into treatments such as MST. Moreover, investigating the conditions under which violent youth enter into the adult mental health system with diagnoses such as antisocial personality disorder may help to inform interventions that are directed at this latter population.

Increasing awareness and understanding of current trends in youth violence should result in additional research efforts directed toward the refinement of effective treatment and prevention programs. These studies should focus on discovering which specific interventions (e.g., family, school, peer, individual) are effective in reducing violence with various populations (i.e., analyzed by age, gender, race, onset of violent behavior). It is possible, for instance, that certain interventions are actually gender-specific or race-specific. If so, then only the most effective interventions with particular subgroups of violent youth would promote rapid therapeutic change and enhance chances of generalization to other contexts.

Another important area for future research is the investigation of how mental health researchers can best disseminate their findings to professionals in other areas (e.g., directors of child protective services, juvenile justice personnel, professionals in the school system). Indeed, there appears to be a great discrepancy between empirically supported interventions and prevention programs and the services that are actually delivered to violent youth. Research needs to determine the most efficient and effective way to persuade professionals outside of academia to implement empirically supported programs in their communities.

Finally, long-term longitudinal studies (i.e., ones that span a decade or more) that evaluate the effectiveness of various prevention and treatment approaches are needed. When such studies are conducted, researchers should calculate the extent of the financial savings to our society. This information can then be used to motivate legislators and service delivery personnel to implement effective programs on a more widespread basis.

CONCLUSION

Violence committed by youth is a pervasive social problem in the United States that has deleterious effects on the current and future lives of youth committing the violent acts, on many victims, and on common citizens. This is a somber picture for the country that serves as the world's superpower and as an ideal to many other industrialized countries. The recognition of psychosocial risk factors for youth violence has begun to guide the development and implementation of prevention and treatment strategies for violent youth and their families.

Indeed, a number of comprehensive primary and secondary prevention programs have been developed in an attempt to forestall or lessen violent behavior among youth. However, with few exceptions, many of these programs currently lack systematic evaluations of their efficacy. Prevention programs, whether conceived by mental health professionals or government personnel, should be based on the extant literature pertaining to youth violence and should be empirically evaluated. Once effective prevention programs are identified, it then becomes the responsibility of lawmakers, mental health professionals, and community leaders to coordinate efforts and implement these programs in their communities. With respect to tertiary prevention, MST is recognized as the most promising treatment approach to date for chronically delinquent and violent youth, from both a cost-effective and recidivism perspective. Experts (see Loeber & Farrington, 1998; Ollendick, 1996) agree that MST is successful because it simultaneously addresses multiple psychosocial risk factors associated with violent behavior in youth (e.g., individual youth characteristics, family relations, parenting behavior, peer relations, school functioning) and because interventions are delivered in the youth's natural environment (e.g., home, school, and neighborhood). To assist mental health professionals, juvenile justice and law enforcement personnel, and school staff who come into frequent contact with violent youth, a treatment manual is now available (Henggeler et al., 1998).

A final implication of our conclusions is that managed health care companies and agencies must recognize their role in treating violent youth. These companies must no longer simply approve one or two visits by the individual and a parent to a mental health professional. Rather, to behave responsibly, these companies must consider the pervasiveness and dangerousness of youth violence and authorize only the most effective treatment approaches. We hope that case managers in managed care companies use readily available information, such as that reviewed in this article, to justify the low expenses needed for the innovative, home-based, and intensive services that violent youth require. These alternatives are much less expensive, and much more effective, than the more common forms of incarceration or inpatient treatment currently authorized.

About the Authors

JAVAD H. KASHANI, MD, is a professor and chief, Division of Psychiatry, and professor of pediatrics and psychology at the University of Missouri–Columbia. He is also director of children's services at Mid-Missouri Mental Health Center. **MICHAEL R. JONES**, MA, is a graduate student seeking a PhD in clinical psychology at the University of Missouri Columbia. His current scientific and clinical interests are in forensic psychology, and the assessment and the treatment of juvenile delinquency, adolescent sexual offending, child abuse, and child neglect. **KURT M. BUMBY**, PhD, is the clinical director for the Missouri Division of Youth Services and is a clinical assistant professor of psychiatry and medical psychology at the University of Missouri–Columbia School of Medicine. In addition, he is the director of sexual offender services at Behavioral Health Concepts, Inc., in Columbia, Missouri. Presently, his professional practice, research interests, and publications involve the assessment and management of sexual offenders, juvenile delinquency, parricide, and child maltreatment. **LISA A. THOMAS**, MD, is finishing her child and adolescent psychiatry fellowship at the University of Missouri–Columbia, where she also completed medical school and residency in general psychiatry. She holds a master's degree in clinical psychology from Washington University in St. Louis. Address: Javad H. Kashani, Case Western Reserve University at Laurelwood Hospital, 5900 Euclid Ave., Cleveland, OH 44094.

References

Alexander, J. F., Holtzworth-Munroe, A., & Jameson, P. B. (1994). The process and outcome of marital and family therapy: Research review and evaluation. In A. E. Bergin & S. L. Garlfield (Eds.), *Handbook of psychotherapy and behavior change* (4th ed., pp. 595–630). New York: Wiley.

Alexander, J. F., & Parsons, B. V. (1982). *Functional family therapy*. Monterey, CA: Brooks/Cole.

American Psychiatric Association. (1994). *Diagnostic and statistical manual of mental disorders* (4th ed.). Washington, DC: Author.

Arbuthnot, J., Gordon, D. A., & Jurkovic, G. L. (1987). Personality. In H. C. Quay (Ed.), *Handbook of juvenile delinquency* (pp. 139–183). New York: Wiley.

Bandura, A., Ross, D., & Ross, S. (1961). Transmission of aggression through imitation of aggressive models. *Journal of Abnormal and Social Psychology, 63,* 575–583.

Barbaree, H. E., Marshall, W. L., & Hudson, S. M. (1993). *The juvenile sex offender.* New York: Guilford.

Barkley, R. A. (1997). *Defiant children: A clinician's manual for assessment and parent training* (2nd ed.). New York: Guilford.

Borduin, C. M., Heiblum, N., Jones, M. R., & Grabe, S. A. (in press). Community-based treatment for serious antisocial behavior in adolescents. In W. E. Martin (Ed.), *Person–environment psychology: Clinical and counseling applications for adolescents and adults.* Hillsdale, NJ: Erlbaum.

Borduin, C. M., & Henggeler, S. W. (1987). Post-divorce mother-son relations of delinquent and well-adjusted adolescents. *Journal of Applied Developmental Psychology, 8,* 273–288.

Borduin, C. M., Mann, B. J., Cone, L., Henggeler, S. W., Fucci, B. R., Blaske, D. M., & Williams, R. A. (1995). Multisystemic treatment of serious juvenile offenders: Long-term prevention of criminality and violence. *Journal of Consulting and Clinical Psychology, 63,* 569–578.

Borduin, C. M., & Schaeffer, C. M. (1998). Violent offending in adolescence: Epidemiology, correlates, outcomes, and treatment. In T. P. Gullotta, G. R. Adams, & R. Montemayor (Eds.), *Delinquent violent youth: Theory and interventions* (pp. 144–174). Newbury Park, CA: Sage.

Bownes, D., & Ingersoll, S. (1997). *Mobilizing communities to prevent juvenile crime.*

Washington, DC: Office of Juvenile Justice and Delinquency Prevention.

Bureau of Justice Statistics. (1996). *Sourcebook of criminal justice statistics–1995.* Washington, DC: U.S. Government Printing Office.

Burkstein, O. G. (1994). Substance abuse. In M. Hersen, R. T. Ammerman, & L. A. Sisson (Eds.), *Handbook of aggressive and destructive behavior in psychiatric patients* (pp. 445–468). New York: Plenum Press.

Crick, N. R., & Dodge, K. A. (1994). A review and reformulation of social information processing mechanisms in children's social adjustment. *Psychological Bulletin, 115,* 74–101.

Dodge, K. A. (1983). Behavioral antecedents of peer social status. *Child Development, 54,* 1386–1399.

Dodge, K. A., Coie, J. D., & Brakke, N. P. (1982). Behavior patterns of socially rejected and neglected preadolescents: The roles of social approach and aggression. *Journal of Abnormal Child Psychology 10,* 389–410.

Donnerstein, E., Slaby, R. G., & Eron, L. D. (1994). The mass media and youth aggression. In L. D. Eron, J. H. Gentry, & P. Schlegal (Eds.), *Reason to hope: A psychosocial perspective on violence and youth* (pp. 219–250). Washington, DC: American Psychological Association.

Dunford, F. W., & Elliott, D. S. (1984). Identifying career offenders using self-reported data. *Journal of Research in Crime and Delinquency, 21,* 57–86.

Durant, R. H., Getts, A. G., Cadenhead, C., & Woods, E. R. (1995). The association between weapon carrying and the use of violence among adolescents living in and around public housing. *Journal of Adolescent Health, 17,* 376–380.

Eron, L. D. (1992). Gender differences in violence: Biology and/or socialization? In K. Bjorkqvist & P. Niemela (Eds.), *Of mice and women: Aspects of female aggression* (pp. 89–97). San Diego: Academic Press.

Farrell, A. D., & Bruce, S. E. (1997). Impact of exposure to community violence on violent behavior and emotional distress among urban adolescents. *Journal of Clinical Child Psychology, 26,* 2–14.

Farrington, D. P. (1991). Childhood aggression and adult violence: Early precursors and later life outcomes. In D. J. Pepler & K. H. Rubin (Eds.), *The development and treatment of childhood aggression* (pp. 5–29). Hillsdale, NJ: Erlbaum.

Farrington, D. P., Loeber, R., Elliot, D. S., Hawkins, J. D., Kandel, D. B., Klein, M. W., McCord, J., Rowe, D. C., & Tremblay, R. E. (1993). Advancing knowledge about the onset of delinquency and crime. In B. B. Lahey & A. E. Kazdin (Eds.), *Advances in clinical child psychology* (Vol. 13, pp. 283–342). New York: Plenum Press.

Federal Bureau of Investigation. (1989). *Uniform crime reports.* Washington, DC: U.S. Government Printing Office.

Federal Bureau of Investigation. (1990). *Uniform crime reports.* Washington, DC: U.S. Government Printing Office.

Federal Bureau of Investigation. (1991). *Uniform crime reports.* Washington, DC: U.S. Government Printing Office.

Federal Bureau of Investigation. (1992). *Uniform crime reports.* Washington, DC: U.S. Government Printing Office.

Federal Bureau of Investigation. (1993). *Uniform crime reports.* Washington, DC: U.S. Government Printing Office.

Federal Bureau of Investigation. (1994). *Uniform crime reports.* Washington, DC: U.S. Government Printing Office.

Federal Bureau of Investigation. (1995). *Uniform crime reports.* Washington, DC: U.S. Government Printing Office.

Federal Bureau of Investigation. (1996). *Uniform crime reports.* Washington, DC: U.S. Government Printing Office.

Federal Bureau of Investigation. (1997). *Uniform crime reports.* Washington, DC: U.S. Government Printing Office.

Federal Bureau of Investigation. (1998). *Uniform crime reports.* Washington, DC: U.S. Government Printing Office.

Feldman, R. A., Caplinger, T. E., & Wodarski, J. S. (1983). *The St. Louis conundrum: The effective treatment of antisocial youths.* Englewood Cliffs, NJ: Prentice Hall.

Frude, N., & Gault, H. (1984). *Disruptive behavior in the schools.* Chichester: Wiley.

Gorman-Smith, D., Tolan, P. H., Zelli, A., & Huesmann, L. R. (1996). The relation of family functioning to violence among inner-city minority youth. *Journal of Family Psychology, 10,* 115–129.

Hammond, R. (1991). *Dealing with anger: Givin' it. Takin' it. Workin' it out.* Champaign, IL: Research Press.

Hammond, R., & Yung, B. (1993). *Evaluation and activity report: Positive adolescent choice training* (Unpublished grant report). Washington, DC: U.S. Maternal and Child Health Bureau.

Hawkins, J. D. (1995). Controlling crime before it happens: Risk-focused prevention. *National Institute of Justice Journal, 229,* 10–18.

Henggeler, S. W. (1989). *Delinquency in adolescence.* Thousand Oaks, CA: Sage.

Henggeler, S. W. (1997). *Treating serious antisocial behavior in youth: The MST approach.* Washington, DC: Office of Juvenile Justice and Delinquency Prevention.

Henggeler, S. W., & Borduin, C. M. (1990). *Family therapy and beyond: A multisystemic approach to treating the behavior problems of children and adolescents.* Pacific Grove, CA: Brooks/Cole.

Henggeler, S. W., Melton, G. B., & Smith, L. A. (1992). Family preservation using multisystemic therapy: An effective alternative to incarcerating serious juvenile offenders. *Journal of Consulting and Clinical Psychology, 60,* 953–961.

Henggeler, S. W., Melton, G. B., Smith, L. A., Schoenwald, S., & Hanley, J. H. (1993). Family preservation using multisystemic treatment: Long-term follow-up to a clinical trial with serious juvenile offenders. *Journal of Child and Family Studies, 2,* 83–93.

Henggeler, S. G., Schoenwald, S. K., Borduin, C. M., Rowland, M. D., & Cunningham, P. B. (1998). *Multisystemic treatment of antisocial behavior in children and adolescents.* New York: Guilford Press.

Hinshaw, S. P. (1992). Externalizing behavior problems and academic underachievement in childhood and adolescence: Causal relationships and underlying mechanisms. *Psychological Bulletin, 111,* 127–155.

Howell, J. C. (1995). *Guide for implementing the comprehensive strategy for serious, violent, and chronic juvenile offenders.* Washington, DC: Office of Juvenile Justice and Delinquency Prevention.

Jouriles, E. N., Bourg, W. J., & Farris, A. M. (1991). Marital adjustment and child conduct problems: A comparison of the correlation across samples. *Journal of Consulting and Clinical Psychology, 59,* 354–357.

Kashani, J. H., & Allan, W. D. (1998). *The impact of family violence on children and adolescents.* Thousand Oaks, CA: Sage.

Kashani, J. H., Darby, P. J., Allan, W. D., Hartke, K. L., & Reid, J. C. (1997). Intrafamilial homicide committed by juveniles: Examination of a sample with recommendations for prevention. *Journal of Forensic Sciences, 42,* 873–878.

Kazdin, A. E. (1996). *Conduct disorders in childhood and adolescence* (2nd ed.). Thousand Oaks, CA: Sage.

Kingery, P. M., McCoy-Simandle, L., & Clayton, R. (1997). Risk factors for adolescent violence. *School Psychology International, 18,* 49–60.

Kruesi, M. J. P., Rapoport, J. L., Hamburger, S., Hibbs, E., Potter, W. Z., Lenane, M., & Brown, G. L. (1990). Cerebrospinal fluid monoamine metabolites, aggression, and impulsivity in disruptive behavior disorders of children and adolescents. *Archives of General Psychiatry, 47,* 419–426.

Lahey, B. B., McBurnett, K., Loeber, R., & Hart, E. L. (1995). Psychobiology. In G. P. Sholevar (Ed.), *Conduct disorders in children and adolescents* (pp. 27–57). Washington, DC: American Psychiatric Press.

Loeber, R., & Farrington, D. P. (1998). *Serious and violent juvenile offenders.* Thousand Oaks, CA: Sage.

Loeber, R., & Stouthamer-Loeber, M. (1986). Family factors as correlates and predictors of juvenile conduct problems and delinquency. In N. Morris & M. Tonry (Eds.), *Crime and justice: An annual review of research* (Vol. 7, pp. 126–152). Chicago: University of Chicago Press.

Lyons-Ruth, K. (1996). Attachment relationships among children with aggressive behavior problems: The role of disorganized early attachment patterns. *Journal of Consulting and Clinical Psychology, 64,* 64–73.

Melton, G. B., Petrila, J., Poythress, N. G., & Slobogin, C. (1997). *Psychological evaluations for the court: A handbook for mental health professionals and lawyers* (2nd ed.). New York: Guilford Press.

Moss, H. B., & Kirisci, L. (1995). Aggressivity in adolescent alcohol abusers: Relationship with conduct disorder. *Alcoholism: Clinical and Experimental Research, 19,* 642–646.

Mulvey, E. P., Arthur, M. A., & Reppucci, N. D. (1993). The prevention and treatment of juvenile delinquency: A review of the research. *Clinical Psychology Review, 13,* 133–167.

Murphy, E. F. (1981). *2,715 one-line quotations for speakers, writers, and raconteurs.* New York: Crown.

Office of Juvenile Justice and Delinquency Prevention. (1997). Race and weapon use. *Juvenile Justice, 3,* 21.

Ollendick, T. H. (1996). Violence in youth: Where do we go from here? Behavior therapy's response. *Behavior Therapy, 27,* 485–514.

Olweus, D., Mattsson, A., Schalling, D., & Low, H. (1988). Circulating testosterone levels in adolescent males: A causal analysis. *Psychosomatic Medicine, 50,* 261–272.

Parker, J. G., & Asher, S. R. (1987). Peer relations and later personal adjustment: Are low-accepted children at risk? *Psychological Bulletin, 112,* 357–389.

Patterson, G. R. (1982). *Coercive family process.* Eugene, OR: Castalia.

Pepler, D. J., & Slaby, R. G. (1994). Theoretical and developmental perspectives on youth and violence. In L. D. Eron, J. H. Gentry, & P. Schlegal (Eds.), *Reason to hope: A psychosocial perspective on violence and youth* (pp. 27–58). Washington, DC: American Psychological Association.

Pratt, T. (1973). Positive approaches to disruptive behavior. *Today's Education, 62,* 18–19.

Raine, A., & Jones, F. (1987). Attention, autonomic arousal, and personality in behaviorally disordered children. *Journal of Abnormal Child Psychology, 15,* 583–599.

Reno, J. (1995). *Juvenile offenders and victims: A national report.* Washington, DC: U.S. Department of Justice.

Roth, J. A., & Moore, M. H. (1995). *Reducing violent crimes and intentional injuries. Research in action.* Washington, DC: U.S. Department of Justice.

Ryan, G. D., & Lane, S. L. (Eds.). (1997). *Juvenile sexual offending: Causes, consequences, and correction* (Rev. ed.). San Francisco: Jossey-Bass.

Scarpa, A., & Raine, A. (1997). Psychophysiology of anger and violent behavior. *Psychiatric Clinics of North America, 20,* 375–394.

Seguin, J. R., Pihl, R. O., Harden, P. W., Tremblay, R. E., & Boulerice, B. (1995). Cognitive and neuropsychological characteristics of physically aggressive boys. *Journal of Abnormal Psychology, 104,* 614–624.

Sickmund, M., Snyder, H. N., & Poe-Yamagata, E. (1997). *Juvenile offenders and victims: 1997 update on violence.* Washington, DC: Office of Juvenile Justice and Delinquency Prevention.

Sloan, J. H., Kellermann, A. L., Reay, D. T., Ferris, J. A., Koepsell, T., Rivara, F. P., Rice, C., Gray, L., & LoGerfo, J. (1988). Handgun regulations, crime, assaults, and homicide: A tale of two cities. *New England Journal of Medicine, 319,* 1256–1262.

Snyder, H. N., & Sickmund, M. (1995). *Juvenile offenders and victims: A national report.* Washington, DC: Office of Juvenile Justice and Delinquency Prevention.

Stephenson, P., & Smith, D. (1989). Bullying in the junior school. In D. Tattum & D. Lane (Eds.), *Bullying in schools.* Stoke-on-Trent, UK: Trentham.

Stoff, D. M., Breiling, J., & Maser, J. D. (1997). *Handbook of antisocial behavior.* New York: Wiley.

Thornberry, T. P. (1994). *Violent families and youth violence.* Washington, DC: Office of Juvenile Justice and Delinquency Prevention.

Walker, H. M., Kavanagh, K., Stiller, B., Golly, A., Severson, H. H., & Feil, E. (1998). First step to success: An early intervention approach for preventing school antisocial behavior. *Journal of Emotional and Behavioral Disorders, 6,* 66–80.

Walker, M. L., Schmidt, L. M., & Lunghofer, L. (1997). Youth gangs. In M. I. Singer & L. T. Singer (Eds.), *Handbook for screening adolescents at psychosocial risk* (pp. 400–422). New York: Lexington.

White, H. R. (1997). Longitudinal perspective on alcohol use and aggression during adolescence. *Recent Developments in Alcoholism, 13,* 81–103.

Widom, C. S. (1989). Does violence beget violence? A critical examination of the literature. *Psychological Bulletin, 106,* 2–28.

Zigler, E., Taussig, C., & Black, K. (1992). Early childhood intervention: A promising preventative for juvenile delinquency. *American Psychologist, 47,* 997–1006.

Preventing School Violence:

The Use of Office Discipline Referrals to Assess and Monitor School-Wide Discipline Interventions

GEORGE SUGAI, JEFFREY R. SPRAGUE, ROBERT H. HORNER,
AND HILL M. WALKER

Confronted by increasing incidents of violent behavior in schools, educators are being asked to make schools safer. Schools, however, receive little guidance or assistance in their attempts to establish and sustain proactive discipline systems. One area of need lies in directions for use of existing discipline information to improve school-wide behavior support. In this article, we describe how office discipline referrals might be used as an information source to provide an indicator of the status of school-wide discipline and to improve the precision with which schools manage, monitor, and modify their universal interventions for all students and their targeted interventions for students who exhibit the most severe problem behaviors.

I N SEPTEMBER OF 1998 SCHOOLS IN the United States received a document from the U.S. Secretary of Education entitled *Early Warning, Timely Response: A Guide to Safe Schools,* recommending concerted attention to the increasing violent and disruptive behavior of students (Dwyer, Osher, & Warger, 1998). The document was compiled in response to the recent series of shootings in schools across the country. An impressive task force of national experts assembled current knowledge related to school safety and prepared the report with the direct goal of providing guidance for school-wide discipline reform. The compelling theme of the document was that important efforts must be made to respond in cases of violence, but the real solution lies in prevention of violent behavior. Schools that are safe, effective, and controlled are not accidents. They are environments where considerable effort has been made to build and maintain safe school cultures. School administrators were encouraged in *Early Warning, Timely Response* to assess safety in their schools and implement proactive steps to build safe schools.

The purposes of this article are to suggest one model for understanding the discipline challenges facing elementary, middle, and junior high schools and to provide an example of how office discipline referrals may be a useful index, both to assess school discipline needs and to monitor the effects of reform efforts. School administrators and their faculty face a plethora of advice on how to make schools safer but little help integrating what are often conflicting messages (Murray & Myers, 1998; Sprague, Sugai, & Walker, 1998; Walker, Colvin, & Ramsey, 1995; Walker, Irvin, & Sprague, 1997).

Recently, however, a three-tiered analysis of violence prevention has been recommended as a method for linking information about the physical school environment, administrative and management practices of the school, neighborhood and family characteristics, and the characteristics of the student population to recommendations for improving school discipline and safety (Gresham, Sugai, Horner, Quinn, & McInerney, in press; Walker et al., 1996). The key to the argument is that violent and disruptive behavior takes many forms and functions. The strategies used by schools for preventing and responding to violence need to be tailored to the features of the behavior and the environmental context in which the behavior is observed. The three-tiered model depicted in Figure 1 defines the discipline challenge for schools as combining the needs of three groups of students and linking each of these groups to a different level of discipline intervention (Universal Interventions, Selected Interventions, and Targeted Interventions).

A major error defined by this model is to assume that a single intervention or approach will meet all the behavioral needs within a school. As depicted in Figure 1, an assumption is that one group of students (85%–90%) will arrive at school already having learned important social skills. An important part of any school-wide discipline system is to ensure that the skills of these students are embedded in the behavioral culture of the school (Taylor-Greene et al., 1997).

The intervention need is for an efficient system of instruction that can be delivered universally (i.e., to all students). Universal interventions constitute a primary prevention strategy. A universal in-tervention is efficient to deliver and is provided to all students without prior individual assessment. Universal interventions for elementary and middle school students often take the form of direct social skills training in class (Committee for Children, 1997; Langland, Lewis-Palmer, & Sugai, 1998), rules instruction for specific settings (e.g., playgrounds) (Colvin, Sugai, Good, & Lee, 1997; Lewis, Sugai, & Colvin, 1998), or all-day workshops to teach expected school behavior (Taylor-Greene et al., 1997). The central message is that schools must avoid the tendency to ignore students who currently are not engaging in problem behavior. The foundation of all effective school-wide discipline efforts lies in systematic attention to the universal training, monitoring, and reinforcement of expected social behavior (Colvin, Kameenui, & Sugai, 1993; Taylor-Greene et al., 1997).

Not all students, however, respond to universal interventions. Students with chronic patterns of problem behavior require either more selected support or highly individualized and targeted support. The level and intensity of support is dictated by the level and complexity of the behavior problem (Sugai & Horner, 1999; Walker, Colvin, & Ramsey, 1995; Walker et al., 1996). Targeted interventions often involve support from related services personnel—including counselors, special educators, and school psychologists—and focus additional school resources on the needs of small groups of students. Efforts such as extra academic support, extra adult attention, scheduling changes, and more frequent access to school rewards can be used to improve the overall likelihood of school success and reduce levels of problem behavior. For the 3% to 5% of students who do not even respond to selected group support, intensive, targeted intervention based on functional behavioral assessment procedures (O'Neill et al., 1997; Sugai, Lewis-Palmer, & Hagan, 1998; Walker et al., 1996) is required.

Research and demonstration efforts are focusing on each of the three tiers of behavior support, and new and improved strategies for implementing universal, targeted, and intensive behavior support are emerging. The most important message, however, is that a continuum of behavior support comprised of 3 very different levels of intervention is needed. The intensity of the intervention must match the intensity of the problem behavior and the complexity of the context in which problem behavior occurs. Universal interventions focus on improving the overall level of appropriate behavior of most students but will have limited impact on the 10% to 15% of students with chronic patterns of problem behavior. Selected interventions that deliver more intense procedures, but are packaged for efficiency and implemented similarly across many students, are designed to address the needs of many of these students but will not prove effective for the 3% to 5% of students with the most intense and chronic patterns of problem behavior and for whom highly

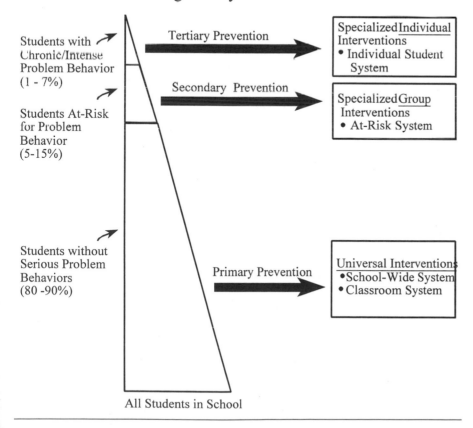

FIGURE 1. Multilevel system of school-wide discipline strategies.

individualized, targeted interventions are needed. The challenge faced by schools is not to identify the one perfect strategy for improving school discipline. Rather, all schools need at least three different discipline efforts: universal, selected, and targeted.

Schools wishing to follow the advice from *Early Warning, Timely Response* should begin by assessing their current school safety and behavior support status and then build an efficient, three-tiered discipline system based on the Walker/ Gresham model. This effort should focus on the implementation of procedures that fit the specific needs of the school rather than adopting a single intervention package in hopes the package will solve all problems. It is as important to define what a school does well and to retain those features of the existing discipline system that "work" as it is to define what is most lacking and to respond to those needs. We propose that an efficient and effective response to the recommendations in *Early Warning, Timely Response* requires a practical ongoing strategy for assessing and monitoring school-wide discipline systems. Patterns of office discipline referrals may prove a simple, available, and useful data source to aid in assessment, monitoring, and planning.

Office Discipline Referrals

Office discipline referrals are used throughout the nation as a method for managing and monitoring disruptive behavior in schools. As a data source, an office discipline referral is an atypical metric. An office discipline referral represents an event in which (a) a student engaged in a behavior that violated a rule or social norm in the school, (b) the problem behavior was observed or identified by a member of the school staff, and (c) the event resulted in a consequence delivered by administrative staff who produced a permanent (written) product defining the whole event. Office discipline referrals are more than an index of student behavior, they are an index of the discipline systems within a school. The major advantage of discipline referrals is that they already are collected in most schools and provide an efficient source

of information for documenting whether reform efforts result in systems change (Skiba, Peterson, & Williams, 1997; Tobin, Sugai, & Colvin, in press; Walker, Stieber, Ramsey, & O'Neill, 1993; Wright & Dusek, 1998). An important limitation of office discipline referrals lies in the unique manner in which each school defines and applies referral procedures. The same student behavior may evoke different responses from teachers in different schools, or differences in the relationship between teachers and the school's administration may alter the use of discipline referrals across schools. As such, the value of student office discipline referrals as a measure of school-wide discipline must be embraced with caution (Wright & Dusek, 1998).

Existing research suggests, however, that office discipline referrals may prove a useful metric when used as a within-school systems metric (Skiba, Peterson, & Williams, 1997; Tobin & Sugai, 1999a, 1999b; Tobin, Sugai, & Colvin, 1996; Tobin, Sugai, & Colvin, in press). Office referral and suspension data have been useful in identifying abnormally high patterns of discipline for minority students (McCarthy & Hoge, 1987; Skiba, Peterson, & Williams, 1997), identifying discipline patterns of students with and without disabilities (Wright & Dusek, 1998), and more recently, for identifying improvements in school-wide systems (Biglan, Metzler, Rusby, & Sprague, 1998; Taylor-Greene et al., 1997) and staff training needs (Tobin, Sugai, & Colvin, in press).

We propose that the information school personnel are already collecting in the form of office discipline referrals may be of substantial value as they attempt to plan for violence prevention. During the past 5 years, we have monitored office discipline referrals from elementary and middle (junior high) schools and learned that by combining a few pieces of data, useful information may be obtained. We have found it useful to blend information from office discipline referrals with suspension, detention, and expulsion data but to date have found office discipline referrals to be the most sensitive index and have chosen to focus attention on this data source in the present article.

Linking Office Discipline Referral Data to School-Wide Discipline

Administrators and faculty committed to improving the school-wide discipline systems in their school may find value in examining (a) the total number of office discipline referrals for a school year; (b) the number of students enrolled during the school year; (c) the number of school days in the year; and (d) the allocation of office discipline referrals by student, location, and date. We find that most schools have these data, although not many use the data for decision making. In light of the three-tiered model of school-wide discipline defined by Gresham (Gresham et al., in press) and Walker (Walker et al., 1996) the data listed above can be used to determine whether to focus school discipline reform efforts on universal interventions, selected interventions, and/or targeted, individualized interventions. See Figure 2 for a simple application of the discipline referral data.

For school faculty members to use their information to the best advantage, multiple years of information should be compared. Examining the results from a single school with general patterns from similar schools also can be useful. With this comparison in mind, we provide office discipline referral data from elementary and middle (junior high) schools collected between 1994 and 1998.

METHOD

Schools/Students

Office discipline referral data were collected from 11 elementary (Grades K–6) schools and 9 middle/junior high (Grades 6–9) schools across seven school districts in two western states. Six schools provided referral data for multiple years. Because of schools with multiple years, a total of 21 academic school years of data were available for a total of 18,598 students (9,070 elementary and 9,528 middle/junior high).

Schools were selected for inclusion in the database based on their interest in improving their school discipline systems, the existence of an established system for collecting and maintaining office dis-

Reform of universal, school-wide behavior support systems is needed if:

1. Total number of referrals per year per student is high;
2. Average number of referrals per day is high;
3. The proportion of students with at least one referral is high.

Reform of selected support systems is needed if:

The proportion of students with at least one referral is low, but the proportion of students with 1 to 10 referrals is comparatively high.

Reform of individualized, targeted student behavior support systems is needed if:

1. There are students who have received 10 or more referrals during the year.
2. The 5% of students with the most office discipline referrals account for a high percentage of all referrals.

FIGURE 2. Application of the discipline referral data.

cipline referrals, and their willingness to provide the data for inclusion in a broad database. Four schools provided data for the year prior and following advent of school-wide discipline reform efforts. Several of the schools reported their data, considered their systems adequate, and did not use reforms. Other schools reported unacceptable levels of problem behavior and are in the process of using the referral data to plan and implement reforms.

Measures

Each of the schools maintained an office referral database developed from individual written office referrals. Each written referral indicated a student, date, location, referring teacher, primary rule violation, and consequence for the student associated with the referring incident. Although different terms were applied, the schools used a surprisingly consistent set of problem behaviors to initiate office discipline referrals.

Each school was asked to report the following:

1. the grade levels in their school;
2. the number of students per school year;
3. the number of office discipline referrals per school year;
4. the number of school days per school year;
5. the number of students with 1 or more office referrals, 5 or more office referrals, and 10 or more office referrals; and
6. the number and proportion of referrals from the 5% of students with the most office referrals.

These raw data were used to calculate the following:

1. the mean number of office discipline referrals per student attending school,
2. the mean number of office referrals per student who received at least one referral,
3. the average number of office discipline referrals per school day,
4. the proportion of students with 1+ (one or more) and 10+ (10 or more) referrals, and
5. the proportion of all referrals accounted for by the 5% of students with the most office discipline referrals.

Data on the proportion of students with 1+ and 10+ referrals were unavailable for two elementary and two middle schools.

RESULTS

Results are separated for elementary and middle/junior high schools and are summarized in Table 1. Where data were available from one school for multiple years, the results for each year are reported (letter name plus number indicates a school and the year) and means and standard deviations were computed based on all school years (e.g., 16 for elementary and 15 for middle/junior high schools). Elementary schools averaged 567 students per year (range 240–1,065) with a mean of only 0.5 office discipline referrals per student per year, and a mean of 1.7 office discipline referrals per school day. On average, only 21% of the student body of the elementary schools received one or more office discipline referrals per year, and only 3 of the schools reported more than 1% of their students with 10+ referrals. The 5% of the student body with the highest level of discipline referrals contributed, on average, 59% of the total referrals for the elementary schools reporting top 5% data. Schools B, I, and K reported impressively low levels of discipline referrals per student (≤ 0.4), and low proportions of students with 1+ referrals (≤ 17%). These 3 schools compared favorably against Schools A and J1.

Elementary school administrators using these data for planning discipline systems reform may see Schools A and J1 as candidates for universal, school-wide interventions and Schools F and J as candidates for intensive, targeted systems reform. School F also may need selected interventions, based on the fact that more children had 10+ referrals than can be addressed via targeted, individualized interventions.

The discipline referral picture changes when middle/junior high schools are compared. The middle schools averaged 635 students per year (range 204–1,194) with an annual mean of 1,535.5 office discipline referrals. On average, each student in the middle schools received 2.4 office discipline referrals, with schools averaging 8.6 discipline referrals per school day. An average of 47.6% of the students in participating middle schools were referred to the office at least once, and 5.4% were referred 10 or more times. The 5% of students with the most office referrals accounted for an average of 40.4% of all referrals.

An analysis of these data sets gives schools direction as they plan and imple-

School	Grade	Total		Referrals		% of students		
		Enrolled students	Discipline referrals	Per enrolled student	Per school day	1 or more referrals	10 or more referrals	% of referrals from 5% with most referrals
				Elementary schools				
A	4-6	240	208	0.9	1.3	32	0.4	41
B	K-5	469	163	0.4	0.9	17	0.1	60
C1	K-5	430	313	0.7	1.9	24	0.1	55
C2	K-5	430	304	0.7	1.8			
C3	K-5	451	201	0.5	1.2			
C4	K-5	485	233	0.5	1.4			
D1	K-5	586	171	0.3	1.1			
D2	K-5	450	94	0.2	0.6			
E	K-6	991	579	0.6	3.4	20	0.4	56
F	K-6	713	331	0.5	1.9	12	1.5	82
G	K-6	648	268	0.4	1.6	18	0.3	64
H	K-6	1,065	445	0.4	2.6	21	0.2	55
I	K-6	451	124	0.3	0.7	13	0.4	70
J1	K-5	573	607	1.1	3.5	39	1.2	42
J2	K-5	638	409	0.6	2.4	25	1.1	51
K	K-5	450	79	0.2	0.4	9.6	0	73
M		566.9	283.1	0.5	1.7	21	0.5	59
SD		212.3	154.7	0.24	0.9	8.4	0.5	12
				Middle/junior high schools				
A	6-8	550	663	1.2	4.1	41	2	35
B	7-8	635	1,274	2	7.1	23	5	72
C	6-8	478	1,708	3.6	10	66	11	29
D1	6-8	530	2,644	5	14.9	57	8	38
D2	6-8	535	1,564	2.9	8.5			
D3	6-8	540	1,234	2.3	6.7	37	7	41
D4	6-8	570	1,348	2.4	7.3			
E1	6-8	618	1,747	2.8	10	50	6	39
E2	6-8	628	1,256	2	7.2	37	4	36
F	7-8	695	1,768	2.5	10.3	52	8	35
G	7-8	1,194	3,520	3	20.6	65	1	35
H	7-8	204	136	0.7	0.8	33	1	44
I1	7-9	815	1,259	1.5	4.8			
I2	7-9	723	1,552	2.1	9			
I3	7-9	813	1,360	1.7	8	15	1	
M		635.2	1,535.5	2.4	8.6	47.6	5.4	40.4
SD		206.6	748.2	1	4.4	16.3	3.3	11

ment discipline systems reform. For example, Schools C, D1, D2, E1, and G reported higher than average levels of both office discipline referrals per student and percentages of students with 1+ referrals. These schools might consider universal school reform efforts targeting all students in the school.

School G reported a high proportion of students with 1+ referrals but a low proportion with 10+ referrals. School G not only may need careful attention to school-wide efforts but also may benefit from school reform focused on selected interventions. Schools C, D1, and F had more students with 10+ referrals than typically can be addressed through the resources available for targeted individualized support. These schools also would be encouraged to consider more efficiency-focused, selected intervention systems.

Schools C, D1, E1, and F reported higher than average levels of both 1+ referral and 10+ referral patterns. These schools may benefit from attention to intensive, targeted intervention systems. School B had a lower than typical level of students with 1+ referrals but a high proportion of students with 10+ referrals, and these students accounted for an impressive 72% of all referrals. School B also would be a candidate for careful attention to targeted, individualized intervention systems reform.

DISCUSSION

School administrators face significant challenges in their efforts to establish and maintain safe and positive environments that allow all teachers to teach and all students to learn. Clearly, prevention-based approaches to school-wide discipline and the management of students with severe problem behavior are preferred because of their potential to reduce the development of new cases of problem behavior (incidence) and the number of current cases of problem behavior (prevalence). A well functioning school-wide system improves the efficiency and effectiveness with which classroom and individual behavior support systems function. However, proactive efforts are difficult to establish and maintain because students with significant learning and behavioral difficulties are so unresponsive to universal interventions, have such a dramatic impact on the overall and daily functioning of classrooms and schools, respond so slowly to even targeted interventions, and demand such intensive and ongoing behavioral support.

When behavioral difficulties are dangerous or harmful to others or property, the first reaction is a call for dramatic school reforms that include installation of metal detectors, hiring security guards, conducting random drug tests, and instituting school uniform policies. Because of the tragic nature of recent violent

school acts, these kinds of reactions are predictable and understandable. The immediate and natural response is to remove the source of the discomfort and to use structural modifications to prevent similar acts from recurring. Unfortunately, these reactive approaches do not provide positive and preventative measures that are based on careful and ongoing assessment of multiple school systems and for changes in the ways in which teachers behave and school systems operate.

Given the need for a proactive, assessment-based approach to school-wide discipline and behavior support, the purposes of this article are to suggest one approach for understanding the discipline challenges facing elementary, middle, and junior high schools and to provide an example of how one data source (office discipline referrals) might be a useful index to both assess reform needs and monitor the effects of reform efforts. Office discipline referral data from 20 elementary and middle schools were summarized to illustrate how referral patterns might be used to guide school intervention decisions regarding selection of potential areas for system modification or reform, and indicators of change across time.

Office discipline referral patterns were suggested as a means of assessing the need for development of universal, selected, and targeted intervention systems. Specifically, preliminary data for the elementary schools suggest that universal intervention support reform is needed when (a) the referral per student ratio exceeds 0.5 or (b) the percentage of students receiving one or more referrals per year exceeds 20. Reform of selected behavior support systems would be warranted if the school had more than 10 children with 10+ referrals, and reform of the targeted intervention systems would be called for if (a) there are more than 0.5% of the students with 10+ referrals or (b) the 5% of students with the most referrals accounted for greater than 60% of all referrals.

The results from middle schools suggests that universal interventions would be the focus of reform if (a) the number

of referrals per student exceeded 2.5, (b) the number of referrals per day exceeded 8, and/or (c) the percentage of students with 1+ referrals was greater than 45%. Selected intervention systems would be recommended if more than 10 students received 10+ referrals. Targeted intervention systems would be indicated if the percentage of students with 10+ referrals exceeded 5%, and/or if the percentage of referrals from the top 5% of students with referrals exceeded 40%.

Cautions

We consider this use and analysis of office discipline referrals as an important first step and direction in improving the way schools make decisions about increasing effectiveness of their school-wide discipline efforts. However, a number of cautions must be considered in this regard. First, we selected schools that (a) had existing and established systems for collecting and maintaining office discipline referrals and (b) were in the initial stages of developing or initiating a plan to improve their school-wide discipline procedures. As the integrity of the office discipline referral monitoring system is weakened, so is the integrity of the data to inform decision making. Future investigations should involve collection of other types of data (e.g., attendance, tardies, arrests, direct observation) to serve as a concurrent measure of the usefulness of office discipline referral data. Previous research by Walker, Tobin, Sugai, Peterson, and others has supported the use of these types of archival data as an indicator of the status of school-wide discipline practices (Colvin, Kameenui, & Sugai, 1993; Lewis-Palmer, Sugai, & Larson, 1999; Taylor-Greene et al., 1997; Tobin & Sugai, 1999a, 1999b; Tobin, Sugai, & Colvin, 1996).

Second, a relatively small number of schools were represented in the study. Clearly, the addition of more data sets from a larger number of schools would improve the identification of data set patterns. An examination of data set patterns from schools with diverse characteristics (e.g., SES, rural/urban, size) also should be conducted. In addition, the office discipline referral patterns from high schools should be investigated.

Finally, we proposed a model that considered office discipline referral data as a means of directing the selection of universal, selected group, and targeted individual school-wide efforts. Whether these data patterns actually result in improved school reform efforts should be tested.

Implications

Given these limitations, we believe this study is important and encouraging because it represents one of the first attempts to link a systematic analysis of office discipline referral data to inform discipline program reform efforts (Tobin & Sugai, 1999a, 1999b; Wright & Dusek, 1998). Clearly, more work needs to be done in this area; however, a number of implications are indicated. First, office discipline referral data are collected in most schools to document major behavioral incidents and represent an economical and readily available source of data.

Second, a regular summary and analysis of discipline data may help identify where individual schools should invest their reform efforts. Rather than relying on impressions or time to guide decisions to maintain or modify discipline policy and procedures, schools could use patterns in discipline referral data at least to direct attention to universal, targeted group, or targeted individual programming.

Third, schools should not assume that a single system will meet all the needs/challenges associated with school-wide discipline practices and policies. At minimum, disciplinary practices can be divided into four subsystems: (a) school-wide, (b) classroom management, (c) non-classroom setting (e.g., cafeteria, hallways, playground) supervision and management, and (d) individual student programming (Sugai & Horner, 1994, 1999). A continuum of behavior support (universal to targeted) needs to be applied to these subsystems; however, data and data decision rules must be identi-fied to guide how supports are assigned and associated within and across these subsystems.

Fourth, school-wide discipline systems are the foundation from which all other efforts are based and directed. If school-wide discipline systems are not in place and functioning effectively and efficiently, the establishment of sustainable systems of support for students with significant behavioral challenges is difficult because they require significant human and material resources, time, and financial costs.

Finally, students with significant problem behavior present major challenges to schools at the school-wide, classroom, and individual programming levels. The problem is not having a technology for identification, assessment, and intervention. The real challenge for the future will be increasing the contextual fit between what we know about effective practices and our ability to adopt and sustain these practices. The data-directed improvement of school-wide discipline systems and practices could improve this contextual gap.

About the Authors

GEORGE SUGAI, PhD, is a professor of special education in the College of Education at the University of Oregon. His areas of expertise include classroom and behavior management, school-wide discipline, functional assessment-based behavior support planning, and educating students with emotional and behavioral disorders. Dr. Sugai conducts applied school and classroom research and works with schools to translate research into practice. He is currently co-director of the Center on Positive Behavior Interventions and Supports at the University of Oregon. **JEFFREY R. SPRAGUE,** PhD, is an associate professor of special education and co-director of the University of Oregon Institute on Violence and Destructive Behavior. His research activities include applied behavior analysis, severe behavioral disorders, school safety, school violence prevention and intervention, special education teacher training, school-to-work transition, and social integration. **ROBERT H. HORNER,** PhD, is a professor of special education at the University of Oregon, director of the Specialized Training Program, department head of the Depart-ment of Special Education and Community Resources, and the Oregon UAP technical assistance coordinator. Currently, Dr. Horner serves as co–project director of the Center for Positive Behavior Intervention and Supports established by the Office of Special Education Programs, U.S. Department of Education, to give schools capacity-building information and technical assistance for identifying, adapting, and sustaining effective schoolwide disciplinary practices. **HILL M. WALKER,** PhD, is a professor of special education, director of the Center on Human Development, and co-director of the Institute on Violence and Destructive Behavior in the College of Education at the University of Oregon. His research interests include social skills assessment, curriculum development and intervention, longitudinal studies of aggression and antisocial behavior, and the development of early screening procedures for detecting students who are at risk for social–behavioral adjustment problems and/or later school dropout. Address: George Sugai, College of Education, University of Oregon, 5262 University of Oregon, Eugene, OR 97403-5262.

Authors' Note

The development of this paper was supported in part by a grant awarded by the Office of Special Education Programs, U.S. Department of Education, Grant No. H326S980003. Opinions expressed herein do not necessarily reflect the position of the U.S. Department of Education, and such endorsements should not be inferred.

References

Biglan, A., Metzler, C. W., Rusby, J. C., & Sprague, J. R. (1998). *Evaluation of a comprehensive behavior management program to improve school-wide positive behavior support.* Manuscript submitted for publication.

Colvin, G., Kameenui, E. J., & Sugai, G. (1993). School-wide and classroom management: Reconceptualizing the integration and management of students with behavior problems in general education. *Education and Treatment of Children, 16,* 361–381.

Colvin, G., Sugai, G., Good, R. H., III, & Lee, Y. (1997). Using active supervision and precorrection to improve transition behaviors in an elementary school. *School Psychology Quarterly, 12,* 344–363.

Committee for Children. (1997). *Second step: Violence prevention curriculum.* Seattle, WA: Author.

Dwyer, K. P., Osher, D., & Warger, W. (1998). *Early warning, timely response: A guide to safe schools.* Washington, DC: U. S. Department of Education.

Gresham, F. M., Sugai, G., Horner, R. H., Quinn, M. M., & McInerney, M. (in press). *Classroom and schoolwide practices that support students' social competence: A synthesis of research.* Washington, DC: Office of Special Education Programs at the U.S. Department of Education.

Langland, S., Lewis-Palmer, T., & Sugai, G. (1998). Teaching respect in the classroom: An instructional approach. *Journal of Behavioral Education, 8,* 245–262.

Lewis, T. J, Sugai, G., & Colvin, G. (1998). Reducing problem behavior through a school-wide system of effective behavioral support: Investigation of a school-wide social skills training program and contextual interventions. *School Psychology Review, 27,* 446–459.

Lewis-Palmer, T., Sugai, G., & Larson, S. (1999). Using data to guide decisions about program implementation and effectiveness. *Effective School Practices, 17*(4), 47–53.

McCarthy, J. D., & Hoge, D. R. (1987). The social construction of school punishment: Racial disadvantage out of universalistic process. *Social Forces, 65,* 1101–1120.

Murray, B. A., & Myers, M. A. (January 1998). Avoiding the special education trap for conduct disordered students. *NASSP Bulletin,* 65–73.

O'Neill, R. E., Horner, R. H., Albin, R. W., Sprague, J. R., Storey, K., & Newton, J. S. (1997). *Functional assessment and program development for problem behavior: A practical handbook* (2nd ed.). Pacific Grove, CA: Brookes/Cole.

Skiba, R. J., Peterson, R. L., & Williams, T. (1997). Office referrals and suspensions: Disciplinary intervention in middle schools. *Education and Treatment of Children, 20,* 295–315.

Sprague, J., Sugai, G., & Walker, H. (1998). Antisocial behavior in schools. In S. M. Watson & F. M. Gresham (Eds.), *The handbook of child behavior therapy* (pp. 451–474). New York: Plenum Press.

Sugai, G., & Horner, R. (1994). Including students with severe behavior problems in general education settings: Assumptions, challenges, and solutions. In J. Marr, G. Sugai, & G. Tindal (Eds.), *The Oregon conference monograph* (Vol. 6, pp. 102–120). Eugene: University of Oregon.

Sugai, G., & Horner, R. H. (1999). Discipline and behavioral support: Preferred processes and practices. *Effective School Practices, 17*(4), 10–22.

Sugai, G., Lewis-Palmer, T., & Hagan, S. (1998). Using functional assessments to develop behavior support plans. *Preventing School Failure, 43*(1), 6–13.

Taylor-Greene, S., Brown, D., Nelson, L., Longton, J., Gassman, T., Cohen, J., Swartz, J., Horner, R. H., Sugai, G., & Hall, S. (1997). School-wide behavioral support: Starting the year off right. *Journal of Behavioral Education, 7,* 99–112.

Tobin, T., & Sugai, G. (1999a). Predicting violence at school, chronic discipline problems, and high school outcomes from sixth graders' school records. *Journal of Emotional and Behavioral Disorders, 7,* 40–53.

Tobin, T., & Sugai, G. (1999b). Discipline problems, placements, and outcomes for students with serious emotional disturbance. *Behavioral Disorders, 24,* 109–121.

Tobin, T., Sugai, G., & Colvin, G. (1996). Patterns in middle school discipline records. *Journal of Emotional and Behavioral Disorders, 4*(2), 82–94.

Tobin, T., Sugai, G., & Colvin, G. (in press). Using discipline referrals to make decisions. *NASSP Bulletin.*

Walker, H. M., Colvin, G., & Ramsey, E. (1995). *Antisocial behavior in school: Strategies and best practices.* Pacific Grove, CA: Brookes/Cole.

Walker, H. M., Horner, R. H., Sugai, G., Bullis, M., Sprague, J. R., Bricker, D., & Kaufman, M. J. (1996). Integrated approaches to preventing antisocial behavior patterns among school-age children and youth. *Journal of Emotional and Behavioral Disorders, 4,* 193–256.

Walker, H. M., Irvin, L. K., & Sprague, J. R. (1997). Violence prevention and school safety: Issues, problems, approaches, and recommended solutions. *Oregon School Study Council Bulletin, 41*(1).

Walker, H. M., Stieber, S., Ramsey, E., & O'Neill, R. E. (1993). Fifth grade school adjustment and later arrest rate: A longitudinal study of middle school antisocial boys. *Journal of Child and Family Studies, 2*(4), 295–315.

Wright, J. A., & Dusek, J. B. (1998). Research into practice: Compiling school base rates for disruptive behaviors from student disciplinary referral data. *School Psychology Review, 27*(1), 138–147.

Designing Schools to Meet the Needs of Students Who Exhibit Disruptive Behavior

This article offers an evaluation of a school-wide program designed to increase the institutional capacity of elementary schools to educate students who exhibit disruptive or externalizing behavior. The project included four elements: school organizational practices, a school-wide classroom management intervention, individual behavioral programs, and an advisory board. Two elementary schools serving large numbers of disadvantaged students were studied over a period of 2 years. Comparisons with two matched elementary schools indicated strong positive effects on the disciplinary actions of the schools and on the teachers' perceptions of their ability to work with children who exhibited disruptive behavior. Additionally, comparisons between target students (i.e., those who exhibited disruptive behavior) and criterion students indicated positive effects on the social adjustment, academic performance, and school survival skills of target students.

THE HARSH TRUTH IS THAT GROWING numbers of children in the United States are exhibiting disruptive behavior or externalizing behavior (also referred to as antisocial, challenging, defiant, noncompliant, aggressive, and acting-out behavior) beyond the occasional minor incident typical of most children during the normal course of development. Such behavior has become one of the most pressing issues in schools (Bullock, Reilly, & Donahue, 1983; Evans & Evans, 1985; Hranitz & Eddowes, 1990). The National Center for School Safety reported that 28,200 students and 5,200 teachers are physically attacked in our nation's secondary schools each month, and 19% of these victims require hospitalization (Greenbaum & Turner, 1989). Further, growing numbers of students and teachers reported that they were seriously concerned for their safety at school (Hranitz & Eddowes, 1990). These staggering statistics do not include the almost 5 million students eligible for special education services who exhibit higher rates of deportment problems relative to their nondisabled peers (e.g., Kerr & Nelson, 1983) or the over 300,000 teachers employed to serve these students (Office of Special Education Programs, 1995). There is little question that

educators across the country must address violent and disruptive behavior. This is especially important to schools because of the well-established relationship between academic underachievement and poor social adjustment (Kazdin, 1987; Patterson, 1982). Indeed, although addressing the growing level of violent and disruptive behavior in schools may be a subordinate objective of the broader academic goals of schools, doing so may be a necessary condition for achieving academic excellence (Nelson, Colvin, & Smith, in press).

Disruptive or externalizing behavior not only confronts schools and society with a serious challenge, it also has an adverse impact on individuals. Disruptive behavior may interfere with aca-

demic and vocational success as well as chronic maladjustment and unhappiness (Kazdin, 1987). Additionally, much literature has pointed to the increasing stability of such behavior from early childhood (approximately age 8) to late adolescence and adulthood (e.g., Huesmann, Eron, Lefkowitz, & Walder, 1984). Retrospective studies found that problem behavior in adulthood is invariably preceded by a pattern of such behavior in childhood (Robins, 1981). Longitudinal research also supported this position (Huesmann et al., 1984). Although the specific behavior may change with development, the relative standing of a child with conduct problems compared to his or her peers remains consistent (Huesmann et al., 1984).

The postschool outcomes of students with emotional and behavioral disorders (EBD) who exit school programs is rather bleak (Edgar & Levine, 1987; Neel, Meadow, Levine, & Edgar, 1988; Wagner & Shaver, 1989). School dropout rates among these students range from 50% to 60%. Unemployment runs between 30% and 40%; if these individuals are employed, the work secured is low paying and menial. Few enter any type of postsecondary educational training, and many are arrested at least once in the 2 years following their exit from school. The most recent data from the SRI National Longitudinal Transition Study documented that the EBD group experienced the highest unemployment, poorest work history, and highest number of social adjustment problems post–high school of any disability group.

The statistics and issues mentioned above, as well as the human and fiscal costs associated with disruptive behavior alone, make the case for new directions and strategies to address such behavior in schools. This article presents the evaluation of a project designed to increase the institutional capacity of schools to work with students who exhibit disruptive or externalizing behavior in its two elementary school sites over a 2-year period. The primary goal of the project was to develop a school environment that was both preventative and remedial in nature. We focused on disruptive behavior because the results of our needs assessment indicated that such behavior was increasing in local schools and the community (Nelson, 1992). The project was preventative in that its central goal was to ensure that disruptive behavior did not commence or become more entrenched as a result of school practices. The project was remedial in nature in that it sought to change disruptive behavior. Additionally, the project was unique in that the goal of the project centered on identifying and changing school and classroom organizational practices that foster disruptive behavior. The project was also unique in that its focus was on universal strategies and organizational structures—both classroom and school-wide—rather than on individualized in-terventions for students. Thus, the staff development activities centered on the implementation of the school-wide and classroom strategies and organizational structures rather than on general strategies and interventions for students who exhibit disruptive behavior.

PROGRAM ELEMENTS

The project included four main elements. The first element centered on structuring school-wide organizational practices to promote positive social behavior. A school-wide classroom management intervention for disruptive behavior was the focus of the second element. The third element consisted of individual behavioral interventions to address students' curricular and behavioral problems. An advisory committee to direct the development, implementation, maintenance, and evaluation of the program was the final element. The program elements are presented in Figure 1 and are described below.

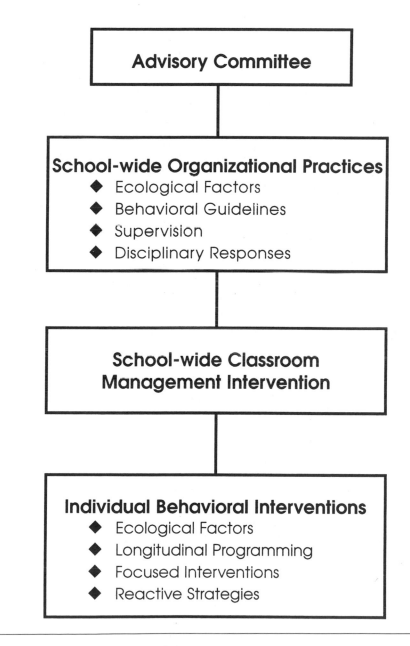

FIGURE 1. Primary elements of the project.

School-Wide Organizational Practices

The first element of the project focused on structuring school-wide organizational practices to promote positive social behavior. The basic framework used was based on research on family–child bonding (e.g., Bowlby, 1988; Pianta & Steinberg, 1992) and child and family guidance (e.g., Patterson, 1982; Patterson & Forgatch, 1987). In brief, this research indicated that the social development of children is enhanced in environments in which there is predictability in the moment-to-moment interactions between adults and children and where it is clear to the child which behaviors are acceptable and which are not. Schools must establish clear and consistent behavioral guidelines, supervise or monitor the guidelines, and establish consequences both for meeting and not meeting those guidelines to achieve such conditions.

The framework used for achieving a school environment that reduces disruptive behavior and promotes the social development of students had four interrelated components: (a) the ecological arrangements of the common areas of the school (e.g., hallways, cafeteria, restrooms, playground); (b) the establishment of clear and consistent behavioral guidelines or expectations for common area routines; (c) supervision of the common area routines to prevent disruptive behavior from occurring and to respond effectively when it did occur; and (d) the creation of effective disciplinary responses with which to respond to disruptive behavior in a timely and effective manner. (We focused on establishing effective disciplinary responses because the strategies used by schools typically were poorly designed whereas the reinforcement strategies they employed to promote positive social behavior were relatively well designed.)

Ecological Arrangements. There were numerous opportunities for ecological arrangements to contribute to the productive management of student behavior in the common areas of the school.

Typical modifications to the ecological arrangements in these areas included (a) eliminating or adjusting unsafe physical arrangements, or (b) improving the scheduling and use of space. Eliminating or adjusting unsafe physical arrangements involved actual structural changes and adjustments in the use of the space. Although each site plan was unique, following are examples of four of the most common problems. First, campus and specific area borders were sometimes poorly defined. Even when fencing was used, it was sometimes obscured by foliage that shielded the campus from natural surveillance. Second, undifferentiated campus areas (e.g., a hidden corner of the playground) presented opportunities for informal gathering areas that were out of sight of adult supervisors. These areas were not only used for prohibited activities but had a tendency to increase the incidence of disruptive behavior and victimization. Third, building layout and design often produced isolated spots (e.g., end of a hallway) where students gravitated and either committed prohibited activities or exposed themselves to victimization. Finally, bus loading areas were often in direct conflict with traffic flow or created conflict and congestion with automobile parking areas. These zones also tended to be in direct conflict with the flow of students leaving the school grounds or entering for extracurricular activities. Congestion created by traffic and student flow provided the occasion for disruptive behavior and raised safety concerns.

One of the most effective ecological strategies for promoting positive social behaviors centered on improving the scheduling and use of space. For example, it not only took longer to get groups through the lunch line because of congestion, but it also provided the occasion for more physical and undesirable social interactions between and among students. One class passed through a doorway to exit the cafeteria while another class entered the cafeteria at the same time. Separating the cafeteria entrance and exit by space, and staggering the start and end of the lunch period helped facilitate movement in and out of the

area. Although there were no set rules, the following guidelines were used to improve the scheduling and use of space: (a) The density of students was reduced by using all entrances and exits to a given area, the space between groups/lines/classes was increased, and the age spread of students was increased as the density of students increased; (b) wait time was kept at a minimum; (c) travel time and distance was decreased as much as possible; (d) movement was controlled through the use of such physical signs as clearly marked transition zones that indicated movement from less controlled to more controlled space or indicated behavioral expectations for the common areas of the school; and (e) the sequence of events in the common areas were designed to facilitate the type of behavioral momentum desired (e.g., going to recess before lunch rather than going to lunch before recess helped students to calm down before returning to the classroom).

Behavioral Guidelines. Behavioral guidelines or expectations for the common area routines of the school were systematically designed and taught. The process of establishing these guidelines was based on Project PREPARE (Proactive, Responsive, Empirical, and Proactive Alternatives in Regular Education; Colvin, Sugai, & Kameenui, 1993) and included identifying specific routines or what students should accomplish, task analyzing the routines, and teaching and maintaining the routines.

Determining what the students should accomplish in a given common area was the first step in establishing behavioral guidelines for the school's common area routines. A task analysis of these routines was then used to specify, in a precise manner, the behavior required of students. These discrete, sequential, and observable behaviors were outlined in specific teaching plans for each common area. Finally, a three-phase process was used to teach students the routines. In the first phase, students were taught the routines under high levels of supervision. This supervision continued through the first 2 to 3 weeks of school and, when necessary, included high rates of social reinforcement and corrective feedback. The second phase involved conducting periodic reviews during the first 2 months of the school session under reduced levels of supervision. "Booster sessions" were conducted throughout the remainder of the year in the third phase (i.e., as needed and after holidays).

Supervision. The school staff actively supervised students to maintain the behavioral expectations and to respond to disruptive behavior in a timely and effective manner. (Supervision was conducted primarily by uncertified school staff with the support of certified school staff.) Although there were no set guidelines, the ratio of supervisors to students was maintained at a level necessary to promote positive social behavior. This required varying levels of support from the certified teaching staff (see discussion on establishing behavioral guidelines above) and reducing the density of students (see discussion on ecological factors above). Established patterns of supervision were developed to enable staff to provide a more complete and balanced coverage of the common areas. Staff also understood which disruptive behaviors warranted an office referral and which behaviors they needed to manage themselves. Staff were given systematic training in the supervision of common areas and in the implementation of responses to disruptive behavior.

Disciplinary Responses. Teaching common area routines at the beginning of the year and actively working to maintain and supervise them encouraged appropriate behavior. However, the fact remained that students exhibited disruptive behavior in spite of these proactive strategies. Thus, it was necessary to develop disciplinary responses for both minor and challenging disruptive behavior. Although it is beyond the scope of this article to fully describe the range of disciplinary responses schools employed to address these behaviors, the following factors were considered when developing them.

The basic response to disruptive behavior was corrective in nature (i.e., staff

responded to students in a constructive and positive manner so that the disruptive behavior was identified and the students were directed to follow the common area routines). The disciplinary responses were carefully designed to ensure that they achieved their intended effect. The major issues considered in designing the disciplinary responses included (a) ensuring that the response enabled staff to respond to disruptive behavior in a timely and decisive manner, (b) employing the response that was appropriate for each individual child rather than standard progressive responses to disruptive behavior, (c) ensuring that the disciplinary response was developed on the basis of its effect on students and not on the basis of its convenience to school staff, (d) delineating and actively teaching the students which behaviors warranted the use of the disciplinary responses, and (e) developing an informed-consent process such as a student/parent manual and individual communication structure to ensure that students and their guardians fully understood the potential disciplinary responses that were employed.

School-Wide Classroom Management Intervention

One of the greatest challenges to working effectively with students who exhibited disruptive behavior was that many of the classroom management systems or strategies used by teachers for disruptive behavior were ineffective, paralleling ineffective family management practices. Indeed, it was not uncommon for many teachers to respond to disruptive behavior by ignoring it or by using elaborate warning systems such as checks after a name or pulling different-colored cards. Commonly used classroom management strategies for disruptive behavior, unlike effective family management practices (Patterson, 1982), do not appear to give central status to the seemingly "innocuous" disruptive behaviors that are commonly found in classrooms. Research on families (Patterson, 1982) has demonstrated that these seemingly innocuous behaviors begin a process that leads to

chronic (repetitive, low-level disruptive) behavior and, under certain conditions, dramatic behavior (e.g., physical assault). Research conducted with families (Patterson, 1982) has suggested that low-level disruptive behaviors in classrooms may *not* be innocuous, and that they should not be ignored because such behaviors may be the basic building blocks for chronic and dramatic behaviors. In contrast to research on families, it appears that educators have not traditionally viewed the low-level disruptive behaviors that are commonly found in classrooms as the building blocks for chronic and dramatic behaviors. Although researchers have demonstrated that a teacher's behavior influences students' behavior (Shores, Jack, Gunter, Ellis, DeBriere, & Wehby, 1993), they appear not to have explored whether low-level disruptive behavior underlies chronic and dramatic behavior (see Doyle, 1986).

Given that commonly used classroom management strategies do not give central status to low-level disruptive behaviors, one of the most important elements of the project centered on establishing a school-wide classroom management intervention for disruptive behavior (Think Time; see Note 1). The framework for the intervention was based on time-out (e.g., Drabman & Spitalnik, 1973; Gard & Berry, 1986; Miller, 1986) and debriefing (Sugai & Colvin, 1996) or providing students with opportunities for feedback and for planning about their performance (Sprick, Sprick, & Garrison, 1993; Walker, Colvin, & Ramsey, 1995). Think Time is essentially a cognitive–behavioral time-out designed to (a) deliver a negative consequence when the student engages in a disruptive behavior, (b) provide the student with feedback and planning for a subsequent performance, and (c) enable the teacher and student to cut off a negative social exchange and initiate a positive one. Think Time includes three elements: (a) reducing or eliminating warnings and/or repeated requests with early intervention—essentially heightening the behavioral sensitivity of the teacher and raising the behavioral expectations for the students,

(b) using a time-out procedure or contingent withdrawal of attention when a disruptive behavior occurred, and (c) employing a debriefing process to help students achieve self-directed behavior and to ensure that every misbehavior was viewed by the teachers as an instructional opportunity.

This intervention required teamwork between two or more teachers—the homeroom teacher and a cooperating teacher(s) who provided the designated Think Time area. Teachers prepared their class for the implementation of the school-wide classroom intervention by actively teaching the students the intervention. The specific steps in Think Time included the following:

1. *Catching disruptive behavior early.* It was critical that teachers catch the disruptive behavior early and that they reduce (in the case of minor problem behavior) and eliminate (in the case of more serious disruptive behavior) threats and ultimatums as well as warnings. In the case of minor behavior (e.g., off-task), the student was reinforced by the teacher if the student complied with a request or prompt to adjust his or her behavior. If the student did not comply, the teacher directed the student to a designated classroom for Think Time. In the case of more serious disruptive behavior (e.g., profanity), the teacher simply directed the student to a designated classroom for Think Time. The communication by the teacher in both cases was limited, unemotional, and matter-of-fact.

2. *Moving to and entering the designated Think Time classroom.* Students typically moved independently to the designated Think Time classroom. In the case of those students who were most problematic (this was a rare event), teachers used a variety of strategies (tracked the amount of time the student took to arrive at the designated classroom, sent the student with an escort, etc.) to ensure that the student moved quickly to the classroom. Once the student arrived, he or she stood by the classroom door and waited until the cooperating teacher directed the student to a designated Think Time desk. The desk was located in an area that was free from

distractions, and it limited the ability of the student to engage the teacher or other students.

3. *Think Time/debriefing process.* After the teacher had observed the student sitting in a calm manner, the student was approached by the cooperating teacher, who initiated the debriefing process. The debriefing was conducted at the convenience of the cooperating teacher and ideally after allowing the misbehaving student a minimum of 5 to 10 minutes to "think about" his or her behavior and to gain "self-control." The time-out was behavior dependent (not time dependent). Teachers initially asked students to describe their behavior objectively prior to providing them the debriefing form to complete independently. If the student was responsive to the opening question regarding the behavior, he or she was asked to complete the form. If not, the teacher responded by saying "I'll be back to you" and returned to his or her regular duties until another appropriate break arrived (and the student was sitting in a calm manner). Throughout this process the teacher did not cajole or was not drawn into a discussion with the student. Behavioral debriefing (for older students) included the following questions in sequential steps: (a) identify their inappropriate behavior; (b) identify what they wanted (e.g., revenge, attention, avoidance of schoolwork); (c) indicate whether or not they got what they wanted; (d) identify what they needed to do (replacement behavior) when they got back to work in their classroom (e.g., follow directions if they did not follow directions); and (e) indicate whether or not they thought they could do the new action(s). A shortened debriefing sequence (Steps a, d, and e) and associated pictorial debriefing form were used with younger students and in some individual cases in which parents did not want their children to be asked "what they wanted." Again, the interaction was limited, unemotional, and matter-of-fact.

4. *Checking students' debriefing responses.* After the student had completed the behavioral debriefing form, he or she waited for the teacher to check if the form had been completed correctly (be-

haviors were stated in objective terms; the debriefing teacher did not know which disruptive behavior the student had actually exhibited at this point). If correct, the student was directed to go back to the classroom with the completed form. If incorrect, the student remained in Think Time. The teacher responded by saying, "I'll be back to you" and returned to his or her regular duties until another appropriate break arrived (and the student was sitting in a calm manner).

5. *Rejoining the class.* When the student reentered the classroom, the student stood by the door and waited until he or she was acknowledged by the teacher. The teacher then assessed the accuracy of the completed behavioral debriefing form. If accurate, the teacher (in a positive manner) directed the student to join the class. Teachers used a variety of reentry procedures (e.g., peer assistance, assignment sheet) to ensure that the student was able to make up work missed. If the debriefing form was inaccurate, the student was directed to return to the designated classroom to repeat Think Time.

6. *Use of other consequences.* The use of Think Time was not the only response to disruptive behavior. It was used flexibly with other classroom strategies (e.g., proximity, eye contact, and consequences). Think Time in itself was a powerful enough response to most minor disruptive behaviors. However, additional contingencies such as parent contacts and response cost were established in the case of chronic disruptive behavior or challenging behavior (e.g., profanity and physical aggression).

Individual Behavioral Interventions

Individual behavioral interventions were taught to teachers to address students' curricular and behavioral problems. Developing effective behavioral programs for disruptive behavior was based on recent work by researchers who studied maintaining contingencies for disruptive behavior (Carr & Durand, 1985; Horner, Day, Sprague, O'Brien, & Heathfield, 1991; Iwata, Vollmer, & Zarcone, 1990).

Teachers used an informal behavioral assessment to identify the function of the behavior (i.e., attention-seeking, escape/avoidance, sensory stimulation, and multiple functions) because it was found that the formal assessment procedures recommended by researchers (e.g., O'Neill, Horner, Albin, Storey, & Sprague, 1990) tended to restrict unnecessarily the development of effective behavioral interventions. School staff were unwilling to conduct analog conditions primarily because of time constraints.

Teachers informally identified the conditions under which the disruptive behavior occurred and formulated a hypothesis regarding the function of this behavior. In addition, the stable response to disruptive behavior created by the school-wide classroom intervention assisted teachers in making an accurate determination regarding the function of the disruptive behavior. There was a high probability that any student who continued to exhibit high rates of disruptive behavior was engaging in escape/avoidance behaviors or sensory behavior (e.g., children with attention-deficit/hyperactivity disorder [ADHD]). This typically enabled teachers to develop effective interventions directly targeted at the function of the behavior. Teachers typically included four types of interventions in their individualized behavioral plans: ecological factors, longitudinal programming, focused interventions, and disciplinary responses.

Ecological Factors. Ecological factors were those physical, interpersonal, and programmatic factors that provided a better fit with the student's characteristics and needs. Key ecological factors included the physical arrangement of desks in the classroom, the orderliness of the room, the position of the student, the interpersonal interactions between teacher and student, and the interventions that address the specific needs of the student.

Longitudinal Programming. Longitudinal programming involved teaching the student fundamental skills and competencies to facilitate behavioral change for the purpose of long-term academic and social success. The most common longitudinal programming interventions used by teachers included social skills training; social problem solving; anger management/conflict resolution; counseling services (individual, group, and family); and intensive academic skills instruction. Additionally, this programming also included medical intervention, when necessary.

Focused Interventions. Focused interventions concentrated on the replacement behavior (e.g., increasing the number of math problems completed and on-task behavior) rather than on the disruptive behavior to be eliminated. Focused interventions included direct, positive intervention strategies designed to help change students' behaviors. Although teachers were trained to implement a number of focused interventions (e.g., differential reinforcement procedures), they typically implemented self-management procedures and behavioral contracts.

Disciplinary Responses. Disciplinary responses included situation management techniques that were used when disruptive behavior occurred. Although teachers relied on the school-wide classroom management intervention described above as the primary disciplinary response, adjustments were made when necessary. This typically occurred in the case of extreme instances of escape/avoidance and sensory behavior (e.g., children with ADHD). In addition, disciplinary responses used in the common areas of the school were adjusted as necessary.

Advisory Committee

An advisory committee was established to direct the development, implementation, maintenance, and evaluation of the program elements. The composition of the committee was representative of the school staff (i.e., certified teachers and special services, administration, and classified personnel). It also included parent representatives. Although the committee directed and guided the program, members maintained a joint venture with staff at all levels. Thus, the role of the committee members was not to represent staff, but to develop plans, which were reviewed and accepted by the school staff. This was critical to ensure the implementation and maintenance of the program.

A five-step process was used by the committee to implement and maintain the program elements. The first step involved the development of draft proposals, which contained descriptions of the current program and descriptions of the revised program element(s), including a discussion of the rationale for the changes (pros and cons). In the second step, the draft proposals were presented to all staff for discussion. The committee provided copies of the draft proposal a few days prior to the formal presentation of the proposal and explained the process and the assumptions that the staff used to review and revise the current program. In the third step, the draft proposal was revised based on staff feedback and recommendations. The second and third steps were repeated until consensus was achieved. The fourth step involved presenting the final proposal to staff for approval, including a staff development plan to ensure the implementation of the program element(s). The final step involved the development of an evaluation plan to assess the effects of the program element(s).

EVALUATION DESIGN

Design

A pre– posttest comparison group design was used to assess the effects of the project (Campbell & Stanley, 1963). The two project schools were selected by school district officials to participate in the data collection from an original pool of six elementary schools receiving project services. These schools were selected prior to the implementation of the program elements. Two matched schools (i.e., enrollment, SES) served as comparison schools.

The experimental and comparison schools were located in the same poverty tract (an area designated by the U.S. Census as a poverty area) in a midsize city in the Northwest and served high numbers of students at risk for school failure. The schools were similar in their total school enrollment ($M = 590$; range = 540 to 630), percentage of students receiving free lunch ($M = 75\%$; range = 74% to 85%), minority enrollment ($M = 18\%$; range = 12% to 27%), historical percentile achievement level (e.g., fourth grade: $M = 36$; range = 24 to 50), and on other factors such as referrals to Child Protective Services and curriculum practices (i.e., schools used the same curriculum materials and were designated Title I schools). Comparison schools continued to implement their traditional school-wide organizational practices and classroom management strategies, and no obvious changes were made in these practices and strategies.

Measures

Various measures were used to assess the effects of the project on the school climate, teachers, and students. A description of the specific measures and associated data collection methods used follows.

School Climate

Information was collected on the number of expulsions, suspensions, and emergency removals. This archival information was obtained for the 1992–1993 (preproject) and 1994–1995 (final year of the project) school years from the annual disciplinary reports submitted to the district's Research and Evaluation Office. The procedures for developing the disciplinary reports were standardized across all of the elementary schools by the local school district and had been ongoing for a number of years.

Teachers

Teachers at the experimental and comparison schools were administered three self-report measures in the fall of the 1993–1994 school year (September; pre-

implementation of program elements) and the spring of the 1994–1995 school year (May; postimplementation). Teachers in the experimental schools also completed a consumer satisfaction survey at the completion of the project. All of the measures were completed individually by teachers, and all responses were anonymous. Four respondents (1 comparison and 3 experimental) were not included in the analysis because of attrition across the assessment period. Ninety-eight teachers (45 comparison and 53 experimental) completed the pre- and posttest measures. Of the 98 respondents, 84 were female and 14 were male. The mean for average years experience of the respondents was 11.2. There were no statistically significant differences between the comparison and experimental groups in the ratio of males to females and in the mean years of experience. In addition, there were no statistically significant differences in the responses of female and male teachers across the measures. Thus, gender was dropped from all subsequent analyses. A description of the three self-report measures follows.

Working Alliance Among Staff Regarding Problem Behavior. A 20-item self-report measure (Working Alliance for Problem Behavior Inventory; WAPBI), based on the Working Alliance Inventory (WAI; Horvath, 1982), was developed to assess the extent to which teachers believed that there were shared or agreed-upon goals among school staff for working with problem behavior. Teachers indicated their level of agreement with each of the items on a 5-point Likert-type scale (1 = *strongly disagree,* 2 = *disagree,* 3 = *undecided,* 4 = *agree,* and 5 = *strongly agree*). The WAPBI provided a total scale score. As that score increased, teachers' belief that there are shared goals for working with disruptive behavior among staff increased. The coefficient alpha for the WAPBI was .88.

Ability to Work with Problem Behavior. A 40-item self-report measure containing three scales (Ability to Work with Problem Behavior Inventory; AWPBI), based on the Devereux Behavior Rating

Scale (Naglieri, LeBuffe, & Pfeiffer, 1993), was developed to assess the extent to which teachers believed that they were capable of working with students who exhibit internalizing, externalizing, and disturbed (e.g., psychotic) behavior (see Note 2). The AWPBI provides a scale score for each of the three scales: Externalizing (E, 12 items), Internalizing (I, 20 items), and Disturbing (D, 8 items). Because the project focused primarily on externalizing behavior, the I and D scales served as a manipulation check. For each item in the three scales, teachers indicated their level of agreement on a 5-point Likert-type scale (1 = *strongly disagree,* 2 = *disagree,* 3 = *undecided,* 4 = *agree,* and 5 = *strongly agree*). Thus, as the score for each scale increased, teachers were more likely to support the proposition that they are capable of working with a student who exhibits the particular type of problem behavior (externalizing, internalizing, and disturbing). The coefficient alphas for the Externalizing, Internalizing, and Disturbing scales were .88, .86, and .85, respectively.

Effects of Stress. The 18-item Effects of Stress Inventory (ESI) of the Pullis Inventory of Teacher Stress (Pullis, 1992) was used to assess the incidence of occupational (i.e., emotional and physiological) stress exhibited by teachers on a 4-point frequency scale (1 = *never,* 2 = *occasionally* [once a week], 3 = *frequently* [a few times a week], and 4 = *very frequently* [most of the week]). The ESI provided a scale score. As the scale score increased, teachers reported a higher incidence of occupational stress. The coefficient alpha for this measure was .87.

Consumer Satisfaction. A 4-item survey was used to assess the satisfaction of teachers with the project (see Table 2). Only teachers in the experimental schools completed the survey at the end of the project period. Teachers indicated their level of agreement with each of the items on a 5-point Likert-type scale (1 = *strongly disagree,* 2 = *disagree,* 3 = *undecided,* 4 = *agree,* 5 = *strongly agree*).

Students

The behavioral adjustment and academic performance of a sample of students who exhibited externalizing behavior (target students) and a sample of students who did not exhibit externalizing behavior or other behavioral adjustment problems (criterion students) enrolled in the experimental schools were assessed by teachers in the fall of the 1993–1994 school year (October to December; initial implementation of the program elements) and the spring of the 1994–1995 school year (April to June; postimplementation). Data on an equivalent group of experimental and criterion students in the comparison schools were not collected because of logistical reasons (e.g., time and resources).

A two-stage multiple gating procedure, modified from the Systematic Screening for Behavior Disorders (Walker & Severson, 1990), was used to identify a sample of students who exhibited externalizing behavior. In Stage 1, teachers at each grade (1 through 6) were asked to list the five students who best exemplified externalizing behavior characteristics. Teachers then rank ordered each list from "most characteristic" to "least characteristic" of the externalizing dimension. In Stage 2, teachers completed a teacher rating (Devereux Behavior Rating Scale–School Form for ages 5 through 12 [BRSSF]) of the three students who most evidenced an externalizing characteristic. Based on their total scale standard score, the two highest rated students from each grade (1 through 6) at each of the two experimental schools were selected to participate in the study. This resulted in 4 students from each grade (1 through 6) for a total of 24 (21 boys and 3 girls) target students.

The respective teachers of the target students were then asked to identify four equivalent (i.e., gender and age-same year) students at each grade who did *not* exhibit externalizing behavior or other behavioral adjustment problems. Teachers were asked to identify typical students rather than those students who demonstrated the best behavioral adjust-

ment. This resulted in a matched sample of 24 criterion students (21 boys and 3 girls) with which to compare the performance of the target students.

Nine percent of the cases were dropped because of attrition over the course of the assessment period. This resulted in 21 target students (20 boys and 1 girl) and 20 criterion students (18 boys and 2 girls). Eight of the target students were receiving special education services (three were classified as having learning disabilities and five were classified as having behavioral disorders). None of the criterion students were receiving special education services. The mean ages of the students in years at each grade (1 through 6) were 6.4, 7.3, 8.6, 9.5, 10.7, and 11.5, respectively. There were no statistically significant differences in the mean ages of the target and criterion students. Thus, grade and gender (because of insufficient numbers of female students) were dropped from all subsequent analyses. Additionally, there also were no statistically significant differences in the mean pre- and post-test BRSSF total scores of the target and criterion students across the grades. Description of the measures used to assess the behavioral adjustment and academic performance of target and criterion students follows.

Behavioral Adjustment. The behavioral adjustment of all students was rated independently by their respective teachers on the BRSSF. The 40-item BRSSF includes four subscales: Interpersonal Problems (IP), Inappropriate Behaviors/Feelings (IBF), Depression (D), and Physical Symptoms/Fears (PSF). The IP subscale assesses the extent to which the student is able to develop or maintain satisfactory interpersonal relationships with peers and teachers. The IBF subscale assesses the extent to which the student exhibits inappropriate behaviors or feelings under normal conditions. The D subscale assesses the extent to which the student exhibits a general pervasive mood of unhappiness or depression. The PSF subscale assesses the extent to which the student tends to develop physical symptoms or fears associated with

personal or school problems. The overall coefficient alpha for the BRSSF was .91. The coefficient alphas for the IP, IBF, D, and PSF subscales were .85, .87, .82, and .83, respectively.

The BRSSF provides a total scale standard score and separate subscale standard scores. The total scale standard score quantitatively describes the student's behavior in relation to the standardized mean of 100. As a total standard score increases beyond 100, the rating obtained for that student becomes less typical and more like those earned by students with emotional or behavioral problems. A cutoff score of 115 (1 *SD* above the standardized mean) indicates that a student's total standard score on the BRSSF departs substantially from the standardized mean and that significant problems are reported by the rater. The BRSSF subscale standard scores quantitatively describe a student's behavior in relation to the standardized mean of 10. As a subscale standard score increases over 10, the rating obtained for that individual becomes less typical and more like scores earned by students with emotional or behavioral problems in that area. A cutoff score of 13 (1 *SD* above the standardized mean) indicates that a student's subscale standard score departs substantially from the standardized mean and that significant problems are reported by the rater.

Academic Performance and School Survival Skills. The school district's Academic, Work Habits, and Social Growth scales of the Skill Development Matrix (SDM) was used to assess the academic performance and the school survival skills of the students. Teachers rated the academic performance of students relative to the established objectives in each given content area on a 4-point scale. Specifically, teachers rated the extent to which the student (a) was meeting objectives and performing independently, (b) was working toward objectives with continuing assistance, (c) required considerable assistance when working toward established objectives in four content areas (reading, language development, mathematics, and science), or (d) needed more time to develop. Music and arts scale scores were not included in this analysis. In the case of school survival skills, teachers rated the work habits and social growth of students using a 4-point Likert-type scale (1 = *very good*, 2 = *satisfactory*, 3 = *shows improvement*, and 4 = *needs work*). These rating systems provided an objective measure of the extent to which the student was meeting the established objectives under each content and school survival area for his or her respective grade level. In all cases, the lower the scale scores, the closer the student was to meeting the established objectives under each of these areas.

RESULTS

Schools

The percentage of change in administrative disciplinary actions for the 1992–1993 and 1994–1995 school years was computed to assess the effects of the project at the school level (see Figure 2). Inspection of Figure 2 reveals that there were clear decreases in the disciplinary actions of the experimental schools following the implementation of the project. For example, the number of suspensions decreased over 40% during the course of the project. In contrast, the number of disciplinary actions in the comparison schools increased. This increase reflects a continuation of the consistent growth over the past 10 years in the use of such actions in schools across the district, including the experimental schools prior to the implementation of the project.

Teachers

Working Alliance Among Staff Regarding Problem Behavior. The pre- and post-test mean total scores for the teachers in the experimental and comparison schools on the WAPBI and associated *F* values for the one-way analysis of covariance (ANCOVA), using the pretest means as the covariate, are presented in Table 1. Inspection of Table 1 reveals that there was a statistically significant difference in the posttest WAPBI

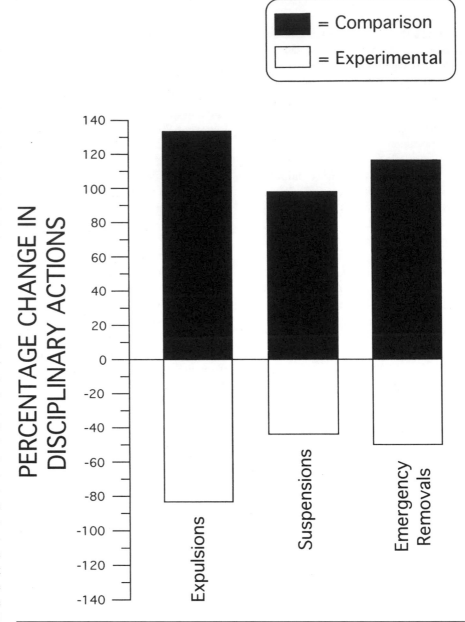

FIGURE 2. Percentage change in the disciplinary responses of the experimental and comparison schools.

mean scores of the teachers in the experimental and comparison schools. Teachers in the experimental schools were more likely to support the proposition that there were shared or agreed-upon goals for working with problem behaviors among school staff than were teachers in the comparison schools.

Ability to Work with Problem Behavior. The pre- and posttest mean AWPBI

scale scores for the teachers in the experimental and comparison schools and associated F values for the one-way ANCOVAs, using the pretest means as the covariate, are presented in Table 1. Inspection of Table 1 reveals that there was a statistically significant difference in the posttest mean E scale scores of the teachers in the comparison and experimental schools. Teachers in the experimental schools were more likely to indicate that they were capable of working with students who exhibited externalizing behavior than were the teachers in the comparison schools. There were no statistically significant differences in the posttest mean I and D scale scores of the teachers in the comparison and experimental schools. This was expected, given that the I and D scales served as a manipulation check because the project focused on externalizing behavior.

Effects of Stress. The pre- and posttest mean scores for the teachers in the experimental and comparison groups on the ESI and associated F values for the one-way ANCOVA, using the pretest means as the covariate, are presented in

Table 1. The results of this analysis revealed that there was not a statistically significant difference in the posttest ESI mean scores of these teachers (see Table 1). Teachers in the experimental and comparison schools reported the same levels of occupational stress.

Consumer Satisfaction. The mean average and associated standard deviation for each question on the consumer satisfaction survey are presented in Table 2. It was important to establish whether teachers were significantly in favor of, or opposed to proposals rather than being neutral or undecided. Therefore, the 95% confidence interval for each mean was computed to determine whether it en-

compassed the midpoint of the scale. Those means in which the midpoint of the response scale (undecided) deviated from the 95% confidence interval are underlined in Table 2. In all cases, teachers reported that they were satisfied with the project (see Table 2).

Students

Behavioral Adjustment. The pre-and posttest mean total and subscale standard scores of the target and criterion students on the BRSSF and the associated pre- and posttest effect size comparisons between these students are presented in Table 3. One-way ANCOVAs were conducted on the posttest BRSSF mean total

TABLE 1
Teachers' Pre- and Posttest Mean Total Scale Scores on the WAPBI, AWPBI, and ESI

| Inventory/scale | Comparison condition[a] | | | | Experimental condition[b] | | | | |
| | Pretest | | Posttest | | Pretest | | Posttest | | |
	M	SD	M	SD	M	SD	M	SD	F (1, 95)
Working alliance for problem behavior	42.07	7.31	40.00	5.55	40.91	5.88	80.17	4.65	16.79*
Ability to work with problem behavior									
Internalizing behavior	30.00	4.55	29.63	3.38	29.50	4.47	29.01	5.45	2.40
Externalizing behavior	59.40	15.45	57.04	16.44	57.00	16.07	78.10	13.13	12.08*
Disturbed behavior	22.40	3.87	21.33	4.96	18.01	4.62	20.60	5.11	2.59
Effects of stress	39.60	7.34	40.67	10.47	41.25	8.45	38.60	9.22	1.22

Note. In all cases, increasing scores indicate that teachers were more likely to support a given matter. WAPBI = Working Alliance for Problem Behavior Inventory; AWPBI = Ability to Work with Problem Behavior Inventory; ESI = Effects of Stress Inventory.
[a]n = 45. [b]n = 53.
*p > .001.

TABLE 2
Mean Average Responses of Teachers in the Experimental Schools on the Consumer Satisfaction Survey

Question	X	SD
1. The project has enhanced my ability to teach students who exhibit disruptive behavior.	4.45	.49
2. I found the techniques and strategies easy to use.	4.37	.61
3. The project addressed the educational needs of all students, including those who exhibit disruptive behavior.	4.46	.51
4. I would recommend the project to others.	4.51	.41

Note. Responses ranged from 1 (*strongly disagree*) to 5 (*strongly agree*). For the means, the 95% confidence interval did not encompass the midpoint (3 = *undecided*) of the scale.

TABLE 3
Students' Pre- and Posttest Mean Total and Subscale Standard Scores on the BRSSF and
Mean Scale Scores on the SDM

	Criterion condition[a]				Target condition[b]				Effect size	
	Pretest		Posttest		Pretest		Posttest			
Measure/scale	M	SD	M	SD	M	SD	M	SD	Pretest	Posttest
BRSSF	107.93	13.79	108.92	15.05	116.44	13.45	108.83	11.47	−.62	.01
Interpersonal problems	11.61	3.13	12.38	3.45	14.63	3.73	11.43	3.72	−.96	.27
Inappropriate behaviors/ feelings	10.86	3.93	11.31	3.81	13.84	3.41	10.78	4.02	−.76	.14
Depression	12.50	3.97	12.92	4.01	16.59	5.12	12.43	3.39	−.91	.12
Physical symptoms/fears	12.96	3.80	13.31	4.12	16.38	5.05	12.19	3.39	−.90	−.27
SDM										
Language development	12.24	5.40	13.37	3.44	16.05	4.49	14.93	4.68	−.71	−.45
Reading	10.20	4.03	11.50	4.14	13.14	5.33	10.71	4.51	−.73	.19
Math	13.76	8.35	9.60	4.28	18.27	9.82	10.86	8.17	−.54	−.29
Work habits	10.28	3.30	8.67	2.66	16.26	5.49	9.07	4.95	−1.80	−.40
Social growth	7.75	2.42	8.17	2.99	13.48	4.25	8.93	4.32	−2.37	−.25

Note. In all cases, decreasing scores indicate enhanced performance in the given area. There were statistically significant differences in all areas ($p > .001$) in the pretest mean scores of the target and criterion students. There were no statistically significant differences in any of the posttest means scores of these students. BRSSF = Devereaux Behavior Rating Scale–School Form (Naglieri et al., 1993); SDM = Skill Development Matrix.
[a]$n = 20$. [b]$n = 21$.

and subscale standard scores using the pretest means as the covariate. In all cases, there were no statistically significant differences in the posttest BRSSF mean total and subscale standard scores.

Inspection of Table 3 shows that the pretest mean total and subscale standard scores of the target students departed substantially from the standardized mean scores (total standardized mean score = 100 and subscale standardized mean scores = 10). In contrast, the pretest mean total and subscale standard scores of the criterion students did not depart substantially from the standardized mean scores. Additionally, the pretest effect size comparisons between the target and criterion students ranged from −.62 to −.96 (see Table 3). The formula used to compute the effect sizes was as follows:

$$\text{Effect size} = (M_{\text{target students}} - M_{\text{criterion students}})/ SD_{\text{criterion students}}$$

Inspection of Table 3 reveals that the posttest mean total and subscale standard scores of the criterion students remained relatively stable across the assessment period. In contrast, the posttest mean total and subscale standard scores of the target students decreased, indicating improvements in their behavioral adjustment. Additionally, the posttest mean total and subscale standard scores of the target and criterion students did not depart substantially from the standardized mean scores provided by the BRSSF interpretation guidelines (Naglieri et al., 1993). The posttest effect size comparisons between the target and criterion students ranged from .01 to −.27

Academic Performance and School Survival Skills. The pre- and posttest mean scale scores of the target and criterion students on the SDM and the associated pre- and posttest effect size comparisons between these students are presented in Table 3. ANCOVAs were conducted on the posttest SDM mean scale scores using the pretest means as the covariate. There were no statistically significant differences in the posttest mean scale scores of the target and criterion students in all areas.

Inspection of Table 3 reveals that teachers' pretest ratings of the academic performance, work habits, and social growth of the target students were consistently higher (indicating less skill development) than those for the criterion students. The effect sizes for the pretest comparisons between the target and criterion students ranged from −.54 to −2.37. In contrast, teachers' posttest ratings of the academic performance, work habits, and social growth of target and criterion students were more similar. The effect sizes for the posttest comparisons between the target and criterion students ranged from −.19 to −.45 (see Table 3).

DISCUSSION

The management of problem behavior or the lack of discipline has been identified by the public as the most persistent and troublesome issue facing schools (Center & McKittrick, 1987; Cotton, 1990; Elam, Rose, & Gallup, 1992; Jones, 1993). Although many children and adolescents occasionally exhibit aggressive and antisocial behaviors in the course of development, an increase is taking place in the number of youth who confront their teachers and schools with persistent threatening and destructive behaviors (Rutherford & Nelson, 1995). The purpose of the present study was to increase the institutional capacity of schools to work with students who exhibit disruptive or externalizing behavior. The project focused on developing universal school-wide strategies rather than implementing individualized interventions for students' behavior problems.

In general, the outcomes of the project were positive on school climate, teachers, and student. These positive outcomes suggest that educators must look closely at the effectiveness of their school-wide and classroom organizational structures and practices prior to the implementation of individualized interventions for students. The project also had positive effects on the number of administrative disciplinary actions used by school officials. Over the course of the project, the numbers of suspensions, expulsions, and emergency removals substantially decreased in the experimental schools, whereas they increased in the comparison schools. Although a formal cost analysis in terms of time associated with the use of the administrative disciplinary actions was not conducted, administrators in the experimental schools reported that the downward shift in the number of administrative disciplinary actions greatly reduced the amount of time they devoted to discipline issues in their schools. These findings are consistent with previous research conducted on the effectiveness of instructionally based proactive school-wide management models (Colvin, Kameenui, & Sugai, 1994).

Consistent with the effects on overall administrative disciplinary actions, the project had positive effects on the behavioral adjustment of target students who exhibited externalizing behavior. These effects appear to be due in large part to the school-wide classroom management intervention (Think Time) element of the project. In all cases, individualized intervention programs were not implemented. Across all measures, teachers noted significant problems in the social adjustment of the target students *prior* to the implementation of the project. The effect sizes ranged from −.96 to −.62. In contrast, teachers' ratings of the social adjustment of the target students fell within the normal range *following* the implementation of the project. The effect sizes ranged from .01 to −.27. These findings are consistent with previous research that has demonstrated that students' classroom behavior is most appropriate when a combination of positive and negative consequences are maintained (e.g., Rosen, O'Leary, Joyce, Conway, & Pfiffner, 1984).

Similar evidence was reported from teachers' rating of the school survival skills of the target students. Prior to the implementation of the project, teachers noted problems in the work habits and social growth of students. The effect sizes for the Work Habits and Social Growth scales on the SDM were −1.80 and −2.37, respectively. In contrast, teachers' ratings of the work habits and social growth of the target students improved following the implementation of the project. The effect sizes for the Work Habits and Social Growth scales on the SDM were −.40 and −.25, respectively.

The academic performance and school survival skills of the target students also improved substantially. Teachers noted problems in the extent to which the target students met the established objectives in the four academic content areas prior to the implementation of the project (effect sizes ranged from −.71 to −.54). In contrast, teachers' ratings of the academic performance of the target students improved in each of the academic content areas following the implementation of the project (effect sizes ranged from .19 to −.45). Taken together, improvements in the social adjustment and academic performance of the target students support previous research indicating that social adjustment and academic performance are linked (Kazdin, 1987).

The project also had generally positive effects on teachers. Teachers in the experimental schools were more likely to support the proposition that there were shared or agreed-upon goals for working with problem behavior among school staff than were teachers in the comparison schools. This finding is not surprising, given that the primary focus of the school-wide organizational practices element was establishing consistent behavioral guidelines or expectations. Additionally, teachers in the experimental schools were more likely to indicate they were capable of working with students who exhibit disruptive behavior than were teachers in the comparison schools. Confidence in this finding is strengthened by the nonsignificant differences in the experimental and comparison teachers' ratings of the extent to which they were capable of working with children who exhibit internalizing and disturbing behavior. Because the project focused on students who exhibited externalizing behavior, these scales served as a check for potential rater bias due to participation in the study.

The project did not appear to have an effect on the occupational stress levels of the teachers. Teachers in the the experimental and control schools reported the same levels of occupational stress at both the pre- and posttest assessments. This finding supports previous research on occupational stress of teachers in which it was shown that school setting factors such as career issues and workload variables were more stressful than direct contact with students who exhibit disruptive behavior (Pullis, 1992).

Despite the positive outcomes of this investigation, several caveats should be mentioned. First, the evaluation of the project included only two elementary schools in one geographic location; therefore, it is not clear whether the program would be as effective in other schools and inferences regarding the generality of the findings must be made cautiously until further research is conducted in other schools. Second, because formal data on treatment fidelity, or the extent to which the project elements were implemented as specified, were not collected, it is not entirely clear whether the changes in children's social behavior were directly related to the implementation of the project. Further, because the project included a number of elements, it is not entirely clear which of these components is necessary to promote positive social behavior in schools. Conclusions regarding the effectiveness of any of the elements must be made cautiously until further research is conducted.

IMPLICATIONS

The results of this study make it possible to discuss implications of the model in several areas. The primary importance of research on the project is on demonstrating that the social adjustment and academic performance of children who exhibit disruptive behavior can be improved with the application of universal strategies and interventions. This is in contrast to common practice in the field in which the focus is on developing individualized intervention programs (Allessi, 1988). Additionally, focusing on universal strategies and interventions may lead to a school environment that is both preventative and remedial in nature. The generally positive effects of the project on the behavioral adjustment and academic achievement of students who exhibit disruptive behavior suggest that the school and classroom environments may not only play a large role in the level of disruptive behavior that students exhibit, but also may be necessary to effectively address the needs of these students. This is not to say that individual students may not need considerable school staff time and attention that go beyond the universal strategies. Rather, that the implementation of the universal strategies may reduce the need for individualized programs, and may be necessary to provide a stable context in which to develop effective individualized intervention programs. Although the acceptance of the universal interventions was not directly assessed, there is little question that teachers will view such interventions more positively than individualized interventions.

Related to the above issues, research on the project demonstrates that the school environment plays a large role in the types and levels of disruptive behavior that students exhibit. Although there are many factors (e.g., family needs and peer influences) that must be addressed to effectively work with students who exhibit disruptive behavior, there is little

schools can do to address such factors. Thus, focusing on those factors under the control of schools and on practices that are effective for most students may lead to better outcomes for students who exhibit disruptive behavior. For example, researchers have demonstrated that teachers may be able to work more effectively with students with emotional and behavioral problems simply by adjusting their social interactions (Gunter, Denny, Jack, Shores, & Nelson, 1993; Shores et al., 1993) and teaching practices (Nelson, Johnson, & Marchand-Martella, 1996). Additionally, the importance of focusing on the school environment is highlighted by evidence that even a child's personality is context-specific (Harris, 1995).

Another implication of the project centers on policy and training issues. Research on the project suggests that school administrators need to establish policies and practices to ensure that schools provide a school environment that is conducive to learning. Such policies and procedures should play a larger role in educational reform efforts in the future. The bleak outcomes of students who exhibit emotional and behavioral disorders suggest that schools must rethink how they serve such students. Related to this issue, the results of this study indicate that staff development efforts in regards to meeting the needs of students who exhibit disruptive behavior might be better focused around the particular practices of each individual school. The school based problem-solving approach utilized in this study not only enhanced teachers' perceptions of their ability to work with students who exhibit disruptive behavior, but resulted also in improvements in the behavioral adjustment and academic performance of such students. Indeed, it may be necessary to treat the policies and procedures centering on the school environment much like curriculum issues, reviewing them on a regular basis.

Finally, the practical importance of the research on the project would be minimal if it depended on conditions unlikely to exist outside of the two experimental schools. The consumer satisfac-

tion ratings of the teachers indicate that they believed that the project would be viewed as useful to other professionals. Additionally, as of this writing, the project exists in 15 additional elementary schools not served by the project within the district and over 50 schools in the region. A number of school districts have implemented the project in all of their K-8 schools and are conducting small-scale pilots in high schools. Effective implementation of the project does not appear to depend on federal funding or unusually effective administrators or outstanding staffs.

About the Author

J. RON NELON, PhD, is an associate professor in the Department of Applied Psychology at Eastern Washington University. Address: J. Ron Nelson, Department of Applied Psychology, Eastern Washington University, Cheney, WA 99004.

Author's Notes

1. This article, and the work that it represents, is dedicated to the many professionals, parents, advocates, and children who participated in the project.
2. Preparation of this article was supported in part by Grant No. H237D20011 from the U.S. Department of Education, Office of Special Education Programs. Opinions expressed herein do not necessarily reflect the position of the U.S. Department of Education, and no endorsement should be inferred.

Notes

1. Teachers received training in, and implemented, a wide variety of strategies designed to prevent disruptive behavior from occurring.
2. A confirmatory factor analysis was conducted to identify the three scales.

References

Allessi, G. (1988). Diagnosis diagnosed: A systemic reaction. *Professional School Psychology, 3*(2), 145–151.

Bowlby, J. (1988). *A secure base.* New York: Basic.

Bullock, L. M., Reilly, T. F., & Donahue, C. A. (1983). School violence and what teachers can do about it. *Contemporary Education, 55,* 40–44.

Campbell, D. T., & Stanley, J. C. (1963). *Experimental and quasi-experimental designs for research.* Boston: Houghton Mifflin.

Carr, E. G., & Durand, V. M. (1985). Reducing behavior problems through functional communication training. *Journal of Applied Behavior Analysis, 18,* 11–126.

Center, D. B., & McKittrick, S. (1987). Disciplinary removal of special education students. *Focus on Exceptional Children, 20*(2), 1–9.

Colvin, G., Kameenui, E., & Sugai, G. (1994). Reconceptualizing behavior management and school-wide discipline in general education. *Education and Treatment of Children, 16,* 361–381.

Colvin, G., Sugai, G., & Kameenui, E. (1993). *Curriculum for establishing a proactive school-wide discipline plan.* Eugene: University of Oregon, Project PREPARE, Division of Learning and Instructional Leadership, College of Education.

Cotton, K. (1990). *School improvement series, Close-up #9: School wide and classroom discipline.* Portland, OR: Northwest Regional Educational Laboratory.

Doyle, W. (1986). Classroom organization and management. In M. C. Wittrock (Ed.), *Handbook of research on teaching* (pp. 392–431). New York: Macmillan.

Drabman, R. S., & Spitalnik, R. (1973). Social isolation as a punishment procedure: A controlled study. *Journal of Experimental Child Psychology, 16,* 236–249.

Edgar, E., & Levine, P. (1987). *Special education students in transition: Washington state data 1976–1986.* Seattle: University of Washington, Experimental Education Unit.

Elam, S. E., Rose, L. C., & Gallup, A. M. (1992). The 24th Annual Gallup/Phi Delta Kappa poll of the public's attitudes toward public schools. *Phi Delta Kappan, 74*(1), 41–53.

Evans, W. H., & Evans, S. S. (1985). The assessment of school violence. *Pointer, 2*(1), 18–21.

Gard, G. C., & Berry, K. K. (1986). Oppositional children: Taming tyrants. *Journal of Child Psychology, 15,* 148–158.

Greenbaum, S., & Turner, B. (Eds). (1989). *Safe schools overview: NSSC resource paper.* Malibu, CA: U.S. Department of Justice, U.S. Department of Education, and Pepperdine University.

Gunter, P. L., Denny, R. K., Jack, S. L., Shores, R. E., & Nelson, C. M. (1993). Aversive stimuli in academic interactions between students with serious emotional disturbance and their teachers. *Behavioral Disorders, 18,* 265–274.

Harris, J. R. (1995). Where is the child's environment? A group socialization theory of development. *Psychological Review, 102*(3), 458–489.

Horner, R. H., Day, H. M., Sprague, J. R., O'Brien, M., & Heathfield, L. T. (1991). Interspersed requests: A nonaversive procedure for decreasing aggression and self-injury during instruction. *Journal of Applied Behavior Analysis, 24,* 265–278.

Horvath, A. O. (1982). Working alliance inventory (revised). *Instructional Psychology Research Group, 82*(1). Burnaby, British Columbia, Canada: Simon Fraser University.

Hranitz, J. R., & Eddowes, E. A. (1990). Violence: A crisis in homes and schools. *Childhood Education, 67,* 4–7.

Huesmann, L., Eron, L., Lefkowitz, M., & Walder, L. (1984). Stability of aggression over time and generations. *Developmental Psychology, 20,* 1120–1134.

Iwata, B. A., Vollmer, T. R., & Zarcone, J. R. (1990). The experimental (functional) analysis of behavior disorders: Methodology, applications, and limitations. In A. C. Repp & N. N. Singh (Eds.), *Perspectives on the use of nonaversive and aversive interventions for persons with developmental disabilities* (pp. 301–330). Sycamore, IL: Sycamore.

Jones, V. (1993). Assessing your classroom and school-wide student management plan. *Beyond Behavior, 4*(3), 9–12.

Kazdin, A. (1987). *Conduct disorders in childhood and adolescence.* Beverly Hills, CA: Sage.

Kerr, M., & Nelson, C. M. (1983). *Strategies for managing behavior problems in the classroom.* Columbus, OH: Merrill.

Miller, D. E. (1986). The management of misbehavior by seclusion. *Residential Treatment of Children and Youth, 4,* 63–73.

Naglieri, J. A., LeBuffe, P. A., & Pfeiffer, S. I. (1993). *Devereaux behavior rating scale–School form.* San Antonio, TX: Psychological Corp.

Neel, R., Meadow, N., Levine, P., & Edgar, E. (1988). What happens after special education: A statewide follow-up study of secondary students who have behavioral disorders. *Behavioral Disorders, 13*(3), 209–216.

Nelson, J. (1992). *Increasing the capacity of schools to meet the needs of students who exhibit disruptive behavior.* Proposal to the U.S. Department of Education from Eastern Washington University, Cheney.

Nelson, J., Colvin, G., & Smith, D. J. (in press). The effects of setting clear limits on the social behaviors of students in the common areas of the schools. *Journal for At-Risk Issues.*

Nelson, J. R., Johnson, A., & Marchand-Martella, N. (1996). A comparative analysis of the effects of direct instruction, cooperative learning, and independent learning practices on the disruptive behaviors of students with behavior disorders. *Journal of Emotional and Behavioral Disorders, 4*(1), 53–63.

O'Neill, R., Horner, R., Albin, R., Storey, K., & Sprague, J. (1990). *Functional analysis of problem behavior: A practical assessment guide.* Sycamore, IL: Sycamore.

Office of Special Education Programs. (1995). *Seventeenth annual report to Congress on the implementation of The Individuals with Disabilities Education Act.* Washington, DC: U.S. Department of Education.

Patterson, G. R. (1982). *Coercive family process.* Eugene, OR: Castalia.

Patterson, G. R., & Forgatch, M. (1987). *Parents and adolescents: Living together.* Eugene, OR: Castalia.

Pianta, R. C., & Steinberg, M. (1992). Teacher-child relationships and the process of adjusting to school. *New Directions for Child Development, 57,* 61–80.

Pullis, M. (1992). An analysis of the occupational stress of teachers of the behaviorally disordered: Sources, effects, and strategies for coping. *Behavioral Disorders, 17,* 191–201.

Robins, L. (1981). Epidemiological approaches to natural history research: Antisocial disorders in children. *Journal of the American Academy of Child Psychiatry, 20,* 556–580.

Rosen, L. A., O'Leary, S. G., Joyce, S. A., Conway, G., & Pfiffner, L. J. (1984). The importance of prudent negative consequences for maintaining the appropriate behavior of hyperactive students. *Journal of Abnormal Child Psychology, 12,* 581–604.

Rutherford, R. B., & Nelson, C. M. (1995). Management of aggressive and violent behavior in schools. *Focus on Exceptional Children, 27*(6), 1–16.

Shores, R. E., Jack, S. L., Gunter, P. L., Ellis, D. N., DeBriere, T. J., & Wehby, J. H. (1993). Classroom interactions of children with behavior disorders. *Journal of Emotional and Behavioral Disorders, 1,* 27–39.

Sprick, R., Sprick, M., & Garrison, M. (1993). *Interventions: Collaborative planning for students at risk.* Longmont, CO: Sopris West.

Sugai, G., & Colvin, G. (1996). *Debriefing: A proactive addition to negative consequences for problem behavior.* Manuscript submitted for publication.

Wagner, M., & Shaver, D. (1989). *Educational programs and achievements of secondary special education students: Findings from the National Longitudinal Transition Study.* Menlo Park, CA: SRI.

Walker, H. M., Colvin, G., & Ramsey, E. (1995). *Antisocial behavior in school: Strategies and best practices.* Pacific Grove, CA: Brooks/Cole.

Walker, H. M., & Severson, H. H. (1990). *Systematic screening for behavior disorders user's guide and administration manual.* Longmont, CO: Sopris West.

First Step to Success:

An Early Intervention Approach for Preventing School Antisocial Behavior

Hill M. Walker, Kate Kavanagh, Bruce Stiller,
Annemieke Golly, Herbert H. Severson, and Edward G. Feil

This article reports results of a 4-year study designed to develop and initially evaluate a combined home and school intervention approach to preventing school antisocial behavior. The First Step to Success program targets at-risk kindergartners who show the early signs of an antisocial pattern of behavior (e.g., aggression, oppositional-defiant behavior, severe tantrumming, victimization of others). First Step to Success consists of three interconnected modules: (a) proactive, universal screening of all kindergartners; (b) school intervention involving the teacher, peers, and the target child; and (c) parent/caregiver training and involvement to support the child's school adjustment. The major goal of the program is to divert at-risk kindergartners from an antisocial path in their subsequent school careers. Two cohorts of at-risk kindergartners, consisting of 24 and 22 students, were identified and exposed to the First Step to Success program during the 1993–1994 and 1994–1995 school years, respectively. A randomized, experimental, wait-list control-group design was used to evaluate intervention effects. Cohort 1 and 2 subjects were followed up through Grades 2 and 1, respectively, with differing teachers and peer groups. Results indicated a measurable intervention effect for both cohorts and persistence of gains into the primary grades.

ANTISOCIAL BEHAVIOR, ADOLES-cent delinquency, vandalism, drug and alcohol involvement, access to weapons, association with anti-social peers, and interpersonal violence are strongly linked dimensions of a life path that increasing numbers of children and youth are adopting (American Psychological Association, 1993). Researchers have shown that antisocial behavior patterns that begin early in a child's life and are severe, occur across multiple settings, and are expressed in diverse forms constitute a powerful risk factor for a host of negative, long-term outcomes (Patterson, 1982; Robins, 1966, 1978). These outcomes often include, but are not limited to, school failure and dropout, rejection by teachers and peers, involvement in delinquent activities, bad conduct discharges from the military, unemployment, lifelong dependence on social service systems, adult criminality, and higher hospitalization and mortality rates (Kazdin, 1987; Patterson, Reid, & Dishion, 1992).

Simcha-Fagan, Langner, Gersten, and Eisenberg defined antisocial behavior as "recurrent violations of socially pre-scribed patterns of behavior" (1975, p.7). This behavior pattern nearly always in-volves severe violations of accepted so-cial norms across a range of settings (e.g., classroom, playground, neighbor-hood, community, home; see Patterson et al., 1992; Walker, Colvin, & Ramsey, 1995). Antisocial children and youth fre-quently victimize others through bully-ing and coercion processes, yet they themselves are very often victimized by hostile, environmental reactions to their aversive behavior patterns (Hollinger, 1987; Patterson et al., 1992).

Researchers now distinguish two forms of antisocial behavior patterns re-ferred to as early versus later starters or *life-course-persistent* versus *adolescent-limited* antisocial behavior (Moffitt, 1994). The prognosis for life-course-persistent antisocial behavior is far more grim than for the adolescent-limited form. Children and youth manifesting life-course-persistent antisocial behavior are socialized to this behavior pattern by their families and primary caregivers; in contrast, youth manifesting adolescent-limited antisocial behavior are socialized to it primarily by their peers (Patterson et al., 1992).

Larger and larger numbers of school-age students are manifesting the more se-vere form of life-course-persistent anti-social behavior, with correspondingly destructive effects on the school setting. Children with life-course-persistent antisocial behavior tend to bring it with them to the schooling process. Patterson and his colleagues have conducted the seminal work on the family processes, dynamics, and mechanisms that produce child antisocial behavior patterns (Patterson & Bank, 1989; Patterson, DeBaryshe, & Ramsey, 1989). Educators must target this student subpopulation as early as possible in their school careers in order to have a chance of diverting them from a destructive, antisocial path during their lives.

Kazdin (1987) argued that if children manifesting severe antisocial behavior patterns are not successfully intervened with by the end of third grade (age 8), then this disorder should be regarded much like a chronic disease such as diabetes. At present, no cure for diabetes exists, but diabetes' debilitating effects can be managed and attenuated over its progressive course through a sensible regimen of diet, medication, and exercise. Researchers in the area of antisocial behavior seem to agree that early, effective intervention is essential for successfully affecting this disorder (Cicchetti & Nurcombe, 1993; Greenwood, 1995; Reid, 1993).

Although a cure for well-established, severe forms of antisocial behavior remains elusive, promising practices have been developed for diverting at-risk children from a path that propels them toward a set of increasingly destructive outcomes (Bierman et al., 1992; McCord, 1993; Patterson et al., 1992; Reid, 1993). The case for early intervention with this population and other at-risk child populations is compelling (Reid, 1993; Zigler, Taussig, & Black, 1992). The key, in this regard, is to detect such vulnerable children as early as possible and to involve them in appropriate, comprehensive interventions. However, it is often difficult to find such at-risk children until they encounter a school-like setting and begin reacting to the structure and teacher- and peer-mediated demands that are characteristic features of such settings. They also experience considerable difficulty in negotiating the social tasks that are so necessary for friendship making and the development of social support networks (Coie, 1994; Gresham, 1986; Hollinger, 1987).

Preschoolers with aggressive, antisocial behavior patterns have been a growing concern of early childhood educators in the past decade. A substantial empirical literature now documents that the early signs of conduct disorder can be seen in the preschool years. We are seeing mature acts of deviance among younger and younger children (Bierman et al., 1992).

It is ironic that, despite the hundreds of millions of dollars that have been invested to date in early childhood programs at federal, state, and local levels, effective models and approaches for intervening at the preschool level with aggressive, antisocial children are in desperately short supply. In this article we report the development and testing of a comprehensive model intervention, called First Step to Success, for detecting and remediating antisocial behavior patterns at the point of school entry (Walker et al., 1997). First Step to Success is a combined home and school intervention that also contains a universal screening procedure to identify kindergartners showing early signs of involvement in an antisocial path. The program targets the three social agents having the greatest influence on the developing child (i.e., parents or caregivers, teachers, and peers; Reid, 1993). First Step to Success is an early intervention program, designed for achieving secondary prevention goals, that was developed and evaluated over a 4-year period (Simeonsson, 1991). The primary goal of First Step to Success is to divert antisocial kindergartners from an antisocial behavior pattern during their subsequent school careers and to develop the competencies needed to build effective teacher- and peer-related, social–behavioral adjustments (Walker, Severson, & Feil, 1995).

METHOD

Study Design

The First Step to Success program was implemented and evaluated over a 2-year period with a total of 46 kindergartners, divided into two cohorts, who were identified as being at risk for developing serious antisocial behavior patterns. A cohort design with participating students randomly assigned to experimental and wait-list control groups was used to evaluate the intervention's effects and to establish a causal relationship between the First Step to Success intervention and documented changes in child behavior. Within each cohort, a group of at-risk kindergartners, who met study participation criteria, were randomly assigned to either the experimental or wait-list control conditions. Baseline performance measures (i.e., adult ratings and in vivo behavioral observations) were recorded on the students assigned to each condition (i.e., experimental or wait-list control) in order to assess effects due to the intervention versus the passage of time or other extraneous factors. An identical set of measures was then recorded for both groups immediately following completion of the First Step to Success intervention. These assessments served as postintervention measures for the experimental participants and as a second set of baseline measures for the wait-list control participants. These procedures were replicated identically for Cohort 2 participants.

Cohort 1 consisted of 24 kindergartners at risk for the development of antisocial behavior, and their families, who were screened and exposed to the intervention during the 1993–1994 school year. Cohort 2 consisted of 22 kindergartners who were similarly screened and exposed to the intervention during the 1994–1995 school year. The study design allowed for the examination of both replication and cohort effects across school years.

The major advantage of this design is that it provides for establishing causal relationships between independent variables and dependent measures but does not deny access to the intervention for wait-list control participants. These participants are exposed to the intervention following its termination for experimental participants and the recording of postintervention measures. This design's primary limitation is that it eliminates the possibility of a control group that would enable more rigorous assessment of long-term maintenance and durability effects. On balance, the authors felt that the use of a wait-list control (or delayed treatment) design was most appropriate for this study given the contextual factors surrounding it (e.g., parental and school district pressures for access to the First Step to Success intervention for all qualifying kindergartners).

Approximately half of the 46 study subjects were followed up into Grade 2 (i.e., $n = 24$ for Cohort 1), whereas the subjects in Cohort 2 ($n = 22$) were followed up into first grade only. In all cases, the kindergarten students in this study were with different teachers and peers from their kindergarten placements during the Grade 1 and 2 follow-up periods. Follow-up consisted of recording the identical measures that were administered at baseline and postintervention time points. No attempts were made to bolster maintenance effects during follow-up by reinstituting the intervention or providing consultant assistance.

Study Participants

As noted, a total of 46 antisocial kindergartners and their families participated in the study across 2 school years. Twenty-six percent of the study participants were female, 33% were receiving supplemental school services, 7% were children of minority status, and 37% lived in families with low incomes (i.e., they received either reduced or free lunches). All 46 participants appeared to be in the normal range of intelligence; however, measures of intelligence were not administered as part of this study.

None of the 46 participants had received a diagnosis of mental retardation or been certified as such for special education eligibility. However, 11 of the participants were certified as eligible for special education services; 8 were in Cohort 1 and 3 were in Cohort 2. Five were labeled as learning disabled, 4 as speech–language impaired, and 2 as severely emotionally disturbed.

All 46 participants were rated across multiple occasions by their kindergarten teachers on the Aggression subscale of the Child Behavior Checklist (CBCL; Achenbach, 1991). Thirty-three of the 46 participants scored in the clinical range on this instrument; 14 in Cohort 1 and 19 in Cohort 2.

Intervention Procedures

Over approximately a 3-month implementation period, all 46 participants were exposed to the First Step to Success early intervention program (Walker et al., 1997). Details of the three components comprising this program (screening, school intervention, parent/caregiver training) are described in Appendix A. The intervention was delivered by a consultant in cooperation with the kindergarten teacher and parents or primary caregivers. Serving in the consultant role were graduate students, fellow teachers, counselors, and teacher aides.

The program content of the intervention to which kindergartners, teachers, and parents were exposed is identical to that described in Appendix A. Issues and procedures in the actual delivery of the intervention are described later in the section "Training and Implementation Procedures."

The First Step to Success program provides four screening options for the user's consideration. The fourth and most comprehensive of these options involves use of the Early Screening Project (ESP; Walker et al., 1994) procedure, which was implemented in this study.

Participant Selection and Baseline Data Collection

The instruments and procedures of the ESP were used to provide universal screening and identification of target students in this study. Details of these screening and identification tasks are described below.

The ESP is a downward extension and adaptation of The Systematic Screening for Behavior Disorders (SSBD) procedure (Walker & Severson, 1990). Like the SSBD, the ESP is a multimethod,

multiagent, and multisetting screening procedure that integrates teacher rankings, teacher ratings, and in vivo behavioral observations across the sequential screening stages. The ESP is designed for use with child populations enrolled in preschool and kindergarten settings within the 3- to 5-year-old age range.

The development and psychometric properties of the ESP have been reported extensively in the professional literature (Feil & Becker, 1993; Feil, Severson, & Walker, in press; Feil, Walker, & Severson, 1995). The national norm sample for the ESP consisted of 2,853 children in the 3- to 6-year-old age range. Interrater reliability estimates have been established for ESP Stage 1 and 2 measures. Interrater estimates ranged from .42 to .70; for Stage 2 measures, they ranged from .48 to .79. Test–retest reliabilities for the Stage 2 instruments ranged from .75 to .91 from fall to spring ratings. Interrater agreement coefficients for academic engaged time (AET) observations are consistently in the high 80s and low 90s.

To date, content, concurrent, and discriminative forms of validity have been estimated for the ESP. Correlations with the Preschool Behavior Questionnaire (Behar & Stringfield, 1974) and Conners Rating scales (Conners, 1989) ranged from .19 to .95, with a median of .69. The ESP has shown high levels of sensitivity and specificity with regard to discriminative validity.

Screening Stage 1. In the fall of the 1993–1994 and 1994–1995 academic years, all kindergarten teachers in Eugene School District 4J were invited to participate in the study. At a follow-up meeting, a complete overview of the intervention program, and the teacher's role in it, were presented. Next, teachers were asked to list the five children in their respective kindergarten classrooms whose behavior best matched a standardized description of externalizing characteristics, and the five children who best fit the standardized description of internalizing characteristics. The two lists were mutually exclusive, so a child could be put on only one list. Then the teachers rank ordered the children on each list from most characteristic (highest rank) to least characteristic (lowest rank) in relation to the externalizing or internalizing dimension.

Screening Stage 2. Based on these rankings, teachers completed ESP Stage 2 rating scales on those children from Stage 1 who were the three students ranked highest for externalizing behavior and the three students ranked highest for internalizing behavior. Stage 2 comprised three behavioral measures: (a) the ESP Adaptive Behavior Rating Scale (eight items), (b) the ESP Maladaptive Behavior scale (nine items), and (c) the Aggression subscale of the Child Behavior Checklist–Teacher Report Form (33 items; CBCL-TRF; Achenbach, 1991).

Stage 2 teacher ratings provided important information regarding the specific content of target participants' behavioral adjustment problems. Instruments at this stage are nationally normed and provide a means for comparing individual participant profiles to appropriate age and sex normative scores.

Screening Stage 3. Those students from Stage 2 whose scores exceeded ESP normative criteria moved on to screening Stage 3. In Stage 3, the target students were observed by project coordinators and implementation agents in their respective kindergarten classrooms on the dimension AET. AET is an important correlate of academic performance and provides a sensitive and reliable measure of classroom behavioral adjustment (Rich & Ross, 1989). As coded in this study, AET was a duration recording of the child's approximate proportion of time spent attending to teacher-led, structured activities, such as story time, or being appropriately engaged in teacher-assigned tasks and activities. AET comprised the following: (a) attending to the teacher, (b) making appropriate motor responses (e.g., following directions), (c) asking for assistance in an appropriate manner, (d) cooperating with others, and (e) being appropriately involved in teacher-assigned tasks and activities.

Baseline observations used to select the target subjects for study participation were completed by coordinators and project consultants following training to criterion by expert observer trainers from the Oregon Research Institute (ORI; see the section "Observer Training and Monitoring Procedures"). Project consultants did not participate in recording or collecting either postintervention or long-term follow-up observations. These observations were completed by a cadre of observers recruited, trained, supervised, and maintained by ORI as part of a related set of research projects. Consultants recorded the baseline AET observations in order to (a) familiarize themselves with the students, (b) provide a partial basis for selecting study participants, and (c) establish a baseline, preintervention database. Independent observers, kept blind to the status (treatment or wait-list/control) of observed participants in order to control for observer bias and dem and characteristics, completed all postintervention and follow-up observations.

Criteria for Participant Selection

The pool of kindergarten students observed in ESP screening Stage 3, whose baseline AET levels averaged 65% or lower, and/or who scored one or more standard deviations above the CBCL Aggression subscale's normative mean, were selected for possible inclusion in the study. These students' parents were then contacted for purposes of explaining the First Step to Success intervention, their roles in it, what they could expect from the study, and how their children were nominated and selected. Completion of these tasks resulted in the selection of 24 at-risk kindergartners who formed Cohort 1 and who participated in the study during the 1993–1994 school year. These screening, identification, and selection procedures were replicated exactly in selecting Cohort 2 participants ($n = 22$) who participated in the study during the 1994–1995 school year.

Cohort 1 participants' CBCL Teacher Aggression subscale scores averaged

20.3; for Cohort 2 participants, the average score on this measure was 24.8. The average AET levels of Cohort 1 and 2 participants were, respectively, 62.5% and 59.6%. Normative levels for academic engaged time as recorded by direct observations in regular classroom settings are considered to be in the range of 75% to 85% (Rich & Ross, 1989; Walker & Severson, 1990).

Cohort 1 participants were screened and selected during the first 3 months of the 1993–1994 school year; Cohort 2 participants were screened and selected near the beginning of the 1994–1995 school year. For Cohort 1, 31 kindergarten classes, involving 25 teachers and 679 kindergartners, were screened in ESP screening Stage 1. A total of 186 of the 679 Stage 1 participants were rated by their teachers in Stage 2. Of these, 55 were selected for AET observations in Stage 3, resulting in the final selection of 24 participants for Cohort 1. These screening procedures were duplicated for Cohort 2, resulting in the selection of 22 participants for the 1994–1995 school year.

Training and Implementation Procedures

In most cases, the intervention required approximately 3 months for full implementation in both school and home settings. A trainer-of-trainers model was used to deliver the intervention procedures. That is, the developers of the First Step to Success program recruited and trained a cadre of eight program consultants (i.e., graduate students, teachers, school counselors, teacher aides) to implement the intervention for each cohort of children and their families. Program consultants were assigned two to three cases each, which they ran in succession. The consultants were supervised in this process by two project coordinators (Stiller, Golly) who are also codevelopers and coauthors of the program. These project coordinators ran cases in addition to performing their supervisory and monitoring responsibilities during the implementation period.

First Step to Success consultants were responsible for implementing and coordinating the school and home components of the intervention for each case they ran. They were supervised and monitored continuously in their implementation of the program through weekly meetings, program visitations, individual debriefing sessions with coordinators, and telephone contact(s). Training procedures to build in consultant mastery of the school and home components of First Step to Success procedures included lectures, videotaped demonstrations, role playing, skill practice/feedback sessions, materials distribution, discussion, study and review, and coordinators' evaluation(s) of their acquisition of key implementation skills and tasks. The program consultants were paid and also provided with inservice staff development credit, at either university or school district levels, for their participation in the study.

At the beginning of the 1994–1995 school year, all program consultants were contacted, and those wishing to participate again were given a refresher retraining course. New consultants were recruited to replace those who did not continue; they were exposed to an intensive training and mentoring regimen to bring their implementation/coordination skills up to criterion. Returning program consultants also participated in this process as peer coaches.

Several methods were used to help build in implementation fidelity of the intervention procedures in addition to the training, monitoring, and supervisory processes described (Gresham, Gansle, Noell, & Cohen, 1993). The CLASS (Contingencies for Learning Academic and Social Skills) program, for example, contains a consultant daily record form in which the child's progress through the program is recorded and monitored. Measures that are recorded daily on this form include the number of points earned out of the total number available, whether the school and/or home rewards were earned, the number of consultant and teacher praises delivered, the number of regular and bonus points earned, and so forth. This measure provides in-

dices of each participant's pattern of responding to the intervention procedures. A similar measure has not been developed, as yet, for the homeBase component of the intervention.

Consultants were also asked to keep written logs of critical events—and their impressions of them—that occurred during implementation. These included special circumstances that emerged with either the school or home interventions and the strategies consultants used to respond to them. Program consultants were debriefed regularly about these logged items, and they became a focus of problem solving for regularly scheduled meetings between the consultants and coordinators.

Each target child, teacher, and family was exposed to the school and home intervention components in a standardized fashion. Considerable structure was built into the CLASS and homeBase intervention components (e.g., schedules for praising and awarding points, prepared scripts, daily task lists, guidelines for application). The monitoring, debriefing, and problem-solving efforts were valuable both in creating a knowledge base regarding implementation issues and barriers and in maximizing coordination of the First Step to Success intervention components.

Dependent Measures

Five dependent measures were used in this study to record participants' performance at the following four time points: baseline, postintervention, first-grade follow up, and second-grade follow up. Cohort 2 participants were followed up only through Grade 1 due to expiration of the grant supporting this study; Cohort 1 participants were followed up in both Grades 1 and 2. Three of the dependent measures were derived from and are included in the ESP procedure: (a) Teacher Ratings of Adaptive Behavior, (b) Teacher Ratings of Maladaptive Behavior, and (c) AET Observations. These three measures were completed, respectively, by kindergarten teachers and the cadre of trained observers who recorded AET observations in kindergar-

ten classrooms. The remaining two measures—the Aggression and Withdrawn subscales—were part of the TRF. The technical and psychometric characteristics of these measures can be found, respectively, in Walker et al. (1994) and Achenbach (1991).

The authors also recorded participants' playground social behavior as part of this study. However, this variable was not formally included as an analyzed dependent measure herein because of a change in the coding criteria and recording procedures used in the ESP Peer Social Behavior (PSB) code from Cohort 1 to Cohort 2. This change produced substantial, unanticipated differences in the level of negative/alone behavior for the two cohorts. For example, average percentages on this measure for Cohort 1 participants across the four evaluation time points were, respectively, 42.7%, 38.1%, 14.5%, and 23.1%. In contrast, the corresponding percentages for the three evaluation time points of Cohort 2 participants were 17.0%, 1.7%, and 2.9%.

Classroom teachers of Cohort 1 participants received copies of the rating instruments at the four evaluation time points of the study as well as instructions to complete them within a 2-week period. Behavioral observations were recorded during approximately the same time period. Each target participant was observed once in a structured classroom-like situation and once during a free-play situation using the AET and PSB codes and recording procedures, respectively. These observations were typically 15 minutes in duration, but in unusual circumstances they were somewhat shorter (10–12 minutes). These procedures were repeated for Cohort 2 participants.

Observer Training and Monitoring Procedures

A three-component procedure was used to train and monitor observers for this study. First, videotape recordings of young children in classroom settings displaying examples and nonexamples of academic engaged time were used to initially train observers and to familiarize them with both the AET coding definitions and recording procedures. Using a stopwatch, observer trainees initially coded the behavior of selected target participants in these videotaped situations and compared their codings with the observer trainer and each other. The stopwatch was allowed to run as long as the child was academically engaged and stopped whenever he or she was not so engaged during the observation period. The time on the stopwatch was then divided by the amount of time observed and then multiplied by 100 to derive an AET percentage score. Discrepancies between AET percentage estimates were discussed and resolved before proceeding with a subsequent observation period or trial. Using repetitions of this procedure, training continued until all observers' interrater agreement levels with the trainer–calibrator and each other averaged 80% or higher.

In the next training phase, each observer trainee was scheduled to independently record AET observations, along with the observer trainer–calibrator, within natural kindergarten settings. Each observer trainee was also required to achieve an interrater criterion of 80% or better with the observer trainer–calibrator in this setting. After having achieved this standard, the observer was allowed to begin recording usable AET observation data in order to document the performance of target participants. These training procedures were repeated in order to record negative and alone behavior in free-play settings.

Observers were regularly monitored by the observer trainer–calibrator in order to maintain a standard of acceptable interrater agreement. Any observer whose agreement level dropped below the 80% reliability standard during these monitoring sessions was dropped from the observer pool, recalibrated, and then allowed to begin recording again after having achieved the 80% standard. The level of interobserver agreement across all four observation time points for AET recordings was approximately 90%.

RESULTS

Intervention Effects

The average scale scores of the teacher rating instruments and mean AET percentages across four evaluation time points for Cohort 1 participants (preintervention, postintervention, first grade, second grade) and three evaluation time points for Cohort 2 participants (preintervention, postintervention, first grade) are presented in Table 1, which shows substantial average gains for Cohort 1 and 2 participants across four of the five dependent measures from pre- to postintervention time points. Gains for Cohort 1 and 2 subject groups, from pre- to postintervention, were quite similar.

Table 2 presents analyses of covariance for each of the five dependent measures where baseline or preintervention measures were used as a covariate. For purposes of these analyses, experimental participants, who were exposed to the intervention, and wait-list control partici-

TABLE 1
Raw Score Intervention and Follow-Up Results: Means and Standard Deviations by Cohort
(1993–1994 and 1994–1995)

Measure (Teacher ratings)	Evaluation time points' Mean (SD)			
	Kindergarten		1st grade[c]	2nd grade[d]
	Preintervention[a]	Postintervention[b]		
1993–1994 Cohort 1				
ESP Adaptive	21.96% (4.57)	28.83% (6.25)	25.43% (4.70)	26.72% (5.66)
ESP Maladaptive	32.58% (7.61)	22.26% (8.86)	23.48% (6.50)	23.83% (9.37)
CBCL Aggression	20.33% (11.10)	11.04% (8.31)	14.19% (10.06)	14.55% (11.79)
CBCL Withdrawn	7.04% (4.87)	4.50% (4.41)	4.62% (4.05)	6.11% (4.08)
AET Observations	(n = 24)	(n = 24)	(n = 20)	(n = 17)
	62.54% (16.35)	79.83% (22.16)	90.65% (10.62)	83.67% (14.02)
1994–1995 Cohort 2				
ESP Adaptive	21.73% (5.26)	26.68% (4.86)	26.47% (5.78)	—
ESP Maladaptive	31.45% (6.97)	26.27% (8.04)	23.67% (6.95)	—
CBCL Aggression	24.82% (10.41)	16.77% (10.56)	17.27% (9.17)	—
CBCL Withdrawn	4.00% (3.49)	2.64% (3.40)	1.20% (1.90)	—
AET Observations	(n = 22)	(n = 22)	(n = 13)	—
	59.64% (14.41)	90.77% (6.71)	81.85% (10.31)	

Note. CBCL = Child Behavior Checklist (Achenbach, 1991); ESP = Early Screening Project (Walker, Severson, & Feil, 1995).
[a] n = 24 for Cohort 1, n = 22 for Cohort 2. [b] n = 23 for Cohort 1, n = 22 for Cohort 2. [c] n = 21 for Cohort 1, n = 15 for Cohort 2. [d] n = 18 for Cohort 1, na for Cohort 2.

TABLE 2
Analyses of Covariance with Experimental and Wait-List/Control Groups Across Five Dependent Measures

Measure and group	Baseline		Postintervention (Experimental) or 2nd baseline (Control)		F value	p value
	M	SD	M	SD		
Adaptive Teacher Rating scale[a]						
Experimental	22.68	(5.03)	28.8	(4.19)	22.91 (1,45)	< .001
Wait-list/control	20.86	(4.56)	22.24	(5.00)		
Maladaptive Teacher Rating scale[b]						
Experimental	32.40	(6.74)	23.52	(8.70)	18.54 (1,45)	< .001
Wait-list/control	31.62	(7.97)	31.86	(7.13)		
Teacher Ratings on the CBCL Aggression subscale[c]						
Experimental	22.24	(10.92)	13.08	(9.42)	16.85 (1,44)	< .001
Wait-list/control	22.76	(11.12)	23.71	(9.35)		
Teacher ratings on the CBCL Withdrawn subscale[d]						
Experimental	5.00	(3.83)	3.08	(3.39)	0.23 (1,44)	= .63
Wait-list/control	6.28	(5.18)	4.09	(4.32)		
Classroom observation(s) of AET[e]						
Experimental	64.00	(10.59)	87.32	(12.54)	5.65 (1,45)	< .05
Wait-list/control	57.76	(19.33)	69.05	(20.44)		

Note. CBCL = Child Behavior Checklist (Achenbach, 1991).
[a]Effect size (ES) = 1.17. [b]ES = 0.93. [c]ES = 0.99. [d]ES = 0.26. [e]ES = 0.97

pants, who were not, were combined across Cohorts 1 and 2 in order to maximize statistical power. Means and standard deviations for each condition by group are presented in Table 2 along with F ratios, degrees of freedom, significance levels, and effect sizes for each dependent variable. The mean differences were statistically significant for four of the five dependent variables. Correlations between the covariate and these same dependent variables ranged from .11 (AET) to .66 (CBCL Withdrawn). These results indicate that four of the five dependent measures were sensitive to the intervention and document a causal relationship between behavior changes and exposure to the intervention, beyond the effect of initial baseline scores.

Effect sizes were calculated for each dependent measure by subtracting postintervention scores for the experimental group from second baseline scores for the wait-list controls and then dividing by the pooled standard deviations (Glass & Hopkins, 1984). The obtained effect sizes (see Table 2) ranged from robust (ESP adaptive teacher ratings) to modest or small (CBCL Withdrawn; Cohen, 1988). Across the five dependent measures used in the study, the effect sizes averaged .86, which Cohen (1988) classified as a large effect (> .8).

Durability Effects

Cohort 1 participants were followed up into the first and second grades, and Cohort 2 subjects were followed up only into Grade 1. Twenty-one of the 24 Cohort 1 participants were located and assessed during Grade 1, and 18 of 24 were located and assessed when they were in Grade 2. Fifteen of the 22 participants in Cohort 2 were followed up and assessed in Grade 1.

The effects of the First Step to Success intervention proved relatively durable across different school years, classroom settings, teachers, and peer groups for Cohort 1 and 2 participants. For both groups, the mean levels on the four statistically significant dependent measures were quite similar between follow-up and postintervention time points. A series of difference analyses, using ANOVA, were conducted between postintervention and follow-up occasions for Cohorts 1 and 2. These analyses showed no significant differences between postintervention and follow-up occasions for either Cohort 1 or Cohort 2 groups ($p > .05$ for all comparisons). Although not statistically significant, one apparent anomaly in this pattern of results is the substantially higher average AET level for Cohort 1 in Grade 1 than for the same participants at postintervention (see Table 1). The authors have no plausible explanation for this unexpected result other than to suggest the possibility that Cohort 1 participants may have been enrolled in highly structured Grade 1 classrooms having correspondingly high levels of AET. However, no data were collected that could confirm this hypothesis.

Cohort Equivalence

The two cohorts of this study appeared to be relatively equivalent. The initial baseline levels, magnitude of behavior change(s) achieved during intervention, and durability of behavioral gains across school years were quite similar for the two groups. Each of the dependent measures was assessed for equivalence using t tests conducted between Cohort 1 and 2 participants at preintervention, postintervention, and follow-up time points. All t tests were nonsignificant except for the CBCL Withdrawn measure at first-grade follow-up (4.62 vs. 1.20, $p < .005$) and academic engaged time at postintervention (81.85% vs. 90.77%, $p < .001$).

Normative Gender Comparisons

As noted earlier, across Cohorts 1 and 2, the study sample comprised approximately three quarters boys and one quarter girls. Table 3 provides means and standard deviations by gender from pre- to postintervention study phases for Cohort 1 and 2 participants combined.

The top half of Table 3 provides information by gender on normative ranges for the four teacher rating instruments that were used in this study. The normative range for AET is considered to be between 75% and 85% of observed time. The authors have no information on gender-specific normative levels for AET.

The results in Table 3 indicate very similar profiles for male and female subjects on the teacher report measures across pre- and postintervention study phases. Across these measures girls appeared to have slightly more problematic profiles than did boys; however, it is doubtful that these differences are statistically significant. Post-CBCL aggression scores were in the normal range for both boys and girls, whereas ESP Maladaptive scores were still outside the normal range at postintervention for both genders. On the ESP Adaptive scale, the

TABLE 3
Normative Gender Comparisons on Teacher Report Measures Across Evaluation Time Points

Normative Ranges by Teacher Report Measure

Dependent measure	Normative range (t score)	Raw score equivalents
CBCL Aggression subscale	50 to 67	Boys = 7 to 19 Girls = 6 to 17
CBCL Withdrawn subscale	50 to 67	Boys = 1 to 6 Girls = 1 to 6
ESP Adaptive	50 to 59	Boys = 35 to 26 Girls = 35 to 28
ESP Maladaptive	50 to 59	Boys = 14 to 19 Girls = 13 to 19

Gender Comparisons Across Pre–Post Study Phases for Combined Cohorts

	Male[a]				Female[b]			
	Preintervention		Postintervention		Preintervention		Postintervention	
Dependent measure	$\overline{X}$	SD	$\overline{X}$	SD	$\overline{X}$	SD	$\overline{X}$	SD
CBCL Aggression subscale	23.3	(10.5)	13.4	(9.2)	20.1	(12.2)	15.3	(12.0)
CBCL Withdrawn subscale	5.1	(4.3)	3.5	(4.1)	7.1	(4.9)	3.8	(3.9)
ESP Adaptive	22.2	(4.7)	28.6	(5.2)	20.8	(5.3)	25.4	(6.5)
ESP Maladaptive	31.5	(7.1)	23.3	(7.5)	33.5	(7.8)	27.1	(11.2)

Note. CBCL = Child Behavior Checklist (Achenbach, 1991); ESP = Early Screening Project (Walker, Severson, & Feil, 1995).
[a]$n = 34$. [b]$n = 12$.

scores for boys were just within the normal range, and for girls were just below it.

Responses to the School Intervention

An analysis was conducted to assess how Cohort 1 and 2 participants who scored in the clinical versus nonclinical range on the CBCL Aggression subscale responded to the recycling feature of the school intervention (see Appendix A). Participants who did not meet the criterion, or appropriate behavior level, for a given program day had to repeat that day and/or an earlier successfully completed program day having a less demanding criterion for success. Across Cohorts 1 and 2, 33 participants scored in the clinical range on the CBCL Aggression subscale. Of these cases, 19 repeated one or more program days, and 14 did not. In contrast, of the 13 participants who scored in the nonclinical range on the CBCL, 3 repeated one or more program days, and 10 did not. A chi-square test of the differences in these frequencies yielded a significant chi-square of 4.44 ($p < .03$). Thus, participants scoring in the clinical range were more likely to be CLASS program day repeaters than were nonclinical participants.

A profile of the clinical and nonclinical groups on the four dependent measures, showing statistical significance from pre- to postintervention time points, is provided in Table 4. Results in this table indicate that the two groups showed similar patterns of responding to the intervention procedures. As expected, the clinical group had less favorable profiles on the study measures than did the nonclinical group at pre- and postintervention time points. However, this was not true for AET.

Figure 1 displays the average number of days repeated, by each program day, during the school intervention for Cohorts 1 and 2 combined. Figure 2 displays the mean percentage of available daily points earned for all participants. These data indicate that the reward criterion becomes more difficult to meet and the proportion of daily points

TABLE 4
Pre- to Postintervention Changes on Dependent Measures
for Nonclinical and Clinical Range Scoring Participants

| | Time point | | | |
| | Preintervention | | Postintervention | |
Group and measure	$\overline{X}$	SD	$\overline{X}$	SD
Nonclinical participants[a]				
ESP Adaptive	24.84	(4.63)	30.15	(6.56)
ESP Maladaptive	26.77	(7.58)	20.15	(8.59)
CBCL Aggression	11.77	(10.70)	8.31	(7.55)
AET observations	61.54	(11.43)	82.15	(18.73)
Clinical participants[b]				
ESP Adaptive	20.67	(4.77)	26.81	(5.03)
ESP Maladaptive	34.12	(6.06)	25.88	(8.18)
CBCL Aggression	26.70	(7.68)	16.09	(9.82)
AET observations	61.00	(16.80)	86.21	(17.00)

Note. CBCL = Child Behavior Checklist (Achenbach, 1991); ESP = Early Screening Project (Walker, Severson, & Feil, 1995).
[a]$n = 13$. [b]$n = 33$.

earned decreases as participants progress through the school intervention portion of the First Step to Success program.

DISCUSSION

Based on results of this investigation, the First Step to Success program appears to be a promising approach to the reduction of antisocial behavior patterns among at-risk kindergartners who were selected on the basis of having high rates of aggressive, oppositional behavior. The impact of First Step to Success, in some respects, is consistent with existing literature on the case for early intervention with at-risk children as reviewed by Zigler et al. (1992). That is, comprehensive early interventions, especially those involving parents, appear to (a) teach relationships between choices and their resulting consequences, (b) develop the social-behavioral and academically related competencies that allow children to cope effectively with the demands of friendship making and the performance requirements of teachers and instructional settings, and (c) reduce the long-term probability that at-risk children will

adopt a delinquent lifestyle in adolescence. Effective interventions of this type are currently in great demand by the early childhood community due to changes in the presenting behavioral characteristics of preschool populations. However, it should be noted that First Step to Success has not been judged against the standard of long-term follow-up used in the longitudinal follow-up studies cited by Zigler et al. (1992).

The First Step to Success intervention was particularly encouraging in that it moved target students to within the normative range on two of the most important measures used to evaluate the program (i.e., the CBCL Aggression subscale and AET). Measures of aggression are a marker for antisocial behavior patterns and for a host of social adjustment problems (Constantino, 1992). AET is a strong correlate of academic performance and also provides a relatively sensitive measure of a student's ability to meet the academic demands of instructional settings, including structured activities within preschool-type settings. On average, scores on the CBCL Aggression subscale at preintervention

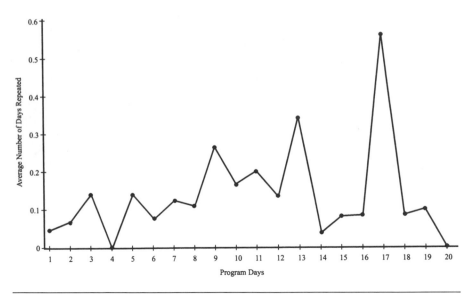

FIGURE 1. Average number of days repeated by program day—
Cohorts 1 and 2 combined.

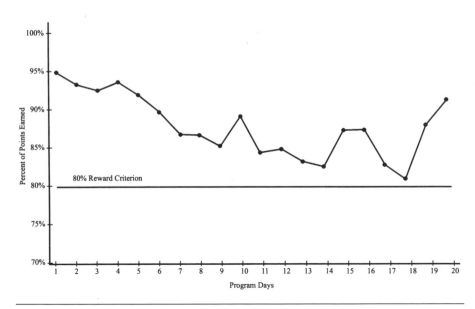

FIGURE 2. Mean percentage of points earned per program day—
Cohorts 1 and 2 combined.

tive levels on the two ESP measures of adaptive and maladaptive behavior at postintervention and slightly below this range at follow-up. The CBCL Withdrawn subscale was not sensitive to the intervention. This finding is not surprising because the First Step to Success program is geared toward reducing antisocial forms of student behavior. Target students were not selected for having socially withdrawn behavior patterns in this study.

The durability of the behavioral gains achieved from pre- to postintervention time points across school years, for both Cohorts 1 and 2, was both gratifying and largely unexpected. The empirical literature on longer-term maintenance effects associated with changes in social-behavioral status suggests pessimism rather than optimism in this regard (Du-Paul & Eckert, 1994). Cohort 1 and 2 participants maintained a substantially greater proportion of their pre- to postintervention gains across kindergarten and Grade 1 and 2 placements than expected. It is possible that participant attrition could partially account for this positive outcome. A major limitation of this finding is the absence of cohort control groups to account for the influence of time, setting, and extraneous factors in evaluating these results. In the absence of this design feature, it is difficult to know what to make of these relatively durable behavioral gains. That is, the achieved maintenance effects cannot be attributed to the First Step to Success intervention in the follow-up periods, and we do not know if the experimental–control group differences at postintervention would have been replicated in follow-up.

Data recorded for all participants on their response(s) to the school intervention procedures indicate that the program becomes more challenging as students progress through it (i.e., there are more program day failures and a smaller percentage of available points earned). These effects are expected because the school intervention is designed to be more demanding of the child in its later stages before it is faded out altogether after approximately 3 months. As a rule, target children adapt to the program's increas-

were in the marginally at-risk band for Cohort 1 and 2 participants, respectively, with average levels of 20 and 24. At postintervention, Cohort 1 and 2 CBCL average scores were reduced to 11 and 16, respectively. Similarly, normative levels for AET, based on in vivo observational data, are considered to be in the range of 75% to 85% of time observed when recorded within regular classroom

settings (Rich & Ross, 1989). Cohort 1 students averaged 62% and Cohort 2 students 59% AET at preintervention; their levels at postintervention were 79% and 90%, respectively.

Although statistically significant improvements were recorded for target participants on their teacher-rated behavioral levels at postintervention and follow-up, they were just within norma-

ing demands (e.g., less direct monitoring and feedback, larger amounts of time occurring between available reward opportunities) relatively well as they move through it. However, results of this study showed, as expected, that participants scoring in the CBCL clinical range at preintervention had more difficulty with the program's demands on them than did nonclinical scoring participants. Except for AET, the clinical sample had less favorable profiles across the dependent measures at postintervention than did the nonclinical sample.

Based on results of the current investigation, the First Step to Success program appears to have promise for achieving secondary prevention outcomes for kindergartners who are at risk for developing antisocial behavior patterns. As such, we consider it worthy of further replication, elaboration, and systematic evaluation over the long term but absent some of the limitations of the current study. In this context, it will be important in future studies to establish the separate and combined effects of the school and home components of the intervention. At present, it is not clear how much of the variance in intervention outcomes is accounted for by each of these components.

In addition, the authors believe it is very important to monitor, track, and support kindergartners exposed to interventions such as those in First Step to Success over the long term, as Tremblay, Pagani-Kurtz, Masse, Vitaro, and Pihl (1995) did so impressively. These authors exposed a sample of disruptive kindergarten boys to a coordinated school and home intervention over a 2-year period and followed them into mid-adolescence using control-group comparisons to assess long-term durability effects. Tremblay et al. recommend "booster shots" (i.e., brief reexposure to the intervention) to help preserve long-term gains for all disruptive students exposed to such interventions. The role of follow-up booster shots in preserving behavioral gains in this regard has shown substantial promise in research to date and would be an important feature of future studies conducted on the First Step

to Success program (DuPaul & Eckert, 1994). Due to resource limitations in the current study, we were unable to provide such booster shots.

To date, the dimensions of *dosage* (degree of exposure to the intervention or intervention components) and *durability* (long-term persistence of achieved treatment effects), and the interactions between them, have not been systematically investigated in studies of early intervention programs for at-risk children. We have planned research involving the First Step to Success that would examine the short- and long-term effects of three delivery options: (a) exposure to the school-only procedures of First Step to Success, (b) school and home procedures combined, and (c) school and home procedures plus follow-up booster shot sessions.

By the standards used in other fields, the First Step to Success program is a relatively brief and inexpensive intervention (Reid & Eddy, in press; Tremblay et al., 1995). Teacher and parental responses to the program have been generally positive, perhaps because the demands on them during implementation are relatively low level compared to the gains achieved. In addition, parents are enlisted as partners with the school in improving their children's school success, rather than blamed for the children's adjustment problems.

More research is needed on the attributes associated with effective consultant delivery of the First Step to Success program. The less formal training the implementation agent has, the more likely that a 1- to 2-day inservice plus follow-up supervision (e.g., as in the case of teacher aides) will be required in the First Step to Success procedures. Graduate students generally require 8 to 10 hours of inservice in the program plus regularly scheduled supervision.

The resources of the current investigation were strained by the training and implementation demands associated with the First Step to Success intervention and by its associated data-collection requirements. Future investigations of the program's efficacy should incorporate more in-depth and diverse data-

collection efforts. These could involve the (a) rating of target students' performance by teachers other than those involved in the intervention who are in a position to make informed rating judgments to assess for cross-setting generalization effects; (b) collection of parent reports of child behavior in the home setting; (c) recording of three to four observation sessions per participant (collected on separate days) at each evaluation time point, in both classroom and playground settings; and (d) analysis of archival school records data as participants are tracked through their subsequent school careers (Tremblay et al., 1995; Walker, Block-Pedego, Todis, & Severson, 1991).

First Step to Success is but one of a growing list of promising practices in early intervention for at-risk kindergartners having serious behavior problems (Coie, 1994; Reid, 1993; Reid & Eddy, in press; Tremblay et al., 1995). Mounting universal screening procedures to detect emerging antisocial behavior patterns among kindergartners and infusing these interventions into the regular offerings of kindergarten and primary grade–level programs represents one of the best options available for reducing the rising tide of antisocial behavior in schools (Bierman et al., 1992; Greenberg, Kusche, Cook, & Quamma, 1995; Walker, Horner, Sugai, et al., 1996).

Allocation of intervention resources has become a critical issue for professionals in coping with the burgeoning at-risk population and shows no signs of abating. For example, the cost-efficiency of the distribution between initial intervention dosage and booster shots provided over time is not clear at present. Are we better off having a relatively small initial dosage up front and regularly scheduled booster sessions over the long-term, or a large initial dosage followed by only occasional boosters? We also need solid information on the efficacy and cost-efficiency of school-only versus combined home and school interventions for this population. Answers to these and related questions will have a strong impact on future school-based prevention initiatives for antisocial populations at the point of school entry.

Powerful evidence suggests that antisocial children and youth follow a developmental trajectory in which the antisocial acts they engage in become more serious (Patterson, Reid, & Dishion, 1992; Reid & Eddy, in press). Their early identification and exposure to interventions designed to divert them from this path is clearly in the public interest. As public policy, this strategy could save millions of dollars in later incarceration costs. However, it requires major changes in how schools respond to this population. Part of this change, if it is to be effective, will necessitate a concentration of prevention-intervention resources at the point of school entry.

About the Authors

HILL M. WALKER, PhD, is codirector of the Institute on Violence and Destructive Behavior in the College of Education at the University of Oregon. **KATE KAVANAGH,** PhD, is a research associate at the Oregon Social Learning Center in Eugene. **BRUCE STILLER,** PhD, is a school psychologist and behavior consultant with Eugene School District 4J in Eugene. **ANNEMIEKE GOLLY,** PhD, is a special education teacher, K–5, and coordinator and trainer for the First Step to Success Program. **HERBERT H. SEVERSON,** PhD, is an associate professor of counseling psychology at the University of Oregon and a research scientist at the Oregon Research Institute. **EDWARD G. FEIL,** PhD, is an adjunct research scientist at the Oregon Research Institute. Address: Hill M. Walker, Center on Human Development, 5252 University of Oregon, Eugene, OR 97403-5252.

Authors' Notes

1. The authors are indebted to the pioneering, ground-breaking work of the Oregon Social Learning Center in antisocial behavior and to John Reid and Jerry Patterson for sharing their expertise and for their support of research relating to the development and testing of the First Step to Success program.
2. This research was partially supported by Grant No. P50 MH46690 from the Prevention Research Branch, National Institute of Mental Health, U.S. Public Health Service, to the Oregon Social Learning Center, John Reid, principal investigator.
3. The authors wish to express appreciation to the Eugene School District kindergarten teaching staff and especially to Tom Henry, director of instruction, whose invaluable support made this study possible.
4. The First Step to Success program is published by and available through Sopris West, Inc., 4093 Specialty Place, Longmont, CO 80504; 800/547-6747. Information about the program and staff training opportunities can be obtained from the publisher or by contacting the senior author at The Institute on Violence and Destructive Behavior, 1265 University of Oregon, Eugene OR 97403-1265.
5. Thanks are due to James Kauffman, Jo Webber, and Frank Gresham for critically reviewing this manuscript.

References

Achenbach, T. (1991). *The Child Behavior Checklist: Manual for the teacher's report form.* Burlington: University of Vermont, Department of Psychiatry.

American Psychological Association. (1993). *Violence and youth: Psychology's response.* Washington, DC: Author.

Behar, L., & Stringfield, S. (1974). *Manual for the preschool behavior questionnaire.* Durham, NC: Behar.

Bierman, K., Coie, J., Dodge, K., Greenberg, M., Lochman, J., & McMahon, R. (1992). A developmental and clinical model for the prevention of conduct disorder: The FAST Track program. *Development and Psychopathology, 4,* 509–527.

Cicchetti, D., & Nurcombe, B. (Eds.). (1993). Toward a developmental perspective on conduct disorder (Special issue). *Development and Psychopathology, 5*(1/2).

Cohen, J. (1988). *Statistical power analysis for the behavioral sciences* (2nd ed.). Hillsdale, NJ: Erlbaum.

Coie, J. (1994, July). *Antisocial behavior among children and youth.* Keynote address presented at the OSEP National Research Director's Conference, Washington, DC.

Conners, C. K. (1989). *Manual for the Conners' rating scales.* North Tonawanda, NY: Multi-Health Systems.

Constantino, J. (1992). On the prevention of conduct disorder: A rationale for initiating preventive efforts in infancy. *Infants and Young Children, 5*(2), 29–41.

Dishion, T., Patterson, G., & Kavanagh, K. (1992). An experimental test of the coercion model: Linking measurement, theory and intervention. In J. McCord & R. Trem-blay (Eds.), *The interaction of theory and practice: Experimental studies of intervention* (pp. 253–282). New York: Guilford.

DuPaul, G., & Eckert, T. (1994). The effects of social skills curricula: Now you see them, now you don't. *School Psychology Quarterly, 9*(2), 113–132.

Feil, E. G., & Becker, W. C. (1993). Investigation of a multiple-gated screening system for preschool behavior problems. *Behavioral Disorders, 19*(1), 44–53.

Feil, E. G., Severson, H. H., & Walker, H. M. (in press). Innovations in the screening of young children for emotional/behavioral delays: Results from the Early Screening Project. *Journal of Early Intervention.*

Feil, E. G., Walker, H. M., & Severson, H. (1995). The Early Screening Project for young children with behavior problems. *Journal of Emotional and Behavioral Disorders, 3*(4), 194–202.

Glass, G. V., & Hopkins, K. D. (1984). *Statistical methods in education and psychology* (2nd ed.). Englewood Cliffs, NJ: Prentice Hall.

Greenberg, M., Kusche, C., Cook, E., & Quamma, J. (1995). Promoting emotional competence in school-aged children: The effects of the PATHS curriculum. *Development and Psychopathology, 7,* 117–136.

Greenwood, P. W. (1995). *The cost effectiveness of early intervention as a strategy for reducing violent crime.* Paper prepared for the University of California Policy Seminar Crime Project, RAND, Santa Monica, CA.

Gresham, F. (1986). Conceptual issues in the assessment of social competence in children. In P. S. Strain, M. J. Guralnick, & H. M. Walker (Eds.), *Children's social behavior: Development, assessment, and modification* (pp. 143–179). New York: Academic Press.

Gresham, F., Gansle, K. A., Noell, G. H., & Cohen, S. (1993). Treatment integrity of school-based behavioral intervention studies: 1980–1990. *School Psychology Review, 22,* 254–272.

Hollinger, J. (1987). Social skills for behaviorally disordered children as preparation for mainstreaming: Theory, practice and new directions. *Remedial and Special Education, 8*(4), 17–27.

Hops, H., & Walker, H. M. (1988). *CLASS: Contingencies for learning academic and social skills.* Seattle, WA: Educational Achievement Systems.

Hops, H., Walker, H. M., Fleischman, D., Nagoshi, J., Omura, R., Skinrud, K., & Taylor, J. (1978). CLASS (Contingencies for learning academic and social skills): A standardized in-class program for acting-out children (Part II): Field test evaluations. *Journal of Educational Psychology, 70*(4), 636–644.

Kazdin, A. (1987). *Conduct disorders in childhood and adolescence.* London: Sage.

Larson, J. (1994). Violence prevention in the schools. A review of selected programs and procedures. *School Psychology Review, 23*(2), 151–164.

McCord, J. (1993). Conduct disorder and antisocial behavior: Some thoughts about processes. *Development and Psychopathology, 5*(1/2), 321–330.

Moffitt, T. (1994). Adolescence-limited and life-course-persistent antisocial behavior: A developmental taxonomy. *Psychological Review, 100,* 674–701.

Patterson, G. R. (1982). *Coercive family process: Vol. 3. A social learning process.* Eugene, OR: Castalia Press.

Patterson, G. R., & Bank, L. (1989). Some amplifying mechanisms for pathologic processes in families. In M. R. Gunnar & E. Thelen (Eds.), *Systems and development: The Minnesota symposia on child psychology* (Vol. 22, pp. 167–209). Hillsdale, NJ: Erlbaum.

Patterson, G. R., DeBaryshe, B. D., & Ramsey, E. (1989). A developmental perspective on antisocial behavior. *American Psychologist, 44,* 329–335.

Patterson, G. R., Reid, J., & Dishion, T. (1992). *Antisocial boys.* Eugene, OR: Castalia Press.

Reid, J. (1993). Prevention of conduct disorder before and after school entry: Relating interventions to developmental findings.

Development and Psychopathology, 5(1/2), 243–262.

Reid, J., & Eddy, M. (in press). The prevention of antisocial behavior: Some considerations in the search for effective interventions. In D. M. Breiling & J. D. Maser (Eds.), *Handbook of antisocial behavior.* New York: Wiley.

Rich, H., & Ross, S. (1989). Students' time on learning tasks in special education. *Exceptional Children, 55*(6), 508–515.

Robins, L. (1966). *Deviant children grown up.* Baltimore: Williams & Wilkins.

Robins, L. (1978). Sturdy childhood predictors of adult antisocial behavior: Replications from longitudinal studies. *Psychological Medicine, 8,* 611–622.

Simcha-Fagan, O., Langner, T., Gersten, J., & Eisenberg, S. (1975). *Violent and antisocial behavior: A longitudinal study of urban youth.* (OCD-CB-480). Unpublished report of the Office of Child Development.

Simeonsson, R. (1991). Primary, secondary and tertiary prevention in early intervention. *Journal of Early Intervention, 15,* 124–134.

Tremblay, R., Pagani-Kurtz, L., Masse, L., Vitaro, F., & Pihl, R. (1995). A bimodal preventive intervention for disruptive kindergarten boys: Its impact through mid-adolescence. *Journal of Consulting and Clinical Psychology, 63*(4), 560–568.

Walker, H. M., Block-Pedego, A., Todis, B., & Severson, H. (1991). *School archival records search (SARS): User's guide and technical manual.* Longmont, CO: Sopris West.

Walker, H. M., Colvin, G., & Ramsey, E. (1995). *Antisocial behavior in school.* Pacific Grove, CA: Brooks/Cole.

Walker, H. M., Hops, H., & Greenwood, C. R. (1984). The CORBEH research and development model: Programmatic issues and strategies. In S. Paine, G. T. Bellamy, & B. Wilcox (Eds.), *Human services that work* (pp. 57–78). Baltimore: Brookes.

Walker, H. M., Horner, R. H., Sugai, G., Bullis, M., Sprague, J. R., Bricker, D., & Kaufman, M. J. (1996). Integrated approaches to preventing antisocial behavior patterns among school-age children and youth. *Journal of Emotional and Behavioral Disorders, 4,* 194–209.

Walker, H. M., Kavanagh, K., Stiller, B., Golly, A., Severson, H., & Feil, E. (1997). *First Step to Success: An early intervention program for antisocial kindergartners.* Longmont, CO: Sopris West.

Walker, H. M., & Severson, H. (1990). *Systematic screening for behavior disorders (SSBD).* Longmont, CO: Sopris West.

Walker, H. M., Severson, H., & Feil, E. (1994). *The Early Screening Project: A proven child-find process.* Longmont, CO: Sopris West.

Walker, H. M., Severson, H., Stiller, B., Williams, G., Haring, N., Shinn, M., & Todis, B. (1988). Systematic screening of pupils in the elementary age range at risk for behavior disorders: Development and trial testing of a multiple gating model. *Remedial and Special Education, 9*(3), 8–14.

Zigler, E., Taussig, C., & Black, K. (1992). Early intervention: A promising preventative for juvenile delinquency. *American Psychologist, 47*(8), 997–1006.

APPENDIX A: OVERVIEW OF THE FIRST STEP TO SUCCESS PROGRAM

First Step to Success is an early intervention program designed for at-risk kindergartners who show clear signs of emerging antisocial behavior patterns (e.g., aggression toward others, oppositional-defiant behavior, tantrumming, rule infractions, escalating confrontations with peers and adults) at the point of school entry (see Walker et al., 1997). The at-risk kindergartner is the primary focus of the First Step to Success intervention; however, teachers, peers, and parents or caregivers participate in the intervention as implementation agents, under the direction and supervision of a school consultant who has overall responsibility for coordinating the intervention. The First Step to Success intervention requires 2 to 3 months, from start to finish, per application, and is applied to only one child at a time in a kindergarten classroom.

Reid (1993) argued persuasively that in order to successfully divert at-risk children and youth from a path leading to antisocial behavior, it is necessary to directly involve the three social agents who have the greatest influence on the developing child's life: parents, teachers, and peers. The coordinated involvement of primary caregivers, teachers, and peers in the intervention process is a key feature of the First Step to Success program. The intervention specifies clear roles and duties for each of these social agents during implementation.

The First Step to Success program was developed through a 4-year federal grant (1992–1996) to the senior author from the Office of Special Education Programs of the U.S. Department of Education. Year 1 of the project was devoted to planning, design, trial testing, and refinement of the three First Step to Success component modules, as well as development of the necessary working relationships with the participating school district. Years 2 and 3 focused on implementing, evaluating, and refining the First Step to Success intervention. The final project year was devoted to long-term follow-up assessments, packaging, field testing, dissemination, and staff training at the development site and beyond.

First Step to Success consists of three modules designed to be applied in concert with each other. These are (a) *the proactive, universal screening of all kindergarten populations* (Walker, Severson, & Feil, 1995), (b) *consultant-based school intervention involving the target child, peers, and teachers* (Hops & Walker, 1988), and (c) *parent training in caregiver skills for supporting and improving the child's school adjustment performance*. The two primary goals of the First Step to Success intervention program are to teach the at-risk child to get along with others (teachers and peers) and to engage assigned schoolwork in an appropriate, successful manner. The intervention is designed to achieve secondary prevention outcomes; that is, to divert at-risk children already showing clear signs of antisocial behavior from a path leading to a host of destructive outcomes (Larson, 1994; Simeonsson, 1991).

The three modules of First Step to Success are based on extensive research on school and home intervention procedures with aggressive, antisocial youth and over a decade of work related to the universal, proactive early screening of at-risk children to provide early detection (Hops & Walker, 1988; McCord, 1993; Patterson & Bank, 1989; Patterson, Reid, & Dishion, 1992; Walker et al., 1988). Each of these modules is described below.

Screening Module

The screening component of First Step to Success is designed to (a) evaluate each kindergarten child in relation to behavioral indicators of emerging or extant antisocial behavior patterns and (b) identify those who show an elevated risk status and could benefit from exposure to early intervention. Kindergartners so identified are possible candidates for the First Step to Success school and home intervention. Four options, varying in their complexity and required effort, are contained within this component to accomplish these screening-identification tasks. The most comprehensive of these options, the Early Screening Project (Walker, Severson, & Feil, 1995), was used in this study.

The four screening options range from a single stage of screening, in which the homeroom teacher nominates and rank orders at-risk students in relation to standardized behavioral definitions of externalizing and internalizing dimensions (ESP Option 1), to a three-stage screening procedure with multimethod and multiagent features, including nominations, rank ordering, adult ratings, and direct observations (ESP Option 4). Walker et al. (1997) provided specific details of these screening options.

School Intervention Module (CLASS)

The School Intervention Module of First Step to Success is an adapted version of the CLASS Program for Acting-Out Child developed by Hops and Walker (1988) for use with conduct-disordered students in the primary elementary grades. CLASS is a consultant-based intervention for remediating the behavior problems of disruptive, aggressive children in the primary grades and requires 30 program days for successful completion. Each program day has a built-in

performance criterion that has to be met before the participant can proceed to the next day of the intervention program; if the criterion is not met, that program day is then repeated, and/or the student is recycled to an earlier, successfully completed program the day before proceeding. Most students require a minimum of approximately 2 months to complete the CLASS program because of this built-in recycling procedure. It is relatively rare for a target child to progress through the program without having to repeat 1 or more program days.

CLASS is divided into three successive phases: consultant, teacher, and maintenance. The consultant phase (Program Days 1–5) is the responsibility of an adult, trained as a First Step to Success consultant, who coordinates the implementation process. This role is normally assumed by a school counselor, an early interventionist, a school psychologist, a resource teacher, or a behavioral specialist, but can be the responsibility of a trained assistant, a parent volunteer, or a graduate student. The role requires someone who can directly implement the program for brief portions of the school day and monitor, supervise, and support participating teachers as they assume control of the program. The consultant also performs the following key program tasks: (a) explains the CLASS program to the teacher, parents, target child, and peers; (b) secures the cooperation and consent of all parties to participate in the program's implementation; (c) operates the program in the classroom for the first 5 program days during two 20- to 30-minute sessions daily; (d) negotiates earned school and home privileges with the child, teacher, and parents; (e) demonstrates the program's operation and trains the teacher in how to apply it; and (f) turns the program over to the teacher and supervises his or her operation of it during the teacher phase of the CLASS program.

The consultant phase is the most critical part of the intervention program. The CLASS program begins with two 20-minute periods daily, usually scheduled during morning and afternoon sessions, and is eventually extended to the entire school day. Initially, the consultant, in close proximity to the target child, monitors her or his classroom behavior using a red and green card on which one point is awarded every 30 seconds. If the child's behavior is appropriate when the point award interval occurs, the point goes on the green side of the card; if not, it goes on the red side. To meet the criterion, 80% or more of the available points during the 20-minute period have to be awarded on the green side. A brief free-time activity involving the target child and peers is made available immediately following the 20-minute period. If the reward criterion for both morning and afternoon sessions is met, the child also earns a home privilege that has been prearranged with parents or caregivers.

Over the course of the program, use of the red and green card is phased out completely by Program Day 15, and the interval in which points and praise can be earned is gradually extended from 30 seconds to 10 minutes. In addition, in the later stages of the program, the target student has to work in blocks of multiple days in order to earn a single reward of higher magnitude. Thus, the program becomes more demanding as the student progresses through it, and the student must sustain acceptable performance for progressively longer periods of time in order to be successful.

The teacher phase (Program Days 6–20) is operated by the classroom teacher in whose room the CLASS program is initially implemented. The homeroom teacher assumes control of the program's operation on Program Day 6 but with close supervision and support provided by the CLASS program consultant. The consultant provides monitoring and technical assistance on an as-needed basis for the regular teacher throughout the remainder of the teacher phase. Teacher phase implementation tasks include (a) operating the program daily, (b) awarding praise and points according to program guidelines and contingent on child performance, (c) supervising delivery of group activity and school rewards, and (d) communicating with parents on a regular basis regarding the target child's performance. The teacher works closely with the program consultant, child, parents, and peers throughout the total implementation period.

The maintenance phase of the CLASS program lasts from Program Days 21 to 30 after which the school intervention is terminated. In this final program phase, the target child is rewarded primarily with praise and expressions of approval/recognition from the teacher at school and the parents at home. An attempt is made during this phase to reduce the child's dependence on the program by substituting adult praise for points, reducing the amount of daily feedback given, and making occasional rewards available contingent on exemplary performance. In the majority of cases, target students who successfully complete the teacher phase of the program are able to sustain their improved behavior in this phase despite these program changes. However, for students who cannot, the CLASS program contains suggested strategies for preserving long-term maintenance effects.

The CLASS program was initially developed, tested, and validated over a 5-year period and has been extensively researched (Hops & Walker, 1988; Walker, Hops, & Greenwood, 1984). Another 3 years of research has been invested in the adapted kindergarten version of the program. CLASS accomplishes powerful behavior change outcomes for acting-out students at the point of school entry (Hops et al., 1978).

Home Intervention Module (homeBase)

The *homeBase* component of First Step to Success consists of a series of six lessons designed to enable parents and caregivers to build child competencies and skills in six areas that affect school adjustment and performance. The target skills that parents are asked to teach their children are as follows: *(a) communication and sharing in school, (b) cooperation, (c) limits setting, (d) problem solving, (e) friendship making, and (f) development of confidence.* homeBase contains lessons, instructional guidelines, and parent–child games and activities for directly teaching these skills. homeBase requires 6 weeks for implementation and begins after the target child has completed Program Day 10 of the CLASS program.

The First Step to Success program consultant visits the parents' home weekly and conducts the homeBase lessons in that setting. Following each session, materials are left with the parents that facilitate daily review and practice of each skill with the target child. The homeBase lessons require approximately 1 hour each. Parents are en-couraged to work with their children 10 to 15 minutes daily and to focus on practicing the homeBase skills being taught.

An important, shared goal of First Step to Success and the home-Base component is to build a strong, positive link between home and school. homeBase is designed to strengthen parenting skills in developing child competence in key performance areas related to school success. Parents and caregivers are enlisted as partners, with the school, in helping the child get the best possible start in his or her school career. Its ultimate goal is to get educators and parents/caregivers on the same side in helping vulnerable children experience early school success. If achieved, this outcome can be a key protective factor in diverting them from an antisocial path in their subsequent school careers.

It is important to note that parents are *never* blamed for the problems their children may be experiencing in school. Instead, developing a collaborative home and school working relationship whose focus is on joint problem solving and the development of school success is emphasized. This skill-building approach is based on the belief that parents are children's best natural resource for achieving school success. Using this approach, the authors have rarely encountered parents who are not interested in participating in and supporting the *First Step to Success* intervention program.

Program content for HomeBase is based on more than 25 years of research at the Oregon Social Learning Center (OSLC), involving hundreds of families who have contributed to our current knowledge of the family-based factors related to children's competent social adjustment (Patterson, 1982; Patterson, Reid, & Dishion, 1992). The approach used in teaching parents how to improve their children's school success in homeBase reflects numerous OSLC clinical trials and research efforts to study the processes inherent in family-based behavior change processes (Dishion, Patterson, & Kavanagh, 1992; Patterson, 1982; Patterson & Bank, 1989). It also stresses the importance of developing a collaborative relationship with parents and tailoring the delivery and implementation of the target skills to meet the family's existing skill level(s) in applying them. Attempting to buffer family stress levels and providing supports to improve coping skills are two strategies used by OSLC investigators to improve the family's ability to respond to parenting training. The OSLC knowledge base on parent training and intervention is derived from families of diverse socioeconomic conditions and social and emotional resources.

The authors of the First Step to Success program attempted to incorporate these values, experiences, and generic strategies into the homeBase program component. It should be noted, however, that the specific effects of homeBase have not, as yet, been tested separately from the CLASS program in accounting for First Step to Success program outcomes.

Second Step:

Preventing Aggression by Promoting Social Competence

KARIN S. FREY, MIRIAM K. HIRSCHSTEIN, AND BARBARA A. GUZZO

Childhood aggression predicts later high-risk behaviors. In this article, we describe *Second Step,* a primary prevention program designed to deter aggression and promote social competence of children from preschool through Grade 9. The curriculum is organized around three areas of social–emotional competency: empathy, social problem solving, and anger management. Theory and findings related to these core competencies are described, as are features of lessons, teacher training, and classroom instruction that promote learning and use of specific behavioral skills. Classroom, school, and family contexts that support student use and transfer of skills are also discussed. A review of formative and outcome evaluation studies of *Second Step* highlights challenges and recommendations related to program implementation.

AGGRESSIVE BEHAVIOR IN CHILD-hood predicts later delinquency, substance abuse, depression, school dropout, and early parenthood (Cairns, Cairns, Neckerman, Ferguson, & Gariepy, 1989). It is estimated that 30% of adolescents consistently engage in multiple high-risk behaviors, and an additional 35% engage at least occasionally in these behaviors (Dryfoos, 1997). Clearly, the societal and individual benefits of interrupting the progression from childhood aggression to future risk-taking behavior are considerable.

Prevention requires promoting constructive behavioral alternatives to aggression. Young people at risk for behavior problems typically lack the core social and emotional competencies necessary for success in school (Wentzel & Wigfield, 1998), family relationships (Gottman, Katz, & Hooven, 1996), and the workplace (Spencer & Spencer, 1993). The research described herein shows that social and emotional skills can be taught and, more importantly, that acquisition of core social and emotional competencies reduces aggressive behavior in youth.

SECOND STEP: A UNIVERSAL PRIMARY PREVENTION PROGRAM

Second Step is a violence-prevention curriculum created with the dual goals of reducing development of social, emotional, and behavioral problems and promoting the development of core competencies (Committee for Children, 1991, 1992a, 1992b, 1997). First published in 1986, *Second Step* is widely used in the United States and Canada. The program has been adapted for use in Australia, Germany, New Zealand, Norway, and the United Kingdom. Danish- and Japanese-language versions are currently in development. A Spanish-language supplement is available for English as a second language (ESL) classrooms.

Classrooms, teachers, or counselors are primarily responsible for delivering the program to students from preschool to middle school. In providing training to all school staff, parents, and on-site trainers, the program seeks to cultivate a whole school environment that addresses children's social problems and supports the learning and ongoing use of positive social behaviors.

The aim of a universal program like *Second Step* is to foster development of the social–emotional skills necessary for students to lead successful and satisfying lives. Even young people who do not evince behavior problems are often limited by social–emotional skill deficits (Weissberg & Greenberg, 1997). It is estimated that adjustment problems of 75% to 85% of students can be addressed by well-implemented primary prevention strategies (Reid, 1993). Participation in universal prevention programs is also important for children in need of more intensive behavioral interventions. Children with behavior problems can benefit by watching more competent children use targeted language, strategies, and skills. Moreover, teacher and peer reinforcement of socially competent behavior is more likely to occur if all children use the same vocabulary and problem-solving strategies. Otherwise, a participant in a "pull-out group" may initiate a strategy that is not recognized or valued by classmates. Students are better able to respond appropriately and notice improvements in their more challenging classmates if they have received similar coaching themselves.

PROGRAM FOUNDATIONS

Grounded in social learning theory, *Second Step* emphasizes the importance of observation, self-reflection, performance, and reinforcement in the acquisition and maintenance of behavioral repertoires (Bandura, 1986). The curriculum draws liberally from other conceptual frameworks as well, including social information–processing (Dodge, Pettit, McClaskey, & Brown, 1986), cognitive–behavioral therapy (Kendall & Braswell, 1985), and Luria's (1961) model of self-regulation through verbal mediation. Concepts and strategies from these frameworks are integrated into a developmental sequence of social–emotional skill acquisition.

Competence in the areas of empathy, social problem solving, and impulse control have been identified as factors that buffer students from risks, such as early problem behavior and poor relationships with peers (Walker et al., 1996). The three units of the *Second Step* program address these core competencies in conjunction with the teaching of specific behavioral skills. Research suggests that combining the teaching of general competencies and domain-specific skills (e.g., resisting peer pressure to victimize an unpopular peer) in this manner is effective in preventing psychosocial problems (Durlak, 1983) and in reducing specific problem behaviors such as aggression (Lochman, Burch, Curry, & Lampron, 1984).

By applying perspective-taking, problem-solving, and anger management strategies, children decide *what* to do; in behavioral skills training children rehearse specific steps for *how* to do it. To illustrate how these processes go hand in hand, imagine that Miriam wants to shoot baskets with a ball that Karin is using. Attempting to solve the problem prosocially, Miriam proposes they take turns with the ball. She knows *what* to do. Yet before Karin has a chance to agree, Miriam impulsively grabs the ball.

A fight ensues, and Miriam is mystified: "I picked a good solution! Why didn't it work?" Although she correctly used the problem-solving steps, she didn't know *how* to execute them, which derailed her good intentions. The real life consequences of conflict with Karin will be unlikely to reinforce Miriam's attempt at prosocial behavior.

In behavioral skills training, a solution, such as trading or sharing, is practiced through role plays in which students apply steps for negotiating a successful exchange (e.g., Step 1: Think of something the other student might like to play with; Step 2: Establish eye contact; Step 3: Ask if he or she would like to share or trade). Other specific skills students practice include joining in group activities, taking turns, interrupting politely, and apologizing. Behavioral skills training is infused throughout the three units on empathy, problem solving, and anger management. Unit contents are displayed in Table 1.

Empathy

Social–emotional competence requires the ability to detect, understand, and appropriately respond to the feelings of others. These processes are closely linked with empathy, the capacity to share the emotional state of another (Eisenberg, 1986). Empathy predicts altruistic behaviors (Strayer & Schroeder,

---

TABLE 1
Lesson Titles for *Second Step*, Grade 1

Empathy	Impulse control (problem solving)	Anger management
Introduction to empathy training	Introduction to problem solving	Introduction to anger management
Identifying feelings	Identifying the problem	Anger triggers
Looking for more clues	Choosing a solution	Calming down
Similarities and differences	Evaluating a solution	Self-talk
Feelings change	Is it working?	Reflection
Predicting feelings	Ignoring distractions	Keeping out of a fight
Communicating feelings	Interrupting politely	Dealing with name-calling and teasing
	Dealing with wanting something that's not yours	

1989) and elementary students' prosocial classroom behaviors (Litvack-Miller, McDougal, & Romney, 1997). Further, empathy has been found to negatively correlate with aggression (Miller & Eisenberg, 1988). Aggressive children typically have difficulty taking another person's perspective and "reading" emotional cues (Hudley & Graham, 1993). For example, a child accidentally hit by a ball on the playground might fail to detect the responsible child's expression of concern or to accurately infer the child's intentions. Thus, an unintentional act may be viewed as hostile provocation.

The first unit of the *Second Step* curriculum focuses on three components of empathy: recognizing feelings in self and others, considering others' perspectives, and responding emotionally to others. The program begins with students' discussing and identifying physical, facial, verbal, and situational cues related to six basic emotions: feeling happy, sad, angry, surprised, scared, and disgusted (Ekman & Friesen, 1975). Students practice communicating and accurately interpreting emotional expressions, and they discuss how expression of emotion may vary for different households and communities. Lessons include short stories that illustrate key concepts in emotional understanding; the stories demonstrate, for example, that feelings change over time (e.g., changing schools makes Angela sad at first and happy later) or that people's feelings about the same experience may differ (e.g., Juan is scared to climb a tree, whereas Marco is excited). Other lessons involve discriminating between accidental and intentional actions and determining fairness.

To practice perspective-taking skills, students participate in role playing scenes of common social problems, and they share personal experiences and reactions to hypothetical situations (e.g., the different perceptions of students who have competing claims to the same table in the lunch room). Recognizing individual differences in perspectives and emotional reactions is fundamental to perspective taking and construction of knowledge about emotion (Saarni, 1999). Students learn how to respond to others' feelings by role playing empathetic behavior (e.g., what to say and do when a friend feels disappointed).

Social Problem Solving

Aggressive children show deficits in several aspects of social problem solving (Dodge & Frame, 1982). Typically they are inattentive to relevant social cues, presuming hostile intent in ambiguous situations. They generate more aggressive and inept responses to social problems than their nonaggressive peers (Rubin, Bream, & Rose-Krasnor, 1991), and they expect aggressive solutions to yield positive outcomes (Crick & Ladd, 1990). Moreover, aggressive children tend to lack behavioral skills required to enact competent responses to social problems (Dodge et al., 1985). Many children who are frequent targets of aggression manifest similar deficits in conflict resolution skills (Olweus, 1993).

Meta-analyses indicate that social problem-solving skills can be substantially improved through intervention (Denham & Almeida, 1987). Dodge, Pettit, McClaskey, and Brown's (1986) social information–processing model describes the processes that contribute to socially competent behavior: accurate encoding and interpretation of relevant social cues, generation and evaluation of potential responses, and behavioral enactment of a selected response. The five-step problem-solving strategy in *Second Step* addresses each of these processes. Students are taught to (a) identify the problem; (b) brainstorm solutions; (c) evaluate solutions by asking, "Is it safe?" "Is it fair?" "How might people feel?" "Will it work?"; (d) select, plan, and try the solution; and (e) evaluate if the solution worked and what to do next. Students apply this strategy first to simple hypothetical problem situations and later to real life problems. They practice using verbal mediation or "self-talk" (Meichenbaum, 1977) as a strategy to remind them to control impulses, think about consequences of actions, and reinforce their own behaviors.

Lessons provide structured opportunities for students to practice identifying problems by using story and context clues. They then brainstorm potential solutions to a problem. Evaluating solutions, the third step in the problem-solving sequence, is critically important, as it establishes four basic values or norms for behavior: safety, fairness, people's feelings, and effectiveness. Establishing clear values by which to evaluate behavior is important because children's social values and goals influence their problem-solving abilities. Studies suggest that establishing positive norms enhances children's problem-solving skills (Lochman, Coie, Underwood, & Terry, 1994), thus protecting young people from becoming embroiled in the dynamics of peer aggression and victimization. The positive norms used to evaluate solutions in *Second Step* highlight the incompatibility of antisocial goals with valued outcomes such as fairness.

Based on how well a solution meets *Second Step* criteria, students select and practice problem-solving behaviors that are likely to succeed. Finally, in Step 5 of the problem-solving strategy, students reflect on how well a solution worked, revisiting previous steps to evaluate other solutions as warranted. Kazdin (1987) has shown that improvements in problem solving correspond to significant reductions in aggression.

Anger Management

Graham (1993) has suggested that emotions account for much of the relationship between cognition and aggressive behavior. Specifically, individuals experience anger when they attribute hostile intent to others, and anger lowers inhibitions that might otherwise moderate one's aggressive responses. Young people who are able to manage their emotions and emotion-related behavior are less likely to behave aggressively (Underwood, Coie, & Herbsman, 1992) and more likely to behave in socially competent ways (Eisenberg et al., 1997).

Anger management techniques (Novaco, 1975) are, therefore, naturally paired with problem-solving and behavioral skill development. Strategies to reduce stress and manage anger have been successful at decreasing disruptive and aggressive behavior in aggressive young boys (Lochman, Nelson, & Sims, 1981) and adolescents (Lochman et al., 1984). Investigation of long-term effects found that compared to untreated aggressive boys, those who received instruction in anger-coping strategies maintained gains in problem-solving skills and had lower rates of drug and alcohol involvement (Lochman, 1992).

The *Second Step* anger management unit teaches strategies to help students recognize anger cues in their bodies (e.g., feeling hot or cold) and use positive self-statements and other stress-reduction techniques (e.g., counting backwards) to avert uncontrolled angry behavior. Children identify their personal "triggers," those situations that typically arouse intense, angry feelings (e.g., name-calling) and then generate and practice strategies to inhibit automatic and impulsive responding. Skill steps include the use of "self-talk" to cool down in the moment, to later reflect on the incident, and to evaluate one's response to the situation. Domain-specific behavior skills training focuses on events that are typically stress-inducing for many people, such as dealing with criticism, being left out, or making a complaint. Students practice skills through repeated modeling and rehearsal of problem-solving and stress reduction steps.

PROGRAM FEATURES

The Lessons

Program lessons are typically taught twice a week by regular classroom teachers or counselors trained in the use of the curriculum. At the early childhood and elementary levels, lessons are structured around large black-and-white photo cards depicting children in various social–emotional situations. On the reverse side of the card, teachers are provided with key concepts, objectives, and a suggested lesson script. Teachers read the lesson story accompanying the photographs and guide whole group discussion.

Second Step also provides video-based lessons, skill-step posters to display in classrooms and throughout the school, and a Family Overview Video to engage parent support. Lessons are accompanied by notes to teachers about child development, transfer-of-training ideas, and extension activities, such as children's literature that illustrates *Second Step* concepts. The most popular feature of the pre-K curriculum may be "Impulsive Puppy" and "Slow-Down Snail," two stuffed puppets used to teach impulse control skills to younger children.

Although similar in content to the preschool and elementary programs, *Second Step* for middle school/junior high (Committee for Children, 1997) places more emphasis on student attitudes and beliefs about aggression. Discussions focus on social dilemmas germane to older students (e.g., the dynamics of dating relationships). The format relies more heavily on use of videos, classroom activities, group discussion, and overhead transparencies for lesson presentation. Video components emphasize specific behavioral skills and particularly address student attitudes and motivation. The first module in this series, referred to as "Level 1: Foundation Lessons," provides the basic vocabulary and strategy skills for the first year of implementation. Levels 2 and 3, presented in subsequent years, focus more on one's motivation to act prosocially and the attitudes that contribute to prosocial actions.

Teacher Training

The *Second Step* training model consists of a 1-day teacher workshop and a half-day workshop for noninstructional school staff. In the teacher workshop, trainers impart the conceptual underpinnings of the program and provide teachers opportunities to discuss and practice specific instructional strategies. The training for teachers focuses on two critical aspects of the program: conducting lessons for student skill development and improving the environmental context in which those skills are expected to be used. The training for noninstructional staff is designed

to familiarize school personnel with vocabulary and skill steps used in the program.

Many teachers are uncomfortable with the interactive teaching methods that social–emotional learning requires, fearing that their use will lead to "out of control" classrooms (Rohrbach, D'Onofrio, Backer, & Montgomery, 1996). Teachers' fears can be assuaged by providing information and practice regarding effective strategies for dealing with potential disruptions. For example, teachers can learn to respond to silly or antisocial "solutions" during brainstorming by using the evaluative criteria laid out in the skill steps ("Is it safe?" "Is it fair?" "How might people feel?" "Will it work?") as one would with the most serious offering. This provides students with essential practice in evaluating inappropriate behaviors and their consequences. Classmates can also enjoy the provocation without having their attention "hijacked" by one student's challenge to authority. Specific tips such as these can help motivate teachers to try more interactive teaching methods.

Instructional Strategies for Teaching Lessons

Teachers who provide students more opportunities for discussion, role play, and opportunity to solve real classroom problems tend to be most successful with the program. Teacher training and *Second Step* teacher manuals focus on several key strategies to facilitate student learning in these activities.

Discussion. Group discussions play a key role in *Second Step* instruction, both as integral parts of lessons and as responses to real classroom events. Students are encouraged to talk about feelings and differing points of view and discuss potential consequences and obstacles to implementation of their ideas. Discussion prompts guide students to relate events on the photo card to their own life experience (e.g., "Have you ever felt frustrated like Dennis? What did you do about it?"). Teachers' nonevaluative responses to students' contributions can create a climate that encourages a range of solutions and viewpoints. In fact, it is advantageous for teachers to suggest an inappropriate solution, if students do not, so the class might evaluate the solution and see why it is a debatable choice. These discussions set the stage for practicing student-generated solutions and skill steps in role plays.

Role Plays. Many *Second Step* lessons conclude with opportunities for students to rehearse specific behavioral skills by role playing hypothetical situations. In a typical lesson, a class may generate two to three skill steps for a solution that will be modeled in a role play. For example, steps for apologizing might include (a) stating what happened, (b) saying "I'm sorry," and (c) offering to make amends. Students discuss the context and nuances of the behavioral steps (e.g., choosing an appropriate time and place, making eye contact, carefully choosing voice tone, and projecting sincerity). Next, the teacher and a student model the solution, calling attention to skill steps as they are performed. They might present multiple versions of how steps could be enacted. This provides examples of how solutions and skill steps generated by students "look" in real life. For example, a teacher might model the facial expression and "voice" appropriate for apologizing. Conversely, a teacher might use a sarcastic tone and ask students to evaluate whether this would be successful. The class critiques the nuances of the performance and how well it adhered to the steps.

Although modeling is an effective strategy for teaching prosocial skills, these skills will not be retained without practice. Students are next given simple scenes to act out. Typically, they might practice in dyads or small groups for 10 minutes while the teacher roams, coaches, and advises. Students then perform their scenes for one another. Initially, students require considerable coaching, particularly when role playing in front of the whole class. Teachers develop a variety of coaching strategies (e.g., using "action" or "freeze" as director-like cues to student actors or providing shy actors with peer coaches to assist them with dialogue). Teachers and students can then offer specific feedback (e.g., "You did a good job of looking the person in the eyes") and coach students through difficult areas (e.g., "Try this part again using a confident voice").

GENERALIZING SECOND STEP SKILLS

However well conceived, lessons in a social skills curriculum provide only part of the social and emotional learning equation in any classroom. The way a teacher organizes and manages a class vividly communicates that teacher's values. Daily classroom life may, therefore, provide in situ *Second Step* training or pose incompatible constraints on that learning (Brewer, Hawkins, Catalano, & Neckerman, 1995). Unlike the lessons, there are no easy-to-follow "scripts" for creating an environment that supports student use of problem-solving and other skills. In *Second Step* training, trainers describe and model strategies to create a classroom environment that supports use of social–emotional skills. They also assist teachers in thinking about how to use real life events to model and practice skills steps, as teachers must be constantly alert to opportunities when they can model or prompt individual use of the skills and exploit the "teachable moment."

Generalization of social and emotional skills is the ultimate goal of any prevention program. A number of specific instructional practices support generalization of social–emotional skills. These include teachers' (a) modeling valued behaviors; (b) cueing, coaching, and reinforcing skills; and (c) creating opportunities for student decision making (Consortium, 1994). Such practices can help infuse *Second Step* skills and language into daily classroom life.

Modeling

Perhaps nothing communicates a teacher's values and beliefs about program efficacy as much as modeling—in other words, the extent to which a teacher "walks the talk" of a social–emotional curriculum. Unfortunately, teachers sometimes model aggressive and coercive behavior. An exchange observed in a third-grade class by the first author illustrates this dynamic. Tom was a new student who entered school on the third day of the school year. Students had just returned from lunch recess when the teacher with playground duty came in and spoke to the classroom teacher, who then left the room. The playground teacher proceeded to berate Tom aggressively, pointing into his face at close range, for not lining up immediately after the bell rang. The classroom was silent during this extremely menacing exchange. After she left, students pointed at one another and avidly reproduced the teachers' tone and gestures, shouting, "She'll kick your ass!" The door opened, and the class quieted immediately as the regular teacher returned. Unfortunately, intimidation tactics often result in a momentary inhibition of aggressive or disruptive responses, and teachers who model aggression may remain unaware that their behavior encourages imitation.

In contrast, effective *Second Step* teachers model perspective taking and impulse control. For example, a teacher might model self-talk in recognizing feelings ("My stomach is in knots because I'm feeling frustrated") and managing anger ("I'll take three deep breaths to calm down"). Students see an adult faced with a real life dilemma successfully using steps to cope. Thus, teacher modeling provides students with information about how strategies "look," appropriate contexts for using skills, and possible consequences of different strategies.

By demonstrating acceptance, concern, and respect for each student, teachers also provide powerful modeling of prosocial and caring behavior. Middle school students describe caring teachers as those who are fair and show concern for student well-being (Wentzel, 1997). These characteristics of caring correspond to students' endorsement of prosocial goals and their cooperation with classroom rules and norms (Wentzel, 1995).

Cueing, Coaching, and Reinforcement

Classroom social dynamics and conflicts can serve as fortuitous opportunities for teachers and other school personnel to cue students to use developing skills and to provide coaching and feedback as needed (Weissberg, Caplan, & Sivo, 1989). If there is a conflict over taking turns at a class computer, for example, a teacher might cue a student to use recently learned negotiation skills (e.g., "Remember those steps we put up on the board?"). This allows the teacher to coach and provide feedback to the student regarding tone of voice, body language, and what words to use ("How do you think you could say that?"). By reinforcing use of skills across situations, a teacher increases the likelihood that students will be able to make reasoned choices about behavior as opposed to being overrun by strong feelings (Greenberg & Snell, 1997).

Teachers can also create feedback structures by using a three-point plan, described in the *Second Step* teacher's manuals, to bring the curriculum into daily activities. Teachers can do this by (a) prompting, (b) reinforcing, and (c) remembering behaviors. "Imagine the Day" activities at the beginning of the school day prompt students to identify times when they might use specific skills and attend to prosocial behaviors like giving compliments and joining groups. Reinforcement can occur throughout the day with teachers emphasizing the natural reinforcement inherent in socially competent behavior (e.g., "How did you feel when she said you had a good idea?"). "Remember the Day" activities take place at the conclusion of the school day when teachers prompt students to review, discuss, and celebrate occasions when targeted skills were used. In the example above, classmates might recall and reinforce their peer's earlier attempt to appropriately request a turn at the computer.

Student Participation in Decision Making

Social–emotional learning programs encourage teachers to make use of students' developing skills by enlisting them as responsible partners in class-

room management. This starts at the beginning of the school year, when students are asked to create class rules in the first *Second Step* lesson. Internalization and commitment to rules increases when the reasons for rules are discussed (Deci & Ryan, 1987) and students have played a part in creating them.

Student input can be sought to solve class problems throughout the year. Teachers may solicit student thinking about a range of situations, from relatively minor problems (e.g., "We seem to be using up our paper supplies quickly. What can we do?") to larger conflicts (e.g., "Some people are being left out. How can we solve this problem?"). Students view teachers who use democratic practices as caring (Wentzel, 1997), and children who view their teacher as caring tend to place greater value on social responsibility and prosocial goals (Wentzel & Wigfield, 1998).

It takes time and repeated practice for students, as well as staff, to adopt skills and strategies as part of their daily, natural practice. By involving students in problem solving on a regular basis and using classroom situations as opportunities to practice and reflect on social skills, teachers increase the likelihood that students can access these skills in times of emotional stress, when it is more difficult to think clearly and act responsibly (Nummela & Rosengren, 1986). However, for teachers with more reactive or controlling teaching styles, *Second Step* requires changing basic classroom patterns and practices. Such teachers may require extensive support and coaching in order to adopt more interactive approaches.

SUPPORTIVE SCHOOL CONTEXTS

The type of long-term relationship that sustains this level of teacher investment is possible only if schools and districts provide adequate resources, support, and commitment. Principals and *Second Step* trainers are pivotal in creating a whole school climate that supports implementation of a social–emotional learning program.

School-Wide Commitment

Social–emotional competencies are most likely to flourish in schools making long-term commitments to school-wide implementation (Weissberg & Greenberg, 1997). With school-wide implementation, students receive some aspect of the program every school year. Equally important, they regularly interact with adults who understand and reinforce program elements. Children benefit most from classroom instruction when all school personnel consistently provide coaching and recognition for constructive problem solving. Confusion and disappointment can result if a student attempts to use a problem-solving strategy that is not understood by school staff. For example, a student's effort to use steps to evaluate a solution to a recess conflict ("Is it fair?" "Is it safe?" "How will people feel?" "Will it work?") may be unintentionally "shut down" by a playground monitor's hasty intervention. Because playground monitors, school nurses, office managers, and bus drivers are often on the "front lines" when conflicts occur, the Committee for Children provides trainers with materials for training non-teaching staff. (The Committee for Children is a non-profit organization that develops and evaluates social emotional learning programs for children, families, and communities. The organization provides training in use of *Second Step* to school staff and on-site trainers. In addition, implementation specialists at Committee for Children assist school, district, and agency personnel in determining their needs and developing plans for successful whole-school implementation.)

Principal Support

Imparting healthy skills and preventing behavior problems in children requires ongoing commitment to school-wide implementation (Elias et al., 1997). Principals are pivotal figures who guarantee a long-term commitment by demonstrating support for the program and holding staff accountable for its implementation. The most successful principals seek training and experience with *Second Step* because their understanding and practical knowledge of the program can aid greatly in resource planning and obtaining teacher "buy-in." Principals are more likely to secure the support of their teaching staff if teachers have had input into the decision-making process and are confident the principal will commit adequate resources for planning, training, and curricular materials (Rohrbach et al., 1996).

Principals also play a vital role in implementation by appointing skilled individuals to be on-site trainers and by allowing them planning and consultation time to do this well. Principals can demonstrate program support by consistently talking about the program at staff meetings, by observing *Second Step* lessons during teacher evaluations, and by setting time aside once a month to discuss what is working and what is problematic in implementation. They also demonstrate their commitment by using the problem-solving strategies with students and staff and by making program elements visible in posters, assemblies, newsletters, and special events. In sum, successful principals make sure that the program "acts proud" (Elias et al., 1997) and remains a visible, valued component of the school culture.

Second Step Trainers

Although Committee for Children trainers conduct on-site training for teachers and staff, they also offer a "training for trainers" model. This model works to create infrastructure and an on-site knowledge base to sustain initial and long-term training needs in districts and schools. School personnel with experience teaching *Second Step* and training adults are the best candidates for being trainers. Following an intensive 3-day workshop, participants are provided with training videotapes, manuals, and ongoing consultation with staff at the Committee for Children. Having on-site expertise presents advantages for schools. In addition to conducting the initial training of teachers, trainers can coach individual teachers, train nonteaching staff, and provide "booster" sessions to motivate and enhance program implementation. This level of support is possible

when trainers are given time to provide assistance as an integral part of their jobs. In sum, the training for trainers model is a cost-effective strategy to create an on-site knowledge base to support implementation over time.

THE FAMILY GUIDE TO SECOND STEP

Although research demonstrates *Second Step*'s effectiveness in changing children's behavior at school in the absence of parent education (Grossman et al., 1997), there is ample evidence that behavioral changes are more likely to transfer to other domains of children's lives with parent training (Simon & Johnston, 1987). Overall, prevention works best when teachers, peers, and families are all targeted.

A Family Guide to Second Step (Committee for Children, 1995) is designed for use with parents and caregivers of children in preschool through Grade 5 who are receiving *Second Step* in their classrooms, youth groups, or after school programs. The guide consists of six video-based instruction modules. Throughout the sessions, parents and caregivers discuss and practice the same vocabulary, concepts, and strategies that children learn through *Second Step*. For example, parents are introduced to the concept of anger "triggers" and use of self-talk to cope with strong feelings.

Family Guide materials can be implemented in several ways. In some schools, sessions are led by the school counselor or social worker. Parents and caregivers attend all six facilitator-led family sessions, during which they have opportunities to view videos and discuss, practice, and ask questions about *Second Step* strategies. Alternatively, parents can attend a 1-night overview session that serves as an introduction to the school program. Another option is for schools to train a cadre of parents to conduct outreach, as well as copresent video-based sessions. This is especially useful in schools with diverse immigrant populations. Parent attendance is supported by provision of child care, refreshments, and, most importantly, a lively, interac-

tive presentation style on the part of the facilitator(s). Nonetheless, many parents will not attend meetings. An introductory take-home videotape, included with the curriculum, provides a general overview of the *Second Step* program for these families.

PROGRAM EVALUATION

The effects of the *Second Step* program have been evaluated in several ways. First, formative studies of prepublished and revised versions of the program were conducted to assist in program development and revisions. Second, researchers at the University of Washington, funded by the Centers for Disease Control and Prevention, undertook a 1-year experimental study of *Second Step* to ascertain program effects on aggressive and prosocial behavior of students (Grossman et al., 1997).

Formative Studies

A series of formative studies of the program for students in pre-K through Grade 8 were conducted in a total of twelve public and two private schools located in urban and suburban districts in the Pacific Northwest (Beland, 1988, 1989, 1991; Moore & Beland, 1992). To assess knowledge gains, children in *Second Step* and control classrooms completed pre- and postinterviews (preschool- and kindergarten-level) and surveys (all other levels). Children who participated in the *Second Step* program significantly improved their verbal perspective taking and social problem–solving abilities. In contrast, children in control classrooms showed no improvement from Time 1 to Time 2. Thus, initial evaluation of *Second Step* indicates that children who receive the program display significantly higher social skills knowledge (e.g., how to calm down when angry) than children who do not.

In formative studies, teachers rated prototype and revised versions of lessons and the overall program. Teachers gave high ratings to the overall program, the lesson format, and the teacher's guide.

They rated the lessons as easy to prepare and to incorporate into other subjects, and they reported that the lessons effectively stimulated student interest.

Unfortunately, lack of random assignment to groups is a limitation of the formative studies just described. Consequently, it is possible that the advances in learning found in students who received *Second Step* could be due to general practices characteristic of their teachers, rather than to participation in the *Second Step* program. Results of these formative studies cannot be completely dismissed, however, given the improvements observed in aggression and positive social behavior in the more rigorous outcome evaluation study conducted by Grossman et al. (1997).

Outcome Evaluation

Grossman and his colleagues examined the impact of *Second Step* on aggression and positive social behaviors of second- and third-grade students in 49 classrooms (*N* = 790). Twelve schools from urban and suburban areas of western Washington state were paired on the basis of (a) school district, (b) proportion of students receiving free or reduced-cost school lunch, and (c) proportion of minority school enrollment. One school from each matched pair was randomly assigned to receive the *Second Step* intervention. Teachers in the control group were given their choice of implementing classroom materials in areas that did not include the social–emotional skills addressed by *Second Step* (e.g., self-esteem).

Classroom teachers taught *Second Step* lessons twice a week during a 4- to 5-month period. Data were collected three times: (a) in the fall of 1993, prior to the start of *Second Step* lessons in intervention schools; (b) in the spring of 1994, 2 weeks after completion of the curriculum; and (c) in the fall of 1994, 6 months after completion of the curriculum. Outcome data included teacher ratings, parent ratings, and direct behavioral observations by trained observers blind to condition. Twelve students from each participating classroom (*n* = 588)

were selected at random to be observed in classroom, lunchroom, and playground settings. Using the *Social Interaction Observation System* (Neckerman, Asher, & Pavlidis, 1994), observers recorded physical and verbal aggression and prosocial and neutral behaviors.

Behavioral observations revealed that physical aggression decreased from autumn to spring among students in the *Second Step* program, but not in the control group (see Figure 1). Reductions were greatest in the least structured settings—the playground and lunchroom—where aggression most frequently oc-

curs. A similar but nonsignificant trend was found for hostile and aggressive comments (e.g., name-calling). Friendly behavior, including prosocial (e.g., "I'll share my snack with you") and neutral interactions (e.g., "Whose turn next?") increased from autumn to spring in the *Second Step* classes but remained constant in the control classes. As with physical aggression, differences between the groups were greatest on the playground and in the lunchroom. In the 6-month follow-up, students in the *Second Step* classes continued to show significantly lower levels of physical aggression than

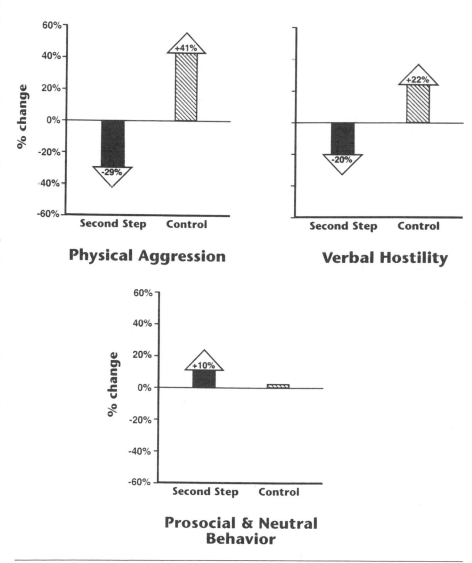

FIGURE 1. Changes, from autumn to spring, in children's social behaviors in playground and lunchroom settings (based on data from Grossman, Neckerman, Koepsell, Ping-Yu, Asher, Beland, Frey, & Rivara, 1997).

those in control classes, and their higher levels of positive interaction were maintained.

This is the first large-scale experimental study examining program effects using systematic observations in class and on the playground. The results provide encouraging evidence that use of *Second Step* reduces children's levels of aggressive behavior and increases socially competent behavior. The findings further suggest that these changes endure over time. Rosenberg, Powell, and Hammond (1997), at the National Center for Injury Prevention and Research, commented on the practical significance of these findings: "At 22 students per classroom and six school hours per day, the changes amount to about 30 fewer acts of 'negative physical behavior' and more than 800 more acts of 'neutral/ prosocial behavior' per class every day" (p. 1641).

In light of results from Grossman et al. (1997), it is somewhat surprising that ratings of student behavior provided by teachers and parents did not show any differences between intervention and control groups in the study. Neither the improvements observed in the *Second Step* students nor the problems observed in the control schools were reflected in ratings of individual students. Grossman et al. (1997) speculate that teachers may not notice small changes in students' behaviors in the context of a whole class. Teachers may also be unaware of aggressive behaviors that take place outside the classroom. Similarly, because parents tend to be more attuned to children's behaviors at home, parent ratings may not reflect behavioral changes that occur between peers in school settings.

Challenges for Long-Term Implementation

The discrepancy between teacher reports of student behavior and observations by trained personnel identifies a potential problem for educators: benefits are not always obvious. In the Grossman et al. (1997) study, *Second Step* students showed modest decreases in aggression, whereas control students showed *increases* over the school year. This trend in the control schools, which has been observed by other researchers (Reid et al., 1997), suggests a natural rise in students' aggressive behaviors over the course of a school year. Teachers who are presenting a program, however, will not have access to both sets of information. That is, they will not know what their students would be like if the program were *not* taught. This poses an important challenge because teachers need to know that their time and effort are paying off if they are to persist.

Lack of visible benefits may be a particular problem in the first year of a program when teachers are still learning program elements and have not yet devised efficient ways of integrating them with academic curricula and daily classroom life. At this tender stage, a social skills program may be viewed as an "add-on," something that requires learning new material, takes time away from academics, and, therefore, adds to teacher stress. Teachers are under ever-increasing pressure to assume wider responsibilities, and these aspects of teachers' experiences pose challenges to ongoing implementation of *Second Step*. Social skills lessons are sometimes viewed as "frills," particularly at the outset of using a new program. Although some teachers report that *Second Step* reduces class disruption so that eventually there is *more* time for academics, teachers who have yet to reap these rewards will be at risk for dropping the program. Unfortunately, it is doubtful that benefits will persist beyond the six months noted in the *Second Step* outcome evaluation if there is no program continuity (Weissberg, Caplan, & Sivo, 1989).

A major challenge for administrators and researchers, therefore, is finding ways to document positive effects of social skills programs in order to garner the committed, long-term support of teachers and parents. In one school adopting *Second Step,* the principal kept yearly records of referrals to the principal's office. As a result, she was able to inform her staff that referrals did *not* increase in the spring as they had in the years prior to teaching the program. This information helped marshal teacher motivation in the initial year of implementation. In subsequent years, commitment was sustained by growing staff awareness of program effects, as teachers reported they could tell which of their incoming students had received *Second Step* instruction and which had not.

SUMMARY

Second Step is a universal violence prevention and social–emotional learning program based on sound research foundations. The program provides (a) classroom lessons to teach core competencies and behavior skills, (b) teacher and staff training to encourage student generalization of skills and create consistency throughout the school, (c) follow-up support and preparation of on-site trainers to sustain ongoing implementation, and (d) a family component to encourage complementary home practices. Although more work in the area of program evaluation is needed, studies reviewed in this article suggest *Second Step* can effectively decrease physical aggression, change attitudes that support aggression, and increase sociable interaction between students.

Well-designed programs alone are not sufficient to produce these changes, however. Districts or schools that fail to allocate sufficient time or resources to implementing a social skills curriculum will likely fall short of desired results. School-wide commitment, strong administrative leadership, and ongoing training of staff are critical factors in sustaining efforts to prevent violence and promote behavioral alternatives to violence in schools. The challenge for developers of *Second Step* and other interventions is to continue identifying new ways to support schools' and practitioners' efforts to nurture development of social–emotional competencies and behavioral skills of all students.

About the Authors

KARIN S. FREY, PhD, is the director of research at the Committee for Children and an associate research professor of education at the University of Washington. Her basic research has focused on peer interaction in school settings, the integration of mastery and social motivation, and the impact of maternal depression on self-regulation and mastery behavior. Her applied work examines the effects of school-based interventions on student aggression, negotiation behavior, and teachers' support of problem-solving strategies. **MIRIAM K. HIRSCHSTEIN,** PhD, is a research psychologist at the Committee for Children. Her research interests include social–emotional development, motivation, and interpersonal processes in classroom settings. She is currently investigating the longitudinal effects of social skill interventions on children and teachers. **BARBARA A. GUZZO** is the director of client support at the Committee for Children. She has extensive experience as an educator and developer of curricula. Currently, she consults with schools, districts, and agencies about effective implementation of the social–emotional learning program. Address: Miriam Hirschstein, Research and Evaluation, Committee for Children, 2203 Airport Way S., Suite 500, Seattle, WA 98134; Web site: www.cf.children.org

Authors' Note

The development of this article was supported, in part, by the Committee for Children. This article reflects the views of its authors. Committee for Children is a not-for-profit organization that researches and develops social–emotional learning programs to reduce aggression and the victimization of children.

References

Bandura, A. (1986). *Social foundations of thought and action: A social cognitive theory.* Englewood, NJ: Prentice Hall.

Beland, K. (1988). *Second Step, grades 1-3: Summary report.* Seattle, WA: Committee for Children.

Beland, K. (1989). *Second Step, grades 4-5: Summary report.* Seattle, WA: Committee for Children.

Beland, K. (1991). *Second Step, preschool-kindergarten: Summary report.* Seattle, WA: Committee for Children.

Brewer, D. D., Hawkins, J. D., Catalano, R. F., & Neckerman, H. J. (1995). Preventing serious, violent, and chronic juvenile offending: A review of evaluations of selected strategies in childhood, adolescence, and the community. In J. C. Howell, B. Kris-

berg, J. J. Wilson, & J. D. Hawkins (Eds.), *A sourcebook on serious, violent, and chronic juvenile offenders* (pp. 61–141). Newbury Park, CA: Sage.

Cairns, R. B., Cairns, B. D., Neckerman, H. J., Ferguson, L. L., & Gariepy, J. L. (1989). Growth and aggression: I. Childhood to early adolescence. *Developmental Psychology, 25,* 320–330.

Committee for Children. (1995). *A family guide to Second Step.* Seattle, WA: Author.

Committee for Children. (1992a). *Second Step: A violence prevention curriculum; Grades 1-3.* Seattle, WA: Author.

Committee for Children. (1992b). *Second Step: A violence prevention curriculum; Grades 4-5.* Seattle, WA: Author.

Committee for Children. (1997). *Second Step: A violence prevention curriculum; Middle school/junior high.* Seattle, WA: Author.

Committee for Children. (1991). *Second Step: A violence prevention curriculum; Preschool-kindergarten.* Seattle, WA: Author.

Consortium on the School Based Promotion of Social Competence. (1994). The school based promotion of social competence: Theory, research, practice, and policy. In R. J. Haggerty, L. R. Sherrod, N. Garmezy, & M. Rutter (Eds.), *Stress, risk, and resilience in children and adolescents: Processes, mechanisms, and interventions* (pp. 268–316). New York: Cambridge University Press.

Crick, N. R., & Ladd, G. W. (1990). Children's perceptions of the outcomes of aggressive strategies: Do the ends justify being mean. *Journal of Developmental Psychology, 29,* 612–620.

Deci, E. L., & Ryan, R. M. (1987). The support of autonomy and the control of behavior. *Journal of Personality and Social Psychology, 53,* 1024–1037.

Denham, S. A., & Almeida, M. C. (1987). Children's social problem-solving skills, behavioral adjustment, and interventions: A meta-analysis evaluating theory and practice. *Journal of Applied Developmental Psychology, 8,* 391–409.

Dodge, K. A., & Frame, C. L. (1982). Social cognitive biases and deficits in aggressive boys. *Child Development, 53,* 629–635.

Dodge, K. A., McClaskey, C. L., & Feldman, E. (1985). A situational approach to the assessment of social competence in children. *Journal of Consulting and Clinical Psychology, 53,* 344–353.

Dodge, K. A., Pettit, G. S., McClaskey, C. L., & Brown, J. (1986). Social competence in

children. *Monographs of the Society for Research in Child Development, 44* (2, Serial No. 213).

Dryfoos, J. G. (1997). The prevalence of problem behaviors: Implications for programs. In R. P. Weissberg, T. P. Gullotta, R. L. Hampton, B. A. Ryan, & G. R. Adams (Eds.), *Healthy children 2010: Enhancing children's wellness* (Vol. 8, pp. 17–47). Thousand Oaks, CA: Sage.

Durlak, J. A. (1983). Social problem solving as a primary prevention strategy. In R. D. Felner, L. A. Jason, J. N. Moritsugu, & S. S. Farber (Eds.), *Preventive psychology: Theory, research, and practice* (pp. 31–48). New York: Pergamon.

Eisenberg, N. (1986). *Altruistic emotion, cognition, and behavior.* Hillsdale, NJ: Erlbaum.

Eisenberg, N., Fabes, R., Shepard, S. A., Burphy, B. C., Guthrie, I. K., Jones, S., Friedman, J., Poulin, R., & Maszk, P. (1997). Contemporaneous and longitudinal prediction of children's social functioning from regulation and emotionality. *Child Development, 68,* 642–664.

Ekman, P., & Friesen, W. (1975). *Unmasking the face.* Palo Alto, CA: Consulting Psychologists Press.

Elias, M. J., Zins, J. E., Weissberg, R. P., Frey, K. S., Greenberg, M. T., Haynes, N. M., Kessler, R., Schwab-Stone, M. E., & Shriver, T. P. (1997). *Promoting social and emotional learning: Guidelines for educators.* Alexandria, VA: Association for Supervision and Curriculum Development.

Gottman, J. M., Katz, L. F., & Hooven, C. (1996). Parental meta-emotion philosophy and the emotional life of families: Theoretical models and preliminary data. *Journal of Family Psychology, 10,* 243–268.

Graham, S. (1993, March). *Peer-directed aggression in African American youth from an attributional perspective.* Paper presented at the biennial meeting for the Society for Research in Child Development, New Orleans, LA.

Greenberg, M. T., & Snell, J. L. (1997). Brain development and emotional development: The role of teaching in organizing. In P. Salovey & D. J. Sluyter (Eds.), *Emotional development and emotional intelligence: Educational implications* (pp. 93–119). New York: BasicBooks.

Grossman, D. C., Neckerman, H. J., Koepsell, T. D., Liu, P. Y., Asher, K. N., Beland, K., Frey, K., & Rivara, F. P. (1997). Effectiveness of a violence prevention curriculum among children in elementary school:

A randomized controlled trial. *Journal of the American Medical Association, 277,* 1605–1611.

Hudley, C., & Graham, S. (1993). An attributional intervention to reduce peer-directed aggression among African American boys. *Child Development, 64,* 124–138.

Kazdin, A. E. (1987). Treatment of antisocial behavior in children: Current status and future directions. *Psychological Bulletin, 102,* 187–203.

Kendall, P. C., & Braswell, L. (1985). *Cognitive-behavioral therapy for impulsive children.* New York: Guilford.

Litvack-Miller, W., McDougal, D., & Romney, D. M. (1997). The structure of empathy during middle childhood and its relationship to prosocial behavior. *Genetic, Social, and Genetic Psychology Monographs, 123,* 303–324.

Lochman, J. E. (1992). Cognitive-behavioral interventions with aggressive boys: Three-year follow-up and preventive effects. *Journal of Counseling and Clinical Psychology, 60,* 426–432.

Lochman, J. E., Burch, P. P., Curry, J. F., & Lampron, L. B. (1984). Treatment and generalization effects of cognitive-behavioral and goal setting interventions with aggressive boys. *Journal of Counseling and Clinical Psychology, 52,* 916–926.

Lochman, J. E., Coie, J. D., Underwood, M. K., & Terry, R. (1994). Effectiveness of a social relations intervention program for aggressive and nonaggressive, rejected children. *Journal of Consulting and Clinical Psychology, 61,* 1053–1058.

Lochman, J. E., Nelson, W. M. III, & Sims, J. P. (1981). A cognitive behavioral program for use with aggressive children. *Journal of Clinical Child Psychology, 13,* 527–538.

Luria, A. (1961). *The role of speech in the regulation of normal and abnormal behaviors.* New York: Liberight.

Meichenbaum, D. (1977). *Cognitive-behavior modification: An integrative approach.* New York: Plenum.

Miller, P. A., & Eisenberg, N. (1988). The relation of empathy to aggression and psy-

chopathology. *Psychological Bulletin, 103,* 324–344.

Moore, B., & Beland, K. (1992). *Evaluation of Second Step, preschool-kindergarten: A violent prevention curriculum kit. Summary report.* Seattle WA: Committee for Children.

Neckerman, H. J., Asher, K., & Pavlidis, K. (1994). *Social interaction observation system.* Seattle, WA: Harborview Injury Prevention and Research Center.

Novaco, R. W. (1975). *Anger control: The development and evaluation of an experimental treatment.* Lexington, MA: D. C. Health.

Nummela, R., & Rosengren, T. (1986). What's happening in students' brains may redefine teaching. *Educational Leadership, 43,* 49–53.

Olweus, D. (1993). Bullies on the playground: The role of victimization. In C. H. Hart (Ed.), *Children on playgrounds* (pp. 85–128). Albany: State University of New York Press.

Reid, J. (1993). Prevention of conduct disorder before and after school entry: Relating interventions to developmental findings. *Development and Psychopathology, 11,* 209–223.

Rohrbach, L. A., D'Onofrio, C. N., Backer, T. E., & Montgomery, S. B. (1996). Diffusion of school-based substance abuse prevention programs. *American Behavioral Scientist, 39,* 919–934.

Rosenberg, M. L., Powell, K. E., & Hammond, R. (1997). Applying science to violence prevention. *Journal of the American Medical Association, 277,* 1641–1642.

Rubin, K. H., Bream, L. A., & Rose-Krasnor, L. (1991). Social problem-solving and aggression in childhood. In D. J. Pepler & K. H. Rubin (Eds.), *The development and treatment of childhood aggression* (pp. 219–248). Hillsdale, NJ: Erlbaum.

Saarni, C. (1999). *The development of emotional competence.* New York: Guilford Press.

Simon, D. J., & Johnston, J. C. (1987). Working with families: The missing link in behavior disorder interventions. In R. B.

Rutherford, C. M. Nelson, & S. R. Forness (Eds.), *Severe behavior disorders of children and youth* (pp. 447–460). New York: Wiley.

Spencer, L. M., & Spencer, S. M. (1993). *Competence at work: Models for superior performance.* New York: Wiley.

Strayer, J., & Schroeder, M. (1989). Children's helping strategies: Influences of emotion, empathy, and age. In N. Eisenberg (Ed.), *Empathy and related emotional responses* (pp. 85–105). San Francisco: Jossey-Bass.

Underwood, M. K., Coie, J. D., & Herbsman, C. R. (1992). Display rules for anger and aggression in school-age children. *Child Development, 63,* 366–380.

Walker, H. M., Horner, R. H., Sugai, G., Bullis, M., Sprague, J. R., Bricker, D., & Kaufman, M. J. (1996). Integrated approaches to preventing antisocial behavior patterns among school-age children and youth. *Journal of Emotional and Behavioral Disorders, 4,* 194–209.

Weissberg, R. P., Caplan, M. Z., & Sivo, J. P. (1989). A new conceptual framework for establishing school-based social competence promotion programs. In L. A. Bond & B. E. Compas (Eds.), *Primary prevention and promotion in the schools* (pp. 255–296). Newbury Park, CA: Sage.

Weissberg, R. P., & Greenberg, M. T. (1997). School and community competence-enhancement and prevention programs. In I. E. Sigel & K. A. Renninger (Eds.), *Handbook of child psychology: Vol. 5. Child psychology in practice* (5th ed., pp. 45–56). New York: Wiley.

Wentzel, K. R. (1995). *Teachers who care: Implications for student motivation and classroom behavior.* Washington, DC: Office of Educational Research and Improvement, QERI Fellows Program.

Wentzel, K. R. (1997). Student motivation in middle school: The role of perceived pedagogical caring. *Journal of Educational Psychology, 89,* 411–419.

Wentzel, K. R., & Wigfield, A. (1998). Academic and social motivational influences on students' academic performance. *Educational Psychology Review, 10,* 155–175.

Inside Multisystemic Therapy:

Therapist, Supervisory, and Program Practices

SONJA K. SCHOENWALD, TAMARA L. BROWN,
AND SCOTT W. HENGGELER

In this article, we highlight key features of Multisystemic Therapy (MST) and of the supervisory, consultation, and program practices that support therapist implementation of MST in community-based settings. The article begins with a summary of the theoretical and empirical foundations of MST and of evidence supporting the effectiveness of the model. The remaining sections of the manuscript focus on therapist implementation of the model, supervisory practices, the use of consultation, and program (e.g., organizational, interorganizational) practices.

MULTISYSTEMIC THERAPY (MST; Henggeler, Schoenwald, Borduin, Rowland, & Cunningham, 1998) is an empirically-based treatment that focuses on changing the known determinants of youth antisocial behavior, including characteristics of the individual youth, family, peer relations, school functioning, and family–neighborhood interactions. The ultimate goal of MST is to empower primary caregivers with the skills and resources needed to independently address the difficulties that arise in rearing youth with behavioral problems and to empower youth to cope with family, peer, school, and neighborhood difficulties. To date, MST is one of the few treatments to demonstrate long-term effectiveness with youth presenting serious clinical problems and their families. MST has enjoyed this success because it is well-specified, is based on solid empirical research, and uses quality assurance mechanisms to ensure that the treatment is delivered as intended.

As might be expected, the capacity of MST to reduce the recidivism of serious juvenile offenders at cost savings has provoked considerable interest in the dissemination of MST programs. Child-serving agencies in 15 states, Canada, and Norway are attempting to implement MST, and pressures to increase the rate of MST dissemination are mounting. Although the growth of MST programs is encouraging to the field of mental health services, in which empirically-validated intervention models are both scarce and seldom used by community-based practitioners, challenges have become apparent in the attempt to successfully implement MST in community settings. Chief among these challenges is identifying the supervisory, organizational, and extra-organizational factors that support clinician fidelity to MST interventions. Thus, manuals documenting MST clinical supervision (Henggeler & Schoenwald, 1998), consultation (Schoenwald, 1998), and key aspects of organizational and interagency practices supportive of MST (Strother, Swenson, & Schoenwald, 1998) have been developed, and extensive training is used to promote therapist adherence to the MST protocol. The purpose of this article is to give readers a glimpse of what it means to "do MST" by describing elements of MST that support the integrity of implementation. A case example is used to illustrate central points throughout the article. First, a brief description of the theoretical and empirical foundations of MST is provided, and empirical evidence supporting the effectiveness of the model is summarized.

THEORETICAL AND EMPIRICAL FOUNDATIONS OF MST

MST is based on a social–ecological theoretical model (Bronfenbrenner, 1979) in which behavior is viewed as multidetermined by individual, family, school, peer, and community systems that are interconnected and have reciprocal influences. According to the social ecology model, (a) behavior is best understood when viewed within its naturally occurring context; and (b) to maximize the probability of achieving change, treatments must have the capacity to address various subsets of the factors conbributing to identified problems. Thus, the scope of MST interventions is not limited to the individual adolescent or the family system but includes difficulties between other systems, such as the family–school and family–peer mesosystems. This perspective is consistent with empirical evidence regarding the multiple risk and protective factors associated with the development of emotional and behavioral problems in youth. To summarize, evidence from multivariate cross-sectional and longitudinal studies indicate that a combination of individual (attributional bias, antisocial attitudes), family (low warmth, high conflict, harsh and/or inconsistent discipline, low monitoring of youth whereabouts, parental problems, low social support), peer (association with deviant peers), school (low family–school bonding, problems with academic and social performance), and neighborhood (transience, disorganization, criminal subculture) factors are linked with serious antisocial behavior in adolescents (for reviews see Elliott, 1994; Henggeler, 1997; Huizinga, 1995; Loeber, Keenan, & Zhang, 1997). Recent reviews of the etiology of adolescent substance abuse/dependence (Henggeler, 1998), juvenile sex offending (Becker, 1998), and the symptoms (disruptive behavior disorders, anxiety, depression, substance abuse, attention-deficit disorder) and functional impairments (school failure, peer relations problems, trouble with the law) encompassed under the label "serious emotional disturbance" suggest that these types of serious clinical problems are also multidetermined (Costello, Angold, Burns, & Behar, 1998; Mash & Dozois, 1996; Quinn & Epstein, 1998).

An important feature of the MST treatment model is the integration of empirically-based treatment approaches (e.g., strategic and functional family therapy approaches, behavioral parent training, cognitive behavior therapies), which have historically focused on a limited aspect of the youth's social ecology

(e.g., the cognitions or problem-solving skills of the individual youth; the discipline strategies of a parent) into an ecological framework that addresses pertinent factors across family, peer, school, and community contexts. In addition and as appropriate, biological contributors to identified problems are identified and psychopharmacological treatment is integrated with psychosocial treatment. In contrast with "combined" (e.g., Kazdin, 1996; Kazdin, Siegel, & Bass, 1992) and multicomponent approaches to treatment (e.g., Liddle, 1996), however, the different types of interventions are not delivered as separate elements or self-contained modules. Rather, throughout treatment, interventions are strategically selected and integrated in ways thought to maximize synergistic interaction. Although techniques are individualized to the strengths and needs of each youth and family, the MST principles constrain the range of options a clinician may consider. Thus, much of the eclectic practice that characterizes community-based professionals is prohibited in MST.

EFFECTIVENESS OF MST

Several outcome studies have been conducted to evaluate the clinical- and cost-effectiveness of MST with youth who engage in serious antisocial behavior (Borduin, Henggeler, Blaske, & Stein, 1990; Borduin et al., 1995; Brunk, Henggeler, & Whelan, 1987; Henggeler et al., 1991; Henggeler, Melton, Brondino, Scherer, & Hanley, 1997; Henggeler, Melton, & Smith, 1992; Henggeler, Pickrel, & Brondino, in press; Henggeler et al., 1986). For example, a randomized clinical trial comparing MST with usual services (Henggeler et al., 1992) in the treatment of serious juvenile offenders at imminent risk of incarceration showed that youths receiving MST had substantially reduced recidivism and out-of-home placement rates at 59-week follow-up and substantially reduced re-arrest rates at a 2.4-year follow-up (Henggeler, Melton, Smith, Schoenwald, & Hanley, 1993). A randomized trial comparing MST with individual therapy

(Borduin et al., 1995) in the treatment of serious juvenile offenders showed, at a 4-year follow-up, decreases in arrest rates, other criminal offenses, and substance related offenses. A third randomized trial with violent and chronic juvenile offenders (Henggeler et al., 1997) demonstrated the effectiveness of MST in reducing out-of-home placements and demonstrated the importance of therapist adherence to the MST principles in obtaining favorable outcomes. Finally, an ongoing trial of MST as an alternative to emergency psychiatric hospitalization is showing that MST can safely reduce rates of psychiatric hospitalization and other out-of-home placements while improving youth and family functioning in comparison with psychiatric hospitalization (Henggeler, Rowland et al., in press; Schoenwald, Ward, Henggeler, & Rowland, in press).

Evidence also indicates that MST may be more cost-effective than the services provided to "difficult to treat" youth and their families in most communities (Schoenwald, Ward, Henggeler, Pickrel, & Patel, 1996). Indeed, a study conducted by the Washington State Institute on Public Policy identified MST as the most cost-effective intervention for juvenile offenders among 16 programs evaluated (Washington State Institute for Public Policy, 1998). In sum, MST has a strong track record in demonstrating favorable long-term outcomes for youth presenting serious clinical problems and their families.

INSIDE MST: IMPLEMENTATION

The Home-Based Model of Service Delivery

The core feature of MST is its emphasis on changing the social ecology of youth and families in ways that promote positive adjustment and attenuate emotional and behavioral difficulties. Because accomplishing this goal requires a high level of involvement in the natural environments of youth and their families, the home-based, or family preservation, model of service delivery is ideally suited for MST. Despite some commonalities among various home-based or family preservation programs (i.e., low caseload, services delivered in home), they vary considerably in purpose, treatment delivered, and outcomes achieved (for reviews, see Fraser, Nelson, & Rivard, 1997; Schoenwald & Henggeler, 1997).

As applied to MST, the home-based model of service delivery is used to provide very intensive and comprehensive treatment that prevents out-of-home placement. As such, caseloads are low, with about four to five families per full-time therapist. Treatment is provided in the families' natural environments (i.e., home, school, and neighborhood settings) at hours and times convenient for the family, such as evenings and weekends. Treatment is time-limited, lasting 3 to 5 months per family, depending on the seriousness of the problems and success of interventions. Therapists are available 24 hours per day and 7 days per week, with the frequency, duration, and intensity of face-to-face contact varying in accordance with the needs and treatment gains experienced by families. Thus, daily contact is common early during treatment and when periodic setbacks occur, with contact reduced to several times per week as treatment progresses.

The Principles and Process of MST

Nine principles guide the MST assessment and intervention process:

1. The primary purpose of assessment is to understand the fit between the identified problems and their broader systemic context.
2. Therapeutic contacts emphasize the positive and should use systemic strengths as levers for change.
3. Interventions are designed to promote responsible behavior and decrease irresponsible behavior among family members.
4. Interventions are present-focused and action-oriented, targeting specified and well-defined problems.
5. Interventions target sequences of behavior within and between multiple systems that maintain the identified problems.
6. Interventions are developmentally appropriate and fit the developmental needs of the youth.
7. Interventions are designed to require daily or weekly effort by family members.
8. Intervention effectiveness is evaluated continuously from multiple perspectives with providers assuming accountability for overcoming barriers to successful outcomes.
9. Interventions are designed to promote treatment generalization and long-term maintenance of therapeutic change by empowering caregivers to address family members' needs across multiple systemic contexts.

The MST treatment process entails interrelated steps that connect the ongoing assessment of the "fit" of referral problems with the development and implementation of interventions. Supervisors encourage clinicians to engage in hypothesis testing when they have hunches, beliefs, or theories about (a) the causes and correlates of particular problems in a family, (b) the reasons that improvements have occurred, and (c) barriers to change. This iterative Analytical Process, depicted in Figure 1, has been dubbed the "MST Do-Loop." Throughout the course of treatment, clinicians conceptualize the many interactions and developments that occur in any given case during a week in terms of the steps in this process. These steps are summarized on paper prior to each supervisory session. Specifically, written summaries provide information about the following:

- the overarching/primary goals of MST;
- the intermediary goals (i.e., goals that represent steps toward achieving the overarching goals);
- advances toward achieving the intermediary goals;
- barriers to achieving the intermediary goals that were not met;
- the fit of advances made and of identified barriers (i.e., factors that contribute to successful achievement of the goal, factors that contribute to identified barriers to goal attainment); and
- new intermediary goals for the upcoming weeks that build upon treatment advances and address observed barriers to treatment progress.

As depicted in Figure 1, the ongoing MST assessment and intervention process begins with a clear understanding of the *reasons for referral*. The next task is to develop *overarching treatment goals* that reflect the goals of the family and other key stakeholders in the youth's ecology (e.g., teachers, probation officers). Following the development of overarching treatment goals, a preliminary multisystemic conceptualization of the fit of referral problems—of how each referral problem "makes sense" within the ecology of the youth—is developed. This *initial conceptualization of fit* encompasses strengths and weaknesses observed in each of the systems in the youth's ecology and becomes more detailed as the clinician gathers information and observations about interactions within and between each system that directly and indirectly influence the referral behavior. Next, the treatment team delineates *intermediary treatment goals*—goals that are logically linked to overarching goals, reflect steps toward achieving the overarching goals, and are achievable in the short term. With initial intermediary goals defined, the team identifies the range of treatment modalities and techniques that might be effective toward meeting the intermediary goals and tailors these to the specific strengths and weaknesses of the targeted client system (e.g., marital, parent–child, family–school).

As *interventions are implemented* and their success is monitored, barriers to favorable outcomes may become evident at several levels. For example, at the family level, previously unidentified parental difficulties such as marital problems, parental depression, or parental drug use might emerge. Likewise, clinician limitations (e.g., inexperience in marital therapy, poor repertoire of engagement

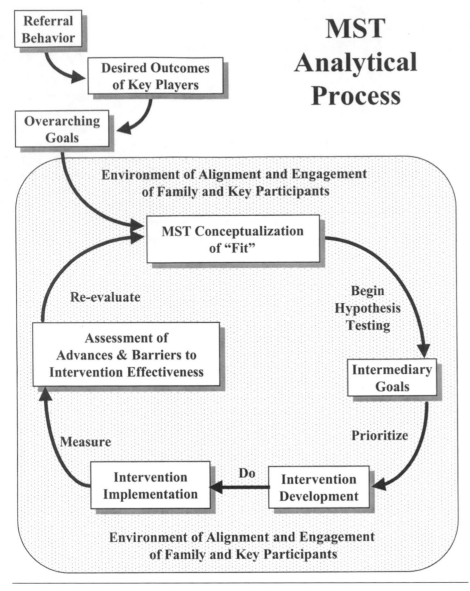

MST
Analytical
Process

FIGURE 1. The MST "Do-Loop."

strategies) may present barriers to change. Then, in an iterative process, *strategies for overcoming the barriers* are developed and implemented. Refinement continues until the desired results are achieved. Throughout this process, the MST consultant provides the ongoing training necessary to help the clinical supervisor and therapists think critically, adhere to the MST principles, and increase the probability that the desired outcomes are achieved quickly and in ways that are sustainable by the family and others in the youth's natural ecology.

Therapist Implementation of Principles and Process— Case Example

The case example of the Hodges family will be used to illustrate the application of the MST principles and analytic process (the "Do-Loop"). Figure 2 shows the Initial Contact Sheet for the Hodges family. The Initial Contact Sheet is a tool used to organize information about the strengths and needs of the youth's ecology obtained by the practitioner through direct observation in multiple settings (home, school, neigh-

borhood) and from multiple sources, including family members, teachers, peers, and archival records. This form is updated with new information throughout the treatment process.

James Hodges is a 14-year-old Caucasian male who lives alone with his mother. James was referred for MST treatment by the probation department following charges for truancy, theft, and assault and battery. The school had contacted the Department of Juvenile Justice regarding the truancy and noted that James had received multiple disciplinary notices and in-school and out-of-school suspensions during the previous semester. The disciplinary and suspension actions were taken in response to James's verbal and physical aggression with peers and increased verbal aggression with teachers. James's mother reported that he was becoming more verbally aggressive toward her at home, that he seemed to be increasingly irritable, and that he sometimes appeared somewhat depressed and isolated himself in his room. Additionally, James only intermittently complied with the medication regimen prescribed by a child psychiatrist for ADHD.

As illustrated in Figure 2, the therapist recorded the following information about her initial contacts with the Hodges family:

- mental health/juvenile justice history of James and his family (i.e., placements, treatments received);
- family structure and history;
- strengths and weaknesses that characterize the family, adolescent, peer group, school, neighborhood, and social support context; and
- treatment goals of the parents, youth, and referring agencies.

In the Hodges case, the referral problems were truancy; theft; assault and battery; verbal and physical aggression toward peers at school; verbal aggression with teachers; noncompliance with Ritalin; and increased irritability, verbal aggression, and isolation at home. The therapist gathered the perspectives of both of James's parents and of several teachers and the principal at the school regarding desired outcomes. She also contacted James' probation officer for input. As seen in Figure 2, Ms. Hodges wanted James to attend and behave in school, bring up his grades, comply with her rules at home, and take his Ritalin. The school wanted James to attend school regularly, stop his verbal and physical aggression toward peers, and stop his verbal aggression toward teachers. The probation officer wanted James to meet the terms of probation, which included attending school daily, unless ill, and meeting a weeknight curfew of 8 pm and a weekend curfew of 10 pm.

The therapist identified several important strengths (MST Principle 2) of James and others in his ecology. At the *individual* level, he had almost average intelligence, enjoyed sports until middle school, and, when regularly taking Ritalin, responded fairly well to behavioral contingencies in school. In terms of his *family,* James's mother had a part-time job in a hospital cafeteria and genuinely cared about James. Members of the extended family lived in the neighborhood and were willing to help the mother in some ways, and the family had a phone and owned a car. Regarding *peers,* James had one acquaintance from elementary school days who was relatively prosocial. One teacher and a coach at *school* were concerned about James and willing to try to help him. A strength in the *community* was the availability of organized athletic opportunities through an inner-city recreation center.

In addition to these systemic strengths, several weaknesses were identified in each of these systems. At the *individual* level, James had been accurately diagnosed with ADHD by a child psychiatrist at the age of 7, was verbally and physically abusive toward individuals in multiple contexts (e.g., mother, teachers), had recently stopped engaging in athletic activities, and had stopped taking Ritalin. In terms of the *family,* Ms. Hodges' parenting style was permissive (i.e., she established few rules, capitulated easily when James complained, backed down when he became verbally aggressive), she experienced symptoms of depression (feeling overwhelmed and hopeless at

times, increased social isolation, halting involvement in activities that used to be of interest, problems sleeping), and she self-medicated for the depression with alcohol several times a week. After use of alcohol, Ms. Hodges was less able to monitor James's whereabouts, overslept in the morning (therefore not detecting whether James actually got to school), and missed work periodically. James's father, who lived two miles away, had serious substance abuse (cocaine) problems, and had been physically abusive toward James prior to the couple's separation of 2 years. Although the couple had no interest in reconciling, Mr. Hodges periodically dropped in on Ms. Hodges and complained about the way she was raising their son. He often threatened to "beat some sense" into James. Ms. Hodges often drank to excess following one of these visits. Although James had periodic contact with one or two peers with whom he had been fairly close in elementary school, he had no other *peer* relations and, consequently, was socially isolated. The majority of the teachers at *school* were not supportive of James and were unwilling to help him. School personnel were inconsistent in handling James's medication adherence and behavioral problems, and communications between the mother and school were more often negative than positive. Finally, at the *community* level, the family lived in a neighborhood characterized by criminal activity.

Given this preliminary picture of the ecology, and significant evidence that the permissive parenting practices, depression and alcohol use, poor school–parent linkage, and combination of social isolation and poor peer relations were among the most powerful and proximal contributors to James' truancy and aggression, the MST consultant helped the supervisor, therapist, and team to identify several initial intermediary goals:

1. Decrease Ms. Hodges' depression and alcohol use because they were related to one another and contributed significantly to her permissive parenting practices, inability to consistently monitor James' school

attendance, and apprehension about meeting with school officials.
2. Alter the permissive parenting style to increase effective discipline and monitoring of school attendance and James' whereabouts at all times.
3. Bolster social support for Ms. Hodges to decrease depression and alcohol use, change parenting practices, and enable Ms. Hodges to assertively manage her estranged husband's disruptive visits.
4. Mend fences between school personnel and Ms. Hodges so that home–school coordination of interventions for truancy and aggression could be developed.
5. Identify, and increase contact with, prosocial peers for James.

Following the therapist's discussions with Ms. Hodges regarding the desirability of these intermediary goals, the consultant suggested to the team that (a) the first four goals required attention before the fifth goal, and (b) some aspects of the first four goals should be pursued simultaneously and others sequentially. The goal regarding prosocial peers was considered slightly less urgent for two reasons: First, James was mostly getting into trouble by himself (not with deviant peers), and, second, it seemed likely that Ms. Hodges would need to make at least some progress toward achieving Goals 1 through 4 before being able to engage in the types of strategies needed to facilitate his interaction with prosocial peers. The consultant explained to the team that, within the conceptual framework of MST, decisions about the simultaneous and sequential pursuit of one or more goals follow from evidence regarding the extent to which the problems targeted by the goals build upon one another (i.e., marital conflict that undermines parental consistency may need to be resolved before parenting practices can improve) or are interrelated (i.e., a parent's depression contributes to alcohol use, which exacerbates depression, and the combination of the two compromises the parent's ability to engage in effective discipline strategies).

Date of Intake: _____ **Referral Agency:** <u>Department of Juvenile Justice</u>

Reasons for Referral:
1. truancy
2. theft
3. assault and battery
4. verbal & physical aggression with peers at school
5. verbal aggression with teachers
6. irritability or verbal aggression w/ mother & isolation (depression?) at home

Summary of Mental Health, Juvenile Justice, and Placement History

Participant
Youth   — Probation previously—age 13—for truancy, theft, and assault
     — Outpatient psychiatry visits for aggression, medication management of ADHD
     — Never placed out of home
Parent Figures — Biological father in drug rehab for 9 months last year
     — Mother has no history of mental health treatment
Others

Initial Goals/Desired Outcomes

Participant   *Goals*
Primary Caregiver   For James to attend and behave in school, bring his grades up, comply with rules at home, and take his Ritalin. Also want to determine whether James' sullenness is normal, reflects depression, or indicates drug use.
Secondary Caregiver   N/A
Youth   Get school teachers "off my back."
Referral Agencies   **School:** For James to attend school regularly, stop verbal & physical aggression toward peers, and stop verbal aggression toward teachers
     DJJ: For James to attend school daily and comply with weekday (8 pm) and weekend (10 pm) curfews.

Overarching MST Goals

1. Attend all classes in school every day as evidenced by attendance records
2. Stop theft as evidenced by no further charges
3. Decrease verbal aggression toward teachers as evidenced by school reports
4. Decrease physical and verbal aggression toward peers as evidenced by school reports
5. Decrease verbal aggression and irritability at home as evidenced by parent reports
6. Have DJJ case closed

_____   _____   _____   _____
Therapist   Date   Supervisor   Date

Systemic Strengths	**Systemic Weaknesses/Needs**
Family	
Ms. Hodges has part-time job	Ms. Hodges' permissive parenting style
Ms. Hodges genuinely cares about James	Ms. Hodges' symptoms of depression
Extended family in neighborhood are willing to support Ms. Hodges	Ms. Hodges' alcohol use interferes with parenting 2 to 3 times per week
Family has telephone	Mr. Hodges is physically abusive toward James
Family owns a car	Mr. Hodges is verbally abusive & physically threatening toward Ms. Hodges
School	
One teacher and a coach are concerned about James and are willing to help him	Little support from most teachers
	School personnel are inconsistent in handling James' medication adherence & behavior problems
	Negative school–parent linkage
Peers	
Periodic contact with one prosocial peer from elementary school	Peers respond to aggressive behavior by challenging James to fight
	Poor peer relations
	Socially isolated

(figure continues)

FIGURE 2. Initial contact sheet for the Hodges family.

FIGURE 2 *(continued)*

Systemic Strengths *(cont.)*	Systemic Weaknesses/Needs *(cont.)*
Individual	
Almost average intelligence	Noncompliance with medication regimen for ADHD
Enjoys sports	Recently stopped engaging in athletic activities
Responds well to behavioral contingencies when taking Ritalin	Verbally & physically abusive toward others (mother, teachers, peers)
Neighborhood/Community	
Availability of organized athletic opportunities	High crime area
Inner-city recreation center	

The therapist provided evidence that Ms. Hodges' depressive thoughts and feelings and visits from Mr. Hodges were consistent triggers for Ms. Hodges' alcohol use, which in turn compromised her ability to monitor James and his school attendance and behavior. As the team was fairly new to MST, the consultant provided the coaching and training materials needed by the therapist to execute cognitive–behavioral interventions for depression and recommended strategies to the supervisor to help the therapist and team practice these interventions. As recommended by the MST consultant, the team also identified how the therapist could garner different types of social support to help Ms. Hodges deal with Mr. Hodges. Specifically, the therapist and Ms. Hodges reinstated a previously enjoyed activity of going to the farmer's market weekly with an aunt and made contact with a church group Ms. Hodges formerly attended (she stopped going as she became more depressed). In addition, the therapist facilitated several discussions between Ms. Hodges and her mother (because there had been a history of negative interaction between Ms. Hodges and her mother over James's behavior), during which the mother agreed, for a 3-week period, to monitor James on the night of Ms. Hodges' church meetings. At the same time, all family members were gathered together by the therapist and Ms. Hodges to devise strategies to help Ms. Hodges manage Mr. Hodges' unwanted drop-ins. These strategies included calling family members when Mr. Hodges dropped in, practicing assertive responses to his visits (via role-

plays), and, later in treatment following his negative responses to these changes, filing a restraining order, and seeking legal aid regarding divorce proceedings.

Although permissive parenting practices were a significant contributor to James's problems, the MST consultant suggested to the team that it would be difficult for Ms. Hodges to make major changes in discipline and monitoring strategies when she was depressed and/or drinking. Ms. Hodges and the team concurred with this assessment. Consequently, incremental interventions to change parenting practices were made initially (e.g., ignoring James' verbal banter, not following him to his room during arguments, calling the school daily to see if he was in attendance) and more substantive changes (developing rules and consequences, enforcing curfew, establishing home consequences for truant or aggressive behavior at school) were implemented several weeks after treatment began. The first face-to-face meeting between Ms. Hodges and school personnel did not take place until the fourth week of treatment, when some of the symptoms of depression had begun to decrease, although the therapist engaged in role-played practice of such meetings as part of the initial cognitive–behavioral interventions for depression (i.e., thought-stopping for all-or-nothing thinking about the school and James's prognosis there, practice of effective problem-solving strategies). Until the meeting was held, Ms. Hodges and the therapist worked with school personnel via phone calls scheduled at the convenience of the

school, and the therapist held one initial meeting with several of the teachers and principal to elicit initial cooperation with MST (with Ms. Hodges' approval, of course).

As is often the case, barriers to intervention success emerged as the therapist and Hodges family worked together. Examples of therapist/team detection of barriers to intervention success, determination of the "fit" of these barriers (factors that contribute to the barrier's existence), and implementation of strategies to overcome them are provided next.

SUPERVISORY PRACTICES

MST supervision sessions are the primary forum in which supervisors obtain evidence of clinicians' development and implementation of the conceptual and behavioral skills required to implement MST effectively (see Note 1). As such, supervision serves three interrelated purposes: (a) development of case-specific recommendations to speed progress toward outcomes for each client family, (b) monitoring of therapist adherence to MST treatment principles in all cases, and (c) advancement of clinicians' developmental trajectories with respect to each aspect of the ongoing MST assessment and intervention process. Clinician adherence to the MST principles is linked with favorable outcomes (Henggeler et al., 1997), and supervisors are primarily responsible for helping clinicians adhere. Thus, just as therapists are encouraged to "do whatever it takes" to achieve treatment goals with families, supervisors must be prepared to expend considerable effort in promoting clinicians' adherence to the MST protocol. When supervisors are new to MST, the MST consultant carries more of the supervisory burden, with ongoing training and consultation to the supervisor directed toward enabling her or him to do so. This section provides information on the structure of MST supervision and on how MST supervision is used to facilitate therapists' acquisition and implementation of the conceptual and behavioral skills required to achieve adherence to the MST treatment model.

Assumptions Underlying MST Supervision

Because seasoned clinicians are typically accustomed to practicing independently, compulsory supervision is often perceived as a foreign experience when they begin to work with MST programs. Thus, MST consultants discuss several assumptions about MST supervision to facilitate the adaptation of clinicians and supervisors to active supervision of cases. These assumptions follow:

1. Each clinician implementing MST is a hard-working, competent professional who brings unique personal strengths and professional experiences to the treatment process.
2. Ongoing clinical supervision is necessary to monitor adherence to MST and to achieve positive, sustainable outcomes with youth presenting serious clinical problems and their families.
3. The purpose of clinical supervision is to enable clinicians to adhere to the nine principles of MST in all aspects of treatment—engagement of client families, case conceptualization, intervention design and implementation, and evaluation of outcomes.
4. The process of clinical supervision should mirror the process of MST. That is, supervision is present-focused and action-oriented and targets specific and well-defined problems that the clinician appears to be having in (a) conceptualizaing the "fit" of referral problems with the

family's ecological context, (b) identifying and using strengths as levers for change, (c) designing interventions, (d) implementing interventions adequately, and (e) overcoming barriers to intervention implementation or success. Supervision should also enable clinicians to sustain MST-like conceptualizations and intervention skills across cases (generalization).
5. Clinicians and clinical supervisors (and the provider organization that houses the MST program) are accountable for outcomes (see Note 2).

Format of Supervision

Group Supervision. MST supervision typically occurs in a small group format (i.e., treatment teams). As described earlier, MST treatment teams typically include three to four therapists, and supervisors are responsible for the conduct and outcomes of all supervision sessions. Group supervision provides several advantages. First, team members have the opportunity to learn from each others' successes, mistakes, and dilemmas. Moreover, when the team brainstorms about how to solve a clinical problem, a variety of solutions may be generated, thus increasing the probability that therapists will possess a greater repertoire of responses when faced with similar barriers in treatment. Second, team members have the opportunity to practice (role play) clinical interventions, especially those that are difficult to implement, in a safe setting. Third, the group supervisory process can facilitate the types of collaboration among team members that lead to better outcomes for families. For example, when progress has been slow and barriers to progress are elusive, another team member may attend one or more treatment sessions to attain direct family contact. This second practitioner often develops new hypotheses about the barriers to progress as a result of having a "fresh" perspective. Fourth, MST programs must be prepared to meet the needs of families in crisis (a) who have not yet made the necessary ecological changes that will prevent out-

of-home placement and (b) whose therapist is not available (e.g., vacation). If team members have helped in the conceptualization and development of interventions for that family through group supervision, these individuals will be in a stronger position to ameliorate crises while "covering" for their colleague who is unavailable.

Individual Supervision. Although group supervision is the norm in MST, some circumstances warrant individual supervision. These include the emergence of a case crisis between scheduled supervision sessions, development of a specific clinical competency by a particular clinician, and assessment and remediation of consistently poor adherence to the model by a particular clinician. For example, in the Hodges case the therapist stayed with Ms. Hodges the first time she asked Mr. Hodges to stop his drop-in visits, and nothing untoward occurred. When Ms. Hodges handled the situation alone for the first time, however, Mr. Hodges threatened physical violence, and Ms. Hodges paged the therapist. Group supervision, however, was not scheduled to occur for 3 days. Thus, the therapist and supervisor met individually to develop a safety plan for Ms. Hodges. A similar meeting might have occurred had the school threatened immediate explusion after an intervention plan failed before group supervision was scheduled to occur.

Few clinicians join an MST program possessing all the requisite clinical skills (i.e., accurate detection and labeling of complex interaction sequences among family members, mastery of marital interventions, cognitive–behavioral interventions for adults and youth, parent–child management techniques, parent–peer interventions, effective school consultation). The MST training package is designed to promote the development of skills needed to implement MST effectively and includes 5 days of orientation training, quarterly booster training sessions, weekly expert consultation, and on-site group supervision. Additional training and consultation is sometimes required to enable clinicians to competently execute techniques introduced via the MST training package. In such cases, the MST consultant collaborates with the supervisor to provide the clinician with the needed resources (e.g., clinical writings, opportunities to practice in group and individual supervision, field observation as the clinician attempts the newly learned skills).

When a particular clinician is not adhering to MST principles and making little progress in most of her or his cases, individual supervision may be needed to assess the "fit" of the lack of adherence and poor progress. A variety of factors may contribute to poor adherence, including poor understanding of the model, continued allegiance to and practice of treatment orientations antithetical to the model, lack of experience with certain intervention techniques, and personal problems. The supervisor's response to lack of experience has already been discussed. Discussion of allegiance to other treatments or personal problems is generally best facilitated in individual supervision. When a practitioner's personal problems interfere with his or her performance, the supervisor does not become the practitioner's "therapist." However, the supervisor is responsible for treatment adherence and, as such, must take steps to identify, discuss, and conjointly develop strategies to increase therapist effectiveness. The supervisor's role is to evaluate the extent to which a therapist's difficulties impede adherence to the MST protocol. Thus, the supervisor may not meet individually with a therapist experiencing personal problems who can adhere to MST and obtain outcomes but may meet with the therapist whose personal problems are interfering with adherence and outcomes.

Use of Supervision Time. Efficiency requires that more time be devoted to cases that are in the beginning stages of treatment—when "fit" is still being determined—and to cases that are not progressing satisfactorily. For the latter, the efforts of team members are directed at understanding the barriers to clinical progress and at designing interventions to overcome those barriers. Extended time may also be needed to devote to a

family that is in an immediate crisis. On the other hand, in cases where progress is satisfactory and the family and clinician are on the intended trajectory for favorable outcomes, relatively little time will be devoted to discussion of the case. MST supervision is not a time to "chit chat" or to discuss administrative issues; the task of supervision is to facilitate therapist adherence and family outcomes. If supervision ends early because the tasks are completed, that is fine.

Supervision usually begins with the supervisor taking inventory of the cases that will need some extended discussion from the perspectives of each clinician for the first 10 minutes of a 90-minute session. Each clinician, for example, might identify one to three cases that he or she wants to discuss for the reasons noted above. The supervisor then allocates time proportionate to need. At the end of the supervision session, each therapist should have a plan to put into place until the next session. In addition, questions and concerns the team and supervisor wish to raise in the next telephone consultation with the MST consultant are identified. If all cases have not been covered, however, the supervisor might meet with the pertinent clinician for a short while longer while excusing the other team members from the session.

Duration and Frequency. MST supervision sessions are held as often as needed to achieve treatment fidelity and favorable outcomes for children and families but not more frequently than is productive. Supervision is a set duration of time, and all efforts should be made to keep within the time frame to maximize efficiency. Depending on the nature of the clinical population and the number of sessions held per week, the duration of supervision may range between 1 and 2 hours, with the typical duration being about 1 hour and 30 minutes. If sessions are extending beyond the time limit, one of two circumstances has probably come into play. Perhaps the supervision time is not being used efficiently (e.g., story telling for its own sake, extended debate without coming to closure, asides that are not relevant to outcomes). Alter-

natively, if supervision is being used efficiently, the complexity of the cases may require more frequent sessions each week for a time-limited period. The MST consultant helps supervisors to identify and remedy possible sources of difficulty with the management of supervision time.

The frequency of sessions may also vary with the maturity of the MST program and nature of the clinical population. In new MST programs, supervision may occur more often than in mature programs because therapists (and supervisors) are just beginning to "learn the ropes." With increased experience, weekly feedback from MST consultants, and program maturity, however, team members generally develop the capacity to address complex clinical problems independently and require less feedback and consultation. Typically, new MST programs treating youth presenting serious clinical problems and families may have two supervision sessions per week, whereas mature programs may only require one session per week to maintain fidelity.

The Process of Supervision

To effectively facilitate adherence to MST and the rapid progress of cases toward favorable outcomes, group supervision requires advance preparation on behalf of the clinicians and supervisor, effective management of the group supervision time by the supervisor, and pertinent follow-up on behalf of the supervisor and clinicians. Although time should be used efficiently and the goals of supervision are serious, supervisors endeavor to make supervision as enjoyable as possible. Therapists who dread supervision are apt to be less productive clinicians, less satisfied employees, and less likely to contribute to the goals of the MST program. Thus, to promote therapist engagement in supervision, supervisors focus on the positive (just as families are more responsive to a strength-focused approach, so, too, are clinicians), view therapist deficits as opportunities to become more effective at implementing a complex clinical model, and help clinicians take their work seriously but not too seriously (taking a job too seriously can lead to burnout, staff turnover, program inefficiency, and failure). Moreover, supervisors facilitate the development of effective analyses of problems and generation of solutions, as few things make people more satisfied with their work than success.

Preparation. For increased efficiency and continuity of care, the clinician and supervisor arrive at supervision prepared to discuss pertinent issues regarding each case. Clinicians come to supervision prepared with their Initial Contact Sheets and weekly progress updates completed. In the case of the Hodges family, for example, the therapist completed the Initial Contact Sheet (see Figure 2) prior to the supervision session, although some additions and changes were made during the session as a result of the team's discussion of information the therapist described in the session.

Weekly Progress. Throughout the course of treatment, clinicians summarize key aspects of case progress in terms of steps in the Analytic Process (i.e., "Do-Loop") prior to each supervision session. The Weekly Case Summary form (see Figure 3) is used for this purpose. The supervisor assures that team input and plans developed in supervision are consistent with the principles of MST. That is, barriers are not described in intra-psychic terms; the "fit" of ad-

---

Family: Hodges   **Therapist:** _____   **Date:** Week 5 of treatment

I. Overarching/Primary MST Goals
1. Attend all classes in school every day as evidenced by attendance records.
2. Stop theft as evidenced by no further charges.
3. Decrease verbal aggression toward teachers as evidenced by school reports.
4. Decrease physical and verbal aggression toward peers as evidenced by school reports.
5. Decrease verbal aggression and irritability at home as evidenced by parent reports.
6. Have DJJ case closed.

II. Previous Intermediary Goals

	Met	Partially	Not
1. Decrease Ms. Hodges' depression and alcohol use.		✔	
2. Alter the permissive parenting style—list of rules, consequences.			✔
3. Bolster social support for Ms. Hodges.		✔	
4. Mend fences between school personnel and Ms. Hodges.		✔	
5. Identify, and increase contact with, prosocial peers for James.			✔

III. Barriers to Intermediary Goals
1. Mr. Hodges responded negatively to intervention designed to manage his behavior, so Ms. Hodges used alcohol again.
2. Therapist did not ensure adequate implementation of intervention re: rules and consequences. Also, Ms. Hodges expressed fear of James' response.

IV. Advances in Treatment
1. Family gathered to problem-solve how to handle Mr. Hodges.
2. Ms. Hodges agreed to list rules, consequences, and rewards.
3. Ms. Hodges began attending women's group at church again and engaging in previously fun activities with aunt. Grandmother agreed to monitor James while Ms. Hodges is at church meetings.
4. Ms. Hodges and therapist did call school and do role plays in session.

V. How has your assessment of the fit changed with new information/interventions?
Failure to change permissive parenting is due partly to fear of son's reaction and partly to therapist failure to implement intervention properly.

VI. Goals/Next Steps for the Week
1. Continue practicing ignoring James' verbal banter and not following him to his room during arguments.
2. Revisit rules and consequences intervention.
3. Problem-solve with Ms. Hodges and family members as to why intervention to manage Mr. Hodges failed.
4. Continue with plan for Ms. Hodges to begin calling school daily to monitor James' attendance.
5. Role play meeting with school personnel with Ms. Hodges, and schedule meeting.
6. Continue to increase and monitor prosocial contacts for Ms. Hodges.
7. Continue to monitor cognitive–behavioral interventions for depression and frequency of alcohol use.

FIGURE 3. Weekly case summary form for the Hodges family.

vances and barriers is described in terms of multiple contributing factors; and interventions capitalize on strengths, target interactions within and between systems, focus on specific problems, and so on. Moreover, the supervisor ensures that steps in the "Do-Loop" are not missed.

Often, the MST consultant's input is needed to help the supervisor retain her or his focus on adherence to the principles and process, as the multiple demands facing each therapist and family during treatment can seem overwhelming to therapists and supervisors alike. During the fifth week of the treatment with the Hodges family, for example, interventions actively targeting changes in discipline and monitoring strategies were introduced. The therapist continued to implement the cognitive–behavioral and social support interventions implemented with Ms. Hodges during the second week of treatment. During week 6, the therapist noticed that Ms. Hodges had only intermittently completed homework assignments pertaining to parental monitoring or discipline. Ms. Hodges had identified the five household and school rules that were most important to her, for example, but did not identify or implement possible rewards or consequences for following or breaking these rules. Similarly, she had established a curfew time for James but did nothing to enforce the curfew after he broke it twice. Thus, the supervisor suggested that the therapist and Ms. Hodges try to identify barriers to completing these homework assignments. Some of the barriers pertained to a lack of practice and fear of James's negative response to limit-setting. The MST consultant focused, in addition, on the extent to which the therapist implemented the interventions properly. As it turned out, the therapist had not taken the appropriate steps to ensure that Ms. Hodges had sufficient understanding and skills to execute the homework tasks. Thus, the consultant recommended that the therapist practice the desired parenting behaviors in sessions with Ms. Hodges and that the supervisor follow up to ensure that the therapist had sufficient experience to do so.

Follow-up. Following supervision, the supervisor notes each therapist's status with respect to each of the assessment and intervention tasks identified in case summaries: the ongoing engagement of key players, the ongoing MST "fit" conceptualization, how the intermediary goals are logically linked with overarching outcomes, how interventions will achieve intermediary goals, and so on. Supervisors also note strategies recommended to enhance clinician and family progress with respect to these steps in the MST treatment process. Such notations help supervisors effectively monitor therapist and family progress toward (and barriers to) identified goals. These notations are also used to help prepare the team for weekly telephone sessions with the MST consultant.

Consultation Practices

MST consultation is designed to support therapist and supervisory fidelity to the MST treatment model on an ongoing basis (see Note 3). For this reason, weekly consultation from an MST expert is a central component of the comprehensive training and quality assurance package developed for use with providers who wish to establish MST programs. Although an adequate understanding of the nature of child and family behaviors and problems is important, the consultation process is directed more at the behavior of the clinicians and supervisors than at the behavior of youth and families referred to MST programs. The purpose of this section is to describe the objectives and structure of MST consultation.

Objectives

The overarching objectives of expert MST consultation are as follows:

- To facilitate clinician learning and application of MST principles to cases when both the clinicians and the on-site supervisor are novices at MST.
- To facilitate logical and critical thinking throughout the ongoing assess-

ment and intervention process, as depicted in the MST Analytic Process (see Figure 1).
- To monitor and support clinician and supervisor adherence to the MST treatment principles as teams become more seasoned in MST.
- To coach supervisors in the effective use of the MST supervision protocol (see Henggeler & Schoenwald, 1998) and monitor the consistency of their supervisory practices with this protocol.
- To provide guidelines to clinicians and supervisors for incorporation of specific treatment modalities into MST intervention plans.
- To provide updated information as needed regarding research relevant to MST, empirically supported treatments subsumed within MST, and the etiology of problems experienced by target populations serviced by MST programs.
- To identify organizational and service system barriers to the effective implementation of MST and to assist the team, and organizational leadership as needed, in addressing those barriers.

The expertise of the MST consultant lies in two general categories—expertise in MST and expertise in teaching clinicians to think and act in accordance with MST principles at every step of the way in every case. Thus, the MST consultant must teach clinicians and supervisors to assess complex clinical problems by focusing on interactions within and between systems in the youth's natural ecology, to design interventions consistent with the nine MST treatment principles, and to use the MST Analytic Process automatically. At this time, fewer than a dozen individuals have served in the consultation role, and these individuals have all been directly trained by faculty involved in the ongoing research and development of MST. In the interest of helping communities develop the capacity to implement MST programs successfully, dissemination projects that involve training therapists to become supervisors, and supervisors to become consultants, are just beginning. The findings from these projects will illuminate the extent to which the combination of therapist, supervisory, and consultation practices can effectively sustain fidelity to the MST treatment model.

Structure

As with supervision, consultation occurs in a small group format. The purpose of the small group format for consultation is to create opportunities for team members to learn from one another's cases and from the recommendations made by the consultant regarding those cases, increase the resources available for problem solving, and provide support for one another that is consistent with both supervisory and consultation recommendations. Each team of three to four clinicians and the on-site supervisor receive consultation on a weekly basis for 1 hour. All team members attend each session.

When MST programs first start, clinicians typically have a caseload of only one or two families for several weeks, until referrals to the new program begin to increase. This low caseload allows consultants the opportunity to spend more time talking through engagement, assessment, and intervention strategies during these early weeks of program operation. However, as clinician caseloads fill, the consultant restructures the level of detail covered in consultation so that team members are able to address the major areas of concern in each case. The responsibility for management of the consultation hour is increasingly shared with the supervisor and clinicians as the team gains more experience with MST cases, MST on-site supervision, and the role of consultation.

Consultants provide on-site training and telephone consultation to supervisors regarding the structure and process of supervision, increasing adherence to MST among clinicians, and facilitating the development of particular competencies in the supervisor and/or clinicians. Such consultation also includes review of group supervision audiotapes by the consultant. In addition, a supervisor may request a brief consultation for one or more team members between regularly scheduled consultations if particularly challenging developments arise with a case. Consultants also track clinician attendance at consultation, cases discussed, and recommendations made during each consultation. When recommendations are not followed, the consultant ascertains why and concurs with, reissues, or revises the recommendation, depending upon the evidence regarding progress in the case.

PROGRAM PRACTICES

Context is important when implementing an intervention—particularly a complex community-based intervention like MST—in real world settings. It seems that MST programs are most appealing to communities in which stakeholders (i.e., juvenile justice, mental health, family court, the schools, social welfare) and funders arc interested in decreasing rates of out-of-home placements by seeking alternatives to incarceration and residential treatment (Henggeler, 1998). A manual (Strother et al., 1998) and other publications (see, e.g., Henggeler, Mihalic, Rone, Thomas, & Timmons-Mitchell, 1998; Schoenwald & Henggeler, in press) describe in detail the community and intraorganizational practices thought to facilitate effective implementation of MST. Highlights from these more extensive works are provided below.

Interagency Collaboration

Collaboration of the MST program with individuals and agencies that have legal mandates for youth or are involved in their lives is critical. For example, to be effective and retain accountability for achieving clinical outcomes—a central tenet of MST—MST clinicians must be able to take the lead in clinical decision making. Thus, prior to developing an MST program, significant efforts are devoted to obtaining community support and acceptance from all key stakeholders. Failure to garner support from any one agency and/or individual can limit the viability of an MST program.

Funding

Financing strategies and fiscal incentives (e.g., third-party reimbursement rates and practices, availability of flexible funding) influence provider motivation to develop an MST program, as well as referral patterns to the program (Schoenwald & Henggeler, in press). For example, if residential treatment programs are reimbursed at higher rates than home-based services, there is little incentive for providers to shift from residential to home-based services. Or, when referral agencies have to pay a portion of the cost for home-based services but do not have to pay any of the costs associated with services such as outpatient treatment and residential placements, referral rates for MST programs tend to be low, a problem which threatens the economic viability of the MST program (Schoenwald & Henggeler, in press). Several mechanisms for funding have been used in MST projects at different sites across the nation, including using Medicaid reimbursement, shifting state children's services monies allocated for residential treatment programs or other out-of-home placements (e.g., foster care) to the MST program, and making MST a component of the continuum of care provided by a managed care organization that treats youth with serious emotional disturbance under a capitated rate from the state. As mentioned previously, the cost savings realized with effective MST programs can be substantial, particularly when one considers that tremendous amounts of financial resources are being devoted to services for serious juvenile offenders who have no demonstrated effectiveness.

Organizational Context

The importance of organizational context in attaining positive outcomes cannot be overstated. In fact, a recent study examining relationships between organizational variables, service system variables, quality of service, and outcomes for youth in state custody, found that organization variables (i.e., organizational climate) were more important than service system variables in predicting children's improved psychosocial functioning (Glisson & Hemmelgarn, 1998). This finding is consistent with our anecdotal observations that several organizational factors seem linked with the successful dissemination of MST. These organizational factors are discussed below.

1. *Organizational Treatment Philosophy.* Some mental health service provider organizations have treatment philosophies (e.g., children are best treated in out-of-home placements) or theoretical orientations (e.g., psychodynamic) that impede an MST program's ability to provide clinically-effective, family-based services with high levels of provider accountability for outcomes. Thus, the functional mission statement of the agency that is to house an MST program must be examined during initial site visit assessments to make sure it is compatible with the MST treatment philosophy. There must be a clearly articulated "fit" between MST and the goals and mandates of the host agency, and the organizational leadership (not just the clinicians and supervisors) must be in agreement with the nature and importance of MST to the provider organization's mission and success.

2. *Program Specification and Design.* The provider organization must be accountable for achieving outcomes. Thus, when new MST programs are being developed, assistance is provided with, for example, reviewing RFP (requests for proposals) documents, all MST-related job descriptions, and hiring advertisements; making recommendations about clinical record keeping practices; and specifying program discharge criteria. Additionally, ongoing assistance is provided in helping new programs overcome barriers to achieving successful clinical outcomes by, for example, tracking treatment fidelity and adherence, promoting the MST program within the broader service community, and developing program-level interventions to increase referrals, reduce staff attrition, and/or restructure program funding mechanisms.

3. *Commitment to Outcomes Measurement.* The host agency must be willing to examine outcomes objectively (e.g., arrest and out-of-home placement rates) and systematically. Without measuring outcomes, it is impossible to know whether the program is having the desired clinical effect.

4. *Staffing and Supervision.* MST is conducted by master's level therapists (and sometimes highly competent bachelor's-level professionals) who receive on-site supervision from doctoral level mental health professionals. Therapists are selected on the basis of their motivation, flexibility, common sense, and "street smarts," with the master's degree being viewed more as a sign of motivation than as evidence of a particular type or level of clinical expertise (Henggeler, 1998). Although the specifics of MST supervision have already been discussed, what is relevant here is that the provider organization must be conducive to the requisite team structure, and the person who is to serve as the clinical supervisor must have credible authority regarding clinician activities.

5. *Training.* Training is provided on-site using essentially the same protocol that has been used in successful clinical trials of MST with violent and chronic juvenile offenders. Although a description of the training protocol has already been provided (e.g., 5-day initial training, 1.5-day quarterly boosters, weekly phone consultation with MST experts), what is important to emphasize here is that all staff who can influence treatment (e.g., a consulting psychiatrist) must be trained in and support MST.

6. *Concrete Support of Treatment Team.* Concrete support of the treatment team must be evident (e.g., personnel, salary, administrative support doing MST, beepers, cellular phones, and so on). For example, MST therapists should not be paid lower salaries simply because their caseloads are significantly lower than those of their coworkers. MST therapists provide high-intensity services, work flexible hours, are available 24 hours per day, 7 days per week, and are held accountable for outcomes. Therefore, they must be paid well. As well, agency paperwork/documentation requirements must dovetail with MST needs. To avoid unnecessary duplication of paperwork, sometimes this means that the provider organization changes its paperwork requirements to conform to MST needs.

7. *MST Program Must Be Distinct.* Organizations must be able to support MST as a distinct program with its own dedicated staff. In other words, staff working for an MST program cannot work part-time with other youth or on other projects, as it is impossible to maintain the high level of clinical intensity required to attain positive outcomes using MST while simultaneously providing other services to other populations. Moreover, organizations must have a commitment to implement MST fully. It is impossible for MST providers to do part of the training protocol or only implement those aspects of the treatment that fit with existing practices. In short, MST is a package deal; there is no "MST light" (Rosenblatt, 1996, p. 106). Thus, assistance is made available to help provider organizations develop the capacity to support the full MST package, which includes modifying policies and practices, and dedicating the resources needed to achieve outcomes. Anything less would likely compromise the clinical- and cost-effectiveness of the program.

CONCLUSION

As pressures to disseminate MST continue to mount, it is becoming clear that even with a well-specified treatment protocol, a specified supervisory process, and additional quality control mechanisms (clinical consultation, program support practices), clinician adherence to MST can vary widely from program to program. We have illustrated practices at the level of the therapist, supervisor, consultant, and program, which is designed to limit variation and support quality implementation and positive outcomes. Empirical investigations of the relations between these practices are being supported by the Office of Juvenile Justice and Delinquency Prevention and the National Institutes of Mental Health. The results of these investigations will help inform future efforts to enable families, therapists, and service systems to implement MST with the fidelity needed to achieve positive outcomes.

About the Authors

SONJA K. SCHOENWALD is assistant professor of psychiatry and behavioral sciences and associate director of the Family Services Research Center at the Medical University of South Carolina. Her research focuses on the validation and dissemination of clinically- and cost-effective treatments for children and adolescents with serious clinical problems and their families. **TAMARA L. BROWN** is assistant professor of psychology at the University of Kentucky. Her collaboration with the Family Services Research Center has focused on the evaluation of community-based treatment for children and adolescents with serious clinical problems and their families. Her ongoing research focuses on the examination of environmental factors that lead to successful outcomes in adolescents and on the cultural competence of therapeutic interventions for minority adolescents and their families. **SCOTT W. HENGGELER** is professor of psychiatry and behavioral sciences and director of the Family Services Research Center at the Medical University of South Carolina. His career has focused on the development and validation of clinically-effective and cost-effective treatments for children and adolescents with serious clinical problems and their families. Address: Sonja K. Schoenwald, Family Services Research Center, Department of Psychiatry and Behavioral Sciences, Medical University of South Carolina, 67 President Street—Suite CPP, PO Box 250861, Charleston, SC 20425; e-mail: schoensk@musc.edu

Authors' Note

Preparation of this article was supported by Grant No. R01DA08029 from the National Institute on Drug Abuse and Grant Nos. R18MH48316 and R01MH51852 from the National Institutes of Mental Health, and by the Annie E. Casey Foundation.

Notes

1. Information in this section has been excerpted from Henggeler, S. W., & Schoenwald, S. K. (1998). *The Multisystemic therapy supervision manual: Promoting quality assurance at the clinical level.* Charleston, SC: MST Institute. Copyright 1998 by S. W. Henggeler & S. K. Schoenwald. Used with permission.

2. The assumptions underlying MST clinical supervision have been reproduced from Henggeler, S. W., Schoenwald, S. K., Borduin, C. M., Rowland, M. D., & Cunningham, P. B. (1998). *Multisystemic treatment of antisocial behavior in children and adolescents* (pp. 46–47). New York: Guilford Press. Copyright 1998 by Guilford Press. Reproduced with permission.

3. Information in this section has been excerpted from Schoenwald, S. K. (1998). *Multisystemic therapy consultation manual.* Charleston, SC: MST Institute. Copyright 1998 by S. K. Schoenwald. Used with permission.

References

Becker, J. V. (1998). What we know about the characteristics and treatment of adolescents who have committed sexual offences. *Child Maltreatment, 3,* 317–329.

Borduin, C. M., Henggeler, S. W., Blaske, D. M., & Stein, T. (1990). Multisystemic treatment of adolescent sexual offenders. *International Journal of Offender Therapy and Comparative Criminology, 35,* 105–114.

Borduin, C. M., Mann, B. J., Cone, L. T., Henggeler, S. W., Fucci, B. R., Blaske, D. M., & Wilson, R. A. (1995). Multisystemic treatment of serious juvenile offenders: Long-term prevention of criminology and violence. *Journal of Consulting and Clinical Psychology, 63,* 569–578.

Bronfenbrenner, U. (1979). *The ecology of human development: Experiments by design and nature.* Cambridge, MA: Harvard University Press.

Brunk, M., Henggeler, S. W., & Whelan, J. P. (1987). A comparison of multisystemic therapy and parent training in the brief treatment of child abuse and neglect. *Journal of Consulting and Clinical Psychology, 55,* 311–318.

Costello, E. J., Angold, A., Burns, B. J., & Behar, L. (1998). *Improving mental health services for children in North Carolina: Agenda for action.* Durham, NC: Author.

Elliot, D. S. (1994). Serious violent offenders: Onset, developmental course, and termination—The American Society of Criminology 1993 Presidential Address. *Crimnology, 32,* 1–21.

Fraser, M. W., Nelson, K. E., & Rivard, J. C. (1997). The effectiveness of family preservation services. *Social Work Research, 21,* 138–153.

Glisson, C., & Hemmelgarn, A. (1998). The effects of organizational climate and interorganizational coordination on the quality and outcomes of children's service systems. *Child Abuse and Neglect, 22,* 401–421.

Henggeler, S. W. (1998). Multisystemic therapy. In D. S. Elliott (Ed.), *Blueprints for violence prevention.* Boulder, CO: Center for the Study and Prevention of Violence.

Henggeler, S. W., Borduin, C. M., Melton, G. B., Mann, B. J., Smith, L., Hall, J. A., Cone, L., & Fucci, B. R. (1991). Effects of multisystemic therapy on drug use and abuse in serious juvenile offenders: A progress report from two outcome studies. *Family Dynamics of Addiction Quarterly, 1,* 40–51.

Henggeler, S. W., Melton, G. B., Brondino, M. J., Scherer, D. G., & Hanley, J. H. (1997). Multisystemic therapy with violent and chronic juvenile offenders and their families: The role of treatment fidelity in successful dissemination. *Journal of Consulting and Clinical Psychology, 65,* 821–833.

Henggeler, S. W., Melton, G. B., & Smith, L. A. (1992). Family preservation using multisystemic therapy: An effective alternative to incarcerating serious juvenile offenders. *Journal of Consulting and Clinical Psychology, 60,* 953–961.

Henggeler, S. W., Melton, G. B., Smith, L. A., Schoenwald, S. K., & Hanley, J. H. (1993). Family preservation using multisystemic treatment: Long-term follow-up to a clinical trial with serious juvenile offenders. *Journal of Child and Family Studies, 2,* 283–293.

Henggeler, S. W., Mihalic, S. F., Rone, L., Thomas, C., & Timmons-Mitchell, J. (1998). Blueprints for violence prevention multisystemic therapy. D. S. Eilliott (Series Ed.), University of Colorado at Boulder, Center for the Study and Prevention of Violence. Blueprints Publications.

Henggeler, S. W., Pickrel, S. G., & Brondino, M. J. (1999). Multisystemic treatment of substance abusing and dependent delinquents: Outcomes, treatment fidelity, and transportability. *Mental Health Services Research, 1,* 171–184.

Henggeler, S. W., Rodick, J. D., Borduin, C. M., Hanson, C. L., Watson, S. M., & Urey, J. R. (1986). Multisystemic treatment of juvenile offenders: Effects on adolescent behavior and family interactions. *Developmental Psychology, 22,* 132–141.

Henggeler, S. W., Rowland, M. D., Randall, J., Ward, D. M., Pickrel, S. G., Cunningham, P. G., Miller, S. L., Edwards, J., Zealberg, J. J., Hand, L. D., & Santos, A. B. (1999). Home-based multisystemic therapy as an alternative to the hospitalization of youths in psychiatric crisis: Clinical outcomes. *Journal of the American Academy of Child and Adolescent Psychiatry, 38,* 1331–1339.

Henggeler, S. W., & Schoenwald, S. K. (1998). *The multisystemic therapy supervision manual: Promoting quality assurance at the clinical level.* Charleston, SC: MST Institute.

Henggeler, S. W., Schoenwald, S. K., Borduin, C. M., Rowland, M. D., & Cunningham, P. B. (1998). *Multisystemic treatment of antisocial behavior in children and adolescents.* New York: Guilford Press.

Huizinga, D. (1995). Developmental sequences in delinquency: Dynamic typologies. In L. J. Crockett & A. C. Crouter (Eds.), *Pathways through adolescence* (pp. 15–34). Mahwah, NJ: Erlbaum.

Kazdin, A. E. (1996). Problem solving and parent management in treating aggressive and antisocial behavior. In E. D. Hibbs & P. S. Jensen (Eds.), *Psychosocial treatments for child and adolescent disorders: Empirically based strategies for clinical practice* (pp. 377–408). Washington, DC: American Psychological Association.

Kazdin, A. E., Siegel, T. C., & Bass, D. (1992). Cognitive problem solving skills therapy and parent management training in the treatment of antisocial behavior in children. *Journal of Consulting and Clinical Psychology, 60,* 733–747.

Liddle, H. A. (1996). Family-based treatment for adolescent problem behaviors: Overview of contemporary developments and introduction to the special section. *Journal of Family Psychology, 10,* 3–11.

Loeber, R., Keenan, K., & Zhang, Q. (1997). Boys' experimentation and persistence in developmental pathways toward serious delinquency. *Journal of Child and Family Studies, 6,* 321–357.

Mash, E. J., & Dozois, D. J. A. (1996). Child psychopathology: A developmental-systems perspective. In E. J. Mash & R. A. Barkley (Eds.), *Child psychopathology* (pp. 3–60). New York: Guilford Press.

Quinn, K. P., & Epstein, M. H. (1998). Characteristics of children, youth, and families served by local interagency systems of care. In M. H. Epstein, K. Kutash, & A. J. Duchnowski (Eds.), *Outcomes for children and youth with emotional and behavioral disorders and their families: Programs and evaluation best practices* (pp. 81–114). Austin, TX: PRO-ED.

Rosenblatt, A. (1996). Bows and ribbons, tape and twine: Wrapping the wraparound process for children with multi-system needs. *Journal of Child and Family Studies, 5,* 101–117.

Schoenwald, S. K. (1998). *Multisystemic therapy consultation manual.* Charleston, SC: MST Institute.

Schoenwald, S. K., & Henggeler, S. W. (1997). Combining effective treatment strategies with family preservation models of service delivery: A challenge for mental health. In R. J. Illback, H. Joseph, Jr., & C. Cobb (Eds.), *Integrated services for children and families: Opportunities for psychological practice* (pp. 121–136). Washington, DC: American Psychological Association.

Schoenwald, S. K., & Henggeler, S. W. (in press). Services research and family based treatment. In H. A. Liddle, G. Diamond, R. Levant, J. Bray, & D. Santisteban (Eds.), *Family psychology intervention science.* Washington, DC: American Psychological Association.

Schoenwald, S. K., Ward, D. M., Henggeler, S. W., Pickrel, S. G., & Patel, H. (1996). Multisystemic therapy treatment of substance abusing or dependent adolescent offenders: Costs of reducing incarceration, inpatient, and residential placement. *Journal of Child and Family Studies, 5,* 431–444.

Schoenwald, S. K., Ward, D. M., Henggeler, S. W., & Rowland, M. D. (2000). MST vs. hospitalization for crisis stabilization of youth: Placement and service use 4 months post-referral. *Mental Health Services Research, 2,* 3–12.

Strother, K., Swenson, C. C., & Schoenwald, S. K. (1998). *Multisystemic therapy organizational manual.* Charleston, SC: The MST Institute.

Washington State Institute for Public Policy. (1998). *Watching the bottom line: Cost-effective interventions for reducing crime in Washington.* Olympia, WA: Evergreen State College.

A Prevention Program for Students with or At Risk for ED:

Moderating Effects of Variation in Treatment and Classroom Structure

DEBRA KAMPS, TAMMY KRAVITS, JODEE RAUCH, JODI L. KAMPS, AND NATASHA CHUNG

In a recent report, positive outcomes were described for use of a prevention program serving students with behavioral and emotional disturbance and those at risk for emotional disturbance (ED) in urban elementary schools. This primarily school-based prevention program consisted of social skills activities, peer tutoring, and individual and classwide behavior management components. Improved behaviors and decreased aggression were noted for the experimental group in treatment for approximately 1½ school years, compared to a control-wait group. This report is a further analysis of the prevention program investigation, including (a) findings from implementation across multiple school years with longitudinal student outcome data; (b) replication effects for the prevention program for the second cohort; (c) effects of variations in program implementation; specifically, strength of treatment and classroom structure; and (d) individual cases of treatment successes and failures. Results for two cohorts indicated that inappropriate behaviors decreased (i.e., aggression, out of seat, negative verbal behaviors) and positive behaviors increased (academic engagement, behavioral compliance) under conditions of strong implementation of program components and in the context of high classroom structure. Individual case studies further confirmed that students exposed to more treatment in each year of the program and in classrooms with more structure had better outcomes. Implications of these findings supporting early, multiyear, high-quality prevention and the adverse effects of weak treatment efforts and low structure are discussed in the context of current practice and the need for additional research.

DISCIPLINE AND SCHOOL SAFETY ARE at the forefront of current educational reform efforts. These issues are particularly pertinent for professionals who work with students with disabilities and the students themselves, as legislators and school administrators wrestle with two critical issues: (a) least restrictive placement for students with emotional disturbance (ED) and behavior disorders; and (b) the commitment to a free, appropriate education, including the need for intervention for inappropriate behaviors that are a manifestation of the disability (see Katsiyannis & Maag, 1998 for a review of the IDEA amendments [1997] and the case law). One promising area has been the use of early prevention programs, including the use of proactive strategies for positive behavior support (see Kamps & Tankersley, 1996; Larson, 1994; Lewis, 1998; Walker, Colvin, & Ramsey, 1995 for reviews). Most practitioners would agree with longitudinal research indicating that antisocial patterns start at a young age and without intervention, continue to escalate for many children (Campbell, 1994; Walker et al., 1995). Although general agreement exists on the need for early intervention, there are a limited number of data-based intervention studies documenting positive outcomes for prevention efforts for young children. A critical need exists: to go beyond documentation of the need (e. g., repeated counts and media coverage of the incident of violence, abundant assessments identifying high-risk students) to a demonstration of what prevention/intervention can do to improve student outcomes (Epstein et al., 1998; Nelson, 1997).

In two prior investigations, we have reported data-based studies demonstrating that early prevention efforts can affect student classroom performance for Head Start children (Kamps et al., 1995; Tankersley, Kamps, Mancina, & Weidinger, 1996) and for elementary-age students with behavior problems (Kamps, Kravits, Stolze, & Swaggart, 1999). In our most recent investigation, findings demonstrated that a multicomponent prevention program (i.e., social skills, peer tutoring, classroom management) reduced inappropriate behaviors and improved academic engagement for the experimental group compared to a control-wait group with similar behavioral problems (Kamps et al., 1999). The purpose of this study was to provide further analysis of the prevention program by reporting findings for intervention across multiple years, and replication to the second cohort. Research questions were as follows:

1. To what degree did implementation of the prevention program and class structure vary for students over multiple school years?
2. What were the observed outcome effects for two groups of students with ED and behavior problems in the prevention program?
3. What did teachers report regarding changes in student behaviors?
4. What was the relationship of strength of treatment and classroom structure to student outcomes (i.e., appropriate and inappropriate behaviors)?
5. What were intervention characteristics of individual successes and failures from the group?

Key components to the program included social skills training, reading peer tutoring, and behavioral interventions.

METHOD

Participants and Settings

A total of 38 students participated in the investigation. Cohort 1 was recruited in Year 1, with student performance monitored over 4 school years. Cohort 2 was recruited in Year 2 and monitored over 3 school years.

Cohort 1. Twenty students—19 boys and 1 girl (16 African American and 4 Euro American)—participated in the program over a 4-year period. Students ranged in age from 5 to 11 years old at the onset of the investigation (mean age = 98 months), with the ages ranging from 8 to 13 during the final probes. Students were selected in Year 1 for participation in the prevention program based upon procedures outlined in the Systematic Screening for Behavior Disorders (SSBD; Walker & Severson, 1992). Scores for the adaptive scale ranged from 17 to 41 (M = 30); for the maladaptive scale, scores ranged from 28 to 52 (M = 38). Eight of the students were identified as having ED, with 5 of those also identified as having Attention-Deficit/Hyperactivity Disorder (ADHD), and 1 also identified as having mild cognitive disabilities. Two of the 20 students were identified as having a learning disability, both also with ADHD and 1 as having mild cognitive disabilities. In addition, 4 students were tested but determined ineligible for special education; however, 2 qualified for accommodations based on having ADHD. Only 4 of the 20 students had not been tested for special education. These 20 students (63%) were part of a larger group (32 originally selected), with approximately one third of the sample dropping out primarily due to mobility prior to the end of the 4-year period.

Settings included general and special education classrooms in a large urban school district in the Midwest. Nine students spent all 4 years in general education, 3 in general education classrooms with special education pull-out services during a portion of the time. For the students with ED, 4 spent the majority of time in special education classes, and 4 were in special classes during the first year, with 2 of the students receiving services in general education classrooms for the final 2 years and 2 in general classes 25% to 50% of the time over the period.

Cohort 2. Eighteen students—16 boys and 2 girls (11 African American, 2 Hispanic, and 5 Euro American)—participated in the Cohort 2. This second group served as a control group to Cohort 1 for a 1-year period and were then introduced to components of the prevention program in the subsequent 2 years. Thus, Cohort 2 students were monitored for 3 years.

Students ranged in age from 5 to 9 years at the onset of the investigation (mean age = 97 months), with ages ranging from 8 to 13 during the final probes. As with Cohort 1, students were selected based upon procedures in the SSBD protocol (Systematic Screening for Behavior Disorders; Walker & Severson, 1992). Scores for the adaptive scale ranged from 20 to 49, with a mean of 32; scores for the maladaptive scale ranged from 26 to 47, with a mean of 37. Three students were identified as having ED, 5 students as having ADHD, 2 students with learning disabilities, and two students with mild cognitive disabilities.

Settings again included special and general education classrooms in the same urban school district. Fourteen of the 18 students spent the majority of the 3 years in general education classrooms, with 1 in special education for half days during the final probe. Two students spent 2 years in special education classrooms, and 2 other students were in self-contained special education classes for the entire 3-year period.

Case Studies. Nine students from Cohort 1 were selected at the end of the study as illustrative case studies. Six were selected (three students with ED, three students at high risk) as examples of successes. The two criteria used in the selection process were that students had received adequate levels of prevention intervention over multiple years and that observation data indicated reliable changes in behaviors over time. Three additional students were selected as examples of program failures; that is, inadequate intervention had been provided across school years and inappropriate levels of behavior problems continued over time. Representative of the cohort, students' ages were from the kindergarten to third-grade level at the beginning of the study, with two students served in ED or learning center classrooms throughout the study, two served in ED classes in Year 1 with general classroom placement in Years 2 through 4, and three served primarily in general education classrooms. Demographic information and program implementation data for Cohorts 1 and 2 and for the individuals identified for case study analysis are presented in Table 1.

Experimental Design and Data Analysis

A delayed control group experimental design (Barlow, Hayes, & Nelson, 1984) was used in the investigation, with experimental control group analysis (reported earlier in Kamps et al., 1999), repeated measures analysis, and pre–post analysis of differences within and across groups. Advantages of this design are (a) control for the treatment variable (i.e., intervention for one group of students is implemented, with the second group of students serving as the control, and with desirable behavior change, treatment is implemented for the second group as a test for replication of effects), and (b) school staff are willing to participate in the research because they have

access to treatment in subsequent years. Six principals were sent written information regarding the study, based upon referral data to special education services. The first two principals who responded were then interviewed and agreed to participate. Two additional principals responded later in that same year, with parent permissions accrued in the spring and early fall of the second year. Thus, the schools were voluntary participants rather than randomly selected. Information was gathered to ensure the samples were matched (a) for demographics, including similar racial and SES characteristics; and (b) to ensure that initial scores of participating students (SSBD ratings) were similar.

In this study, implementation of the prevention program (teacher training and classroom use of social skills, peer tutoring, and management strategies) occurred in Years 1 through 4 for Cohort 1, with selection and monitoring for Cohort 2 in Year 2, followed by prevention/intervention in Years 3 and 4. Analysis of experimental and control group effects from Year 2 showed positive differential

effects for students in early prevention (see Kamps et al., 1999). Two statistical analyses were conducted for the multiyear data (reported herein) to note trends over time for the two cohorts: (a) a multivariate repeated measures analysis, and (b) a paired samples t test noting differences from the first year's data to Year 4 data across cohorts. In order to run these analyses, several rules were followed. First, statistical analyses were conducted for each cohort separately because of unequal numbers of data points (Cohort 1, 12 observations; Cohort 2, 8 observations). Second, this analysis, using the SPSS® General Linear Model test, eliminates cases with missing data; thus estimates were used on 11% of the data, with estimates being the adjacent most recent data point.

Two additional analyses were conducted upon completion of the study. The first was analysis of behaviors based on (a) levels of intervention, and (b) classroom structure. Experimenters determined this to be a critical analysis of the longitudinal data in that both variables changed within and across school years.

TABLE 1
Demographics and Levels of Intervention Across Cohort 1, Cohort 2, and Case Study Participants

Group	Age	Adaptive SSBD	Maladaptive SSBD	Social skills frequency (%)[a]		Tutoring frequency (%)[a]		Behavior support frequency (%)[a]	
Cohort 1 N = 20	98	30	38	147	(69)	95	(44)	123	(58)
Cohort 2 N = 18	97	32	37	102	(76)	79	(59)	31	(23)
ED successes[b]									
Carl	107	41	31	7	(58)	7	(58)	7	(58)
Mike	86	36	32	12	(100)	5	(42)	7	(58)
Lamar	73	35	32	10	(100)	5	(50)	10	(100)
Risk successes[b]									
John	62	32	40	10	(83)	10	(83)	3	(25)
Anthony	74	36	30	5	(45)	7	(64)	2	(18)
Ronnie	86	22	48	9	(82)	5	(42)	5	(42)
ED/Risk failures[b]									
Maurice	95	18	47	8	(72)	3	(27)	11	(100)
Kyle	103	31	39	4	(33)	2	(17)	7	(58)
Daniel	67	26	45	8	(67)	9	(75)	5	(42)

Note. SSBD = Systematic Screening for Behavior Disorders (Walker & Severson, 1992); N = total number in a sample.
[a]Frequency of observation probes showing engagement in each prevention component, social skills, tutoring, management (total probes for Cohort 1 = 215, for Cohort 2 = 135). [b]Six cases from Cohort 1 were selected as having successful outcomes, showing effects of prevention, with 3 treatment failures.

This provided an opportunity for analysis similar to an alternating treatments design (Burke, 1992). A multivariate analysis of variance (MANOVA) using SPSS was thus conducted. Estimates were again used for the analysis for missing data (11%) and outlier data (i.e., 3% at 3+ standard deviations from the mean).

The second post hoc analysis was case study analysis conducted for a smaller group of students from Cohort 1 ($N = 9$), with visual inspection of trend lines over time for aggression as directly observed by experimenters and reported by teachers. Student performance in terms of observed on-task behavior and compliance to teachers' behavioral requests (e.g., please return to your seat, line up, stop talking) was also reviewed to note progress, or lack thereof, over time.

Prevention Program Components

The prevention intervention was guided by findings from prior studies and best practices recommendations (e.g., Del'Homme, Kasari, Forness, & Bagley, 1996; Forness, Serna, Kavale, & Nielsen, 1998; Kamps et al., 1999; Lewis, 1998; Walker et al., 1995), which indicated that children with ED or at risk need early intervention programs to help reduce problem behaviors, learn positive social skills, and improve academic engagement and cooperative school behaviors. Thus, the prevention program primarily consisted of interventions designed to provide social skills instruction, peer tutoring, and classroom management programs. Currently, recommended best practices include the use of "universal interventions," such as school-wide implementation of social skills and unified discipline (rules and consequences) in all schools serving high risk groups, such as classrooms in urban, low-SES areas (Lewis, 1998; Walker et al., 1995).

Social Skills. Social skills instruction typically occurred once a week and consisted of lessons selected from several published curriculum, including the following: *Skillstreaming the Elementary School Child* (McGinnis & Goldstein, 1984; 1997), *The ASSIST Program-Affective/Social Skills: Instructional Strategies and Techniques* (Huggins, 1995), and *Second Step: A Violence Prevention Prayer* (Committee for Children, 1991). Skills taught included those to promote appropriate peer interactions (e.g., joining a group, appropriate play, conversations, problem solving, anger management) and acceptable classroom behaviors (e.g., following instructions, completing assignments, accepting consequences). All social skills lessons were approximately 30 minutes in length and were conducted by the classroom teachers on a weekly basis (more frequently in special education classes). Many teachers also used incidental teaching to reinforce skills, redirect inappropriate behaviors, and apply consequences for use or misuse.

Peer Tutoring. A variety of peer tutoring formats were used. All teachers received training for the Classwide Peer Tutoring developed at the Juniper Gardens Children's Project (Greenwood, Delquadri, & Carta, 1997). This model for structured peer tutoring consisted of students paired with a partner with reciprocal tutor/tutee roles. In the case of reading, oral reading of text passages to the partner was conducted followed by comprehension questions, awarding of points on a tutoring score card, reversing roles, and tallying team or class point totals. Depending upon academic need, spelling or reading peer tutoring was used. In the case of spelling, word lists were tutored for correct spelling and definitions, again with the error correction procedure and the awarding of points. Other peer tutoring formats were also used, including partner reading strategies, cross-age tutoring, and adult tutoring. Nearly all students received the Greenwood et al. tutoring in reading for 1 year with approximately 50% receiving it for 2 years. Students across both cohorts received peer or individual tutoring 44% to 50% of the project period.

Positive Behavior Management. Classroom management systems included token systems with students earning points, tickets, and other positive reinforcements for on-task and appropriate behaviors, with access to social and tangible reinforcers. Many classrooms used warning systems for behaviors, with consequences administered in a hierarchy for instances of behavior (e.g., warnings, loss of recess minutes, office referral, parent call). Student contracts, self- and group-management programs, and home–school notes programs were implemented 58% of the time for Cohort 1 and 23% of the time for Cohort 2. Teacher training in the use of management systems included an inservice (provided by the university staff on the prevention project and/or district personnel), along with intermittent individual consultation from the project staff regarding key information such as assessment data, probable functions/contributors to behavior problems, and examples of specific management systems. Consulting involved designing programs with input from the teacher and support staff, assisting in implementation of the program if requested, and following up on student performance with revisions. Procedures included recommendations from prior research and written resources, including the following: *The Tough Kid Book: Practical Classroom Management Strategies* (Rhode, Jenson, & Reavis, 1992, 1998), *Antisocial Behavior in School: Strategies and Best Practices* (Walker et al., 1995), and *Applied Behavior Analysis for Teachers* (Alberto & Troutman, 1995, 1999).

Dependent Variables and Data Collection

As part of the prevention program, students were monitored over the 4-year period (3 years for Cohort 2) using direct observation data and teacher reports.

Direct Observation Data. Key dependent variables analyzed for this report consisted of appropriate and inappropriate behaviors indicative of a preponderance to learn, follow directions, and so on or, conversely, of an antisocial, nonproductive nature. Direct observations using paper-and-pencil recordings of frequency counts of behaviors were conducted by project staff. Inappropriate behaviors noted included aggression, negative verbal remarks to peers (e.g., teasing, insulting, arguing, threatening) and adults (e.g., arguing, threatening, refusals to comply), and out-of-seat behavior. Appropriate behaviors analyzed for the report consisted of behavioral compliance (responses to adult directions to correct inappropriate behaviors within 5 seconds) and academic engagement as defined using the SSBD protocol (i.e., on-task behavior, including attending, reading, writing, and so on). Academic engagement was measured during 20- to 30-minute blocks of time using a stopwatch to note the amount of time the student was on task, typically four to six times during each observation probe. Behavioral compliance checks were completed based on opportunities (i.e., each instance a request was given). Also included were teacher praise and reprimands to target students and the class. Additional definitions, reliability data, and observation procedures were provided in prior reports (Kamps et al., 1995; Kamps et al., 1999).

Teacher Behavior Report Form (TBRF). Teacher ratings also provided information for analysis of student performance. Ratings were requested from teachers on a weekly basis during 8 to 20 weeks of the school year using the TBRF. This instrument was developed by the experimenters with questions designed to provide estimates of the frequency of disruptive behaviors over the week and ratings of appropriate classroom behavior as well. Items used for this report included the following inappropriate behaviors: acting aggressively, not following directions, and arguing with peers. Estimates of frequency were circled on the form by teachers (0, 1, 2 , 3, 4, 5+, 10+, 20+). Ratings of two behaviors were also included (i.e., appropriate peer interaction and completion of work) using a scale of 5 (*always*), 4 (*usually*), 3 (*frequently*), 2 (*sometimes*), 1 (*rarely*), and 0 (*never*).

Data Collection Schedules. Project staff served as observers for the study, with initial training consisting of joint observations until 80% agreement across behaviors was achieved for two sessions. Twelve direct observation probes were scheduled for Cohort 1 over the 4-year period, with each observation consisting of two occasions of $2\frac{1}{2}$ to 3 hours each. The total number of direct observations conducted was 215, approximately 1,100 hours. Eight direct observation probes of the same duration were scheduled for Cohort 2 over a 3-year period, for a total of 135 and approximately 638 hours.

Teachers were asked to complete the weekly TBRFs for 8 to 16 weeks of each school year. TBRF scores were then averaged to form a probe for the first half of each year and again for the second half of each year (6 total). A total of 114 TBRFs were collected for Cohort 1 and 75 for Cohort 2.

Reliability. Prior reports indicated early reliability across direct observation variables ranging from 87% to 94%. During Years 3 and 4, reliability data were collected for approximately 10% of the observations, with means for Cohorts 1 and 2, respectively, for the following: behavioral compliance—90.1% and 86.9%, academic engagement—95.4% and 95.9%, aggression—95.1% and 99.4%, negative verbals—95.9% and 97.7%, and out of seat—97.8% and 95.8%.

Independent Variable Measures

Implementation Levels. Levels of implementation for prevention program components were noted across the project period for both cohorts. This information was derived primarily from teacher reports to the project staff, as well as from observations of program components. At each observation point, it was noted if the student received social skills instruction at least once a week, if peer tutoring occurred at least twice a week, and if an individual behavior management program was being used. The percentage of implementation was then

computed by the percentage occurrence across observation periods across cohorts. Limited formal procedural checks were conducted for the interventions— 8 occasions for social skills and 20 occasions for peer tutoring. For social skills, checks were simple yes or no's for defining and modeling the skill from the curriculum, student discussion, student practice of skill, and teacher feedback. The percentage implementation averaged 83% with student-to-student practice of skill and teacher feedback most frequently omitted. For peer tutoring, the procedural checklist (Greenwood et al., 1997) in the training manual was used, with procedures implemented an average of 91% ($R = 82\%$–100%).

In order to quantify the *strength of treatment* (dosage) for each student, a simple metric was derived (Yeaton & Sechrest, 1981). A rating of 1 was assigned for use of one intervention component (i.e., social skills, peer tutoring, behavior management) or inconsistent use, a rating of 2 if two interventions were used during the period, and a rating of 3 if all three prevention programs were in place. The data were summarized in relationship to the observation schedules, with the corresponding number at each point (i.e., low to high levels of intervention).

Project staff also completed ratings of the level of classroom structure (i.e., rules in place, organized schedules, variance in lesson formats, student productivity expectations). Ratings consisted of a simple Likert scale (1 = *low structure,* 2 = *moderate structure,* 3 = *high structure*). Ratings matched to the observation probes, with 215 ratings for Cohort 1 and 135 for Cohort 2.

RESULTS

What Were Levels of Prevention Program Implementation and Classroom Structure?

Table 1 presents information regarding the levels of implementation for prevention program components and structure ratings over time for the students. For

Cohort 1, the level of implementation for social skills was 69% (i.e., once a week implementation was noted for 147 out of the 215 total probe periods), 44% for peer tutoring, and 58% for behavior management (counted only if specifically designed for individual student needs). In addition, 12 of the students received one-to-one tutoring during 58% of probes. For Cohort 2, social skills implementation occurred for 76% of the period, 59% for peer tutoring, and 23% for individual behavior management programs. Eleven of the 18 students were delayed academically, with 41% of the probes indicating adult tutoring intervention. Data from class structure ratings indicated that 25% of the observations for Cohort 1 were in classrooms with low structure, 45% indicated moderate structure, and only 30% indicated highly structured, organized classrooms. For Cohort 2, 19% indicated low, 36% moderate, and 45% high structure (also see Tables 3 and 4).

What Were the Prevention Program Effects for Student Outcomes?

Analysis of direct observation data of student behaviors over the project period showed that prevention programs reduced problem behaviors and increased student performance.

Repeated Measures Analysis. Results from analysis of trends in student behaviors over time are presented in Table 2. Direct observation data showed decreasing trends for aggression and out-of-seat behaviors. For Cohort 1, there were significant within-subject main effects for time of measurement and inappropriate variables, with student aggression showing a significant decrease over time. Out-of-seat behavior showed slightly lower trends but no significant change. Negative verbal remarks to peers unfortunately showed increasing trends over time. For Cohort 2, moderate but nonsignificant decreases in aggression, out-of-seat behaviors, and negative verbals were noted. Increases in academic engagement and behavioral compliance were noted for both cohorts. Significant within-subject main effects for time of measurement and appropriate behaviors were noted for both cohorts, with improvements for engagement and compliance.

First Year to Final Year Differences. Pre–post longitudinal effects showed similar findings to the repeated measures test of effects for use of the prevention intervention program. Figure 1 shows means across observations for Cohorts 1 and 2. Aggression decreased from frequencies of 7.2 to 1.7 from Year 1 to Year 4 for Cohort 1 ($p = .011$). Aggression also decreased for Cohort 2, 6.1 to 2.8, but the difference was not statistically significant. Decreases were found for out-of-seat behavior for both cohorts, although these were not significant (14.4

TABLE 2
Summary of Repeated Measures Analysis of Variance for Time Across Cohorts

Cohort	Multivariate					Univariate				
	Value	F	Hypothesis df	Error df	p	SS[a]	df	MS	F	p
Cohort 1										
Time effects										
Inappropriate	.410	2.847	33.000	594.000	.000					
Appropriate	.239	2.440	22.000	396.000	.000					
Variable										
Aggression						1087.368	11	98.852	3.988	.000
Verbals						1904.469	11	173.134	2.500	.006
Out of seat						1422.088	11	129.281	1.536	ns
Engagement						13838.930	11	1258.085	4.257	.000
Compliance						3114.456	11	283.132	1.397	.177
Cohort 2										
Time effects										
Inappropriate	.144	.857	21.000	357.000	ns					
Appropriate	.297	2.968	14.000	238.000	.000					
Variable										
Aggression						394.222	7	56.317	1.425	ns
Verbals						374.556	7	53.508	1.009	ns
Out of seat						778.882	7	111.269	.608	ns
Engagement						9350.938	7	1335.848	4.778	.000
Compliance						1717.972	7	245.425	1.700	.115

[a]Type III.

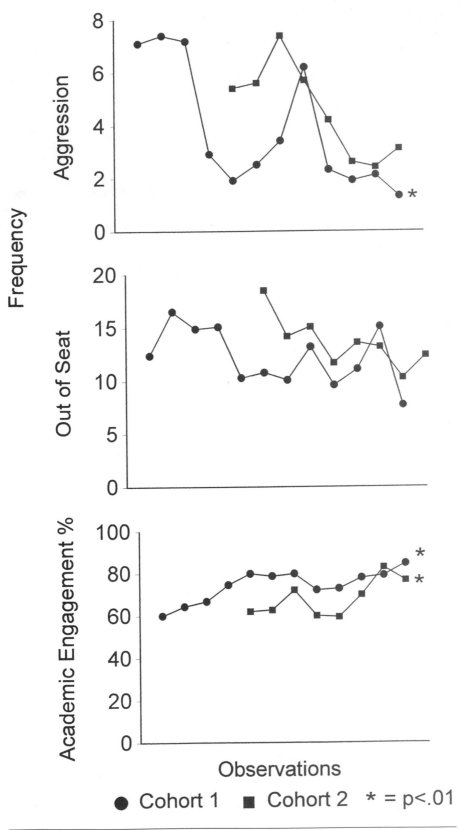

to 11.4 for Cohort 1, 16.4 to 11.4 for Cohort 2). An increase over time was noted for arguing with peers (not in figure) for Cohort 1 (6.6 to 9.2), with a decrease noted for Cohort 2 (8.4 to 6.8). Academic engagement time was significantly increased in both cohorts, with increases from 63% to 81% ($p = .008, .003$). Behavioral compliance (not in figure) also showed slight improvement, with mean increases from 73% to 78% and from 77% to 84%, respectively, for the two cohorts.

What Did Teachers Report for Student Behavior Changes?

Teachers reported lower aggression levels overall than those noted in observations. On the TBRF, aggression decreased for Cohort 1 (2.2 to 1.9) and remained stable for Cohort 2 (1.8 to 1.9). Instances of not following directions remained about the same for Cohort 1 (4.0, 4.7) and significantly decreased for Cohort 2 (10.4, 4.8). Teachers also reported lower estimated frequencies for negative verbals to peers than those observed by staff. These behaviors remained unchanged for Cohort 1 (3.6, 3.7) but were significantly improved for Cohort 2 (7.9, 4.9).

How Did Strength of Treatment and Classroom Structure Change Student Behaviors?

Tables 3 and 4 present mean frequencies of appropriate and inappropriate behaviors across direct observation periods for Cohorts 1 and 2 (see Note). Overall, better outcomes were attained with strong intervention and high structure. Behaviors were evaluated as to their occurrence during (a) low, moderate, and high levels of intervention (prevention components), and (b) low, moderate, and high levels of classroom structure using MANOVA statistical tests.

Table 3 presents behaviors in relationship to the *levels of intervention,* with significant findings for aggression, out-of-seat behavior, academic engagement, behavioral compliance, and teacher

FIGURE I. Observation means across the project period depicting trends for aggression, out-of-seat behavior, and academic engagement for Cohorts I and 2.

reprimands for Cohort 1 and, again, significant differences for aggression, out-of-seat behavior, academic engagement, behavioral compliance, and reprimands for Cohort 2. Aggression was consistently lower in classes with the highest levels of intervention across both cohorts. Means for no or limited intervention environments were 5+, with decreases of 1 to 2 with multiple interventions in place (i.e., classes with social skills, behavior management, and peer/adult tutoring programs). More intervention (i.e., Level 3) also set the occasion for significantly lower frequencies of out-of-seat behavior for Cohorts 1 and 2 ($M = 6$–7) compared to low intervention means of 16 to 20 in a 5- to 6-hour block of time. Intervention effects were also noted for academic engagement and behavioral compliance across groups, with significant differences related to more intervention. Classes with moderate levels of intervention also showed improve-

ment over those with minimal prevention components in place. Minimal changes were noted, however, regarding intervention and negative verbals to peers (see Table 3 for means by intervention levels).

Regarding observed teacher behaviors, significantly more reprimands were observed in classes with limited intervention ($Ms = 25$–30) than in classes with moderate to high levels of intervention ($Ms = 16$–19). Minimal differences were noted, however, for teacher praise.

As mentioned previously, *classroom structure* was noted by observers to also play a key role in the occurrence of inappropriate student behaviors. Structure had a significant impact for aggression, out-of-seat behaviors, academic engagement, behavioral compliance, and teacher reprimands for Cohort 1 and for aggression, out-of-seat behaviors, academic engagement, teacher praise, and reprimands for Cohort 2 (see Table 4). Ag-

gression was significantly lower in classes with high structure (2 to 4), compared to low structure (5 to 9), with significantly lower out-of-seat behavior as well. Lower levels of negative remarks to peers were noted with higher structure but were not significant.

For academic engagement, both moderate and high structure classrooms were equally better than classes with low structure for both cohorts. Behavioral compliance was significantly better with high structure for Cohort 1, with relatively equal levels of compliance across all levels of structure for Cohort 2 (see Table 4). Teacher reprimands were much higher in classrooms with limited structure, with significant differences at the moderate and high levels of structure. No significantly different levels of teacher praise were noted for Cohort 1 in relation to structure; for Cohort 2, however, praise was significantly higher with more structure.

TABLE 3
Levels of Intervention and Effects on Behaviors Noted in Direct Observations

Behavior	Level 1 intervention (M)	Level 2 intervention (M)	Level 3 intervention (M)	F[a]	p value[b]
Aggression C1	5.58	3.01	1.77	8.344	1, 2 p = .006; 1, 3 p = .001
Aggression C2	5.84	4.84	1.35	3.096	1, 3 p = .043
Negative verbals C1	9.09	9.74	5.93	2.291	ns
Negative verbals C2	8.77	7.86	7.80	0.207	ns
Out of seat C1	16.51	10.63	6.84	12.77	1, 2 p = .001; 1, 3 p = .000
Out of seat C2	20.05	11.05	6.65	7.116	1, 2 p = .009; 1, 3 p = .001
Engagement C1	67.06	79.60	79.29	12.509	1, 2 p = .000; 1, 3 p = .001
Engagement C2	65.58	67.16	80.70	4.472	1, 3 p = .013; 2, 3 p = .031
Compliance C1	74.29	78.71	86.85	8.316	1, 3 p = .000; 2, 3 p = .016
Compliance C2	76.75	85.59	82.90	7.183	1, 2 p = .001
Teacher praise C1	20.08	23.33	22.55	.774	ns
Teacher praise C2	15.02	15.35	21.60	1.635	ns
Reprimand C1	25.12	16.82	19.75	6.185	1, 2 p = .002
Reprimand C2	30.02	19.03	16.20	14.161	1, 2 p = .000; 1, 3 p = .000

Note. Direct observations averaged 5 to 6 hours; behaviors tallied for frequency of occurrence; Level 1 = no intervention or limited; inconsistent use of behavior management strategies, social skills, peer tutoring programs; Level 2 = some intervention including social skills and tutoring programs; Level 3 = strong interventions in behavior management, social skills, tutoring; Cohort 1: Level 1—$n = 73$ of 215 data probes; Level 2—$n = 94$; Level 3—$n = 44$; Cohort 2: Level 1—$n = 57$ out of 135 data probes; Level 2—$n = 58$; Level 3—$n = 20$.
[a]$df = 2$. [b]Significance between levels of intervention.

TABLE 4
Levels of Classroom Structure and Effects on Behaviors Noted in Direct Observations

Behavior	Level 1 structure (M)	Level 2 structure (M)	Level 3 structure (M)	F^a	p value[b]
Aggression C1	5.54	3.38	2.47	4.900	1, 3 p = .007
Aggression C2	8.76	3.61	4.02	5.312	1, 2 p = .008; 1, 3 p = .012
Negative verbals C1	10.19	9.20	6.83	1.839	ns
Negative verbals C2	10.88	7.43	7.80	1.632	ns
Out of seat C1	15.75	13.11	6.89	11.205	1, 3 p = .000; 2, 3 p = .001
Out of seat C2	21.92	16.27	9.38	5.954	1, 3 p = .004
Engagement C1	65.18	78.13	79.84	12.951	1, 2 p = .000; 1, 3 p = .000
Engagement C2	60.36	66.33	73.91	4.507	1, 3 p = .016
Compliance C1	71.52	77.74	86.74	14.489	1, 3 p = .000; 2, 3 p = .001
Compliance C2	77.12	81.71	82.89	1.759	ns
Teacher praise C1	22.81	20.82	23.27	0.459	ns
Teacher praise C2	11.20	13.65	20.15	4.584	1, 3 p = .029
Reprimand C1	26.44	19.52	16.23	6.754	1, 2 p = .025; 1, 3 p = .001
Reprimand C2	34.48	24.78	17.43	16.847	1, 2 p = .006; 1, 3 p = .000; 2, 3 p = .008

Note. Direct observations averaged 5 to 6 hours; behaviors tallied for frequency of occurrence; Level 1 classroom structure indicates situations with disorganized schedules, chaotic learning conditions, problems with compliance and discipline; Level 2 structure indicates moderate levels of structure, generally well-managed environments; Level 3 structure indicates very well organized and structured schedules, smooth/brief transitions, effective management with minimal disruptions to learning, N = 64; Cohort 1: Level 1—n = 52 out of 215 data probes; Level 2—n = 95; Level 3—n = 64; Cohort 2: Level 1—n = 25 out of 135 data probes; Level 2—n = 49; Level 3—n = 61.
[a]df = 2. [b]Significance between levels of intervention.

Teacher Ratings by Intervention/Structure. The relationship of behaviors as reported by teachers was also analyzed in terms of the levels of (a) prevention intervention and (b) classroom structure. Regarding *levels of intervention,* as depicted in Figure 2, aggression decreased for both cohorts with more intervention (p = .005 for Cohort 1). Minimal changes were noted for not following directions and arguing with peers for either group across intervention levels. Peer interaction and work completion ratings (not in figure) averaged 3+ across groups (a rating of "sometimes"), with minimal reported intervention change by teachers.

Significant differences were noted for both cohorts when analyzing *classroom structure.* High structure resulted in significantly less aggression and increased following directions than during periods of low structure. Arguing with peers declined, but not significantly, for both cohorts. Teachers also rated students' appropriateness of peer interactions and work completion on a scale of 0 (*never*) to 5 (*always*), with no differences noted for levels of classroom structure and means indicating "sometimes to frequent" levels of appropriateness.

Case Studies

Results for case studies are presented in Figures 3 and 4, with the first two panels (Carl, Mike, Lamar, John, Anthony, and Ronnie) presenting means for successful students and the third panel showing treatment failures for Maurice, Kyle, and Daniel. For all students, aggression occurred more frequently during initial probes (first 3 data points), with highest data points indicating serious aggression for Mike (15), John (76), Ronnie (21), Anthony (19), Maurice (42), Daniel (13), and Kyle (23). Trends for the successful students showed decreases over time, with many probes indicating minimal aggression. Conversely, Maurice, Kyle, and Daniel continued to have higher levels of aggression during at least half of the probes.

As depicted in Figure 4, academic engagement probes generally reflected improvements over time (80% +) for Carl, Mike, John, Anthony, and Ronnie (five of the six successes), with Lamar continuing to need teacher proximity or one–to–one instruction to ensure attention to task. For students viewed as treatment failures (Panel 3), Maurice exhibited some periods of high academic engagement; however one-to-one instruction was nearly always necessary to maintain performance, and Kyle and

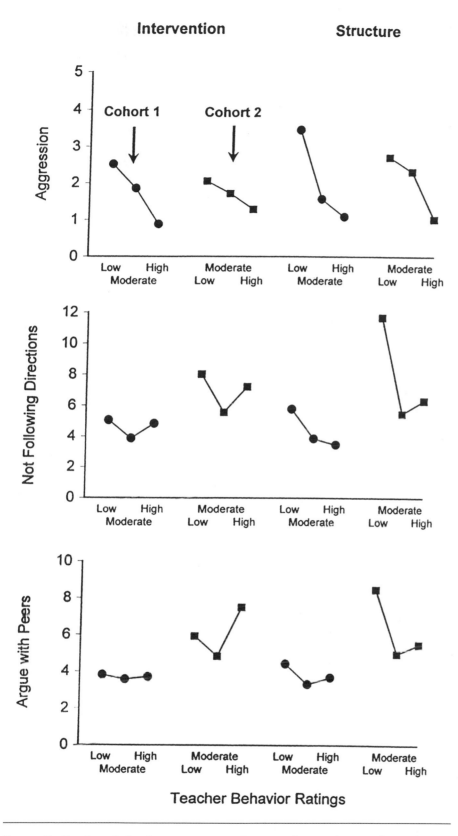

Intervention   **Structure**

FIGURE 2. Student behaviors as reported on teacher ratings and in relation to intervention levels and classroom structure. Low = low structure/minimal intervention, moderate = moderate structure/two interventions, and high = high structure/three interventions.

Daniel continued to show many instances of low task persistence.

DISCUSSION

Overall, the use of universal prevention programs over 3 to 4 years was found to (a) reduce the frequency of physical aggression toward peers for elementary school students with ED and high-risk students, (b) reduce other inappropriate behaviors that interfere with classroom performance, and (c) increase behavioral compliance and academic engagement. These findings concur with other reports recommending prevention and prereferral interventions (e.g., Del'Homme et al., 1996; Walker et al., 1995). Results were replicated with two groups of students with ED and at high-risk, one group monitored over a 4-year period and the second group monitored over a 3-year period. Significant differences were noted in some instances and not in others. Trend analysis of student outcome data for 38 participants indicated decreased aggression and out-of-seat behavior and increases in academic engagement and behavioral compliance for both groups. For the Years 1 to 4 comparison (pre and post data), decreases in aggression and out-of-seat behaviors were noted, and improvements in academic engagement were significant for both Cohorts (see Figures 1 and 2). Given these findings, a disappointment was the lack of improvement in negative verbal behaviors (arguing with peers, name calling, teasing) for Cohort 1. It was relatively more resistant to change even with prevention intervention in place.

The second analysis, reviewing the data by levels of intervention and classroom structure, allowed for a more thorough understanding of student outcomes. For example, when viewing periods of more intervention (individual behavior support, social skills, peer tutoring), for Cohorts 1 and 2, aggression and out-of-seat behaviors were significantly lower and academic engagement and behavioral compliance were significantly higher. Likewise, when viewing periods of high classroom structure, ag-

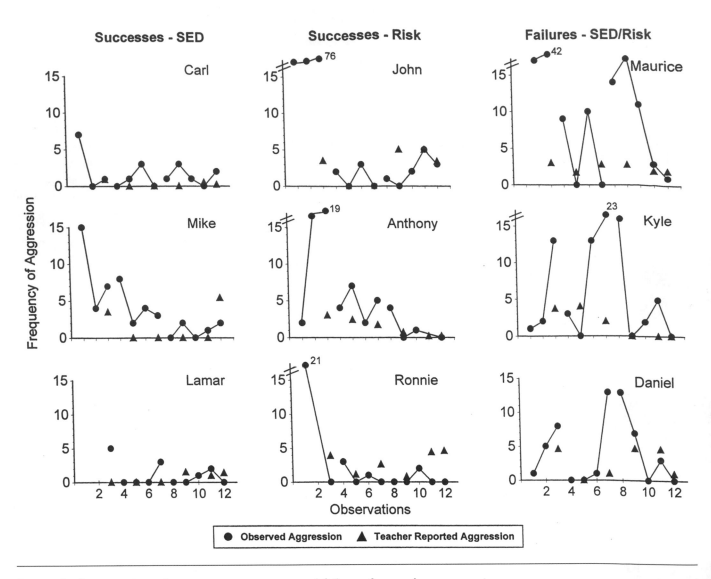

FIGURE 3. Case studies of treatment successes and failures for student aggression.

gression and out-of-seat behaviors were significantly lower, and academic engagement was significantly higher for both groups. Behavioral compliance was significantly higher for Cohort 1 during high structure, but no significant difference was noted for Cohort 2. Having noted that both intervention and structure influenced student behaviors, it is further suggested that the level of classroom structure influenced the feasibility of treatment and, in some cases, teachers' ability to implement consistent, quality interventions. The intervention in this study did not appear robust or consistent enough to decrease negative verbal remarks (e.g., arguing, teasing) with adults or peers, nor did the level of classroom

structure appear to influence these behaviors. Although less serious in nature than physical aggression, these behaviors also contribute/predict tendencies to violence, thus indicating the need for further investigation into effective intervention for negative verbal behaviors (Braun, Kirchner, Hartman, Overton, & Caldwell, 1998). Of related interest in this study were the verbal behaviors of participating teachers. First, the frequency of praise was not noticeably different than teacher reprimands, in spite of continued recommendations for praise rates to be at least on a 2-to-1 ratio. Second, teacher reprimands were significantly higher in classes with low structure and low levels of intervention. It is

uncertain as to the relationship of these findings to the knowledge base on school climate and positive behavior support for students (Kauffman & Hallahan, 1997).

In addition to effects for the groups, individual cases provided further insight as to the influences of the prevention/ intervention program. Functional assessment techniques in particular, including observation data, teacher interviews, and parent conferences, provided key information for summarizing variables contributing to individual successes and factors maintaining poor performance for other cases. All six successful cases (see Panels 1 and 2 in Figures 3 and 4) were initially enrolled in a selected "prevention" school with a strong commitment

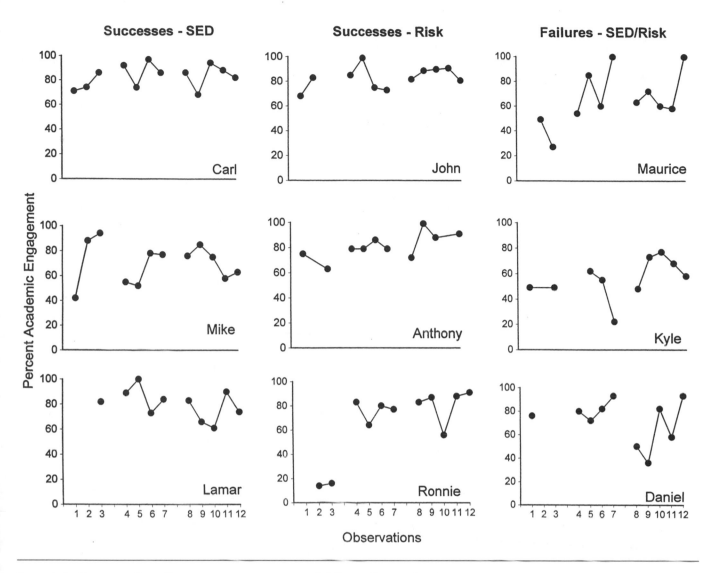

FIGURE 4. Case studies of treatment successes and failures for academic engagement.

to the use of social skills and peer tutoring. In addition, the school implemented a peer mediation program during recess. Carl, Mike, and Lamar (Panel 1) were also served in a self-contained ED class during Year 1, receiving small-group social skills instruction with consistent reinforcement for appropriate behaviors. Carl and Lamar were transferred for subsequent school years, with both in new settings with highly organized classrooms and consistent use of proactive management and social skills. Carl and Mike were increasingly served in general education classrooms with special education support/case management and consistent home support (frequent phone calls, home–school notes, stable family conditions).

Panel 2 presents data for high-risk students who experienced general improvements over time. John and Ronnie remained at their initial school with continued school-wide social skills and with John in structured classes and receiving peer tutoring for reading. John's parents maintained school contact and participated in parent support activities (parenting classes, frequent school contacts, home tutoring). Anthony and Ronnie received varying levels of prevention components with periods of time counterproductive to positive behavioral support.

Maurice, Kyle, and Daniel were considered treatment failures in the study (Panel 3). Maurice received intensive services in ED classes beginning in Year 2,

with much of his instruction provided on a one-to-one basis, thus improving his engagement and academic performance. Effective behavior support, however, fluctuated greatly, with high levels of attention for inappropriate behaviors, which tended to escalate their occurrence. Second, traumatic home events continued to occur for this student (e.g., sibling gang involvement, including one instance of gun violence; removal from the home on two occasions; parental substance abuse; extreme poverty), with all variables contributing to periods of anxiety, depression, and acting out behavior. For Kyle and Daniel, home variables also were detrimental to progress, including variance in parental contact (e.g., refusals to school requests for conferences and assistance) and noncompliance to physician's recommendations for medication for ADHD for both students. School variables further appeared to maintain some behavioral problems for Kyle and Daniel (e.g., periods with no positive behavior management program, unstructured classrooms, inconsistent instruction for academic deficits for Kyle). These findings and those from the groups overall demonstrated two important issues related to strength of intervention: (a) some children may need intensive intervention over long periods of time, and (b) students need at least moderate levels of intervention and structure to maintain improvements.

Limitations and Future Directions

In spite of generally positive findings, there were limitations to the study. First, the fidelity of treatment was not consistently or formally monitored. Project staff did provide training, ongoing classroom visits, and consultation to assist with implementation. More steadfast attention and documentation of prevention programs would, however, greatly enhance replication of programs and perhaps assist in higher levels of implementation in new settings (Nelson, 1997; Witt, Noell, LaFleur, & Mortenson, 1997). A second limitation was the small size of the groups, 20 and 18 for the two cohorts. A third limitation was mobility; many students moved, with approximately a one-third dropout rate over 4 years. Project staff did continue to track some students who moved within district; however, this reduced the time available for staff to assist teachers and restricted the success of school-wide maintenance of procedures.

Several conclusions can be drawn from these findings and limitations. Prevention can make a difference for elementary school students, and efforts should be made for all schools to implement consistent programs. Recommendations include school-wide implementation of social skills with direct instruction of classroom and interpersonal skills, peer tutoring and mentoring by positive role models, and classwide management programs supportive of student success (Kamps & Tankersley, 1996; Lewis, Sugai, & Colvin, 1998; Montague, Bergeron, & Lago-Delello, 1997; Strayhorn, Strain, & Walker, 1993). Additional attention is needed to define components of "structured" classrooms and determine methods for reliably instructing and training teachers in how to improve structure and organization. This element was shown to be as critical as the levels of interventions for increasing performance and reducing antisocial behaviors in this sample. The chaotic, disruptive environments frequently encountered in urban, low-SES areas are an ongoing issue for parents, teachers, and society at large (Walker et al., 1998). In addition, more applied intervention research is needed to determine strategies for successful management of behaviors on a classwide basis and for individual students needing intensive support. Promising interventions in this study included individual and classwide self-management, reinforcement schedules, home–school notes, and social skills instruction tied to specific behaviors with reinforcement for performance in generalization settings.

An additional area for investigation includes strategies for increasing positive collaboration with families in support of improving student behaviors at school and home (e.g., Epstein et al., 1998; Kay & Fitzgerald, 1997). The most successful cases in this study were those in which (a) parents were supportive of school efforts (e.g., responsive to phone calls, conferences) with frequent communications; (b) families accessed needed services for themselves and their children (e.g., mental health); and (c) home/community life was stable (consistent residence, protection from exposure to violence, stable parental employment).

In conclusion, implementation of prevention programs, with adequate family and school-based support, may greatly enhance the academic engagement of students with behavioral problems/ED and assist in the reduction of violence-related behaviors in urban schools.

About the Authors

DEBRA KAMPS, PhD, is a senior scientist with the University of Kansas, Schiefelbusch Institute for Life Span Studies. Professional interests include prevention and intervention research and instructional programming in the areas of autism, behavior disorders, and high-risk populations. She is currently a principal investigator at the Juniper Gardens Children's Project, a community-based research facility. **TAMMY KRAVITS,** MA, is a behavioral consultant for Professional Behavior Management, Inc. Professional work interests include school- and family-based intervention for children with autism, developmental disabilities, and behavior disorders. **JODEE RAUCH** is a school psychologist in the Wichita Public Schools. Professional areas of interest include assessment and intervention for students at risk and with learning and behavior difficulties and services for students in urban communities. **JODI L. KAMPS,** MA, is a fourth-year doctoral student in the Clinical Child Psychology Program at the University of Kansas. She is primarily interested in pediatric psychology but has enjoyed working with children exhibiting behavior problems through the Juniper Gardens Children's Project. Currently, she is investigating problems with adherence in children with asthma. **NATASHA CHUNG,** MA, is a psychology intern at the Child Development and Rehabilitation Center at Oregon Health Sciences University's Doernbecher Children's Hospital. Her current professional work and interests include intervention and assessment with children with developmental disorders, as well as culturally competent assessment and delivery of psychological services to children with emotional and behavioral disorders. Address: Debra Kamps, Juniper Gardens Children's Project, 650 Minnesota Ave., 2nd Floor, Kansas City, KS 66101.

Authors' Notes

1. The authors extend their sincere appreciation to the teachers and students who participated in this project in the Kansas City, Kansas Public Schools. Special thanks are credited to Dr. Laura Clark, director of Special Education Services and principals who supported prevention efforts: Mrs. Willia Crawford, Ms. Stephanie Bland, Mrs. Gloria Soldon, and Mrs. Flora Anderson.

2. This research was supported by Grant No. H237F50019 from the U.S. Department of Education. The views expressed are those of the authors, not necessarily the funding agency.

Note

Upon request, a more complete table with means and standard deviations may be requested from the first author.

References

Alberto, P., & Troutman, A. (1999, 1995). *Applied behavior analysis for teachers.* Upper Saddle River, NJ: Prentice Hall.

Barlow, D., Hayes, S., & Nelson, R. (1984). *The scientist practitioner: Research and accountability in clinical and educational settings.* Elmsford, NY: Pergamon Press.

Braun, N. A., Kirchner, L. A., Hartman, M. S., Overton, K. J., & Caldwell, T. E. (1998). Establishing a descriptive database for teachers with aggressive students. *Journal of Behavioral Education, 8*(4), 457–470.

Burke, J. (1992). *Decreasing classroom behavior problems: Practical guidelines for teachers.* San Diego: Singular.

Campbell, S. (1994). Behavior problems in preschool children: A review of recent research. *Journal of Child Psychology and Psychiatry, 36,* 113–149.

Committee for Children. (1991). *Second Step®: A violence prevention program.* Seattle, WA: Author.

Del'Homme, M., Kasari, C., Forness, S., & Bagley, R. (1996). Prereferral intervention and students at-risk for emotional or behavioral disorders. *Education and Treatment of Children, 19,* 272–285.

Epstein, M., Jayanthi, M., Dennis, K., Hardy, R., Fueyo, V., Frankenberry, E., & McKelvey, J. (1998). Educational status of children who are receiving services in an urban family preservation and reunification setting. *Journal of Emotional and Behavioral Disorders, 6,* 162–169.

Forness, S., Serna, L., Kavale, K., & Nielsen, E. (1998). Mental health and Head Start: Teaching adaptive skills. *Education and Treatment of Children, 21,* 258–274.

Greenwood, C., Delquadri, J., & Carta, J. (1997). *Together we can! Classwide peer tutoring to improve basic academic skills.* Longmont, CO: Sopris West.

Huggins, P. (1995). *The ASSIST program—Affective/social skills: Instructional strategies and techniques.* Seattle: Washington State Innovative Education Program.

Kamps, D., Ellis, C., Mancina, C., Wyble, J., Greene, L., & Harvey, D. (1995). Case studies using functional analysis for young children with behavior risks. *Education and Treatment of Children, 18,* 243–260.

Kamps, D., Kravits, T., Stolze, J., & Swaggart, B. (1999). Prevention strategies for students at risk and identified as serious emotionally disturbed in urban, elementary school settings. *Journal of Emotional and Behavioral Disorders.*

Kamps, D. M., & Tankersley, M. (1996). Prevention of behavioral and conduct disorders: Trends and research issues. *Behavioral Disorders, 22*(1), 41–48.

Katsiyannis, A., & Maag, J. W. (1998). Disciplining students with disabilities: Issues and considerations for implementing IDEA '97. *Behavioral Disorders, 23*(4), 276–289.

Kauffman, J. M., & Hallahan, D. P. (1997). On creating a climate of classroom civility. *Phi Delta Kappan, 79,* 320–325.

Kay, P., & Fitzgerald, M. (1997). Parents + teachers + action research = real involvement. *Teaching Exceptional Children, 30,* 8–11.

Larson, J. (1994). Violence prevention in the schools: A review of selected programs and procedures. *School Psychology Review, 23*(2), 151–164.

Lewis, T. (1998). *Responsible decision making about effective behavioral support: A handbook for educators.* Eugene, OR: The National Center to Improve the Tools of Educators.

Lewis, T. J., Sugai, G., & Colvin, G. (1998). Reducing problem behavior through a school-wide system of effective behavioral support: Investigation of a school-wide social skills training program and contextual interventions. *School Psychology Review, 27,* 446–459.

McGinnis, E., & Goldstein, A. (1984). *Skillstreaming the elementary school child: A guide for teaching prosocial skills.* Champaign, IL: Research Press.

McGinnis, E., & Goldstein, A. (1997). *Skillstreaming the elementary school child: New strategies and perspectives for teaching prosocial skills.* Champaign, IL: Research Press.

Montague, M., Bergeron, J., & Lago-Delello, E. (1997). Using prevention strategies in general education. *Focus on Exception Children, 29*(8), 1–12.

Nelson, M. C. (1997). Aggressive and violent behavior: A personal perspective. *Education and Treatment of Children, 20*(3), 250–262.

Rhode, G., Jenson, W., & Reavis, H. (1998). *The tough kid book: Practical classroom management strategies.* Longmont, CO: Sopris West.

Strayhorn, J., Strain, P., & Walker, H. (1993). The case of interaction skills training in the context of tutoring as a preventive mental health intervention in schools. *Behavioral Disorders, 19,* 11–26.

Tankersley, M., Kamps, D., Mancina, C., & Weidinger, D. (1996). Social interventions for Head Start Children with behavioral risks: Implementation and outcomes. *Journal of Emotional and Behavioral Disorders, 4,* 171–181.

Walker, H., Colvin, G., & Ramsey, E. (1995). *Antisocial behavior in school: Strategies and best practices.* Boston: Brookes/Cole.

Walker, H. M., Forness, S. R., Kauffman, J. M., Epstein, M. H., Gresham, F. M., Nelson, C. M., & Strain, P. S. (1998). Macrosocial validation: Referencing outcomes in behavioral disorders to societal issues and problems. *Behavioral Disorders, 24*(1), 7–18.

Walker, H., & Severson, H. (1992). *Systematic screening for behavior disorders: Observer training manual.* Longmont, CO: Sopris West.

Witt, J. C., Noell, G. H., LaFleur, L. H., & Mortenson, B. P. (1997). Teacher use of interventions in general education settings: Measurement and analysis of the independent variable. *Journal of Applied Behavior Analysis, 30*(4), 693–696.

Yeaton, W. H., & Sechrest, L. (1981). Critical dimensions in the choice and maintenance of successful treatments: Strength, integrity, and effectiveness. *Journal of Consulting and Clinical Psychology, 49,* 156–167.

An Elementary School–Based Prevention Program Targeting Modifiable Antecedents of Youth Delinquency and Violence:

Linking the Interests of Families and Teachers (LIFT)

J. Mark Eddy, John B. Reid, and Rebecca A. Fetrow

Linking the Interests of Families and Teachers (LIFT), a prevention program designed for delivery to children and parents within the elementary school setting, is described. The LIFT targets for change those child and parent behaviors thought to be most relevant to the development of adolescent delinquent and violent behaviors, namely child oppositional, defiant, and socially inept behavior and parent discipline and monitoring. The three major components of the LIFT are (a) classroom-based child social and problem skills training, (b) playground-based behavior modification, and (c) group-delivered parent training. The results of a randomized controlled evaluation of the LIFT are reviewed. To date, the program has positively impacted the targeted antecedents. Most importantly, during the 3 years following the program, the LIFT delayed the time that participants first became involved with antisocial peers during middle school, as well as the time to first patterned alcohol use, to first marijuana use, and to first police arrest.

DELINQUENCY HAS BEEN A SERIOUS problem in the major cities of the eastern United States since the beginning of the Industrial Revolution (Eddy & Swanson Gribskov, 1997). In these locales, policymakers and laypeople in each successive generation have spoken out against the increasing dangerousness of youth and the pressing need for solutions. Despite the plethora of "preventive" measures that have followed, delinquency has persisted and spread and is now a topic of debate not only in cities and towns throughout the United States but in many rural areas as well. Even criminal gang activity, which was once the sole province of the most densely populated cities, was a phenomenon reported by police departments in over 750 locales in 1992 (Klein, 1995).

HISTORICAL BACKGROUND

Through most of the history of the United States, prevention meant incarceration as early as possible in the life of a child perceived to be "delinquent." The actual commission of a delinquent act was not a requirement for delinquency classification. Thus, during the nineteenth century, many incarcerated children were from impoverished, immigrant families who were considered "unfit" to properly raise a child. After the creation of the juvenile court at the turn of the twentieth century, psychological techniques began to be used to assess youth brought before the court. These techniques, as well as various forms of psychological intervention, were disseminated throughout the country via a burgeoning network of child guidance clinics. Not until the 1930s did preventive attempts begin to incorporate some of the techniques that are popular today. For example, the use of community boards in the development of interventions was pioneered in Chicago neighborhoods (Sechrest, 1970) and a multimodal preventive intervention program began to be employed in "high risk" neighborhoods in Boston (McCord, 1992).

Early studies of the effectiveness of these interventions suggested that they were less than promising. For example, youth who received services in child guidance clinics appeared to be unaffected in terms of their delinquent behavior (Glueck & Glueck, 1934). A large-scale randomized controlled study of Boston-area prevention efforts (i.e., a casework mentoring program) found that the program not only failed to have an impact (Powers & Witmer, 1951), but may have increased the likelihood that participants displayed problem behaviors (McCord, 1981).

Although concerns about delinquency were eclipsed during World War II, in the years following the war, police arrests of youth due to their antisocial behavior rose at an astounding rate. By the end of the 1950s, public concern was so intense that the federal government and several private foundations began to finance a new generation of delinquency prevention efforts. Unfortunately, the impact of most of these programs was as unclear as that of those that preceded them. Most simply failed to make a difference (Berleman & Steinburn, 1969).

During this same period of time, psychological researchers throughout the country began to use and study the effect of a new set of intervention techniques based on behavioral principles. These researchers moved away from the individual and clinic-based treatments that were popular at the time and instead intervened directly in the classroom, in the home, or both (e.g., Hops & Walker, 1988; Meichenbaum & Goodman, 1971; Patterson, 1974; Schweinhart & Weikart, 1988; Shure, Spivack, & Jaeger, 1971; Walker, Hops, & Greenwood, 1993). The promise of these new intervention strategies helped inaugurate a new wave of preventive efforts. By the late 1970s, researchers such as Hawkins and colleagues (Hawkins, Von Cleve, & Catalano, 1991) were implementing elementary school–based preventive programs that targeted child aggression and antisocial behavior through the use of a variety of techniques in multiple settings. A plethora of studies on the effectiveness of similar multimodal prevention programs have followed (e.g., Conduct Problems Prevention Research Group, 1992; Kellam et al., 1991; Tremblay, Pagani-Kurtz, Masse, Vitaro, & Pihl,

1995). At a minimum, most of these new programs combined parent training and child social skills training.

One of the programs developed during this most recent round of preventive activity was the Linking the Interests of Families and Teachers (LIFT), a multimodal prevention program targeting the antecedents of youth delinquency and violence and designed for use in elementary school settings. The LIFT comprised three components: (a) a classroom-based child social and problem skills training component, (b) a playground-based behavior modification component, and (c) a group-delivered parent training component. In this article, we describe the LIFT in detail, overview our findings on the efficacy of the program, and conclude with a set of recommendations for practice.

THEORETICAL BACKGROUND

The major difference between recent and earlier preventive efforts is the degree to which the new programs have been informed by basic scientific research on the development of delinquency. During the past several decades, a variety of parent and child behaviors during early and middle childhood have been consistently linked to delinquent behaviors during adolescence (see Stoff, Breiling, & Maser, 1997). One of the most promising theories based on this research, and the theory upon which the LIFT is based, is coercion theory (Patterson, 1982; Patterson, Reid, & Dishion, 1992).

In coercion theory, the key mechanism hypothesized to drive the development of child problem behaviors is negative reinforcement. "Negative reinforcement" is the association of certain behaviors with the termination or delay of aversive situations, such as a person hitting the "snooze" button when his or her alarm rings in the morning. In contrast, the more familiar "positive reinforcement" or reward paradigm is the association of certain behaviors with a preferred occurrence or situation, such as a child receiving a piece of candy with lunch because he did not fight with his sister in the car on the way to school. In either reinforcement situation, over time,

the behaviors that are most effective at leading to the desired outcome in a given situation become the most likely to occur when that situation occurs (e.g., alarm rings → button pressed → alarm off).

Negative reinforcement is a particularly common learning paradigm in family interaction. For example, a father asks his son to clean up his room immediately because company is coming over for dinner. The child complains and dawdles, and the parent feels frustrated. The parent then asks again, and the child continues to delay. The parent now feels angry and yells at the child to "get moving." The child yells back and says, "Leave me alone" and runs outside to play with his friends. The parent, now distraught and exhausted, quickly picks up his son's room and then begins to cook dinner.

The final outcome of a scenario such as this is that child refusal to cooperate is inadvertently reinforced by parent acceptance of the refusal. In effect, the child's refusal is rewarded. If repeated again and again, this type of seemingly innocuous social interaction is hypothesized to serve a major role in the genesis and maintenance of child behavior problems. If aversive behavior effectively ends undesirable situations with parents, children are likely to display the same type of behavior when they encounter undesirable circumstances in other relationships (i.e., child–peer, child–teacher). Insidiously, most instances of such negative behavior are probably not the result of a conscious act by the child, but rather are the display of an acquired relationship skill. The more frequently these interactions end in the reinforcement of child misbehavior, the more likely the child will continue to behave in similar ways in the future.

The consequences of this pattern of child behavior are severe. Children who display frequent defiance and opposition to those around them are likely to be disliked and shunned. As adults and peers alike withdraw from contact with a child, he or she is less likely to receive reinforcement for the positive behaviors that are displayed. A lack of adult engagement places a child at risk for exposure to other rejected peers who are willing to engage the child. It is often through relationships with these "deviant peers" that a youth with a history of troubled relationships begins to commit criminal behaviors. Youth who commit many delinquent behaviors are likely to commit a variety of different kinds of offenses, including violent acts. Notably, the best predictor of violence during adolescence is prior frequent antisocial behavior (Capaldi & Patterson, 1996).

PRACTICAL CONSIDERATIONS

The LIFT targets for change those child and parent behaviors thought to be the most relevant to the development of adolescent delinquent and violent behaviors, namely opposition, defiance, and social ineptitude on the part of the child and disciplining and monitoring on the part of the parent (see Stoff et al., 1997). Antecedents to problems in each of these areas have been identified before birth (see Reid & Eddy, 1997), and interventions that target maternal behaviors during the prenatal period have been shown to impact later delinquency (Olds, Hill, Mihalic, & O'Brien, 1998). Targeting the antecedents of problem behaviors as early as possible in the lifecourse is highly appealing given the correlation between child age and problem complexity. Interventions have been developed for children (see Taylor, Eddy, & Biglan, in press) and for parents (Reid & Eddy, 1997) that appear to positively impact child problem behaviors and parent discipline and monitoring. While these can be delivered to families on a clinical basis during early childhood, it is difficult to provide such programs on a broad, preventative scale in the United States due to the dispersion of young children and parents across numerous service systems.

Elementary school is the first point in the lifespan when the majority of children enter a service system that includes a broad cross-section of the population. In some states, such as Oregon, virtually the entire school-age population attends public elementary school (Oregon Department of Education, 1999). Because of this depth of access, the public school system is an ideal setting for providing a population-level intervention relevant to children.

This type of access is important when targeting delinquency and violence because it is difficult to predict exactly who will become delinquent and/or violent during adolescence (Offord, 1997). While a general group of children can be identified from which the most problematic youth are most likely to arise, providing more intensive individualized services to all such at-risk children would be prohibitive within most states (see Albee & Gullotta, 1997). On the other hand, we hypothesized that a less intensive, theory-based program available to an entire population could decrease the prevalence of delinquency and violence at a cost that most states could afford. Such a program could serve as a useful complement to the existing mental health and juvenile justice systems through decreasing the total number of children in need of the services provided by those systems. In turn, a portion of the cost savings to these systems could be used to fund such a preventive program.

PARTICIPANTS AND COMMUNITY SETTING

The LIFT was designed for delivery to a general population of elementary school–aged boys and girls and their parents. Two major sources informed the LIFT: (a) the scientific knowledge base that has accrued through cross-sectional and longitudinal studies on the development and treatment of antisocial behavior problems and (b) the clinical knowledge base that has accrued at our own and similar centers through outpatient and inpatient clinical work with youth displaying antisocial behavior problems and their families. These sources provided us with a vast amount of information to draw upon in the creation of the LIFT, but they do have their limitations. Each source contains an abundance of information about boys but relatively little of such information about girls. Each source contains scant information about ethnic minority families. We are currently investigating whether the LIFT is more efficacious with boys than girls, and to date, this does not appear to be the case. We are just beginning to explore whether adaptations of the LIFT will be acceptable to and efficacious in populations with different demographic characteristics.

The LIFT was developed within a moderately sized urban area in the Pacific Northwest (i.e., Eugene-Springfield, Oregon). Schools from each of the three major public school districts in the area participated in the program. In 1990, the local metropolitan area population was approximately 200,000, and 92% of residents were White. In that same year, 19% of families in the local area earned $15,000 or less per year, 58% earned from $15,000 to $50,000 per year, and 23% earned over $50,000. In the evaluation of the LIFT reported below, participating schools tended to be located in neighborhoods that were more likely than the metropolitan area at large to have residents with lower incomes (24% with incomes of $15,000 or less) or to have residents who were members of an ethnic minority (12%).

FEATURES AND IMPLEMENTATION PROCEDURES

Classroom Component

LIFT classroom instructors meet with all the students in a classroom for 1 hour twice a week for 10 weeks. Each session follows the same general format: (a) brief lecture and role play on a specific set of social and problem-solving skills, (b) structured small- and large-group skills practice, (c) unstructured free play on the playground, and (d) skills review and presentation of daily rewards. The second weekly session also includes a formal class problem-solving session. The regular classroom teachers assist the LIFT instructors in role plays and group practice. The skills presented in the curriculum are similar for first and fifth graders (see the Appendix); however, the specific content of each lesson is tailored to address the development challenges typically met by the members of each age group. In addition, the fifth-grade curriculum includes a study skills component relevant to academic work in middle school. The instructors who taught the LIFT in our evaluation study were members of our research center staff. However, the program can be taught by classroom teachers, school counselors or psychologists, or trained and experienced laypersons.

Playground Component

The playground component of LIFT takes place during the middle of the free play portion of the classroom component. A modification of the Good Behavior Game (GBG; Barrish, Saunders, & Wolfe, 1969; Dolan et al., 1993) is used to actively encourage positive peer relations on the playground. At the beginning of the program, children within each classroom are divided into small groups. The groups engage in various activities together throughout the program. Through (a) the demonstration of positive problem-solving skills and other prosocial behaviors and (b) the inhibition of negative behaviors while on the playground, group members earn rewards for themselves, their entire class, and their group.

Individual and class rewards are based on the display of positive behaviors. Individual rewards are given by regular playground staff and the LIFT instructor during the recess period. When a staff member observes a child acting in an overtly positive manner toward peers, the child is given an armband and verbally praised. At the end of recess, all armbands earned by class members are put into one class jar. When the jar is full, the entire class earns a special privilege.

In contrast, group rewards depend on the ability of group members to inhibit their negative interactions with peers. Throughout recess, each time a child is observed behaving in a negative manner, his or her behavior is noted in a class log book. At the end of recess, the total number of negative points earned by a group is subtracted from a preset number of "good faith" positive points each group

receives at the beginning of recess. If a group manages to retain a predetermined percentage of their positive points, each member earns a sticker. When the group earns a certain number of total points after several recess periods, each member selects a small prize.

Parent Component

LIFT parent instructors meet with groups of 10 to 15 families once a week for 6 weeks. These sessions are held during the same 3-month period of time that children are participating in the classroom and playground components at school. Like the classroom sessions, each parent session follows a common format: (a) review of the results of the home practice from the previous week; (b) lecture, discussion, and role plays; and (c) presentation of the home practice activities for the following week and attendance drawing. Videotaped scenarios are used in several sessions to present and illustrate certain skills. The basic skills presented in the first- and fifth-grade parent curriculums are similar and linked to the corresponding classroom curricula (see the Appendix), but again the content is modified to address the challenges faced by parents with youth in the respective age groups. Specifically, parents of first graders are taught how to actively encourage positive play between their child and his or her friends, and parents of fifth graders are taught negotiation skills that have been found to be useful for families with adolescents for solving problems.

In the original evaluation of LIFT, the parent curriculum was taught by our center staff. To better represent those who would likely deliver such a program in the field, we deliberately employed instructional staff with a wide range of experiences and training. Our intervention team included experienced parent trainers without a college degree, recent doctoral-level clinical psychology graduates, and experienced psychologists. The curriculum was designed to accommodate such varying levels of clinical expertise.

Family Involvement

As discussed previously, research and clinical information that has accrued during the past several decades was used in the creation of the LIFT program. Prior to developing the curriculum, we had worked with over 1,500 families in our various clinical and research studies. Over the years, the interactions between our staff and these families have shaped our intervention techniques, our intervention materials, and our assessment techniques. This shaping has been both informal, through our day-to-day clinical work, and formal, through research studies designed to investigate how therapists and families influence the behavior of each other (e.g., Patterson & Chamberlain, 1994). The first draft of the LIFT curriculum was, thus, strongly influenced by several decades of family involvement.

Prior to finalizing the LIFT curricula for the evaluation study discussed below, we spent 1 year piloting the entire program. The pilot was conducted in one first-grade class and one fifth-grade class within a rural school district located outside of our local metropolitan area. The majority of families in each class participated (84%), and formal feedback was solicited from parents and teachers at various points during the pilot year. A variety of changes to the first draft of the curriculum were made based on this feedback. For example, the first-grade parents wanted to spend more time focusing on fostering positive peer relationships, and the fifth-grade parents wanted to spend more time on discussion and home exercises related to preparing for adolescence. Both the instructional videotapes and the treatment manuals for the parent component were edited and refined based on such feedback. Edits for the classroom component were based on feedback from students, teachers, and parents.

The primary focus of the LIFT program is on parents and parenting behaviors. Parents are invited to attend six group training sessions at their child's school. To encourage attendance, sessions are offered each weekday evening and one weekday afternoon, free childcare is provided, and a prize drawing is held at the completion of each session. If parents are unable to attend, individual sessions are offered in their home. If family commitments or circumstances make this option unworkable, parents are sent written materials. Additional parent sessions are arranged if necessary to discuss specific family problems and provide appropriate referrals.

Several means of communication are used to maximize the involvement of parents throughout the LIFT program. During the 10 weeks of the classroom component, parents receive weekly newsletters describing LIFT activities at school and providing suggestions for complimentary family activities. To provide more frequent information, a phone and answering machine are installed in each classroom. Teachers are encouraged to leave brief messages about class activities and homework assignments on the "LIFT Line" and to update these daily. Parents are encouraged to call for these messages and then to leave a message for the teacher. To ensure that each family has regular personal contact, parents are called once each week by the staff member leading their parent group. During the call, the staff member checks in on family progress on home exercises and addresses any specific questions or concerns. Each of these parent contacts is intended to assist in the integration of the home and school components of the LIFT. We view the family involvement aspects of the LIFT as bringing together the home, playground, and classroom components to "set the stage" for positive child development.

ILLUSTRATIVE CLASSROOM, PLAYGROUND, AND PARENT SESSIONS

Classroom/Playground Session

Lesson 15 of the first-grade classroom curriculum (Ramsey, Lathrop, Tharp, & Reid, 1994) focuses on dealing with teasing and criticism. At the beginning of the session, the classroom teacher and LIFT instructor use animal puppets (one of which is a turtle) to illustrate teasing situations that typically occur among first-grade students. Initially, one puppet teases, and the other responds negatively. The interaction escalates until both puppets are upset, angry, and sad. The instructor probes the class for alternative reactions to teasing. After several alternatives are given, the turtle puppet introduces her "turtle trick":

> The "Turtle Trick" is a trick you can use to help calm yourself down when someone is bothering you. We all get mad when people tease or call us names. When someone bothers you, just imagine you are a turtle and go into your shell. When a turtle is not upset its head is out. What does a turtle do if someone bugs it? It goes into its shell. When the turtle goes into its shell it is safe: no one can hurt it and it can't hurt anybody else.

Children are then asked to imagine that they are a turtle who is being teased:

> Now imagine someone is bugging you and you pull into your safe shell so you don't do or say anything mean. Doesn't it feel good to be in your shell? It's nice and warm and safe. You can't get into trouble and you have time to think about what you can do to keep from getting into trouble. (Ramsey et al., 1994)

Next, the class is divided into two groups, one led by the instructor and one by the classroom teacher. Students are asked to develop a list of situations at school when the "turtle trick" could be helpful. A pair of students is asked to role play a situation on the list, and the other students are asked to shout out "turtle trick!" at the moment when the provoked student might lose his or her temper. The group leader helps the provoked student imagine going into a shell. After the demonstration, all students within each group are asked to role play.

The groups are then brought back together, and the turtle trick is reviewed. Students are encouraged to use the trick not only when they need to calm down, but also when they are being bothered and don't want to get upset. As they employ the trick, students are encouraged to think of solutions to the problem besides responding in negative ways.

The class is then prepared for recess. The list of playground rules is read, and students are reminded that positive behavior on the playground will be rewarded. Students are instructed to use the "turtle trick" on the playground if someone makes them angry. Small groups are reminded about the number of total points they have, the number they need to earn for a daily reward, and the number they need to earn a group reward.

After a 15-minute recess period during which the Good Behavior Game is employed, students reconvene in the classroom. Positive behaviors observed on the playground are reviewed. Students are asked to review their use of the "turtle trick." Finally, observed negative behaviors are reviewed, group progress charts are filled out, and award incentives are given.

Parent Session

Lesson 6 of the first-grade parent curriculum begins with a 20-minute discussion of parent experiences during the past week while using a daily homework/study time, time outs, and a home behavior contract. This discussion is then used to introduce a more formal overview and discussion of successful peer relations. Parents are taught skills for coaching children's peer relationships, including techniques for creating peer situations where children are likely to be successful. Parents are asked to complete a questionnaire on their child's skills with peers and their involvement with their child's peer relationships. A few parents are asked about their specific responses, and the ensuing discussion is used to introduce a videotape on coaching peer relations.

In the videotape, three points important to helping children deal with peer conflict are emphasized:

1. *Assess.* Help your child define the problem in clear and specific terms.

Take your child's point of view into consideration.

2. *Plan.* Make a plan with your child that he or she can use to help solve the problem.
3. *Review.* Stay involved and review with your child how the plan worked.

Parent concerns following the tape are discussed, with the LIFT leader paraphrasing comments and providing ample support of positive parent examples. Four strategies for creating situations where children can be successful are presented:

1. *Suggest activities with a common goal.* Situations for children that have a common goal will increase cooperation and positive play. Individual goals create competition; group goals create cooperation.
2. *Reward group accomplishments.* Whenever possible, it is best to reward the accomplishments of a group of children playing rather than their individual efforts. Singling out one child is likely to create competitive, not cooperative play.
3. *Find your child's strengths, and create situations that build on strengths.* It is important to create peer situations that maximize a child's strengths. Don't try the "sink or swim" method, where a child is placed in a situation where he or she clearly has trouble. For example, if a child has problems playing with children his or her own age, it is okay to have him or her play with younger peers and slowly introduce the child to playing with same-age peers. Such a gradual approach tends to enhance a child's self-confidence and their peer relations.
4. *Pay close attention during transition periods.* When a child is successful with peers most of the time in one type of situation (one-on-one play), it is time to encourage new peer situations (small-group play), monitor these situations, and intervene as necessary with coaching skills.

Since the sixth session is the last in the program, the session closes with thanking parents for their participation, offering parents the option to call the instructor if help is needed in the future, encouraging the continued use of the LIFT Line, and conducting the final attendance drawing. After the session ends, the instructor sets up any final individual meetings to assist families in finding referrals should the problems they are facing require clinical services. In the evaluation study, such services were not provided by LIFT staff members.

FUNDING

The original development and testing of the LIFT was supported by a Prevention Intervention Research Center grant from the National Institutes of Mental Health (NIMH). Follow-ups of the original sample are being funded by additional grants from the NIMH. Examinations and extensions of the LIFT within new settings have been supported by a variety of sources, including the Wyoming Children's Trust Fund, HMO Oregon, and Kaiser Permanente. Work relevant to a broader dissemination effort is currently underway via a grant from the McConnell Clark Foundation.

EVALUATION

In a randomized clinical trial involving more than 600 youth and their families, the LIFT program has been shown to decrease levels of antisocial and other problem behaviors. The trial contrasted the outcomes of participants who received the LIFT (i.e., the intervention group) versus those who did not (i.e., the control group). Complete details of the investigation are provided in Reid, Eddy, Fetrow, and Stoolmiller (1999).

Targeted Schools

All public elementary schools located in high juvenile crime neighborhoods within the Eugene-Springfield, Oregon, metropolitan area were eligible to participate in the study. A "high juvenile

crime" neighborhood was defined as an elementary school catchment area having a higher than average number of households per year with at least one police contact due to juvenile misbehavior. At the beginning of the study, an average of 9% of households in the Eugene-Springfield area had such a contact in a given year.

Research Design

During each of 3 school years of the program phase of the study (1991–92, 1992–93, and 1993–94), four schools from high juvenile crime areas were randomly chosen as LIFT program schools, two as control schools (i.e., no prevention program but $2,000 provided in unrestricted funds), and two as alternatives should one of the assigned schools decline to participate. Over the course of the study, only three schools declined to participate, and two of those declined prior to randomization. Once a school was chosen, either the first or the fifth grade within the school was also randomly chosen to participate. The 12 schools randomly chosen for the study had an average neighborhood juvenile arrest rate of 13% of households, an average yearly student turnover rate of 43%, and an average free-lunch rate of 47% of students.

Assessments

To index the relative impact of the prevention program, all participants were assessed in the fall of the first year of the study, an intervention was conducted in prevention program schools during the winter, and all participants were again assessed in the spring. In subsequent years, all participants were assessed during the middle of the academic year. During each assessment, children, parents, and teachers were interviewed and completed a variety of paper-and-pencil questionnaires. Additionally, school and court records were collected, children were observed in the classroom and on the playground, and parents and child were observed during family problem-solving discussions at home or at our research center.

Participants

All students and their families within the chosen grade at each school were invited to participate in the study. Of the full-time students enrolled in the selected grades at the start of the LIFT program year, parents of 85% of students agreed to participate fully. An additional 3% of parents allowed their children to participate, but they themselves declined participation. The final sample comprised 671 students (51% female), with 382 participants attending intervention schools and 289 participants attending control schools at the beginning of the study. By the third year follow-up assessment, only 3% of participants dropped out of the study. As discussed previously, participants tended to be White and to have families earning lower to middle incomes. Participating parents tended to have completed high school or to have some college education. Approximately 25% of families were receiving some type of government assistance at the beginning of the study. On average, the characteristics of participants were similar to those of the school catchment areas in which they lived.

Program Implementation

Intervention fidelity (i.e., was the program delivered as planned), program utilization (i.e., did families participate), and participant satisfaction (i.e., were participants pleased with the services received) were high. In terms of fidelity, parent and classroom instructional staff were rated by independent observers on the actual content of prevention program sessions. In an average parent group or classroom, 95% of the planned program content was delivered. In terms of utilization, 93% of families received all parent training materials in some manner, either through the planned group sessions, through home visits, or through the mail (i.e., written materials and videotapes). In terms of satisfaction, 94% of families reported they would recommend LIFT to other parents, and 79% reported the program was either "quite helpful" or "very helpful." The majority of teachers also felt extremely positive about the LIFT, especially first-grade teachers (e.g., 100% endorsed the highest ratings for "recommend program to other teachers" and "students acquired better social skills"). Likewise, from 50% to 70% of fifth-grade teachers gave their highest endorsement on these same items.

Complementing these figures, dropout from the prevention program was quite low (7%), due in part to the multiple modes of service delivery (i.e., group sessions, individual sessions, mailings) used to provide materials to parents who did not attend group meetings. However, while the vast majority of participants were exposed to all LIFT program materials, only 28% of parents actually attended all six group parent training sessions. For any given LIFT parent session, an average of 59% of families attended the scheduled group, 23% received information on the session in the mail, 13% accepted a home visit to cover the material, and 5% refused to participate.

Immediate Impact

Significant changes in child and parent behaviors due to the intervention were found (Reid et al., 1999). In accord with our development model of antisocial behavior, we hypothesized that the LIFT would have a significant impact within three domains relevant to future youth problem behavior: child physical aggression toward classmates on the school playground, parent aversive behavior during family problem-solving discussions, and teacher impressions of child positive behaviors with classmates. After controlling for the clustering of children by classrooms, we found statistically significant differences between the control and LIFT program groups on each of these variables. In the spring following the intervention, children in the LIFT group were less aggressive on the playground and were perceived as more positive by their teachers than children in the control group. Further, parents of children in the LIFT group behaved less aversively with their children during family problem-solving discussions.

Interestingly, the effects of the LIFT appeared to be strongest for children who had the highest level of behavior problems prior to the intervention. In this regard, the effect of the LIFT on playground behavior was particularly powerful. Although aggressive children in the control group were equally aggressive toward their peers during the fall and spring of the program year, aggressive children in the prevention program group drastically decreased their aggressive behaviors in the spring following the intervention (Stoolmiller, Eddy, & Reid, 2000).

Three-Year Impact

Because of developmental differences in the first- and fifth-grade samples, we hypothesized different preventive effects of LIFT. During middle school, the most powerful predictors of serious and chronic delinquency are association with deviant peers and police arrest. For fifth graders, we found that intervention participants were significantly delayed during the middle school years in time to first report by teachers that a youth was spending time with peers with various behavior problems and time to first police arrest (see Eddy, Reid, Stoolmiller, & Fetrow, 2000). Intervention participants were also significantly delayed in the exhibition of problem behaviors that often accompany deviant peer association, such as patterned alcohol use and marijuana use. Interestingly, these effects were found for youth regardless of how problematic their behavior was prior to the start of the intervention; even those youth who were behaving in more extreme antisocial ways prior to the start of the program appeared to have benefited.

During elementary school, increases in inattentive, impulsive, and hyperactive behaviors appear to be important markers for later delinquency and other conduct problems, particularly when they are noticed early in the school setting (Loeber, Green, Keenan, & Lahey, 1995). We found that over the 3 years following the intervention, LIFT first graders were significantly less likely than control group children to show an increase in the severity of these types of behaviors as perceived by teachers. The effect size for this difference was 1.5 within group standard deviations, considered "very large" for a psychological intervention (Cohen & Cohen, 1983).

Meaningfulness of the LIFT Program Effect

The statistically significant differences reported above translate into meaningful differences between the groups. For example, observed aggressive behavior on the LIFT playgrounds decreased dramatically following the intervention. Prior to the intervention, a child on an average LIFT control or intervention playground exhibited six aversive physical behaviors during a 30-minute recess period. Following the intervention, children in the intervention group averaged 4.8 aversive behaviors per day, and children in the control group averaged 6.6 per day. On an average playground, these seemingly trivial differences in behavior rates translate into a dramatic decrease in exposure: A youth on an intervention playground was exposed to 1,700 fewer physically aversive events during the spring following the intervention than a youth on a control playground.

In terms of long-term effects, within 3 years following the intervention, youth in the fifth-grade control group were 2.2 times more likely to affiliate with misbehaving peers than youth who received the LIFT program. Fifth-grade control youth were also 1.8 times more likely to be involved in patterned alcohol use and 1.5 times more likely to have tried marijuana than LIFT youth. Finally, fifth-grade control youth were 2.4 times more likely to be arrested during middle school than LIFT youth.

DISCUSSION

The LIFT program was designed to integrate theoretically sound and practically promising preventive intervention techniques into a package that could be easily and inexpensively integrated into the day-to-day activities of an elementary school. In our original evaluation of the program, the parent, classroom, and playground components were well-liked by both parents and teachers, intervention fidelity was maintained across a wide spectrum of staff training and experience, and high participation rates were achieved. Further, under the conditions of a tightly controlled randomized evaluation, the LIFT has been demonstrated to impact the antecedents of delinquent behavior during elementary school and delinquent and other problem behaviors during adolescence. This impact appears to be strongest on the children exhibiting the highest rates of problem behaviors.

As clinical researchers, we are quite aware of the difficulties in changing antisocial behavior patterns. In fact, this awareness was one of the reasons that we, as a research group, began to be more interested not only in preventive work (Bank, Marlowe, Reid, Patterson, & Weinrott, 1991), but also in intensive individualized residential interventions such as Multidimensional Treatment Foster Care (Chamberlain & Reid, 1998). From this base of experience, the impact of the LIFT on high-rate children has been quite surprising to us. On reflection, several possible reasons are noted for this effect. First, children with extreme behavior problems tend to live in a social world that provides a rich array of reinforcers for their antisocial behaviors and few reinforcers for their positive behaviors. In targeting an entire school class in the LIFT, rather than individual children within a class, the density of reinforcement for positive behaviors for each of the individuals within the class becomes much higher. In turn, this behavioral milieu provides children with the highest level of problems the opportunity to develop a new set of behaviors. This opportunity would simply not be possible unless the majority of children and adults in a child's world were "on board" and working together to create a mutually beneficial positive environment. In effect, each of the individuals within the class becomes a treatment agent.

Second, the children with the highest level of problems may simply be more vulnerable to any stimuli in their environment. For these individuals, chaotic environments are particularly damaging (S. Kellam, personal communication, April 18, 1999). The structure that was imposed by the LIFT was apparently enough to assist some of these children in better managing their behaviors. For example, the slight changes in rates of aversive physical behavior on the playground actually led to rather large changes in overall exposure to risk (i.e., 1,700 less physically aversive events on the playground during the spring term). This lessening of cumulative exposure to noxious social interactions may have the largest payoffs for the most behaviorally vulnerable children.

Our findings on the LIFT parallel the recent findings of other researchers using similar techniques. For example, in a randomized controlled investigation of Second Step, a classroom-based skills training program that addresses many of the same issues addressed in the LIFT classroom component, Grossman et al. (1997) found that elementary school students in the prevention program group displayed significantly fewer physically aggressive behaviors at school following the completion of the program. Notably, however, this effect lasted less than 6 months after the program was completed.

More similar to the LIFT, a recent study by Webster-Stratton and Hammond (1997) investigated the joint impact of parent training and child social and problem-solving skills training. In contrast to the school-based LIFT and Second Step investigations, Webster-Stratton and Hammond conducted their investigation in a child clinic, and participants were 4- to 7-year-old children referred for conduct problems and their parents. The researchers contrasted the impact of a well-validated parent training intervention (Webster-Stratton, Kolpacoff, & Hollinsworth, 1988) with combined parent and child training. At 1-year follow-up, the combined intervention resulted in greater reductions in child problem behavior in the home than the parent training intervention alone. Unfortunately, neither of the intervention conditions had an appreciable effect on problem behaviors at school.

These examples illustrate the central shortcoming of many of the more popular "preventive" interventions of today: the bounding of an intervention within a time (e.g., a portion of a school year) or place (e.g., a mental health clinic) that has little relevance to a child soon after the intervention ends. If such interventions were powerful enough to cause fundamental changes within an individual, this bounding would be acceptable, at least in terms of changing the behaviors of the targeted individuals. However, we propose that interventions such as the Good Behavior Game or even child problem-solving and social skills training have their most powerful effects on a given social milieu as a whole, which in turn has effects on individuals within the milieu, rather than vice versa. When the individuals comprising the milieu change, new sets of social relationships and interactional patterns are established that may not provide support for positive behaviors, and the brief intervention that was done with some members of the new group becomes irrelevant. Unfortunately, if some of the new children who enter the milieu have well-developed repertoires of problem behaviors, the new pattern that is developed may be ruled by negative reinforcement patterns such as those discussed earlier. This is especially true in less structured settings such as the playground.

Certainly, an intact social group can carry forward the effects of an intervention (e.g., the families in Webster-Stratton and Hammond's [1997] study). However, we posit that intact social groups are sparse within many school settings. It is not uncommon for many of the classmates of a child and certainly his or her teacher to change on a yearly basis. Some of these changes are attributable to school planning efforts and others simply to the high mobility rate of the U.S. population at large.

For example, from the 12 original at-risk schools in the evaluation reported here, participants had dispersed into more than 70 schools by the beginning of the next school year. Two years later, participants had dispersed into more than 100 schools. Three years later, participants were dispersed into 150 schools. Clearly, many students in LIFT were in completely different peer social environments 1, 2, and 3 years after the intervention than they were during the intervention; thus, we would not expect the classroom and playground interventions to have much relevance in their day-to-day lives any longer. On the other hand, since parents were also involved in the LIFT, we hypothesized that overall we would find a lasting impact of the intervention on children, such as lower rates of involvement with deviant peers and lower arrest rates. To date, we have found support for this hypothesis. Whether the LIFT ultimately impacts the total frequency and content of delinquent behavior, including violence, throughout adolescence remains under investigation. Within the next 3 years, all participants in the fifth-grade cohort of the ongoing evaluation will reach the age of 19 years, so information on this important issue is forthcoming.

RECOMMENDATIONS

Establish and Maintain Preventive Interventions in Key Settings

Programs like the LIFT could be incorporated into school settings with relatively little difficulty. Many schools already provide some type of child problem-solving training within the regular curricula, and many school districts provide parents at least some opportunity during the year to attend parent education classes. All schools provide some type of monitoring of playground behavior and activities, and telephones are becoming increasingly common in classrooms. Through integration of these activities and resources in a standardized program such as LIFT, schools could prevent at least some students on the pathway to delinquency from escalating to more extreme forms of antisocial behavior. The emotional and financial toll saved through the prevention of even a seemingly small percentage of criminal acts can be quite substantial (see Greenwood, Model, & Rydell, 1996).

Such positive effects seem most likely if an entire school district, or a geographically associated set of school districts, provides LIFT-type services (i.e., yearly parent education, yearly child social and problem skills training, and daily playground monitoring, as well as one telephone/answering machine in each class) to students throughout the elementary school years. Given that many family moves are local (within a metropolitan area, a county, or a state), widening the reach of programs in such a manner would ensure that despite relocations, most children and families would receive the intervention. Youth delinquency and violence are behaviors that develop within and are maintained by a dynamic social context. Interventions that fail to attend to context on an ongoing basis are unlikely to have a lasting effect.

Intervene Simply with Theory in Mind

Interventions such as the LIFT are low-cost, simple, straightforward, and theoretically sound solutions to a complex and devastating problem. Certainly, a vast array of such solutions will be needed to address the overwhelming difficulties that youth face in the United States today. In concert, however, we believe that these types of efforts can make a difference. We close with an example that illustrates the importance of theoretically based simplicity.

Anybody who has experienced or studied bullies knows there are three types of participants in the process: the bully, the victim, and the observing nonparticipants. The latter are the ones who typically watch and laugh or who escalate arguments into fistfights with comments like, "Don't let him talk about your mother that way." These "nonparticipants," who rarely get in trouble, can turn cowardly, hurtful, and despicable behavior into high theater.

We once met a police chief in the city of London who described a problem he was having in his precinct. A number of adolescents were hanging out on a busy street corner, smoking, using offensive and sometimes threatening language, and refusing to make way for walkers, forcing them to step into the street in order to pass. Although this situation was frightening to neighborhood residents, and particularly to the elderly, the teenagers were technically within their rights as U.K. citizens to congregate wherever they liked. The police felt frustrated and had no legal power to deal with the problem. As the youngsters became more hostile to the police, the police found themselves tempted to escalate the situation in order to goad the leaders in the group into an illegal act that would justify arrest. Finally, an incident occurred, and a story accusing the police of misconduct appeared in the newspaper. The stalemate continued, and the frustration level of the police increased, as did the number of complaints by residents.

After some talking, we came up with the following plan. Although citizens can congregate where they please without any interference from police, the police have the right to ask anyone for identification, at any time. The officers were instructed to gather the names and addresses of the youth and the residents each time a problem was witnessed or reported. The police officers simply turned in the list of youngsters' names at the end of the shift. A form letter was sent to the home of each youngster, addressed to "The Parent(s) of _____." It was a cordial letter explaining that the youngster had done nothing illegal but that his or her behavior, and that of the group, was frightening to the elderly residents. The parents were asked if they could have a talk with the youngster to explain how the innocent behavior might make older folks uncomfortable.

Over a year later, we saw the officer at a conference, and he told us that the intervention was a complete success. Shortly after the first wave of form letters, the corner gang disappeared. At first glance, it is not obvious why the intervention would have any effects at all on the most antisocial members of the group. Although it is clear from the research literature that parental influence and supervision are powerful deterrents of adolescent delinquency and association with antisocial peers, it is also the case that the most severely delinquent teenagers are usually out of parental control. They spend most of their time and have their most meaningful relationships with kids who do not go to school and enjoy talking about delinquent activities. It is unlikely that the letters directly impacted these youth through their own parents.

However, the most delinquent youth do spend some of their time with less antisocial children, who to a greater or lesser degree might be classified as "wannabes." One could see how the younger and less antisocial kids (i.e., those whose parents still have influence on them) would respond to a strong parental demand to abandon the street corner and to stop harassing people. When the parents of the wannabes keep them home, the hard-core delinquent loses his street corner support system. And, the street corner support system is absolutely vital to the hard-core delinquent.

Chronic delinquents are probably best thought of as generals; take away the young recruits, and it is hard to have a war—or even a drill, for that matter. Thus, by working directly with those in the initial stages of antisocial development, we really are working on those youth who are further up the pipeline, not only by diverting children away from deviant peer involvement but also by decreasing the followers of those who have moved further down the line. Interventions like the LIFT appear to be one way to begin the process of successful diversion.

About the Authors

J. MARK EDDY, PhD, is a research scientist at the NIMH-funded Oregon Prevention Research Center, part of the Oregon Social Learning Center, a nonprofit research center that was formed in 1975 to conduct research on the development of aggression, delinquency, and violent behavior in Eugene. His research focuses on the development and refinement of interventions to prevent parent and child problem behaviors. He is currently the principal investigator of the Paths Project, which is examining the transition to young adulthood for serious juvenile offenders. **JOHN B. REID,** PhD, is currently the executive director of the Oregon Social Learning Center. Dr. Reid has acted as consultant for prisons and detention centers, taught at several universities, served on numerous editorial boards of professional journals, and served on private, state, and federal task forces to try to determine the most effective interventions for delinquency and antisocial behavior. He has chaired committees for NIMH and NIH to evaluate grant applications to do research on the development and prevention of delinquency. **REBECCA A. FETROW,** BS, is a research assistant at the Oregon Social Learning Center. She has been the director of operations for several NIMH-funded research projects at the Oregon Social Learning Center. She is currently overseeing the activities of the Oregon Prevention Research Center and the LIFT Program, which is a research intervention program designed to prevent the development of aggressive and antisocial behavior. Address: J. Mark Eddy, Oregon Social Learning Center, 160 E. 4th Ave., Eugene, OR 97401; e-mail: marke@oslc.org

Authors' Notes

1. Support for the development and evaluation of the LIFT was provided by grants MH 54248 and MH 46690 to John B. Reid from the Prevention and Behavioral Medicine Research Branch, Division of Epidemiology and Services Research, National Institutes of Mental Health, U.S. P.H.S. The opinions expressed are those of the authors and do not necessarily reflect those of the funding agency.

2. Special thanks to the children and their parents in the Bethel, Eugene 4J, and Springfield Public School districts; to district staff members Charles Stevens, Bob Lady, Robert Hammond, and Sue McNair-Gallup; and to the principals and teachers of the 12 participating schools.

3. Thanks to the many OSLC staff and research scientists for their leadership roles in various aspects of the LIFT project, and particularly to Kathy Jordan, Pat Wasp, and Mike Stoolmiller for their work on conceptualization and analyses and Linda Wallenius for her assistance with the manuscript.

References

Albee, G. W., & Gullota, T. P. (1997). Primary prevention's evolution. In G. W. Albee & T. P. Gullota (Eds.), *Primary prevention works: Issues in children's and families' lives, Vol. 6* (pp. 3–22). Thousand Oaks, CA: Sage.

Bank, L., Marlowe, J. H., Reid, J. B., Patterson, G. R., & Weinrott, M. R. (1991). A comparative evaluation of parent-training evaluations for families of chronic delinquents. *Journal of Abnormal Child Psychology, 19*, 15–33.

Barrish, H. H., Saunders, M., & Wolfe, M. D. (1969). Good behavior game: Effects of individual contingencies for group consequences and disruptive behavior in a classroom. *Journal of Applied Behavioral Analysis, 2*, 119–124.

Berleman, W. C., & Steinburn, T. W. (1969). The value and validity of delinquency prevention experiments. *Crime & Delinquency, 15*(4), 471–478.

Capaldi, D. M., & Patterson, G. R. (1996). Can violent offenders be distinguished from frequent offenders: Prediction from childhood to adolescence. *Journal of Research in Crime and Delinquency, 33*, 206–231.

Chamberlain, P., & Reid, J. B. (1998). Comparison of two community alternatives to incarceration for chronic juvenile offenders. *Journal of Consulting and Clinical Psychology, 66*(4), 624–633.

Cohen, J., & Cohen, P. (1983). *Applied multiple regression/correlation analysis for the behavioral sciences*. Hillsdale, NJ: Erlbaum.

Conduct Problems Prevention Research Group. (1992). A developmental and clinical model for the prevention of conduct disorder: The FAST Track Program. *Development and Psychopathology, 4*, 509–527.

Dolan, L. J., Kellam, S. G., Brown, C. H., Werthamer-Larsson, L., Rebok, G. W., Mayer, L. S., Laudolff, J., Turkkan, J. S., Ford, C., & Wheeler, L. (1993). The short-term impact of two classroom-based preventive interventions on aggressive and shy behaviors and poor achievement. *Journal of Applied Developmental Psychology, 14*, 317–345.

Eddy, J. M., Reid, J. B., Stoolmiller, M., & Fetrow, R. A. (2000). *Three year outcomes for a preventive intervention for conduct problems*. Manuscript submitted for publication.

Eddy, J. M., & Swanson Gribskov, L. (1997). Juvenile justice and delinquency prevention in the United States: The influence of theories and traditions on policies and practices. In T. P. Gullota, G. R. Adams, & R. Montemayor (Eds.), *Delinquent violent youth* (pp. 12–52). Thousand Oaks, CA: Sage.

Glueck, S., & Glueck, E. (1934). *One thousand juvenile delinquents: Their treatment by court and clinic*. Cambridge: Harvard University Press.

Greenwood, P. W., Model, K. E., & Rydell, C. P. (1996). *Diverting children from a life of crime: Measuring costs and benefits*. Berkeley: University of California.

Grossman, D. C., Neckerman, H. J., Koepsell, T. D., Liu, P., Asher, K. N., Beland, K., Frey, K., & Rivara, F. P. (1997). Effectiveness of a violence prevention curriculum among children in elementary school: A randomized controlled trial. *Journal of the American Medical Association, 27*, 1605–1611.

Hawkins, J. D., Von Cleve, E., & Catalano, R. F. (1991). Reducing early childhood aggression: Results of a primary prevention program. *Journal of the American Academy of Child and Adolescent Psychiatry, 30*(2), 208–217.

Hops, H., & Walker, H. M. (1988). CLASS: *Contingencies for learning academic and social skills*. Seattle, WA: Educational Achievement Systems.

Kellam, S. G., Werthamer-Larsson, L., Dolan, L. J., Brown, H., Mayer, L. S., Rebok, G. W., Anthony, J. C., Laudolff, J., Edelsohn, G., & Wheeler, L. (1991). Developmental epidemiologically based preventive trials: Baseline modeling of early target behaviors and depressive symptoms. *American Journal of Community Psychology, 19*(4), 563–584.

Klein, M. W. (1995). *The American street gang: Its nature, prevalence, and control*. New York: Oxford University Press.

Loeber, R., Green, S. M., Keenan, K., & Lahey, B. B. (1995). Which boys will fare worse? Early predictors of the onset of conduct disorder in a six-year longitudinal study. *Journal of the American Academy of Child and Adolescent Psychiatry, 34*, 499–509.

McCord, J. (1981). A longitudinal perspective on patterns of crime. *Criminology, 19*, 211–218.

McCord, J. (1992). The Cambridge-Somerville Study: A pioneering longitudinal experimental study of delinquency prevention. In J. McCord & R. E. Tremblay (Eds.), *Preventing antisocial behavior: Interventions from birth through adolescence* (pp. 196–206). New York: Guilford Press.

Meichenbaum, D., & Goodman, J. (1971). Training impulsive children to talk with themselves: A means of developing self-control. *Journal of Abnormal Psychology, 77*, 115–126.

Offord, D. (1997). Bridging development, prevention, and policy. In D. M. Stoff, J. Breiling, & J. D. Maser (Eds.), *Handbook of antisocial behavior* (pp. 357–364). New York: Wiley.

Olds, D. L., Hill, P. L., Mihalic, S. F., & O'Brien, R. A. (1998). *Prenatal and infancy home visitation by nurses*. Boulder, CO: Institute of Behavioral Science.

Oregon Department of Education. (1999). *Statistics and reports*. [On-line]. Available: http://www.ode.state.or.us/stats/index.htm

Patterson, G. R. (1974). Interventions for boys with conduct problems: Multiple settings, treatments, and criteria. *Journal of Consulting and Clinical Psychology, 42*, 471–481.

Patterson, G. R. (1982). *Coercive family process*. Eugene, OR: Castalia.

Patterson, G. R., & Chamberlain, P. (1994). A functional analysis of resistance during parent training therapy. *Clinical Psychology: Science and Practice, 1*, 53–70.

Patterson, G. R., Reid, J. B., & Dishion, T. J. (1992). *Antisocial boys*. Eugene, OR: Castalia.

Powers, E., & Witmer, H. (1951). *An experiment in the prevention of delinquency: The Cambridge-Somerville Youth Study*. New York: Columbia University Press.

Ramsey, E., Lathrop, M., Tharp, L., & Reid, J. B. (1994). *Linking the interests of families and teachers: Classroom social skills component grade 1*. Linking the Interest of Families and Teachers manual.

Reid, J. B., & Eddy, J. M. (1997). The prevention of antisocial behavior: Some considerations in the search for effective interventions. In D. M. Stoff, J. Breiling, & J. D. Maser (Eds.), *Handbook of antisocial behavior* (pp. 343–356). New York: Wiley.

Reid, J. B., Eddy, J. M., Fetrow, R. A., & Stoolmiller, M. (2000). Description and immediate impacts of a preventive intervention for conduct problems. *American Journal of Community Psychology, 27*(4), 483–517.

Schweinhart, L. J., & Weikart, D. P. (1988). The High/Scope Perry Preschool Program. In R. H. Price, E. L. Cowen, R. P. Lorion, & J. Ramos-McKay (Eds.), *14 ounces of prevention: A casebook for practitioners* (pp. 53–66). Washington, DC: American Psychological Association.

Sechrest, D. (1970). *The community approach*. Berkeley: University of California School of Criminology.

Shure, M. B., Spivack, G., & Jaeger, M. A. (1971). Problem solving thinking and adjustment among disadvantaged preschool children. *Child Development, 42,* 1791–1803.

Stoff, D. M., Breiling, J., & Maser, J. D. (Eds.). (1997). *Handbook of antisocial behavior.* New York: Wiley.

Stoolmiller, M., Eddy, J. M., & Reid, J. B. (2000). Detecting and describing preventive intervention effects in a universal school-based randomized trial targeting

delinquent and violent behavior. *Journal of Consulting and Clinical Psychology, 68*(2), 296–306.

Taylor, T. K., Eddy, J. M., & Biglan, A. (in press). *Skills training to reduce aggression, antisocial behavior, and delinquency: A review for practitioners and policymakers in education, mental health and juvenile justice.* Clinical Child and Family Psychology Review.

Tremblay, R. E., Pagani-Kurtz, L., Masse, L. C., Vitaro, F., & Pihl, R. O. (1995). A bimodal preventive intervention for disruptive kindergarten boys: Its impact through mid-adolescence. *Journal of Consulting and Clinical Psychology, 63*(4), 560–568.

Walker, H., Hops, H., & Greenwood, C. (1993). *RECESS: A program for reducing negative-aggressive behavior.* Seattle: Educational Achievement Systems.

Webster-Stratton, C., Kolpacoff, M., & Hollinsworth, T. (1988). Self-administered videotape therapy for families with conduct problem children: Comparison with two cost-effective treatments and a control group. *Journal of Consulting and Clinical Psychology, 56,* 558–566.

Webster-Stratton, C., & Hammond, M. (1997). Treating children with early-onset conduct problems: A comparison of child and parent training interventions. *Journal of Consulting and Clinical Psychology, 65,* 93–109.

APPENDIX:
CONTENT OF LINKING THE INTERESTS OF FAMILIES AND TEACHERS (LIFT) CLASSROOM AND PARENT COMPONENTS

Classroom Component

1. Relationship Fundamentals
   • Listening
   • Identifying feelings
   • Responding appropriately to others
   • Dealing with anger
   • Asking appropriate questions
   • Understanding and following rules
   • Giving and receiving compliments
   • Being flexible

2. Peer Group Skills
   • Joining a group
   • Cooperating within groups
   • Problem solving: Definition, brainstorming, evaluating, and trying solutions
   • Including new people in a group
   • Responding to closed groups

Parent Component

1. Discipline Fundamentals
   • Disengagement
   • Paying attention sooner rather than later
   • Appearing calm
   • Using small positive and negative consequences

2. Family Management Skills
   • Listening and tracking
   • Making effective requests
   • Controlling negative emotions
   • Giving encouragement
   • Defining cooperation
   • Making behavior-change contracts
   • Giving consequences: Time out, work chores, privilege removal
   • Networking with teachers and parents
   • Problem Solving: Definition, brainstorming, evaluating, and trying solutions

Multidimensional Treatment Foster Care:

A Program for Intensive Parenting, Family Support, and Skill Building

PHILIP A. FISHER AND PATRICIA CHAMBERLAIN

The goals, objectives, and philosophy of Multidimensional Treatment Foster Care (MTFC) are outlined in this article. Three specific mechanisms of the MTFC approach known to reduce conflict in the therapeutic milieu and to contribute to successful outcomes for youth and their families are described: a proactive approach to reducing problem behavior, the creation and maintenance of a consistent and reinforcing environment for the participating youth, and the separation and stratification of staff roles. Controlled outcome research comparing MTFC to other community treatment alternatives with similar populations of troubled youth are also described. Additionally, the results of preliminary research evaluating the impact of an MTFC model adapted to meet the needs of maltreated preschool-age children at entry to foster care are presented.

WITH THE ADVENT OF ACCOUNTability-based movements such as managed care, there has been an increased focus on the measurement and examination of the outcomes of community-based mental health and juvenile justice treatment services. This is a much-needed emphasis because currently the most widely used treatment approaches remain largely untested. For example, children and adolescents who are the most severely disturbed and/or delinquent are typically placed in congregate care settings such as group homes and residential treatment centers. This is a common practice in most communities, and the number of such placements is expanding, according to the Select Committee on Children, Youth, and Families (1990). The American Public Welfare Association estimates that approximately 70% of the total funding for children's mental health services is used for residential services.

The rationale for the use of residential placements is intuitively appealing: By removing troubled youth from their families and communities and placing them in settings in which the level of restrictiveness appears quite high, it should be possible to maximally impact their func-

tioning. Yet, little research exists on either the short-term effectiveness or long-term benefits of group-based residential care (Burns & Freidman, 1990; Chamberlain & Reid, 1998). Ironically, compared to other treatment and mental health service models, the least evidence of effectiveness exists for residential services, where the majority of dollars are spent (Burns, Hoagwood, & Maultsby, 1998).

There is reason to believe that children and adolescents with disruptive behavior problems, such as antisocial and aggressive symptoms, are among the most difficult populations to treat in residential settings and that they tend to benefit the least when compared to their nonantisocial counterparts in care (Zoccolillo & Rogers, 1991). A possible set

of explanations for this notion is that placement of such youth together in group settings actually increases their rates of problem behaviors possibly through mechanisms such as modeling and direct reinforcement of aggression. For example, Dishion and Andrews (1995) showed that boys with a history of early arrest were more likely to reinforce each other's antisocial or rule-breaking talk with laughter than were nonarrested boys. Peer support for aggressive behavior in the classroom has been shown to increase aggression (Guerra, Huesmann, Tolan, Van Acker, & Eron, 1995), and interaction with negative peers has been shown to predict later substance use (e.g., Dishion & Andrews, 1995; O'Donnell, Hawkins, & Abbott, 1995). McCord's (1997) reanalysis of the Cambridge-Somerville data showed that youth who attended summer camp with other antisocial boys were more likely to become adult offenders than youth who did not attend summer camp.

There is a growing body of empirical support for the relations between negative peer relations and adverse psychosocial outcomes (e.g., Elliott, Huizinga, & Ageton, 1985). Association with deviant peers has been shown to be a strong predictor of both initial involvement in and escalation of aggressive and delinquent behavior. Research in sociology and developmental psychology over the past 25 years supports the notion that youngsters who have strong bonds with delinquent peers are at far greater risk for becoming delinquent—and for escalating in delinquency over time—than those who associate with nondelinquent peers (Dishion, McCord, & Poulin, 1999; Elliot et al., 1985; Patterson, Reid, & Dishion, 1992).

In spite of this evidence, most community-based treatment models put youngsters with conduct problems or criminal histories together in groups that have the potential to facilitate further bonding and development of common social identities among group members. Clearly, a need exists for alternative treatment strategies. Multidimensional Treatment Foster Care (MTFC) represents such an alternative. MTFC is a model that has been shown to be effective with severely emotionally disturbed, antisocial children and adolescents who would otherwise be treated in congregate care settings (Chamberlain & Reid, 1998). MTFC capitalizes on more than 40 years of research and treatment activities that have supported the notion that families, and particularly parents who are skilled and supported, can have a powerful socializing role and positive influence on troubled youth (Chamberlain, 1994; Patterson, 1982; Patterson, Reid, & Dishion, 1992).

In this article, we provide details on the philosophy, goals, and objectives of MTFC. We also describe three mechanisms within the MTFC approach that contribute to successful outcomes for youth and their families and that are critical to reducing conflict within the therapeutic milieu. These mechanisms involve the following: a proactive approach to reducing problem behavior, the creation and maintenance of a consistent and reinforcing environment for participating youth, and the separation and stratification of staff roles. We describe the populations of troubled youth served through the MTFC model and provide information about the results of controlled outcome research comparing MTFC to other community treatment alternatives. We conclude by describing a recent adaptation of the MTFC model in order to meet the needs of maltreated preschool-age children and by presenting the results of preliminary research evaluating the impact of this program on the initial adjustment to foster care.

PROGRAM PHILOSOPHY, GOALS, AND OBJECTIVES

MTFC is based on the philosophy that for many youth who exhibit antisocial behavior, the most effective treatment is likely to take place in a community setting, in a family environment in which systematic control is exercised over the contingencies governing the youth's behavior. Indeed, families are intricately involved in the implementation of the MTFC model in two ways. First, MTFC parents are the primary treatment agents for program children and adolescents. Second, the youth's own biological/step/adoptive/relative families help shape their youngsters' treatment plan and participate in family therapy and home visits throughout placement to prepare for reunification with their child/adolescent at the program's end.

The objectives of the MTFC program are to provide youth who have serious and chronic problems with delinquency with close supervision, fair and consistent limits, predictable consequences for rule breaking, a supportive relationship with at least one mentoring adult, and limited exposure and access to delinquent peers. The goals are to decrease delinquent behavior and to increase participation in developmentally appropriate prosocial activities. Specific targets of MTFC treatment are listed in Table 1.

A PROACTIVE APPROACH TO REDUCING PROBLEM BEHAVIORS

A primary mechanism within the MTFC model that contributes to positive outcomes is the proactive approach taken to reducing problem behaviors. Several factors account for this effect. For example, program staff members pay close (daily) attention to the individual youth's progress/problems in the foster home and at school. Case managers—whose role is described later—carry smaller caseloads (e.g., 10–12 cases) than may be typical within most social service agencies. Although lower caseloads may raise concerns about cost, the population in treatment is at such a high risk for being a long-term burden to society that these concerns are unwarranted. Indeed, an evaluation of the cost-effectiveness of MTFC revealed that it produced substantial savings in costs to taxpayers because the cost of the program was more than mitigated by criminal justice system costs that were avoided (a total savings of $5,815 per youth; Washington State Institute for Public Policy, 1998). An additional $11,760 was saved per youth in terms of reduced crime victim costs. Thus, cost-effectiveness clearly favors the MTFC approach.

MTFC parents are carefully recruited, and a high level of preservice training as well as ongoing support and supervision is provided to them. Throughout the treatment process, MTFC parents, who are the eyes and ears of the program, maintain close communication with the case manager. The parents help identify target behaviors and formulate treatment plans. MTFC parents are strongly and repeatedly encouraged to call the case manager at any hour of the day or night if they are concerned or have a question about the child placed with them. MTFC parents participate with program staff in daily data collection on child problems/progress and program implementation via the Parent Daily Report (PDR) calls. They participate in weekly supervision/support meetings with their case manager and other MTFC parents. MTFC parents have substantially influenced the

TABLE 1
Areas Targeted by Multidimensional Treatment Foster Care

- Reinforce normative and prosocial behaviors

- Provide the youth with close supervision

- Closely monitor peer associations

- Specify clear and consistent limits and follow through on rule violations with nonviolent consequences

- Encourage youth to develop positive work habits and academic skills

- Support family members to increase the effectiveness of their parenting skills

- Decrease conflict between family members

- Teach youth new skills for forming relationships with positive peers and for bonding with adult mentors and role models

program design and implementation methods over the years.

Foster Parent Recruitment

MTFC parents are recruited through a variety of methods; word-of-mouth and newspaper advertising have been the most successful. Existing MTFC parents are paid a "finder's fee" of $100 for referring new families to the program. Newspaper ads are most successful if they include a description of the age and gender of the child to be placed and the amount of the monthly stipend that MTFC parents will be given. Interested MTFC parents are first screened by telephone for basic eligibility (e.g., adequate space in their home, no previous criminal history). Next, they are sent an application. Following return of the application, the MTFC recruiter conducts a home visit. During the home visit, the recruiter provides a complete explanation of the program and explains the training and certification requirements to prospective MTFC parents. The purpose of the home visit is to meet the prospective family, to see if their home atmosphere is conducive to caring for a disturbed or delinquent youngster, and to give them more information about the program. Many families who are suitable for "regular" foster care are not good MTFC parents. In MTFC, the parents must be

willing to take an active treatment perspective, to work with the program in implementing a daily structured program for the youngster, and to work with a delinquent or disturbed youngster. In the 15 years that we have run the program, we have worked with families from all walks of life. Single parents and married couples with and without children of their own have been successful MTFC parents. Although we have conducted no formal research on selection factors, the individual and family characteristics that seem related to success in working with our most difficult youth include an ability to take another person's perspective, a good knowledge of child and adolescent development (often acquired through raising one's own children), and a healthy sense of humor. The recruiter makes an informal assessment of these characteristics during the home visit. Families who appear to be unsuitable are referred to the local child welfare office to participate in providing "regular" foster care or are discouraged from continuing in the process.

Preservice Training of MTFC Parents

MTFC parents participate in a 20-hour preservice training, which includes an overview of the model. During the preservice training, we teach a four-step ap-

proach to analyzing behavior (knowing when a problem is a problem, developing a clear behavioral description of that problem, identifying what precedes the behavior, and identifying antecedents to the behavior), demonstrate and discuss procedures for implementing an individualized daily program with youth, review methods for working with the child's biological family, and explain MTFC policies and procedures. The training methods used are didactic and experiential. During the training, we place a great deal of emphasis on methods and techniques for reinforcing and encouraging youth. Prospective MTFC parents who are resistant to the idea of giving youngsters extra support and attention for doing what they are supposed to do are discouraged from continuing. Many well-intentioned people feel that providing daily incentives for achievement undermines an individual's basic motivation. Because daily encouragement is such an important component of our MTFC programs, we are insistent that families share or at least do not oppose this philosophy.

Ongoing Consultation, Support, and Supervision

Following the preservice training, a match is made between prospective MTFC parents and youth. The MTFC parents are given all of the information that the program has on the child, including the case file to review, so that they are fully informed about the youth's history. If a match is made, the youth's individualized daily program is developed by the case manager in concert with the MTFC parents.

Throughout the placement, foster parents receive continued support in addressing new problems via weekly support group meetings with program staff and other foster parents, daily telephone calls from program staff members to inquire about behaviors that have occurred in the past 24 hours, and (in the initial stages of treatment) weekly home visits from program staff members. In addition, program staff members are available 24 hours a day to provide back-up support to the foster parents. All staff members carry pagers or cellular phones and will go to the home if the problem cannot be managed over the telephone.

A Consistent, Reinforcing Environment for the Youth

A second mechanism for facilitating positive treatment outcomes is the implementation of an individualized, detailed behavior management program within the foster home. This daily program specifies the schedule of activities and behavioral expectations and assigns a number of points the youth can earn for satisfactory performance. The points are the concrete way that MTFC parents provide the youth with positive feedback about his or her progress. The goal of the behavior management program is to give MTFC parents a vehicle for providing the youngster with frequent, positive reinforcement for normative and prosocial behavior and to give the youngster a clear message about how he or she is doing.

The program implemented in the MTFC home involves the use of a three-level point system by which the youth are provided with structured daily feedback. Points are earned throughout the day for expected activities, including going to class on school days. Points are lost for rule infractions, including small "violations" such as not listening to an adult or having a surly attitude. The economy of the point system is set up to emphasize positive achievements, including participating in the developmental tasks associated with youngsters in this age group. We train MTFC foster parents to take points away in a matter-of-fact or slightly sympathetic way. They are specifically taught to refrain from lecturing or arguing and on methods to disengage if the youngster initiates an argument.

Level 1 lasts for approximately 3 weeks or until the youth earns a total of 2,100 points. On Level 1, the youth earns points for routine daily activities, such as getting out of bed on time in the morning, getting ready for school, doing a short chore, doing homework, having a mature attitude, attending classes at school, having a cooperative attitude in school, and other behaviors that are designated by the MTFC parents and the program staff. Points earned one day are traded for privileges on the following day. On Level 1, daily point totals are also tracked to determine when the youth is eligible for advancing to Level 2. On Level 2, points are accumulated over a week's time and applied to an expanded list of privileges that can be earned during the following week. On Level 3, privileges are expanded further and include opportunities for youngsters to be involved in community activities without direct adult supervision. An example of a daily point chart is shown in Figure 1.

Separation and Stratification of Staff Roles

The third mechanism within MTFC that is aimed at reducing conflict and facilitating positive outcomes involves the separation and stratification of staff roles. In many youth treatment programs, staff members are assigned a "generalist" role; that is, they work across multiple domains that may include youth therapy, family therapy, other agencies providing services, and foster parent consultation. It has been our experience that when working with severely delinquent and/or behaviorally disordered youngsters, this model is often insufficient. Various factors, including the complexity of the families receiving services through MTFC, the high level of conflict among family members, the severity of the youth's behavioral problems, and the likelihood that the family will be involved with multiple other service providers, have a tendency to place generalist staff members in positions in which they must continuously balance opposing needs of different constituencies. Within this context, it is challenging to develop and maintain a trusting relationship with any of the parties involved in treatment; conflict is common between the youth and foster parents, between the biological parents and family therapist, or between other involved parties.

A distinguishing characteristic of MTFC is its use of a treatment team (in which roles are clearly defined) to carry out the treatment plan for each youth. As discussed below, the treatment team includes behavior support specialists, youth therapists, family therapists, consulting psychiatrists, PDR callers, and case managers/clinical team supervisors. Little overlap is found in the responsibilities of team members. This helps to reduce confusion about whose role it is to carry out specific tasks. Staff members advocate the needs of those with whom they work. This ensures that the youth, biological parents, foster parents, and other service providers have a voice in the treatment process.

In addition to a separation of staff roles, there is also stratification, that is, multiple layers of staff involvement with the child, the family, and the foster family. For example, it is common for conflict to arise between youth and their foster parents over a number of issues. If only one staff member is working with the family, that individual must mediate this conflict and try to balance the needs of the child and the foster parents. It is often difficult for staff to emerge from such a situation without angering or offending someone. Within the stratified MTFC model, when a conflict arises, the next layer of involvement might be for the child to phone his or her therapist. Often, the therapist's support provides critical cooling-off time and diffuses the conflict. When it does not, it is possible to involve the case manager/clinical supervisor (another layer of involvement). This staff member can support the foster parents in their efforts to resolve the conflict and can work with the child therapist to better understand the youth's point of view. If it is necessary to meet to discuss the problem, foster parents and youth have an advocate. By slowing down the process and providing support to all involved, conflicts rarely escalate to a point that threatens the foster placement. Moreover, conflicts appear to decrease in frequency over time.

The stratification of staff roles also helps to respond strategically to treatment resistance. Such resistance may re-

SCHOOL DAYS LEVEL II CARD

Name: _____ Day: _____ Date: _____

THINGS TO DO TO EARN POINTS	EARNED	BONUS	TAKEN	TOTAL
UP ON TIME (10 pts.)				
READY IN MORNING (10 pts.)				
MORNING CLEAN-UP (10 pts.)				
GO TO SCHOOL (1 pt./Class)				
CARRY SCHOOL CARD (4 pts./Class)				
BEHAVIOR IN CLASS (5 pts./Class)				
READ AND STUDY (20 pts.)				
ATTITUDE/MATURITY A.M. (15 pts.)				
ATTITUDE/MATURITY P.M. (15 pts.)				
CHORE (10 pts.)				
LAST WORD (2-10 pts.)				
NOT NAGGING (2-10 pts.)				
NOT ARGUING (2-10 pts.)				
COMPLAINING (2-10 pts.)				
VOLUNTEERING (10 pts.)				
BED ON TIME (10 pts.)				

DAILY TOTAL _____

FIGURE 1. Multidimensional Treatment Foster Care behavior management program daily point chart.

side in the youth, the biological parents, or the foster parents. For instance, it is typical for parents to be given homework assignments in family therapy that involve various behavior management strategies. Some parents struggle to complete these assignments. However, it can be counterproductive for the therapist to confront parents about their noncompliance. In these situations, the case manager/clinical supervisor will play an authoritative role, contacting the parents and pushing for them to complete assignments. Throughout this process, the family therapist will continue to support the parents, joining with them to figure out how to comply with the demands of the program. Thus, not only does stratification reduce conflict between the youth and others, but it also helps to reduce conflict between biological/foster parents and program staff. In the section that follows, we provide descriptions of staff roles.

Behavior Support Specialist (BSS)

These staff members teach the youth prosocial behavior and problem-solving skills through intensive one-on-one interaction and skill practice in the community. For example, some delinquent youth attract negative attention and suspicion to themselves as they enter a place of business because of their gait, their style of dress, their lack of eye contact, or their manner in speaking to employees. A BSS would practice the skills for entering a store and asking for help with a youth. The youth would then go out to a store and practice these skills, and the BSS would provide reinforcement and feedback to the youth. School is another setting in which a BSS is useful, especially with youth for whom school has been a generally negative experience. A BSS can help youth learn appropriate classroom behavior and conflict resolution skills.

BSSs are trained to use applied behavior analysis as a way of examining potential antecedents to, and reinforcers for, problem behavior in the youth's environment. They are also instructed in the use of shaping procedures to teach new behaviors. The implementation of BSS interventions often is based on behavioral contracting with the youth, such as a reward for a certain number of days occurring without a particular problem (as reported by the foster parents).

Youth Therapist

Initially, the primary role of this staff member is to serve as an advocate and support person as the youth adjusts to life in the foster home. Many MTFC youth, despite their "tough" demeanor, are highly anxious when they are first placed in the program. Additionally, many youth have poor social skills and are unable to advocate for themselves effectively. The youth therapist also participates in the therapy process with the biological family (see below), again serving primarily as an advocate for the youth. This is especially helpful in families in which there is a great deal of conflict and in which treatment sessions can be very chaotic and emotional. Finally, in some circumstances, youth may address issues of past maltreatment or family of origin with their therapist. However, this typically does not occur until the youth has spent some time in the foster home and his or her behavior has stabilized.

Family Therapist

A key component to the success of the MTFC program is the degree to which the youth can generalize from the gains made during treatment to post-treatment environments. Parents (or other adult guardians) are the primary social agents who determine the quality and consistency of this generalization in aftercare. Our analyses show that to the extent that the youth is not allowed to have unsupervised time with delinquent peers and experiences thorough supervision, he or she is reinforced for appropriate/positive behaviors, and parents are consistent and fair in discipline for rule violations and misbehavior, the youth will engage in less criminal behavior in follow-up. Although it is tempting to think that participation in the program fundamentally changes delinquent youth, the fact is that without continued parental (or adult) support and socialization in follow-up, gains do not remain. Therefore, teaching parents how to effectively supervise, discipline, and encourage their child is a major task undertaken during the placement in MTFC.

The components of the parent management training model (PMT) that we use are adapted from those that have been previously developed and tested with families of antisocial children and adolescents (Taylor, Eddy, & Biglan, 1999). In the MTFC program, we include the basic components of PMT, including first establishing a consulting role with the youth's parents. Many of the families have had multiple experiences with service providers and may be working currently with a number of agencies in addition to the MTFC program. For many of these families, their experiences with social service agencies have ranged from neutral to poor and have involved blame, confrontation, avoidance, and other negative events. Thus, it is important that the therapist develop an alliance with the family and establish a relationship that is supportive and constructive prior to introducing parent training techniques.

The family therapist works with parents to plan and implement strategies that increase reinforcement for positive/appropriate youth behavior. The therapist works with parents to help them understand the necessity of providing their youngster with close supervision and to develop methods for doing so that take into consideration the logistical constraints parents face. Parents are instructed in procedures for following through on rule violations and misbehavior with fair and consistent discipline. Finally, the family therapist emphasizes the necessity for the youth to associate with nondelinquent peers.

As with most PMT models, we emphasize the in-home practice of skills talked about in treatment sessions. As the parent learns particular skills, supervised visits with the child at the treatment center are initiated. As multiple skills are learned, the visits lengthen and then transition to the family's home. Parents have specific practice assignments that they implement during the youth's home visits. Not only do parents and youth have a chance to try out new ways of relating through these assignments, but also the balance of power gradually shifts. Additionally, the youth is more accepting of the guidance and support provided by the parent. Ultimately, home visits extend to overnight and then weekend visits. Provided that this process occurs without further maltreatment of the child, family reunification occurs. The family therapist maintains contact with the family during this transition and for anywhere from 1 to 3 months following reunification.

Consulting Psychiatrist

Many MTFC youth enter the program with multiple diagnoses that include disruptive behavior disorders such as conduct disorder and attention-deficit disorder, as well as posttraumatic stress disorder, depression, dysthymia, bipolar disorder, and obsessive–compulsive disorder. Often, along with these diagnoses come complex medication regimens that have developed as the youth has transitioned from one setting to another. Although it is possible to refer these youth for medication evaluations to providers in the community, the ability to consult directly with a psychiatrist who is familiar with the program elements is extremely useful. It allows for a careful examination of the accuracy of diagnoses as well as a clarification of the specific medications judged most effective for addressing particular symptoms. Working together, the psychiatrist and program staff members are able to evaluate the impact of medication changes on the child's functioning. Consequently, once the child or youth has stabilized in the foster home, it is often possible to greatly reduce the number and dosage of medications.

PDR Caller

Because a high level of contact with foster parents is so critical to the success of treatment, the MTFC model employs a staff member whose role is to contact foster families each day via telephone. During the phone conversation, the staff member reviews a behavior checklist called the Parent Daily Report (PDR; Chamberlain & Reid, 1987). The PDR consists of a list of 40 items that reflect problem behaviors exhibited by disruptive children. Foster parents are asked to indicate which of the behaviors occurred in the past 24 hours. The checklist takes approximately 5 minutes for the foster parent and PDR caller to complete. The information gathered is then sent to the case manager along with notes about any additional information that the foster parent provided during the phone call. PDR information provides a thumbnail sketch of the youth's functioning and can be used to track progress or to identify problematic patterns of behavior. PDR has also been found to be a useful instrument for program evaluation research. Because the PDR interview is highly structured, it is possible to recruit and hire PDR callers with solid interpersonal skills but relatively limited clinical experience.

Case Manager/Clinical Team Supervisor

The case manager/clinical team supervisor pulls together and organizes all aspects of the MTFC treatment. This person is the leader of the treatment team and is the primary advocate for the MTFC parents. Given the disparate roles of the team members, a key role of the case manager is to oversee and integrate the activities of the team. The clinical supervisor works to ensure that all team members are following the same treatment protocol, that team members are informed about the activities of all others, and that the needs and concerns of all parties—youth, foster parents, and biological families—are being heard. Although the treatment team may not maintain a strict hierarchy, the clinical supervisor is the team leader. Therefore, this individual ultimately articulates the treatment plan, resolves disputes among team members, and sets the tone for the treatment process. Within the MTFC model, this individual is typically someone who has had experience in a number of the other roles on the team prior to becoming a clinical supervisor and who can provide insight into the particular tensions involved in providing effective treatment.

Given the multidisciplinary nature of the team, effective communication is essential for treatment to proceed smoothly. This communication occurs through weekly team meetings, through electronic mail (e-mail), and through informal conversations among team members. A strong emphasis is placed on maintaining a high level of information sharing so that consistency of treatment across team members can occur. Although this approach may appear to be somewhat labor- and personnel-intensive, the long-term benefits of effective early intervention may well provide justification for the utilization of these resources. In addition, because of the clarity in which roles are defined and the ability of staff to focus intensively on the needs of the youth and adults involved in treatment, the turnover rate for staff is quite low and morale is quite high.

POPULATIONS SERVED

The population most well-researched by the Oregon Social Learning Center (OSLC) MTFC programs are youth referred from the juvenile justice system because of severe and chronic delinquency problems. Since 1983, over 250

such youth have been served in OSLC's Monitor Program. Monitor participants are 12- to 17-year-olds who have an average of 13 previous arrests, including 4.6 previous felonies. Youth are admitted into the MTFC program from juvenile detention and stay an average of 6 to 9 months. Monitor youth attend public schools with close supervision from the program staff. Their attendance, behavior, and homework completion are carefully monitored on a daily basis. Fifty-five percent are receiving special education services. From 1990 to 1996, we evaluated the Monitor program in a clinical trial in which 79 boys were randomly assigned to the Monitor Program or to one of 11 group homes located throughout the state.

Three years after the beginning of Monitor, in 1986, we conducted a randomized clinical trial with children 9 to 18 years old who were leaving the Oregon State Hospital Child and Adolescent Treatment Program. After referral to the OSLC Transitions program, they were randomly assigned to participate in MTFC or in a "treatment as usual" condition. Based on the results of that study, we continued to accept referrals from our local Child Welfare branch and state offices and received Medicaid funding to provide MTFC services.

In 1994, in response to an increasing number of referrals of young children (ages 3–7), we developed the Early Intervention Foster Care (EIFC) program. The source of these referrals is the state child protective services system; consequently, maltreatment/neglect is a commonality among all cases. The EIFC program targets behavior problems from a perspective that is developmentally appropriate for young children. In addition, interventions are designed to facilitate the development of the child's emotion regulation capabilities and to remediate developmental delays that commonly co-occur with maltreatment. With the exception that a higher rate of sibling groups are referred to this program and that more work is conducted using a home visit model of service delivery, EIFC program elements remain much

the same as MTFC. The EIFC program is described in greater detail in Fisher, Ellis, and Chamberlain (1999).

Another special population that we serve using MTFC are youth who have borderline intellectual functioning and a history of problems with inappropriate sexual behavior, including aggression. These youth are screened and referred through a central committee at the State Child Welfare Office (State Office for Services to Children and Families: SCF).

EVALUATION OF OUTCOMES

The MTFC model has been evaluated in five previous studies. Here we will report findings from one of the two randomized clinical trials (i.e., outcomes for juvenile offenders; Chamberlain & Reid, 1998). The other randomized trial examined the relative effectiveness of MTFC for a group of 9- to 17-year-old youngsters who were leaving the state mental hospital (Chamberlain & Reid, 1991). The matched comparison group design study that we will describe examined the relative effectiveness of MTFC involving young abused/neglected children with severe behavioral and emotional problems.

MTFC for Juvenile Offenders

From 1991 to 1996, a total of 79 boys who the juvenile court mandated to out-of-home care were randomly assigned to MTFC or Group Care (GC). In GC programs, boys lived with from 6 to 15 other boys in family-style group homes, in stand-alone group homes, or in cottages on the grounds of larger institutions. Most boys in GC participated in daily group therapy. Most programs used variations of the Positive Peer Culture model, where peers were expected to participate in daily governance and decision making. Boys' families participated in family therapy in 40% of the cases, and boys participated in individual therapy in 53% of the cases. Eleven group homes located throughout the state of Oregon participated in the study.

Data on official arrest rates at 1 year postdischarge showed that boys in

MTFC had significantly fewer arrests than boys in GC ($M = 2.6$ and 5.4 arrests, respectively). Postdischarge self-reports of delinquent activities also showed that boys in MTFC reported engaging in significantly fewer delinquent activities, including serious and person crimes, than boys in GC ($M = 12.8$ and 28.9 self-reported criminal activities, respectively). Boys in MTFC also spent fewer days incarcerated than did boys in GC ($M = 53$ and 129 days, respectively), and they ran away from their placements less often ($M = 18$ and 36 days, respectively).

Two-year postdischarge data are available from 76% of the sample. So far, results continue to favor boys in MTFC. For example, significantly more boys in MTFC reported to be working in legal jobs, to have positive relationships with their parents, and to have refrained from unprotected sex than did boys in GC. In addition, boys in MTFC reported using hard drugs and marijuana significantly less often than boys in GC. Boys in MTFC continued to be arrested at significantly lower rates than boys in GC.

Analyses are under way to examine the effect(s) of mediating variables on MTFC treatment outcomes. For example, we hypothesized that the boys' rate of contact with delinquent peers during placement would predict criminal behavior in follow-up. In addition, we hypothesized that supervision and consistent discipline during treatment and having a quality relationship with a prosocial adult would be protective factors in terms of subsequent criminality. These analyses will begin to identify which factors or practices are active or are key ingredients in successful versus unsuccessful treatment as measured by the boys' desistance or continuance in criminal activities.

EIFC Evaluation Results

The EIFC program was the subject of a 1-year pilot evaluation, funded by the National Institutes of Mental Health (NIMH) Child and Adolescent Prevention Research Branch. The purpose of this study was to gather preliminary evi-dence of the effectiveness of the EIFC model. The study focused on the transitional period during the 3 months following placement in a new foster home. Of the 30 children who participated in the study, 10 were clients in the EIFC program, 10 were children in regular foster care (RFC), and 10 were typically developing children living with their biological families in a community comparison condition (CC). Results are reported in greater detail in Fisher, Gunnar, Chamberlain, and Reid (1999).

Consistent with MTFC research, the study hypotheses centered on the mediating role that parenting practices play in determining outcomes. It was hypothesized that to the extent that the EIFC foster parents show higher levels of consistent discipline, monitor the child's whereabouts, and provide greater positive reinforcement than RFC foster parents, more positive outcomes would be observed in the EIFC children. Moreover, because of the training, support, and supervision of EIFC foster parents, it was expected that their behavior toward foster children would look similar to that of the CC parents and that the outcomes for EIFC children would look similar to those of CC children.

Although the EIFC program targets specific behaviors, emotion regulation, and developmental delays, we did not examine developmental delays as an outcome variable because we did not anticipate changes in that area during the period of adjustment to the new foster home. However, our results did replicate previous findings that maltreatment of young children results in developmental delays (Landsverk, in press): Children in the EIFC and RFC groups were significantly behind children in the CC group on a measure of developmental status.

Outcome analyses revealed a positive impact of the intervention on foster parents' parenting strategies. At both the initial assessment (3 weeks after the child was placed) and the final assessment (12 weeks later), the EIFC and CC groups were observed to employ similar levels of consistent discipline, positive reinforcement, and monitoring, and their scores on these measures were significantly higher than those in the RFC group. In addition, EIFC foster parents' stress in responding to child behavior decreased from initial through final assessments, whereas RFC foster parents' stress increased. This produced a marginally significant interaction effect ($p = .08$).

In terms of the youth, their scores on a symptom checklist that foster/biological parents reported over time increased for the RFC group, whereas they decreased for the EIFC group (and decreased marginally for the CC group), yielding significant group and Group × Time interaction effects. In order to assess emotion regulation, we collected salivary cortisol at weekly intervals throughout the 12 weeks of participation in the study. Extensive evidence shows that the brain systems involved in the production of cortisol (specifically, the Limbic-Hypothalamic-Pituitary-Adrenal axis) are active in emotional regulatory processes and that they function in response to stress (Stansbury & Gunnar, 1994). Perhaps more relevant to the present study, these systems have been shown to be impacted by maltreatment (Golier & Yehuda, 1998). We thought it was important to examine (a) whether the foster children in our sample had cortisol levels similar to those previously found and (b) whether the intervention might be able to change cortisol levels.

Our results were, in a preliminary manner, consistent with our hypotheses. Both foster care groups had higher cortisol levels than the CC group initially. The EIFC group, which had the most severe maltreatment history, also showed a disruption to their daily release patterns at the initial assessment. Whereas cortisol is typically at highest levels in the morning and decreases throughout the day, EIFC children showed a modified "U-shape" pattern in which scores were highest in the morning, decreased through midday, but then increased slightly by bedtime. Interestingly, this pattern was replaced by the typical pattern by the time of the final assessment. In addition, repeated measures multivariate analyses of variance comparing weekly cortisol levels revealed trends of increasing cortisol for the RFC group and decreasing cortisol for the EIFC group over time.

These results are promising in that they suggest the possibility of bringing about physiological changes related to emotion regulation through an environmental intervention. However, it is important to note limitations to this study. In addition to the small number of participants, we were not able to randomize the EIFC and RFC participants. Thus, participant-specific explanations for these results cannot be ruled out. Further research is planned that will include random assignments, more participants, and a greater study interval.

SUMMARY AND CONCLUSIONS

The evidence gathered thus far suggests not only that MTFC may be an effective approach for treating delinquent adolescents in a community setting but that it may have the flexibility to facilitate positive change in other populations of troubled children as well. The emphasis of our ongoing work is in three areas. First, we continue to follow the youth who have participated in our treatment evaluation studies in order to determine how they progress through various developmental transitions. It is critical that we understand whether these interventions are effective over the long term or whether their impact is relatively short-lived. As noted, the results we have obtained thus far are promising. Second, the MTFC model continues to be extended to other populations. For example, one group that might be especially well suited are teen parents, who might be placed in foster homes along with their children. This context might facilitate the introduction of positive parenting skills in a much more naturalistic milieu than traditional parenting classes. Other populations include infants and toddlers with special needs and youth with dual diagnoses that included substance abuse and some other problem. As with our previous work, a primary goal for extensions of the MTFC model is the development of bases of empirical sup-

port for the use of the approach with a particular population. Understanding the potential and the limits of the MTFC model is important. Finally, we are also committed to the dissemination of the MTFC model to community-based mental health agencies and social service organizations. Clearly, for this approach to have a broad impact, it must prove viable outside of the context in which it was developed. To that end, we are collaborating in partnerships with community organizations around the country to introduce MTFC programs. The individual qualities of specific communities such as rural versus urban location, availability of resources, and ethnic diversity (or lack thereof) will undoubtedly necessitate some adaptations to the model. These in turn will need to be tested empirically. Although these efforts are mostly in a preliminary stage, the process is both interesting and rewarding, and the outlook is promising.

About the Authors

PHILIP A. FISHER, PhD, a research scientist and licensed psychologist, is particularly interested in prevention in the early years of life. He is principal investigator on the Early Intervention Foster Care Project, a 5-year randomized trial funded by NIMH to test the effectiveness of a preventive intervention for maltreated preschool-age foster children that examines how the intervention impacts multiple domains, including behavior, emotions, and neurophysiology (specifically, HPA axis activity, frontal lobe function, and memory). PATRICIA CHAMBERLAIN, PhD, is founder and director of the Oregon Social Learning Center's Treatment Foster Care (TFC) programs, which have served severely disturbed and chronically delinquent youth since 1983. She has published numerous articles on TFC and is currently conducting an NIMH-funded study on the effectiveness of TFC with females referred from the juvenile justice sysem. Address: Philip A. Fisher, Oregon Social Learning Center, 160 E. 4th Avenue, Eugene, OR 97401-2426; e-mail: philf@oslc.org

Authors' Note

Support for this project was provided by Grant No. RO1 MH59780, NIMH, U.S. PHS; Grant No. RO3 MH56932, NIMH, U.S. PYS.; and Grant No. RO1 HD19739, NICHD, U.S. PHS., to the first author. Additional support was provided by Grant No. RO1 MH54257, NIMH, U.S. PHS.; and Grant No. RO1 MH59127, NIMH, U.S. PHS.; to the second author, and by Grant No. P50 MH46690, NIMH, U.S. PHS. The opinions expressed are those of the authors and do not necessarily reflect those of the funding agency.

References

Burns, B. J., & Freidman, R. M. (1990). Examining the research base for children's mental health services and policy. *The Journal of Mental Health Administration, 17,* 87–99.

Burns, B. J., Hoagwood, K., & Maultsby, L. T. (1998). Improving outcomes for children and adolescents with serious emotional and behavioral disorders: Current and future directions. In M. H. Epstein, K. Kutash, & A. J. Duchnowski (Eds.), *Community-based programming for children with serious emotional disturbance and their families: Research and evaluations* (pp. 685–707). Austin, TX: PRO-ED.

Chamberlain, P. (1994). *Family connections: Treatment foster care for adolescents with delinquency.* Eugene, OR: Castalia.

Chamberlain, P., & Reid, J. B. (1987). Parent observation and report of child symptoms. *Behavioral Assessment, 9,* 97–109.

Chamberlain, P., & Reid, J. B. (1991). Using a Specialized Foster Care treatment model for children and adolescents leaving the state mental hospital. *Journal of Community Psychology, 19,* 266–276.

Chamberlain, P., & Reid, J. (1998). Comparison of two community alternatives to incarceration for chronic juvenile offenders. *Journal of Consulting and Clinical Psychology, 6*(4), 624–633.

Dishion, T. J., & Andrews, D. W. (1995). Preventing escalation in problem behaviors with high risk young adolescents: Immediate and 1-year outcomes. *Journal of Consulting and Clinical Psychology, 63,* 538–548.

Dishion, T. J., McCord, J., & Poulin, F. (1999). When interventions harm: Peer groups and problem behavior. *American Psychologist, 54,* 755–764.

Elliott, D. S., Huizinga, D., & Ageton, S. S. (1985). *Explaining delinquency and drug use.* Newbury Park, CA: Sage.

Fisher, P. A., Ellis, B. H., & Chamberlain, P. (1999). Early intervention foster care: A model for preventing risk in young children who have been maltreated. *Children Services: Social Policy, Research, and Practice, 2*(3), 159–182.

Fisher, P. A., Gunnar, M. R., Chamberlain, P., & Reid, J. B. (1999). *Specialized foster care for maltreated preschoolers: Impact on behavior and neuroendocrine activity.* Manuscript submitted for publication.

Golier, J., & Yehuda, R. (1998). Neuroendocrine activity and memory-related impairments in posttraumatic stress disorder. *Development and Psychopathology, 10,* 857–871.

Guerra, N. G., Huesmann, L. R., Tolan, P. H., Van Acker, R., & Eron, L. D. (1995). Stressful events and individual beliefs as correlates of economic disadvantage and aggression among urban children. *Journal of Consulting and Clinical Psychology, 63*(4), 518–528.

Landsverk, J. (in press). Foster care and pathways to mental health services. In P. Curtis & G. Dale, Jr. (Eds.), *The foster care crisis: Translating research into practice and policy.* Lincoln: The University of Nebraska Press.

McCord, J. (1997, April). *Some unanticipated consequences of summer camp.* Paper presented at the meeting of the Society for Research on Child Development Symposium, Washington, DC.

O'Donnell, J., Hawkins, D. J., & Abbott, R. D. (1995). Predicting serious delinquency and substance use among aggressive boys. *Journal of Consulting and Clinical Psychology, 63*(4), 529–537.

Patterson, G. R. (1982). *Coercive family process.* Eugene, OR: Castalia.

Patterson, G. R., Reid, J. B., & Dishion, T. J. (1992). *A social learning approach: IV. Antisocial boys.* Eugene, OR: Castalia.

Select Committee on Children, Youth, and Families, U.S. House of Representatives. (1990). *No place to call home: Discarded children in America.* Washington, DC: U.S. Government Printing Office.

Stansbury, K., & Gunnar, M. (1994). Adrenocortical activity and emotion regulation. *Monographs of the Society for Research in Child Development, 59,* 108–134.

Taylor, T. K., Eddy, J. M., & Biglan, A. (1999). Interpersonal skills training to reduce aggressive and delinquent behavior: Limited evidence and the need for an evidence-based system of care. *Clinical Child and Family Psychology Review, 2,* 169–182.

Washington State Institute for Public Policy. (1998, January). *Watching the bottom line: Cost-effective interventions for reducing crime in Washington.* Olympia, WA: The Evergreen State College.

Zoccolillo, M., & Rogers, K. (1991). Characteristics and outcome of hospitalized adolescent girls with conduct disorder. *Journal of the American Academy of Child and Adolescent Psychiatry, 30*(6), 973–981.

Alternative Education Strategies:

Reducing Violence in School and the Community

TARY TOBIN AND JEFFREY SPRAGUE

Alternative education programs are expanding in the United States due to zero-tolerance policies, changes in the Individuals with Disabilities Education Act, increases in youth violence and school failure, and knowledge of the developmental trajectories leading to antisocial behavior. At the same time, there is little research evidence of the efficacy of these programs due to great diversity in approaches, populations served, and locations of the programs. In this article we provide a review of teaching strategies expected to be effective in alternative education programs for students who are at risk for school failure, dropout, delinquency, and violence. We discuss the need for alternative educational programs for students in both special and general education, describe research-based and recommended alternative education strategies, and offer suggestions for program development.

ALTERNATIVE EDUCATIONAL PROgrams are growing in number and diversity across the United States and vary greatly in their design, philosophy, and effectiveness (Fizzell & Raywid, 1997). Parents or students voluntarily choose some alternative education programs, such as charter, language immersion, or private schools; home schooling provided by parents; and vocational or professional technical education programs that emphasize transitions from school to work. In contrast, enrollment is usually required in alternative education programs designed to remove students who have antisocial or violent behavior, in part to keep expelled and frequently suspended youth off the streets. For students in special education who have serious discipline problems, the 1997 amendments to the Individuals with Disabilities Education Act (IDEA) have stimulated interest in the design of interim alternative educational programs that would be more effective than the common resort to homebound placements with tutoring and other restrictive placements (U.S. Department of Education, 1994). In addition, interest is growing in possibilities for alternative education programs that would serve elementary and/or middle school students

in both special and general education who are at risk for antisocial behavior. As noted by Leone and Drakeford (1999), "Rarely are alternative education programs available as a proactive choice to students or parents before serious problems develop" (p. 86).

The unique characteristics of alternative programs and the diverse populations they serve have made rigorous evaluation very difficult. Few studies on the effectiveness of alternative programs have been conducted. The results of those that have been conducted need to be replicated in new settings (Cox, 1999; Cox, Davidson, & Bynum, 1995; Duke & Griesdorn, 1999; Kochhar, 1998). What evidence is available, however, indicates that well-designed alternative education programs can benefit students at risk for failure in traditional programs

(Guerin & Denti, 1999; Nichols & Utesch, 1998; Raywid, 1990, 1998).

In this article we will focus on teaching strategies and processes expected to be effective in alternative education programs for students who are at risk for school failure, dropout, delinquency, and violence. We discuss the need for alternative educational programs for students in both special and general education, describe research-based and recommended alternative education strategies, and offer suggestions for program development.

THE NEED FOR ALTERNATIVE EDUCATIONAL PROGRAMS

In the United States, we have a strong tradition of valuing public schools where "poor and minority students" may have "access to the full range of educational opportunities" (Stevens & Grymes, 1993, p. 1). In reality, access to resources in education is not equally distributed (Stockard & Mayberry, 1992). For example, although vocational training may be in the best interest of some students (Bullis & Gaylord-Ross, 1991; Edgar, 1991), schools tend to focus on the college preparation track. If alternative educational strategies were more widely used, more students might successfully complete school (Office of Policy and Planning, 1992). The term "alternative education" refers to nontraditional educational services, ranging from separate schools for students who have been expelled to unique classes offered in a general education school building. Although the phrase might refer to any type of program that differs from traditional public schooling, it is commonly used in reference to programs designed for youth with challenging behavior (National Association of State Boards of Education [NASBE], 1994).

In the past, alternative education has focused on adolescents but now is increasingly being extended to younger students for several reasons. First, it has become more common for young students to act out in ways that are dangerous. At the beginning of the 1990s, about 450,000 delinquent youth were being placed in detention centers or training schools each year and another 300,000 sent to adult jails (Leone, Rutherford, & Nelson, 1991). Rates of arrests for young offenders (e.g., preteens and early adolescents) have increased since then, especially for violence related to weapons (Butts & Snyder, 1997). Although violent crimes began to decline in 1994, the overall level remains unacceptably high, and the fact that violence perpetrated by very young offenders continues to be usually high does not bode well for the future ("Declining Violence," 1998). Concern about the human and financial costs of incarceration of juveniles has led many to the conclusion that schools and other community agencies must develop alternative education programs and services (Dryfoos, 1997; Howell, 1995). Second, increasing interest in serving

children is a logical outcome of the findings of longitudinal research on the development of antisocial behavior patterns (see Loeber & Farrington, 1998; Patterson, Reid, & Dishion, 1992), which clearly reveals developmental trajectories starting in early childhood. Early intervention programs for children are more likely to change behavior than later rehabilitation programs for adolescents or adults (Walker & Bullis, 1995; Walker, Stieber, & Bullis, 1997; Walker & Sylwester, 1991). Third, the current trends of (a) under-identification (and late identification) of students with emotional and behavior disorders (Forness, Kavale, MacMillan, Asarnow, & Duncan, 1996; Kauffman, 1997; Tobin & Sugai, 1999a, 1999b), and (b) the inclusion of more students with disabilities in general education classes rather than providing a full continuum of placements (MacMillan, Gresham, & Forness, 1996) has resulted in an increased need for interim and permanent alternative placements.

Special Education Students

With the passage of the IDEA Amendments of 1997 came increasing pressure to develop and use alternative education strategies for students who fail to adjust to the demands of general education. Sec. 300.519 addresses change of placement for disciplinary removals and makes it clear that after a child with a disability has been removed from his or her current placement for more than 10 school days in the same school year, during any subsequent days of removal, the public agency must provide services to the extent necessary. In addition, the days when a student with challenging behavior is "sent home" or "removed" without being formally "suspended" now will have to be included when counting the 10 days.

General Education Students

Students in general education who are having difficulty adjusting to school may be in need of alternative education strat-

egies. Gottfredson and Gottfredson (1985) noted, "Substantial evidence implies that it is youths who do not do well in school who most often drop out early and who engage in more delinquent behavior" (p. 191). Alternative education programs that succeed in helping students at risk of dropping out to obtain educational credentials would be providing a service to society in terms of social, emotional, and financial outcomes. As Alternbaugh, Engel, and Martin (1995) noted, "The benefits of dropout prevention would exceed the costs by a ratio of 9:1."

RECOMMENDED ALTERNATIVE EDUCATION STRATEGIES

Recommended practices were selected on the basis of evidence from a range of educational programs serving students who are at risk for antisocial behavior. Given the lack of research at the middle and high school levels on alternative programs per se, we reviewed research on school-based interventions that have been effective with students who have behavior disorders and/or antisocial behavior. Electronic databases (e.g., ERIC, Expanded Academic Index, First Search) were searched using key words such as *middle school alternative education, behavior disorders, delinquency prevention, dropout prevention,* and *school-based intervention*. In addition, nonelectronic searches were conducted of recent issues (1990–1999) of *The Journal of Emotional and Behavioral Disorders* and *Behavioral Disorders*. Selection criteria were as follows: An educational practice or school-based intervention was described that (a) was applicable to students at risk for antisocial behavior and/or failure in traditional classes, (b) was sufficiently practical to be implemented in local public schools, and (c) had convincing evidence of positive outcomes. An overview of what we identified as best and preferred practices for alternative education of at-risk students is presented in Table 1. In the material that follows, each practice is defined, described, and discussed.

Low Ratio of Students to Teachers

Definition. In the context of alternative education, "low ratio of students to teachers" means reduced class size in comparison with general education.

Description. Class size should be small enough for "substantial opportunities for informal adult–student interactions, where teachers are committed to and interested in working with students, and where students are perusing similar courses of academic study within an environment that is safe and orderly" (Altenbaugh et al., 1995, p. 184). Exact numbers cannot be provided, given that the ratio that is appropriate in a particular setting will be relative to local general education practices and affected by students' needs and available resources. A small class size means teachers and staff have more time for each student than would be possible in a traditional setting, which may improve bonding and commitment to school.

Examples. Stockard and Mayberry (1992) reported that students who were not able to cope with the variety and multiple transitions involved in a typically large middle school would do very well in a "school within a school" setting. Dryfoos (1990) described an educational program based on this type of alternative educational programming that reported behavioral gains that lasted over time for the treatment group.

Discussion Point. While the debate about the value of smaller classes in general education continues, smaller classes are, no doubt, better for students with emotional, social, or behavior problems.

Highly Structured Classroom

Definition. A highly structured classroom is one in which expectations, rules, and schedules are clearly defined, specified, explained, and enforced. Although students may learn to handle choices, free time, and responsibilities over time, initially the adults in the room establish

TABLE 1
Summary of Research-Based Alternative Education Strategies

Low ratio of students to teachers
  More personal time for each student
  Better behavioral gains
  Higher quality of instruction

Highly structured classroom with behavioral classroom management
  Level systems provide predictable structure
  Self-management skills are taught
  High rates of positive reinforcement
  High academic gains
  Students are able to move to less restrictive settings

Positive rather than punitive emphasis in behavior management
  Rewards for acceptable behavior and compliance
  Directly teach clear classroom rules
  Begin with rich reinforcement and then "fade" to normal levels when possible
    (four positives to one negative)

Adult mentors at school
  Mentor must use positive reinforcement
  Mentor takes special interest in child
  Mentor tracks behavior, attendance, attitude, grades
  Mentor negotiates alternatives to suspension and expulsion

Individualized behavioral interventions based on functional behavioral assessment
  Identify causes of the behavior
  Identify what is "keeping it going"
  Identify positive behaviors to replace problems
  Interview and involve the student
  Use multicomponent interventions

Social skills instruction
  Problem solving
  Conflict resolution
  Anger management
  Empathy for others

High-quality academic instruction
  Direct instruction plus learning strategies
  Control for difficulty of instruction
  Small, interactive groups
  Directed responses and questioning of students

Involving parents
  Frequent home–school communication
  Parent education programs, provided either at school or in the community

routines, provide directions, and monitor students' behavior closely. Behavioral classroom management makes use of conditions, such as reminders before an expected behavior is to occur and feedback immediately afterwards, to encourage appropriate behavior.

Description. Typically, the teacher will establish detailed expectations for student behavior throughout the school day and will directly teach and frequently review these expectations. Students learn that appropriate behavior will be noticed, appreciated, and often rewarded in some way. Likewise, inappropriate behavior will be followed by corrective consequences. Prompting and reinforcing are gradually faded as students gain self-management skills.

Examples. In the Franklin-Jefferson Program (Schloss, Holt, Mulvaney, & Green, 1988), behavior control was gained by providing three 15-minute breaks and recreational activities that could be gained or lost according to a point system. The staff monitored their own behavior by holding daily after-school team meetings to see that the point system was being applied consistently. Students in this program reportedly made high academic gains, and many were able to move to less restrictive settings.

Discussion Point. Lipsey and Wilson (1998) found that behavioral programs have positive effects and that the evidence for this—for noninstitutionalized juvenile offenders—is consistent.

Positive Rather Than Punitive Emphasis

Definition. Having a positive rather than a punitive emphasis in behavior management means that positive reinforcement for appropriate behavior is used more often than punishment for inappropriate behavior.

Description. Mayer (1995) describes positive behavior management as increasing praise for constructive classroom behavior, group rewards for acceptable behavior, and rewards for compliance. In addition, Mayer's research indicates that these methods are more effective than punitive methods.

Examples. For very young children, First Step to Success (Walker, Kavanaugh, et al., 1997; Walker et al., 1998) is an alternative educational strategy for very young students that emphasizes positive behavioral support and can be provided in an integrated setting. Students receive positive reinforcement for compliance to teacher requests and for remaining on task. It has been shown to dramatically reduce maladaptive behaviors and increase academic behaviors in at-risk kindergartners and first graders. The Day Treatment Model is an adaptation of the Achievement Place Model

(Hicks & Munger, 1990). Emphasis is placed on reducing inappropriate behavior by teaching and positively reinforcing appropriate behavior. Teachers try to maintain a ratio of four positive consequences for every negative consequence. Better grades, a decrease in problem behaviors at home, and a 65% decrease in police and court contacts were reported as positive gains made by students in this program. The Gateway Program (Davis, 1994) uses a positive, nonpunitive behavior management system in an alternative education program for middle and high school students who have been suspended or expelled from traditional schools for carrying weapons, harassment, aggression, drugs, and other disciplinary problems. In addition to providing support through counseling, the school uses a level system in which students can earn privileges. As Davis noted, "A student can earn *one point each hour for each rule* [italics added] followed during that period" (p. 4). In traditional programs, when a student breaks one rule, generally the teacher's attention is focused entirely on the broken rule. In the Gateway Program, although the student would not earn a point for the rule broken, he or she would still be given credit for the rules followed. In addition, every new hour brings a new start.

Discussion Point. Negative consequences remain the standard approach to management of student behavior in schools across the country (Bear, 1998). In alternative education, the use of positive rather than punitive behavior management could be delivered at high levels and then gradually faded in preparation for reintegration after students learn prosocial responses and attitudes.

Adult Mentors at School

Definition. An adult mentor at school is a staff member or community volunteer who develops an advisory relationship with an individual student and guides the student's progress.

Description. The mentor builds a relationship of trust with the student by

getting to know the student; listening; providing information; making suggestions; noticing and encouraging accomplishments; and, when necessary, functioning as an advocate for seeking community resources.

Examples. Check and Connect (Evelo, Sinclair, Hurley, Christenson, & Thurlow, 1996) reduced dropout and delinquency by providing daily, personal contact between an adult at school and at-risk students. Vance, Fernandes, and Biber (1998) reported that having an adult mentor *at school* (instead of in the community) was a significant protective factor for youth with aggressive behavior or emotional and behavioral disturbance. They noted, "Promoting a school setting that emphasizes finding each high-risk child an adult mentor, who can reach out and take a special interest in that child, may go a long way toward enhancing educational progress" (p. 220).

Discussion Point. According to Catalano, Arthur, Hawkins, Berglund, and Olson (1998), research supports mentoring *only* if mentors are trained to use behavior management and provide positive reinforcement for appropriate behavior (e.g., attending school).

Functional Behavioral Assessments

Definition. Functional behavioral assessments refer to identifying antecedents and maintaining consequences of problem behavior.

Description. In an alternative education program, individualized behavioral interventions based on functional behavioral assessment would provide environmental changes and teaching strategies for a student to reduce inappropriate behavior and increase appropriate behavior (O'Neill et al., 1997).

Examples. When the student is not attending school (or the alternative placement) regularly, school staff may be able to assess the attendance problem by using The School Refusal Assessment

Scale, which has teacher, parent, and student interviews with documented validity for developing behavior support plans that match the functions of replacement and problem behaviors (Kearney & Silverman, 1993; Kearney & Tillotson, 1998). For example, one child might avoid school for fear of doing poorly when asked to speak in front of the class. Another child might make excuses to stay home when doing so would lead to attention from a parent. The solutions that will be effective for each child will be different.

Reports of successful use of functional assessments of behavior problems to develop interventions are encouraging (Dunlap et al., 1993; Kern, Childs, Dunlap, Clarke, & Falk, 1994; Lewis & Sugai, 1996). Student interviews should be a part of the functional assessment process for students who are capable of reporting on the circumstances surrounding their behaviors. Forms for semistructured student interviews are available for use in schools (Kern, Dunlap, Clarke, & Childs, 1994; Reed, Thomas, Sprague, & Horner, 1997).

Discussion Point. Individualized interventions based on behavioral functional assessments are mandated by IDEA 1997 for students with disabilities whose discipline problems have reached the point where alternative educational placements are needed. Many of these students will have multiple problems that are quite serious and likely will need more than one intervention to overcome the difficulties in their lives. Functional assessments could be integrated with the development of wraparound interventions if school staff collaborated with community agency staff and parents in the development of individualized service plans (Eber, Nelson, & Miles, 1997; Sprague, Sugai, & Walker, 1998).

Social Skills Instruction

Definition. Instruction in social skills refers directly to teaching appropriate ways of getting along with other individuals.

Description. Social skills instruction should include the following: (a) interpersonal problem solving (Kazdin, Siegel, & Bass, 1992), (b) conflict resolution (Johnson & Johnson, 1996), (c) anger management (Lochman, Coie, Underwood, & Terry, 1993), (d) vocational social skills assessment and instruction (Bullis, Bull, Johnson, & Johnson, 1994; Clement-Heist, Seigel, & Gaylord-Ross, 1992), and/or (d) social skills needed to replace aggressive behaviors (Goldstein & Glick, cited in Howell, 1995).

Examples. Lipsey and Wilson (1998) reported that for noninstitutionalized juvenile offenders, interpersonal skills training had the greatest equated effect size of all the treatments they reviewed. For institutionalized juveniles, interpersonal skills training was second only to "behavioral program," and both had an effect size more than .40 in reducing recidivism. Kamps, Kravits, Stolze, and Swaggart (1999) included social skills lessons, as well as peer tutoring and a behavioral classroom management program, in a program for at-risk students and students with EBD. The social skills lessons were selected according to individual needs and included content related to a range of interpersonal situations (e.g., following directions, accepting consequences).

Discussion Point. Social skills deficits in school predict future delinquency (Walker, Stieber, et al., 1997). If social skills instruction is to result in a more favorable future outcome, planning for generalization is essential (Walker, 1995). Scott and Nelson (1998) recommend generalization strategies that "emphasize altering student response variables (e.g., teaching replacement behaviors, schedule thinning) and strategies that directly alter generalization settings (e.g., group contingencies, peer coaches)" (p. 269).

Effective Academic Instruction

Definition. Academic instruction refers to lessons in content areas such as arithmetic and reading as well as language arts, social studies, and science. These lessons are considered "effective" when the student demonstrates progress toward meeting expected grade-level standards.

Description. Effective academic instruction should include individualized remediation in addition to small group lessons. Many students will have "gaps" in their understanding of basic skills due to having changed schools frequently and having missed lessons due to being sent to time out or not attending, and so forth. As such, providing increased practice opportunities is critical.

Examples. Swanson and Hoskyn (1998) conducted a meta-analysis of outcomes in 180 experimental studies and determined that the following instructional features are most successful across all subject areas for students with learning disabilities: (a) combining direct instruction and strategy instruction, (b) controlling task difficulty and number of steps, (c) having small interactive groups, and (d) encouraging directed responses and questioning of students. Katsiyannis and Archwamety (1999) found that for 12- to 18-year-old incarcerated males, individualized academic instruction was a valuable rehabilitation tool and concluded, "The results also support the need for intensive academic remediation for incarcerated youths, since academic improvement is associated with lower rates of recidivism" (p. 99).

Discussion Point. Most students in alternative education will need extra academic support. It would be usual to find that many have learning disabilities or other special needs. Even students who are not characterized as having a disability may have fallen behind academically, or not be achieving optimally, if they are having difficulty adjusting to traditional education.

Involving Parents

Definition. School staff can involve parents when school process and climate encourage parents to be active participants in planning and implementing the education of their child.

Description. Parents are involved in a child's education when they take an interest in what the child is learning, communicate with school staff, attend meetings and school functions related to their child's progress, and provide the emotional and material supports needed to be successful at school. This should include frequent communication between the teacher and the parent about the child's homework (Epstein, Munk, Bursuck, Polloway, & Jayanthi, 1999). More importantly, parents should be included in planning behavioral interventions and educational programs.

Examples. School-based parent training can have a positive effect on both parents and students. In a controlled study, an 11-week intervention (Aware Parenting, meeting once a week for 2 hours) with parents of fifth-grade students produced both academic and behavioral gains for students when they were in sixth grade (Bornstein et al., 1998). This model is based on the philosophy that the parent trainer should model the type of nurturing behavior desired by being attentive first to the *parents'* concerns and needs and then addressing expectations for the parents to do more for their children. The five components of the model are (a) support, (b) attentiveness, (c) responsiveness, (d) guidance, and (e) receptivity to emotion. Effective parent training programs aimed at the prevention of juvenile delinquency have emphasized increasing positive interactions and parental involvement in the child's education as well as more active supervision of the child's free time (Patterson et al., 1992; Walker, Colvin, & Ramsey, 1995).

Discussion Point. In general education, school staff may avoid working with parents of students with challenging behavior because home–school interactions have been aversive. A student's inappropriate responses to directions, social situations, and task demands may

have been learned in the home and then generalized from home to school (Patterson et al., 1992; Snyder, Schrepferman, & St. Peter, 1997; Walker, Stieber, Ramsey, & O'Neill, 1991). However, interventions for students who are at risk for conduct disorder need to be implemented in a coordinated manner across school, home, and community settings (Reid, 1993).

ESTABLISHING AN ALTERNATIVE EDUCATION PROGRAM

Who Is Appropriate?

Universal, Proactive Screening. Universal screening for emotional, behavioral, and interpersonal problems should be done when children first start school (Walker, Severson, & Feil, 1994) and repeated at regular intervals (Walker & McConnell, 1988; Walker & Severson, 1992). Regular universal screening monitors excessive internalizing or externalizing behaviors, assesses critical behavioral events (e.g., hurts animals, starts fires), observes attention to task and social interactions, and ensures that all students at risk of problems will be considered. In addition, special education students who are suspended or expelled for weapon or drug offenses will need to be provided educational services (IDEA, 1997).

School Records of Discipline Problems. Discipline referrals are warning signs of more serious problems likely to occur (Tobin & Sugai, 1999b; Walker, Stieber, Ramsey, & O'Neill, 1991, 1993). Rather than waiting for these serious problems to develop before taking action or allowing students to drift into patterns of alienation, educators should take preventive actions quickly in response to these warning signs. In general, students who have referral and suspension rates that are much greater than other students' or who have been referred for violent behavior should be considered as candidates for alternative education. School records could be reviewed

and summarized on the School Archival Records Survey (SARS; Walker, Block-Pedego, Todis, & Severson, 1991). School records of discipline referrals, grades, and attendance are increasingly being entered into computerized databases, making it possible to quickly recognize warning signs (by programming "red flags" in advance; Sprague, Sugai, Horner, & Walker, 1999).

Chronic Victims. In addition to using school records to identify students with disruptive behavior problems, chronic victims' names generally will be recorded in reports of bullying or harassment incidents. According to Hodges and Perry (1996), "About 10% of schoolchildren are chronically abused by peers. Victimization is highly stable over the school years and is associated with a wide variety of negative outcomes for the child, including depression, low self-esteem, and avoidance of school" (p. 23). A study of self-reports of 474 children in Grades 3 through 6 indicated that chronic victims are likely to have "social-psychological adjustment difficulties" (Crick & Grotpeter, 1996). According to Day (1996), teaching children to "assert themselves without verbal or physical violence" (p. 84) would help children to avoid being either victims or bullies, and providing victims at school with "counseling, support, and protection [is important] so that the desire for revenge does not fuel more violence" (p. 92).

Avoiding Iatrogenic Effects

Whenever individuals are identified for prevention or treatment interventions, including alternative education strategies, potential iatrogenic (negative) effects should be considered. The National Association of State Boards of Education found that alternative educational programs serving older students removed from school for disciplinary reasons may be seen as stigmatizing (NASBE, 1994). Educators need to design alternative programs so that the long-term advantages outweigh the short-term disadvantages of the intervention (Hayward & Tallmadge, 1995).

A number of researchers have discussed the sources of iatrogenic effects. Kazdin (1994) asserts that group programs in which children come into contact with deviant peers are most likely to produce unfavorable results with children whose initial problems were not severe and most likely to help children in need of remediation who had severe problems. As for the influence of peers, Kazdin (1994) states, "More active use of non antisocial peers in the treatment process (e.g., as therapeutic change agents) would follow from current research" (p. 371). However, other authors warn that not only may a group intervention "have an adverse effect" on the students it was intended to help, but "the students selected as role models" may be adversely affected (Guerra, Tolan, & Hammond, 1994, pp. 391–392). Potential participants in any preventive program should be screened to "reduce the possibility of iatrogenic effects by offering services only to those youngsters and their families who actually demonstrate problems or deficits in areas targeted by the intervention procedures" (Reid, 1991, p. 867).

Obtain Support, Implement, and Evaluate

Alternative education strategies need to be supported by school administrators and local communities. Although an individual teacher could use some of the strategies discussed above, typical teacher-to-student ratios and resources would make it difficult to fully implement all of them. As the name implies, the alternative education program should be systematically different from traditional education and serve as a "relief valve" for general education. The program needs to be adequately funded, and program staff need to have adequate skills and training to carry out the intervention. Alternative education programs should not serve as dumping grounds for disruptive students or ineffective teachers. Finally, because of the relative lack of research, alternative education programs should be rigorously and continuously evaluated regarding student progress, costs, and family and staff satisfaction.

CONCLUSION

We have reviewed a variety of issues related to the need for alternative education, discussed different models of service delivery, and recommended practices for those programs, and briefly described the components of a promising model. Given the number of students who are dropping out of or being expelled from traditional educational programs, the need for alternative education programs is clear.

Service delivery systems vary in terms of location, approach, and ages served. Although more research is needed on types of delivery systems, specific strategies that have a strong research base can be recommended for alternative educational programs in any setting. These include (a) small class size; (b) highly structured classroom management; (c) positive rather than punitive behavior management; (d) adult mentors at school; (e) interventions based on functional assessments for individual students with serious behavior problems; (f) social skills instruction, especially in the areas of empathy, anger management, and conflict resolution; (g) instructional strategies (i.e., tutoring, direct instruction, and strategy instruction) that will help students who have fallen behind academically to catch up; and (h) parent training programs that provide support for parents before urging parents to do more for their children.

Alternative education programs should be supported by the entire community. Traditional schools serve most students well; for this reason, many administrators feel pressure to maintain the standard programs. In fact, it may seem that the traditional school is more orderly if disruptive students or those who do not "fit in" either leave voluntarily by dropping out or are removed by expulsion or homebound placements or other segregated special educational settings. When this happens, however, it is the community as a whole that suffers as the dis-placed youth attempt to find their place in a society without adequate preparation. Alternative education programs have helped many youth already and, if expanded creatively, hold promise for the future for many more.

About the Authors

TARY TOBIN, PhD, is a research associate at the University of Oregon. Her current interests include school-based prevention programs and positive behavioral interventions. **JEFFREY SPRAGUE,** PhD, is an associate professor of special education and co-director of the University of Oregon Institute on Violence and Destructive Behavior. He has been a classroom teacher, teacher supervisor, behavioral consultant, researcher, and university teacher, and was the director of the Center for School and Community Integration at the Indiana University Institute for the Study of Developmental Disabilities. Address: Tary Tobin, College of Education, Room 241A, 5262 University of Oregon, Eugene, OR 97403-5262; e-mail: ttobin@oregon.uoregon.edu

Authors' Notes

1. This manuscript was developed with support from the United States Department of Justice, Office of Juvenile Justice and Delinquency Prevention to The University of Oregon Subcontract to the Hamilton Fish National Institute on School and Community Violence (OJJDP Award # 97-S22). The opinions expressed are those of the authors and do not necessarily reflect those of the funding agency.
2. We would like to thank Hill Walker, Vicki Nishioka, Michael Bullis, and Debra Eisert for their contributions regarding alternative education strategies and Wendy Weller for document preparation.

References

Altenbaugh, R. J., Engel, D. E., & Martin, D. T. (1995). *Caring for kids: A critical study of urban school leavers.* Washington, DC: The Falmer Press.

Bear, G. G. (1998). School discipline in the United States: Prevention, correction, and long-term social development. *School Psychology Review, 27*(1), 14–32.

Bornstein, P., Duncan, P., Clauson, J., Abrams, C., Yannett, N., Ginsburg, G., & Milne, M. (1998). Preventing middle school adjustment problems for children from lower-income families: A program for aware parenting. *Journal of Applied Developmental Psychology, 19*(1), 129–151.

Bullis, M., Bull, B., Johnson, P., & Johnson, B. (1994). Identifying and assessing the community-based social behaviors of adolescents and young adults with emotional and behavioral disorders. *Journal of Emotional and Behavioral Disorders, 1,* 173–189.

Bullis, M., & Gaylord-Ross, R. (1991). *Moving on: Transitions for youth with behavior disorders.* Reston, VA: ERIC Clearinghouse on Handicapped and Gifted Children.

Butts, J. A., & Snyder, H. N. (1997, September). The youngest delinquents: Offenders under age 15. *Juvenile Justice Bulletin.* [On-line] Available: http://www.ncjrs.org/jjbulletins/jjbul_997/jjb.html

Catalano, R. F., Arthur, M. W., Hawkins, J. D., Berglund, L., & Olson, J. J. (1998). In R. Loeber & D. P. Farrington (Eds.), *Serious and violent juvenile offenders: Risk factors and successful interventions* (pp. 248–283). Thousand Oaks, CA: Sage.

Clement-Heist, K., Seigel, S., & Gaylord-Ross, R. (1992). Simulated and *in situ* vocational social skills training for youths with learning disabilities. *Exceptional Children, 58*(4), 336–345.

Cox, S. M. (1999). An assessment of an alternative education program for at-risk delinquent youth. *Journal of Research in Crime and Delinquency, 36*(3), 323.

Cox, S. M., Davidson, W. S., & Bynum, T. S. (1995). A meta-analytic assessment of delinquency-related outcomes of alternative education programs. *Crime and Delinquency, 41*(2), 219–234.

Crick, J. R., & Grotpeter, J. K. (1996). Children's treatment by peers: Victims of relational and overt aggression. *Development and Psychopathology, 8,* 367–380.

Davis, S. M. (1994). How the Gateway Program helps troubled teens. *Educational Leadership, 52*(1), 17–19.

Day, N. (1996). *Violence in schools: Learning in fear.* Springfield, NJ: Enslow.

Declining violence. (1998, October 9). *The CQ Researcher, 8*(38), 892.

Dryfoos, J. G. (1990). *Adolescents at risk.* New York: Oxford University Press.

Dryfoos, J. G. (1997). Adolescents at risk: Shaping programs to fit the need. *Journal of Negro Education, 65*(1), 5–18.

Duke, D. L., & Griesdorn, J. (1999). Considerations in the design of alternative schools. *The Clearing House, 73*(2), 89.

Dunlap, G., Kern, L., de Perczel, M., Clarke, S., Wilson, D., Childs, K., White, R., & Falk, G. (1993). Functional analysis of classroom variables for students with emotional and behavioral disorders. *Behavioral Disorders, 18*(4), 275–291.

Eber, L., Nelson, C. M., & Miles, P. (1997). School-based wraparound for students with emotional and behavioral challenges. *Exceptional Children, 63*(4), 539–555.

Edgar, E. (1991). Providing ongoing support and making appropriate placements: An alternative to transition planning for mildly handicapped students. *Preventing School Failure, 35*(2), 36–39.

Epstein, M. H., Munk, D. D., Bursuck, W. D., Polloway, E. A., & Jayanthi, M. (1999). Strategies for improving home-school communication about homework for students with disabilities. *The Journal of Special Education, 33*(3), 166.

Evelo, D., Sinclair, M., Hurley, C., Christenson, S., & Thurlow, M. (1996). *Keeping kids in school: Using check and connect for dropout prevention.* Minneapolis: University of Minnesota, College of Education and Human Development, Institute on Community Integration.

Fizzell, R., & Raywid, M. A. (1997). If alternative schools are the answer . . . What's the question? *Reaching Today's Youth: The Community Circle of Caring Journal, 1*(2), 7–9.

Forness, S. R., Kavale, K. A., MacMillan, D. L., Asarnow, J., & Duncan, B. B. (1996). Early detection and prevention of emotional or behavioral disorders: Developmental aspects of systems of care. *Behavioral Disorders, 21,* 226–240.

Goldstein, A. P., & Glick, B. (1994). *The prosocial gang: Implementing aggression replacement training.* Thousand Oaks, CA: Sage.

Gottfredson, G. D., & Gottfredson, D. C. (1985). *Victimization in schools.* New York: Plenum.

Guerin, G., & Denti, L. (1999). Alternative education support for youth at-risk. *The Clearing House, 73*(2), 76.

Guerra, N. G., Tolan, P. H., & Hammond, W. R. (1994). Prevention and treatment of adolescent violence. In L. D. Eron, J. H. Gentry, & P. Schlegel (Eds.), *Reason to hope: A psychosocial perspective on violence and youth* (pp. 383–403). Washington, DC: American Psychological Association.

Hayward, B. J., & Tallmadge, G. K. (1995). *Strategies for keeping kids in school: Evaluation of dropout prevention and reentry projects in vocational education. Final Report.* Washington, DC: U.S. Government Printing Office. (ERIC Document Reproduction Service No. ED 346 082)

Hicks, T., & Munger, R. (1990). A school day treatment program using an adaptation of the teaching family model (TFM). *Education and Treatment of Children, 13*(1), 63–83.

Hodges, E. V., & Perry, D. C. (1996). Victims of peer abuse: An overview. *Reclaiming Children and Youth: Journal of Emotional and Behavioral Problems, 5*(1), 23–28.

Howell, E. C. (Ed.). (1995). *Guide for implementing the comprehensive strategy for serious, violent, and chronic juvenile offenders.* Washington, DC: Office of Juvenile Justice and Delinquency Prevention.

Individuals with Disabilities Education Act Amendments of 1997, 20 U.S.C. § 1400 et seq.

Johnson, D. W., & Johnson, R. T. (1996). Conflict resolution and peer mediation: Programs in elementary and secondary schools: A review of the research. *Review of Educational Research, 66*(4), 459–506.

Kamps, D., Kravits, T., Stolze, J., & Swaggart, B. (1999). Prevention strategies for at-risk students and students with EBD in urban elementary schools. *Journal of Emotional and Behavioral Disorders, 7*(3), 178–188.

Katsiyannis, A., & Archwamety, T. (1999). Academic remediation/achievement and other factors related to recidivism rates among delinquent youths. *Behavioral Disorders, 24*(2), 93–101.

Kauffman, J. M. (1997). *Characteristics of emotional and behavioral disorders of children and youth* (6th ed.). Columbus, OH: Merrill.

Kazdin, A. E. (1994). Interventions for aggressive and antisocial children. In L. D. Eron, J. H. Gentry, & P. Schlegel (Eds.), *Reason to hope: A psychosocial perspective on violence and youth* (pp. 341–382). Washington, DC: American Psychological Association.

Kazdin, A. E., Siegel, T. C., & Bass, D. (1992). Cognitive problem-solving skills training and parent management training in the treatment of antisocial behavior in children. *Journal of Consulting and Clinical Psychology, 60*(5), 733–747.

Kearney, C. A., & Silverman, W. K. (1993). Measuring the function of school refusal behavior: The School Refusal Assessment Scale. *Journal of Clinical Child Psychology, 22*(1), 85–96.

Kearney, C. A., & Tillotson, C. A. (1998). School attendance. In T. S. Watson & F. M. Gresham (Eds.), *Handbook of child behavior therapy* (pp. 143–161). New York: Plenum.

Kern, L., Childs, K. E., Dunlap, G., Clarke, S., & Falk, G. D. (1994). Using assessment-based curricular intervention to improve the classroom behavior of a student with emotional and behavioral challenges. *Journal of Applied Behavior Analysis, 27*(1), 7–19.

Kern, L., Dunlap, G., Clarke, S., & Childs, K. (1994). Student-assisted functional assessment interview. *Diagnostique, 19*(2-3), 29–39.

Kochhar, C. A. (1998). *Alternative schools and programs for chronically disruptive, violent and delinquent youth.* Unpublished manuscript, The George Washington University at Washington, DC, Graduate School of Education and Human Development, Hamilton Fish National Institute on School and Community Violence.

Leone, P. E., & Drakeford, W. (1999). Alternative education: From a "last chance" to a proactive model. *The Clearing House, 73*(2), 86.

Leone, P. E., Rutherford, R. B., & Nelson, C. M. (1991). *Special education in juvenile corrections.* Reston, VA: Council for Exceptional Children.

Lewis, T., & Sugai, G. (1996). Descriptive and experimental analysis of teacher and peer attention and the use of assessment-based intervention to improve the prosocial behavior of a student in a general education setting. *Journal of Behavioral Education, 6*, 7–24.

Lipsey, M. W., & Wilson, D. B. (1998). Effective intervention for serious juvenile offenders: A synthesis of research. In R. Loeber & D. P. Farrington (Eds.), *Serious and violent juvenile offenders: Risk factors and successful interventions* (pp. 313–345). Thousand Oaks, CA: Sage.

Lochman, J. E., Coie, J. D., Underwood, M. K., & Terry, R. (1993). Effectiveness of a social relations intervention program for aggressive and nonaggressive, rejected children. *Journal of Consulting and Clinical Psychology, 61*(6), 1053–1058.

Loeber, R., & Farrington, D. P. (1998). *Serious and violent juvenile offenders: Risk factors and successful interventions.* Thousand Oaks, CA: Sage.

MacMillan, D. L., Gresham, F. M., & Forness, S. R. (1996). Full inclusion: An empirical perspective. *Behavioral Disorders, 21*, 145–159.

Mayer, G. (1995). Preventing antisocial behavior in the schools. *Journal of Applied Behavior Analysis, 28*, 467–478.

National Association of State Boards of Education. (1994). *Schools without fear: The report of the NASBE study group on violence and its impact on schools and learning.* Alexandria, VA: Author.

Nichols, J. D., & Utesch, W. E. (1998). An alternative learning program: Effects on student motivation and self-esteem. *The Journal of Educational Research, 91*(5), 272–279.

Office of Policy and Planning, U.S. Department of Education. (1992). *Transforming American education: A directory of research and practice to help the nation achieve the six national education goals.* Washington, DC: Author.

Patterson, G. R., Reid, J. B., & Dishion, T. J. (1992). *Antisocial boys.* Eugene, OR: Castalia Press.

Raywid, M. A. (1990). Alternative education: The definition problem. *Changing Schools, 18*, 4–5.

Raywid, M. A. (1998). Small schools: A reform that works. *Educational Leadership, 55*(4), 34–39.

Reed, H., Thomas, E., Sprague, J. R., & Horner, R. H. (1997). The student guided functional assessment interview: An analysis of student and teacher agreement. *Journal of Behavioral Education, 7*, 33–49.

Reid, J. B. (1991). Mediational screening as a model for prevention research. *American Journal of Community Psychology, 19*, 867–872.

Reid, J. B. (1993). Prevention of conduct disorder before and after school entry: Related interventions to developmental findings. *Development and Psychopathology, 5*, 243–262.

Schloss, P. J., Holt, J., Mulvaney, M., & Green, J. (1988). The Franklin-Jefferson Program: Demonstration of an integrated social learning approach to educational services for behaviorally disordered students. *Teaching Behaviorally Disordered Youth, 4*, 7–15.

Scott, T. M., & Nelson, C. M. (1998). Confusion and failure in facilitating generalized social responding in the school setting: Sometimes 2 + 2 = 5. *Behavioral Disorders, 23*(4), 264–275.

Snyder, J., Schrepferman, L., & St. Peter, C. (1997). Origins of antisocial behavior: Negative reinforcement and affect dysregulation of behavior as socialization mechanisms in family interaction. *Behavior Modification, 21*(2), 187–215.

Sprague, J. R., Sugai, G., & Walker, H. (1998). Antisocial behavior in the schools. In S. Watson & F. Gresham (Eds.), *Child behavior therapy: Ecological considerations in assessment, treatment, and evaluation* (pp. 451–474). New York: Plenum.

Sprague, J. R., Sugai, G., Horner, R. H., & Walker, H. M. (1999). Using office discipline referral data to evaluate school-wide discipline and violence prevention interventions. *Oregon School Study Council Bulletin, 42*(2). Eugene: University of Oregon, College of Education.

Stevens, F. I., & Grymes, J. (1993). *Opportunity to learn: Issues of equity for poor and minority students.* Washington, DC: National Center for Educational Statistics.

Stockard, J., & Mayberry, M. (1992). *Effective educational environments.* Newbury Park, CA: Corwin Press.

Swanson, H. L., & Hoskyn, M. (1998). Experimental intervention research on students with learning disabilities: A meta-analysis of treatment outcomes. *Review of Educational Research, 68*(3), 277–321.

Tobin, T. J., & Sugai, G. M. (1999a). Discipline problems, placements, and outcomes for students with serious emotional disturbance. *Behavioral Disorders, 24*(2), 109–121.

Tobin, T. J., & Sugai, G. M. (1999b). Using sixth-grade school records to predict violence, chronic discipline problems, and high school outcomes. *Journal of Emotional and Behavioral Disorders, 7*(1), 40–53.

U.S. Department of Education. (1994). *To assure the free appropriate public education of all children with disabilities: Sixteenth annual report to Congress on the implementation of the Individuals with Disabilities Education Act.* Washington, DC: Author.

Vance, J., Fernandez, G., & Biber, M. (1998). Educational progress in a population of youth with aggression and emotional disturbance: The role of risk and protective factors. *Journal of Emotional and Behavioral Disorders, 6*(4), 214–221.

Walker, H. M. (1995). *The acting-out child: Coping with classroom disruption* (2nd ed.). Longmont, CO: Sopris West.

Walker, H. M., Block-Pedego, A., Todis, B., & Severson, H. (1991). *School archival records search (SARS): User's guide and technical manual.* Longmont, CO: Sopris West.

Walker, H. M., & Bullis, M. (1995). A comprehensive services model for troubled youth. In C. M. Nelson, B. Wolford, &

R. Rutherford (Eds.), *Comprehensive and collaborative systems that work for troubled youth: A national agenda* (pp. 122–148). Richmond: Eastern Kentucky University, National Coalition for Juvenile Justice Services, Training Resource Center.

Walker, H. M., Colvin, G., & Ramsey, E. (1995). *Antisocial behavior in school: Strategies and best practices.* Pacific Grove, CA: Brooks/Cole.

Walker, H. M., Kavanagh, K., Golly, A. M., Stiller, B., Severson, H. H., & Feil, E. G. (1997). *First step to success.* Longmont, CO: Sopris West.

Walker, H. M., Kavanagh, K., Golly, A. M., Stiller, B., Severson, H. H., & Feil, E. G. (1998). First Step to Success: An early intervention approach for preventing school antisocial behavior. *Journal of Emotional and Behavioral Disorders, 6*(2), 66–80.

Walker, H. M., & McConnell, S. R. (1988). *Walker-McConnell scale of social competence and school adjustment.* Austin, TX: PRO-ED.

Walker, H. M., & Severson, H. H. (1992). *The Systematic Screening for Behavior Disorders Scale.* Longmont, CO: Sopris West.

Walker, H. M., Severson, H. H., & Feil, E. G. (1994). *The early screening project: A proven child-find process.* Longmont, CO: Sopris West.

Walker, H. M., Stieber, S., & Bullis, M. (1997). Longitudinal correlates of arrest status among at-risk males. *Journal of Child and Family Studies, 6*(3), 289–276.

Walker, H. M., Stieber, S., Ramsey, E., & O'Neill, R. E. (1991). Longitudinal prediction of the school achievement, adjustment, and delinquency of antisocial versus at-risk boys. *Remedial and Special Education, 12*(4), 43–51.

Walker, H. M., Stieber, S., Ramsey, E., & O'Neill, R. E. (1993). Fifth grade school adjustment and later arrest rate: A longitudinal study of middle school antisocial boys. *Journal of Child and Family Studies, 2*(4), 295–315.

Walker, H. M., & Sylwester, R. (1991). Where is school along the path to prison? *Educational Leadership, 49*(1), 14–16.

Searching for Safe Schools:

Legal Issues in the Prevention of School Violence

MITCHELL L. YELL AND MICHAEL E. ROZALSKI

Violence in the United States has reached epidemic proportions, with a predictable spillover into public schools. The national concern over the problem of school violence has led to federal, state, and local efforts to address this issue by creating new laws and policies, which include adopting zero-tolerance approaches, conducting targeted and random searches of students and their property, using metal detectors, and preventing violence through education. In this article, we begin by examining these laws and policies. Then, we separate school district reactions to violence into three categories: tertiary, secondary, and primary prevention and describe procedures within each category. We end by proposing a framework within which school districts may develop legally correct policies and procedures to address school violence.

VIOLENCE IN AMERICAN SOCIETY has reached epidemic proportions. Especially troubling is the increasing violence among young people, with the predictable spillover of effects into the public schools. In fact, violence has become a significant aspect of the public school experience in America. The recent schoolyard murders in Mississippi, Kentucky, Arkansas, Pennsylvania, Oregon, and Colorado have focused the nation's attention on these problems; however, the levels of violence in our schools have been increasing for the past decade (Kopka, 1997). Numbing statistics reveal the extent of the problem: Violence in and around schools has become more common and more serious (Kachur et al., 1996; National League of Cities, 1995). Three million crimes are committed each year on the campuses of America's public schools (Sautler, 1995). In the two-year period from 1992 to 1994, 105 students and 12 teachers died violently at school or during school-related activities (Kachur et al., 1996). Eighty percent of these deaths were homicides; guns were used in 77% of the cases. The remaining 20% of these deaths were suicides. Furthermore, school violence, often associated with impoverished inner-city schools, has moved to suburban and rural schools (Sleek, 1998).

Teachers, students, and administrators recognize the increasing levels of violence. According to a survey issued in 1996 by the Office of Juvenile Justice and Delinquency Prevention of the U.S. Department of Justice, 12% of students reported carrying weapons to school for protection, 28% indicated that they sometimes or never felt safe while at school, and 11% said that they stayed home from school or cut classes because of fear of violence (U.S. Department of Justice, 1996). The survey also revealed that 82% of the school districts reported a rise in violence over the past 5 years, 60% reported weapons incidents, and 75% reported having to deal with violent student-on-student attacks. A 1995 survey of public school teachers showed that 41% of them believed that violence in the schools was a very serious problem (Harris, 1995). The American public

also recognizes the magnitude of the school violence problem. A Gallup Poll conducted in 1997 of attitudes toward public schools revealed that fights, violence, and gangs ranked with lack of discipline as the most significant problems facing America's schools (Rose & Gallup, 1998). The same poll revealed that, nationally, 36% of parents reported concerns about the safety of their children while they were at school.

The national concern over the problem of school violence has led to federal, state, and local efforts to address this issue by creating new laws and policies. These laws and policies include adopting zero-tolerance approaches, conducting targeted and random searches of students and their property, using metal detectors, and preventing violence through education. Our goal in this article is to examine these laws and policies. To do this, we first present an overview of federal and state laws intended to prevent and control school violence. Next, we briefly examine decisions by the U.S. Supreme Court that have had an important effect on the school–student relationship, especially as these decisions pertain to issues of student searches. Then, we separate school district reactions to violence into three categories—tertiary prevention, secondary prevention, and primary prevention—and describe procedures in each of these categories. Finally, we will propose a framework within which school districts may develop legally correct policies regarding violence. In sum, we will focus on legal issues and considerations in America's search for safe schools.

FEDERAL AND STATE LEGISLATION

National concern over the rise in violence in the public schools has led federal and state governments to create laws to address these issues. In this section we briefly review these efforts.

Federal lawmakers have reacted to the problems of violence by passing measures designed to make schools safer. The federal government's powers, however, are limited by the U.S. Constitution. According to the Tenth Amendment, the powers not delegated to the federal government by the Constitution are reserved to the states. Because regulation of education and crime are not

powers expressly given to the federal government in the Constitution, it is a state prerogative to legislate such matters. The federal government, therefore, cannot interfere directly with the states' right to govern public schools. Thus, the federal efforts have primarily involved funding the development of state programs or withholding federal funds if states did not address the particular concerns of Congress. In this way, federal lawmakers are able to influence state legislation of educational matters by tying federal funds to legislation. Table 1 lists and briefly explains some of these federal efforts.

An example of a federal law influencing state laws is evident in the Gun-

TABLE 1
Federal Laws Targeting School Violence

Law	Purpose	Provision related to school safety
The Gun-Free School Zones Act of 1990, 18 U.S.C. § 922(q)(1)(A)	This law made it a federal crime to possess a firearm in a school zone (i.e., within 1,000 feet of a public, parochial, or private school).	• This law was declared unconstitutional by the U.S. Supreme Court in *U.S. v. Lopez* (115 S.Ct. 1624, 1995).
The Gun-Free Schools Act of 1994, 20 U.S.C. § 8921	This law required that all states receiving federal funds require that schools expel any student bringing a gun to school.	• Expulsions had to be for a period of 1 year. • School district administrators were allowed to modify the expulsion on a case-by-case basis.
Safe and Drug Free Schools and Communities Act of 1994, 20 U.S.C. § 7107 et seq.	This law provided federal funding for violence prevention programs. Grants were awarded to educational agencies, institutions of higher education, and nonprofit groups.	• Grants were intended to prevent school violence, provide training and technical assistance, fund violence education programs, and deter the use of illegal drugs & alcohol.
Violent Crime Control and Law Enforcement Act of 1994, 42 U.S.C. § 13701	This law authorized over $30 billion to fund more police officers, new prison construction, and community-based crime prevention efforts. It also imposed severe penalties on violent & repeat offenders.	• Crime prevention efforts were targeted at youth in high-poverty and high-crime areas. • Purpose of funding was to encourage projects involving community participation and school cooperation.
Individuals with Disabilities Education Act Amendments of 1997, 20 U.S.C. § 1400 et seq.	This law reauthorized and amended the Individuals with Disabilities Education Act.	• School district administrators can place students in special education in an interim alternative educational setting (IAES) for 45 days when they bring a weapon to school or a school function. • If a school district can convince a hearing officer that a student in special education presents a danger to self or others, the hearing officer can order the student placed in an IAES for 45 days.

Free Schools Act of 1994 (hereafter the GFSA). The GFSA required that all states receiving federal education funding through the Improving America's Schools Act (IASA; 1994) pass laws mandating that school districts expel, for not less than 1 year, any student who brought a gun to school. States that did not have such a law in place by 1995 faced the cutoff of all federal IASA funds. Congress thus avoided constitutional problems by creating a law that was tied to federal funding rather than imposing federal school and firearms requirements on the states. By October 1995, all 50 states had enacted legislation that met the requirements of the GFSA. In this way, the federal government has been able to exercise some amount of control over the states' legislation with respect to school violence.

States have responded to these federal laws by mandating community- or school-based prevention and education programs and by requiring that school officials expel students who carry weapons onto school grounds. It is important that administrators and educators know the legal requirements in their particular state prior to addressing the problems of school violence.

State and federal courts have also addressed the issue of school safety and violence. As we will see, the courts, while safeguarding students' rights, have generally supported federal and state efforts to ensure the safety of students and staff in the public schools. The most important of these decisions have come from the U.S. Supreme Court.

THE U.S. SUPREME COURT

The U.S. Supreme Court has not heard a case directly addressing violence in the schools. However, the high court has issued rulings in cases that have had a profound effect on the relationship between schools and students, especially those students who may present a danger to the public school setting. The most important of these decisions are included in Table 2.

The U.S. Supreme Court, in these cases, upheld the constitutional rights of students in public schools. However, the high court has also recognized that schools have a duty to educate students in a safe and orderly environment. In these decisions, the Court has attempted to balance the rights of students with the duties of school district personnel. For example, a student's freedom of expression is limited to expression or speech that does not interfere with the school's operation, precisely because schools have a duty to establish standards of student conduct and behavior. Similarly, a student's right to privacy gives way to a school's duty to maintain a safe environment.

TABLE 2
U.S. Supreme Court Cases on the Rights of Students and School Officials

Case	Ruling
Tinker v. Des Moines School District, 393 U.S. 503 (1969)	• School officials could not deny students freedom of expression when such expression did not interrupt the school's operations or activities and did not intrude into school affairs. • Students do not shed their Constitutional rights "at the school-house gate."
Goss v. Lopez, 419 U.S. 565 (1975)	• Students facing temporary suspensions from public school are protected by the due process clause. • These protections include the right to receive written or oral notice of the charges against them and the opportunity to present their version of what happened to cause the suspension.
New Jersey v. T.L.O., 469 U.S. 325 (1985)	• Students are protected by the Fourth Amendment's protection against unreasonable searches and seizures. • School officials, however, are held to a lower standard regarding what is reasonable than are police officers in conducting searches and seizures. • To be reasonable, school officials' searches of students and their property must be justified at inception and should not exceed that which is necessary under the circumstances.
Bethel School District v. Fraser, 478 U.S. 675 (1986)	• Public school students have freedom of speech under the First Amendment, including the right to advocate unpopular and controversial views in school. • However, this right must be balanced against the schools' interest in teaching socially appropriate behavior. • Public schools may legitimately establish standards of civil and mature conduct.
Veronia School District v. Acton, 515 U.S. 646 (1995)	• Public school district's student athlete drug testing policy did not violate students' right to privacy or to be free from unreasonable searches. • Public school students have lesser privacy expectations than the general population. • Courts must balance student privacy interests against schools' legitimate interests.

The two Supreme Court decisions that directly affect how school officials may keep schools safe and orderly while safeguarding the rights of students are *New Jersey v. T.L.O.* (1985) and *Veronia School District v. Acton* (1995). In fact, James (1994) referred to the decision in *New Jersey v. T.L.O.* as a virtual blueprint for designing school safety policies. In this case, the Court noted that the interests of teachers and administrators in maintaining discipline in the classroom would be furthered by a less restrictive rule of law that would balance schoolchildren's legitimate expectations of privacy and the school's equally legitimate need to maintain an environment in which learning could take place. We now discuss these very important cases.

New Jersey v. T.L.O. (1985)

In 1985, the U.S. Supreme Court in *New Jersey v. T.L.O.* (hereafter *TLO*) addressed warrantless searches in the schools. A teacher in a New Jersey high school discovered two girls smoking in the school lavatory. The students were taken to the vice-principal's office. The vice-principal took a purse from one of the girls to examine it for cigarettes. In addition to the cigarettes, the purse also contained cigarette-rolling papers. Suspecting that the girl might have marijuana, the vice-principal emptied the contents of the purse. In it he found a pipe, a small amount of marijuana, a large amount of money in small bills, a list of people owing TLO money, and two letters implicating her in marijuana dealing. The girl's parents were called, and the evidence was turned over to police. Charges were brought by the police, and based on the evidence collected by the vice-principal and TLO's confession, a juvenile court in New Jersey declared TLO delinquent. The parents appealed the decision on the grounds that the search was conducted without a warrant and, therefore, illegal under the Fourth Amendment. Because the search was conducted illegally, the parents argued, the evidence was inadmissible. The case went to the New Jersey Supreme Court, which reversed the decision of the juvenile court and ordered the evidence obtained during the vice-principal's search suppressed on the grounds that the warrantless search was unconstitutional.

The U.S. Supreme Court eventually heard the case. The Court declared that the Fourth Amendment, prohibiting illegal searches and seizures, applied to students as well as adults. The Court also noted, however, that a student's privacy interests must be weighed against the need of administrators and teachers to maintain order and discipline in schools. Furthermore, the Court noted that maintaining security and order in schools required some easing of the requirements normally imposed on police.

The Court ruled that schools did not need to obtain a search warrant before searching a student; however, the Fourth Amendment's reasonableness standard, a standard lower than that of probable cause, had to be satisfied. *Probable cause* refers to a standard to which police are held; that is, police may only conduct a search if it is more than probable that the search will reveal evidence of illegal activities. Based on this standard, police must usually obtain a warrant prior to conducting the search. The reasonableness standard that school officials must meet holds that a reasonable person would have cause to suspect that evidence of illegal activities be present before conducting the search. If these preconditions are met, school officials may conduct the search. The reasonableness standard is much easier to meet than is the standard of probable cause.

The Court also adopted a two-part test to determine whether a search conducted by school officials was reasonable and, therefore, constitutionally valid. The two parts of this test that must be satisfied are that the search must be (a) justified at inception and (b) related to violations of school rules or policies. First, the search must be conducted as the result of a legitimate suspicion. This does not mean that school officials must be absolutely certain prior to conducting a search, but rather that there is a commonsense probability regarding the necessity of a search. A search cannot be justified on the basis of what was found during the search. Situations that justify a reasonable suspicion include information from student informers, police tips, anonymous tips and phone calls, and unusual student conduct (Yell, 1998). Second, the scope of the search must be reasonably related to the rule violation that led to the search in the first place. Because the vice-principal's search of TLO met the Supreme Court's test, it reversed the judgment of the New Jersey Supreme Court and ruled that the marijuana was admissible as evidence.

Veronia School District v. Acton (1995)

A school district in Oregon was experiencing a startling increase in drug use, rebelliousness, and disciplinary problems among its students. School officials identified student athletes as the ringleaders in the drug problem. Following unsuccessful attempts at solving the problem through the use of educational programs, a public meeting was held. During the meeting, school officials received unanimous parent support for adopting a drug-testing program for all students participating in sports. The policy required that if a student wanted to participate in interscholastic sports, the student and his or her parents had to sign a consent form submitting to drug testing. If a student and his or her parents did not sign the consent form, the student was not allowed to participate in sports. A seventh-grade student, James Acton, who wanted to play interscholastic football, refused to sign the consent form. When the school did not allow James to play football, his parents sued the school district, alleging that their son's constitutional rights had been violated. The case, *Veronia School District v. Acton* (hereafter *Veronia*) was heard by the U.S. Supreme Court in 1995. In a six to three decision, the high court ruled in favor of the school district's drug-testing policy. Although the Court's ruling only addressed drug testing of student athletes, the decision has important implications for school districts' search and seizure policies. The Court, citing its decision in *TLO*, stated that the Fourth Amendment to the Constitution required balancing the interests of the student's privacy and the school district's legitimate interest in preserving order and safety. In making this determination, the Court noted that students in school have a decreased expectation of privacy relative to adults in the general population. The Court also considered the relative unobtrusiveness of the drug-testing policy. The primary consideration, therefore, was regarding the special context of public schools, which act as guardians and tutors of the students in their care (Zirkel, 1995). Clearly, this decision indicated that in situations involving such preventive measures, courts will favor the needs of the school over the privacy interests of students when the procedures used are reasonable.

Discussion of the Supreme Court's Rulings

The *TLO* and *Veronia* decisions affirmed the constitutional rights of students to be free of unreasonable searches and seizures and to possess a reasonable expectation of privacy while at school. In both cases, however, the court granted a great deal of latitude to schools because they have a legitimate duty to educate students in a safe and orderly environment. The high court clearly stated that when the rights of students and those of school officials seem to conflict, the law favors the duties of school officials.

According to the *TLO* decision, the law permits educators to respond to school safety problems as the situation dictates, providing the actions are reasonable (James, 1994). In *Veronia*, the high court noted that the privacy expectations of students in public schools are less than those of the general public because school authorities act in loco parentis. In loco parentis is a concept that originated in English common law. According to this concept, when parents place their children in schools, they give

a certain amount of their control of their children to school personnel. The principal and teacher, therefore, have the authority to teach, guide, correct, and discipline children to achieve educational objectives (Yell, 1998).

Nonetheless, these decisions do place some degree of restraint on school personnel. In *TLO* the court held that reasonable grounds must exist to lead school authorities to believe a search is necessary, and the search must be related to the original suspicion. According to Dise, Iyer, and Noorman (1994), this standard requires that school officials weigh the credibility of the information prior to making a decision to conduct a search. Court decisions following *TLO* have recognized situations in which searches and seizures in school environments do not give rise to Fourth Amendment concerns (i.e., searches during which even the standard of reasonable suspicion is not required). These situations include searches (a) to which a student voluntarily consents, (b) of material left in view of the school authorities, (c) in an emergency to prevent injury or property damage, (d) by police authorities that are incidental to arrests, and (e) of lost property (Valente, 1994).

The intrusiveness of the search is also a relevant factor. Considering the nature of the possible offense, the search should not be overly intrusive (e.g., a strip search to locate missing money). When these conditions are met, school officials have a great deal of leeway in conducting searches of students and their property.

In *Veronia*, the court stated that the interest of the school in taking the action (e.g., random searches, drug tests) must be important enough to justify the procedure. The court saw protecting students from drug use and maintaining a safe and orderly educational environment as "important—indeed compelling" (p. 2395).

These decisions are extremely important because they give school officials guidance in using procedures such as targeted and random searches, drug testing, and surveillance. For legal purposes, we

have divided such procedures into three categories. In the next section we summarize tertiary, secondary, and preventive procedures.

PREVENTIVE PROCEDURES

In this section we will discuss school district reactions to violence, specifically focusing on tertiary, secondary, and primary prevention procedures. *Tertiary prevention* procedures are procedures that are applied to a problem that is already out of control. These procedures are responses to crises and are used when the problem has already become severe and protracted (Kauffman, in press). When applied to schools, these problems are a clear threat to its functioning and safety. The goal of tertiary prevention, then, is to keep the problem from engulfing the school and individuals therein. These procedures generally are used to remove the offending student or students from the school environment before they commit violent acts again. Tertiary procedures are reactive; school officials wait until incidents have occurred, identify the violators, and apply disciplinary procedures (James, 1994). *Secondary prevention* procedures are used to keep the problem from becoming severe. Such procedures are designed to arrest the problem and, if possible, reverse or correct it (Kauffman, 1999). When applied to violence in the schools, secondary prevention procedures are used to curb violence or drug use before it occurs. In effect, school officials monitor student behavior for warning signs of trouble and devise plans to respond, hopefully prior to an outbreak of violent behavior (James, 1994). Finally, *primary prevention* includes those procedures that focus on reducing the risk of violence by addressing educational and safety needs (Kauffman, in press). When applied to schools and potential violence, preventive procedures are those procedures that focus on educating students to avoid violence. Such procedures include conflict resolution programs and school-wide behavior management systems.

Tertiary Prevention

Zero-Tolerance Policies. Zero tolerance refers to policies in which any violation of a specified type (e.g., violence, drug use) results in a severe consequence (e.g., expulsion, arrest). Such policies grew out of the drug enforcement policies of the 1980s and in the 1990s began to be adopted by school districts across the country (Skiba & Peterson, 1999). Within the context of the GFSA, zero tolerance is the requirement that local education agencies expel from school for a period of not less than 1 year any students who bring a gun to school (20 U.S.C. § 8921 (b)(1)). GFSA does allow case-by-case modification of the mandatory expulsion by school officials.

All 50 states have enacted zero-tolerance legislation to comply with the GFSA. Some states have taken additional measures in an attempt to toughen the consequences of violating their respective laws. For instance, Arkansas treats violent incidences on school grounds, buses, or bus stops as felonies (Arkansas Code Annotated). In Illinois, minors aged 14 to 16 who carry a weapon to school will have their cases transferred from juvenile to criminal court (Bogos, 1997).

In addition to bringing firearms to school, some states have included additional offenses in their zero-tolerance laws that result in mandatory expulsion. For example, possession of illicit drugs or alcohol in Hawaii (Pipho, 1998), drug possession in Massachusetts (Shepherd & DeMarco, 1996), and rape or arson in Michigan (Michigan Compiled Laws Annotated) are now legal grounds for mandatory expulsion. Massachusetts (Massachusetts General Law Annotated) and a few other states have also broadened the definition of weapons to include knives (Colorado Code).

Additionally, most states have included various modifications of the GFSA in order to make their respective laws more practical. Colorado's law explicitly states that if a student immediately reports to school personnel that he or she possesses a firearm, the 1-year expulsion may be waived (Colorado Code). Although the media quickly highlights cases in which rationality, not school safety, is jeopardized, school boards and school administrators often have the discretion to change the mandatory consequences. For example, recently in South Carolina, a fifth-grade student was expelled for bringing a butterknife in her school lunch box (Roberts, 1998). The school board reviewed the expulsion and decided that the student's action did not constitute an ongoing threat. They reduced the expulsion to a year's probation, although the expulsion was left on her permanent record. However, as Pipho (1998) mentions, with respect to GFSA, case-by-case exceptions cannot be used to avoid overall compliance with the 1-year expulsions.

Unlike New Jersey, where expulsions under zero-tolerance laws require placement in alternative programs, pending a Board of Education hearing (Kopka, 1997), most states do not require schools to provide education to students in general education who were removed for violating zero-tolerance laws. In the highly publicized case of *Doe v. Superintendent of Schools of Worcester* (1995), the Supreme Judicial Court of Massachusetts ruled that the state did not have to provide an alternative education to a student who brought a lipstick case that contained a small knife blade. The court reasoned that neither the federal nor state Constitution guarantees a federal right to education. According to the court, the Commonwealth of Massachusetts has an obligation to educate its children, but students do not have a fundamental right to an education. By bringing a weapon to school, the student forfeited her right to a public education. The expulsion had followed the school's procedural guidelines and, as per Massachusetts State law, the student was expelled for 1 year for bringing a weapon to school. Thus, the school had fulfilled its obligation to provide an education to the student (Rubinstein, 1996).

A second type of tertiary prevention is the targeted search of a student and his or her property. Targeted searches are searches of a particular student who is suspected of committing a crime or violating a school rule. As we saw in *TLO*, school officials should base their decisions to conduct targeted searches on reasonable suspicion. Targeted searches include strip searches and searches of a student's property. The more serious the violation, the wider the scope and the greater the intrusiveness of the search allowed (James, 1994). For example, if a student is suspected of carrying a weapon, reasonable grounds for a strip search would exist because of the seriousness of the situation. However, suspicion of stealing candy from another student would not be reasonable grounds for such an intrusive search.

Strip Searches. Strip searches of students are extremely intrusive. Courts will, therefore, carefully scrutinize such searches. For example, in a decision by the U.S. Court of Appeals for the Seventh Circuit, *Cornfield v. Consolidated High School District No. 230* (1993), a high school student classified as seriously emotionally disturbed brought a suit alleging that a strip search conducted by the teacher and dean was a violation of his constitutional rights. Suspecting that the student was hiding drugs, the dean phoned the student's mother, who refused to consent to a search of the boy. The teacher and dean then escorted the student to the boys' locker room, where they conducted a strip search and physically inspected his clothing. No drugs were found. The student sued the school district, teacher, and dean. The district court ruled in favor of the defendants. On appeal, the circuit court affirmed the decision of the district court, stating that the strip search met the Fourth Amendment standard of reasonableness for searches conducted by school officials. The court noted that prior drug-related incidents involving the student combined with the personal observations of the teacher and aide created a reasonable suspicion that the student was concealing drugs. According to Maloney (1993), this ruling indicates that students, with or without disabilities, who are known to be actively using or dealing drugs can be subjected to similar search procedures. Because of the highly intrusive nature of these types of student searches, they should only be a last resort and only be conducted using the least intrusive means. Furthermore, the search must be based on reasonable suspicion (Miller & Ahrbecker, 1995). When strip searches are necessary, they should be conducted by persons of the same gender as the student and in a private area in the presence of school personnel also of the same gender as the student.

Targeted Searches of Students' Property. Although the U.S. Supreme Court has not heard a case involving targeted searches of student property, the court did uphold searches of government offices, desks, and file cabinets based on reasonable suspicion (*O'Connor v. Ortega,* 1987). Lower courts, using this decision as precedent, have upheld school officials' targeted or random searches of student lockers, if the searches are based on reasonable suspicion (*In the Interest of Isaiah B.,* 1993; *People v. Overton,* 1969). Searches by school authorities may also extend to students' cars and locked briefcases (*State of Washington v. Slattery,* 1990), as well as objects in which contraband may be hidden, such as backpacks (*People v. Dilworth,* 1996).

When school officials use tertiary prevention procedures, such as targeted searches of students and their property, they do not have to wait until the illegal behavior affects the school before taking action. School officials are legally permitted to act in response to reasonable suspicion that a student is violating or may have violated school rules or committed an illegal act. That is, they only need reason to believe that the safety or order of the school environment may be threatened by student behavior.

There is, however, another class of procedures that in many situations do not require reasonable suspicion prior to being undertaken. We refer to these as secondary procedures. Secondary procedures include random searches, use of metal detectors, and surveillance. It is

legally useful to consider such searches separately from targeted searches and other tertiary procedures because the standard that school officials must meet in using secondary procedures is lower. In the next section, we briefly examine the legality of secondary prevention procedures when used by school officials.

Secondary Prevention

Secondary prevention procedures involve school officials' attempts to seize weapons or contraband materials before they can be used. These procedures typically consist of random searches of students' belongings or property (e.g., lockers, automobiles, desks, backpacks). The use of metal detectors and various means of surveillance also fall into this category. Furthermore, the use of metal detectors to search students, even though there is no suspicion or consent to a search, is permitted (*Illinois v. Pruitt,* 1996). To keep weapons, drugs, and contraband off school property, random searches of students and their property are now common occurrences in public schools, especially at the secondary level (Dise et al., 1994). Secondary procedures, like tertiary procedures, are governed by the Fourth Amendment to the U.S. Constitution, which prohibits unreasonable searches and seizures. Unlike tertiary procedures, secondary procedures are directed at all students or are conducted randomly and therefore do not require reasonable suspicion.

A decision that has great importance for school districts conducting random searches was *In the Interest of Isaiah B.* (hereafter *Isaiah B.,* 1993). In this decision, the Wisconsin Supreme Court ruled that a student did not have reasonable expectations of privacy in his school locker. The court based its decision largely on the existence of the Milwaukee Public Schools policy regarding student lockers. According to the school policy,

> School lockers are the property of Milwaukee Public Schools. At no time does the Milwaukee School District relinquish its exclusive control of lockers provided

for the convenience of students. School authorities for any reason may conduct periodic general inspections of lockers at any time, without notice, without student consent, and without a search warrant. (*Isaiah B.,* p. 639)

Unless prohibited by state law, Miller and Ahrbecker (1995) suggested that schools develop policies regarding locker searches, such as the Milwaukee Public Schools policy, that notify students and parents that there is no reasonable expectation of privacy in a student locker and that both random and targeted searches of the locker may be conducted without student or parental consent. Bjorklun (1994), likewise, concluded that random locker searches may be conducted without individualized suspicion.

Secondary procedures include the use of random searches, surveillance cameras, and metal detectors. These procedures are legally proactive because they serve as a deterrent (James, 1994). School officials attempt to seize contraband and weapons before they are used. Unlike tertiary procedures, the *TLO* standard of reasonable suspicion is not as directly applicable in situations involving random property searches and other secondary procedures. That is, school officials do not necessarily need reasonable suspicion to conduct, for example, random locker checks. Rather, school officials must balance their legitimate need to search lockers with the privacy rights of students. When conducting searches of students and their property, it is important that school district officials adhere to established guidelines and policies that correspond with the case law. Students have diminished expectations of privacy while at school; nevertheless, school officials must notify students and their parents that student property may be subjected to random searches and that surveillance measures will be used and that the purpose of such measures is to ensure that students are educated in a safe and orderly environment. As James aptly states, "School officials must announce their intentions to make custodial interests (of the school) a part of a proactive campus safety plan that is communicated to students (and their parents) and consistently enforced" (p. 200). Procedural suggestions for using tertiary and secondary procedures are included in Table 3.

Primary Prevention

Primary prevention strategies are designed to reduce the risk of violence by educating students about violence and how it may be avoided or prevented. Such procedures include school-wide discipline plans, social skills training, conflict resolution programs, and parent training programs. A comprehensive examination of effective violence prevention programs is beyond the scope of this article; however, the legal importance of including such programs in safe school efforts cannot be overemphasized.

For extensive discussion and brief evaluations of 84 violence prevention programs, we refer readers to *Safe Schools, Safe Students: A Guide to Violence Prevention Strategies* (Drug Strategies, 1998). A compilation of best practices that address the prevention of school violence is available in *Early Warning, Timely Response; A Guide to Safe Schools* (Dwyer, Osher, & Warger, 1998).

Schools' efforts to decrease violence have been guided in part by legislation and litigation. Federal and state laws have mandated violence prevention strategies ranging from proactive education programs designed to reduce the risk of violence to reactive policies implemented in order to remove known or potential threats. The courts have consistently safeguarded students' rights while granting school officials the means to ensure school safety. We next examine how to best develop school-based policies and procedures within a legally sound framework.

RECOMMENDATIONS FOR DEVELOPING SCHOOL DISTRICT POLICIES AND PROCEDURES

School district responses to school violence must begin with establishing a priority that recognizes school violence as a significant problem and develops policies and procedures to address these problems. The policies should include careful planning and implementation of tertiary, secondary, and primary prevention procedures. In this section we offer several important considerations for de-

veloping legally sound school district plans to address school violence.

1. *Know the law.* Prior to developing policies and procedures regarding school violence, school district personnel must be aware of federal laws, state laws, and regulations addressing these issues. All 50 states have laws regarding issues of school violence. In some states, these laws mirror the federal requirements, although other states have laws that go far beyond the federal requirements. Developing school policies that are in line with state laws and regulations is essential.

2. *Make prevention of violence a publicly announced priority.* Few issues affect the public as profoundly as the issue of school violence (Kyle & Hahn, 1995). School districts should publicly announce the measures they take to address these problems. Publicly announcing the formation of policies and procedures increases the likelihood of community cooperation and support. In the event of crisis situations, previously announced policies can help minimize both negative publicity and legal liability. School district policies and procedures can be made available through newsletters, pamphlets, school manuals, and mailings to parents, as well as pre-

---

TABLE 3
Developing Tertiary and Secondary Prevention Policies

1. Draft a school district policy regarding tertiary and secondary procedures.
   a. Describe reasons for and purposes of the policy (e.g., need to protect students and maintain a safe and orderly educational environment).
   b. State that lockers are the property of the school and that students have reduced expectations of privacy in lockers. The policy should also address reduced privacy regarding student property on school grounds (e.g., automobiles, backpacks). Students and their parents should sign an acknowledgement form.
   c. Describe circumstances that will lead to targeted and random searches of students and their property.
   d. Specify procedures that will be followed if contraband is found in targeted or random searches (e.g., conduct more intrusive search, call police).
   e. Specify possible sanctions and situations in which the police will be notified.
   f. Notify public regarding school district policy.
2. Prior to conducting targeted searches or seizures:
   a. School officials must have reasonable suspicion (e.g., tips from informants).
   b. The scope of the search must be reasonable given the student's age and nature of the offense.
3. Document targeted and random searches of students and their property and have witnesses sign the record. In the case of targeted searches, the record should indicate how the search was justified at inception and that it was reasonably related to the violation (i.e., not overly intrusive).

---

sentations to the school board and community groups. The general information provided should include programs to train school personnel, school programs to prevent violence, school safety plans, and crisis response procedures.

3. *Involve the community.* School violence is a community problem. The district team should reach out to the community for assistance with violence prevention efforts. For example, the team could bring in local law enforcement, staff from child and family service agencies and mental health service agencies, student and parent groups, and other influential groups in the community.

4. *Assess the physical safety of district schools and implement correction procedures.* School district officials should conduct safety audits of all schools and develop comprehensive plans for maintaining security. Law enforcement officials should be used in assessing and developing these security measures. Safety audits should be conducted annually and be used for both evaluation and planning purposes. These audits should address building security, school-wide discipline, student troublemaker identification, supervision practices, staff screening processes, campus intruder and visitor procedures, school and district communication, and crisis response plans (Stephens, 1994). For resources addressing the characteristics of safe schools and suggestions for making schools safe, readers are referred to Dwyer et al. (1998), Stephens (1994), and Walker and Gresham (1997).

5. *Form school district and individual school teams.* One of the most important elements for establishing legally sound policies and procedures is to designate a school district team to address school violence. Moreover, these teams should be given the resources and the responsibility for identifying and implementing prevention plans for the district. The teams should be comprised of school district administrators, teachers, security personnel, community representatives (e.g., law enforcement personnel), parents, and others. Kyle and

Hahn (1995) suggest that the teams that develop district policy should include representatives from the school district's legal department or someone knowledgeable about federal and state laws.

The primary tasks of the team should be to (a) designate a leader, (b) review the seriousness of violence in the school district, (c) assess the level of school district readiness for dealing with violence, (d) develop a district policy for implementing violence prevention plans, (e) provide training for school district employees, (f) formulate an action plan addressing crisis intervention when a serious incident occurs, and (g) oversee the creation of teams in each of the schools to implement the school district policies and procedures.

6. *Conduct district-wide training of all staff.* School districts could face a lawsuit if they fail to train administrators, teachers, and staff in preventing and minimizing the effects of violent incidences (Kyle & Hahn, 1995). Administrators, teachers, school staff, and other members of the district and school teams should receive ongoing professional development in preventing violent behavior and intervening effectively and safely. Training should include (a) understanding the characteristics of safe and unsafe schools, (b) managing and disciplining students in the classroom, (c) identifying and responding to warning signs of possible violent behavior, (d) using safe and effective intervention procedures, and (e) responding to violence after it has occurred.

7. *Implement prevention programs.* We mentioned the importance of violence prevention through educational programs. School district efforts should be directed at identifying those students at risk of developing behavioral problems and teaching them positive social interaction skills. Programs such as conflict resolution and peer mediation should be a part of these efforts. Violence prevention efforts must involve schools in developing school-wide discipline plans. These plans should include (a) specifying expected

behaviors, (b) communicating these expectations, (c) developing procedures for correcting problem behavior, and (d) establishing a commitment from all school staff to implement the discipline plan (Walker, Colvin, & Ramsey, 1995).

8. *Develop crisis procedures for responding to violent incidents.* Despite efforts to prevent violence from occurring, schools must be prepared to react to such incidents if they occur. School districts, therefore, must have crisis-response procedures in place. Crisis plans should include (a) a clear chain of command, (b) an effective communication system involving both internal and external notification procedures, (c) a process for securing external emergency support (e.g., law enforcement, trauma consultants, counselors), (d) staff training in safe and effective interventions during and following the crisis, (e) investigative procedures, and (f) public relations considerations (Dwyer et al., 1998; Kyle & Hahn, 1995).

9. *Use law enforcement and the courts to address violence when it occurs.* State laws address violent incidents. These laws prohibit juvenile possession of certain weapons and drugs; therefore, a student caught with either drugs or weapons is likely to face charges in a juvenile or adult court system (Shepard & DeMarco, 1996). School district officials should know what legal relief is available when incidences of violence occur. Law enforcement authorities should be called in when violent incidents occur. Furthermore, law enforcement and the courts can act to obtain court orders that may serve to prevent violent incidents.

10. *Formatively evaluate school district policies and procedures.* It is extremely important that violence prevention be an ongoing effort. Therefore, in the initial planning stages, the school district team should address procedures for formative evaluation of the plan. A member of the school district team could be given responsibility to (a) conduct safety audits, (b) develop a system to ensure that the plan is being implemented with fidelity and consistency,

(c) monitor and track incidents of violent behavior, and (d) implement procedures whereby schools can review and revise their violence prevention plans.

SUMMARY

We have attempted to provide legally sound guidelines to effectively prevent violence in the schools. These guidelines are outlined by federal and state legislation and are continuously clarified by litigation. Future court cases and new federal and state laws will continue to redefine the legal framework; therefore, school district officials should monitor such developments and revise their violence prevention strategies when necessary.

About the Authors

MITCHELL L. YELL, PhD, is an associate professor in Programs in Special Education at the University of South Carolina. MICHAEL E. ROZALSKI, MEd, is a doctoral student in Programs in Special Education at the University of South Carolina. Address: Mitchell L. Yell, 235-G Wardlaw, University of South Carolina, Columbia, SC 29208; e-mail: myell@sc.edu

Authors' Note

We wish to thank Dr. Erik Drasgow for his excellent suggestions on an earlier draft of this manuscript.

References

Arkansas Code Annotated §5-73-119 2(A-B).

Bjorklun, E. C. (1994). School locker searches and the fourth amendment. *Education Law Reporter, 92,* 1065–1071.

Bogos, P. M. (1997). "Expelled. No excuses. No exceptions."—Michigan's zero tolerance policy in response to school violence: M.C.L.A. section 380.1311. *University of Detroit Mercy Law Review, 74,* 357–387.

Colorado Code §§ 22-33-106(d) *et seq.*

Cornfield v. Consolidated High School District No. 230, 19 IDELR 1058 (1993).

Dise, J. H., Iyer, C. S., & Noorman, J. J. (1994). *Searches of students, lockers, and automobiles.* Horsham, PA: LRP Publications.

Doe v. Superintendent of Schools of Worcester, 653 N.E.2d 1088 (1995).

Drug Strategies. (1998). *Safe schools, safe students: A guide to violence prevention strategies.* Washington, DC: Author.

Dwyer, K., Osher, D., & Warger, C. (1998). *Early warning, timely response: A guide to safe schools.* Washington, DC: United States Department of Education. http://www.air-dc.org/cecp/cecp.html

Gun-Free Schools Act of 1994, 20 U.S.C. § 8921(b)(1).

Harris, L. (1995). *Violence in America's public schools: A survey of the American teacher.* New York: Metropolitan Life Insurance.

Illinois v. Pruitt, 64 USLW 2575 (Ill. App. 1996).

Improving America's Schools Act, 20 U.S.C. § 6301 *et seq.* (1994).

In the Interest of Isaiah B. 500 N.W. 2d 637 (Wisc. 1993).

James, B. (1994). School violence and the law: The search for suitable tools. *School Psychology Review, 23,* 190–203.

Kachur, S. P., Stennies, G. M., Modzeleski, W., Stephens, R., Murphy, R., Kresnow, M., Sleet, D., & Lowry, R. (1996). School associated violent deaths in the United States, 1992-1994. *Journal of the American Medical Association, 275,* 1729–1733.

Kauffman, J. M. (1999). How we prevent the prevention of emotional and behavioral disorders. *Exceptional Children, 65,* 448–468.

Kopka, D. L. (1997). *School violence.* Santa Barbara, CA: Contemporary School Issues.

Kyle, J. W., & Hahn, B. W. (1995). Violence and the school as a workplace. In *Violence in the schools: Causes, prevention, and crises management.* Conference handbook of the violence in the schools conference, Horsham, PA: LRP Publications.

Maloney, M. (1993, September 15). Strip search for drugs did not violate student rights. *The Special Educator, 9,* 42.

Massachusetts General Law Annotated 71 § 37H.

Michigan Compiled Laws Annotated § 380.1311 *et seq.*

Miller, B., & Ahrbecker, W. C. (1995). Legal issues and school violence. In *Violence in the schools: Causes, prevention, and crises management.* Conference handbook of the violence in the schools conference, Horsham, PA: LRP Publications.

New Jersey v. T.L.O., 469 U.S. 325 (1985).

National League of Cities. (1995). *School violence in America.* Washington, DC: Author.

O'Conner v. Ortega, 480 U.S. 709 (1987).

People v. Dilworth, 661 N.E.2d 310 (Ill. 1996).

People v. Overton, 249 N.E.2d 366 (NY 1969).

Pipho, C. (1998). Living with zero tolerance. *Phi Delta Kappan, 79*(10), 725–727.

Roberts, L. (1998, October 24). Girl expelled from school for possessing a butterknife. *The State Newspaper,* p. B1.

Rose, L. C., & Gallup, A. M. (1998). The 30th annual Phi Delta Kappa/Gallup Poll of the public's attitudes toward the public schools. *Phi Delta Kappan, 80,* 41–56.

Rubinstein, S. (1996). Lipstick case shades education question. *Criminal Justice, 11,* 29–31.

Sautler, R. C. (1995). Standing up to violence. *Phi Delta Kappan, 76,* K1-K12.

Shepherd, R. E., Jr., & DeMarco, A. J. (1996). Weapons in schools and zero tolerance. *Criminal Justice, 11*(2), 46–48.

Skiba, R., & Peterson, R. (1999). The dark side of zero tolerance: Can punishment lead to safe schools? *Phi Delta Kappan, 80,* 372–382.

Sleek, S. (1998). Experts scrambling on school shootings. *APA Monitor, 29*(8), 1–4.

State of Washington v. Slattery, 787 P.2d 932 (Div. 1 1990).

Stephens, R. D. (1994). Planning for safer and better schools: School violence prevention and intervention strategies. *School Psychology Review, 23*(2), 204–215.

U.S. Department of Justice. (1996). *Juvenile offenders and victims: 1996 update on violence.* Washington, DC: Office of Juvenile Justice and Delinquency Prevention.

Valente, R. (1994). *Law in the schools* (3rd ed.). New York: Merrill.

Veronia School District v. Acton, 515 U.S. 646 (1995).

Walker, H. M., Colvin, G., & Ramsey, E. (1995). *Antisocial behavior in school: Strategies and best practices.* Pacific Grove, CA: Brooks/Cole.

Walker, H. M., & Gresham, F. M. (1997). Making schools safer and violence free. *Intervention in School and Clinic, 32*(4), 199–204.

Yell, M. L. (1998). *The law and special education.* Upper Saddle River, NJ: Prentice Hall/Merrill.

Zirkel, P. A. (1995). Courtside: Drug tests passes court test. *Phi Delta Kappan, 77,* 187–188.

Safe School Design

A Handbook for Educational Leaders

Crime Prevention Through Environmental Design (CPTED) is based on a simple premise: the physical characteristics of the setting influence human behavior.

CPTED helps us to understand how the physical environment of schools affects the behavior of students and staff. Using CPTED principles, school architects and designers, and school board members and administrators can improve the management and use of physical spaces in schools, thus making them safer places for the people who work and learn in them.

CPTED has been used extensively in the prevention and deterrence of criminal behavior in a range of community settings, including schools. CPTED asserts that the proper design and use of the built environment can produce three important outcomes:

- reduction in the incidence and fear of crime
- improvements in quality of life
- productive use of space

CPTED concepts and principles are remarkably ignored and underutilized in today's schools. We believe the CPTED approach is one of the most effective tools currently available for creating safer schools and reducing the likelihood of student violence. The purpose of this book is to illustrate how the CPTED knowledge base can be applied productively in the effort to create safer schools.

This guide provides school administrators and school board members with access to the extensive body of knowledge on innovations in the architectural design, use, and supervision of space in our schools.

CONTENTS

1. The Changed Landscape of School Safety and Security
2. The Relevance of CPTED as a Strategy for Improving School Safety and Security
3. Key CPTED Concepts and Principles
4. Site Evaluation: The Foundation for Improving School Safety and Security
5. Case Study Applications of CPTED Principles
6. The Role of Architects in School Design
7. Policy Recommendations for School Districts

The Authors

- **Tod Schneider** is the Eugene, Oregon, Police Department's Crime Prevention Specialist and Crime Prevention Through Environmental Design (CPTED) Analyst.

- **Hill Walker** is codirector of the Institute on Violence and Destructive Behavior at the University of Oregon and has conducted research on students with disruptive behavior disorders in school settings for over three decades.

- **Jeffrey Sprague** is codirector of the Institute on Violence and Destructive Behavior at the University of Oregon and an expert in school safety, violence prevention, delinquency, and evaluation of programs in delinquency prevention and school safety.

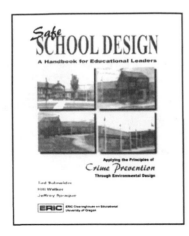

Safe School Design

A Handbook for Educational Leaders

Applying the Principles of Crime Prevention Through Environmental Design

Tod Schneider

Hill Walker

Jeffrey Sprague

2000 • 8 ¹/₂ x 11 inches

xiv + 96 pages

perfect bind

ISBN 0-86552-148-4

$18.00

CODE: EMOSSD

ERIC Clearinghouse on Educational Management
College of Education
University of Oregon

1488

ORDER FORM

Send me _____ copies @ $18.00 each plus $4.00 S&H

Name _____

Position _____

Institution _____

Phone ( ) _____

Address _____

City _____ State _____ Zip _____

Visa/MasterCard No.

⬜⬜⬜⬜ ⬜⬜⬜⬜ ⬜⬜⬜⬜ ⬜⬜⬜⬜

Exp. ⬜⬜⬜⬜ Signature _____

How to Order: You may place an order by sending a check or money order, mailing or faxing a purchase order, or calling with a Visa or MasterCard number. Add 10% for S&H (minimum $4.00). Make payment to University of Oregon/ERIC. Shipping is by UPS ground or equivalent.

You can also order online (with Visa or MasterCard) from our website—Your gateway to information about educational policy and management.

http://eric.uoregon.edu

ERIC Clearinghouse on Educational Management
5207 University of Oregon
Eugene, Oregon 97403-5207

800-438-8841

FAX 541-346-2334

Email: sales@eric.uoregon.edu

HOW did they do that?

motion graphics

ROCKPORT

GLOUCESTER MASSACHUSETTS

HOW
did they do
that?

ROCKPORT
PUBLISHERS

motion graphics

DAVID GREENE

© 2003
Rockport Publishers, Inc.

All rights reserved. No part of this book may be reproduced in any form without written permission of the copyright owners. All images in this book have been reproduced with the knowledge and prior consent of the artists concerned, and no responsibility is accepted by producer, publisher, or printer for any infringement of copyright or otherwise, arising from the contents of this publication. Every effort has been made to ensure that credits accurately comply with information supplied.

First published in the United States of America by
Rockport Publishers, Inc.
33 Commercial Street
Gloucester, Massachusetts 01930-5089
Telephone **(978) 282-9590**
Fax **(978) 283-2742**
www.rockpub.com

Library of Congress Cataloging-in-Publication Data available
ISBN 1-56496-910-X
10 9 8 7 6 5 4 3 2 1

Design **Stoltze Design**
Copyeditor **Pamela Hunt**
Proofreader **Stacey Ann Follin**

Printed in China

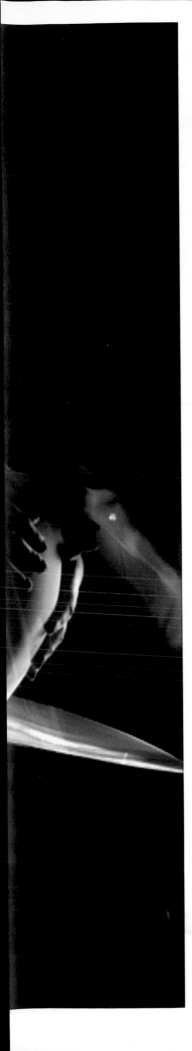

This book
is dedicated to

Kelli, who is the true definition of beauty in motion, and without her love, patience, and assistance this book would never have come to light.

Emma, may you grow strong and happy, and learn to forgive Daddy for being so obsessed with the images that flicker across the screen.

Contents

Introduction

This book endeavors to take an expansive view of motion graphics. We examine projects from a wide range of disciplines, ranging from broadcast to new media, exploring both the creative genesis of the work and the production techniques required to produce the work. Motion graphics can be as subtle as the visual scratching techniques employed by a documentary filmmaker or as apparent as a full-blown special effects extravaganza. Both are highlighted in this book. The objective is to show how dynamic visual communication techniques are employed to convey an underlying message.

The firms and projects represented in this book are only a small sampling of the wide range of talent that exists in the field. Projects were selected based upon creative excellence, relevance, and availability. A sincere debt of gratitude is owed to those who have taken the time to share their vision, creativity, and production expertise to this book.

Prehistoric cave paintings from
the Lascaux Caves in France.
Art Resource, NY

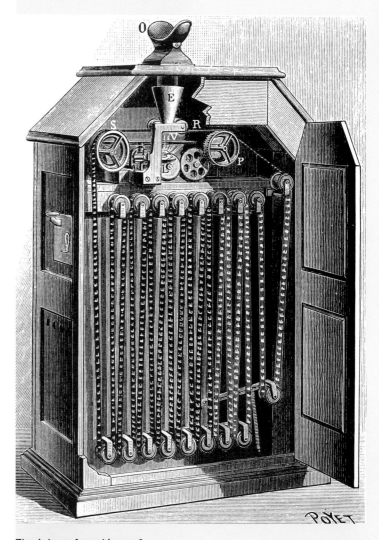

The internal workings of
Edison's kinescope, circa 1894.
Image Select/Art Resource, NY

Overview

Communication is one of the primary tools that differentiates man from the other species inhabiting this planet. Humans have an innate desire to express their thoughts and feelings through visual representations, and motion—whether real or implied—has always been an integral part of this visual communication.

You can see it in the earliest cave paintings—the thrill of the hunt, the motion of the prey, and the pursuit of the hunters. All figures are in action; the degree in which the motion is conveyed is limited only by the technology available.

As society evolved, our ability to convey motion has undergone a similar evolution. Fingertips dipped in red ochre eventually gave way to the intricate brushwork of the Renaissance. In the early 1800s, Frenchmen Joseph Niépce and Louis Daguerre launched the art of photography. For the first time, man could actually capture images exactly how they appear in nature. By the end of the century, motion was introduced to photography by means of a hand crank. Flipbooks, which became all the rage in penny arcades, allowed viewers to flip through a sequence of images and see animated "films," such as the censored *Serpentine Dance* by Annabelle Moore.

Eventually, the flipbook made way for Edison's kinescope, and the age of modern motion graphics was at hand. It has been barely more than a century since that invention, and motion graphics have grown monumentally both in technique and content. Where we were once limited to colorless films without the benefit of sound, we now can create digital fire from small gray boxes that fit underneath our desks.

Marshall McLuhan once said "The medium is the message." That statement is no longer entirely true. The message is in motion, and it refuses to sit still. The transmission device is not important—only the reception. The message does not care if it moves though airwaves, coax-ial cables, telephone lines, or gleaming fiber optics. It only cares about being received and retained.

This is the challenge of the modern motion graphics artist—to cut through the clutter and convey the message, whether it be to entertain or to promote, in the most effective and engaging way possible. There are a myriad of choices and technologies. There is never one clear-cut answer or solution. Often it is not just one technique but several that are intertwined to create the desired effect.

To remain competitive, it is essential to understand and embrace the art of motion in all of its current incarnations: animation, film, CG special effects, and interactivity. That being said, never forget that beyond all of the commerce, the endless meetings, the budgetary constraints, and the technical glitches is the simple need to communicate. This is what drives us as humans.

To put images into motion and ideas into action is a celebration of the human spirit at its most elemental and beautiful

Cinemax packaging ID, circa new millenium.

Chapter 1
Television

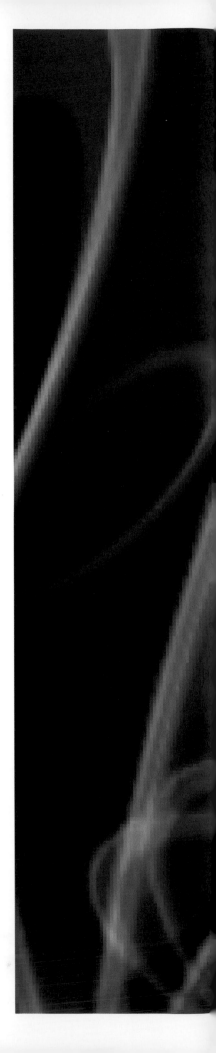

It is difficult to quantify television's influence on modern society. It influences and shapes public opinion and is blamed for everything from the denigration of our moral fiber to our expanding waistlines. In the context of this book, however, what is more interesting than its societal ramifications is television's influence on television.

Gone are the days of three primary networks locked in a gladiatorial struggle for ratings. Cable, digital cable, and satellite connectivity have changed the playing field. More options mean more competition. More competition means more innovation is required to make viewers sit up and take notice.

In essence, television has become a victim of its own success. To leave a lasting impact in the minds of an oversaturated, attention-deficit-driven viewing audience, more and more sophisticated graphics and creative approaches are required. Network packages, interstitials, advertisements, and show openers are all on the front line of the ratings battle. It is simply too easy for the consumer to click the remote and find compelling content elsewhere.

This book examines some of the most unique and effective approaches taken to combat this trend. From the disturbingly beautiful work of German design firm Velvet on the *Horrorskop* campaign to the next-generation virtual broadcast-identity package developed for the BBC Four by Lambie-Nairn, we have sought out examples of excellence in broadcast design.

Although these projects span the globe in terms of origin and the variation of production techniques employed, they share one common thread—they are all effective communications grounded by solid design and exemplary technical implementation.

TechTV
Audiofile
Program
Package

Project Overview

To even the causal viewer, it is obvious that the program package for *Audiofile* was developed by a crew who hold music near and dear to their hearts.

The show revolves around the dual themes of technology and music and their interaction in the modern world. The show package is an original pastiche of bits of technology interlaced with scenes of people caught in the act of both creating music and reacting to it.

The project originated in early 2001, during the transition of ZD TV's relaunch as TechTV. Belief had originally been hired to produce three station IDs. The channel was so pleased with these spots that they offered Belief the opportunity to develop the show package for their flagship program.

The development time was quick—two weeks start to finish—but the visuals show no evidence of anything less than a truly innovative production house operating at a full-tilt boogie of imagination and passion. Their efforts paid off with the main titles winning a regional Emmy and garnering a national Emmy nomination for Best Prime Time Main Title Design.

Mike Goedecke (left)
and Ryan Riccio (right)
constructing a
3-D landscape.

Creative Process

The creative brief was succinct and to the point. TechTV wanted the package to have three main features: be bright and upbeat, show people interacting with musical instruments, and be stylistically reminiscent of the boxes created by Joseph Cornell.

Joseph Cornell was an American artist who began constructing collaged shadow boxes in the 1930s. His works have become collector's items and museum pieces. The works were originally developed as "gifts" to people who had touched his life in some way. His boxes were monuments to the emotions sparked inside him by the recipients, many of whom he never met.

Unfortunately, Cornell's boxes were often fairly dark, and the show package required a lighter color base. Creative director Mike Goedecke explained, "Although the show was broadcast during prime time, they planned to rebroadcast it throughout the day, so they wanted it to have a bright, positive feeling. They really liked the artist Cornell and his boxes, but his style was very antique, and he usually used a fairly dark color palette. So we asked ourselves, 'What if Cornell was making boxes today? What would they look like, and how would he make them?'"

Belief explored a number of different approaches. At one point, they attempted to create the "boxes" in 3-D but found they were spending too much time on the models and that the feeling of the piece was

becoming too "computery." Although the show is about technology, TechTV wanted the show to feel warm—after all, music is an evocative emotional experience; the computer is merely a tool to facilitate that feeling.

To transition the concept of the Cornell boxes into the modern age, Belief experimented with real-world objects. Using Lucite as a base, they constructed a test 3-D landscape of discarded technological and musical equipment. Various lighting effects were applied to the model, and digital stills were taken and posted on the Belief website for the client to review. As Goedecke put it, "Once they approved it, there was no going back."

Production Process

Building The Panels

"For us to build a prop, it's not something that would scare us," said Goedecke. "Most of us have fine art backgrounds, so building these panels was not a big departure for us. We went to different stores and electronic graveyards and dug, picked, and unscrewed things to find interesting shapes and forms that were pieces from the past."

Assembled horizontally onto a 5' x 8' (1.5 m x 2.4 m) Lucite panel mounted on plywood, the keyboards, resisters, knobs, switches, and transistors were transformed into a 3-D landscape. Lucite had been selected for the background so that light would show through the model. Working with Lucite presented unique challenges. It is an unforgiving material, and fingerprints or glue spills would ruin the effect. Therefore, exceptional care was taken with the gluing process, and gloves were worn to prevent unsightly blemishes on the surface.

In addition to the technology, various color swatches were glued on the background. These swatches would be used later in postproduction for tracking the areas to be composited. Although they did not know exactly what images they would place in these locations, they knew where they would like them to be in the model.

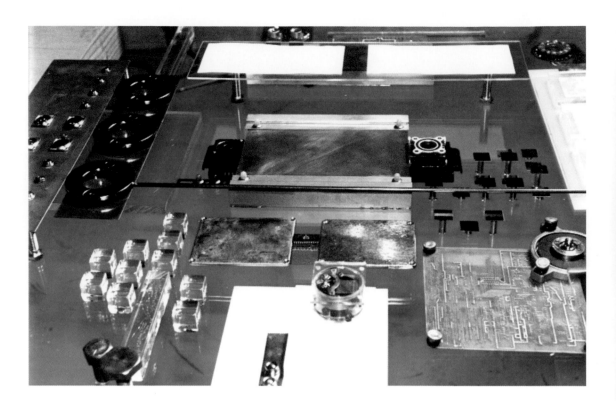

Film Shoot

Day One—Model Shoot

Afraid that the panels were too delicate to transport, Belief photographed them in 35 mm at their studio. The panels were shot using a Frasier lens, which is a specialized piece of equipment used for shooting miniatures. The lens has two primary features. It allows you to shoot close macrophotography while keeping a large depth of field. It can also rotate on any axis to give the illusion of spinning. Goedecke described it as "almost like having a motion-controlled camera, only cheaper."

The panels were shot in a vertical position to allow for more lighting options, and the Belief crew tried numerous variations. They placed panels behind each other and pulled focus to add depth to the shot. For the opening shot, they mounted glass rods on c-stands and placed them in front of the model. They then created dolly shots as they rotated the Frasier lens. They even experimented with different lighting techniques, ranging from pans and wipes, to people casting shadows behind the panels.

The one unforeseen problem with the shoot was with the Frasier lens's lighting requirements. In order to work properly, the lens needed a lot of light—so much light, in fact, that during the shoot, the panels would heat the epoxy in the glue, which would loosen, causing pieces to fall off.

Goedecke explained, "It's all these things you never think about. Then you find yourself in production, and all of a sudden, things start sliding and you go, 'Oh, my God!'" In the end, they found themselves occasionally having to shut down the shoot to let the models cool.

Day Two—Talent

A cast of professional musicians and dancers was assembled at a green-screen studio for the one-day shoot of the compositing elements. The talent were given a high degree of leeway to express themselves, both musically and physically. Even Ryan Riccio, the designer, got into the act, jamming on drums for the spot.

Belief found shooting some of the brass instruments, like the saxophone and trumpet, especially challenging, because of the instruments' highly reflective surfaces. They worked around this problem by almost entirely enveloping the instruments in black cloth to prevent the reflections of the crew in the instruments.

Postproduction

Belief created the final scenes by compositing in After Effects and editing in Media 100. They had a rough audio track to work with and were able to determine the general idea of how long the individual scenes would be. The first step was to edit a version of the spot using only the model shots. Once those were locked, they reviewed the talent footage and determined the placement and order of each shot.

Goedecke explained, "You have to choose all shots before going into compositing because you don't want to be "fiddle-faddling" with the stuff while you're compositing. You have to work really hard to make a shot work, and if that shot changes, you need to completely rework it."

From there, Riccio and Goedecke broke up the scenes and traded off. In a frantic fit of tag-team editing, they completed the project by the deadline. The editing was no easy task—each shot contains multiple live elements. In fact, the opening shot has over 30 pieces of talent footage composited on top of graphics treatments, the panels themselves, and a number of glass tubes moving in the foreground.

Another designer worked on the logo animation for end resolve. The team had already selected the background for the shot, so integration of the final scene was relatively painless. The final touch was the transitions between the scenes. Originally, the spot was intended as a cuts-and-dissolves piece, but in the end, quick 20-frame morphs were used to transition between shots.

Credits

Executive Creative Director **Mike Goedecke**
Live Action Director/Director of Photography **Mike Goedecke**
Designer/Animator **Ryan Riccio**
Model Builders **Ryan Riccio and Mike Goedecke**

Tools

Adobe After Effects
Adobe Illustrator
Adobe Photoshop
Apple Macintosh G4
Media 100

Production Company

Belief
Santa Monica, CA, United States

MTV
Total Request Live
Show Package

Project Overview

Total Request Live (TRL) is currently one of the most influential music programs on television. This program has been responsible for breaking some of the largest acts in the music industry today. The impact of the show is vast, measured not only in the music charts, but also in the fashion and language of today's youth.

Like the music industry, the show is constantly changing. Popular tastes are fickle, especially in the youth-culture marketplace. One of the challenges in designing this show open was not only to develop a brand identity, but also to create an identity that, unlike many of the musical performers featured on the show, would still seem fresh in six months.

Creative Process

On MTV, excitement is the name of the game, and the *TRL* show open is lacking neither movement nor intensity. The open was based on a concept developed by MTV. "Journey to *TRL*" is a fast-paced tour through New York City to the *TRL* set as seen from the fans' point of view.

The aim was to capture the enthusiasm and excitement of the audience members on their way to the show. To achieve this effect, both time-lapse photography and sequenced stills were used. The entire city becomes a billboard for the imagination of the mobile fan. Puff Daddy inhabits the poster next to the escalator in the subway. J.Lo and Jay-Z spring to life on the sides of buildings. Christina Aguilera gives a come-hither smile from the side of a phone booth, and Eminem smirks from a taxi popup. It's as if the viewers' fantasies have come to life on the canvas that is the city.

Art director and designer David Clayton explained, "The biggest issue was that the titles and graphics were going to air twice a day, every day. The show's producer, Adam Freeman, needed us to find a look that could still be interesting after that much saturation on the air. He then sent us a 'mega-mix' that the MTV sound people did for some promo. He loved the idea of a sound collage worked into the open."

The audio collage gives the clip a feeling of urgency, of random thoughts and imagery that might cross the mind of excited fans on their way to their favorite show.

Production Process

This production required a high degree of communication and coordination between The Picture Mill and MTV Studios. MTV's editorial department had to pull clips to use, the legal department needed to clear hundreds of images, and the team had to tailor all of the deliverables to work efficiently with MTV's graphics department and their control booth technology.

Footage

The team took one day to scout for a three-day four-camera shoot around New York City. One of the greatest challenges, it seemed, was driving the loaded cargo van around the city. Luckily, other elements of the city were more accommodating, such as the NYC Film Permit Office, which proved helpful and sympathetic to needs of the crew.

"We generally would set up a time-lapse camera or two in the morning and let them start rolling at one frame every five seconds, all day long," Clayton said. "Then we'd walk around with our director of photography, John Donnelly, and bootleg some uncontrolled action by hiding the camera under a jacket and just letting it run." The combination of time-lapse shots and first-person action footage gives the clip its propulsive sense of motion.

Clearances

One of the largest hurdles in this shoot was the clearance issue. For example, the difficulty in getting clearance to shoot from the building across from the *TRL* studio was unexpected because *TRL* already has a camera installed on the building. Even after a written prearrangement, the team spent an additional four hours to get the security clearances required to shoot above Times Square.

In addition to the difficulty obtaining clearances, the team faced major legal issues regarding signage and buildings around Times Square. More than half of the dailies had to be discarded on legal technicalities. Permission is required to broadcast signs, trademarks, logos, and landmarks. Unfortunately for the team, a trademark exists roughly every two feet in Times Square.

Prior to final delivery, *TRL* did a rehearsal show to test the new open with their in-studio technology, because the show has some very specific requirements for keying and titling. After some minor modifications requested by the technical director at *TRL* were implemented, the identity package was delivered.

Initial design to final delivery of the on-air toolkit took about five weeks.

Credits

Creative Director **William Lebeda**
Producer **Kirk Cameron**
Art Director/Designer **David Clayton**
Director of Photography **John Donnelly**
Editor **Kye Krauter**
Animator/Compositor **Nelson Yu**

Tools

Adobe After Effects
Adobe Illustrator
Adobe Photoshop
Apple Final Cut Pro
Media 100

Production Company

The Picture Mill
Santa Monica, CA, United States

Images courtesy of MTV.

USA Networks
U.S. Open
Promotional Package

Project Overview

Venus Williams serves, Pete Sampras returns, Anna Kournikova backhands, and Andre Agassi makes the shot by the skin of his teeth. The crowd goes wild.

Sound like an unlikely match? Perhaps. But this is no ordinary match— this is a fantasy sequence created to promote the 2001 U.S. Open on the USA network. In this dynamic campaign, the stars of professional tennis meet in a netherworld of competition, defined only by the lines of the court and the limits of their abilities.

The combination of the promotional campaign and the quality of the matches resulted in the 2001 U.S. Open becoming one of the highest-rated tennis events in history.

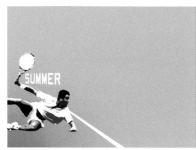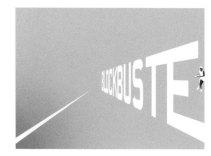

Creative Process

The promotional campaign for the U.S. Open was a true collaboration between the client and the production team at R!OT. Although production and execution of the spots were done at R!OT, a good portion of the creative work came from the network.

Lorenzo de Guttaduaro, the creative director at USA Networks, said, "We didn't think the straight-sports sell was going to work on our air, and quite honestly, we're not CBS Sports. What we wanted to do was present the U.S. Open through our brand lens. We're pretty much about big blockbuster entertainment, and the Open really lends itself to that. Tennis stars today are almost like big movie stars. There is that sexiness to them. It's not a team—it's either one-on-one or couples—but mainly it's like one-on-one, and that's gutsy. We made the illusion of two gladiators in the ring. That's sexy, that has emotional conflict."

The initial look was also developed at USA Networks, where the art director isolated an image of a player falling to his knees with his arms raised in victory. They placed the image on a flat, mossy green background in a poster-sized display. It was from that image that the tenor and tone of the piece sprung forth.

The objective was to lose everything but the star, to maintain focus on the player—everything else was superficial. The spots play out as virtual dream matches in a world that exists only for tennis.

Aggressive tag lines were developed, each focusing on a different theme. "Every Player, Every Triumph…Every Player, Every Upset…Every Player" pointed to the fact that USA Network had more coverage than any other network. CBS may have had most of the final matches, but it didn't broadcast the preliminary matches. For women's tennis, they developed the tag, "They may look nice, but they certainly don't play nice." Another tag plays off the summer blockbuster craze: "The only summer blockbuster that won't have a predictable ending." Yet another tag relays the agony of defeat: "Why is it so fun watching a man's dream getting crushed?"

Production

Director Jeremy Hollister explained, "This was an interesting project because the USA team had already done a lot of conceptualization of what they wanted it to be. They wanted it to be a giant tennis match between all the stars, kind of like a free-for-all. They had come up with the general idea that the space should be green to reflect the color of a tennis court, so that was our jumping-off point. What they wanted us to do was figure out a way to bring it to life and give it that extra bit of special dynamic."

To give it that "special dynamic," Hollister worked out an innovative production process. He took the footage given to him by USA and brought it frame by frame into Flash. Flash has a feature that enables users to transform bitmapped images into vector images. Hollister discovered this feature after playing with the program for a day, and after some initial tests, he decided that this feature would give the piece the look they were after.

"Turning the footage into vectors allowed us the flexibility to make them as large as we wanted to. In video you can't blow stuff up because it loses resolution," said Hollister. "The way we approach things is to figure out what tools are right for the job and how to make the tools do things you don't expect them to do. Everyone was like, 'Oh, wow, we never thought about Flash for that.' I try not to get caught up in the limitations of the tools I'm used to working with. I often ask myself, 'What else is there?'"

Hollister described the process of achieving the final effect as "fairly brutal." First, they needed to identify the footage they wanted to use. Once footage was selected, each frame was output at high resolution. The image was then taken into Photoshop where everything but the player was cropped out. Next, the image was opened in Flash and converted into vectors. To retain smooth motion, the process was done at 30 frames per second. Hollister estimates that they converted nearly 5,000 frames using this process, which took nearly 2 1/2 months with a staff of up to ten people to complete.

The individual frames were exported to After Effects for reassembly. The final piece was composited in Inferno. Spatial items, such as the baselines and net, were created in Inferno. Camera moves were added to give the piece its sense of motion, depth, and drama.

The final element of this production was the soundtrack, which is composed of actual court sounds. Grunts, squeals, and the twang of the racket strings add to the visual effects, culminating in a truly vibrant and engaging "clash of the titans" from the world of tennis.

Credits

R!OT Design
Designers/Directors **Jeremy Hollister** and **Manwai Cheung**
Executive Producer **Connie Griffin**
Producer **Jennifer Hargreaves**

USA Networks
Senior VP On-Air Promotions **Chris McCumber**
Creative Director **Lorenzo de Guttaduaro**

Tools

Adobe After Effects
Adobe Illustrator
Adobe Photoshop
Discreet Inferno
Macromedia Flash

Production Company

R!OT Design
Manhattan, NY, United States

Images courtesy of USA Networks.

Young & Rubicam Damaris
Grupo Leon Jimenes
Water

  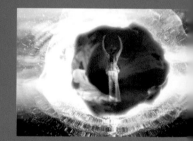

Project Overview

"The *Water* piece for Y&R Damaris is the third in a series of interstitials for their client Leon," explained ViewPoint Studios executive producer Dave Shilale. "The first two revolved around the arts and press. This one was based on water conservation within the Dominican Republic. Our goal here was to illustrate the client's respect toward their country's most basic life-preserving values, using water as a symbolic element."

naturaleza

Creative Process

When Y&R Damaris approached ViewPoint Studios with the spot, they had a very loose framework already in place. The objective was to promote conservation, but outside of the stated objective, the parameters for the spot were fairly vague—to show water as a symbol, to flow seamlessly between scenes without hard edits, and to feature water in a hyperreal, dreamlike environment. Even the exact running time of the spot was left undetermined. The creative brief was open-ended—to explore the concept of water conservation in the Dominican Republic and express it effectively, with artistry and with no specific limits on their imagination.

"Because the Dominican Republic is an island, we thought it would be important to show fresh water in all the forms that the people would actually see: waterfalls, streams, lakes, in agriculture, and as rain water," related design director Michael Frederick. "We wanted to show that people coexist with water, that they need it not only to stay alive, but also for its natural beauty and the lush flora and fauna it brings to their island. That was where our creative idea came from. Additionally, we

determined that it was important for each scene to incorporate a human being interacting with the water. It was that integration of water and humanity that really sold Y&R Damaris on this concept."

With the underlying parameters determined, the team then focused on establishing a basic visual paradigm on how water was to be featured. Water was always to be shown as free-flowing and natural, never dominated by man, as it would be if it were shown in an irrigation system or as tap water.

The piece starts with a single drop, which explodes, giving forth life. From that point, it flows through lush island vegetation and cascading waterfalls. People are choreographed into a symphony of movement that blends humanity with the natural wonders of this island paradise.

Production Process

Footage

The natural beauty of *Water* is the product of a seamless blend of stock and original footage. For convenience and budgetary reasons, the team used stock footage whenever possible. Stock footage included objects such as the waterfalls, time-lapse photography, and palm trees. The talent and any additional elements that were required were shot on 35 mm film at a green-screen stage in Boston.

Computer Graphics

In order to achieve the fluid, dreamlike quality of the piece, CG animator Mike Leone created an extensive number of 3-D elements in Maya.

"Flame artist Dave DiNisco and I worked with each other. I was in contact with him on an hourly basis feeding him bits and pieces. There was a lot of trial and error to get the shots to work. Most of them matured as we went, figuring out what we needed as we went," explained Leone.

A perfect example of the integration of 3-D is the scene where a model is "showering" in a waterfall. For the shot to work it needed to create the illusion that the woman was actually in the waterfall instead of simply standing in front of it. Leone created CGI streams of water that were designed to appear as if they were splashing off the model's head. It is this attention to detail that gives the scene a realistic feeling, although it is actually composed of many disparate elements.

Compositing

The various elements, stock footage, original footage, and CGI were combined in Flame. Numerous effects were used to create the unique look and feel of the spot. The transitions were designed in an organic fashion, with each scene flowing fluidly into the next.

A number of the scenes proved increasingly complex. For example, the scene of the farmer in the field combines oversized CG raindrops with stock footage of clouds and palm trees, original green-screen footage of the farmer, and 3-D fields modeled in Maya.

The editing process was fairly open from the perspective of time limitations. Shilale explained, "Because the Dominican Republic does not have a set time format for spots, the team was free to experiment with different edits. Initially, we were shooting for a spot that lasted between 35 and 45 seconds, but when client saw it, they said, 'Let's open it up a bit and let it breathe and flow.' The final cut was 59 seconds, give or take a few frames."

Credits

Young & Rubicam Damaris
Director of Production **Javier Pena Defillo**

ViewPoint Studios
Creative Director, Design Studio **Glenn Robbins**
Executive Producer **Dave Shilale**
Director/Director of Photography **Austin DeBesche**
Associate Producer **Adrienne Gum**
Design Director **Michael Frederick**
CGI Animator **Mike Leone**
Flame Artist **Dave DiNisco**
Line Producer **Mary Schiarizzi**
Telecine Finish **Boston**
Colorist **Greg Dildine**
Music **Berman & Branco, Boston**
Composers/Arrangers **Steve Berman and Matt Branco**
Sound Design/Mix **One Studio, Boston**
Engineer **Jim Sullivan**

Tools

Adobe Photoshop
Alias|wavefront Maya
Discreet Flame

Production Company

ViewPoint Studios
Needham, MA, United States

Cinemax
Maxtime
Block Packaging

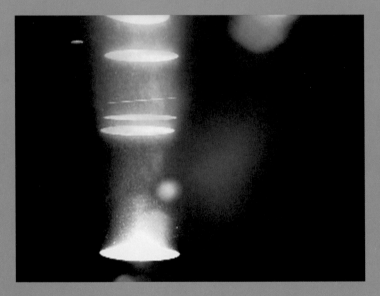 

Project Overview

When Cinemax was looking for a new opening for their prime-time movie, they tapped the creative talents of Hatmaker. The two companies had already established a longtime working relationship. Previous projects included the design for the Cinemax logo and a complete redesign of the channel identity package in 1997.

Creative Process

Prior to the new Maxtime package, the Cinemax brand had always
relied on a flat, 2 D feel targeted for a "pop" underground look. The
new identity initiative for the channel was to upgrade the look and feel
of the prime-time movie opening to a more upscale and sophisticated
mainstream audience.

"We had designed the logo and had always been using it as a flat
graphic. It was never meant to be rendered as a ball; it was always
used as a disk. Part of the new strategy was to open up the z-space and
add dimension to the identity package," explained creative director Chris
Goveia. "We came up with a bunch of ideas that were all complicated
and complex, but in the end, I wanted to bring it back to a very simple
idea, to make it about a feeling."

In the final design, the viewer is in a dark movie theater, where
the Cinemax logo acts as a projector casting a beam of light through
the darkness. The beam illuminates particles in the atmosphere,
and the viewer is transported into this beam of light where "anything
can happen."

Production Process

"Here at Hatmaker, we like things to have somewhat of an organic feel," said Goveia. "We don't like highly rendered 3-D objects. This project could have easily been done in a 3-D software package, but we wanted it to have an ethereal feeling. The piece needed to have soft feel, not a hard one. After all, that is the nature of film. To accomplish this, we decided to get very low-tech about it."

This low-tech approach involved purchasing a fish tank, a flashlight, laundry detergent, a couple of cans of tomato soup, and various other substances. Goveia and the Hatmaker crew then filled the tank with water, draped it in black cloth, and shone the flashlight into the tank to create the shaft of light. They then dropped the different materials into tank and used the footage as the basis for the light beam environment.

They shot the footage using a Hi8 camera. Additional animation elements were created in After Effects and imported into Flame. These elements were treated with a variety of effects and composited with the fish tank footage in Flame.

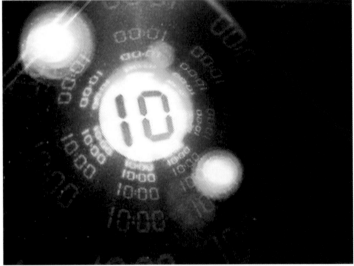

Credits

Client Contact **Mark Davidson and Robert Priday**
Project Manager **Elz Bentley**
Creative Director **Chris Goveia**
Designer **Prang Tharawanich**
Postproduction Manager **Brian Drewes**
Postproduction Company **Brickyard vfx**
Visual Effects Artist **Dave Waller**

Tools

Adobe After Effects
Adobe Illustrator
Adobe Photoshop
Discreet Flame
Media 100

Production Company

Hatmaker
Watertown, MA, United States

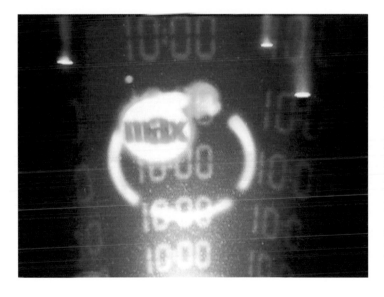

The LifeStyle Channel, Australia
Julie's Baby
Program Package

Project Overview

The LifeStyle Channel's program *Julie's Baby* is a series that follows the life of a young woman going through her first pregnancy. The objective of the show is to capture the emotional aspects of a single woman's experience of having a baby and the accompanying life changes.

The show's producers were determined to focus on the emotional resonance of the situation for the show's packaging rather than taking a "cute" approach. First and foremost, the client didn't want to see any pink, blue, or yellow hues.

Creative Process

TACTIC had worked with Sydney-based designer Dana Rayson, from Robot DNA, for many years. At the time of this project, Rayson happened to be in the midst of her first pregnancy. Her involvement in the project seemed to be a perfect match.

"When we first saw photos of Julie with her baby boy, I was immediately reminded of the pre-Raphaelite painting *Ophelia* by John Everett Millais from 1851. This triggered the ideas, and the piece was developed from there," said Rayson.

From that seed of an idea, the visual style of the piece was born. Mixing time-lapse photography, free-flowing choreography, and a hauntingly beautiful audio track—containing a subtle but continual heartbeat—the show's title sequence is a visually stunning and sensitive piece, which emphasizes the dual themes of growth and the passage of time.

Production Process

"I wanted the opening title sequence to show time passing through the seasons," explained Rayson. "So, I went about collecting leaves and made up batches of fake snow. Julie's dress was custom designed out of silk chiffon to be light and billowy. I wanted her to represent a flower bursting into bloom."

Shot in one day, Julie and her baby were filmed in a tank of shallow water against a black backdrop. Because the opening sequence was shot after Julie had delivered her baby, a stand-in belly was required for the close-up shots of the pregnant stomach.

Postproduction was completed over six days. The footage of Julie and her baby was composited using Flint with both stock and original time-lapse photography.

Two versions of the show open were produced. One featured Julie by herself, and the other included the baby, because the first episodes aired while Julie was pregnant, and the producers wanted to keep the outcome a mystery. By the third episode, her baby boy, Jaya, had been born and was included in the show packaging. The revised elements were introduced in episode three and played for the remainder of the series.

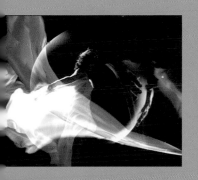   

Credits

TACTIC Creative Services
Creative Director **Diana Costantini**
Design/Director **Dana Rayson**
Producer **Bree Tutena**
Sound Design **Andy Wilson**

The LifeStyle Channel
General Manager **Sandra Hook**
Director of Programming and Production **Trevor Eastment**

Tools

Adobe Photoshop
Discreet Flint

Production Company

TACTIC Creative Services
Sydney, Australia

Haglund Reklam
Make Your Mind Up
Test Spot

Project Overview

Originating as an offhand comment by art director Niclas Haglund, *Make Your Mind Up* was designed as a challenge to the cosmetic industry. The basic premise of this production was to promote cosmetics from a standpoint of self-confidence rather than fear.

Excited by the idea, Haglund approached a local Swedish cosmetics brand with the concept. Although they had never done broadcast advertising campaign before, they were intrigued by the concept and gave director Klas Jonsson a small budget to shoot this test spot.

Creative Process

"This all started when Niclas and I were having a conversation about cosmetics advertising," explained Jonsson. "We agreed that this was one area of the industry where some rethinking should be in order, because most cosmetic advertisements deal with fear. Fear of wrinkles. Fear of growing old. We think people should be concerned about what kind of messages are being put out there, especially with the pressure that is being put on young women. It seems that most of the messages are unhealthy. That is why we decided to focus on using cosmetics to promote self-confidence instead of fear."

Production Process

With its minimal budget, the production for *Make Your Mind Up* was decidedly understated, with most of the cast and crew taking a reduction in their normal rate. Lars Heydecke, director of photography on the shoot, is a fashion photographer by trade, and although he had done a few music videos, he was initially reluctant to do the spot.

To convince him to join the production, Jonsson looked through Heydecke's portfolio, pointed to an image, and said "Can you do this with moving images?"

Heydecke responded, " I think so."

"Great, let's try it. This is a test spot. There's no better place than this to try it out."

Jonsson's ploy worked, and Heydecke joined the production team.

The result is a powerful yet playful take on the joy of cosmetics. The images were shot on film, with effects and typography added in After Effects. Final assembly was done on an Avid editing suite.

Credits

Director/Designer **Klas Jonsson**
Art Director **Niclas Haglund**
Director of Photography **Lars Heydecke**
Model **Karin Adali**
Postproduction **DVP, Stockholm**

Tools

Adobe After Effects
Adobe Photoshop
Avid Media Composer

Production Company

Strobe
Stockholm, Sweden

MTV
2001 Movie Awards
Show Package

Project Overview

MTV has long been known for its innovative show packaging, and the *2001 Movie Awards* package was no exception. Designed by R!OT Manhattan, the packaging has a decidedly retro-'70s kitsch feeling, using classic film icons as the basic design metaphor.

Logos for the award segments were based on the designs from seminal movies of the '70s, such as *The Godfather*, *Saturday Night Fever*, and *A Clockwork Orange*. These movies were matched with appropriate award topics, i.e. Best Dance Sequence was *Saturday Night Fever*, Best Movie was *The Godfather*, and Best Action was *Rollerball*.

Although the clips were produced using modern technology, every effort was made to give the spots an authentic look and feel of state-of-the-art—circa 1974—style of animation.

Creative Process

Jeremy Hollister of R!OT had established a working relationship with MTV prior to being asked to design the *2001 Movie Awards* show package. Hollister said, "They approached us and said, 'Hey, we want you to do the movie award packaging. We are coming up with it from scratch and want you to be involved from the beginning.'"

Being involved from the beginning meant helping to align the overall concept of the package with the show itself. Thematically, they were looking to create a '70s vibe by making the package feel as if it was produced during that time period. That being said, they still wanted the presentation to have a modern twist.

"It's supposed to be playful. It wasn't about being super-slick and super-modern. It was more about saying, 'Let's be really playful.' It's intended to be as if you were in 1974 at the Oscar awards, and you're on acid," said Hollister. "That was the approach, so everything was desaturated as if it was shot in old Technicolor where you'd only have a limited range of colors."

Production Process

One of the challenges of this production was using digital equipment to replicate the idiosyncrasies of the handmade animation style of the '70s. The traditional way involved multiple passes of color screens, which would enhance the flaws of the piece.

Hollister explained, "In the old days, you had to go mat by mat. You'd hold back everything except for one color, and then you'd run it through. Then you'd go back and do it again for the next color. You would do this until you had the finished piece. It was very much like silk-screening, only you would be exposing layers of color directly on film instead of fabric. You would have to do one layer at a time. As a result, every time you exposed the film it would get softer and softer until the edges weren't crisp and would have a bit of bleed to them."

To recreate this old style of animation, Hollister started in the most unlikely of places—3-D modeling software. The first step was to create an element—for example, the stars used in multiple sections of the package. Using Inferno, he took these stars and re-keyed them multiple times, adding a new color each time. He found that by doing this, he could simulate the silk-screened appearance of the '70s style of animation.

Additional 3-D elements were combined with various promotional stills, original photography, and frame grabs of home movies and type treatments to complete the animations. All that remained to perfect the illusion of handcrafted animation was the addition of simple Inferno effects, like simulated film grain, scratches, and dirt.

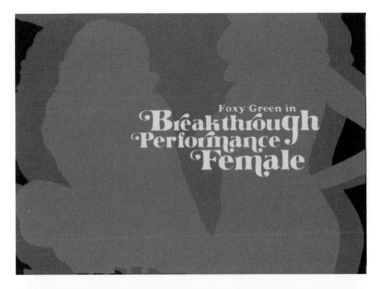

Credits

R!OT
Creative Director/Designer **Jeremy Hollister**
Executive Producer **Connie Griffin**
Producer **Peter Metsopoulos**
Design **Manwai Chueng and Bill McMullen (Orange Network)**
Animator/Designer **Mike McKenna**
3-D Animators **Patricia Heard-Greene and Dylan Maxwell**
Production/Design **R!OT**

MTV
Creative Director **Joel Gallen**
Producer **Rick Austin/Austin Redding**

Tools

Adobe After Effects
Adobe Photoshop
Alias|wavefront Maya
Discreet Inferno
Macromedia Flash
Softimage

Production Company

R!OT Design
Manhattan, NY, United States

Images courtesy of MTV.

Sesame Street
Show Open

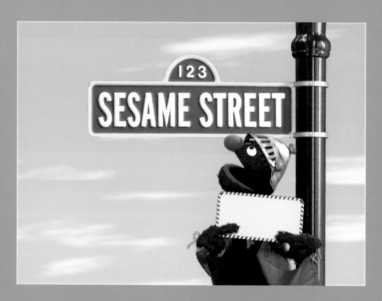

Project Overview

Sesame Street is arguably the most successful children's show ever broadcast. Its success has had a wide impact on how the children of our planet learn to read, write, and relate to each other. The characters from the show—Big Bird, Kermit, Miss Piggy, to name just a few—have become cultural icons, transcending all boundaries of culture and language.

Perhaps one of the more noticeable effects of the program is the trend for children to start learning to read at a much younger age. When the show started 33 years ago, the average age of viewers was five to six years old. Currently, that demographic has shifted toward three- to four-year-olds. Accompanying that shift in demographics has been a retooling of the show's format.

Gone is the freewheeling "anything goes" approach to programming. The new style of the show is modular to reflect the fact that younger children prefer a more regimented, structured format. Regular segments—like the Count, Journey to Ernie, and Elmo's World—now appear at consistent times during the show. In turn, *Sesame Street* turned to Big Film Design (BFD) to create a new show open that would highlight their new modular format.

Creative Process

BFD was no stranger to working with *Sesame Street*, having created a previous version of the show open. The new open would be different from prior versions in that it had a very specific mission: to communicate information about the new format of the show. The open could not simply be a group of children having fun and interacting with the characters. It needed to function as a showcase for the modules of the show.

Even after the team examined a number of ideas and concepts, the final concept remained illusive. Director Randall Balsmeyer explained, "What we were looking for was some kind of device that would allow us to feature the modules in an entertaining way. Eventually, we decided on alphabet building blocks to describe the elements of the show. Building blocks are universal—the 'here's how to learn the alphabet' metaphor that everybody recognizes. It was also something we could easily animate, which would allow us to take existing clips and not have to get Bert, the Count, and the whole cast to a special shoot. It was a flexible device around which to build the sequence."

For additional inspiration, the team also looked to the main refrain from the show's theme song, *Can you tell me how to get to Sesame Street?* Combining the building blocks with the quest to find Sesame Street is what gives the show's opening its shape and story arc.

"Basically you should have the sense that Big Bird and his friends are looking for Sesame Street, and the blocks are leading them there," said Balsmeyer. "That was kind of where we went, and once we had the rules of engagement, the challenge was how to create situations where Big Bird, the kids, and the blocks all have fun."

Production Process

The primary challenge facing BFD on this project was how to fit all of the planned elements into a fixed budget. Accomplishing this task required very careful planning and very thorough storyboards. They realized they would only have one day of live shooting with the remainder of the budget going to 3-D animation and postproduction.

Storyboards

The team assembled tight storyboards, which highlighted the progression of Big Bird and the children on their quest for Sesame Street. From these storyboards they were able to determine what kinds of locations they needed for a playground, a fork in the road, a jungle gym, and so on.

Location Scouting

Although it's common knowledge that *Sesame Street* is produced in New York, the show has a global appeal. Therefore, the show open needed to appear generic in terms of its location. Balsmeyer and co-director Amit Sethi spent weeks scouting the parks of New York. Often they would bring their bikes to work or hop on the subway and scour the parks to find the perfect locations.

Eventually they selected Central Park because it offered the most locations in one compact area. They were careful to ensure that their shots featured generic buildings rather than the easily identifiable landmarks that surround the park. A problem that they encountered was a new zoning regulation that prohibits shooting footage at the park's playground. For the playground shot, therefore, they found a spot at a park across the city that was similar to the landscape found in Central Park.

Casting

Sesame Street wanted the show open to feature the most inclusive group of children possible. Over 30 children were cast for the spot. The children were selected to represent every ethnicity, in addition to children with disabilities and Down syndrome.

Shoot

One Steadicam, 30 children, multiple shooting locations, and a 7-foot (2 m) costumed bird made for one long day of shooting. The shoot started with the playground shot at the alternative park at 7:00 a.m., and the cast and crew arrived at Central Park by 10:00 a.m.

All the shots had been planned in terms of location and number of children, but the exact cast was chosen on the spot from the children available. The 3-D modeling team's need for visual markers to map out the scenes for motion matching added complexity to the shoot. Ping-Pong balls were placed in trees, grass, and other locations as reference points to be used in postproduction.

"The scary part was that the planning had dragged on through fall to the point where we were unable to do the shot until the middle of October," said Balsmeyer. "We were lucky—I think we got the last day there actually were green lawns and green trees. We were really trying to make this a three-season opening, and the fates smiled on us."

Although not officially in the production schedule, *Sesame Street* was able to accommodate BFD and create one custom shot of Super Grover for the show open.

Music

To speed up the pace of new opening, a new arrangement of the show's familiar theme song was developed. Balsmeyer explained, "One of our goals was to shorten the open as much as possible. We couldn't cut the song or its lyrics, so we experimented with speeding up the tempo of the song. We came to the conclusion that 50 seconds was about as short as you could make it without sounding silly."

They mixed a tape of the theme song at the new tempo and sent it to *Sesame Street*'s music composer, Mike Rienzi. He liked the new sound and rescored and rerecorded the theme song at the new tempo.

Postproduction

The footage was edited in Avid to a rough cut of the new soundtrack. The alphabet blocks were created and animated in Softimage. *Sesame Street* provided segment footage for the sides of the blocks. The Ping-Pong balls from the live shoot were used as reference points for the match-motion software. These reference points enabled the modelers to synchronize the blocks' animations with the movement of the Steadicam footage.

This integration between real and 3-D was not always as simple as planned. Sethi explained, "One shot that proved particularly complex was when the blocks the child is playing with spring to life. You would think that something a simple as a cube with a letter carved out of the front would be an ideal thing to make in 3-D, but the outdoor lighting, the grass in front of the cube, the little reflections on the block, and the uneven ground made it take a lot longer than I had originally planned. But I had to get it right because it really would have stood out and blown the whole effect. After all, that's the moment when the magic starts to happen. It was really important to get it right."

And get it right they did, much to the delight of *Sesame Street* producers and children around the world.

Credits

Big Film Design
Director **Randall Balsmeyer**
Director of Photography **Jeffrey Victor**
Producer **Kathy Kelehan**
Storyboarding/3-D Animation/Editing/Co-directing **Amit Sethi**
2-D Compositing **John Corbett**
3-D Animation/Modeling **Alex Jacob**

Sesame Workshop
Executive Producer **Michael Loman**
Executive Producer **Carol-Lynn Parente**
Line Producer **Karen Ialacci**

Tools

Adobe After Effects
Avid
REALVIZ MatchMover
Softimage

Production Company

Big Film Design
New York, NY, United States

Addgel
Achiever
Zero Gravity

Project Overview

A teacher asks her class a simple question: "OK, kids, where do we find zero gravity?" One student responds, "In space." Another says, "On the moon." The next child stares at his pen before declaring, "Right here."

The teacher appears puzzled, and suddenly the child levitates above the classroom.

Simple and amusing, this Indian production demonstrates how a little imagination and a heavy-duty pulley system can go a long way toward crafting an effective advertising message.

Creative Process

When Dilip Ahuja of Xpose Motion Picture Company was approached to develop this spot, the creative brief he was given was to project effortless writing.

To dramatize the concept of effortless writing, he found his inspiration in the 1969 conquest of the moon. After all, what could be more effortless than writing in zero gravity? He believed this concept would be appealing to children and would give the pen a high-tech image.

The team initially presented the concept in script format and soon followed up with storyboards. The client was intrigued, but was concerned the effect could not be pulled off convincingly without spending considerably more money than was budgeted. Upon reviewing Ahuja's plans for the effect and samples of his past work, the client decided to push forward with the spot.

Production Process

A full week of planning was required for the two-day shoot. Every detail of the school was planned for maximum impact. Ahuja even selected the vivid yellow and blue uniform of a local school district to enhance the viewers' identification with the children in the spot.

Casting for the class and teacher was fairly straightforward. The role of the levitating child was given to a boy whose primary skill set consisted of having the ability to maintain a smile while being suspended 30 feet (9 m) off the ground for long periods of time. This skill was important because the levitation effect was achieved through the use of a harness attached to a manual pulley system that was connected to a large crane. Understandably, this was not the most comfortable of setups for the child.

Beyond attending to the care and well-being of the hoisted child, the focus of the crane operator was to keep the harness strings as far out of frame as possible during the shoot to reduce the amount of cleanup work required in postproduction.

The team required a full week of post-production to remove the cables, create the 3-D bubble sequence, and complete the compositing and editing for the piece.

Cast and crew hanging around on the set.

Credits

Creative Director **Vishal Vij**
Producer/Director/Editor **Dilip Ahuja**
Cameraman **Gopal Shah**
Graphics **Animesh**
Agency **Benchmark Communications**

Tools

Discreet Edit
Quantel Edit Box
3D Max
URSA GOLD Telecine

Production Company

Xpose Motion Picture Company
Mumbai, India

Universal Studios Networks, UK LTD
Pulp Sci-Fi
Program Package

Project Overview

Pulp Sci-Fi is the name given to the retro genre of programming played on the Sci-Fi Channel, UK. The Pulp Sci-Fi block includes a mixture of classic shows such as *The Six Million Dollar Man*, *The Bionic Woman*, *The Time Tunnel*, and *Fantasy Island*, with timeless films like *The Brain*, *Bride of the Monster*, and *The Time Travelers*. Pulp Sci-Fi is home to material that's science fiction with a funky retro feel.

The objective of this spot was to create a package that could highlight the genre of retro sci-fi programming with wit, humor, and irreverence.

Creative Process

"The first step, as always, is research," said designer and director Andy Brown. "After spending a week immersing myself in the many classic sci-fi films and TV shows from the '50s, '60s, and '70s, I came up with the concept of mixing up the story conventions found in a lot of these films, conventions such as time travel, manipulations, beauty and beast, strange planets, invasions, little and tall, and mad scientists."

Although the content of the programming was decidedly retro, creative director Diana Costantini wanted to ensure the overall experience wasn't too retro. "I wanted to start and finish in a modern world. We had to come up with a device or a way to enter in and out of our modern worlds."

Brown added, "We came up with the idea of using a futuristic sci-fi girl who observes the Pulp Sci-Fi worlds through an old Viewmaster. The look of these scenes was inspired by the stereoscopic Viewmaster slides, which have a layered, flat, cut-out quality. This led us to use a variety of techniques for each vignette, mixing matte paintings with 3-D and 2-D characters and live action."

Production Process

"Once the idea and storyboards were locked, we had about a week to prep for a one-day shoot," said Brown. "The sequence was to be aired on a 16 x 9 screen, so Allan Koppe, the director of photography, suggested shooting on Super 16 film. The art department built and found props in a very short time. We cast the characters in about two days and spent a few last frantic hours rummaging around a drag queen store looking for a suitable space girl costume."

When asked if the project required any special equipment, Brown responded, "The usual stuff really—two Frisbees to build the UFO, one fake chicken with a diamante-studded leash, fake eyeballs, and a very large cicada."

All the props and characters were shot against a blue, black, or white screen and edited on Final Cut Pro. In postproduction, the TACTIC team used a variety of techniques. They used Softimage to create the Venus's-flytrap, cicada, and fly head. The environments were matte paintings, the eyes were 2-D, and the final composite was created in Flame and After Effects. Sound designer Andy Wilson was brought in early in the production cycle to create retro sci-fi sounds, which were crucial for setting the mood in the different worlds showcased in the Viewmaster.

Costantini said, "This project had so many creative possibilities, we all wanted to keep developing it, taking the viewer into more and more peculiar fantasy worlds. I think one of the biggest challenges we faced was trying to contain ourselves! So, even though the budget and time line were reasonable, it became quite an ambitious project. We pushed the idea as far as we could, and as a consequence, I don't think anyone made a lot of money. But it was lots of fun and the results are stunning."

Credits

Universal Studios Networks, UK, Ltd
Director of Channels **Tor McLaren**
Director of Programming **Mark Staufer**

TACTIC Creative Services
Concept/Creative Director **Diana Constantini**
Sound Design **Andy Wilson**
Production Company **Animal Logic**
Concept/Design/Director **Andy Brown**
Producer **Jackie Allison**
Flame Artist **Stefan Coory**
After Effects Compositor **Shawn Mohammadi**

Live Action Credits

Director of Photography **Allan Koppe**
Art Director **Rebecca Cohan and Joanne Belkoff**
Hair and Makeup **Simona Janek**

Tools

Adobe After Effects
Adobe Photoshop
Apple Final Cut Pro
Discreet Flame
Logic Audio Pro Tools
Softimage

Production Company

TACTIC Creative Services
Sydney, Australia

NHK
(Japan
Broadcasting
Corporation)
Kyouiku Today

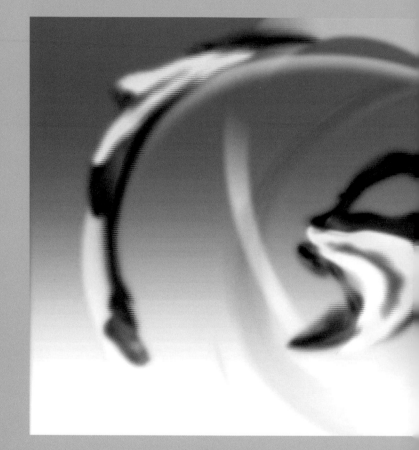

Project Overview

Broadcast on the viewer-supported Japanese public television service NHK (Japan Broadcasting Corporation), *Kyouiku* (Education) *Today* is an informational program targeted toward parents and educators about the changing landscape of the Japanese school system.

The program features information on a range of subjects pertaining to the Japanese educational system. The show is timely because the Japanese educational system is currently in a transitional phase—the Internet is changing the face of the classroom, truancy and disciplinary issues are on the rise, and the system is being challenged from elementary schools to high schools. *Kyouiku Today* provides parents and educators the knowledge to make informed decisions regarding the educational system.

Vehicle + has created a bright and cheerful show open that highlights the joy of children celebrating their youth through movement, smiling, and simply being children.

Creative Process

Vehicle + was brought into the project by a colleague who worked at NHK and recommended their services. They were given some basic parameters for the tone and feeling of the spot.

The objective was to keep an upbeat tone. Happy children were chosen to symbolize the hope for a solution to the current educational problems. Darkness was to be avoided; the vision of a brighter future, despite the setbacks of the present, was to be emphasized.

Vehicle + developed a number of different graphical treatments for the open. These various approaches were created as a series of still images in Photoshop and presented as a PDF file to the client.

Production Process

It took nearly a month of intensive production to create the show open. Extensive casting and a photo shoot were required to find the correct mix of children for the spot.

Once the shoot was complete, the images had to be scanned, manipulated, and color-corrected in Photoshop. The team used After Effects to create the visual effects and animation. The initial storyboards were followed very closely in production, and the end result is a simple yet effective portrait of children caught reveling in the joys of youth.

Credits

Director **Takeshi Yoshida**
Production **Vehicle +**

Tools

Adobe After Effects
Adobe Illustrator
Adobe Photoshop

Production Company

Vehicle + Co., Ltd
Tokyo, Japan

British Broadcasting Company
BBC Four Identity Package

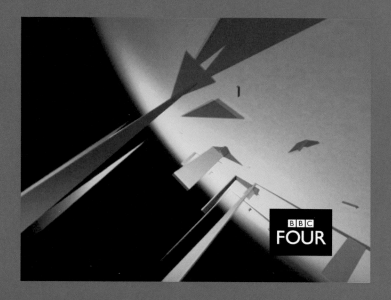

Project Overview

BBC Four is positioned as the most culturally inspiring television and wanted an identity to support this claim. To achieve this effect, Lambie-Nairn created an identity package that is entirely unique and fundamentally different from anything they have previously attempted.

The idea was to create a piece of "living" contemporary art. The resulting identity exists in its own 3-D space, reacting to the sounds and voices of the channel. It was born from the concept of images reacting to sound. In this particular case, the visuals are created in real time, reacting both to music and to live-voiced announcements. In effect, Lambie-Nairn has designed and produced the next stage of broadcast IDs with the first virtual identity package of the broadcast medium.

Creative Process

The Lambie-Nairn team's objective was to create a virtual identity where every sequence broadcast was completely unique, every time it was broadcast.

"Personally, my inspiration has come from one place—Disney's *Fantasia*, in particular, a small segment of the movie that introduces the audience to the soundtrack (who is depicted as a character)," said designer and director Jason Keeley. "This soundtrack, in character, responds to the sounds that are played using different visual interpretations, as conjured up by the animators. The visual style of this sequence is classic Disney—a sequence of great beauty that plays with the idea of a visual reacting to sound."

It took a month to generate and visualize the concept. A combination of Photoshop visuals, After Effects animation, and reference material were presented to the client to explain the concept of a virtual identity package. After approval, the team embarked on seven months of development and production.

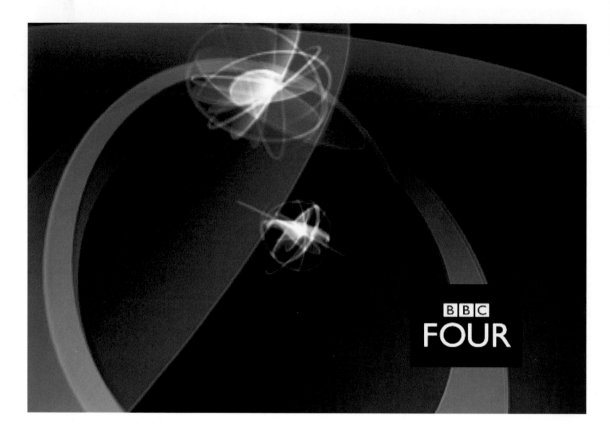

Production Process

The team determined early on that it would be impractical and costly to produce unique IDs using standard production methods. The virtual identity package could only be achieved by pushing the technology envelope.

"To bring this project to life, we commissioned Glassworks—a highly respected facility house, well-versed in high-end production and 3-D animation—to research and develop dedicated computer software that could analyze audio and synchronize and render 3-D graphics to it, in real time," said Keeley. "This software has been written from the ground up and renders the graphics using openGL. Many parameters in the software—such as camera position and speed, shape selection and formation, and lighting—are designed to behave randomly, so that you'll never see exactly the same identity sequence twice. Each sequence is an original—this was key to the concept."

An interesting aspect of this virtual package is that the team used off-the-shelf hardware for development, which would have been unthinkable only a few short years ago. Top-of-the-line computers, tricked-out with state-of-the-art graphics and sound cards, were purchased. The use of off-the-shelf equipment provides the ID package a high degree of flexibility for future expansion. This means as better and faster equipment becomes available, upgrading the system to handle more complex and ambitious visual styles and designs will be possible.

The production team from Lambie-Nairn worked closely with programmers and producers at Glassworks, seeing how far they could push the hardware before it fell over. It was a highly collaborative environment in which the companies crafted a unique and innovative package.

Joe Glasman at Hum composed the musical elements. The team's goal was to record intimate, live solo performances using as many different instruments as possible to create a wide breadth of visual reactions. The team discovered that live sounds caused far better reactions than samples. There are over 40 different performances, each of which interpret and improvise on the BBC Four theme. Instruments ranging from a jazz guitar to a didgeridoo to a Cretan lyra were recorded to give the spots a variable sonic palette.

The way the system works is as follows: At transmission, one of the musical performances is selected randomly by the audio server. Simultaneously, the performance is mixed with an ambient audio background track, which is randomly selected from a choice of four. At this point, the collective audio is sent to the dedicated graphics computer to trigger a visual reaction. When a voiced announcement begins, the computer is able to identify it and switches over its visual reaction from the music to the voice—all in real time.

No taped media was included in the final deliverables. The identity package was delivered as a computer system with preconfigured software and was installed at the BBC Four facility.

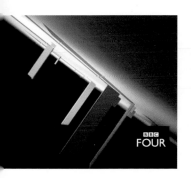

Credits

Lambie-Nairn Team
Creative Director **Gary Holt**
Designer/Director **Jason Keeley**
Producer **Clare Howell**
Technical Adviser **Tom McKerrow**

Glassworks Team
Head of Research and Development **Robin Carlisle**
Software Developer **Pete Reilly**
Managing Director **Hector Macleod**
Director of Special Effects **Bruce Steele**
Postproduction Producer **Liz Roberts**

Hum Team
Composer **Joe Glasman**
Producer **Dan Simmons**

Tools

2 top-end PCs
2 1.7 GHZ Intel processors, each running a GeForce 3
graphics card and professional four-channel digital
sound card

Production Company

Lambie-Nairn
London, England

Statistical Analysis Systems Institute
Flood and *Harvest*

Project Overview

Flood and *Harvest* are the award-winning television commercials for Statistical Analysis Systems's (SAS) recent marketing campaign. What makes these spots so unique are not the spectacular special effects, but the fact that although the spots were sent out for bids from some of the top special effects houses in the world—ILM, Digital Domain, and Rhythm & Hues—the job was given to a single individual rather than to a company.

Remarkable, you might think, but no less remarkable than the person to whom SAS awarded the contract—special effects guru, Richard Taylor. Taylor's achievements are numerous. Along with his partner Kevin Lyman, he founded Rainbow Jam, a light show and graphics company that performed with the Grateful Dead, Santana, and Jethro Tull. In 1973, Taylor helped found Robert Abel and Associates, the pioneer television commercial graphics/special effects studio. In 1978, he moved into film where he designed the models and directed the special effects sequences for *Star Trek, The Motion Picture*. As visual effects supervisor for *Tron*, he virtually created the modern industry of computer-generated motion picture effects. Since *Tron*, Taylor has been working in the advertising world creating some of the most memorable spots of the past two decades.

Richard Taylor behind the camera.

Original image from *Harvest* storyboard.

Green screen model shoot for *Harvest*.

A hard day's work in the fields.

Creative Process

SAS is one of the largest software companies in the world. Started by Dr. Jim Goodnight in the late '70s, the company has grown into a multibillion-dollar entity with over 5,000 employees and a 300-acre campus at its headquarters in Cary, North Carolina.

The company had been so successful that they've never had to seriously advertise their presence in the market prior to this campaign. However, the recent spate of aggressive television marketing campaigns from a new breed of software companies had made SAS rethink their advertising strategy.

The company decided on a more high-profile approach and hired Howard, Merrell and Partners to create a new branding campaign. The centerpiece of this campaign was two television spots, *Flood* and *Harvest*. The agency sent the storyboards to ILM, Digital Domain, and Rhythm & Hues for production bids.

Little did the agency know that Goodnight had asked Alternate Route Studios (ARS) to bid on the job independently. The reason Goodnight had asked ARS to get involved was that they were a subsidiary of SAS and had a considerable amount of production experience and equipment. ARS was a complete production studio with 8 Maya workstations, two sound stages, multiple editing bays, a model shop, and a finishing suite. The problem was that their expertise was in developing games for the Sony PlayStation. They had some commercial production experience, but nothing close to what was required to produce the effects specified in the *Flood* and *Harvest* storyboards.

ARS posted an ad at www.wheresspot.com for "an experienced special effects/live action director" who was freelance or who could work on loan from a production company. The purpose of this search was to see if they could both build their in-house resources and lower the budget.

An associate of Taylor's forwarded the post to him, and he responded. After reviewing his reel and résumé, the head of production at ARS contacted Taylor and sent him the agency boards and a sample reel.

After receiving the materials, Taylor spoke with the head of ARS who asked him to bid on the project. He was instructed to use whatever combination of companies and personnel he wished to use, but was asked to consider using ARS for some part of the production. The degree of their participation was left up entirely to Taylor.

Production Process

Taylor's first concern was developing a working relationship with the advertising agency. He was concerned that this nontraditional bidding approach might adversely affect their working relationship. "This was something I brought up early in the conversations because I needed to know how the agency would respond," explained Taylor. "I wanted to work with the agency writer and art director. I needed their input as a sounding board for my ideas. The original creative material from the agency was exceptionally good, and I didn't want to blow the whole project because of friction between all the diverse parties involved in this unique approach to production. I didn't want the agency to feel that they were getting cut out of the production." He was assured that a suitable working relationship could be established if he was given the contract.

Taylor got to work building a team and designing the effects. One of his first moves was to suggest that they change one aspect of the *Harvest* storyboards. The scene originally showed workers harvesting data from trees in a giant orchard. Taylor's vision was more reminiscent of *Days of Heaven*, with data being harvested from an infinite field.

Additionally, he began to do research for the effects, studying footage of heavy rain and flood patterns from the Weather Channel and other sources. Eventually he determined the best way to achieve the effect needed for *Flood* was to shoot the scenes on location and then overlay the CG data.

The final presentation package to the client included new storyboards, reference materials, a budget, and a shooting schedule. ARS was included in the production to build models, provide sound stages for shooting the models, and to create a number of CG backgrounds for the city in *Flood*.

In the end, it was Taylor's creative process that won him the contract. It also didn't hurt that his budget was $800,000 less than any of his competitors. Taylor attributes the cost differential to his creative approach and the ability to source multiple production resources, including ARS.

To build his vision of *Harvest* and *Flood*, Taylor assembled a bicoastal and international collective of production companies. The production was produced through Film Machine in Miami, Florida. Special effects were to be produced by Simex in Santa Monica, California. As mentioned previously, all model building and additional production services were to be done by ARS in Cary, North Carolina, and all live shooting was to be done on location Vancouver, British Columbia.

As location scouting and initial casting began in Vancouver, Taylor and a storyboard artist created the shooting storyboards. He also began designing the gothic thrasher machines for *Harvest* and the main building for *Flood*. These elements were to be built as models by ARS. The team used the Internet extensively for sharing rough versions of the storyboards and sketches among all involved parties.

Final designs were delivered to the ARS model shop, and reference materials for the CG modeling were presented to the ARS 3-D team. In California, Simex began tests for the data rain sequence of *Flood* and started developing the choreography for *Harvest*. Meanwhile, in Vancouver, construction had begun on the large set pieces required for the live shoot.

Modeled statue on green-screen set and after being composited into spot.

On location in Vancouver.

Shooting Schedule

Day One
Several of the shots required traffic control and could only be shot during specified hours. The team was able to shoot at Vancouver's Public Library complex. Multiple scenes were shot, all requiring water, rain-making equipment, and wind machines. For additional realism, a stream system was rigged for the street gutters.

Day Two
At the Vancouver Art Museum, the team shot the lion and umbrella scene for *Flood*. A small blue screen was set up to shoot actors so they could be added to the *Harvest* spot.

Day Three
Three different locations were shot. The first location was the master shot for *Flood*. The second location was the clock, and the final location was in front of the large gold doors of a bank. These gold doors were used multiple times in the *Flood* spot. It is into these doors that the businessman is pulled from the stream of data.

Day Four
The team shot footage for *Harvest* in a large field on a farm about 30 miles (48 km) east of Vancouver. This was a long and complex day of shooting with numerous extras and some large set pieces.

After principal photography had been completed in Vancouver, Taylor flew to North Carolina to oversee the model shoot. Once all footage was complete, he returned to Los Angeles to begin the editing process.

It took nearly three days to assemble the raw footage into the two 30-second spots. Rough cuts were sent to the agency for approval, and music production began in Los Angeles. Once the rough cuts were approved, final transfer was made of all the film elements and Taylor began making matte paintings and overlays for various scenes in both spots.

For the next eight weeks, the team worked on refining the animation and compositing for both spots. With production in so many disparate locations, the Internet became an essential tool for sharing images, tests, and final cuts. Initially Simex was scheduled to do most of the data animation, but as production progressed, it became apparent that ARS could handle more of the production.

Although the initial specification was for two 30-second spots, the client was interested in expanding both spots to 60 seconds. At that point, the advantage of including ARS in the production mix became truly apparent. Taylor explains, "The benefits of including ARS in the production became clearer as the weeks went by. Because they were, in essence, the client as well as a production company, they could do as many versions or changes to a scene as I wanted. It was soft money inside the company and wasn't under the same budgetary restraints as a company like Simex. Simex had budgeted a definite amount of time and manpower to the job and needed to stick to those numbers for obvious reasons."

After the decision was made to expand the spots to 60 seconds each, Taylor recut the footage and had the music and voiceovers rerecorded. Simex had only been budgeted to work on the 30-second spots, and by this point, ARS had learned enough of the production techniques to complete the spots on their own.

Taylor worked with ARS for another two months to complete the spots. "ARS had no qualms about redoing a scene time and again to add more detail," Taylor said. "It was their chance to shine. It was not a matter of budget at this point, so they were relentless. The new scenes that were added were significant. Some of them required a lot of work in animation, for example, the scene of the foot stepping into the puddle of data. We just kept adding more and more data until it became dense alphabet soup."

In the end, both the production and the spots were resounding successes. Not only has SAS received two 60-second spots for considerably less than what they had initially expected to pay for two 30-second spots, they now had increased the ability and the value of their own internal resources. The spots themselves aired in early 2001, and went on to win three Tellies and second place for effects in the New York show.

Model detail.

Credits

Director **Richard Taylor**

Agency

Howard, Merrell & Partners
Creative Director **Scott Crawford**
Art Director **Scott Ballew**

Production Company

Alternate Route Studios (ARS)
President **Susan Ellis**
Director **Richard Winn Taylor II**
Producer **Deven LeTendre**
Producer **Ray Ellis**
Production Managers **Gary Peterson and Beth High**
Art Director **John Plymale**
CGI Manager **Greg Shank**
CGI Art Director **Jeff McFall**

Vancouver Production

Director of Photography **Conrad Hall, Jr.**
Assistant Director **Lorin Fulton**
Art Director **Bill LeBlanc**
Production Manager **Dru Adams**
Gaffer **Terry Kim**
Key Grip **Lionel Huppee**
Locations Manager **Jon Summerland**

Post Effects

Simex Digital Studios
Creative Director **Alan Yamashita**
Visual Effects Supervisor **Nick Bates**
Editor **Jamie Norton**

ZDF
Aspekte
Program Package

Project Overview

Aspekte, broadcast on the German public television station ZDF, is a culture-based video magazine. The show, which highlights the best in German theater, literature, photography, music, and art, is *Kulture* with a capital K. It provides informative segments that combine a sarcastic tone with in-depth background information, allowing the viewer to place a cultural event in context with social and political events.

When Velvet Design was developing the packaging for the long-standing program, they took a bold, new direction. Believing that culture is not simply an event or artistic endeavor, Velvet focused on the impact of culture on the individual viewing it. Throughout the packaging, individuals are shown with reflective surfaces instead of faces to highlight the fact the culture is reflected back into society by those who view it. Culture impacts the individual as much as the individual affects culture through his or her own unique interpretation and reflection.

Creative Process

When *Aspekte* was looking to revamp their image, they contacted a number of different firms to bid on the project. The objective of the redesign was to show that culture is not the province of a select group of intellectuals; it is an entertainment platform for the public at large. The intent was to inspire a younger audience to experience the program while retaining existing viewers. Velvet Design won the contract with a pitch based on an idea of elegant simplicity.

"Culture is the process of the synapses reflecting life's circumstances and the political environment in which they exist. We took the idea of the brain's reflection, literally, and replaced a man's mind with a mirrored head that reflects its social, cultural, and political environment," said Matthias Zentner, director and creative director. "To add more emphasis to the presentation, we added the abstract step of giving the people's outfits a graphical context of a silhouette. All of the reflections occurring in the heads are accompanied by an animated layer of spilling ideas."

Production Process

After two full weeks of scouting locations in Berlin, the spots were shot in two days. A high degree of planning was required for the shoot. There were multiple locations, and the cast and crew needed to be efficient in order to fit all storyboarded shots within the allocated time frame.

Precise choreography was imperative and required extensive rehearsals because the actors were effectively blind once they were wearing the mirrored faces.

Zentner and the crew used some interesting tools to achieve the shots. Instead of dollies and cranes, which were both inconvenient and expensive, they used skateboards and wheelchairs to add motion to the camera shots.

The final footage took four days to edit in an Avid editing suite. Detailed storyboards were presented to the After Effects animator for the text animation. The team spent another two days on the final edits and compositing of the show open, interstitials, show close, and logo treatment.

Credits

Director/Creative Director **Matthias Zentner**
Director of Photography **Thorsten Lippstock**
Producer **Stefan Müller**
Art Director Set **Frank Neumann**
Art Director for Animation and Design **Peter Pedall**
Logo Designer **Peter Pedall**
Editor **Jochen Kraus**
Animators **Peter Pedall and Hartwig Tesar**
Compositors **Matthias Zentner and Andrea Bednarz**

Tools

Adobe After Effects
Avid

Production Company

Velvet Design
Munich, Germany

Zilo Networks, Inc.
Identity Package

Project Overview

New York City–based Zilo Networks, Inc., is the first integrated multiplatform entertainment network designed specifically for the U.S. college market. Zilo's mission is to provide high-impact original programming via a three-pronged delivery system: on campus though live events; on television, via Zilo TV; and online, accessed though Zilo's website.

Zilo TV broadcasts a roster of original shows created especially for the college audience. Launched in September 2000, Zilo is now seen on more than 200 college campuses. Zilo's original programming runs 12 hours per week in 3-hour blocks, delivered by colleges' own cable networks.

Big Film Design (BFD) was hired to develop the identity package for the television entity. This brand identity would eventually be incorporated as part of the brand package for all of the company's activities.

Zilo wanted to develop a distinct personality for the network. This personality was to be conveyed through a open and close segment for their programming block, accompanied by IDs sprinkled throughout the original programming. When developing a personality for the network, BFD was working with a *tabula rasa*. The channel had no identifiable personalities to leverage. Even the name itself, Zilo, had been intentionally selected as a name that had no meaning whatsoever.

"One thing we had going for us was we knew they were quite irreverent, and the attitude of the programming was 'anything goes,'" said director Randall Balsmeyer. "They said the one thing you never want to do is speak down to college students. They have a very sensitive BS detector. As soon as you make it seem like grown-ups talking to kids, they'll find something else to watch. So we came up with this scenario where two deranged robots stage a guerrilla takeover of the campus TV station."

This guerilla takeover had its origin in some experiments co-director Amit Sethi did in his downtime. BFD showed a number of concepts, but as soon as Zilo saw the dancing robots, the die was cast.

Sethi explained, "I did this dancing robot test for my own amusement. I think it was the personality of the robots that sold them [Zilo, Inc.] on the concept. Basically they asked if they could have more of the same attitude, and I said, 'I can do that all day long—let's go!'"

A rudimentary story line was attached to the characters. Basically, two nameless party-ninja robots decide that they can't watch the normal programs shown on the station, so they take over the station and play Zilo programming, which then plays for the next three hours.

Unfortunately for the robots, they are much better at guerrilla assaults and general mischief than at actually running a television station. In fact, they are quite inept, and by the end of the three-hour Zilo block, they completely lose control and the station explodes. The next night, the same process begins again as Zilo takes over the airwaves.

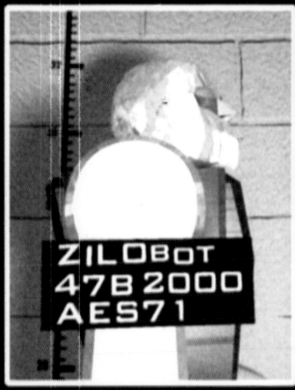

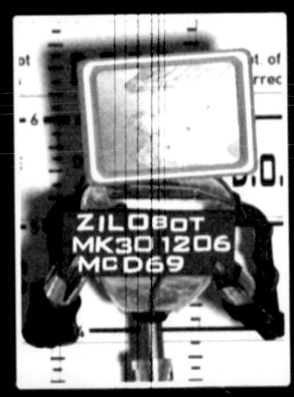

Production Process

Although there was a basic story line, the BFD team did not want the show open to read as a linear story. The story was simply a starting point for the robots' fun.

Balsmeyer elaborated, "Our approach was to basically have specific gags but no linear story line. We sketched up little gags and then cut them up onto pieces of paper. We then spread them out on the table and shuffled them around until it felt like there was a succession of shots that kind of went together without being a linear story. So if you want to make connections between the spots you can, but you are not forced into it."

These "gags" were assembled using Softimage for modeling and animation. A wide variety of effects and numerous graphic styles—ranging from grainy black-and-white to highly rendered metallic shades and neon glows—were employed to give the package its frenetic and action-packed pace.

Credits

Big Film Design Team
Director **Randall Balsmeyer**
Co-director/3-D Animator **Amit Sethi**
Compositor **Fabian Tejada**
3-D Animator **Alex Jacob**
Producer **Kathy Kelehan**

Zilo Networks, Inc. Team
President **Campbell McLaren**
CEO **David Isaacs**
Director of Programming **F.M. DeMarco**

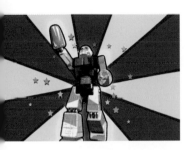  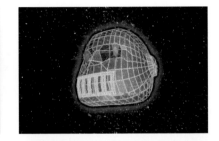

  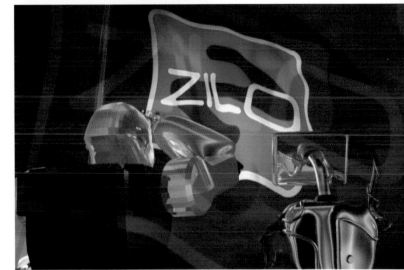

Tools

Adobe After Effects
Adobe Photoshop
Avid
Softimage

Production Company

Big Film Design
New York, NY, United States

Zilo is a registered trademark of Zilo Networks, Inc.

Universal Studios Networks, UK LTD
The Studio News Program Package

Project Overview

The scene is a marvelous cocktail party, and you're invited, dear. Dressed to the nines, the crowd of movers and shakers enjoys a stiff drink and loose conversation. "Love the shoes...hate the dress" is likely to be heard. And the meal on tap for the evening? Movies, darling...served on a silver platter.

That is the vibe presented by the show open for *The Studio News*. *The Studio News* is a weekly show that looks at all that is happening in the world of movies. The show, which airs on the UK channel, The Studio, supports the belief that movies are great, but the business of making movies is wonderfully ridiculous. It is presented with arch humor, passion, and occasional downright bitchiness.

Creative Process

The client requested a title sequence that had a different look and feel than what you'd expect from a show about movies. They were looking for a stylish and elegant open that retained a dash of humor.

Creative director Diana Costantini explained, "My objective was to create a sequence with a few surprising twists, turns, and an element of illusion, using the scene of an A-list movie-star party and TV sets. For example, in one of the setups, you hear clinking sound effects, which you presume to be glasses clinking. As the waiter comes into frame, the viewer learns that the clinking is actually coming from a sword fight that is happening on a telly, which the waiter is wheeling by on his tray. This is followed by a close-up shot of the Hollywood sign burning. As the camera pulls back, we reveal a chichi chick who is having her cigarette lit as another waiter moves in the background with a television showing the image of the Hollywood sign. It is a series of subtle, unexpected scenarios, making viewers think one thing and then leading them somewhere else. My initial idea was to use live action, but the further I developed the concept, the more apparent it became that a chic and stylish illustrative approach would work much better."

Visual reference and inspiration for the style of the piece came from the stunning work of illustrator Anja Kroencke. Classic films, such as *Ben-Hur*, inspired the animation inside the TV monitors.

The client was initially concerned about going with animation for the weekly movie show. It was important that the overall look and feel wasn't too cartoon-like. Although the piece is animated, it is definitely an adult experience, thanks to the fine balance of animation, wit, and style applied by Tactic to both the design and execution of the piece.

Production Process

Completed over the course of six weeks, the project began as a series of hand-drawn silhouette pencil sketches created by designer James Hackett. After the characters had been designed and refined they were scanned and imported into Illustrator. In Illustrator, they were retraced as vectors to be used in After Effects.

Each individual character and element, such as smoke and fire, was animated separately and then composited in After Effects. After the characters and animations were finalized, camera moves were added to give the illusion of depth.

Hackett produced this animation in After Effects 4.1, which doesn't have the parent-and-child animation tools of version 5. He overcame this limitation with an elaborate nesting of compositions within a stage composition.

The end result is simply stunning. Now, could you be a dear and get me some more champagne? The crab puffs were simply dreadful, and I must do something to get this foul taste out of my mouth.

Credits

Universal Studios Networks, UK LTD
Director of Channels **Tor McLaren**
Director of Programming **Mark Staufer**

TACTIC Creative Services
Concept/Creative Director **Diana Costantini**
Designer/Animator **James Hackett**
Animator **Helen Clemens**
After Effects Compositor **James Hackett**
Sound Designer **Andy Wilson**
Producer **Jonathan Davis**
Postproduction House **Engine**

Tools

Adobe After Effects
Adobe Illustrator
Apple Macintosh G3
Logic Audio Pro Tools

Production Company

TACTIC Creative Services
Sydney, Australia

Discovery Digital Networks
Discovery en Español
Relaunch

Project Overview

The identity package for Discovery en Español is a stunning piece of work that bridges both continents and cultures. It mixes humanity with the inherent urge of humans to discover, creating compelling portraits of Hispanic men and women and their individual senses of community and discovery.

Discovery en Español is a network targeted at the Hispanic market in the United States. The challenge of the relaunch was to create an identity for an audience with multiple allegiances and identifications. The programming is in Spanish, but most of households intended to view the programming are decidedly cross-cultural and multilingual.

Inclusiveness and cultural sensitivity were of paramount importance to the Discovery Channel while developing this channel for the Latin American community. The ID package needed to reflect a commitment to those ideals while engaging and entertaining the audience.

Creative Process

PMcD Design is a company that does their homework. For this project, they were deeply involved with marketing and research efforts, even sitting in on a number of focus groups.

Creative director Patrick McDonough explained, "When you attend a focus group and actually hear the people talking, certain things stick in your mind. Things get repeated, and you start to create a direction for the concepts. In this case, it was how people talked about juggling two worlds—living in America but being from someplace else, about living in a home where you speak English but your parents and grandparents speak only Spanish. Balancing of two worlds was very important to these viewers."

The objective was to position Discovery en Español as a channel that can help place these two worlds in context by examining elements that bind them as a community while celebrating their cultural diversity.

While developing concepts for the project, McDonough came across an image that was to become a creative touchstone for the rest of the project. In the photo, a migrant worker in her 60s is pictured with her son. The woman—strong, comfortable with herself and with the decisions she has made—is seated in a chair. What is most evident, perhaps, is the pride she has in her son, who now works for a government agency that is attempting to improve the lives of farm workers.

McDonough said, "It was her sense of determination and strong connection to family that really impressed us. What these people share is their American experience, rooted in progress and dreams of a better life. It is a bond between generations: the sacrifices and responsibilities of the previous are rewarded by the successes of the present and future. From there we were determined to create a series of portraits where people talk about what they would like to discover. This is, after all, a part of the Discovery Network's family."

Production Process

Casting

PMcD Design hired a casting agency to find a cross section of people from Latin American countries. Cuba, Puerto Rico, Mexico, and Colombia were all represented in the final selection.

Together, they looked at over 100 individuals and selected 20 for the spots. Most of the people selected were "real people" with little or no theatrical experience. This was important because Discovery en Español wanted the spots to ring true and sincerely reflect their target audience.

Shoot

The models were asked to bring something that had a strong connection to their culture. One gentleman brought a photo of his mother as a child; another woman brought her dog, Cuca.

The shooting lasted one day. Scenarios were shot on a stark white backdrop. McDonough describes the vibe of the shoot as a party, and by the end of the day, the cast and crew became like "one big family."

Ten tables full of props from different Latin American cultures were laid out for people to use in their portraits. A wide selection of chairs was also provided, and people gravitated toward objects that spoke to them.

Postproduction

The shoot produced a considerable amount of footage. McDonough used an Avid editing suite to group the stories together in a mix-and-match process.

Once the basic edits were complete, Flame was used for compositing images into the frames that appear in the spots. The intended effect was images of things that the person was either thinking about or that he or she might want to discover were hanging on the wall.

The Discovery en Español logo was produced by Neeson Pearl, who did logo redesign for the Discovery channel. To keep icons and elements consistent between the Discovery brands, PMcD Design worked closely with Neeson Pearl. Two different versions of the Discovery logo were modified for Discovery en Español. These elements were assembled with the spots to create the final identity package.

Credits

Creative Director **Patrick McDonough**
Director/Director of Photography **Russell Fine**
Editor **Anne Craddock, Red Car NYC**
Digital EFX **Liquid Light**
3-D Graphics **Neeson Pearl**
Music **Elias & Associates**
Executive Producer **Dana Bonomo**
Producer **Michelle Lockett**
Client **Discovery Digital Networks/Discovery en Español**
VP Marketing **Mary Hicks**
Project Manager **Eliza Booth**

Tools

Alias|wavefront Maya
Avid
Discreet Smoke
Paintbox 8
Spirit DataCine

Production Company

PMcD Design
New York, NY, United States

Discovery En Español® is a registered trademark of Discovery.

UKTV
UK Horizons
Identity Package

Project Overview

UK Horizons is a digital-only channel, which broadcasts the best of the BBC's factual output, including nature and wildlife, travel, men and machines, and "fly on the wall" documentaries.

Positioned as "television that makes life worth watching," UK Horizons was looking for an identity package to support this claim. The resulting identity features a flying camera that relays sounds and images to the viewers while it goes anywhere and sees everything.

Creative Process

Designer and director Jason Keeley explained, "We decided to focus on the concept of watching life, and soon we arrived at the idea of using an eye as a starting point. We took the idea of the eye and extended it to become a flying eye, in that it could be a mobile entity that visited all manner of different environments—like an explorer! The idea of a flying eyeball sounds a bit creepy, so we refined the idea so that the eye became mechanical."

During the conceptual process, the team referred to droids and hovering spacecraft from sci-fi movies like *Star Wars*. Research led them to realize that many of the latest gadgets and commercial products have been taking on characters and personalities of their own—Sony's robot dog, the Smart car, and even the Apple iMac.

Using these products as a base or reference, they developed the visuals for their own character—a flying cameraman who could record both audio and video.

UK Horizons

"The design process began with a visualizer, who came back with a series of rough drawings to give us some thoughts on how our little fellow might fly, work, investigate, and move. This was quite a fun stage. We got back some really weird stuff—some of it good and some that told us where we didn't want to go. However, we eventually arrived at a basic design with input from several designers," said Keeley.

Production Process

Next, the team refined and built the character in 3-D computer graphics. Using Softimage, Keeley worked with Phil Hurrell at SVC, based in London. Together they breathed life into the eye character.

Nicknamed "The Bug" by the production team, the final character comes complete with a blinking protective lens hood, a huge extending zoom lens, a bee-stinger antenna for communication purposes, and a microphone that folds in and out of the main body structure.

The Bug has a transparent shell structure through which the electronic circuit boards and glowing, rotating engine parts are clearly visible. To give the creature a more human feel, a fluorescent plasma-style iris was created for the eye. The external detailing of The Bug includes the channel logo, serial and model numbers, and electrical hazard warnings on the outside casing of the machine.

Once the initial machine was built, the team needed to develop a series of identity spots, one for each of the four program genres—nature and wildlife, travel, men and machines, and "fly on the wall" documentaries.

This project was animated on Softimage and was rendered and composited entirely in CG without any external compositing tools like Inferno or Infinity. Other than digital still shots for texturing purposes, no live action shots were used. The final sequences each took eight days to produce, plus an initial five days to build The Bug.

Credits

Lambie-Nairn Team
Creative Directors **Brian Eley and Marcus Jones**
Designer/Director **Jason Keeley**
Producer **Linda Farley**

SVC Team
Head of CG Animation **Phil Hurrell**
Animator **Howard Bell**
Post-Production Producer **George Isaacs**

Hum Team
Composer **Joe Glasman**
Producer **Dan Simmons**

Tools

Softimage

Production Company

Lambie-Nairn
London, England

Sci Fi Channel
SCInema Feature
Movie Block Package

Project Overview

Shown nightly on the Sci Fi Channel, the *SCInema Feature* movie needed an identity package. The objective of the project was to create a show open and close, as well as other elements, to give the programming block a unique and unified feel.

Director Jeremy Hollister used this opportunity to pay tribute to one of his favorite sci-fi movies of all time, *Tron*.

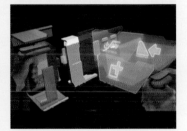

Creative Process

Hollister explained, "We wanted to give it a big epic feel and also tell a
story. Stylistically, it is supposed to feel futuristic, but like *Tron*, it's done
in that kind of flat-shaded 3-D with live action composited into it. The
idea of it is she's on a mission to upload contraband media by
infiltrating the citadel of some unnamed, neofascist, futuristic authority.
You see, in this future society, you can't get good programming, and so
she has to smuggle it in and jack it into the mainframe. Once it's
uploaded into the system, it's broadcast to the waiting masses. That's
her mission, and you watch her progress during the course of the
evening's entertainment."

Telling a story in 20-second blocks interspersed throughout an evening is
no easy task. Our protagonist starts on the roof of the citadel, watching
the skyline of the city. She receives her instructions from the communications pad on her wrist and navigates her way though the labyrinthine
corridors of the citadel, avoiding detection and capture. Finally she locks
into the mainframe control panel and uploads the contraband media,
striking a blow for freedom and better programming.

Production Process

Done on a very tight budget, this spot took four weeks from storyboards to completion. Even though much of the piece has a 3-D look and feel, most was done as flat 2-D images that were manipulated in Inferno. This effect is exemplified when the protagonist runs through the hallways. The walls were simple 2-D painted panels manipulated to simulate a flat-shaped 3-D effect.

The green-screen shoot proved challenging, but not for the reasons you might expect. Bill Denahy, who produced the live action segments, elaborated, "The woman that we used for talent was actually a fitness teacher. She was amazing because we were shooting on a very short stage, and

we literally did not have one foot more of space than we needed. To get the effect we needed for the spot, she had to keep running up to speed, and she would have to stick out her hands before slamming into the wall at the end of her runs! She was a very brave woman."

For the final climactic shot of the protagonist uploading the contraband media into the mainframe, a careful choreography between the live shoot and the 3-D elements was required. The model was given green handles and told to grab onto them and turn, to simulate operating the controls of the machine. The machine was modeled in Softimage and matched precisely to her movements to complete the effect.

Credits

Designer/Director **Jeremy Hollister**
Designer **Victor Newman**
Producer **Peter Metsopoulos**
Executive Producer **Connie Griffin**
Director of Photography **Toshiaki Ozawa**
Colorist **Clive Christopher**
Music and Composition **Ohm Lab**
Clients **Creative Director, Josh Greenberg**
Director of On-Air Promotions **Rick Austin**

Tools

Adobe Illustrator
Adobe Photoshop
Avid
Discreet Inferno
Cinema 4D
MetaCreations Poser
Softimage

Production Company

RIOT Design
Manhattan, NY, United States

Images courtesy of the Sci Fi Channel.

J. Walter Thompson (Hong Kong)
King World Ginseng Commercial

Project Overview

Kayaking though the desert? Impossible, you might say, but not for this ambitious athlete. She navigates the dunes with style and vigor in this exhilarating spot from Hong Kong.

The intended message is that with good health and willpower, anything is possible, that is, if you take a King World ginseng capsule on a daily basis.

Creative Process

The creative brief from the agency defined the objective: "To have a woman skillfully navigate her kayak in sand dunes. Visuals should be powerful and realistic." Initially, the client anticipated a blue-screen shoot combined with a 3-D ocean of sand to create the desired effect.

Director Michael Chu had a different vision of how the effect could be created. He believed that the virtual approach might not be convincing and could potentially detract from the message. His suggestion was to film the spot using a real kayak in a real desert. Chu found his inspiration in the science-fiction classic, *Dune*. He closely studied the movement of sand in the cinematography. His vision of the kayak's motion was directly inspired by the massive sand worms in the film.

To convince the client of the validity of his approach, Chu showed clips from the film in combination with scenes of white-water rafting. His objective was to show how the concept of "sand rafting" could be created using real-world materials. The client agreed that Chu's approach was the better tack and commissioned the project.

Credits

Creative Director **Milka Ho**
Agency Producer **Annie Tong**
Director/Cameraman **Michael Chu**
Producer **Chris White**
Editing Company **Touches (Hong Kong)**
Editor **Teddy Mak**
On-line Facility **Digit Digit**
Telecine **Chan Kwok Choi**
Flame Artist **Derrick Wong**
Music **Drum Music**

Tools

Discreet Flame
URSA Diamond Telecine

Production Company

Cinetech Production Group
Causeway Bay, Hong Kong

Production Process

Shot in one day at Dumont Sand Dunes near Baker, California, the shoot was arduous, to say the least. Most of the shoot involved attaching the kayak to gas-powered winches and a Hummer and dragging it across a wide variety of terrains.

To create the visual of a wake behind the kayak, a special v-shaped rig was developed and attached to the kayak. This rig would travel under the sand, creating the rippled-wave effect as it moved. A bulldozer and air cannon were employed to create turbulence in the foreground of the shot.

A professional female rafting expert was brought in for the more dangerous long shots of the kayak traveling down the steep inclines of the dunes. For the close-up shots, the primary model was placed in the kayak and pulled by the winches.

Chu shot the scene in 35 mm and found that the bright light in the desert required no additional lighting. Most scenes were filmed at 80 to 100 frames per second at a 45-degree camera shutter angle to give the splashing sand a crisper look. To create highlights behind the action, he used 4' x 4' (1.2 m x 1.2 m) mirrors and shiny boards. Many of the angles simulate a sports camera covering a white-water-rafting race.

After the shoot, Chu claimed that cleaning the sand from his nooks and crannies was probably the most time-consuming element of the day. The female model, on the other hand, has vowed never to kayak in the desert again.

Postproduction involved a telecine transfer and two days of compositing in Flame to combine the sand movement with the live action footage. Additional distortion and tracking of sand movement were achieved by using texture maps from the Flame software libraries.

Cosmopolitan Television
Launch Package

Project Overview

The assignment to launch Cosmopolitan's International Television was no easy task. Hatmaker's challenge was to take the magazine's identity to television and give it a unique personality that not only complemented the magazine but was also capable of standing alone as a separate brand.

The initial launch of the network was in Spain, with plans to expand the channel into additional European and Asian markets.

Creative Process

The central tenet of Hatmaker's branding strategy was to divide the network identity into blocks that appealed to specific demographic segments. These blocks were based on the existing *Cosmopolitan* tagline: *Fun Fearless Female*.

Different age demographics were matched with the different statements. *Fun* spots were designed for the teenage market; *Fearless* for 18- to 28-year-old women; and *Female* for women 28 and older.

"The way we designed the channel is that each of these spots would have a relationship to each other, but they would each have their own attitude and look and feel," said creative director Chris Goveia. *Fun* spots were shot using stop-motion animation techniques. *Fearless* spots have a rapid pace and composite 35 mm shoots of live action models into a "Comso World." *Female* spots are specifically designed to move at a slower, more ethereal pace. The spot featured in this book is taken from the *Fearless* category.

Beyond the specific spots and branding strategy were the marketing concerns of Cosmopolitan Television. The channel planned for a rapid expansion into additional markets, requiring the identity package to have a broad appeal and a high degree of flexibility. To address these concerns, Hatmaker specifically choose a culturally diverse selection of women for the spots and took a universal approach to the use of color and design sensibilities, ultimately creating an identity package that can be adapted easily to different cultures by replacing the language and typography.

Production Process

Fearless spots were designed to have an aggressive feeling and are aired in the afternoon and evening. For these spots, Goviea said, "We wanted to create a specific sense of place, a surreal environment where the women can move and react, and the Cosmo logo is behind them. One of the things that we wanted to do was create a sense of seamlessness between the women, the graphics, and the environment."

To enhance the integration of the elements, Goveia and the team shot the live footage of the models against a white background. They choose to shoot against white because they felt that the shadows from a blue-screen shoot might look too "cut out" and detract from the atmosphere they were attempting to create.

This footage was imported into Flame where the models were composited against a white floor created in the program. The white-screen shoot proved to be more of a challenge than expected in the postproduction process. Although most of the white could be keyed out, occasionally certain areas required a substantial amount of cleanup to remove the white completely.

In the end, the extra effort proved worthwhile, giving the spots a seamless appearance and a palpable sense of place.

Credits

Client Contacts **Cynthia Hudson Fernandez and Gustavo Basalo**
Creative Director/Designer **Chris Goveia**
Designer **Prang Tharawanich**
Project Manager **Elz Bentley**
Production Company **Creative Café**
Postproduction Company **Brickyard vfx**
Visual Effects Artist **Dave Waller**
Postproduction Manager **Brian Drewes**

Tools

Discreet Flame
Media 100

Production Company

Hotmaker
Watertown, MA, United States

Discovery Networks International
Animal Planet International's "Whale of a Week" Promotional Package

Project Overview

Animal Planet International's "Whale of a Week" was a weeklong event that featured a lineup of shows about whales and man's relationship to these majestic creatures. The programming aired in the United States, Europe, Latin America, and Asia.

"Our goal," said Molly McCarthy, associate producer of international on-air promotion for Discovery Networks International, "was to create a promo that would travel across all regions of the world and portray the beauty and mystery of whales, while maintaining the international on-air look of the Animal Planet network. We wanted something that would show whales as they are—magnificent, tranquil creatures whose continued existence depends so much on our understanding of how fragile life can be."

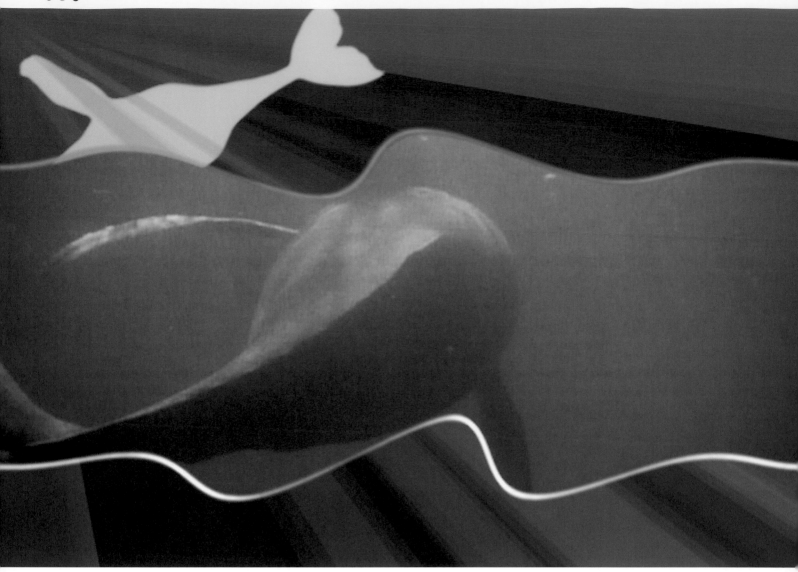

Creative Process

Designer and art director Tom Bik explained, "I wanted to design something that would set it [the event] apart from everything else on the station. The basic objective was to show the grace and grandeur of these animals. I thought, 'How can we do this in a simple way?' So we cut it down to its simplest shapes, leaving out everything, so your main focus is on this unbelievable animal."

Animal Planet provided Bik with raw footage. From this footage, he sought out scenes that he referred to as "signature moves" of whales—actions such as jumping out of the water, breaching the surface, or diving for food. Once he found these key frames, he flattened the images in Illustrator and applied a soothing yet vibrant color palette of light and water. The images were converted into storyboards and placed on-line for approval.

Because this spot was intended for an international audience, regional programming directors for The Discovery Networks reviewed the spot and gave their input. The response from all geographic regions was unanimous: ViewPoint had found the ideal direction and was given the green light to complete the spot.

Production Process

Although the final appearance of the spot is a flat, 2-D look, the piece required a large degree of 3-D modeling and animation. Bik edited the footage he wanted to use in the piece, and ViewPoint's 3-D staff created an exact replica of the whale in Maya. The model's motion was then painstakingly matched frame-by-frame with the original footage. The animation was output as black-and-white flat images.

Color treatment was added during final composing in Flame. To get the effect Bik was looking for, he brought in the original storyboards, and the elements were matched to the original color swatches. Final delivery of the spot included five localized versions—English, Mandarin Chinese, Japanese, Portuguese, Spanish—and a blank edit with no text

The result is a simple yet elegant homage to one of our planet's most enduring and sublime creatures.

Credits

Discovery Networks International
Vice President International Programming and Promotion **Laura Frankel**
Manager of International On-Air Promotion **Holly Roessler**
Associate Producer of International On-Air Promotion **Molly McCarthy**

ViewPoint Studios
Creative Director, Design Studio **Glenn Robbins**
Executive Producer **Dave Shilale**
Producer **Adrienne Gum**
Designer/Art Director **Tom Bik**
Flame Artist **Colleen Dolan-Hastings**

Tools

Adobe Photoshop
Adobe Illustrator
Alias|wavefront Maya
Discreet Flame

Production Company

ViewPoint Studios
Needham, MA, United States

Ten United
Hoover's SpinScrub Advertisement

Project Overview

American Bandstand, a singing gender-bending '80s club diva, and glowing translucent green brushes are not what you usually identify with floor-care product sales pitches, but Hoover's SpinScrub is a unique spot that transcends normal expectations.

Ten United tapped Bill Denahy of R!OT Design for this spot after reviewing a tape of his groundbreaking work on the VW Turbonium campaign. The agency already had a rough outline of what they were looking for in terms of music and messaging, but they looked to Denahy to give the spot its personality.

Creative Process

"Hoover was a fun project," said Denahy. "Basically, they came to us and said they had the song 'You Spin Me Round' by Dead Or Alive and wanted to make a big deal out of these spinning brushes. I came back to them with the idea of playing off of *American Bandstand*. So we literally recreated *Bandstand* with a virtual camera and created a space for all these green brushes to dance around. We also gave each of them their own character. The thing I always remembered was there was always the really good-looking couple that they'd zoom in tight on. I tried to do that with the dancing brushing as if I were directing an episode of *American Bandstand*."

Production Process

The spot is a seamless blend of 3-D elements combined with real-world motion-controlled footage. Modeled in Softimage, the brushes were programmed with a randomize function that created variations in each brush's dance style. This attention to detail has created a world where each brush is seen as a featured dancer with its own unique personality.

In addition to the 3-D elements of the piece, a motion-control rig was used for a number of the shots, including a 360-degree rotation of the vacuum used in the kaleidoscope effect. The most challenging image of the live shoot was a shot featuring the scrubbing action. This shot was taken from underneath the machine as it moved across a Plexiglas panel, leaving behind a trail of suds. What made this scene so complicated was the creation of a discernable suds pattern using a clear liquid against a white background.

Denahy explained, "Everyone kind of looked at me askew when I said we're going to have clear liquid with a white background. Luckily I had done some tests before with running lights through liquid, and I kind of managed to sell them on the idea. It's basically kind of cross-lit to get the light running through to get those highlights on the liquid and the suds. I think it comes out really nice because it gives you that nice natural suds pattern."

And somewhere, Dick Clark is smiling, or perhaps even steam-cleaning his Persian rug.

Credits

Ten United
Senior Vice President/Associate Creative Director **Steve Smith**
Vice President, Creative Supervisor **Frank Longo**

R!OT Design
Director **Bill Denahy**
Inferno Artist **Matt Reilly**

Tools

Discreet Inferno
Softimage

Production Company

R!OT Design
Manhattan, NY, United States

All images courtesy of Hoover.

Universal Studios Networks, UK Ltd
Short Provokers
Program Package

Project Overview

Short Provokers is a 30-minute program that airs short films on the UK movie channel The Studio. TACTIC had previously worked with the client on a number of projects for both the Sci-Fi Channel and The Studio.

The objective was to establish an entertaining Saturday-night short-film brand that was accessible and humorous without reverting to tired "filmic" icons or an art-house look and feel. To meet these goals, TACTIC took the unique approach of creating an animated 3-D storyboard world for the show package. The effect is both irreverent and enticing, creating an easily identifiable brand presence.

Creative Process

"As the client requested, we had to give the package context without pulling out the ol' flying film strip or clapperboard clichés," said creative director Diana Constantini. "We weren't able to use any visuals from the short films either, so it was a case of starting from scratch."

Designer Marcus Lyall explained, "I started off thinking we could maybe film a small drama that used classic genre scenes. I started sketching these ideas out and realized that the answer was in front of me. Short films are a director's calling cards. Storyboards are a good way of showing the director's input into a film. So I came up with the idea of entering into a storyboard world."

Because of the distance between TACTIC and their client, everything had to be shared via the Internet. The initial concept was presented on-line as a series of JPEG files accompanied by a written description. The approach fit neatly into the identity package that Universal was hoping to develop. The concept was approved nearly instantaneously.

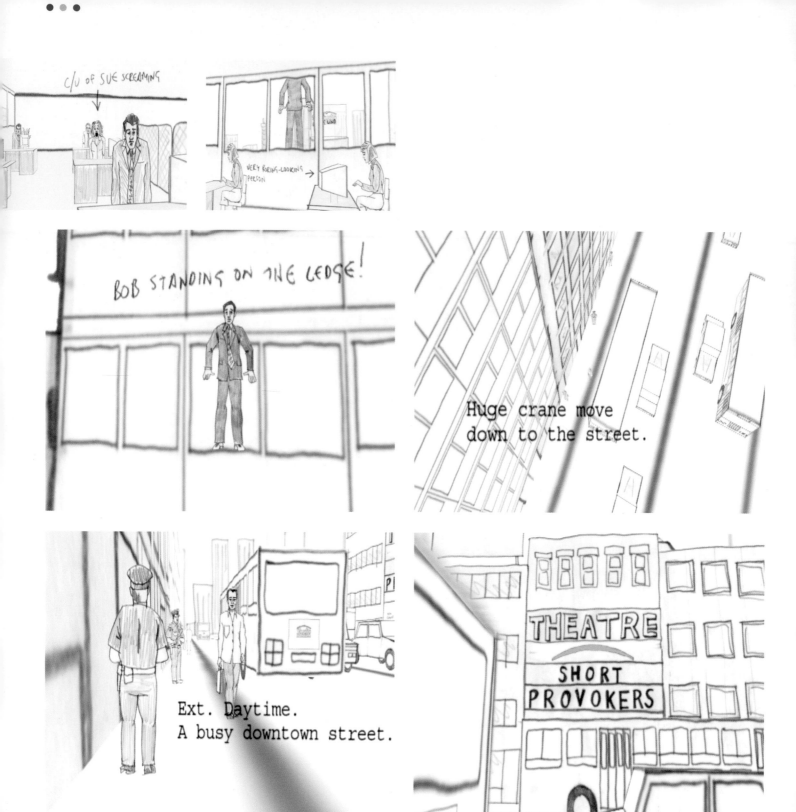

Production Process

Animating and giving depth to the storyboards was not as easy as you might think. For this project, TACTIC did not rely on traditional 2-D animation techniques. They started by writing three short film scenes. The scenes were then drawn as rough sketches. From there they were able to determine what elements would be needed for the animation.

Elements were hand-drawn, scanned, and imported into After Effects. When necessary, elements were drawn as front and side views to achieve a dimensional effect. All the sketches were scanned, graded, and matted in Photoshop. Text overlays were created using Illustrator. The client discouraged attempts to perfect the piece. In fact, an illustrator was hired, but the client preferred the rough style of the initial concept board illustrations.

"We thought the flat white look would allow us to hide some mistakes," said Lyall. "It was the other way round. It was completely unforgiving! We started off using high-resolution scans, but this caused memory problems and 'fizzing' on the video monitor. So we went back and resized all the images. We animated in After Effects, which isn't really a 3-D program. It just lets you use flat planes of video in 3-D space. Making the cars was difficult because we had to build them out of flat planes of video. The After Effects 5 3-D renderer had some issues, so none of the planes could intersect. This meant going through and making sure none of the planes were touching. It was a hard slog in After Effects."

In terms of communicating with the client, Constantini felt that the distance between them actually helped both production and creative processes. "The fact that TACTIC is based in Sydney and our client is in London has never been a hindrance. In fact, we both feel it's a more efficient way to work. While they're sleeping, we're working, so when they arrive at the office in the morning, there's new 'work in progress' QuickTime files waiting for them to check. It really speeds up the process and eliminates meetings, which is always a good thing!"

Credits

Universal Studios Networks, UK Ltd
Director of Channels **Tor McLaren**
Director of Programming **Mark Staufer**

TACTIC **Creative Services**
Creative Direction **Diana Constantini**
Sound Design **Andy Wilson**
Production House **GMD**
Designer/Illustrator **Marcus Lyall**
Producer **Aren Fieldwalker**
After Effects Compositor **Marcus Lyall**

Tools

Adobe After Effects
Adobe Illustrator
Adobe Photoshop
Discreet Flame

Production Company

TACTIC Creative Services
Sydney, Australia

Admerasia
Kohler China
Advertisement

Project Overview

It's Esther Williams—style choreography meets modern plumbing design in this Chinese underwater ballet spot for Kohler.

Creative Process

Director Michael Chu had previously filmed another spot for Kohler for the Chinese market using a similar technique. The response to the first spot was so positive that Kohler requested his participation in the filming of their next spot.

Inspired by Howard Schatz's underwater portrait photography, Chu set about designing a spot that synchronized the movements of sea nymphs with the curves and features of faucets, sinks, toilets, and bathtubs.

Chu explained, "Because there were a lot of products to be featured in the spot, I had to be very careful in the design of scenes—the visual balance and transitions—to avoid making the commercial seem too much like a catalog. I tried to artistically match the formation and actions of the sea nymphs to the shapes of the products, such as transforming the toilets into a pedestal for statues."

For client approval, Chu presented Photoshop-based storyboards, which combined stock mermaid images with Kohler products. Movie clips from early Esther Williams movies were also used as reference points for underwater movements.

Production Process

Casting

Finding water nymphs for this spot proved to be a challenge. Because the spot was to air in China, an all-Chinese cast was required. The team had such a difficult time casting the lead, they almost considered assembling their own synchronized swimming team.

The casting criteria was to find a model who was very attractive and could swim like Ester Williams. Casting calls were done throughout China and Hong Kong. Ultimately, a Hong Kong—based model who had been a champion swimmer in high school was chosen.

Shoot

The next hurdle was to find a suitable swimming pool in Shanghai. Unfortunately, the shooting schedule coincided with a national sporting event. Because all large swimming pools are government operated, Chu's producer had to convince officials to let the crew film in the pool from 8:00 p.m. to 6:00 a.m.

Jordy Klein, an expert in underwater photography, was flown to Shanghai from Florida to assist with the shoot. Special platforms and rigs were built to enable product placement in both the foreground and background of the shots with the water nymphs.

Over the course of three consecutive evenings, Chu shot his water ballet on 35 mm film. The team coach, who also became one of the featured nymphs in the spots, developed the underwater choreography. Klein brought his own underwater speaker system, which proved invaluable for communicating with the dancers and cameramen during the shoot.

A 25-foot Pegasus crane was used for the top-angle wide shot of the swimmers. When lighting through water, it is very difficult to get the appropriate f-stops, and the crew employed numerous high-powered lighting rigs.

Telecine was done with a Spirit and DaVinci 2K Datascan. Compositing took three days of Inferno work at Digit Digit of Hong Kong. Inferno was also used to create a matte for all the products. Chu found that this matte provided more flexibility and control during the compositing phase by separating products from the layers of water.

Credits

Creative Director **Kapo Cheung**
Agency Producer **Jennifer Yeh**
Director **Michael Chu**
Producer **Wendy Chu**
Cameraman **Lam Fung**
Underwater Cameraman **Jordy Klein**
Editing Company **Edit Point (Hong Kong)**
Editor **Garnet Chiu**
On-line Facility **Digit Digit**
Telecine **Leung Ka Kat**
Flame Artist **Kenneth Chung**
Music **Voices**

Tools

Adobe Photoshop
Discreet Inferno
Spirit DataCine

Production Company

Cinetech Production Group
Causeway Bay, Hong Kong

13th Street
Horrorskop

Project Overview

For most, the signs of the astrological wheel are viewed as an amusing daily forecast served up in their morning newspaper. Others look to the stars seeking portents of good fortune or perhaps the realization of their innermost dreams.

But what if the opposite were true?—that is, if the signs were seen through a warped lens where the symbolic creatures were denizens of a subterranean world where they serve as living talismans that represent the worst qualities of human nature. Infinitely compelling, grotesquely beautiful, and ultimately disturbing, *Horrorskop* is every tarot card reader's nightmare come true.

Originally planned as a simple highlight-trailer promotional package for 13th Street, a European action and suspense channel, the concept proved so powerful that it was implemented as a total network campaign, complete with print collateral, Internet presence, and coordinated on-air events.

CAPRICORN
22·12 - 19·01

AQUARIUS
20·01 - 18·02

PISCES
19·02 - 20·03

ARIES
21·03 - 19·04

TAURUS
20·04 - 20·05

GEMINI
21·05 - 2 ·06

CANCER
22·06 - 22·07

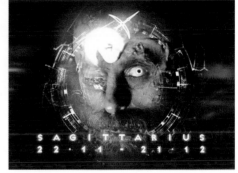

Creative Process

Allie Schropp, a freelance producer from 13th Street, conceived the initial concept for *Horrorskop*. His idea was for a series of highlight trailers to feature the channel's upcoming movies. The basic premise was to reference the upcoming movies in a way that is similar to a horoscope prediction. The twist is that that the prediction would be a "horror-scope," and the focus would be on all the bad things—nothing good or positive, only the things in life that are potentially fearful or dangerous.

13th Street had three design companies submit proposals for the spots, and eventually selected Velvet. Velvet not only developed a compelling creative package, they also pushed the concept not only as a series of highlight trailers, but also as an overall branding strategy for the channel.

"After the client saw our proposal, they realized the possibilities that *Horrorskop* offered across all departments," said director Matthias Zentner. "The room was buzzing—programming, PR, and marketing all generated ideas of how to use the *Horrorskop* idea in their areas. Suddenly, this was not an on air promotion project anymore! It became a project for the whole channel that was tailor-made to communicate their brand values."

Creatively, *Horrorskop* acknowledges the dark side and toys with the idea of how every sign either meets its death or brings death to others. The plots and the behavior of the characters are directly connected to death, murder, attack, or danger. The signs are always one of two stereotypes: the perpetrator or the victim.

Specific story lines were developed to complement the nature of the astrological signs. For example, Taurus is depicted as a proud bull in the arena, tormented by faceless matadors; Pisces, as a fishwoman, tragically tempted by the lure of a fishing hook; and Sagittarius, as the determined hunter, skillfully placing an arrow in the heart of his prey.

Images from Pisces.

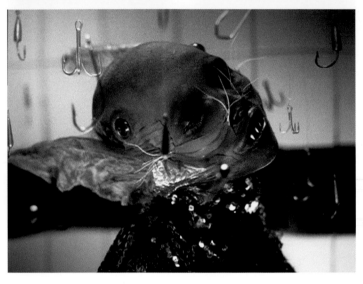

Production Process

Location Shoot

Nearly two and half months of preproduction was required for the shoot in Budapest. A considerable amount of time was needed for location scouting and casting. Initially, the plan was to shoot 12 spots in 10 days, although the final schedule was expanded to 11 shooting days.

Locations ranging from a rotting underground military hospital to a nearly demolished Turkish bathhouse were selected for the final shoot. To avoid constantly moving the production, each location doubled as the background for two spots. Although many of the spots were shot in the same location, extensive set dressing was applied to give each character its own unique environment. A high degree of planning was required because many of the locations had time limitations for their use. The team employed a rotating crew to facilitate the long shooting days.

Visual Effects

Shooting the 12 highly complex shots proved difficult on the limited budget. The team came up with many improvised solutions to achieve the final style of the piece. Shot on 35 mm film, the team attempted to create most of the visual effects in camera by building their own specialized lenses. These lenses were attached to the camera in front of the camera's existing lens and would distort the images in a variety of different fashions, ranging from altered focus to skewed perspectives.

Casting

Zentner found the environment in Budapest ideal for casting the specialized talent needed for the spots. The city is home to a very active arts community, and finding talent without having to go the traditional casting-agency route was not a problem.

The range of talent included a professor of pantomime for the broken puppet character in Libra; an award-winning Hungarian dancer to interpret the goatlike movements of Capricorn; a stuntman who could hold his breath for over two minutes for the Aquarius spot; a techno dancer who suffered though the Taurus shoot in a cumbersome latex costume for 10 hours; a theater actor, who was more than a little freaked out by the flying rig and needed to move through the fire on the set of the Aries spot; a pair of real twins, who mistakenly believed they were going to a photo shoot for Hugo Boss, were cast as Gemini; two performers for Leo—one for the facial shot and one, a circus performer, for the body movements; and a courageous woman who was strapped into a harness 39 feet (12 m) off the ground for the Virgo spot.

Costuming and Makeup

Creating the look of the creatures was a collaborative process between the Velvet team and a makeup artist. Numerous sketches and computer composites were created. Once they reached Budapest, a team of four makeup artists and stylists spent two full weeks attempting to recreate the look and feel of the original designs in the flesh.

For costuming, a special-effects person was teamed with a costume designer to develop functional clothes with an outstanding look. These costumes were all handmade, combining mechanical rigs and organic materials.

Postproduction

Once the final footage had been assembled, a two-month period of intensive Avid editing was required to complete the spots. Matte paintings created in Photoshop and Illustrator were used for planning all of the graphical layouts. The typography effects were created in After Effects, and 3-D graphics were assembled for the Sagittarius spot. The final elements were composited in Flame.

Final Delivery

Final broadcast deliverables included twelve 30-second spots, one- and two-minute teaser campaigns, and a complete promotion package for monthly highlight trailers. Nonbroadcast deliverables included postcards, a calendar, and Internet-specific elements. Additionally, a *Horrorskop* show hosted by German punk rock star Bela B. was produced.

Credits

Creative Director **Matthias Zentner**
Creative Director, 13th Street **Lars Wagner**
Director **Matthias Zentner**
Creator **Allie Schropp**
Art Director **Daniel von Braun**
Production Manager **Anne Böck**
Director of Photography **Torsten Lippstock**
Editor **Jochen Krauss**
1 AD Germany **Felix Föhr**
Cameraman **Thorsten Lippstock**
Assistant Cameraman **Attila Kiss**
Film Loader **Daniel Werner**
Art Direction/Set Designer **Katja Severin**
Makeup Artists **Christian Hoppe. Michele Timana, and Ellen Keller**
Costume Designers **Katharina Ost and Ziad Ragheb**

Production Company

Velvet Design
Munich, Germany

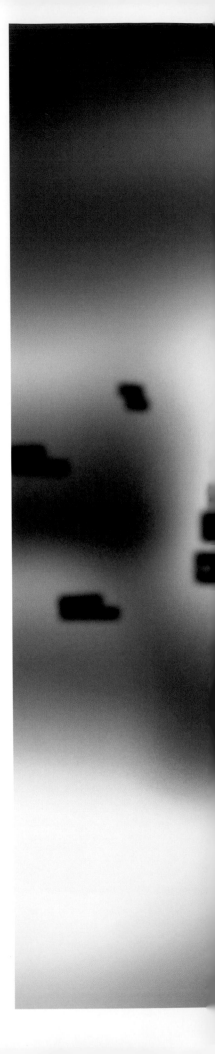

Chapter 2
Film

It's dark. You're waiting—waiting to be taken somewhere, waiting to be entertained, waiting for something worth the price of admission to appear on the screen.

The theater is home to a world of escapism; it's a separation from one's normal existence into one of voyeuristic intent. The characters on the screen play out our deepest fears, longings, desires, and ambitions.

Quality of the work is of paramount importance in this arena—screens are larger, and expectations are higher. Nothing else holds quite the cachet as motion pictures.

The demands placed on motion graphics artists in this specialty are great. Visual effects and title sequences need to be carefully balanced with story concerns. All elements must be harmonized to create the ultimate effect—a seamless entertainment experience that takes the viewer on a journey.

Nothing is more important to that journey than setting the proper tone. Title sequences provide an entrée to the world the viewer will inhabit for the next few hours. They can either be integrated into the story line, such as in *Spy Game*, or they can serve as an evocative series of images designed to lay the proper mood and setting, as was done with the Swedish film *Dream*.

Beyond the introductory sequences, motion graphics for film encompasses a wide range of techniques and intentions. From an animated short developed for 3-D IMAX to a short film celebrating the Portuguese explorers of the 16th century to a modern documentary on the DJ culture, we will examine how filmmakers are using motion graphics to add emphasis, create drama, and add to the emotional resonance of their films.

Now...please pass the popcorn, and enjoy the show.

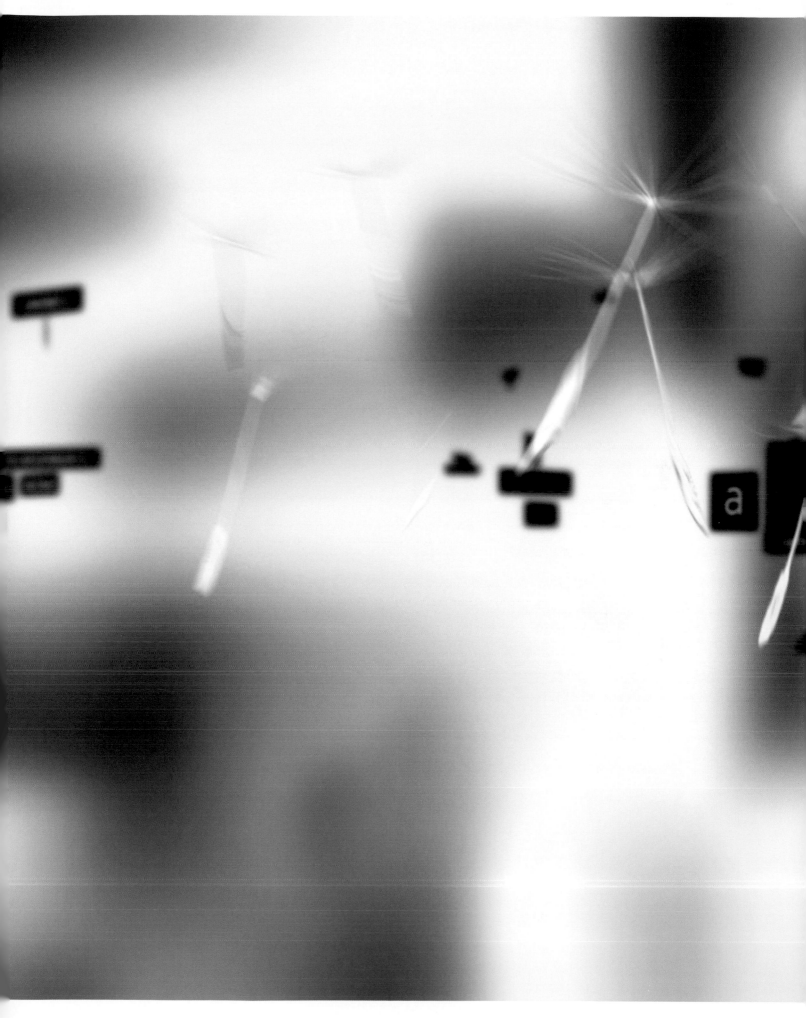

IMAX Corporation
Cyberworld
"Tonight's Performance"
3-D (IMAX) Project

Project Overview

Cyberworld was the first all-CG 3-D film in IMAX's 30-year history. Hosted by "Phig" (voiced by actress Jenna Elfman), *Cyberworld* is a fusion of eight animated shorts, consisting of both original and previously released material from DreamWorks, Fox, and Sony Pictures Imageworks. The effect is a modern-day *Fantasia* presented in 70 mm stereoscopic 3-D.

Included in the piece is a two-minute short developed by Hollywood-based graphic design and animation studio REZN8. Entitled "Tonight's Performance," the piece is a Jules Verne—inspired modern-day opera in the clouds.

Intended to engage audiences in a visual world of wonder, "Tonight's Performance" spotlights a number of abstract and ambiguous elements. The surreal piece centers on a young female performer in a fantasy ballet and is structured to convey the multiple stages of a circus—from setup to the grand performance. Whale-like reptiles, high-wire lighting gaffers, and stilt-walking electrical engineers inhabit this amazing world where a circus in the clouds seems not only feasible but eminently real.

Creative Process

"I met Hugh Murray of IMAX at a large-format convention," says executive producer and creative director Paul Sidlo. "In our conversation, he mentioned this idea he had of IMAX creating a stereo 3-D film comprising a collection of high-end CGI shorts, in the style of Disney's *Fantasia*. He asked if REZN8 would submit a concept for a short. We had a meeting with our creative team, and through some brainstorming, we developed the core concept of 'Tonight's Performance.' Essentially, we proposed a 'musical opera' of sorts—a fantasy theater in the clouds—where it would be more about the experience rather than being a narrative."

"Tonight's Performance" is a combination of classic and futuristic influences, seamlessly meshing art deco with science-fiction motifs. Stylistically, the design was inspired by influences as diverse as Cirque du Soleil; the films *The Fifth Element*, *Metropolis*, *City of Lost Children*, and *Brazil*; and the visionary architecture of Lebbus Woods.

First presented as a series of sketches and renderings, the piece was quickly turned to an animatic to illustrate the blocking and the complete vision of the scene. IMAX was enthusiastic about its inclusion in the larger work. Some modifications were required to integrate the piece with the overall project. Although "Tonight's Performance" was initially to be a stand-alone animation, alterations were made eventually to the scene's ending to tie the clip to the overall story line of the larger *Cyberworld* piece.

Production Process

"Tonight's Performance" proved to be an ambitious undertaking, taking nearly six months to produce. The project was so ambitious, in fact, that as the team began production, they purchased a rack of 20 dedicated rendering PCs. Despite all of this rendering firepower at their command, they found that they still required machines running 24 hours a day throughout the entire production.

Large-format filmmaking requires meticulous production. REZN8 had to ensure that the scale was correct and that every piece of geometry was point accurate. Producer Ileana Garcia-Montes elaborated, "With IMAX, the format is less forgiving. By that I mean, with large format, mistakes are more easily noticed, so it requires precision."

Technical director David Humpherys added, "The size of IMAX was a considerable challenge in terms of rendering and texturing. Each texture map had to be of a exponentially higher resolution than normal. This required more time to paint each map and more scrutiny up front to ensure that the final image didn't degrade. Due to the increased scale, render times were also an issue. With several other large projects happening in-house at the same time, render servers had to be managed carefully to ensure that all the renders were completed on schedule."

Complicating the challenges of developing 3-D for IMAX was the addition of stereoscopic 3-D effect. With stereo IMAX, you have the latitude to adjust the distance between two virtual cameras, which in effect changes how close or how far an object appears in 3-D space. Many of the environments were outdoors with an infinite background, and foreground objects were at times 100 feet (30.5 m) or more away. Many 3-D tests were required to achieve the proper balance and perspective that give "Tonight's Performance" its timeless quality and dramatic impact.

Credits

Executive Producer/Creative Director **Paul Sidlo**
Producer **Ileana Garcia-Montes**
Art Directors/3-D Artists **Bill Dahlinger, Mannix, and David Necker**
Technical Director/3-D Artist **David Humpherys**
Editor/Consultant **Sheldon Kahn**
Animators/Modelers **John C. Woo and Jeremy Appelbaum**
Visual Effects **Tim Montijo**
Character Facial Animation **Marjorie Hebrard**
Modeler **Fred Haro**
Paint and Texture Artists **John Ryan O'Keefe and Seton Kim**
Modeler **Tom Palmer**
Systems Administration **Bob Cazzell**
Accounting **Jake Klejna**
Tape Operation **Gregory Ivens**
Production Secretary **Alisen Nihill**

Tools

Adobe Photoshop
Afterburn Plugin for 3D Max
Eyeon Digital Fusion
Nothing Real Shake
3D Max

Production Company

REZN8
Hollywood, CA, United States

Mirabai Films
Monsoon Wedding
Title Sequence

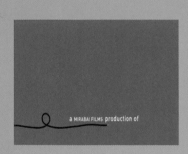

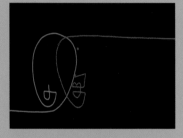

Project Overview

An animated line snakes its way across a swatch of color. Type springs forth to form various loops and curlicues on the screen. Eventually the line meets its mate, and they intersect in an image of two intertwined faces. The camera zooms into the bindi on the woman's forehead, and the credits continue.

Simple and colorful, the title sequence for *Monsoon Wedding* effectively engages the viewer in this tale of an arranged marriage in contemporary India.

Creative Process

When developing the title for her whimsical new film, Indian director Mira Nair was clear in her vision. She was looking for something colorful, something that "felt very Indian," and appeared as one continuous line. To materialize her vision, she opted to work with Trollbäck and Company, with whom she had worked on a number of previous projects.

"We did a lot of research on Indian culture, looking for forms, shapes, and colors," explained art director Jasmin Jordi. "Jakob [Trollbäck] also had an illustrator friend, Laura Ljungkvist, who does illustrations using one continuous line, never taking the pen off the page. We decided to take such an illustration and animate it. To symbolize the arranged marriage at the center of the film, the illustration has two intertwined faces. The falling dots reference the falling marigolds at the beginning of the film, linking the title into the opening sequence."

MUSIC BY **mychael danna**

EDITOR allyson c. johnson

EXECUTIVE PRODUCERS jonathan sehring
caroline kaplan

AND roshan seth
soni razdan

DIRECTOR OF PHOTOGRAPHY declan quinn

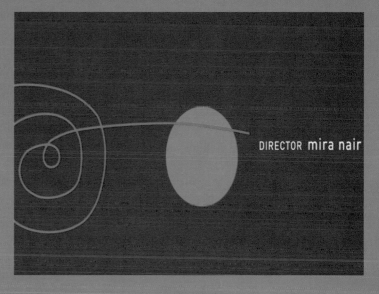

DIRECTOR **mira nair**

Production Process

The primary challenge of this production was keeping people intrigued for two minutes using only the most rudimentary geometric shapes—dots and lines. A number of different approaches were attempted, including producing the bindi in 3-D. Adding the third dimension allowed the team to rotate perspective, but in the end, they found the most entertaining option was to keep the animation on a flat 2-D plane.

Crediting an espresso machine as one of their primary production tools, the team at Trollbäck spent nearly five weeks completing this spot. The sequence was created using a paper and pencil and After Effects, in addition to the caffeine.

Sketches were scanned and animations were created in After Effects to mimic the shape and motion of the lines. After the team had completed a preliminary version of the animation, Nair returned to India and recorded a marching street band as the music for the sequence. The titles were then reworked to match the timing of the final soundtrack

Credits

Art Director **Jasmin Jordi**
Creative Director **Jakob Trollbäck**
Creative Director **Antoine Tingueley**
Director **Mira Nair**
Illustrator **Laura Ljungkvist**
Producer **Jesse Wann**

Tools

Adobe After Effects
Pencil and paper

Production Company

Trollbäck and Company
New York, NY, United States

Palm Pictures
Scratch
Documentary Film

elements

Project Overview

Scratch is a feature-length documentary film that explores the world of the hip-hop DJ. With interviews, dynamic live performances, and archival footage, the movie reveals how DJs invented hip-hop in the late '70s and recently reemerged as "turn-tablists," or musicians who manipulate vinyl with their hands by scratching, "beat-juggling," and blending recordings together to create entirely new compositions.

Scratch features such "old-school" pioneers as Afrika Bambaataa and Grand Wizard Theodore (who invented the concept of scratching), as well as a group of world-class DJs, such as Qbert, Mix Master Mike (Beastie Boys), DJ Shadow, DJ Premier (Gang Starr), Cut Chemist and Numark (Jurassic 5), DJ Krush, and others.

The independently produced film premiered at the Sundance Film Festival 2001, was nominated for a 2002 Independent Spirit Award by the IFP, and was distributed throughout the United States by Palm Pictures in the spring of 2002 and internationally by Intermedia.

What makes this film interesting from a motion graphics perspective is how director Doug Pray used a combination of analog and digital technology in the editing process to mimic the scratching style of the performers. By adopting this technique, Pray enhanced the effectiveness of the editorial content by using a visual style that is similar to the featured subject matter.

Creative Process

Producers Brad Blondheim and Ernest Meza developed the concept of *Scratch* and solicited financing from independent investors (through their production company Firewalk Films). Pray, Blondheim, and Meza had complete creative control of the film. Once it was complete, the film was picked up for distribution.

"I'm a musician, and music has always been central to my life since birth," said Pray. "But instead of pursuing music as a career, I've made it central to my filmmaking, in subject and emphasis. Furthermore, in documentary films—more than dramatic—I believe that sound is more important to the audience than imagery. A mentor once taught me that when editing documentaries, to edit audio first, then worry about the imagery later. This rule defines my work from the filming and production phase—when emphasizing sound recording—to the cutting and into the sound mix, when I feel like the movie becomes a movie for the first time. *Scratch* was all about sound and about musicians who search for and manipulate sound to a high degree."

Pray had previously worked with a number of musicians on musical documentaries and music videos. His last feature, *Hype!*, was about the rise and fall of the Seattle grunge music scene of the late '80s and early '90s. *Scratch*, although a stylistic departure, was a continuation of that exploration.

"I approach theatrical documentaries with the goal of making them as entertaining as possible. I feel an obligation to let artists speak fully for themselves—no host or narrator—to make their musical performances as loud and clear as possible, no matter how raw the music is, and to make the film feel like the music sounds—hence, the hip-hop DJ-style chopping of the images and DJ-style segues between scenes," explained Pray. "This latter editorial choice was my favorite part about working on *Scratch*. Hip-hop DJs essentially create new music by clipping, cutting, looping, playing backward, and playing different recordings together to make new creations. I've never edited a piece that allowed me more freedom to cut and juxtapose my own source material in so many unexpected ways. I was so inspired by the DJs themselves that I had great fun 'scratching' the film, playing it backward, splicing in random insert shots, and working all of my transitions in a way that felt more musical than visual. In the end, I feel that documentary editing is the closest thing to hip-hop DJing there is. DJs use source vinyl; we use uncut, raw footage. DJs find the 'break'—the funkiest, best part of a song—and expand and exaggerate it to create an evening of danceable entertainment. We spend hours finding the best quotes and sound bites from a long interview and cut them back-to-back to force a dynamic narrative. The selection process—records versus footage—the idea of finding a flow or a dramatic structure, the goal of affecting people's emotions and moods, all of these are similar."

Production Process

The film was shot entirely in 16 mm film with an Arriflex SRII camera. The crew was minimal: director of photography and operator Rob Bennett and second unit Brian Knappenberger, gaffer and grip Keith Barefoot, and a sound person—Kelly Vandever, Jason Blackburn, Eric Meza, or Doug Pray. Two cameras were used for some of the live performances. Occasionally, Pray used his 1950s wind-up Bolex camera (16 mm) for extra pick-up shots, including the blue close-up shots of vinyl and needles that were used as backgrounds for the chapter headings. These were filmed with a set of extension tubes and a turntable on Pray's dining room table.

The shooting was spread over the course of one calendar year, with only about five full weeks of true production: two weeks in New York City, two weeks in San Francisco, and a number of days in Los Angeles. Editing began halfway through the shooting process. To Pray, editing is 90 percent of the work that goes into a documentary, because he feels that "you're essentially writing it as you go."

Believing that great sound is essential for any music documentary, most performances were recorded onto DA88s (digital 8 or 16 tracks) with direct feeds from the mixers on the turntables themselves or off the house soundboard. In all cases, room sound was recorded onto digital audio tape (DAT) separately (ambience, crowd, music from the speakers) to be used sparingly during the mix later. That recorder also supplied visible time code to the slate for syncing to the camera dailies. All interviews were recorded onto DAT with time code.

All 45 hours of original 16 mm footage were transferred in a telecine bay (film to video) to Betacam SP masters and ¾" (2 cm) off-line masters (with time code, Kodak key code, audio time code, and camera roll information in each corner of the frame). These were digitized at low resolution into an Avid editing system. Editing took approximately seven months, and the final cut was translated into an EDL (time code "edit-decision" list) and redigitized onto a 1:1 Avid Symphony (full resolution online).

The online master was color-corrected (in a tape-to-tape telecine bay) by Kelly Reese at Matchframe, and then all of the identifying subtitles (over 100) and main titles were superimposed in a final online video pass. The finished DigiBeta master was transferred digitally by E-Film in Hollywood to 35 mm film and printed by CFI.

That final process, in which the 525 video lines are digitally enhanced to several thousand "lines" of resolution and then "film-out" to 35 mm photographic negative, is very expensive. It is also being done more and more by people who need a film to be theatrically projectable, but can't afford traditional cinema technologies. In the case of *Scratch*, because they began with 16 mm, 24-fps film, and ended up back in 24-fps film, it is almost impossible to tell that video was an intermediate step. (The grain structure and frame rate are there again.)

Audio was translated from the Avid or reloaded from the original DATs into a Pro-Tools audio editing system. It was then "cleaned" and reconfigured for mixing by David Bartlett. The final print master was recorded to a Dolby Digital 5:1 format. "5:1" is shorthand for a six-channel theatrical speaker configuration where you have left/right/center (your main sound) and left surround/right surround (for the rear of the theater). The "1" is the subwoofer, or boom channel, that adds those deep rumbling sounds that make your stomach vibrate. An optical sound element was struck (NT Audio), and the lab (CFI) married the optical to the 35 mm picture print. Minutes later, it premiered at the Sundance Film Festival.

Credits

Director/Editor **Doug Pray**
Producers **Brad Blondheim and Ernest Meza**
Executive Producers **Allen and Albert Hughes**
Director of Photography **Robert Bennett**

Production Company

Firewalk Films
Los Angeles, California, United States

Filmlance
En Häxa I Familjen (Witch in the Family) Title Sequence

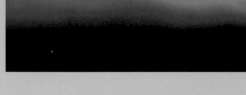

Project Overview

Simple and effective, Strobe's title sequence for *Witch in the Family* sets an evocative and foreshadowing atmosphere for this Swedish children's horror film.

Creative Process

Witch in the Family is a film about a young girl who is raised by her grandmother. As her grandmother tells her a story, the girl begins to believe that her grandmother is actually a witch and intends to boil her in a pot. Director Jonas Hallberg read the script and designed the sequence to set the mood for the film.

"The sequence is about putting the children in the appropriate atmospheric feeling in the theater," said Hallberg. "This is a bit of a horror film, but it was made specifically for children. Our idea was to connect the opening to the story. It is done from a child's perspective, where we focus on the most frightening elements of the girl's imagination—the fire and the pot—and try to build a sense of impending doom."

Production Process

The sequence was shot on 35 mm film in a studio using colored lights and dry ice. Hallberg described the shoot as "pretty simple." The challenge for this project came in postproduction.

Simple typography tests were created in After Effects. These tests were used to establish the basic parameters for the animation, which was created in Inferno. The problem came during the rendering phase of production. Because the typography animation made use of numerous layers with multiple effects, the render times for the piece were inordinately long. In the end, it was simply a matter of patience to create the moody, foreshadowing effect they were after.

Credits

Director **Lars Sköllerhom**
Designer **Jonas Hallberg**
Director of Photography **Olof Johnsson**
Producer **Josh Thorne**
Post-Production **The Chimney Pot, Stockholm**

Tools

Adobe After Effects
Discreet Flame
Discreet Inferno

Production Company

Strobe
Stockholm, Sweden

Beacon Pictures
Spy Game
Title Sequence

Project Overview

Balancing plot points with intricate typography, the title sequence of *Spy Game* immerses the viewer into the tension of the film from the first frame.

In this spy thriller, Robert Redford is a spymaster attempting to save a young agent (Brad Pitt) from execution in China. The structure of the film is nonlinear storytelling at its finest, shifting back and forth through different locations and time frames to give an overall scope and emotional context to the main story.

The title sequence was a collaborative effort between designer Garson Yu and director Tony Scott. The two have a long-standing relationship, which began in 1996, when Yu designed the title sequences for the Robert De Niro film *The Fan*. Since then, Yu has been Scott's designer of choice, crafting the openings for *Enemy of the State* and *Spy Game*.

Creative Process

The two men worked closely together when designing this sequence. "For this project, Tony had cut the beginning background sequence the way that he wanted this movie to open," explained Yu. "He wanted the beginning to tell the audience what the mission is—to go to China to rescue Brad Pitt. The sequence sets the tone for the story and explains why Brad Pitt is in China. After Tony did the rough cut, he brought me in and showed it to me. What I did was develop an on-screen type of graphic treatment to enhance his editorial style."

The treatment he developed was specifically geared toward magnifying the dramatic tone by starting slowly and intertwining with the edits. As the cuts increase in intensity, the typography responds with additional speed and complexity, ultimately culminating in building the tension and anxiety of the scene.

Production Process

After viewing Scott's first pass on editing, Yu imported the footage into Inferno and applied type treatments. As production progressed, Yu would ask for specific sections to either have additional frames or be reduced in size. Scott would rework the background plates to accommodate the changes and would ask for modifications to the typography. Multiple edits were sent between the designer and the director.

Yu said, "We were back and forth on that. The first time that we met, the editing wasn't completely done. We presented some ideas, and then he revised it. Then we revised our animations, and then we went back and forth on it, because there were lots of tight, very sensitive timing issues in his cut that didn't allow us to create a legible animated title. So we went back and forth, changing the timing or the background, extending the lengths, and shortening some other parts. It was a process—going back and forth. He worked on the background, sent it to me, and then I would work on the timing on the title."

Once they agreed on the final edits and typography, the final cut of the background plate was converted and color-corrected in telecine. It was then brought into Avid and composited with the typography from Inferno. After compositing, the completed sequence was output back onto film for inclusion in the final print.

Credits

Director **Tony Scott**
Designer/Creative Director **Garson Yu**
Designers/Animators **Benjamin Cuenod and Etsuko Uji**
Typographer **Martin Surya**
Inferno Artist **Todd Mesher**

Tools

Avid
Discreet Inferno

Production Company

Yu + Co
Hollywood, CA, United States

Portuguese Pavilion
Expo '98
A Viagem
Short Film

Project Overview

The Trip (*viagem* is Portuguese for "trip") was commissioned for the Portuguese Pavilion at the 1998 World Exhibition in Lisbon. Initially, it was supposed to be a restricted international contest. In the end, 10 filmmakers of diverse nationalities—Belgian, Canadian, French, and Portuguese—were invited to submit notes of intention and budgets for the project.

Following these submissions, the exhibition directors asked five candidates to prepare a minute of film. This phase turned out to be the determining factor. Writer and director Christian Boustani and his team were the only ones to propose a composited approach, mixing real characters and computer graphics with a design based on the intricate details of the infamous Namban screens.

This innovative and dynamic approach won Boustani the contract. The film has taken on a life outside the confines of the Pavilion and has won numerous international awards.

Creative Process

The year is 1543. A Portuguese vessel is bound for Japan for the first time. The sailors will be the first Europeans ever to set foot on the island and will shepherd in the next age of commercial and cultural exchange.

Japanese artists painted the Namban folding screens to document the arrival of these Portuguese explorers. The meeting of these two cultures is recorded in complex images on panels gilded in fine gold. These images show the wonder, amusement, and distrust of these strange visitors with their peculiar habits and long noses. These travelers, with their unfamiliar objects—such as rifles—forever changed the course of Japanese history.

"I conceived the film as a diary of that first voyage," said Boustani. "A crossing during which the navigators learned to face their own demons, to pass certain tests, and to reach an understanding of the other culture. But with *A Viagem*, I also wanted to tell the story of two opposing worlds: a feudal Japan isolated by its secular traditions and a Portugal in full renaissance, well-versed in the domains of science, technology, and religion. Thus, the film navigates between historical reality, imagination, and legend. It explores the mutual influences, mixing lots of stylized scenes and descriptions, juxtaposing the naive universe of the Japanese folding screens and the epic literature of 16th-century Portugal, and confronting the landscape and architectural vision of the East presented in flat tints with the perspective added by the West."

The film's visual approach is directly inspired by the Japanese folding screens. The people, especially the Portuguese, are portrayed as symbols, caricatures equipped with prominent noses and ridiculous trousers, distorted by a painter both amused and disdainful of their foreign guests.

The Lisbon street scene shown as storyboard, blue-screen shoot, and final composited image.

Japanese artist painting the Namban screens on which *A Viagem* is based.

Production Process

A 13-month production cycle was required to make *A Viagem*. The production began with two months of drafting the scenario and designing the storyboards. During this time, the team employed historians to validate each detail: the veracity of the facts, the choice of the characters, the costumes, the accessories, and the decorations.

Once the directors approved the storyboards, preparation of the shoot took three weeks. The primary footage was shot in Belgium on 35 mm. The majority of the sequences were shot against blue screen in 12 days. Shooting days were separated into sections. One day was allocated for shooting animals—a horse (costumed as a unicorn), peacocks, dogs, Chinese pigs, and an Asian cock. One day was set for motion-controlled shooting of the boat models. Another day was devoted for Alain Escalle, the CG artist, to create the animation elements. Finally, two extra days were needed to shoot the boat models and Japanese actors.

"The choices concerning the casting were easy to make, in that I was looking for interesting faces with pronounced features," said Boustani. "It was not so important that I choose professional actors, because I wanted to obtain a result somewhere between pantomime and choreography. As for the costumes, designer Lenja van der Laan and I were inspired to remain faithful to the Japanese folding screens. We wanted to retain that caricature style of the puffy pantaloons. Lenja had the brilliant idea to fill them with tulle. Some costumes were rented, but Lenja designed others, such as those worn by the slaves."

The rhythm and structure of the film were determined during a 15-day stretch of digital editing on an Avid. The heaviest part of the work was in postproduction and was conducted over a nine-month period. Escalle lead the team in developing the modeling, doing the 2-D and 3-D animation, preparing the various elements of set decoration, and integrating the people into the sets. Four powerful computers running Flame and Inferno ran 24 hours a day, seven days week to composite the live footage with the CG backgrounds, boat models, 3-D sea serpent, and elements of traditional animation required to composite these 10 minutes of film.

A shortened version—around four minutes—was shown in high-resolution video at the Portuguese Pavilion. Beyond the exposition, the film received additional exposure in its full-length, 35 mm version, which ran with honors at a number of international festivals and was broadcast on television in both France (Canal +) and Portugal (RTP).

The Namblan screens were crafted by 16th century Japanese artisans to commemorate the arrival of the Portuguese in Japan. Four centuries later these screens provided the inspiration for "A Viagem".
Top: Scala/Art Resource, NY

Credits

Writer/Director **Christian Boustani**
CG Artist **Alain Escalle**
Music **Manuel Faria**
Sound Effects **Vitor Mingates and Manuel Faria**
Costume Designer **Lenja van der Laan**
Prosthetic Makeup Effects **Lif Reymer**
Light and Camera **Emmanuel Soyer**
Editor **Franck Magnant**
Assistant Director **Emmanuelle Legrand**
CG **Trix (Belgium)**
Production **D&D Audiovisuais (Portugal)**

Tools

Adobe Photoshop
Alias|Wavefront Maya
Avid
Composer et Matador
Discreet Flame
Discreet Inferno

Production Company

D&D Audiovisuais S.A.
Lisbon, Portugal

HBO Films
Hysterical Blindness
Title Sequence

GENA ROWLANDS

HBO FILMS PRESENTS

A KARUNA DREAM /
BLUM ISRAEL PRODUCTION

Project Overview

The film *Hysterical Blindness* is based on Laura Cahill's adaptation of the stage play of the same name. It is a story about the search for meaning and love in New Jersey in the '80s. At the beginning of the film, Uma Thurman discusses sitting at her computer and losing her sight. She had been rushed to the hospital and was diagnosed with "hysterical blindness."

In the film, she regains her sight, but the phrase serves as a metaphor for the general state of the characters in the film. Design firm Trollbäck and Company created a powerful and visually stimulating title sequence based on subtle uses of light and form in combination with the experience of an eye exam.

Creative Process

The company has a long-standing relationship with the film's director, Mira Nair, and was given a high degree of creative freedom. Designer and director Antoine Tinguely explained, "This project was very exciting for us. We have a great relationship with the director, Mira Nair. She believes in our skills and lets us do what we do best."

Although the film does not show an actual eye exam, the team felt that this would be a powerful image with which to set the tone for the film. A one-day film shoot, specifically for the title sequence, was scheduled with one of the stars of the film, Uma Thurman.

After establishing the basic parameters for the shoot, the team got to work creating the storyboard. They used the eye exam as a starting block and composed the final sequence as a combination of the exam, beams of light with typography, and layout designs inspired by Swiss designer Josef Muller-Brockman.

HYSTE RICAL BLIND NESS

JULIETTE LEWIS

EXECUTIVE PRODUCERS
UMA THURMAN, JASON BLUM, AMY ISRAEL

SCREENPLAY BY
LAURA CAHILL

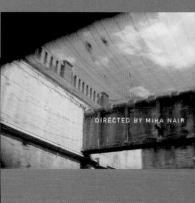

DIRECTED BY MIRA NAIR

Production Process

After the initial footage was shot on 35 mm, the dailies were imported into After Effects. The primary challenge facing the designers was that with only a day's worth of footage, they had to generate additional material with light effects to fill out the piece. A rough cut was submitted for approval. Once approved, the footage was scanned and composited in After Effects. Final output was transferred back to film. The final sequence is a stunning combination of light and mundane images with the inherently disconcerting experience of an eye exam.

Credits

Designers/Directors **Laurent Fauchere, Jakob Trollbäck, Antoine Tinguely, Greg Hann, and Jasmin Jordi**
Editor **Nicole Amatto**

Tools

Adobe After Effects
Avid

Production Company

Trollbäck and Company
New York, NY, United States

Finalcut Entertainment
Dream
Title Sequence

Project Overview

Dream is the first title sequence created for an international film by the Stockholm-based production company Strobe. Finalcut Entertainment commissioned Strobe after viewing their demo reel of past work for the Swedish film industry.

The sequence's objective was to convey a visual metaphor for the content of the film, where a working-class girl dreams of living the glamorous life of a fashion model while dealing with the reality of an unexpected pregnancy.

Creative Process

Finalcut wanted the title sequence to be engaging but remain true to the nature of the film by not appearing too slick or too "Hollywood." "We wanted to give a foreshadowing of the film in this sequence," explained director Klas Jonsson. "Initially, we had talked about using sperm, but then moved to other ideas that conveyed this concept without being so literal. You have a lot of dreams, but only one will land somewhere where it is fertile and can grow. That's how we came up with the dandelion idea. It was not until much later on that we found that the word *dandelion* means 'dream flower' in a number of languages."

Production Process

The initial presentation of the concept was done as still frames created in Photoshop using a very simple 3-D model of the dandelion created by Jonsson. Strobe intended to shoot the sequence in a studio, but budgetary constraints proved prohibitive for a real-world production.

Finalcut had become attached to the dandelion concept and asked Strobe to explore alternative production methods that would work within the existing budget. To accomplish this goal, Strobe went to an all-digital production and brought in 3-D animator Robert Karlsson.

While Karlsson refined and animated the model in Maya, the rest of the Strobe team worked on developing the background for the sequence. The first attempts involved animating the seedpods against a photorealistic background with a very shallow depth of field. These images were discarded after it was determined that they didn't match the feel of the film.

The final solution involved hiring photographer Vince Reichart to shoot out-of-focus abstract images. These images were then texture-mapped onto a sphere in Maya. The final rendered pieces were assembled using After Effects.

Credits

Director/Designer **Klas Jonsson**
3-D Animator **Robert Karlsson**
Producer **Josh Thorne**
Texture Photography **Vince Reichart**
Postproduction **The Chimney Pot, Stockholm**

Tools

Adobe After Effects
Adobe Photoshop
Alias|wavefront Maya
Discreet Inferno

Production Company

Strobe
Stockholm, Sweden

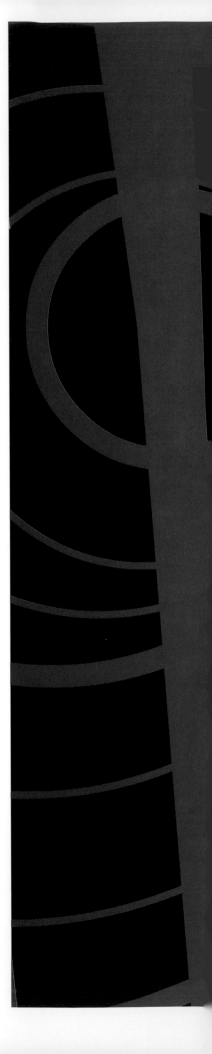

Chapter 3
New Media

By definition, motion graphics are never static. Neither is technology. The two complement each other in a symbiotic dance. Technology provides the tools to build and deliver compelling content, while high-impact graphics entice consumers to purchase the latest technology with which to view them. The dance is never-ending, feeding off itself and pushing the demand for advanced graphics to new levels.

Only a few short decades ago, the Internet, CD-ROMs, DVDs, interactive kiosks, PDAs, and specialized gaming platforms were the province of science-fiction writers. They are now simply accepted elements of the modern landscape, inhabiting our homes and shopping malls.

With the advent of these new delivery platforms, motion graphics artists are finding new challenges and opportunities. Interactivity has been added to the mix, allowing for the user to make choices that affect the content and context of what is shown on the screen. Flash technology has both created a vast audience through the Internet and expanded the range for digital expression. Existing skill sets can be transported to new marketplaces, expanding the creative and financial potential for motion graphics professionals.

It is impossible to anticipate what is on the horizon for emerging technologies—the scope of their impact and depth of their cultural significance is simply too great. We can, however, be certain of one thing: Whatever the technology may be, from biological implants to flexible liquid plasma screens, motion graphics will be there.

The following projects are examples of how motion graphics artists are using today's technology for a wide array of communications. From the innovative Internet music videos by Pixelwurld to the outrageous viral marketing of the Swedish milk brand Fjällfil and the eminently practical process animations of Pivia, the new media-based motion graphics presented here are indicative of the range of creative expression and commercial opportunities available to the modern motion graphics artist.

139

Fjällfil
Milko Music Machine

Project Overview

Little did local Swedish milk brand Fjällfil know that when they contacted the FarFar agency to build their website, they would become one of the most successful viral marketing campaigns ever to appear on the Internet.

With a spartan budget, a song in their heart, and a willingness to learn stop-motion animation, FarFar created a site that has received eight international awards, been selected as Macromedia's Shocked Site of the day, and has increased the sales of Fjällfil milk products by 23 percent.

To date, the Milko Music Machine site has attracted over two million visitors. Even after 16 months, the site still receives between 3,000 and 5,000 unique visitors a day.

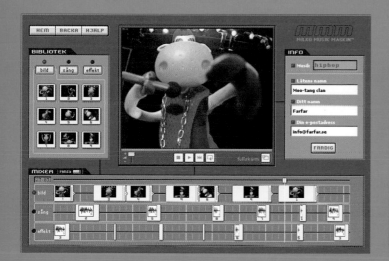

Creative Process

The Milko Music Machine initially started out as a much larger project pitched to Fjällfil. The original concept was to take the Fjällfil "Mountain Cow" on an adventure. According to the story, the cow lives in Stockholm, works as an IT professional, and wants to return to the country to visit her friends. FarFar proposed a "game" situation where the cow had to accomplish a number of tasks to afford the trip. Fjällfil found the initial project too ambitious, but liked the "song and dance" aspect of the proposal.

FarFar reworked the pitch to focus on the musical element. The result is the Milko Music Machine, a real-time online music-video mixer. The Milko Music Machine is an intuitive environment where the user can select from a number of different video clips and audio effects and drag them onto the time line to create a 30-second video.

"We designed the piece as a branding experience," said Nicke Bergstrom, art director for the project. "We figured if we keep people playing for five minutes, they are watching a five-minute commercial, but they are making the commercial themselves, which is more interesting than just watching."

The Milko Music Machine is subtle about the branding. In fact, the only true branding is the cow drinking Fjällfil's milk prior to going on stage. Beyond that, the company's products are decidedly downplayed.

Promotion for this site also proved to be a challenge because there was no budget for either online or traditional media advertising. To overcome this obstacle, FarFar decided to incorporate a viral marketing strategy into their creation. Once users have finished creating a video, they can e-mail it to their friends. The initial promotion campaign for the site started with the staff of FarFar e-mailing videos they had made with the Milko Music Machine to their friends. From there, it blossomed, and within a few weeks, the site had over 100,000 hits, which is not bad for a country of only eight million people.

Fjällfil was so pleased with the results that they commissioned another version of the site where users can lead the Mountain Cow through a workout video.

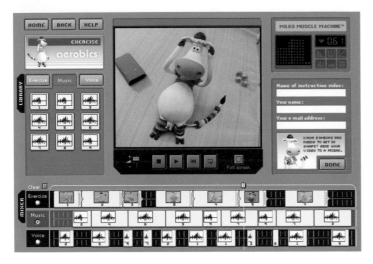
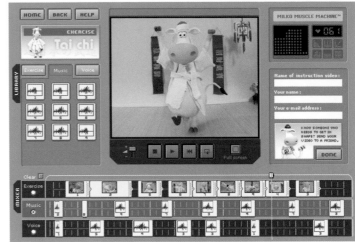

Production Process

Stop-Motion Animation

"We went with stop-motion because everything on the web at that time looked like old computer games. We always try to do something that stands out graphically," related Bergstrom. "So, we said, 'Let's do stop-motion.' Unfortunately, no one at the company had ever done anything like it before. But we figured, it's only 12 frames per second, so... let's bend a cow and try it out."

The first step was to have a Norwegian company produce a 5-inch (13 cm) bendable plastic model of the cow. From there, it was all trial and error. Bergstrom says, "The first tests did not work very well and made us think, 'Why did we ever try this?' But the second test worked perfectly, and made us think, 'We can do this!'"

Due to the limited budget, all sets and costumes were made in-house. The set was built in their studio, and the animation was filmed on a digital video camera with the frame capture done in Premiere.

The most complicated element of the animation was how to make the cow's motion synchronize with the beat. This was imperative, because the cow is always in motion. They accomplished this by matching the beats per minute (BPM) of the songs with the frame rate. The frame rate used on the project was 12 frames per second, so the BPM for the music was either 96, 120, or 144.

The coordination between the visuals and the music was facilitated by the fact that all the production, including the sound, was done in-house by FarFar's staff. Anders Gustavsson, producer of the project and a veteran musician, scored the music to meet the requirements of the stop-frame animation.

Programming

The Milko Music Machine programming was developed in Director with playback through the Shockwave browser plug-in.

For the purpose of sharing the videos, when a user creates a "video," it is assigned a unique ID and stored as a text sequence in an online database. When the "video" is e-mailed to another individual, he or she is sent a web link, which references the unique ID and plays back the video created by the original user.

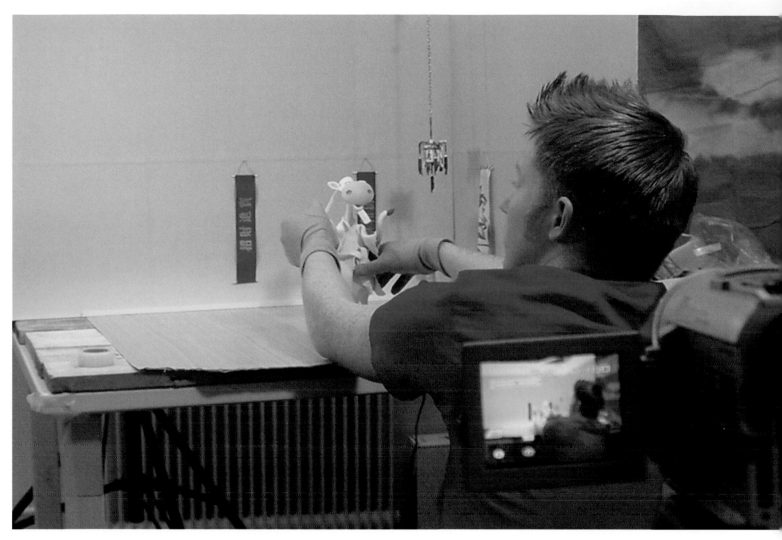

Per Hansson, pixel pusher and stop-motion artist, in action.

Credits

Account Manager **Matias Palm-Jensen**
Art Director **Nicke Bergstrom**
Production Manager **Per Nasholm**
Producer **Anders Gustavsson**
Pixel Pusher **Per Hansson**
Developer **Pontus Kindblad**

Tools

Adobe After Effects
Adobe Illustrator
Adobe ImageReady
Adobe Photoshop
Adobe Premiere
Macromedia Director
Macromedia Flash
Protools Free

Production Company

FarFar
Stockholm, Sweden

Supreme Beings of Leisure
"Never the Same"
Internet/Broadcast
Flash Video

Project Overview

Originally, the Supreme Beings of Leisure (SBL) were simply looking for an e-card to promote their new single. They turned to their web developer, Pixelwurld, who had previously produced similar projects for Madonna, Tricky, Apex Twin, and Orbital.

Fortunately for SBL, Pixelwurld had more up their sleeve than a simple card. They were interested in pushing the limitations of Flash technology as both an art form and as a promotional vehicle. After seeing the creative possibilities that Pixelwurld presented for a multipurpose production encompassing both broadcast and Internet versions, SBL opted in.

Although the creative possibilities were what initially tempted SBL, what made this project viable from an economic standpoint was the extreme flexibility of the Flash development platform. The same production can be output into a variety of playback options. In this case, the same animation was output as both broadcast-quality video and as a web version optimized for playback through the Flash browser plugin.

This type of multipurpose production is the wave of the future. Production dollars are stretched by leveraging the same production into multiple marketplaces. The marketing implications for this type of production are astounding. No less astounding is the creative vision and technical achievements that went into the production of "Never the Same."

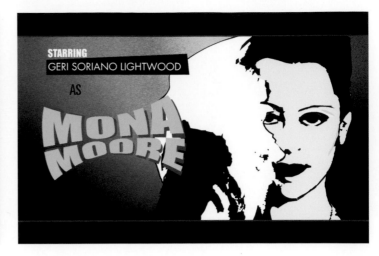

Creative Process

"Never the Same" was a true collaboration between the band, their label, and Pixelwurld. The concept of a Flash-enabled Internet video was very appealing to both the band and their label, because their marketing objective was to promote SBL as the Internet band. They wanted to be the first band to break it big through the Internet. They quickly realized the benefits of creating an integrated package where the music video seen on TV was identical to the experience available online.

Director Andres Moreta worked very closely with lead singer and producer, Geri Soriano-Lightwood, on the creative development of the project. Taking their inspiration from posters designed by Saul Bass for Alfred Hitchcock's classic films, they crafted a clever mix of film noir clichés and modern intrigue. One of the reasons they selected Saul Bass as an inspiration was the nature of his graphic style. His style was very linear and would translate well into the vector-based development environment of Flash. By selecting this approach, they could play to the strengths of Flash and ultimately would be able to create smaller and faster-playing animations for the web.

One of the unique features of the online version is the integration of interactivity within the story line and the visuals. For viewers accessing the video with slower connections, a "spy game" was placed at the start of the video to keep their attention. Moreta explained, "We hated the loading screens on most Internet videos, so we asked ourselves, 'What can we do to keep it interesting?' Then Miles, our main tech guy, said, 'I have a simple game that we can start off with.' So we created this game so that there is something to do while you're waiting for the video."

This game provides viewers with more than a time killer. At the end of the video, viewers can print out SBL posters based on the video. There are four different posters—which poster is printed is determined by the viewer's actions in the game. This clever ploy has proven successful in terms of attracting repeat viewings. Users need to capture different items in the game and view the video again to print different posters. Curses! You have uncovered my evil plans!

Production Process

Although this was a Flash production, Pixelwurld approached it as a music video. The band was shot on a green screen with full makeup and costuming.

"The lighting was important, because some of the details can get pretty ugly once you make them high contrast," explained Moreta. "We took time with the lighting, making sure that nobody had weird shadows. This was especially important for the lead singer. On the guys, shadows kind of give them some character, but on a girl, those hard edges and hard shadows don't make them as attractive as they could be. In filming, the lighting was our main priority. "

After shooting the footage, Moreta edited a rough cut in Premiere. From that, he then created sample frames in Photoshop to show the After Effects artist what effect he was looking for. The After Effects artist duplicated the effect and exported the video scene-by-scene into different folders as a series of numbered image files.

Once they had the series image files, they created Quick Keys shortcuts for batch processing. To translate them from bitmap into vectors, the images were individually processed by a combination of Streamline, Illustrator, and Freehand before being imported into Flash.

A considerable number of images are required to create a four-minute video at 12 frames per second. To remain organized, the team placed the vectorized images into an extensive cataloging system.

The mainframe rate of the piece is 12 frames per second, but the lip-syncing effect was created at eight frames per second to keep sync for slower connections. Compensation for the difference between the frame rates was accommodated by cleverly placed duplicate frames.

Moreta says, "Lip-synching was the thing that we really wanted. That was our main focus. We said to ourselves, 'Let's have the singer actually sing.' So I discovered that if you had enough frames in between and it's streaming, you could get something fairly accurate or pretty damn close to lip-synching."

In the end, the effect is stunning, taking the viewer into a world of intrigue, deceit, villainy, and dance beats. The final version has been broadcast on MTV2, on Much Music, and in clubs throughout Europe. It is currently waiting for you online at www.pixelwurld.com.

Credits

Producer **Geri Soriano-Lightwood**
Director **Andres Moreta**
Technical Director **Miles Lightwood**
Videographer **Marcos Soriano**
Art Direction **Andres Moreta**
Design/Flash Animators **Andres Moreta, Sabrina Soriano, and Rico Enomoto**
Design/Motion Graphics Artist **Sabrina Soriano**
Flash Action Scripting **Miles Lightwood**

Tools

Adobe After Effects
Adobe Illustrator
Adobe Photoshop
Adobe Premiere
Adobe Streamline
Macromedia Flash
Macromedia Freehand
Mini DV Camera
Quick Keys

Production Company

Pixelwurld
Los Angeles, CA, United States

Stills from "Never the Same" performed by Supreme Beings of Leisure
Courtesy of © 2001, Palm Pictures, LLC. All rights reserved.

hillmancurtis
"Simple Simon"
Flash Narrative Short

Project Overview

It is a sad fact that often we become too entangled in the marvels of our technology to acknowledge their true value as tools for communication. It is too easy to get caught up in the latest lens flare effect, 3-D filter, or animation technique. This is not a matter of blame; it is an economic reality. In our attention-deficit-driven society, consumers are attracted to designs that lean toward eye candy. In turn, clients push their designers for the latest, newest, flashiest presentations possible.

But what if we ignored all of that for a moment and tried to use the latest technology as a means for true communication, as a method for storytelling with sincere emotional resonance. Using a digital video camera and Flash, Ian Kovalik of hillmancurtis, inc., has created such a piece.

"Simple Simon" is a Flash narrative short, which can only be described as a labor of love. It is both a tribute to the narrative prowess of this grandfather and to the power of modern storytelling when stripped to its basic technological elements.

Creative Process

Kovalik was the number-two person signed to hillmancurtis, inc. He and Hillman Curtis met through a client and struck a bond, which has led to some of the most innovative and unique Flash communications on the web today.

Beyond the corporate work of their firm, the two had always been interested in film and storytelling and were searching to find a way to use Flash as a tool to communicate in a similar fashion to short film. They already had definitive ideas on how to approach the project from a technical perspective. The only thing missing was the appropriate story to tell.

In the end, the inspiration for this piece came from Kovalik's own grandfather. His grandfather, Simon, had always been a teller of tales and the keeper of the family history. His failing health, however, had confined him to a nursing home. The footage for "Simple Simon" was shot during the course of a family meal.

"It was really kind of a special evening, because at the time, my grandfather had been in a nursing home for about a year. He'd had a couple of strokes and really wasn't all that talkative for a while, so this dinner was a big deal for him," said Kovalik. "It was a chance for him after a year to come out, spend the evening with us at home, and just sort of get to be a little bit normal again."

Kovalik kept the tape for a few months before he and Curtis decided to create "Simple Simon." Their objective was to take something shot in digital video and translate it into a quick-loading Flash movie, while maintaining the original tone of the storytelling by using streaming voiceover and still images.

Production Process

Kovalik's brother and sister shot the raw footage on digital video over the course of a two-hour meal. The actual story of "Simple Simon" was told during a 20-minute stretch and included many digressions, including requests for potato salad.

The first stage of production involved bringing the footage into Premiere. Once Kovalik had done a rough edit, he took the audio track into Sound Forge. There he edited the audio track down to its final length of one minute and 10 seconds.

"Finally, I had this great story that I could start hanging images on. That was the next challenge—to find the visuals that would match up and push the story along. The main footage that you see was created by taking sections from the actual dinner and my grandfather telling the story. We used an old trick to give it that video feel. We took 10 sequential frames of him moving and pulled those out in Premiere frame-by-frame. Then we turned them into sequential bitmaps. After that, I imported that into a symbol in Flash, where I was able to reuse it in different dimensions and speeds. It is great technique that allows me to really fill up a piece visually without costing the piece a lot in terms of file size," relates Kovalik.

To fill out "Simple Simon" from a visual perspective, Kovalik went to the National Archive and found a number of royalty-free images originally shot by Thomas Edison. To maintain the nostalgic feel of the piece, he took additional images from the National Archive and supplemented them with some images from his grandfather's favorite comic book art of the 1930s.

Kovalik explained, "He was a big fan of Flash Gordon and a lot of the early 1930s comics. I just went for something like that and sort of filled out the action part of the story. That's really why I chose the images that I did, to sort of build in that sense of nostalgia and sort of color the time that he was growing up in."

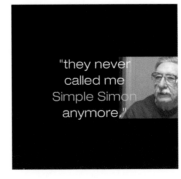

The images were imported into Flash. They were placed on the main time line along with the video clips and animated to the streaming audio track. One of the advantages of creating this type of visual montage was not being tied to a precise lip-synch. The visuals of his grandfather are treated more as color and reference to the piece than as actual narrative images. This technique is also beneficial for both a smaller file size and more leeway in the playback over the Internet—if a few frames are missed due to network congestion, the overall impact of the piece is in no way diminished.

"Simple Simon" is available for viewing at www.hillmancurtis.com in their web motion section.

Credits

Concept/Director/Editor/Animator **Ian Kovalik**
Additional Direction **Hillman Curtis**
Camera **Laryn and Adam Kovalik**
Talent **Simon Kovalik**
Project Management **Homera Chaudhry**

Tools

Adobe Photoshop
Adobe Premiere
Macromedia Flash
Sonic Foundry Sound Forge
Sony DCR-TRV9

Production Company

hillmancurtis, inc.
New York, NY, United States

"What...?"

"MERCY!"

"finally... I let 'em go."

"...and then
I named my son"

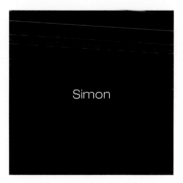

Simon

Simon Kovalik
Munhall, PA

iOasis
Interactive Hotel Services Interface

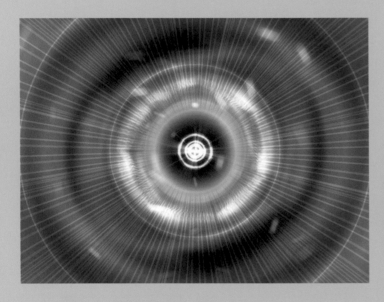

 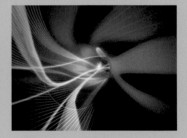

Project Overview

iOasis is a new technology developed for the hotel industry as an alternative to the current in-room video-on-demand systems, which are usually a series of static screens with minimal interactivity and branding.

iOasis is the next generation of in-room ordering services, which combines a full-motion identity package with dynamic interactivity. From a technical perspective, the iOasis technology revolves around a transparent browser that is displayed on the customer's television. This browser accesses a server that displays HTML pages with MPG 4 backgrounds and an overlay of Flash Generator content for room-specific information.

Belief joined the production team while the technology was still in development. The challenge for Belief was to develop a brand identity for a technology package that was still in flux. They had been given basic specifications for the format of the deliverables, but were unsure of the exact methodology for which the elements would be assembled.

Creative Process

"They said that it was going to be full-motion technology, and so we designed it given those parameters and didn't really worry about how they were going to be implemented," said executive creative director Mike Goedecke. "They assured us that whatever the final playback device would be—MPG 4, whatever—it would play full-motion, and we should design it as such."

Once it was established that full-motion was the order of the day, the Belief team examined the project from a both technical and a creative perspective. From the creative perspective, they determined that the project was similar to developing a network identity package. They approached the creative development by asking themselves, "How do we brand this as the iOasis network?"

They determined that the programming would start with an iOasis intro. Then the user would determine which "world" they wanted to enter—on-demand movies, room service, Internet access, or an environment in which they could check the status of their bill. Each world would be given a unique visual identity, similar to specific programming blocks on a network, but still remain in the overall brand package of iOasis.

Visually, the identity is very liquid. Goedecke explained, "For us, the name iOasis resonated with the notion of waves and water, almost like an oasis in the desert. Then we thought, 'What if it was an oasis of light?' So the design is very wavelike, using light instead of liquid as the water source."

From a development perspective, Belief found the project similar to DVD development. Belief had previously produced a number of DVDs and found the technical requirements of the project to be very similar.

"We looked at it as similar to a DVD, where you have these one-minute loops. You create transitional segues from section to section. Once a viewer is in a section, he or she sees a one-minute animation that would just stay on-screen and loop infinitely. Then once the viewer makes a decision, he or she will see the next segue that brings them to the next loop, which plays until the next selection is made," said Goedecke.

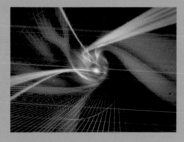
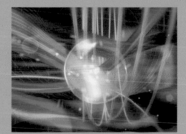

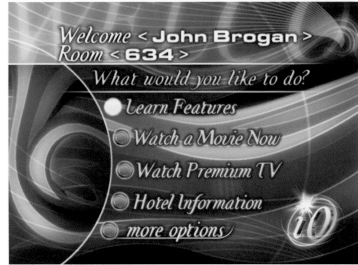

Welcome < John Brogan >
Room < 634 >

What would you like to do?

○ *Learn Features*

○ *Watch a Movie Now*

○ *Watch Premium TV*

○ *Hotel Information*

○ *more options*

iO

Search Confirmation

You are looking for movies

Staring: Sean Connery

Rating: ANY

Genre: ANY

○ *Add More*   ○ *Show Me*

iO

Purchase Confirmation

Title: **The Rock**
R/ Action
Sean Connery & Ed Harris

Price: **$8.95**

Security Code:

Buy this movie now?

Yes   *No*   *iO*

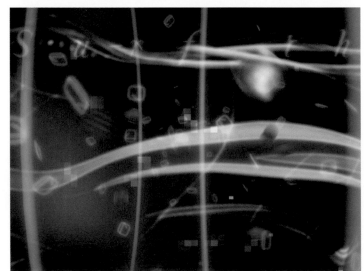

Production Process

Although the final production would involve numerous individual clips, the first phase of production was to create a six-minute linear animation of simulated user experience. This animation was used by iOasis as a fund-raising tool. It proved successful, and once iOasis had raised the next round of financing, the project moved into the final round of production.

Final production took nearly three months. The team needed to create multiple 3-D worlds, as well as the specific transitions to connect the worlds.

The production was built primarily in 3D Max. The piece has a unique look that was created by rendering multiple passes out of 3D Max. For example, on one scene they rendered out just one lighting effect, a strand tunnel effect, and then another strand tunnel effect. These elements would be composited together in After Effects with different plug-ins and different overlays to create the final look.

The final pieces were delivered to iOasis as MPG 4 files and were integrated into the final product by the iOasis team.

Credits

Executive Creative Director **Mike Goedecke**
Designer/Animator **Chris Pagani**

Tools

Adobe After Effects
Adobe Illustrator
Adobe Photoshop
Apple Macintosh G4
Integraph NT Box
Media 100
3D Max

Production Company

Belief
Santa Monica, CA, United States

All images courtesy of iOasis.

Red Sky
Red Sky on the Frontier
Promotional CD-ROM

Project Overview

Imagine a website with no limits—an ideal world with no bandwidth restrictions, no browser incompatibilities, and no fumbling for the perfect JavaScript, a world where the only thing that mattered was conveying the brand values of a company without the technology imposing artificial boundaries on human creativity.

This is the exact approach that Red Sky took when designing this promotional disk. The objective was simple—to feature the Red Sky portfolio while providing an engaging interactive experience. They started by asking themselves a deceptively simple question: What would our company website look like if it were free from the present limitations of the online world?

The resulting CD-ROM is a work that transcends the normal expectations of a promotional piece. The disk succeeds on a number of levels, accomplishing its marketing objectives while celebrating the unyielding creative vision of a team dedicated to pushing the boundaries of the interactive genre.

Creative Process

The Red Sky team, lead by director Joel Hladecheck, is unique in their development approach to interactive products. They have developed a series of basic tenets that define and shape their creative approach to any interactive production.

High Idle

Usually when you think of interactivity, you envision users interacting with the product, but what if the user doesn't interact? Does the presentation come to a screeching halt, remaining static until the user makes some form of decision, or does it continue to entertain until the user decides they would like to divert the course?

"We had a brain trust on this piece where we decided that choosing not to interact was a valid interactive choice. On the surface, this is may seem like a very simple idea, but it is profound when you start thinking about what the requirements are for the interactive developer," said Hladecheck. "It means that the interactive developer has to plan a program for when the user chooses not to interact. A high idle is a way of making an interactive piece appear to be alive. There's never a point where you feel like the piece is broken. As you expand the concept of a 'high idle' out into the broadband world, you find that this puts you directly in competition with television, films, and real entertainment-based products."

With that understanding in mind, Red Sky specifically designed this piece to provide a continuous and captivating story line, whether you as the user choose to be involved or not. The interactivity allows the user to switch the focus of the piece toward his or her area of interest, but the entertainment and branding value is never diminished by noninteraction.

Embrace the Limitations of the Technology

Probably the most frequent mistake that interactive designers make is overestimating the power and stability of the tools in their arsenal. Many productions work wonderfully in the lab but perform poorly in the real world. When designing *Red Sky on the Frontier*, the team at Red Sky looked very hard at what potential issues could affect their production outside of a controlled environment.

"Be realistic about what the technology can do and develop creative conceits that behave the way the technology forces you to go. It's a very Zen way to work, but it also means that the weakness of the technology will not show through the content," advised Hladecheck. "It's a little of the chicken and the egg. You have to accept the way the technology works, but create an idea that looked like it was intended to be that way in the first place."

They realized early on that—because of the layers of interactivity and amount of content on the disk—they were anticipating a fairly low frame rate. Once they understood the frame-rate issue, they decided to develop a creative construct to explain it. Their solution was to develop the underlying theme of the work—that this is an interactive movie being played on an imaginary interactive movie machine, circa 1930.

Once they established the basic parameters for explaining the limits of the technology, the rest of the piece fell into place. Cowboy movies were very popular in the '30s, and the cowboy theme dovetailed nicely with the Red Sky brand concept. Black and white was chosen as the color theme, because it is more forgiving during compositing and is smaller in file size. As the user interacts with the works, a "film splice" easily explains the jump cuts that happen to Gus Gilroy, the cowboy, as the mechanics of the fictional machine switches reels.

The team even built in a layer of hidden interactivity that few people ever see. Throughout the presentation, users can shoot items on screen—everything from the birds in the sky to Gus Gilroy himself. The characters have specific behaviors they exhibit when shot.

What the team realized was that if users become carried away and shoot too frequently, they can overload the system and cause the disk to crash. To prevent this from happening, they built in a safeguard. When the user's clicks become intense enough to cause a potential breakdown, the program automatically shifts to a different path. On this path, it appears as if the interactive projector is overloaded, the user sees the "film" on screen melt, and Cookie, the crotchety old interactive projectionist, cusses the user as he reloads the machine. This solution is a perfect example of taking the limitations of the technology and weaving it into the overall creative structure to create a truly engaging and integrated presentation.

Production Process

Casting

While casting for the cowboy on the spot, Hladecheck observed that getting good actors to act poorly was fairly difficult. Many professional actors auditioned for the part, but none achieved the slightly awkward and stunted acting style of the cowboys of the early days of film.

The solution was found when a friend of one of Red Sky's staff members auditioned for the part. He was not a professional actor; he was just a person who liked to play the part of a cowboy and even had the wardrobe. For the shoot, Hladecheck simply put up cue cards and instructed him to "just read them as best he could."

Shoot

The video was shot on a green screen in the Red Sky office space. Extensive planning was required to shoot all of the necessary elements for the production, and the team developed an elaborate flowchart to catalog all of the various elements in the script. This flowchart was necessary because each user interaction would create different dialog or actions to be displayed on screen.

Programming and Postproduction

Although the presentation appears to be QuickTime movies layered over a background, *Red Sky on the Frontier* is actually a frame-based animation piece authored in Director. The video was first imported into Premiere and exported as sequences of single frames. These frames were then imported into Photoshop and composited with the background images. Finally, they were imported into Director.

Early in the process Hladecheck decided that to make the virtual old-fashioned interactive movie machine work, the visuals needed to be similar to those seen in old films. He decided to use three primary effects to achieve this visual style—the flicker, the dust, and the occasional jitter. Of the three, the flicker was found to be the most important.

By placing the images as frame animations in Director, the team was able to programmatically switch between two different color palettes between the frames. Basically, every other frame has a slightly different color palette, which when viewed mimics the flicker of an old-style projection machine. The reason this method would not work with QuickTime is

that it is overlaid on top of the Director stage. For this effect to work, everything on the stage needed to be attached to the main color palette while it cycles through the different color palettes.

The additional effects of dust and the jitter were implemented programmatically, with the dust being randomly selected from six different dust animations. The jitter was basically a piece of code that randomly jiggles the entire frame either up and down or left and right.

Speaker Support Area

This area of the interface was designed for members of Red Sky to use for presentations at speaking engagements. It is hidden from casual users and can only be accessed by a special key code. In this area, a series of Power Point–like presentations were created with the same visual style as the rest of the work. Using this feature, members of the Red Sky staff can make integrated presentations using the same visual metaphor as *Red Sky on the Frontier*.

Credits

Director **Joel Hladecek**
Producers **Deirdre McGlashan and Amy Lee**
Technical Lead **Marc Blanchard**
Engineering Director **John Kim**
Senior Engineer **Jeff Miller**
Director of Production **Jessica Burdman**
Production Manager **Christina Neville**
Sound & Music **Jeff Essex**
Writer **Richard Ciccarone**
Speaker Support/Creative Director **Clay Jensen**
Work Screen/Creative Director **Genevieve Moore**
Designer **Rob Brown**

Tools

Adobe After Effects
Adobe Photoshop
Adobe Premiere
Macromedia Director

Production Company

Red Sky
San Francisco, CA, United States

Pivia
The Intelligent Solution
Animation

Project Overview

In the end it's all about communication. Motion graphics is about conveying information. Whether it be presenting a branding statement for a network, setting the proper tone and atmosphere for a cinematic experience, or explaining the features and benefits of a specific product, motion graphics is the most effective method to get the message across.

Pivia, a California-based startup company, had a marketing need to explain a very complex product quickly and efficiently to both a technical and a nontechnical audience. This explanation needed multiple playback options ranging from the Internet to a CD-ROM for use in sales presentations and tradeshows to an executable file, which could be sent as an e-mail attachment.

The decision was made to produce this animation in Flash due to its Internet animation capabilities and the ability to leverage a single production into multiple playback formats.

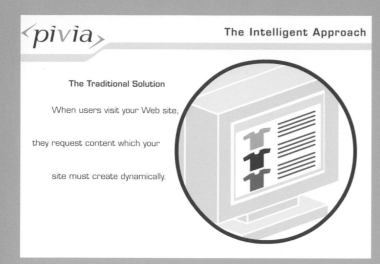

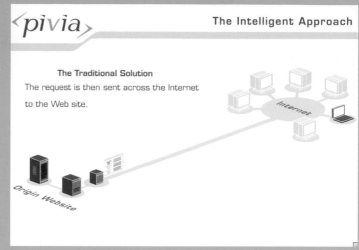

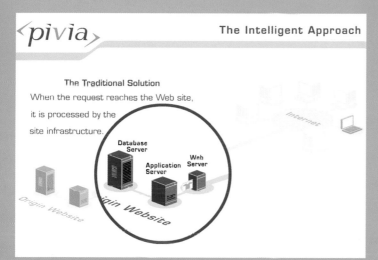

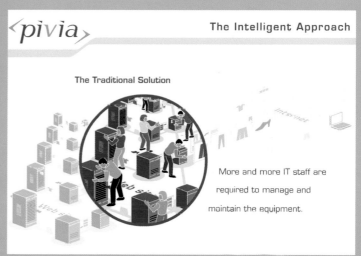

Creative Process

Pivia's Dynamic Application Caching software is a technical solution to a complex problem. Initially, Ray Marshall was given a diagram of this process, which he and animator David Greene used as a starting point.

"After viewing this diagram, we distilled the process down to its most rudimentary form," relates Marshall. "The Pivia software is based on stored bits of code called Pivlets. The process leant itself easily to a machine metaphor, where pages go through a metal-stamp machine that makes them into Pivlets, and a second machine stamps the Pivlets into web pages when the same content is requested again."

The final animation consists of two sections. The first illustrates the problems and limitations of the traditional solution. The second presents the same scenario but highlights the benefits of the Pivia "machine" as the solution.

Production Process

Illustration

"To make the design more interesting, I choose to create the illustrations at a 20-degree angle up from the horizontal plane," explains Marshall. "This made the animation much more dynamic and visually stimulating than either a side-on or top-down perspective."

Although he normally hand-sketches an image, scans it, and then traces over it in Illustrator, Marshall opted to create these images directly in the program. His first step was to create a grid of the 20-degree perspective and then draw the objects on top of it. These illustrations were used as storyboards, which were reviewed by the client. Once finalized, the illustrations were sent to the animator for use in the finished piece.

Animation

The complexity of this animation required it to be locked at a fixed size. This was necessary because, although Flash is capable of full-screen playback, the animation speed is affected by a number of factors, including processor speed, the number of items animated, and screen size. At times, this animation contains over 65 discreet elements in motion simultaneously, and the full-screen playback was unacceptable. A fixed size was set at 760 x 500 pixels.

Setting the animation at a fixed size had ramifications, which required modifications to the original storyboards. The original illustrations were done at a much larger size in Illustrator. When the animation was played back at the fixed size, some of the details were difficult to discern. To overcome this issue, pullouts were employed to focus attention on specific information as needed.

The final web animation clocks in at over seven minutes in length and is optimized for both low- and high-bandwidth connections. The animation was also converted into a CD-ROM—based presentation, an executable file suitable for delivery as an e-mail attachment, and a screensaver. The Intelligent Approach animation is available for veiwing at www.piva.com.

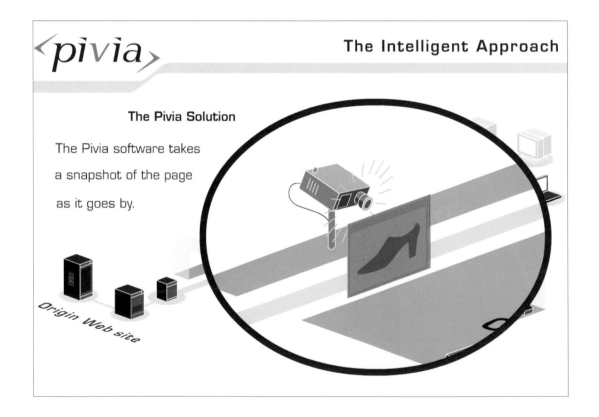

Credits

Creative Directors **Ray Marshall and David Greene**
Illustration **Ray Marshall**
Animation **David Greene**
Audio Production **Nick Peck**
Producer **Heidi Palmer**
Executive Producer for Pivia **Neil Selvin**

Tools

Adobe Illustrator
Macromedia Dreamweaver
Macromedia Fireworks
Macromedia Flash
ScreenTime for Flash

Production Company:

Ray Marshall Design
Emeryville, CA, USA

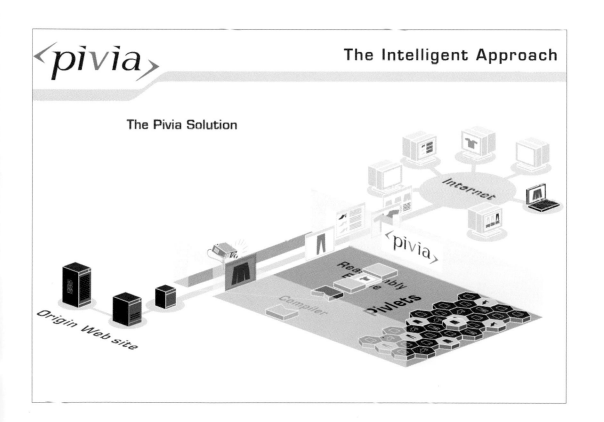

Palm Pictures
Skindive
"Tranquilizer"
(Internet/Broadcast
Flash Video)

Project Overview

Images of an innocent child overwhelmed by a barrage of contemporary images merge with a homeless man's undetermined quest on the gritty streets. All of the images intertwine with the viewers' own hopes, fears, and self-images. The effect of this piece can only be described as unsettling.

"Tranquilizer" is that rare piece of media that transcends the standard viewing experience by drawing the viewer into a strange yet familiar world where his or her own predilections and subconscious are as important, if not more so, than the story being unveiled.

A production designed for both broadcast and Internet playback, "Tranquilizer" takes the Flash video format to the next level. It is a carnival of anxiety, a customized Rorschach test, and a window into the very soul of the viewer.

CALM

sharp teeth

CALM

lost

Creative Process

Skindive share the same label—Palm Pictures—with the Supreme Beings of Leisure. Through the label, they were introduced to Pixelwurld's vision of multipurpose broadcast/Internet videos using Flash technology. Excited by the prospect, the band developed the initial treatment for "Tranquilizer."

"The band had an initial treatment with the old homeless man, but it wasn't fully realized," said director Andres Moreta. "We felt that he needed a purpose. By brainstorming and throwing it back and forth with the band, we came up with the homeless man who's collecting TVs and building a monument with them. We then combined it with the innocent child who's watching the TV. Maybe the old man is in his position because of watching TV. Maybe the old man is the same child, years later. In truth, even I don't know. After we had the basic premise, the band asked, 'What's going to happen after he builds his monument?' We threw out the idea that he gets sucked into the TV. The band loved it, and we went in that direction."

For the online Flash version, the team added a customization section where viewers answer questions about themselves and take a Rorschach test. Their responses are intertwined with the visual playback, and they see their own responses and personality seamlessly integrated into the video.

"It's a very personal, introspective song, and we thought the personality test would be an interesting way to involve viewers in a more active role," said technical director Miles Lightwood. "We came up with a bunch of different questions throughout the development process. The objective of the final questions is to make it an analytical thing. There are some multiple-choice questions, fill-in-the-blank questions, and Rorschach inkblots. When you type in an interpretation of the inkblots, it becomes part of the visual noise that is going on in the background of a number of scenes. When viewers select different options to questions—like 'What is your favorite movie?'—depending on which movie is selected, quotes from that movie are displayed throughout the video."

Additional elements from the viewers' selections are played throughout the video, such as slogans for a fictional hamburger stand and imagery for the viewers' dream vacations displayed on billboards and street signs.

A subtext to "Tranquilizer" is the effect of subliminal messages in the media. The personality test is a tool for making these subliminal messages personalized for each viewer, and the ultimate effect is that of incorporating the viewer into the visual experience itself.

Production Process

Production for this project first focused on the creation of the broadcast version with playback at 30 frames per second. The frame rate was then scaled back to 8 frames per second for Internet playback.

Moreta explained, "I did the video first, but I wanted to have a Flash feel to it. Even though I'm using bitmaps, sometimes there's a layer of vectors overlaid on them. Basically, I did the video first in After Effects at 30 frames per second. After the video was completed, I exported it out at a smaller size—at 8 frames per second. We had all the elements already treated in After Effects, and all we did was export it to different layers and recompiled it in Flash."

This recompiling in Flash was no easy task. At times, Moreta found the files so large that they became unwieldy and difficult to work with.

The footage of the homeless man was shot on the street in Los Angeles. The look and feel of the piece is fairly rough, so the masking of the homeless man into a separate layer contains some harsh edges, which display elements of the original background. Moreta felt it would fit the vibe of the song and would help in expediting production. The footage of the child was taken in a more controlled environment—on a set with the televisions.

Moreta edited the footage in After Effects into the way that he envisioned the final piece would look. This rough cut was exported into a series of numbered image files. The image files were batch-processed in Streamline and Illustrator. The processed files were then imported back into After Effects. Moreta alternated frames between bitmapped images and vector-based images to give the video its unique look and style. This effect also was developed in anticipation of the Internet playback of the video.

"The problem that I was running into was that I had all these bitmaps," said Moreta. "I was thinking that I was going to run into lots of problems, just streaming-wise. So what I did was for every other frame, I added a vector—a vector is smaller than a bitmap—to prevent the movie clips from being too big."

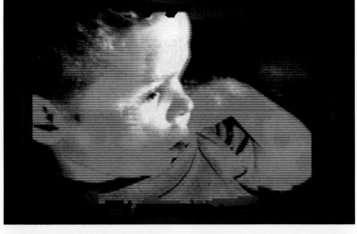

The broadcast version of the video was a straight, linear piece, but the Internet version incorporates a high degree of personalization from the personality test. ActionScript, the programming language of Flash, saves the answers from the test as variables. These variables are then displayed as they are called in the video.

Flash can save this information internally. Although viewers have the option of entering their own personal information to customize the viewing experience, it is not required.

Even without viewer interaction, the Flash video plays differently each time because of a randomize function implemented by Lightwood. This function automatically cycles through a list of preprogrammed responses to questions and creates new visual combinations for each time the file is played back.

"Tranquilizer" is available for viewing at www.pixelworld.com.

Credits

Executive Producer **Brian Sutnick**
Producer **Geri Soriano-Lightwood**
Director **Andres Moreta**
Technical Director **Miles Lightwood**
Videographer **Andres Moreta**
Art Direction **Andres Moreta**
Design/Flash Animators **Andres Moreta and Sabrina Soriano**
Design/Motion Graphics Artist **Sabrina Soriano**
Flash Action Scripting **Miles Lightwood**

Tools

Adobe After Effects
Adobe Illustrator
Adobe Photoshop
Adobe Premiere
Adobe Streamline
Macromedia Flash
Macromedia Freehand
Mini DV Camera

Production Company

Pixelwurld
Los Angeles, CA, United States

RollingStone.com
"60 Seconds With Sum 41"
Online Video

Project Overview

It is a generally accepted proposition that in the future most forms of media will eventually be available on demand through some form of online delivery mechanism. Unfortunately, we do not live in that world; full-frame, full-speed online video is still the providence of fantasy. Eventually, the technology will advance to the point where online video delivery will be viable, but for the foreseeable future, the Internet climate is still mired in slow connection speeds, and videos are presented with reduced frame rates, color palettes, and proportions.

This is why, in comparison to traditional broadcast productions, there are still relatively few Internet-only video productions. "60 Seconds with..." is a series of web-based video interviews created for RollingStone.com. The interviews—conceived, shot, and edited by the team at hillmancurtis, inc.—run the gamut from classic rockers to new talent talking about love, life, alcohol, and their latest albums.

Creative Process

RollingStone.com originally called hillmancurtis, inc. to help them with a website makeover. That consulting job led to a larger conversation about the role of video on the web and the impact it could have on a website. When Curtis came up with the idea for "60 Seconds with...," RollingStone.com loved it. Before long, the crew was racing to various backstages at a moment's notice, camera in hand to film whatever footage they could.

Because of the success of the original consulting job, RollingStone.com trusted the team's vision and gave them a high degree of creative freedom. Their most binding creative directive was, "The band has 20 minutes free before they go on at 8:00 tonight. Can you make it?"

Director of photography and interviewer Ian Kovalik explains, "On the web, shorter is better, and that forces us to keep what is important and lose what is boring or irrelevant. The interviews are fast-paced. We realize that we only have a minute to profile each artist, so we identify the absolute essential ingredients of each piece and stick to them from the filming to the editing."

Credits

Director/Editor Hillman Curtis
Director of Photography/Interviewer Ian Kovalik
Gaffer Matt Horn
Project Manager Homera Chaudhry
Producer for RollingStone.com Doug Gottlieb

Tools

Adobe After Effects
Adobe Illustrator
Adobe Photoshop
Apple Final Cut Pro
Canon XL1
RealSystem Producer
Smartwater
Sorenson Video 3

Production Company

hillmancurtis, inc.
New York, NY, United States

Production Process

"60 Seconds with..." has featured many artists, ranging from Stevie Nicks to Monster Magnet. The featured interview was with the Canadian punk quartet Sum 41.

"For a punk band, they're surprisingly respectful," said Kovalik. "We set them up in front of a white screen in our studio and had them change positions every couple of questions. Despite being painfully hung over— it was the bass player's birthday the night before—they obliged, and it was a blast. Most of the interviews we had done previous to Sum 41 were focused on one person, usually seated backstage before a show, with little time for preparation and plenty of time for chaos. For the Sum 41 shoot, the band had a little more flexibility in their schedule and were able to come out to our studio, where we could set them up however we wanted. It was the most control we had yet during an interview."

The spot took 20 minutes to shoot, followed by a few days of post-production. Once the footage was gathered, it was imported it into Final Cut Pro, and the crew went to town.

"We get a lot of our inspiration on the streets of New York. On his walk to work, Hillman noticed a poster in a SoHo fashion store that featured enlarged type splashed at funky angles across the photography. He loved it, and taking an immediate cue, began laying out type and images directly in After Effects for later import into Final Cut Pro," said Kovalik.

The video was processed at full-size, full-motion. To down-sample the size to 320 x 240 pixels and reduce the frame rate, the movie was run through Sorenson 3 video compression technology. The final movie was delivered to RollingStone.com as both a QuickTime file and as a Real Media file.

Available for viewing online at www.hillmancurtis.com in the broadcast section, the spot is a graphically appealing rocket ride, which reveals the mischievous and engaging personality of Sum 41 in just under 60 seconds.

Chapter 4
Out of the Box

From the skyline of Times Square to the floor of an automotive trade show, modern motion graphics seem to be ubiquitous. They sell us products, inform us of the vital statistics of the player at bat, explain processes, and influence our options and purchasing behaviors. In other words, motion graphics have become inextricably woven into the fabric of our lives.

Gone are the confines of the television, theater, or computer screen. Motion graphics are portable and now appear in nontraditional playback environments too numerous to list.

The intent is the same—to impart information, to motivate, to educate, and to entertain; only the venue has changed. The skills required to create these graphics are nearly identical to those used in broadcast, film, and new media. However, new concerns influence the design and production of this type of work. Questions such as "How will this image read when the sun is over the outfield wall?" and "What kind of message would appeal to individuals walking at approximately 4 miles per hour (6.4 km) through an overstimulating urban environment?" enter the mix.

More often than not, the solutions are as fascinating as the challenges. The work featured in this section ranges from a custom animation projected onto an 8 foot (2.4 m) balloon floating over the floor of a convention center in Japan to a California sports stadium to what is referred to as "the world's oddest format" located in the heart of Times Square—all nontraditional, all motion graphics, and all custom-designed to work within the limitations of their unique playback environments.

Advanced Fibre Communications, Inc.
Nasdaq MarketSite Tower

Project Overview

Soaring over the heart of Times Square is the Nasdaq MarketSite Tower. This massive light-emitting diode screen is contoured to the cylindrical shape of the Nasdaq building and measures 90 feet (27.4 m) in width and 120 feet (36.6 m) in height.

In June 2000, Advanced Fibre Communications (AFC) president and CEO John Schofield was invited to open the day's trading. As part of the invitation, Nasdaq offered to play a 90-second spot on the MarketSite Tower.

Creative Process

Creating an effective message on what executive producer Kim Salyer calls "the world's oddest format" was no easy task. Creative director Chris Blum had to take into consideration a number of limiting factors: the odd aspect ratio (the screen has dimensions similar to those of a soup can), the development of a strong branding message without a soundtrack, and a highly mobile and distracted audience.

The objective of the AFC spot was to establish brand awareness and to stimulate demand for their DSL services. To meet these objectives and overcome the inherent limitations of the format, Blum and Salyer developed the core concept—*Stop Growing Old Waiting for Broadband*.

This message was conveyed by watching a baby morphing through his life cycle, ultimately resulting in an image of an old man accompanied by the tag line. This sequence was then played in reverse with a new tag line, *Reverse the Aging Process...Get Broadband ASAP*.

Faces were chosen because, according to Salyer, "they are what we respond to as humans, and we wanted to make sure we had a strong message that was easy to grasp." The final spot was a stunning piece of work, proving effective from both a branding and an artistic perspective.

Production Process

Casting

More than 100 people were in the initial casting call. Polaroids were taken of each of the models using the same background and light. Blum then used these Polaroids to create a storyboard of the morph and select the final models.

Photo Shoot

A digital camera was chosen for the photo shoot for both efficiency and budgetary reasons. For the morphing effect to work smoothly, the shoot required careful preplanning. Identical outfits were purchased in sizes ranging from newborn to adult. A metal brace was developed to help the models keep their heads in place. Additionally, a grease pen was used to mark the eye position on the viewfinder of the digital camera. By doing this, the photographer was able to create a series of photos where the models all had a uniform head position, which led to greater efficiency during the postproduction process.

Layout

Initially, the project had a slightly different layout. This layout was changed after Nasdaq played a test version on the big screen while the Video Arts crew viewed it live through the Nasdaq Webcam. What they found was that the window placement was interfering with some of the elements. A slight redesign was required to increase legibility of the typography and improve the playback of the morph.

Postproduction

In the final production, 17 still-frame images were used. Modifications were necessary to some of the images to smooth transitions between models. These modifications included sharing eyes and ears between models and, in one case, using the same hairline for three different images.

For final delivery, Video Arts created a special digital Betacam master where the video was compressed to two-thirds by three-fifths of its original size. The reason for this is although the screen has an odd aspect ratio, the playback device does not. Therefore, the video needed to be compressed to a size that will expand correctly when it is shown in Times Square.

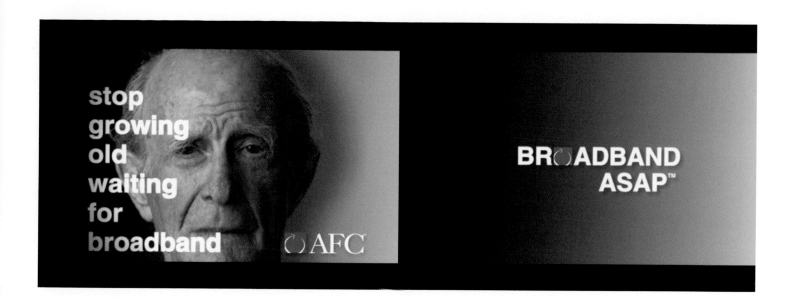

Credits

Executive Producer **Kim Salyer**
Director/Creative Director **Chris Blum**
Producer **Marilyn Warner**
Senior Effects Designer/Compositor **Mark Singles**
Editor and Text Animations **Zac Pineda**
Photoshop Artist **Michael Endlich**
Photography **Holly Stewart**
Casting **Nancy Hayes Casting**
Project Manager for Advanced Fibre Communications **Ted Meister**

Tools

Digital camera
Adobe Photoshop
Discreet Flint
Discreet Smoke
Digital linear online edit suite

Production Company

Video Arts, Inc.
San Francisco, CA, United States

Volvo
Trade Show
XC90 Launch—*Provoke*

Project Overview

The collaboration between architects Zeilon & Partners and Strobe resulted in an integrated trade show package that strikes a stunning balance between architecture and communication.

The objective was to design a fitting launch for Volvo's XC90, a new all-weather vehicle, at international car shows in Detroit and Los Angeles. Working together closely, the companies developed a visually compelling identity package, which builds on the Lifecycle concept that Strobe previously developed for Volvo.

The resulting display booth creates a unified presentation, integrating the visual communications with the space itself. The showcase of the space is the launch film, which combines the abstract imagery of the Lifecycle concept with a powerful performance by the Swedish dance troupe Bounce.

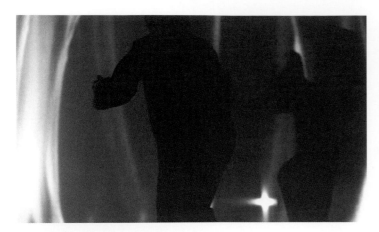

Creative Process

In 2001, Strobe developed a concept to house the Volvo product line. The concept was called Lifecycle, and it separated the Volvo product line into four distinct categories: Emerge/Birth—concept cars; Discovery/Curiosity—family cars; Peak/Adventure—adventure cars; and Insight/Experience—luxury cars. This approach is typical of Strobe's development process. Director Jonas Hallberg explained, "That's the way we work. When we create any communication, we start with an emotional concept. Our objective is to translate the client's brand values into an emotional platform."

When asked to develop the launch film for the XC90, Strobe reverted to the creative brief for the Peak section of the Lifecycle concept. Peak values had been identified as intense, powerful, thrilling, and passionate.

To emphasize these themes, Strobe decided to create an abstract journey through a tornado. What differentiates their piece from those of other carmakers was the decision to use humans to represent the car instead of using the actual car.

In *Provoke*, the dancers become an abstraction of the car, traveling through chaos and emerging safely. They take the journey the car would have taken in real life, and their successful excursion through the heart of the storm conveys a sense of safety and security.

Strobe's creative process is precise, breaking down the abstract journey into five specific sections. First is Rise. The dancers start in normal condition. Movement is added to build expectation that something is about to occur. Second is Search. The first wave of the storm hits, trying to uproot dancers, trying to throw them off balance, but they remain in control. Third is Vacuum. It is the eye of the storm, a brief respite, giving dancers time to rest, but they are aware that they still have to face the second part of the storm. Fourth is Chaos. The dancers are thrown back into the storm, which is similar to the first wave, only more intense. The motions of the dancers are accelerated to indicate the intensity and fury of the storm. The final section is Release. The dancers have made it through the storm safely. They have survived the tornado, and the XC90 is revealed.

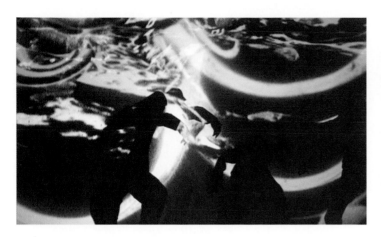 

Production Process

Music

Hallberg considers the music essential, not only to set the mood of the piece but as an integral part of the storytelling. "Music is the carrier telling you where you are in the story. Graphics and dancers react to the music to visually tell you where you are in the story, but music is where it all begins," said Hallberg. Prior to the video production, a rough cut of the music was created.

Initial Visual Production

The first stage of production was to reedit the original source files used for Peak section of Lifecycle. Hallberg cut pieces together in Avid using the new music for *Provoke*. The edited footage was then color-corrected in Inferno and exported to Beta.

Choreography

The Swedish dance troupe Bounce was selected for the spot for its unique urban style. "If you look at the car, it's a street car. That's why we used street dancers. They have a lot in common. In *Provoke*, all the dancers' movements were coming from a low center of gravity, just like the car, giving the appearance that they are sturdy, impossible to flip," explained Hallberg.

Live Shoot

One interesting aspect of this production is that most of the visual effects were shot in camera. This was achieved by building a stage surrounded by transparent fabric. The edited Peak footage was projected onto the fabric from two projectors as the dancers performed. This created an environment intended to feel like an abstract world based on the Peak visual style.

The stage took one day to prep and two days to shoot. Minimal lighting beyond what was generated by the two projectors was used. The footage was shot on 35 mm using a Steadicam rig.

Postproduction

After the telecine transfer of the film, it was edited on Avid to the final music track. The edited footage was then imported into Inferno and Fire for further effects and color-correcting.

For the final shot, Strobe wanted the car to drive through the dancers' environment. Unfortunately, that was not possible—the XC90 was not yet in production and all available models were on their way to Detroit for a car show. Instead, the team was given footage of the car shot against a white screen. To achieve the effect of the car driving through the dancers' environment, they took the white-screen footage and composited it with the multiple layers of the Peak footage.

The final effect is a piece in which the dancers and the car inhabit a world of beauty and fury that dovetails perfectly with the trade show booth and Volvo's overall product positioning strategy.

Credits

Creative Directors **Jonas Hallberg and Lars Sköllerholm**
Producer **Josh Thorne**
Directors **Jonas Hallberg and Lars Sköllerholm**
Director of Photography **Linus Sandgren**
Visual Consultant **Vince Reichardt**
Production Designer **Bengt Frödeberg**
Choreographer **Bounce Street Dance Company**
Colorist **Edward Frithiof [film to video]**
Avid Artist **Gregers Dohn, Nostromo**
Fire Artist **The Chimney Pot**

Tools

Avid
Discreet Fire
Discreet Flame
Discreet Inferno

Production and Brand Communication Company

Strobe
Stockholm, Sweden

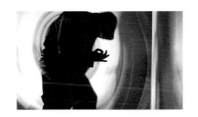

THE NEW VOLVO **XC90**

Canon Inc. (Tokyo)
Expo 2000

Project Overview

In the autumn of 2000, Canon held Canon Expo 2000, a global exhibition of the company's technologies, products, and vision for the 21st century. Exhibitions were held in New York, Paris, and Tokyo.

For the Tokyo exhibition, Environmental Planning Laboratory, Inc., was hired to design and plan the exhibit space. The centerpiece of the exhibit space was a video greeting designed and produced by Vehicle +. This greeting was an animated video loop projected onto an 8-foot (2.4-m) tall balloon floating over the center of the exhibition space.

Creative Process

The objective of the animation was to set the general atmosphere of the convention hall while expressing the themes and global vision of Cannon. A balloon was selected as the display screen because of its dynamic appearance and visibility from anywhere in the hall.

Vehicle + chose a circle metaphor for the look and feel of the piece to enhance the unique visual possibilities offered by projecting images onto the surface of a balloon. Themes and faces intertwine in a continual loop, with circular transitions to give the appearance of ripples in a fountain floating casually above the heads of the exhibition visitors.

Much care was taken to achieve this effect, and many tests were done. The first tests were done on smaller balloons. Eventually, tests were projected on a beach ball for the client as part of the approval process.

Production

Models were selected both for diversity and facial expression. The focus of the exhibition was the bold new vision for the future, and expressions were selected that conveyed both anticipation and exhilaration.

Images were scanned and treated in Photoshop and After Effects. The focus was blurred slightly along the outside edges to complement the distortion caused by the playback on the curved surface of the balloon.

The final presentation was burned into a DVD, which allowed for smooth looping. In the exhibition hall, two 800-lumen projectors were set up, both front and back, to cover as much as possible of the balloon with the video greeting.

Credits

Exhibit Planning **Environmental Planning Laboratory, Inc.**
Production **Vehicle + Co., Ltd.**

Tools

Adobe After Effects
Adobe Illustrator
Adobe Photoshop
NewTek LightWave 3D

Production Company

Vehicle + Co., Ltd.
Tokyo, Japan

Oakland Athletics
Game Open and Lineup

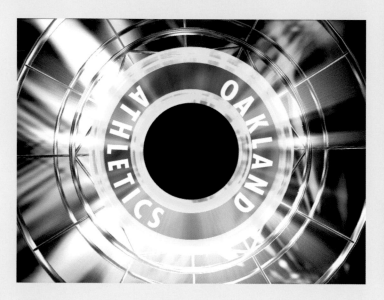

Project Overview

The Oakland Athletics and Video Arts have been working together since 1986, when Video Arts produced *Dot Racing*, a "between innings" entertainment feature for Oakland's new DiamondVision screen and the launch of their in-stadium entertainment initiative. *Dot Racing* turned out to be a huge success with the fans, and Video Arts and the Oakland Athletics have been producing new in-stadium entertainment pieces every season since.

Originally envisioned as the open to the 2001 highlight video, the featured graphics are the in-stadium graphics for the 2002 season. Shown at the start of the game on the DiamondVision screen, these graphics both set the tone for a day at the ballpark and introduce the A's lineup.

Creative Process

The 2002 Open animation feature was the brainchild of Video Arts senior designer and Flint artist Mark Singles. To research this project, Singles was forced to endure many afternoons at the stadium watching the ball game. In his spare time, he studied the DiamondVision screen and took notes on what images were effective on the screen. He found that high-contrast, brightly colored designs read best in the daylight glare in the stadium

From a design perspective, he wanted to create a dynamic network sports—style presentation with a strong logo treatment. The general look of the piece was inspired by the circular shape of the A's logo and the type of scaffolding and metallic framework that one usually associates with grandstands.

Inherent in the design brief was the need to reconfigure the lineup on an as-needed basis. To accommodate this requirement, Singles created a consistent wipe pattern at the end of each player's introduction. This wipe would enable the lineup to be seamlessly reassembled for each game.

Production Process

Singles's first step was to work with 3-D artist Michael Endlich on the design of framework models that could be used as the structural foundation for the animation. Endlich worked in 3D Max to create a basic double-wagon-wheel-strut–based structure that was then imported into Flint. Singles used that structure to hang a semitransparent "wall" on which video windows could be "hung."

The result is a stack of shallow, rotating cylinders with action clips projected onto the cylinder walls. A column of light connects the structures at their hubs. At the top of the column of light is another stack of columns that are revealed to be the A's logo.

Once the basic design was developed and approved, game footage was acquired and plugged into the set. Because the player roster is subject to change at any time, a strategy was developed to allow Smoke editor Zac Pineda to incorporate the camera and lighting data used in Flint so that video clips could more easily be swapped out. Player clips and headshots were shot by the A's and Fox Sports early in spring training to create an archive of images that could be resourced through-out the season.

The final animations were delivered on a DigiBeta master and placed on the A's server. From their server, the in-stadium production crew can reconfigure the clips into the daily lineup and broadcast them on the DiamondVision screen on an as-needed basis.

Credits

Video Arts
Designer/Animator/Flint Artist **Mark Singles**
Smoke Editor/Compositor **Zac Pineda**
3-D Artist **Michael Endlich**
Executive Producer **Kim Salyer**

Oakland Athletics
Director of Stadium Entertainment/Co-Producer **Troy Smith**
Director of Multimedia Services/Co-Producer **David Dons**

Tools

Discreet Flint
Discreet Smoke
3D Max

Production Company

Video Arts, Inc.
San Francisco, CA, United States

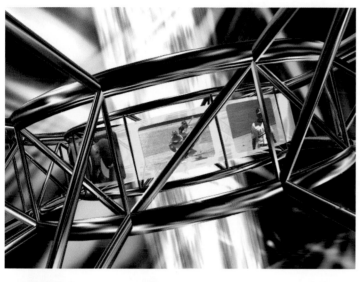

Directory of Production Compa

Alternate Route Studios
One Research Drive
Cary, NC 27513
www.alternateroutestudios.com

Belief
1832 Franklin Street
Santa Monica, CA 90404
www.belief.com

Big Film Design
137 Varick Street
New York, NY 10013
www.bigfilmdesign.com

Creative Spark
150 Henry Street
San Francisco, CA 94114
www.creative-spark.com

Cinetech Production Group
15/F. Professional Building
19–23 Tung Lo Wan Road,
Causeway Bay, Hong Kong
www.cinetech.com.hk

D&D Audiovisuais S.A.
Rua das Trinas, nº 14-46
1200 Lisbon, Portugal

FarFar
Kocksgatan 50
116 29 Stockholm, Sweden
www.farfar.se

Firewalk Films
Los Angeles, CA
www.scratchmovie.com

Hatmaker
63 Pleasant Street
Watertown, MA 02472
www.hatmaker.com

hillmancurtis, inc.
447 Broadway, 5th Floor
New York, NY 10013
www.hillmancurtis.com

Lambie-Nairn
Greencoat House
Francis Street
London, England
SWIP 1DH
www.lambie-nairn.com

Ray Marshall Design
4053 Harlan Street
Emeryville, CA 94608
www.raymarshalldesign.com

Palm Pictures
601 W. 26th Street, 11 Floor
New York, NY 10001
www.palmpictures.com

The Picture Mill
5620 Hollywood Boulevard
Hollywood, CA 90028
www.picturemill.com

PMcD Design
484 Greenwich Street
New York, NY 10013
www.pmcddesign.com

nies

Pixelwurld
www.pixelwurld.com

Red Sky—San Francisco
921 Front Street
San Francisco, CA 94111
www.redsky.com

REZN8
6430 Sunset Boulevard, Suite 100
Hollywood, CA 90028
www.rezn8.com

R!OT Design
545 5th Avenue
New York, NY 10017
www.riotingmanhattan.com

Strobe
Kyrkslingan II
S III 49 Stockholm
Sweden
www.strobe.se

TACTIC Creative Services
43 Bucknell Street
Newtown NSW 2042
Sydney, Australia
www.tactic.com.au

Richard Taylor
www.richardtaylordesign.com

Trollbäck and Company
915 Broadway
New York, NY 10010
www.trollback.com

Vehicle +
C/o vehicle+ Hills-Daikanyama #201
1-34-15 Ebisu-nishi, Shibuya-ward
Tokyo, Japan #150-0021
www.vehicle-plus.co.jp/web/

Velvet Mediendesign Gmbh
Osterwalsstrasse 10
80805 Munich, Germany
www.velvet.de

ViewPoint Studios
140 Gould Street
Needham, MA 02494
www.viewpointstudios.com

Video Arts, Inc.
724 Battery Street, 2nd Floor
San Francisco, CA 94111
www.vidarts.com

Xpose Motion Picture Company
F/18, Everest, Tardeo
Mumbai 400 034
India
www.xposeindia.com

Yu + Co
941 North Mansfield Avenue
Hollywood, CA 90038
www.yuco.com

Acknowledgments

First and foremost, I would like to thank Larry Kay, because if his dance card was not full at the time, I would not have been given the opportunity to write this book. To Paula Munier, my editor, thank you for your wisdom, guidance, and patience. Many thanks to Winnie Prentiss, David Martinell, Pamela Hunt, and all of the good people at Rockport who have worked so hard to make this book a reality. A special thank-you to fellow Syracuse alumnus Steve Curran whose assistance has been invaluable.

A sincere thank-you to all of the people from the design and production houses who have given so willingly of their time, their images, and their thoughts. It has been a privilege to work with so many talented and dedicated professionals. Special appreciation to the following individuals without their support and this book would not have been possible: Adrienne Gum, David Shilale, Michael Frederick, Michael Leone, Thomas Bik, Glenn Robbins, Randall Balsmeyer, Amit Sethi, Kathy Kelehan, Alexandra Grüneberg, Andres Moreta, Miles Lightwood, Luellen Renn, Garson Yu, Miki Kawahara, Meghan O'Brien, Mike Goedecke, Brian Eley, Jason Keeley, Mark Mirsky, Carol Ricks, Matthias Zentner, Sandra Schwittau, Clay Jensen, Joel Hladecheck, Caroline Marshall, Melissa Holden, Danon Hinty, Patrick McDonough, Dana Bonomo, Michelle Lockett, Ian Kovalik, Hillman Curtis, Homera J. Chaudry, Michael Chu, Kim Salyer, Chris Blum, Mark Singles, Michael Endlich, Ileana Garcia-Montes, Julie Bedford, Paul Sidlo, David Humpherys, Julie Siemens, Richard Taylor, Chris Goveia, Elz Bently, Christian Boustani, David Clayton, William Lebeda, Kirk Cameron, Rick Probst, Per Hansson, Nicke Bergstrom, Per Nasholm, Anders Gustavsson, Chris Snyder (Dude), Lisa Cleff, Lorenzo de Guttadauro, Sari Rosen, Bill Denahy, Diana Constantini, James Hackett, Dana Rayson, Andy Brown, Dilip Ahuja, Doug Prey, Brad Blondheim, Karol Martesko Fenster, Joyce Dollinger, Jonas Hallberg, Klas Jonsson, and the good people at Resfest. My sincerest thanks to one and all.

I owe a debt of gratitude to the following people who have enriched my life and without whom I would never have the courage and support to write anything, much less this book: my parents, Dr. Roberta Sacks, Dr. Alan & Susan Greene; my sisters, Deborah, Judybeth, and Lisa; my extended family—Madeline Chappelle (The NaNa); Ed & Lois Zachary; Dr. Bruce Zachary; Lisa & David Fain; Joyce Barron & Wayne Nyberg; Missy & Steven Barron; Dr. Fred & Merle Greene; Danielle Greene (ABD); Paul,

Evey, Collin & Zac Pinkham; Mac Bernstein; Tony, Lisa, Tahra & Julia Knudsen; Samantha & Eric Carson; Brandon Stroughter (The Buddha Boy); Eileen, Bill, and DeeDee, and their wonderful family; the Sacks clan—Laura, Gwen, Robert, Jessica, and Naomi; Robert DeBrauwere (for his sage legal advice and faithful renditions of Barry White songs), and his wonderful family, Cayrn, Tyler, Ethan, and Tristan; Andy, Anna & Dylan Kahan; Ray, Lorraine, Gemma & Zoe Marshall; Marissa Berger; Zac Mathews; Dr. Deborah Lowe (what can I say—You Rock); Christo & Brad; Annabelle Breakey (thank you for everything); Jim and Moxie; Andy Carson; Olivia Clayton (my musical better half) and her wonderful husband, Greg; Jonathan & Matt Hoffberg; John Samsel (My Guru); John Dubois; David Fischer; Bob, Ann, Sarah, Julia, and Alexandra Grace; Leroy Hasen, Willow Older & Max, the wonder child; Steve, Phyliss, Haley, and Sammie Hasen; the Kedsons of Philadelphia; Robert Faust; Terry Keegan; Connie, Edgar, and Clara; Steve Rappaport (who got me into this mess), his new wife, Candyce & Collin; Randy Kremlacek & Mary Finley; the gang at the Roanoke Company; Chris Blum; Laurence Levy (for helping me maintain); Tim Modok Pearson; Claudia Brenner; Daniel Pine; Lauri Rose, Joe, Kerstin, and Mark Connelly; Will Roland; Ed Schultz; Nathan Vogel; Laura Victoria (Mueller); Holly Park; Megan, Marc & Hayley Akers; Joel Delude (wherever he may be); Ed Wolh (may we hang out again soon); Sam, Geri, Samuel III, and Gillian Skidmore; and Rita, Chris, and Melissa Tracy.

To the previous generation:
For Edna, Abraham, and Herman, who I will never forget,
and to Charlotte, who can't remember for herself. All my love.

To those who are no longer with us:
Stanley Sacks, a man whom I loved and was sincerely wonderful
to my mother.
Steve Lester, a man who had a heart bigger and stronger than his body
was aware of.

Finally, to anyone I have forgotten, please forgive the oversight—
I haven't slept in a while.

About the Author

Designated a "multimedia guru" by *Entertainment Weekly*, David Greene has been at the forefront of interactive computer technology for over nine years. He was a cofounder of Tribeca Interactive, where he served as project originator and lead game designer for the hallucinogenic game title Nine (rated "A" by *Entertainment Weekly*). Entertainment clients include Aerosmith, Geffen Records, Real McCoy, and Arista Records. Most recently, Mr. Greene has opened Creative Spark, a San Francisco design and production agency that focuses on creating compelling Internet and interactive experiences for corporate clients.

Mr. Greene also has an extensive background in education, teaching, and guest lecturing on the Internet and interactive production at San Francisco State University, The Art Academy (San Francisco), Full Sail Recording Institute (Orlando, FL), and California Recording Institute (San Francisco).

Mr. Greene lives in San Francisco with his wife Kelli and daughter Emma Rose.

Photo: Annabelle Breakey Photography